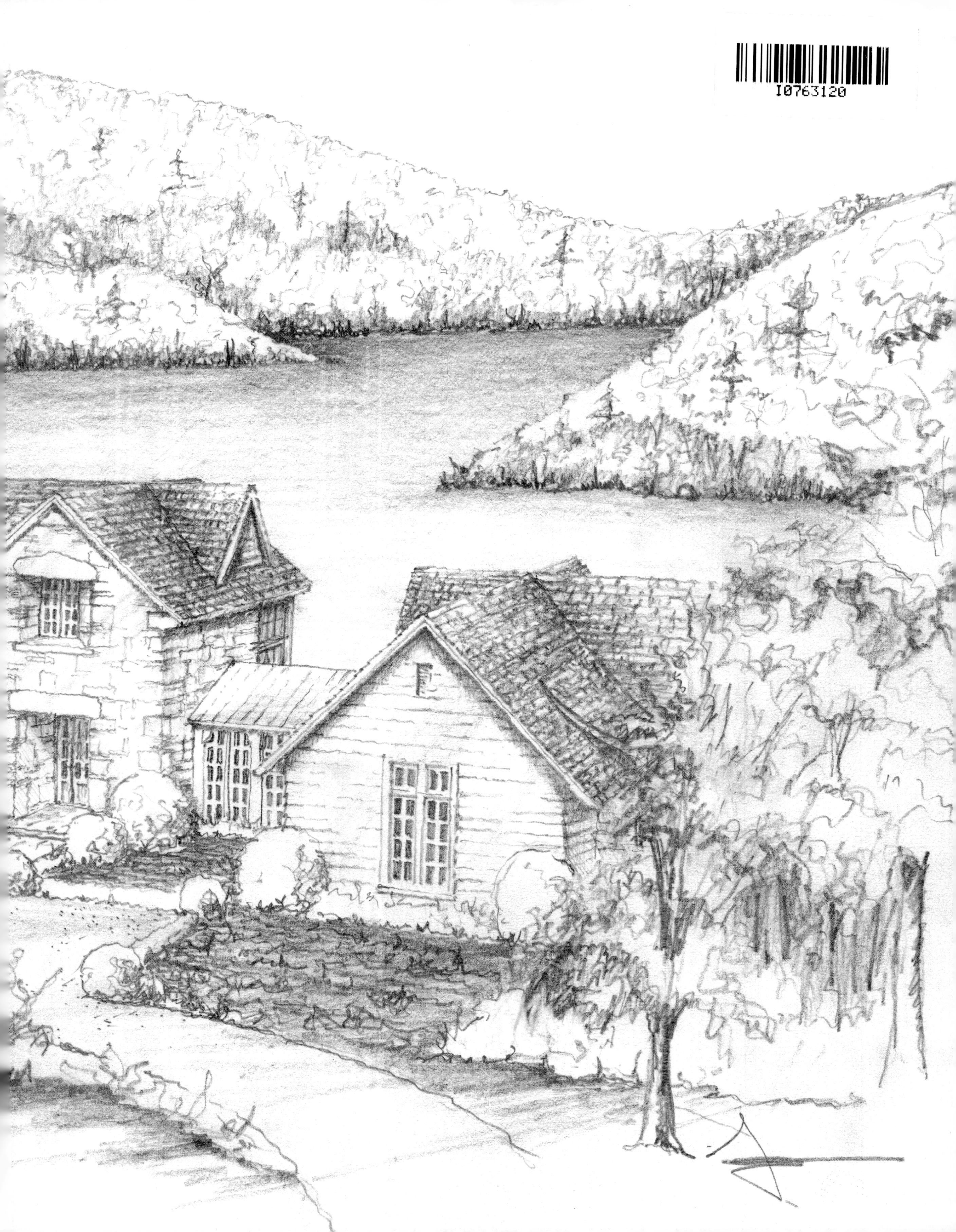
I0763120

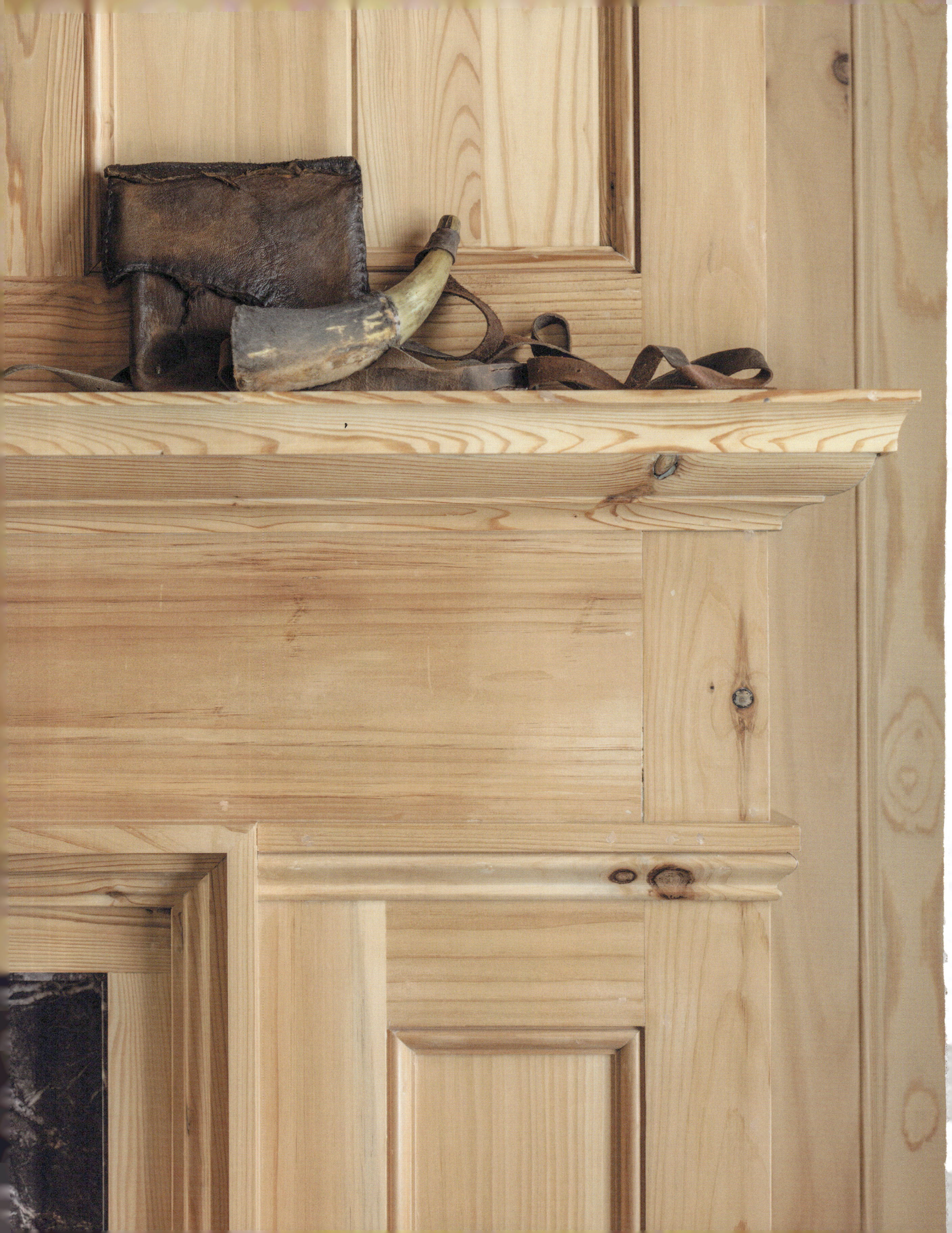

TRADITION MADE NEW

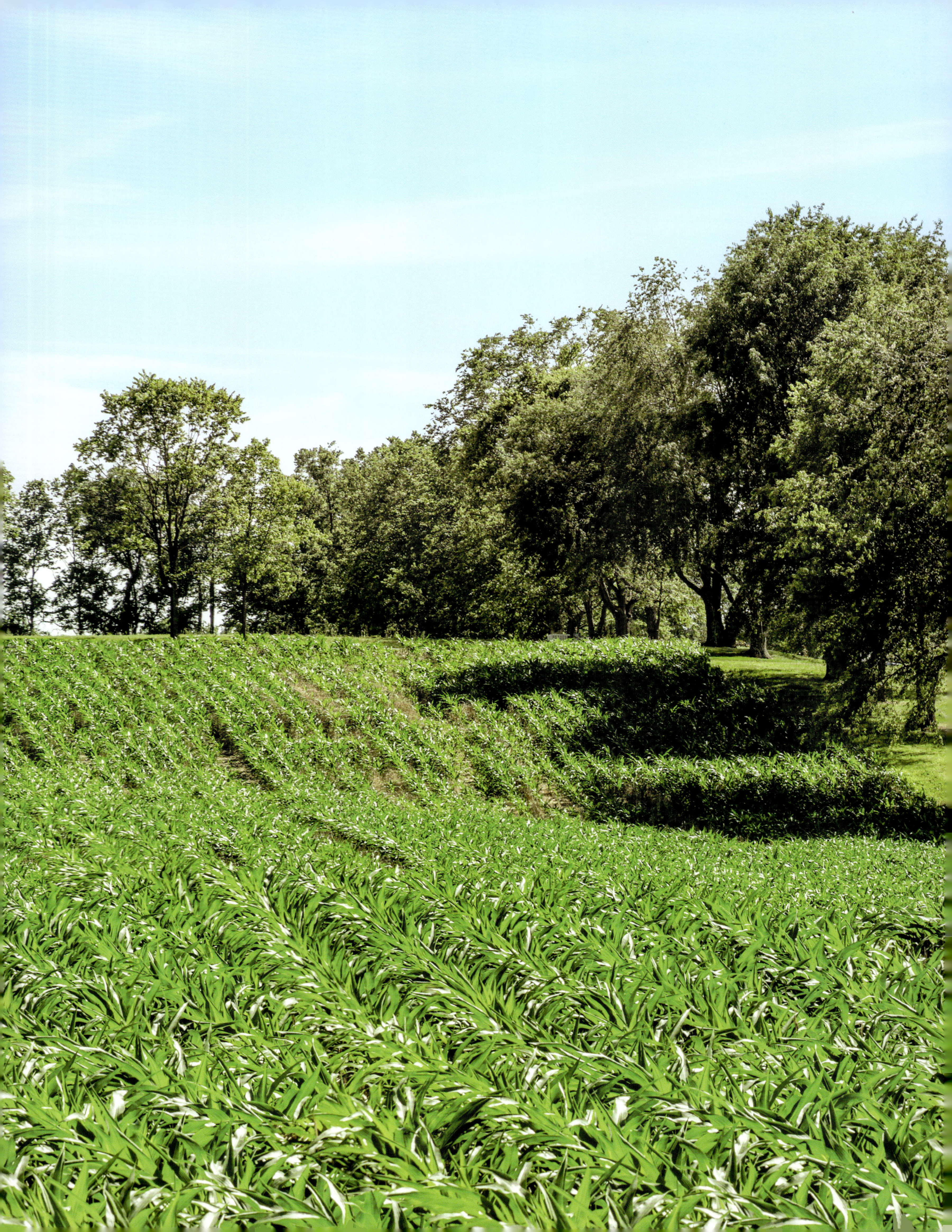

TRADITION MADE NEW

HOUSES WITH A SENSE OF SOUL AND HISTORY

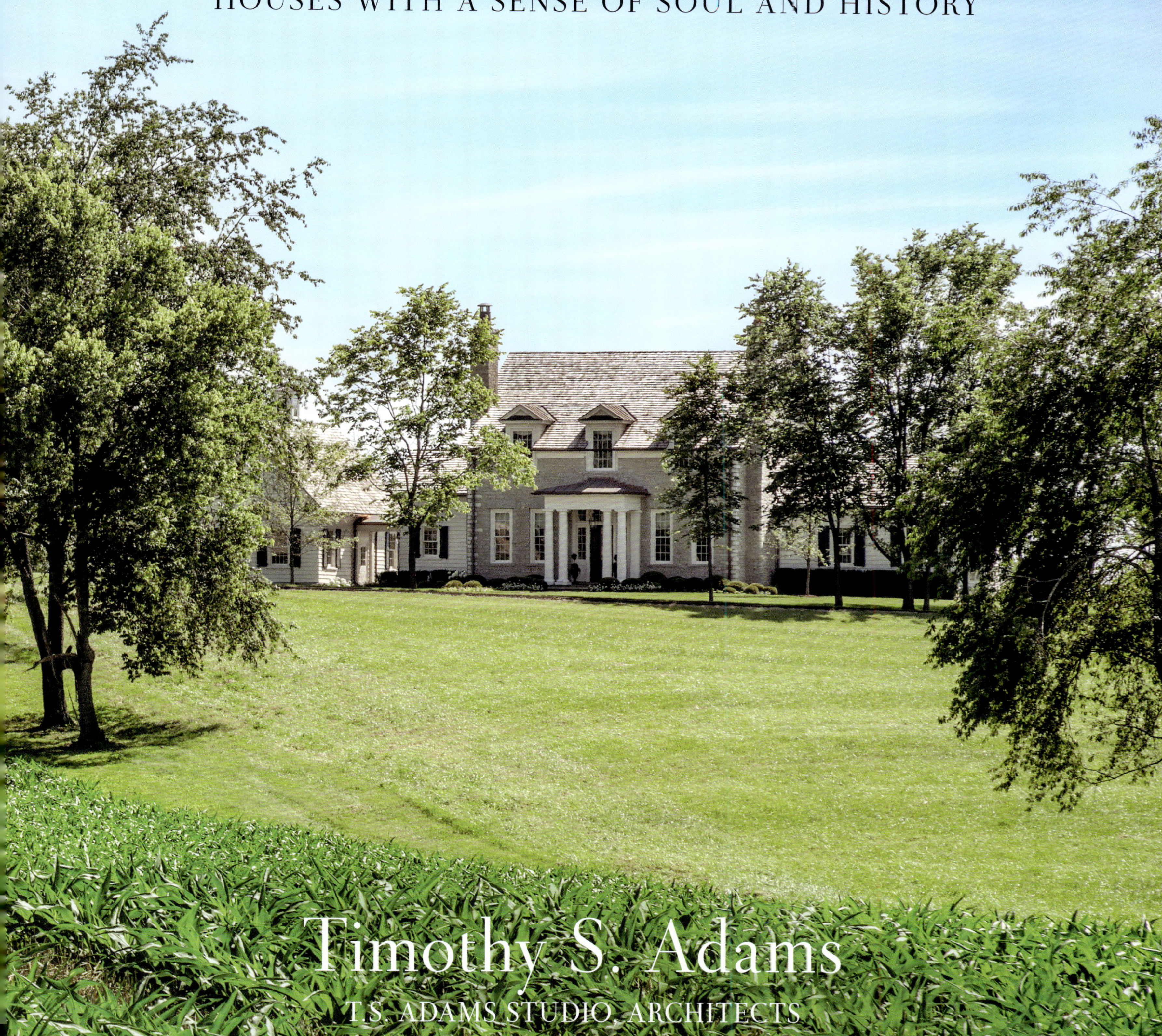

Timothy S. Adams

T.S. ADAMS STUDIO, ARCHITECTS

FOREWORD BY BETH WEBB

PRINCIPAL PHOTOGRAPHY BY LISA ROMEREIN

WRITTEN WITH KYLE HOEPNER

RIZZOLI NEW YORK

New York Paris London Milan

To my wife, Kelli, for your unwavering support,
and to my children—Will, Ben, and Caroline—my biggest fans.

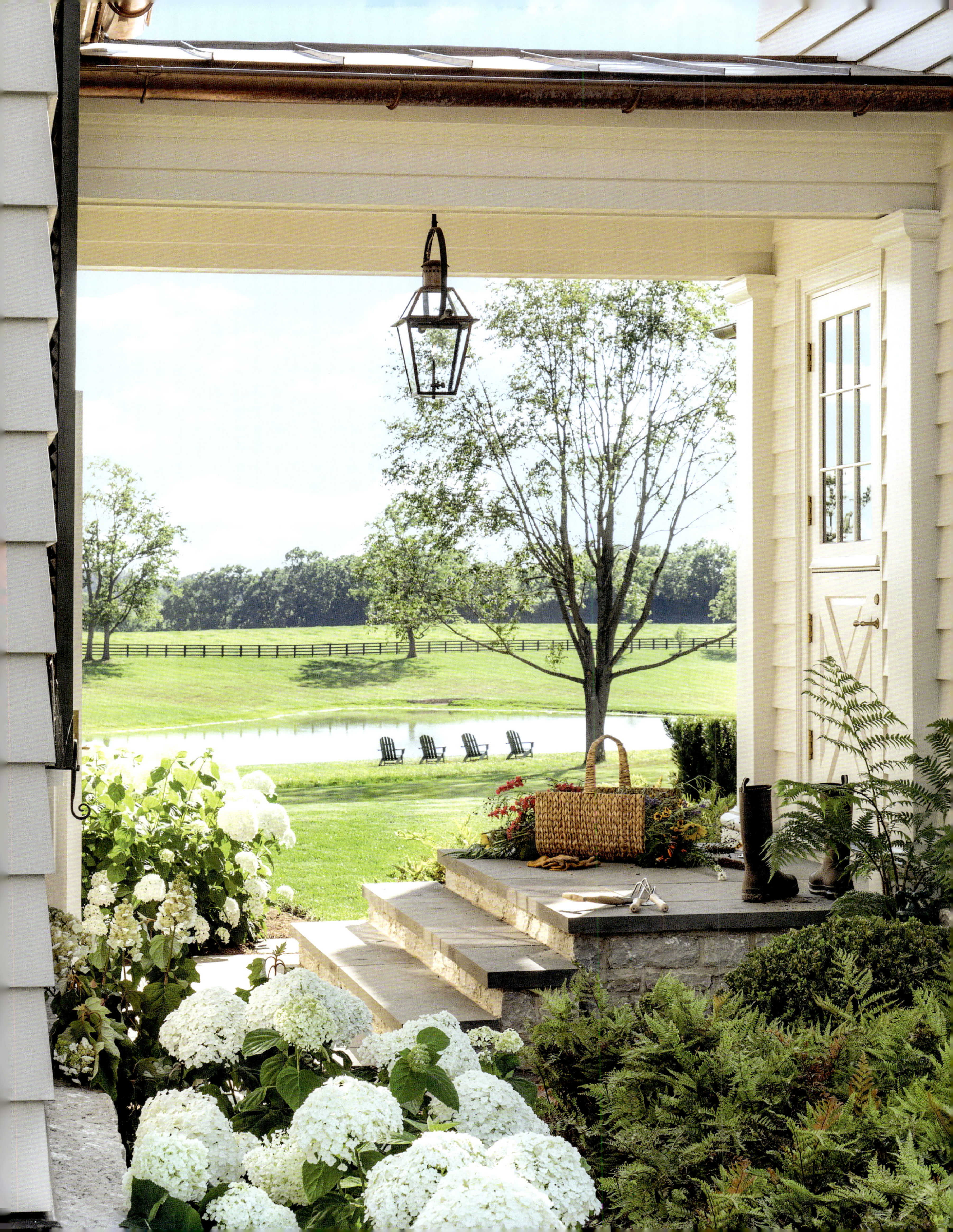

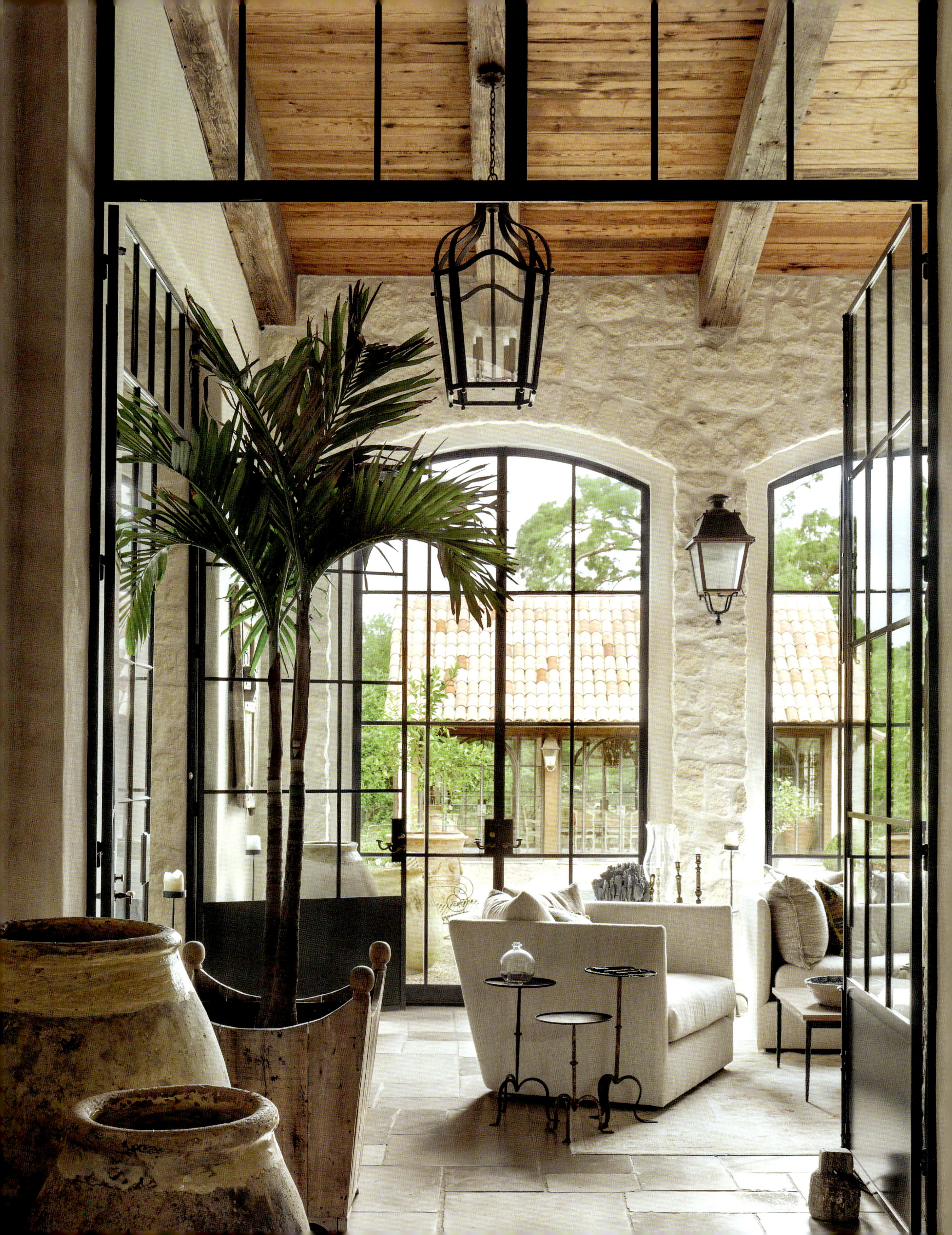

CONTENTS

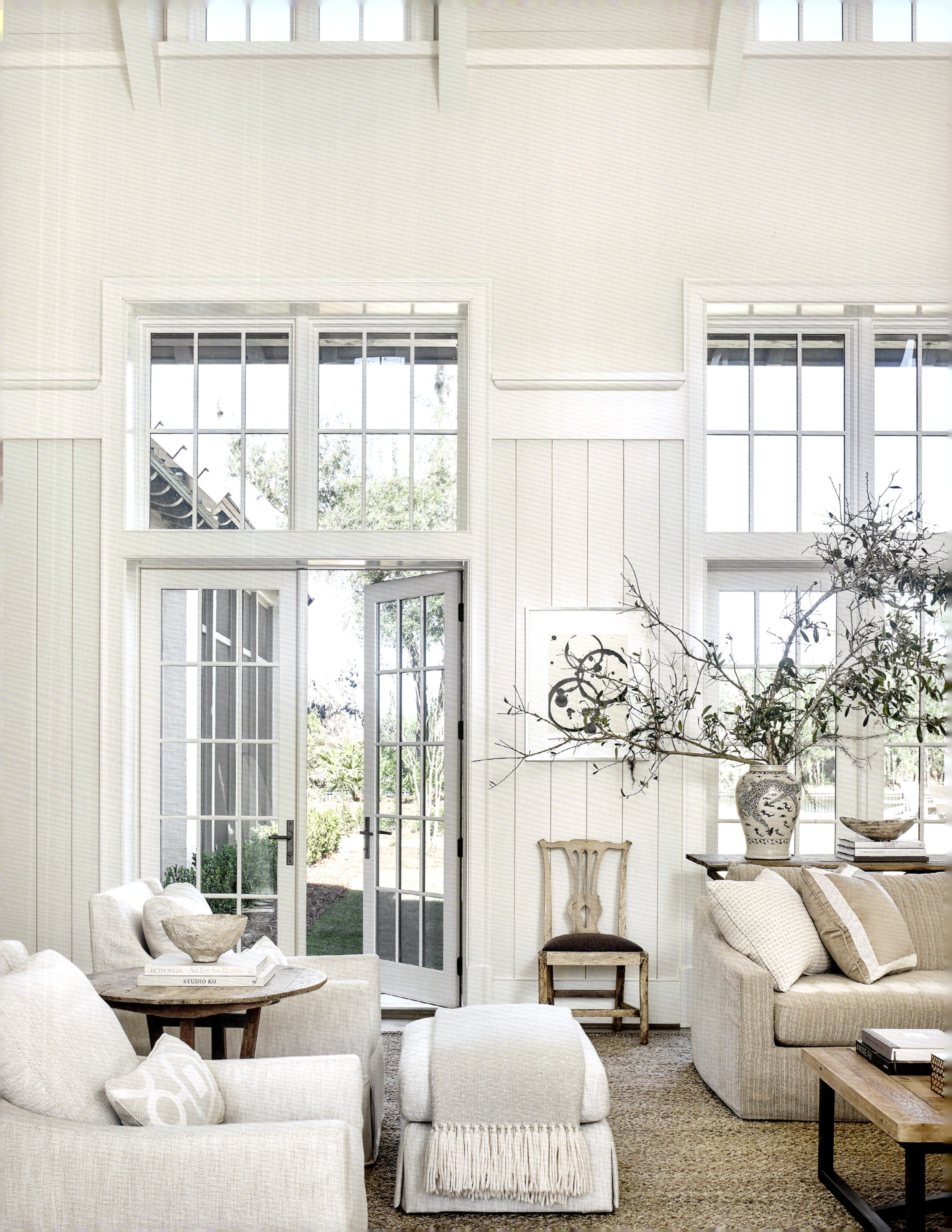
BETH WEBB An Eye for Beauty
STUDIO KO

FOREWORD

by Beth Webb

For over two decades Tim Adams and I have had the pleasure of collaborating on many projects together. Having met each other early in our careers when we were both fledgling architect and designer, we formed a bond. He is a man who not only seeks collaboration but embraces it, with both his staff of talented project architects and a team of like-minded professionals that he intentionally creates for every home he crafts.

Tim is one of those architects who wholeheartedly enjoys the process of designing a home from beginning to end. He is an excellent listener who carefully and considerately interprets his clients' hopes, wishes, and dreams to create a final realization by drawing upon a vast library of resources, craftspeople, and artisans. His thoughtful attention to detail doesn't stop at simply drafting the big picture, but rather he delights in the minutiae of all components making up the home—no element goes unnoticed nor unattended. Nothing is too menial or unworthy of his unerring eye. I remember vividly the first time Tim handed me a complete set of his plans; there were pages and pages of carefully drawn designs—the complete set must've weighed twenty-five pounds!

Tim Adams has become known for creating not only beautiful homes but comfortable, livable spaces with an inherent sense of timelessness—the benchmark of his work. He combines the perfect mix of form and function. Incorporated into all his work is a profound understanding of and respect for historical precedents, authentic proportions, and considered features. Tim remains naturally and intensely curious and is constantly expanding his repertoire.

Tim's Southern roots help define his vernacular. Having grown up on a farm in Asheville, North Carolina, he has a deep and abiding connection to the land—another passion we share. An avid sportsman, he loves the outdoors and all that goes along with a sporting life. First and foremost, though, Tim is a family man and makes a priority of spending as much time as he can with his wife and children on their farm in Georgia. In any free time he has, Tim can be found quail hunting in South Georgia with friends, fishing off the coast of Costa Rica, or pursuing his other passions of painting, drawing, or gardening on the farm. He is a Southern gentleman at heart, steadfast and loyal to his friends, gregarious and welcoming to all who have the pleasure of making his acquaintance. His lifestyle and intrinsic appreciation of all things pertaining to the art of a well-lived life inform his architecture and aesthetic sensibilities, which in turn are what truly make a house a home.

INTRODUCTION

The practice of architecture is a natural fit for me, and I was lucky enough to realize it early on. I grew up on a small farm outside of Asheville, North Carolina, where my family was always building things: storage and equipment sheds converted from old log cabins, say, or a gambrel-roofed horse barn. My dad and grandfather even built our house, with my mom taking charge of the interiors. She embodied creativity, with her love of painting and crafts; my father was the nuts-and-bolts, pragmatic one. I seem to have inherited both genes, if you will, and am unusually adept at uniting the aesthetic and the practical—an ideal combination for an architect.

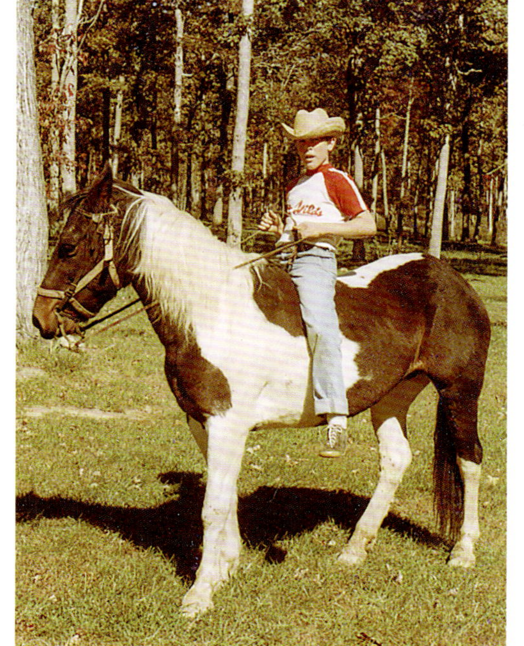
Me on my pinto quarter horse, Patches.

This is not to say that I didn't also love all the other aspects of agrarian life: keeping horses and cows, hunting, fishing, and generally being out on the land. Even today, if you don't find me in our Atlanta office, there's a good chance I'll be out at my own farm in Georgia's Meriwether County, where we grow vegetables and raise both miniature and standard cattle. It's mostly a weekend spot, a place to get away and think and spend evenings around the firepit with my family, free from twenty-first-century distractions—but if I hadn't pursued architecture, I would almost certainly be a full-time farmer now.

Drawing was another passion that I discovered as a kid. In elementary school I won an art competition with a drawing of a barn that included all its details, down to the knots and grain of the wooden walls. Throughout middle school and high school, I was constantly doodling and sketching—to the point where some teachers would confiscate my pencils in an attempt to make me pay better attention in class. Drawing, I gradually came to understand, was my way of processing and assimilating information. And that's still how my mind works. My hand moving across the paper serves to focus my thoughts, making sketching a crucial element in my design method.

I remember always being fascinated by the built environment. Once, I was given a model railroad set for Christmas, and I spent more time using the cardboard boxes to construct a town for the tracks to run through than I did playing with the train itself. My enjoyment

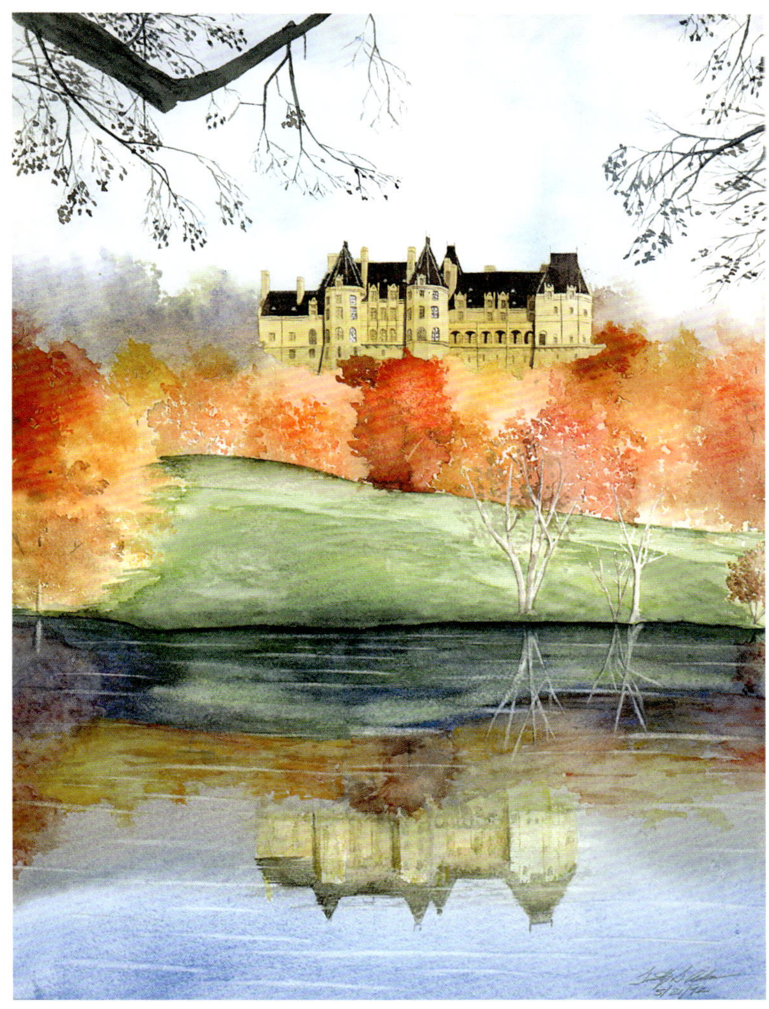

I painted this watercolor of Biltmore while I was at Georgia Tech, as a gift for my mother. The estate was always a meaningful place for us both, and formative in my development as an architect.

came from the process of creating something. I loved it when we'd drive through downtown Asheville, with its wide range of architectural styles. While I didn't yet know the technicalities of what made buildings like the Grove Park Inn special, I was fascinated all the same.

Family vacations often involved touring historic sites such as Colonial Williamsburg, whose streets and houses I found equally captivating. One of our most frequent nearby destinations was Biltmore, George Vanderbilt's huge Renaissance Revival château, where my mother and grandmother took me on many occasions. One trip in particular, when I was maybe ten years old, helped solidify my future career path. During that visit, the architect Richard Morris Hunt's scale model and drawings for the house were on display, and I stood transfixed in front of them. They were a revelation for me, proof that I could combine my love of drawing with my desire to see structures I imagined come to life at a level far beyond a homemade cardboard village.

Biltmore House and similar great buildings of previous centuries persisted in my thinking throughout college, when I lived in Atlanta while earning my bachelor's and master's degrees in architecture at the Georgia Institute of Technology, and through the decade-plus that I spent working for a residential architecture firm before founding my own company in 2001. That childhood exposure to the power that well-thought-out places can exert led directly to the kind of architecture we practice today in my studio. Properly designed buildings, for me, have a soul, an essential quality that is founded on an engagement with the past in the form of historical styles.

When I first meet clients to discuss a new house project, many hours go into understanding their needs and wants and sharing imagery to find out what specific features or qualities truly inspire them. Knowing those things points us in the direction of an appropriate look and feel, be it Tudor or Arts and Crafts, French country or Southern farmhouse. And the boundaries of the chosen aesthetic—its characteristic proportions, materials, and details—inform our design as we move forward. The aim is not to do everything precisely as it would have been done in those earlier periods, but to capture a resonance from tradition that carries with it an impression of lastingness, of solidity.

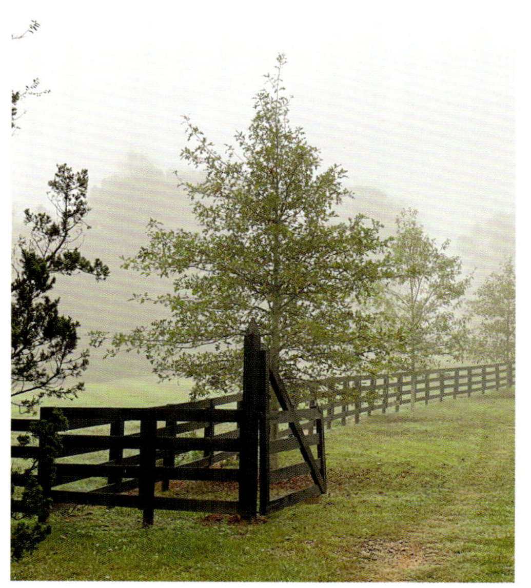

An oak allée at my Georgia farm.

My next step is to visit the site. In our initial meetings, we will have hashed out many of the fundamental spatial relationships in the dwelling—whether the kitchen should be connected to or separate from the main living space, for instance, or whether the principal bedroom suite should go on the home's main level or upstairs. Then, when I actually walk the land in person, taking in the movement of the terrain, the attributes of the natural landscape, and the quality of the light throughout the day, a sort of "bubble diagram" layout of the house-to-be starts to form in my head—thus I'm responding to the property rather than making the property respond to some preset concept. Each home I design is built solely for its exact location. You couldn't move one of my houses to another type of property; it wouldn't embody the same experience.

The homes we create are not one-person undertakings; they're the result of group effort and collaborative input. My company, to begin with, has grown into a collection of gifted and dedicated professionals, all of whose contributions greatly enrich the work we do together. Moreover, every project depends on the partnership of a team: architect, interior designer, builder, and landscape architect—each of them integral to the success of the final outcome. The most beautifully conceived room can nonetheless fail if it doesn't have sensitively chosen furnishings that harmonize with the space they inhabit, and the linking of a home to its natural surroundings by way of plantings, courtyards, gardens, walkways, outdoor living areas, retaining walls, and similar features can

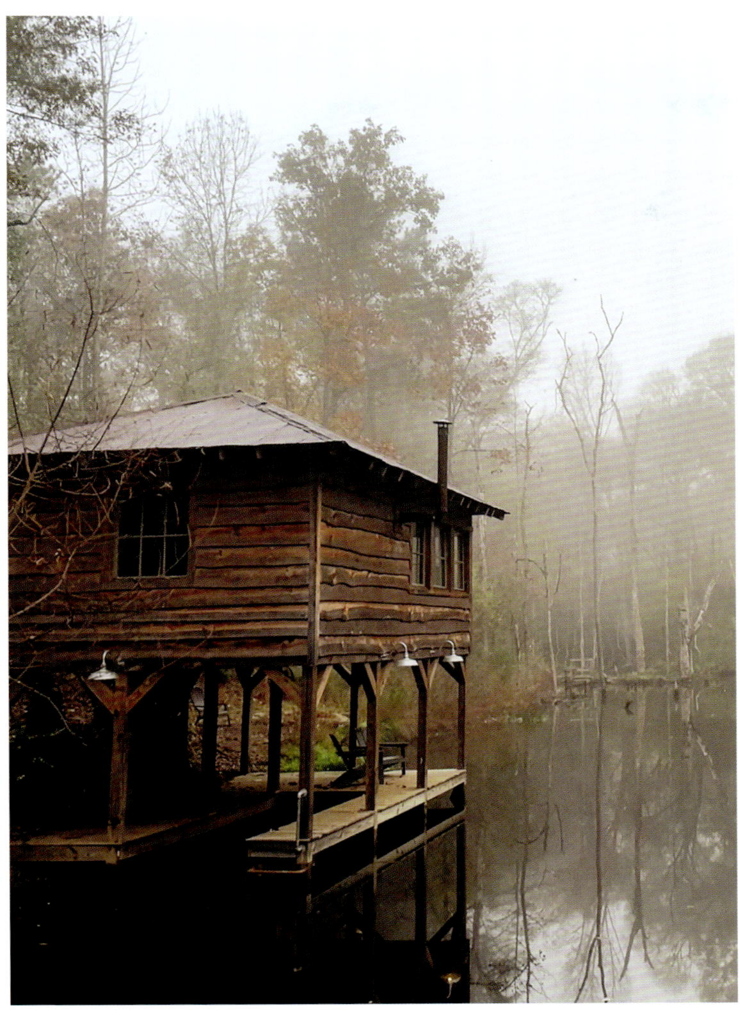

We call the farm's boathouse "the Cajun shack" because its design is based on Louisiana models. Built on the site of an old moonshine still, it extends out over the water with two boat slips underneath.

have a huge impact on the amount of pleasure you'll get from a property.

Clients, too, have a critical duty, not just in providing a vision but in their willingness to do things the right way. This level of architecture requires an investment in the finest craftsmanship and in finishes and materials that are meant to last. I'm a firm believer in wood, stone, copper, and other natural substances that age gracefully, acquiring patina and becoming lovelier with the passage of the years.

After decades in the profession, I'm still excited to see and absorb as much as I can. My library continues to grow, book by book, as I come across a volume on some regional vernacular or track down a historical reference. I continue to travel for the same reason. Often on my trips, I'll intentionally take back roads that wind through smaller towns and out-of-the-way places, because hidden on a residential block or fronting a courthouse square will be an architectural treasure, possibly dilapidated and little noticed yet eminently worthy of being seen and studied. The education is endless.

Architecture, for me, is far from simply a profession. It's a calling. My firm's goal is to make every house a unique and perfect fit for its owners and its site: grounded in the past, designed for the present, and intended to remain beautiful and functional over the long term.

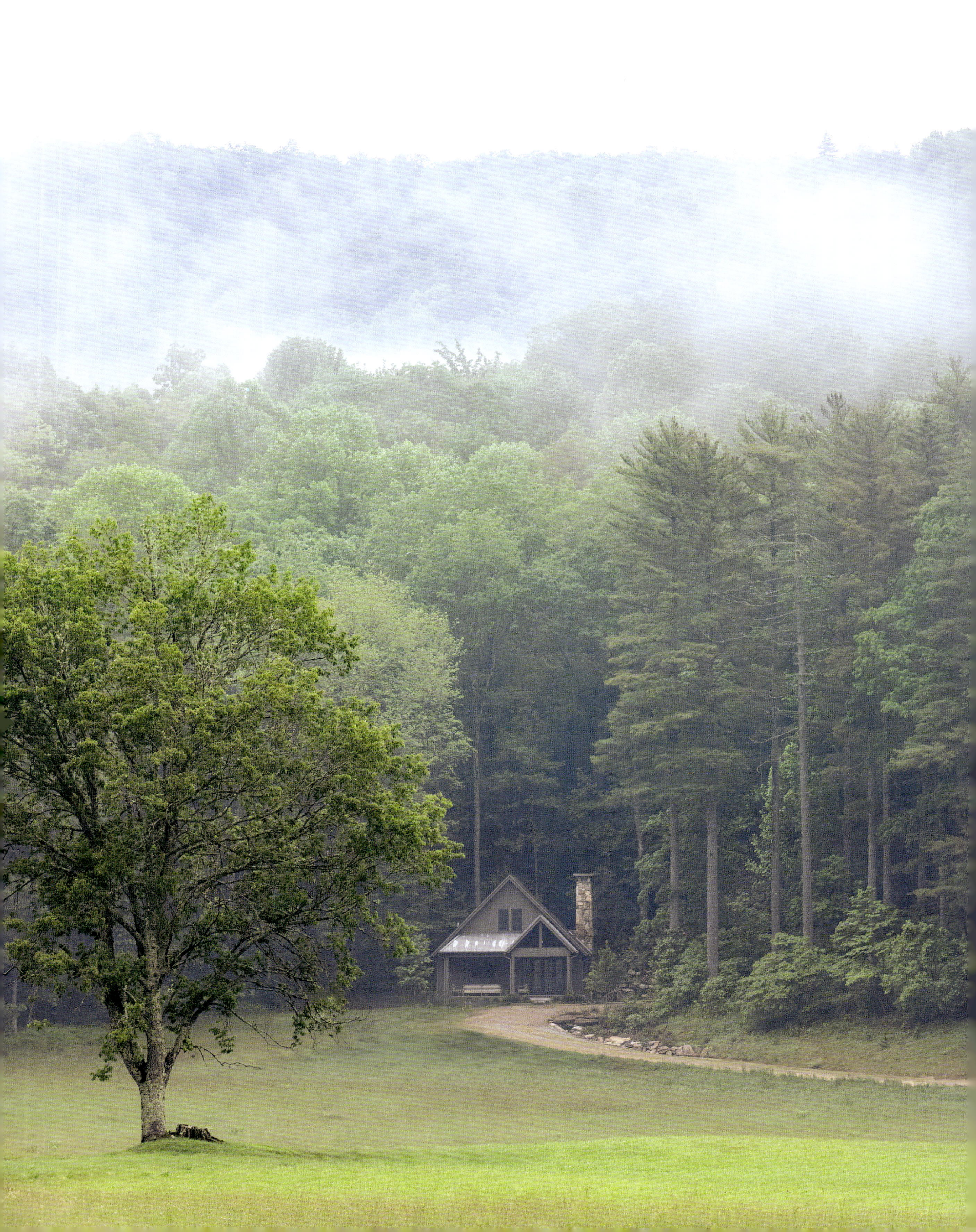

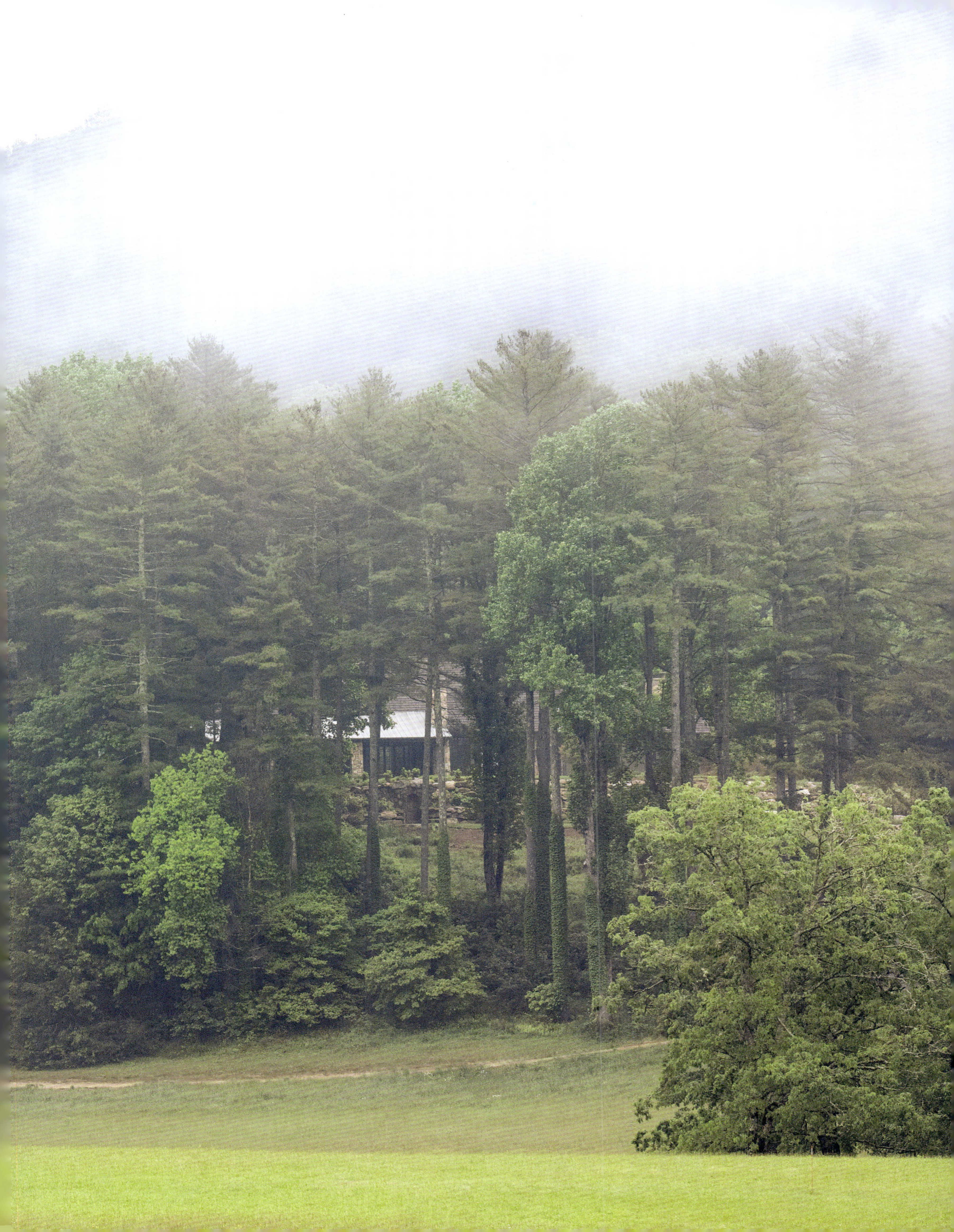

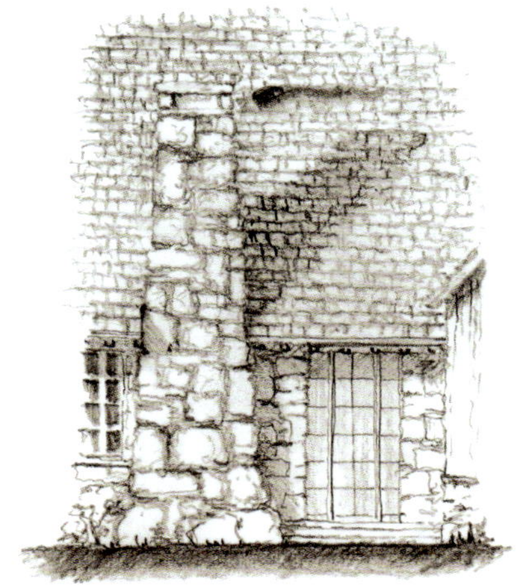

MEADOW'S EDGE

On one side of a mountain valley in western North Carolina, the woods give way to a broad, green meadow with a trout stream wandering through it. Tucked into the fringe of trees is a small building that might be an old farmhouse, its discreet gravel driveway curving off to the right. Beyond, among the trunks of a stand of pines, you catch glimpses of a rugged stone wall and an additional structure—or maybe there are two of them? The terrain higher up is cloaked in the hanging mists that give the Great Smoky Mountains their name, furnishing a wonderfully moody backdrop for the entire scene.

PRECEDING SPREAD: The various elements of this property are visible only in tantalizing glimpses, seeming to be a collection of separate dwellings semihidden in the foothills. OPPOSITE: Landscape architect Alex Smith devised the rugged stone stairway that descends the slope from the main house to one of the guest cabins. FOLLOWING SPREAD: A pair of monumental chimneys add textural interest upon arrival. PAGE 20: Intersecting vaulted ceilings define the living and dining spaces. Relatively sleek, modern furnishings in the home counterpoint the rustic notes of its architecture.

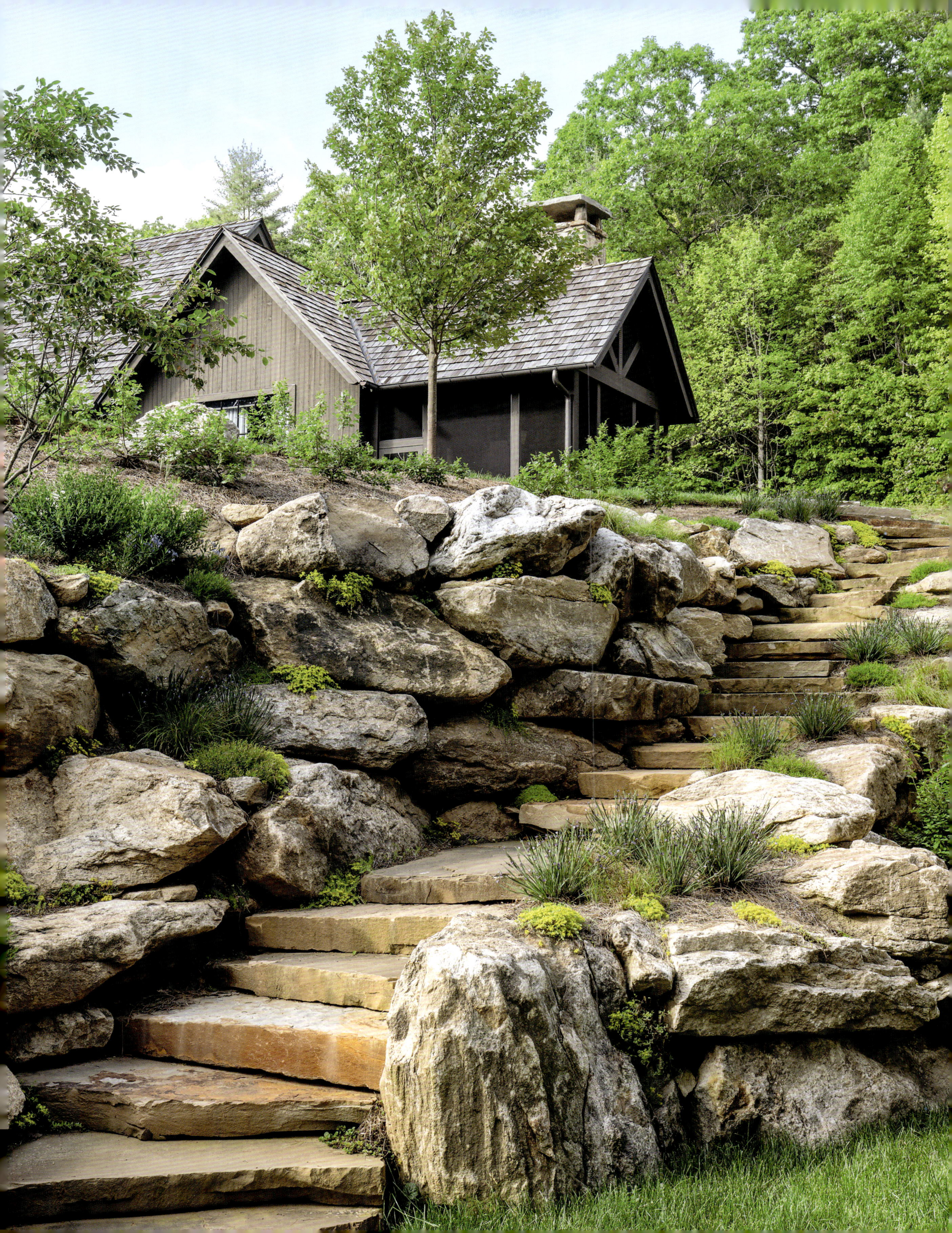

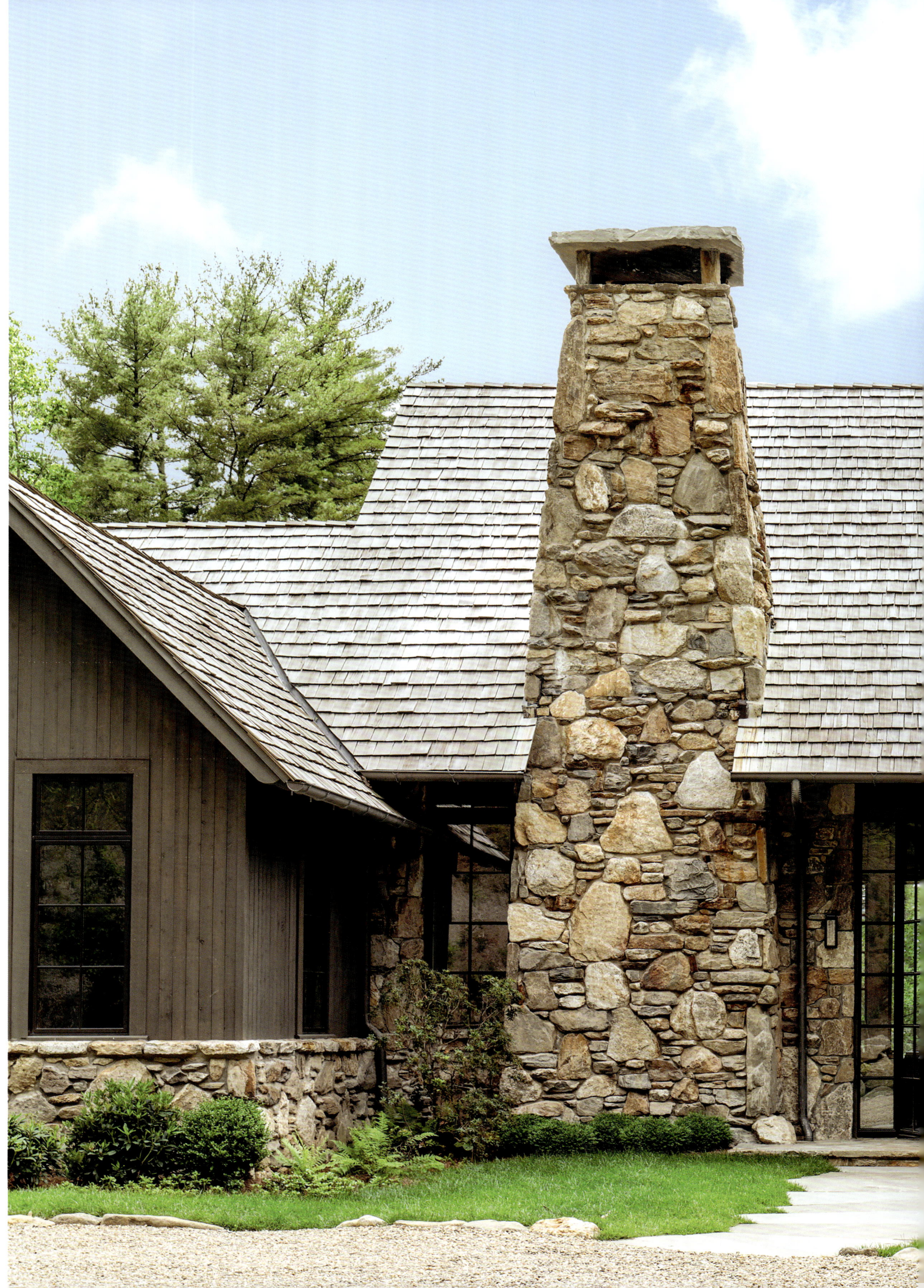

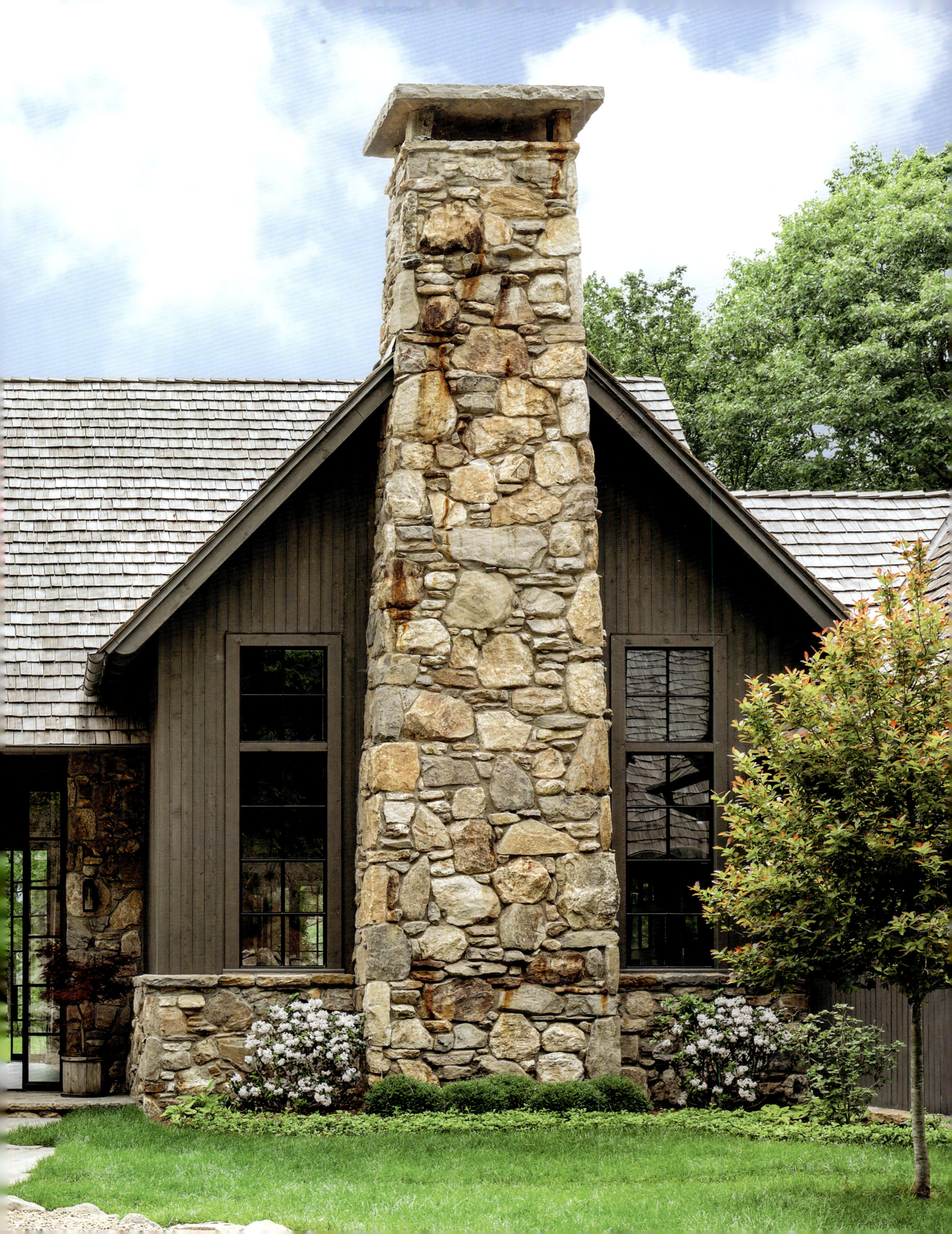

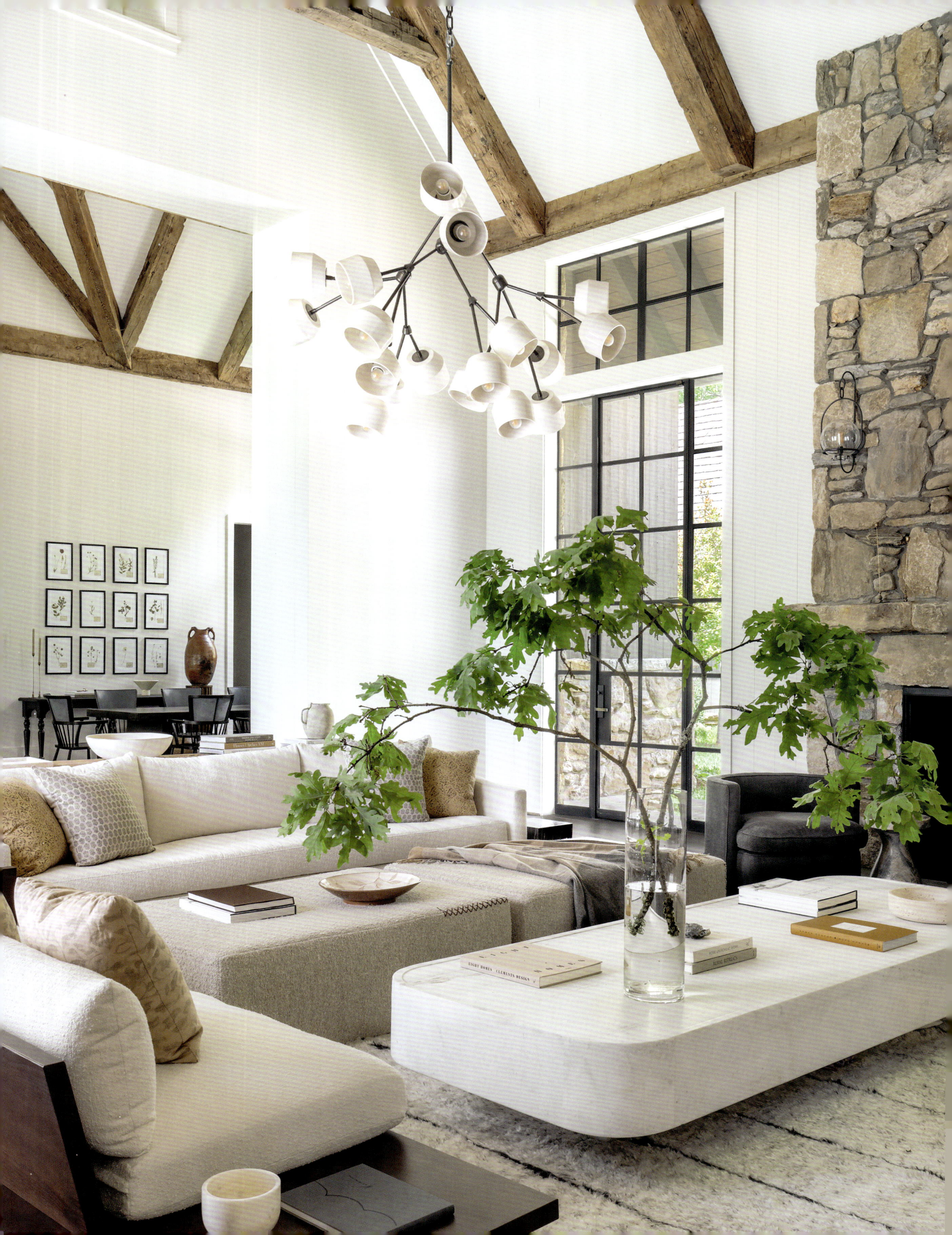
EIGHT HOMES CLEMENTS DESIGN
RURAL RETREATS

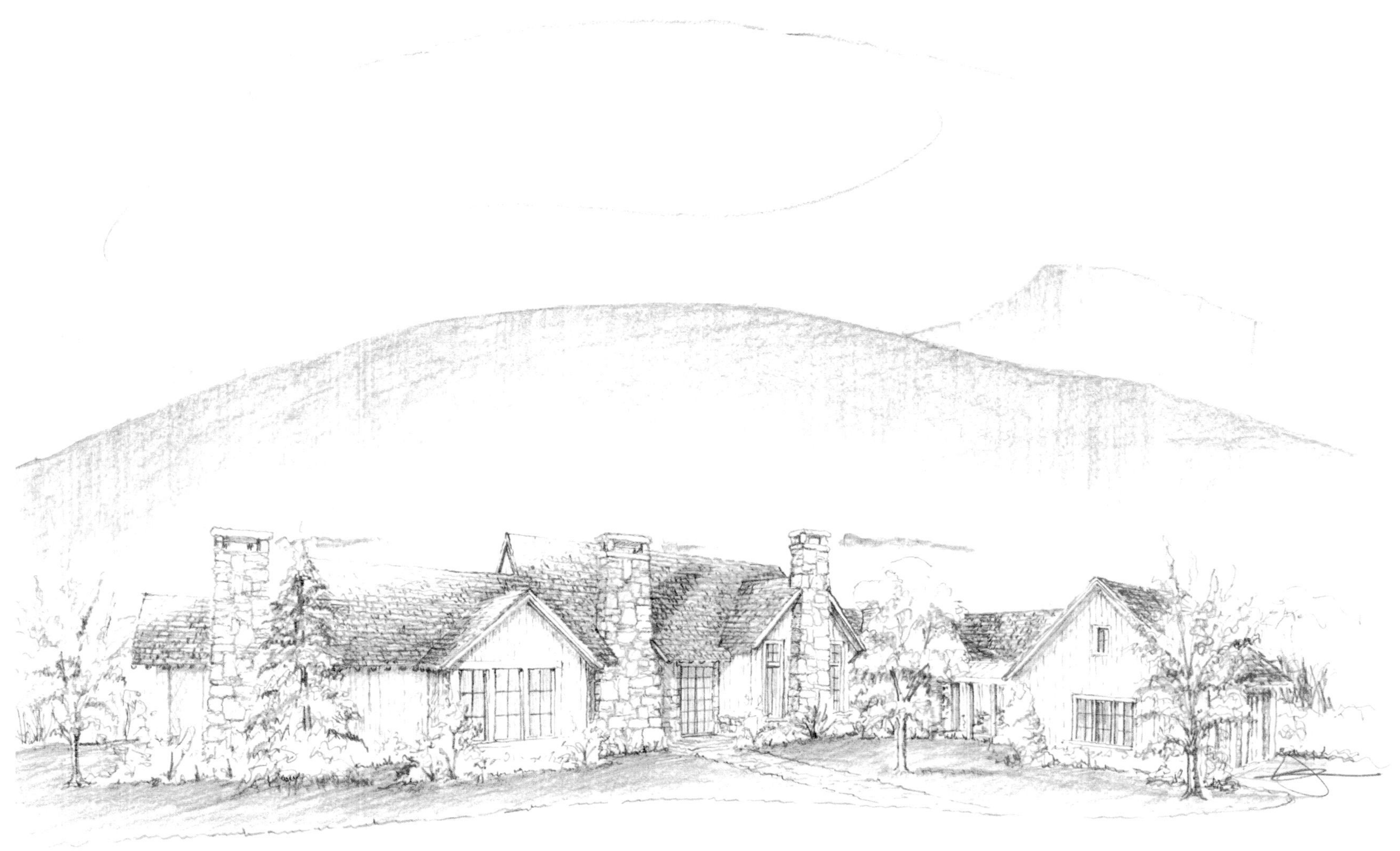

This is the setting for a warm-weather residence for a young family from Atlanta. The property's unobtrusive public face disguises a complex program that brings together four different living experiences: A fully kitted-out main house serves as home base and entertaining venue for the family during the summer. Two guest cabins of differing characters provide quarters for overnight visitors. And, finally, a hidden outdoor terrace and wine cave make for a romantic escape when the mood hits. We took advantage of the contours of the land and the transition from shady forest to sun-drenched grass to imbue each location with its own distinct ambience.

The region around Cashiers, North Carolina, is known for having a lot of steep topography; homes there often include multiple stories embedded in rocky slopes. So by local standards, we were working with a very flat piece of ground. The main house mostly spreads out on one level atop a little plateau that was cleared long ago to plant an apple orchard. Although large pine trees surround the site, they're some distance away, allowing space for a lawn that sweeps completely around the home's back side and offers equally sweeping views toward the meadow below.

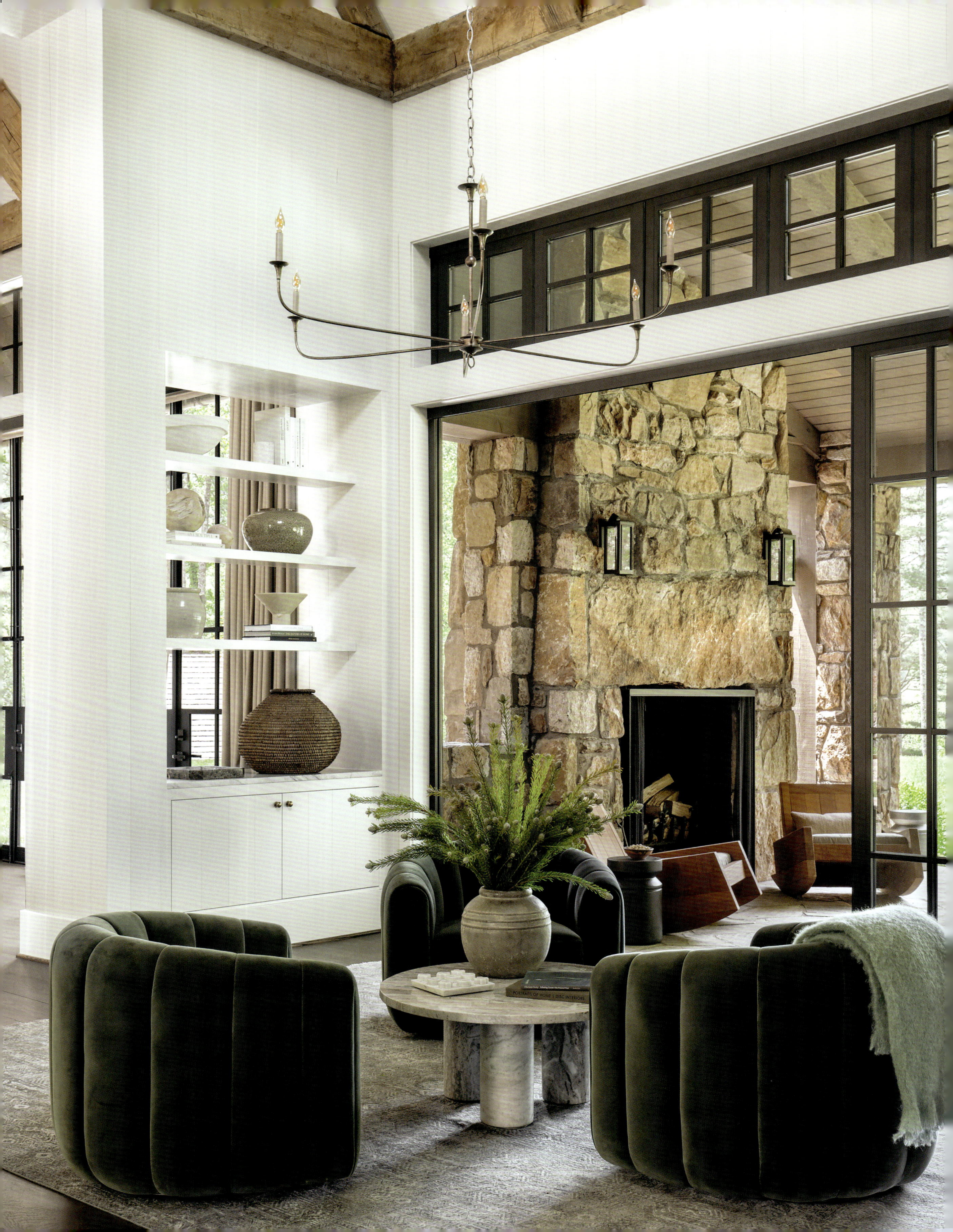

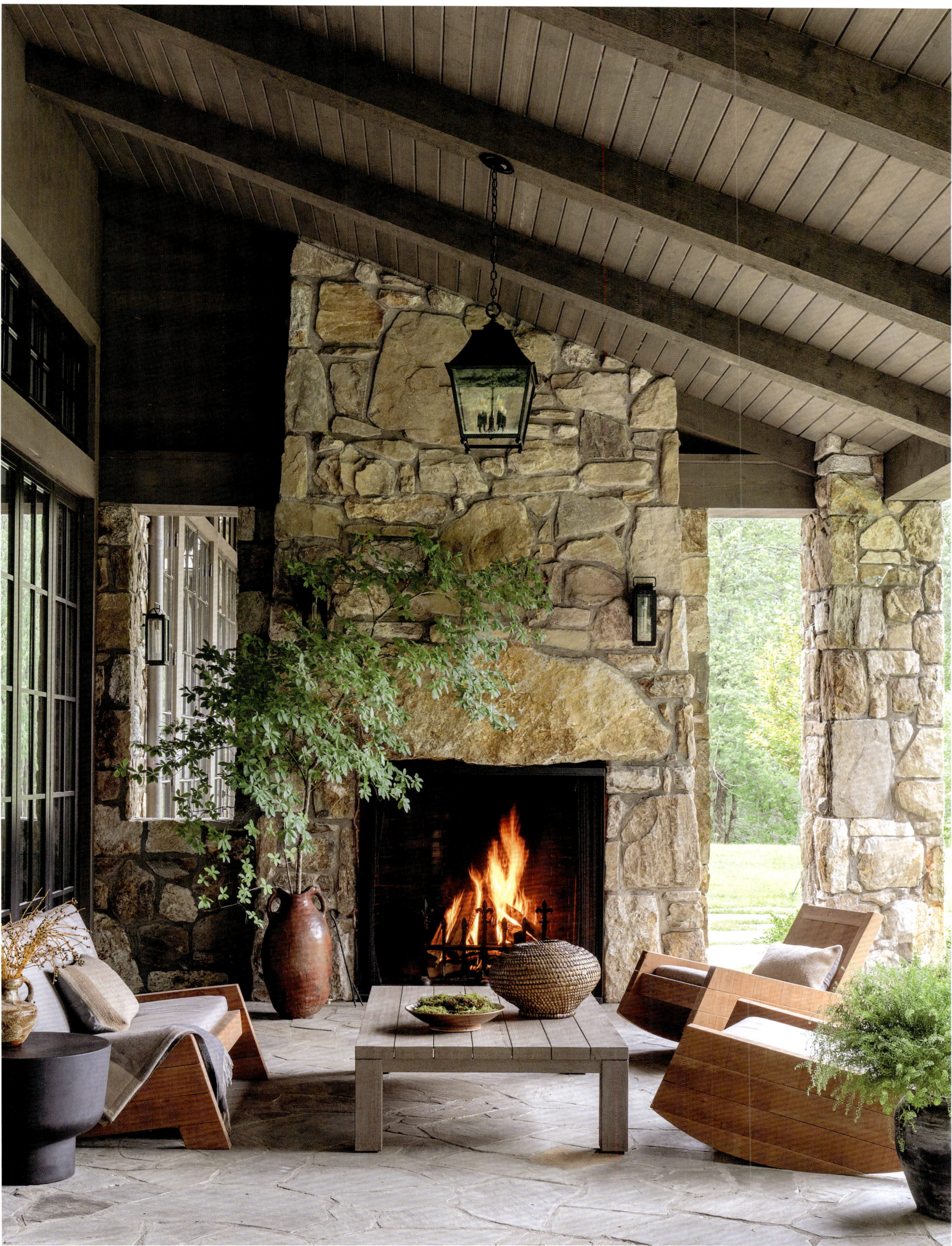

We therefore designed the rear of the home for optimal ease of access between inside and out, both visually and on foot.

Tall steel-and-glass doors capped by transoms in the great room, a big expanse of windows in the principal bedroom, and a private screened porch attached to the primary suite all look out across the lawn. A larger covered porch wraps around the kitchen and a sitting area adjacent to the dining room, reached via a series of bifold doors for effortless traffic flow during parties and barbecues. A monumental fireplace anchors one end of the porch—a reliable source of enticing atmosphere as well as physical warmth—and stone columns frame the landscape.

Approaching the home's entry door from the front, you can see straight through for a glimpse of Whiteside Mountain in the distance. The central core of the house contains the public gathering areas: great room, dining room (with the attached seating I mentioned earlier), and kitchen. I've never been a fan of typical "open-concept" layouts, where living, dining, and cooking functions are all lined up, bang-bang-bang, as a single unit. While the spaces here are interconnected, they're also individually defined by their wall and ceiling treatments and by the cased openings that link them. The dining room and great room, for example, both have vaulted ceilings with reclaimed oak trusses, but in the kitchen, the ceiling beams are laid flat in a coffered pattern for a more intimate scale.

The two guesthouses are near twins in their size, yet not so alike in their surroundings and aesthetics. One, dubbed the "woods cabin," stands on a shady, pine-covered bank slightly downslope from the main house, overlooking a trout pond. It feels rustic and cozy, with an uncomplicated silhouette, board-and-batten siding, and interior finishes predominantly

PRECEDING SPREAD, LEFT: A separate seating area is next to the covered rear porch. Double-sided display shelves within the wall balance separation and connectivity. PRECEDING SPREAD, RIGHT: The back porch ceiling slopes upward, emphasizing the sense of space and allowing ample light to reach the home's interior. OPPOSITE: A fireplace with a carved, monolithic lintel anchors the dining room's lofty ceiling and windows, while flowing draperies add soft formality.

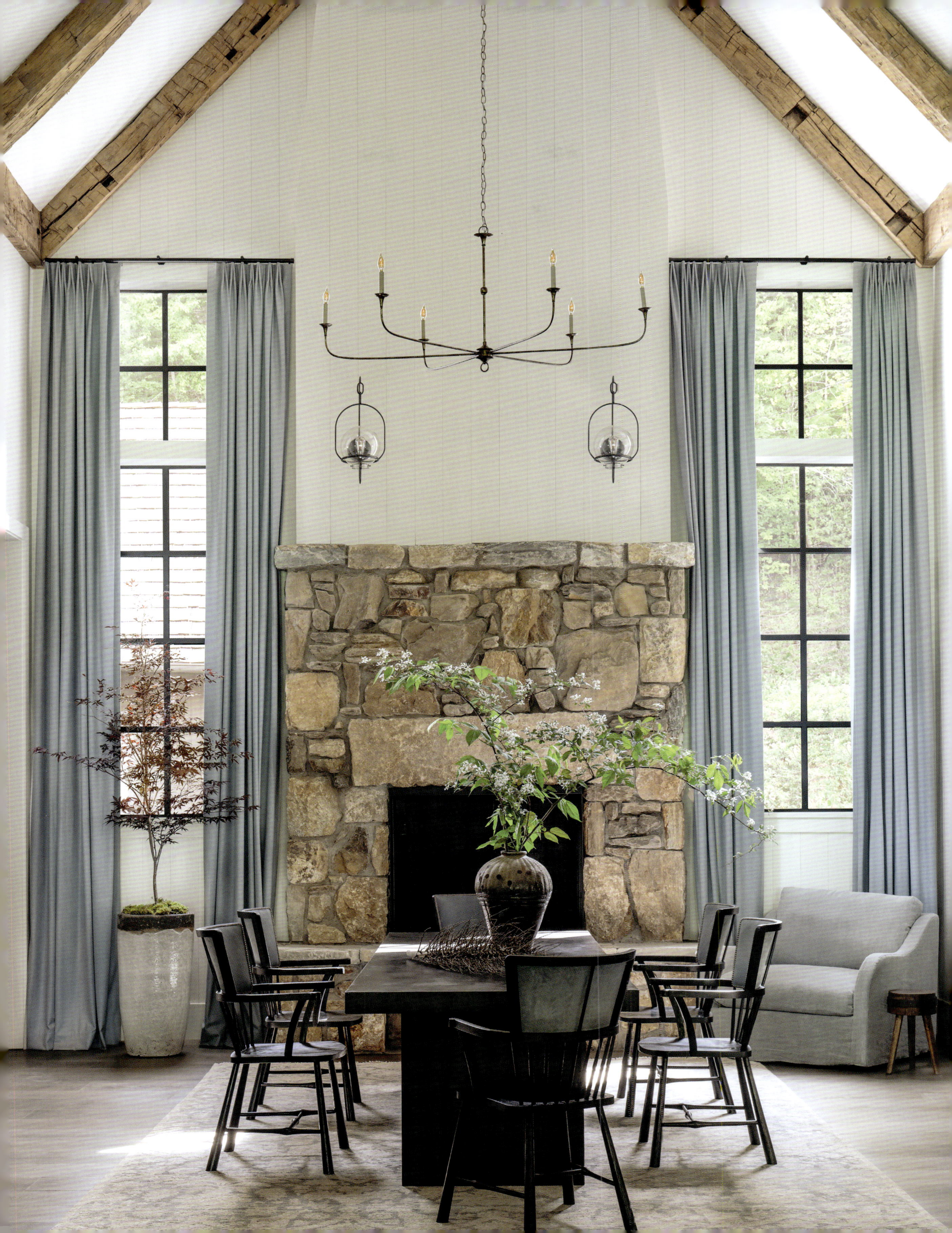

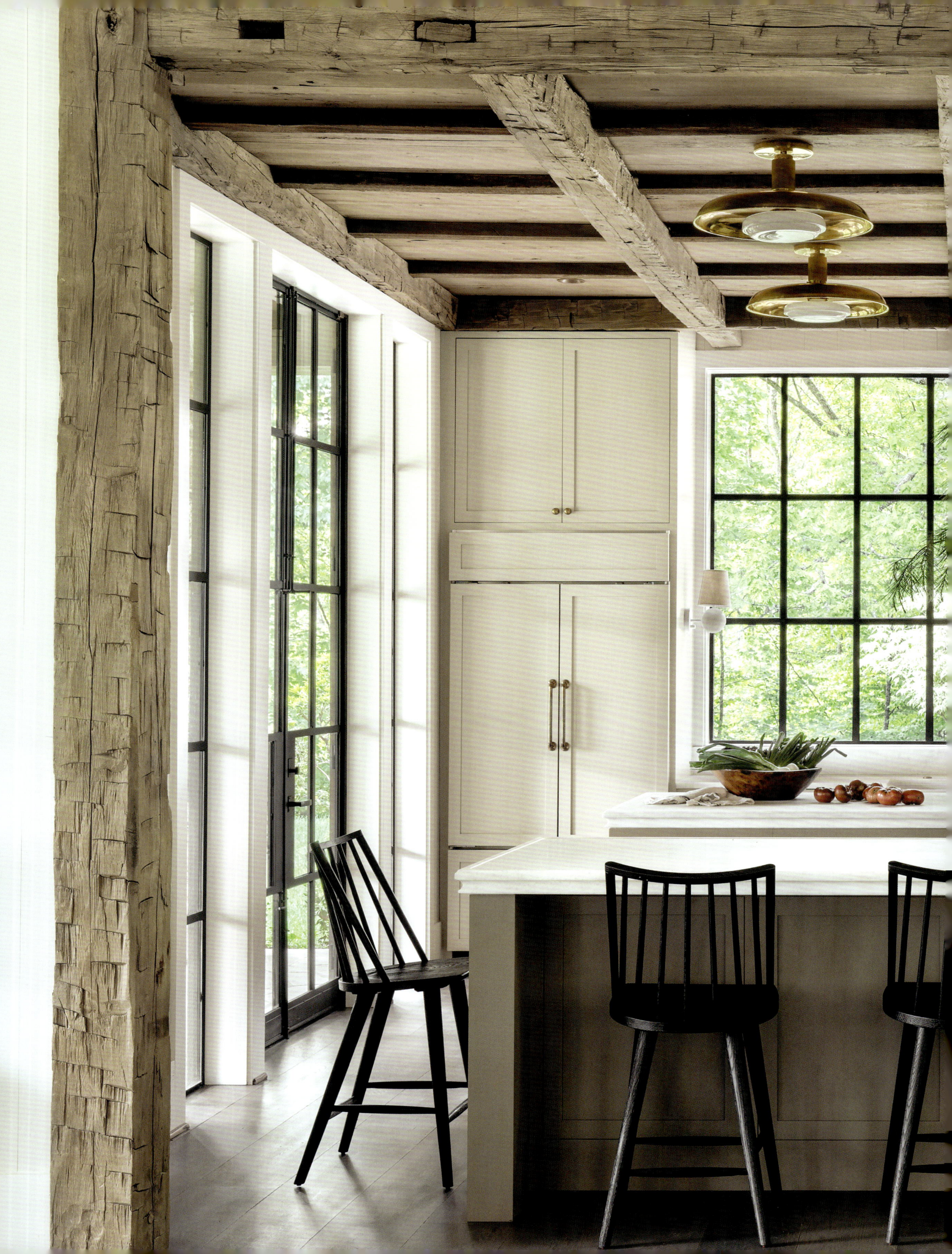

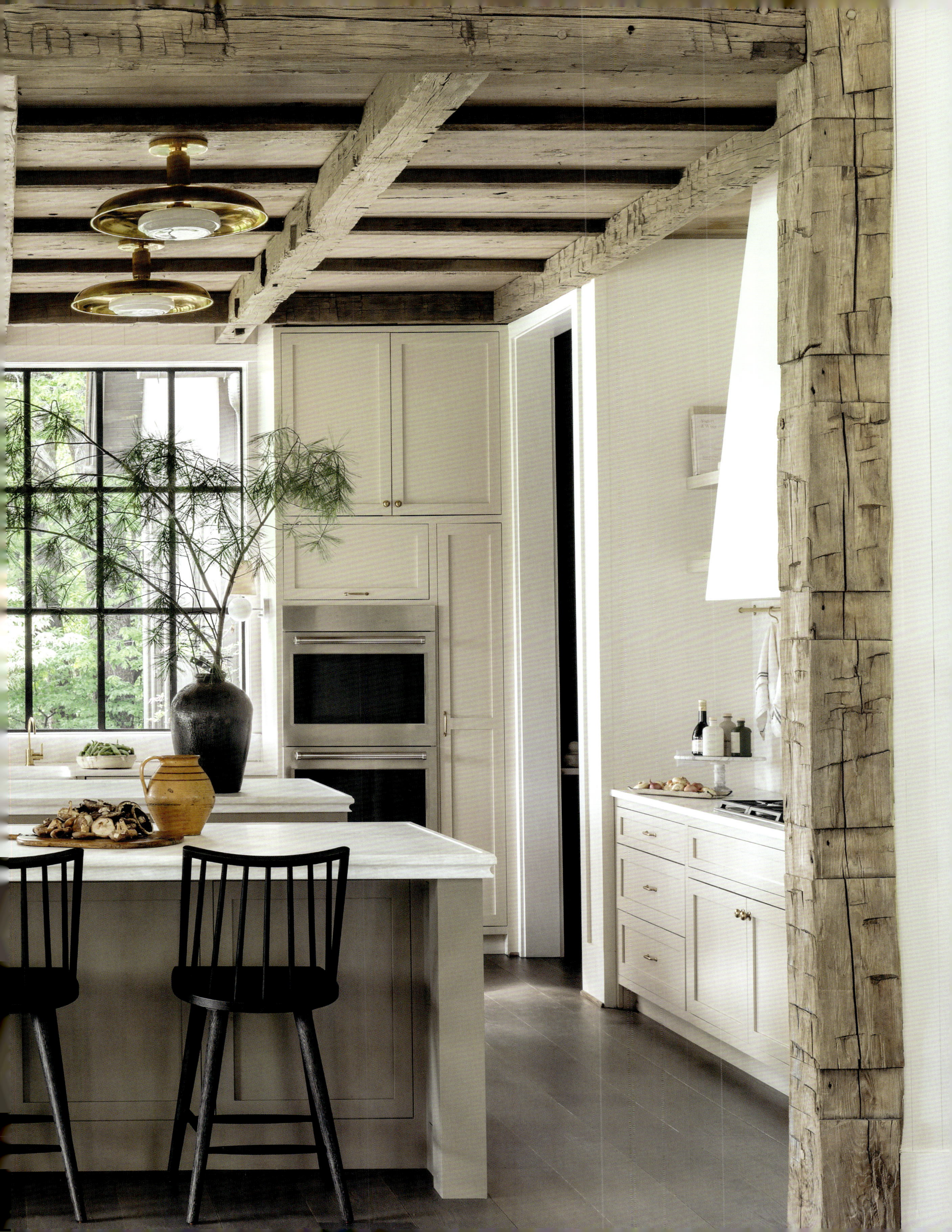

of stained oak. The "meadow cabin" is the little structure placed at the boundary where the trees stop at the edge of the meadow. Its personality is lighter, brighter, and airier.

The main house, in a way, splits the difference between these two poles. The owners didn't want to give it the full-on mountain house treatment—no antlers or birch bark, please—and instead requested a design that was a tad cleaner, neither too traditional nor too contemporary. Our approach was to take the lines and materials of a mountain house and refine them for a greater degree of sophistication. The home's stonework is its loosest, most organic element, seeming as if it has simply thrust up out of the ground to form the tall chimneys. The walls, however, are clad in smooth, butt-jointed planks rather than anything rough-hewn. And the color palette indoors is all whites and creams, with an occasional dab of blue, far from the usual dark hues of a mountain house.

A rugged stone retaining wall borders the long arc of the lawn and hides the final piece of the scheme my clients and I worked out. An underground wine cave, buried in the hillside and invisible from the house itself, opens out to a west-facing pea-gravel terrace that is the perfect spot for watching sunsets and taking in the serenity of the evenings. Sitting at a café table among the plantings, you might imagine you're in Napa or perhaps Italy. It is yet another moment of enjoyment on a property that already has more than its share.

This home performs as admirably when twenty or thirty people have been invited over as when only the couple and their children are in residence. It has a pleasant amount of polish while remaining relaxed enough to fit its natural environment. Where woods and meadow meet, we created a destination that embraces multiple points of interest within it.

PRECEDING SPREAD: A broad opening crafted of reclaimed oak timbers defines the entrance to the kitchen, which extends outward under the low-sloped porch roof. Double islands—one for food prep, one for serving—provide plenty of workspace for entertaining. OPPOSITE: A broad backsplash of warm white marble and a full-length brass rod for hanging towels and tools accent an otherwise simple plaster wall and vent hood.

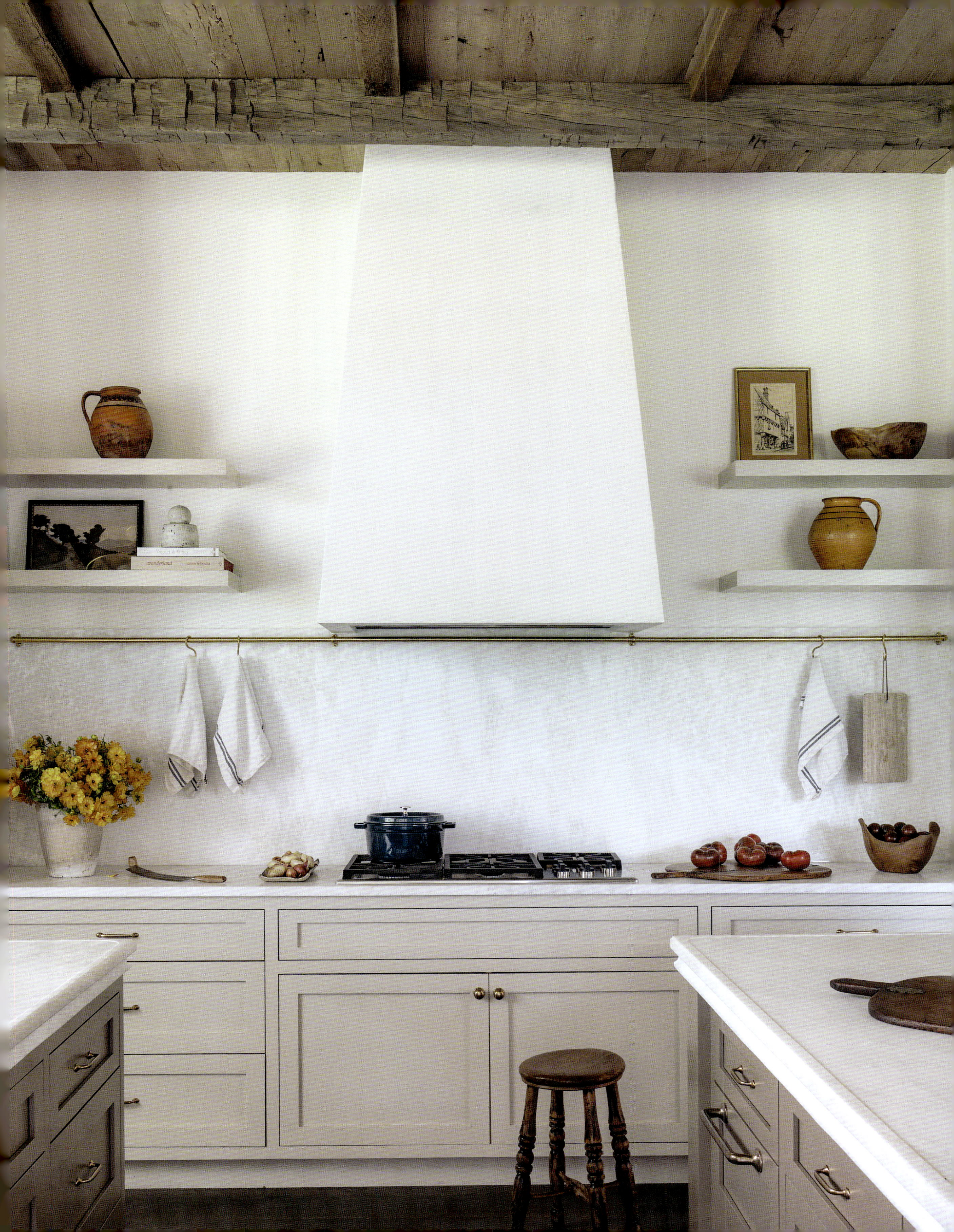

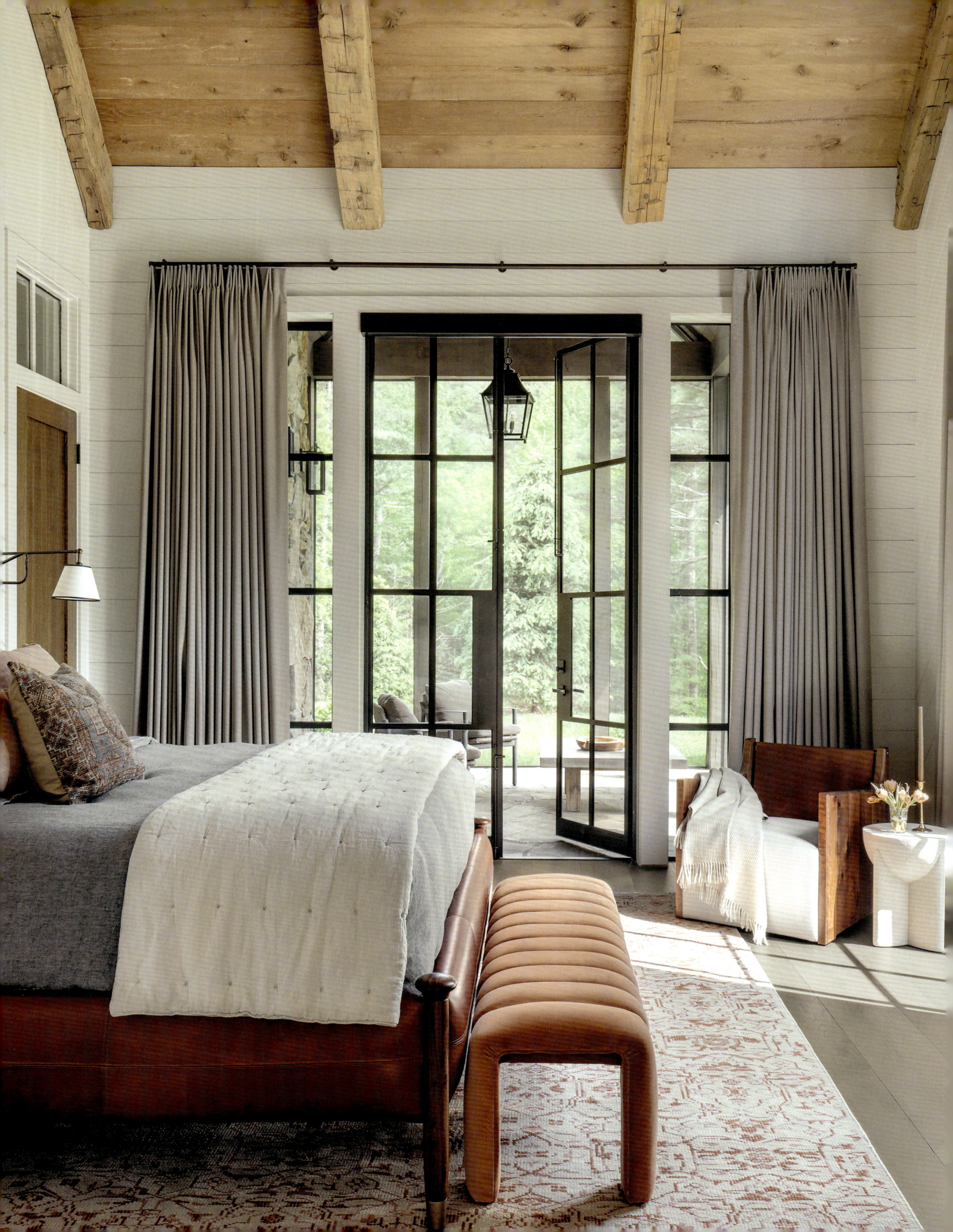

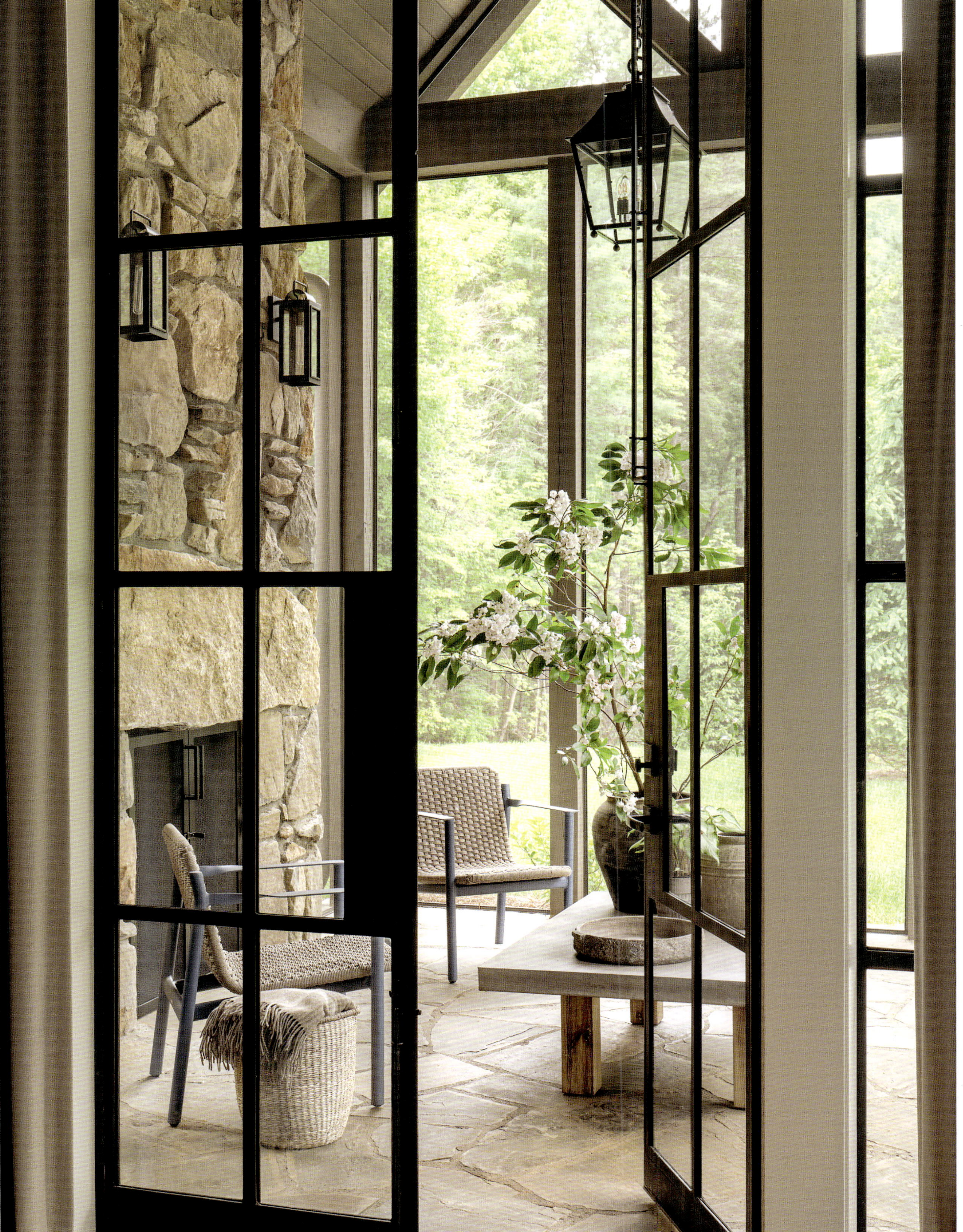

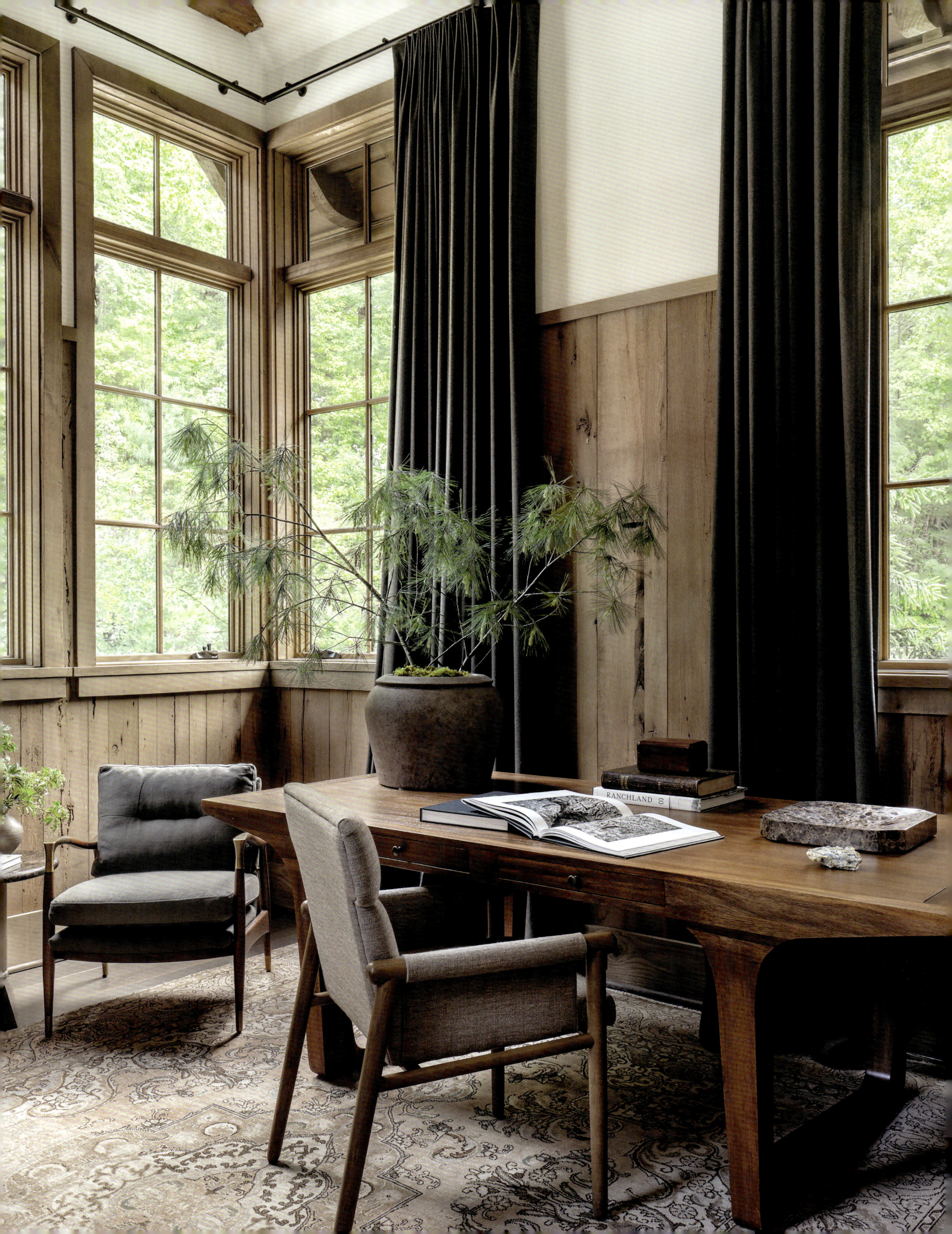
RANCHLAND

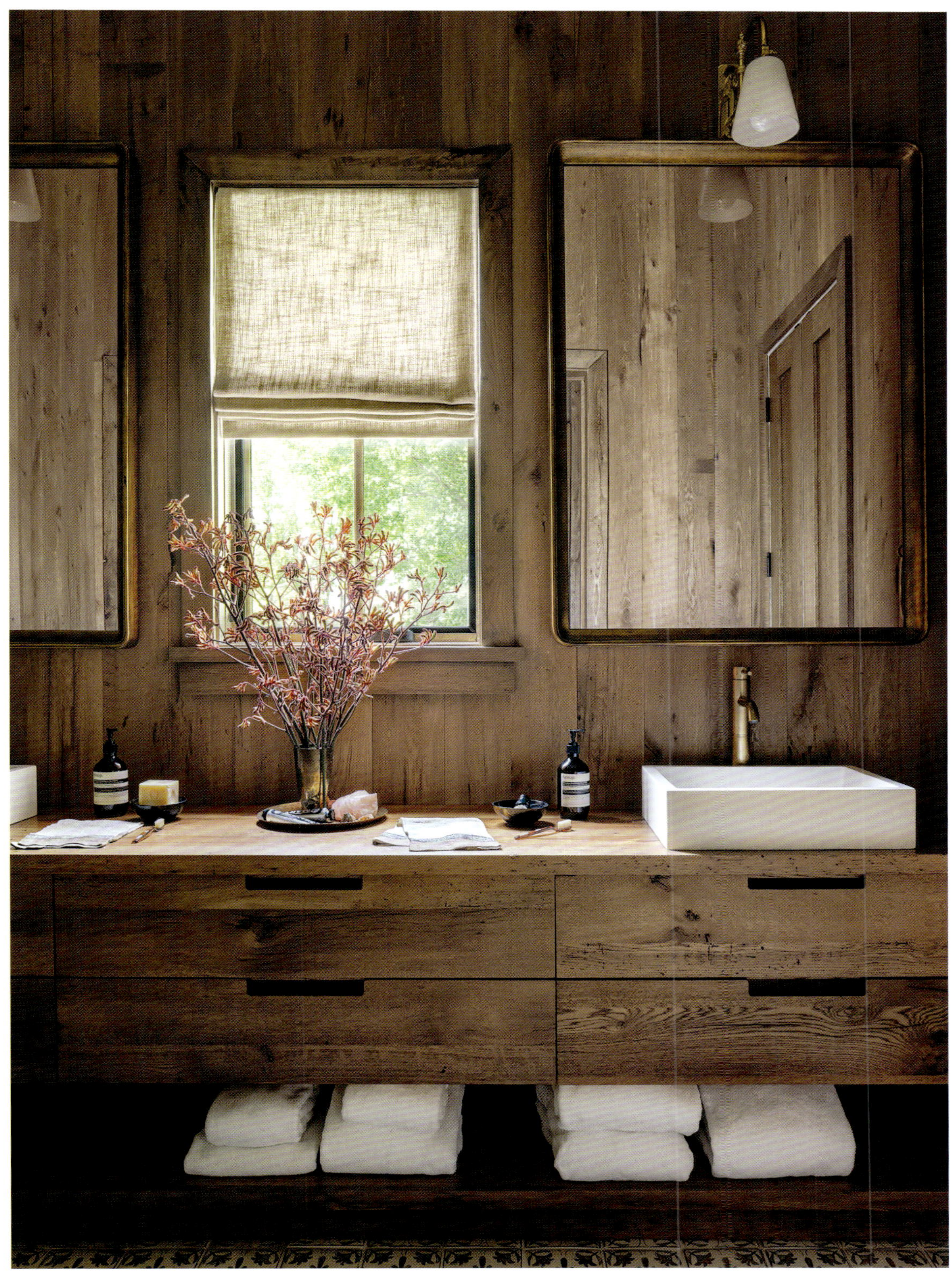

PRECEDING SPREAD, LEFT: In the principal bedroom, the bed faces the recreation lawn and mountain views. PRECEDING SPREAD, RIGHT: The principal suite features a sitting porch—a private spot for the couple to enjoy their morning coffee. OPPOSITE: The husband's office gives him a place to work during long summer stays. ABOVE: A wooden vanity matches the oak walls in this guest bath.

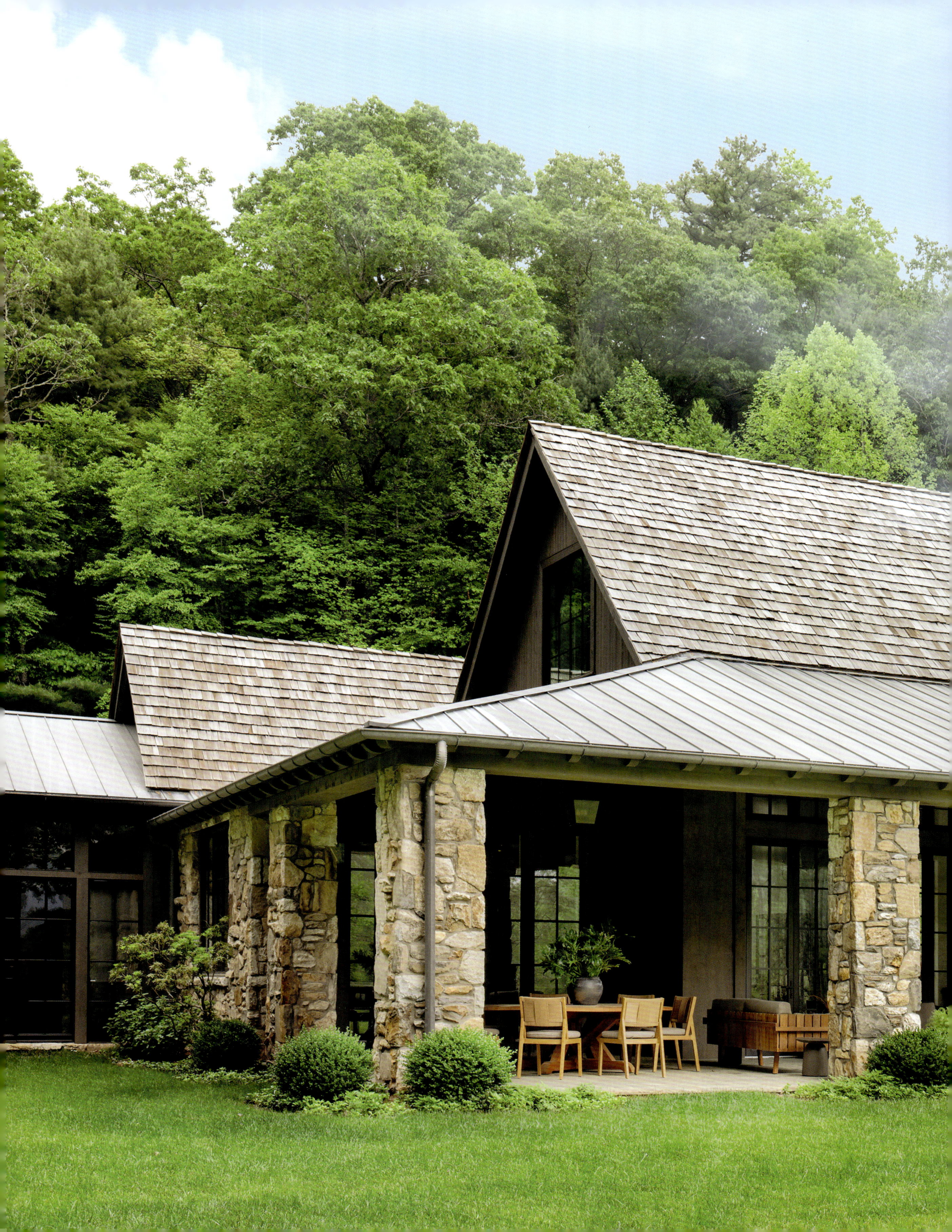

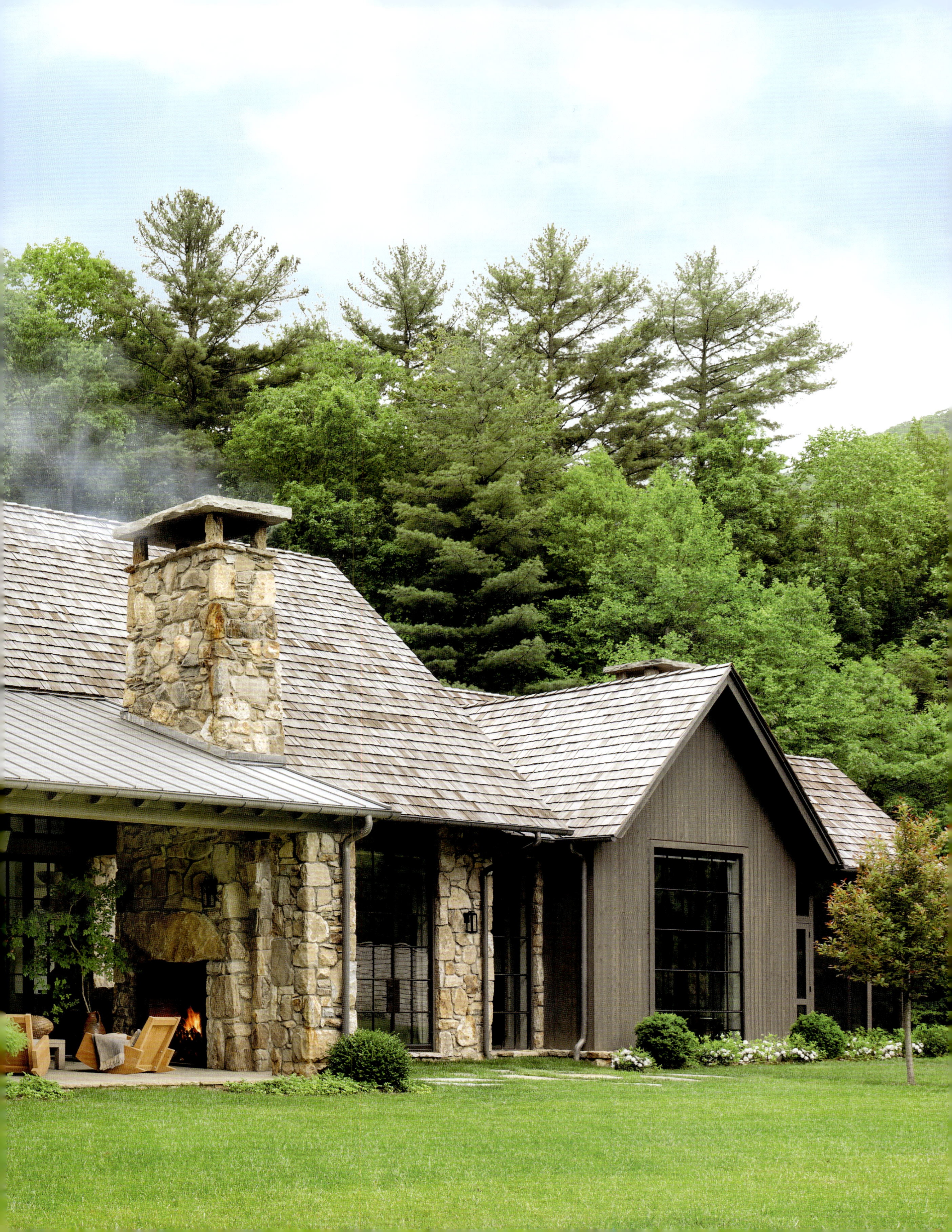

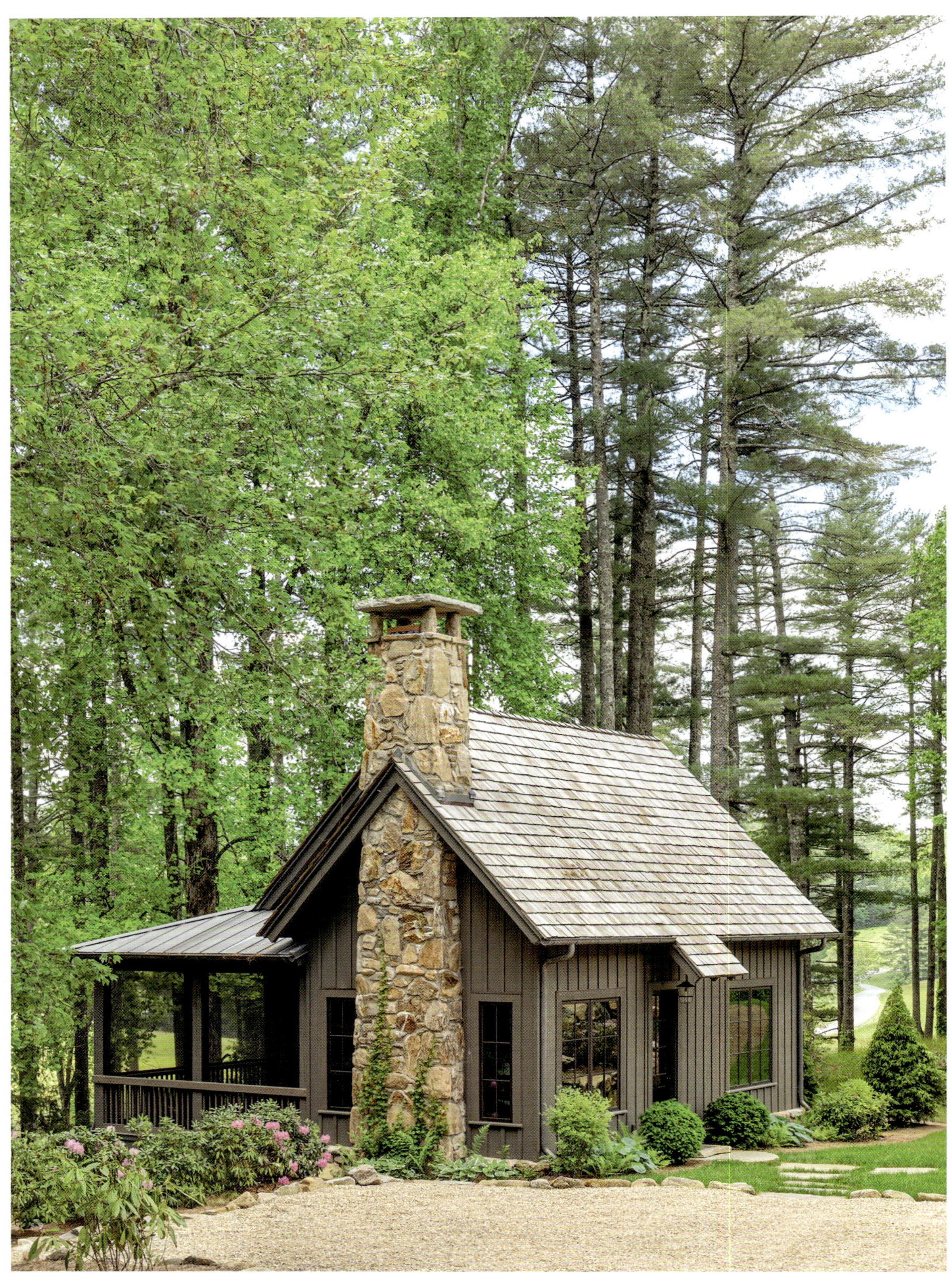

PRECEDING SPREAD: The rear of the home looks out toward a meadow that spreads below. Stone columns supporting the porch roof allow for extrawide openings. ABOVE: The "woods cabin" is simple in form and was built first, giving the family a place to stay during construction on the main house. OPPOSITE: Inside the woods cabin, paneling extends across the ceiling, walls, and chimney breast.

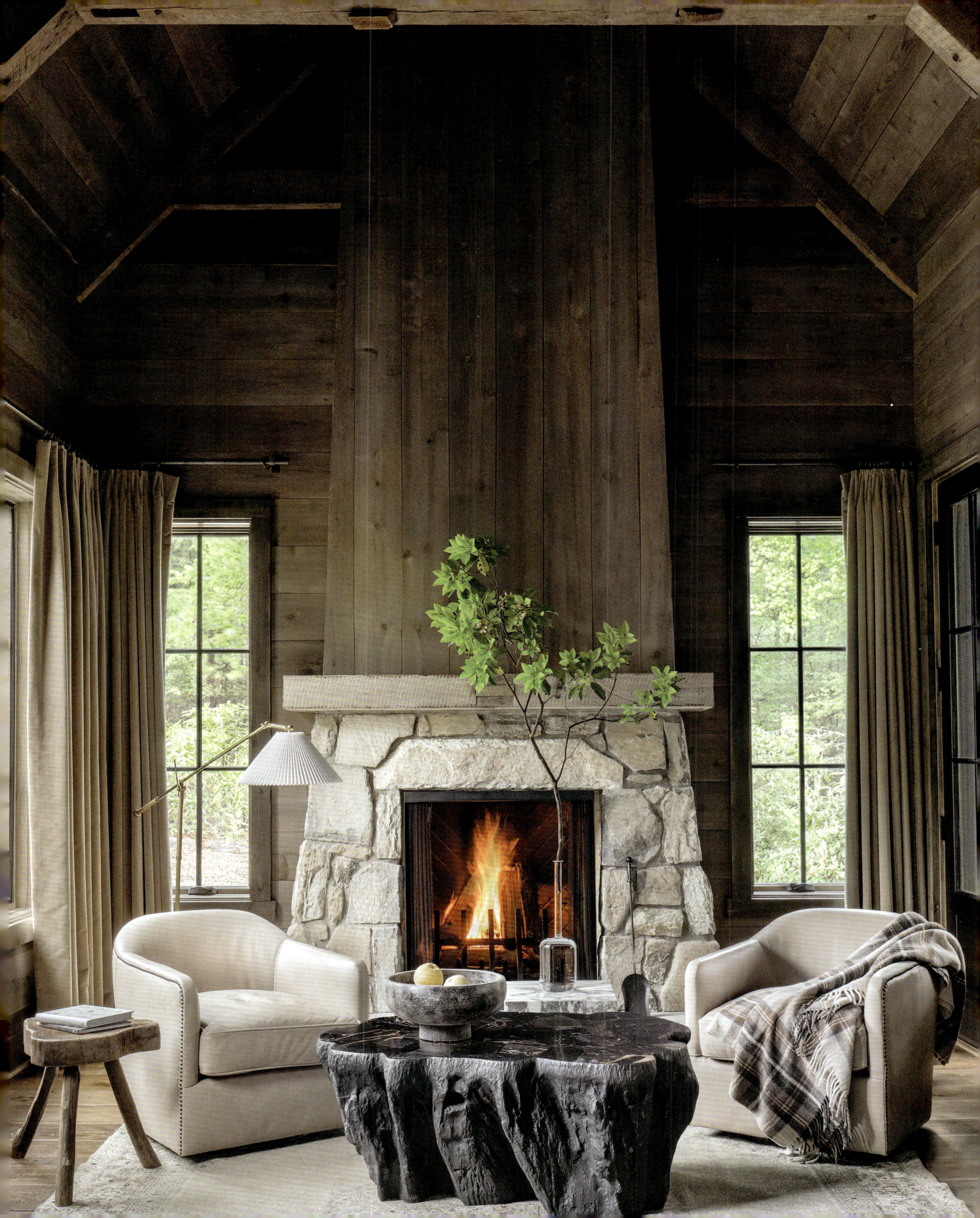

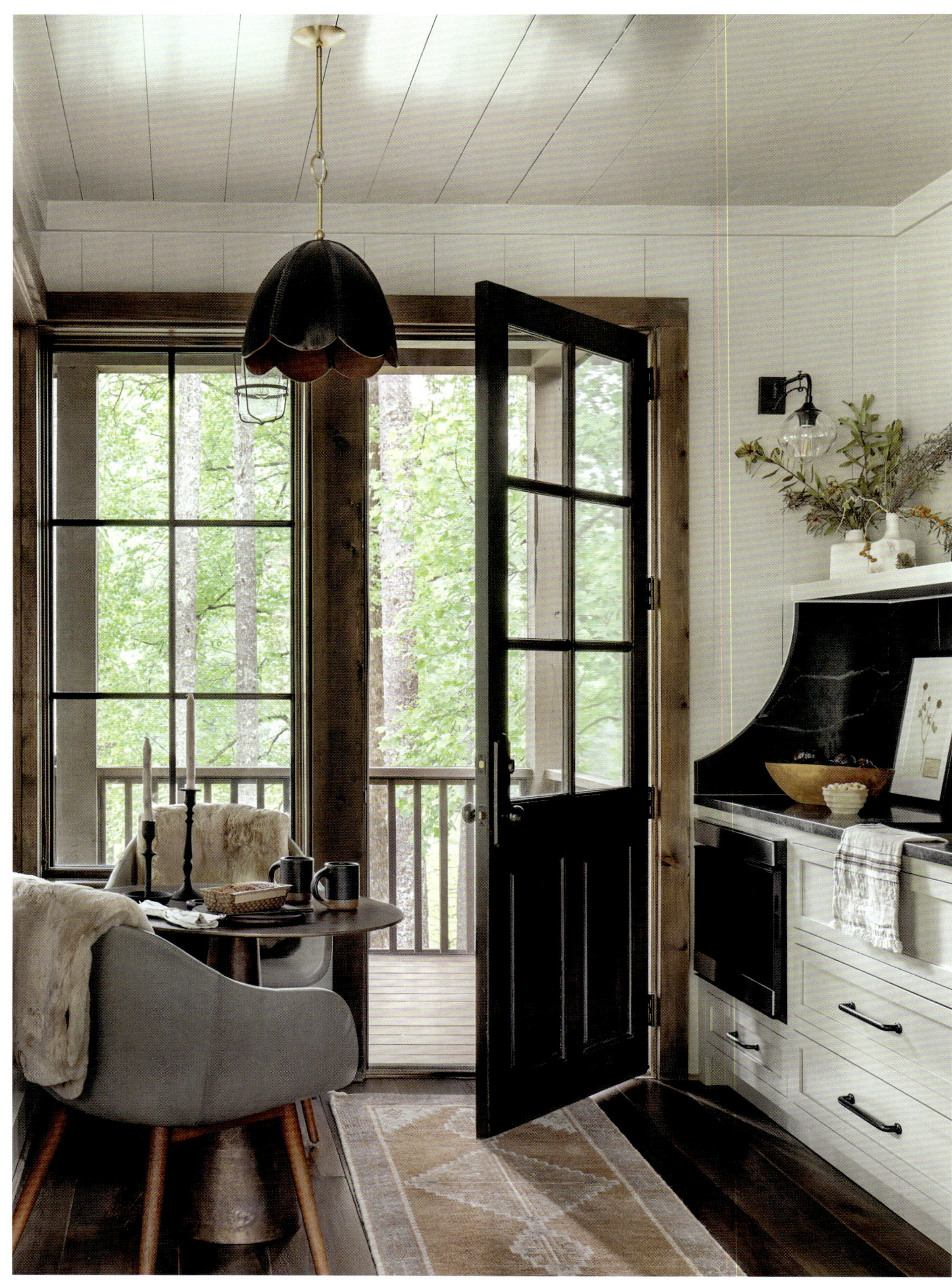

ABOVE: The woods cabin kitchen didn't need to be elaborate—a marble countertop, built-in refrigerator and microwave, and a few drawers are plenty, with a curved apron added for style. OPPOSITE: Doors from the cabin's living room and breakfast room open to an L-shaped porch overlooking a trout pond—a major draw when the weather is nice. Screens all around keep the insects at bay.

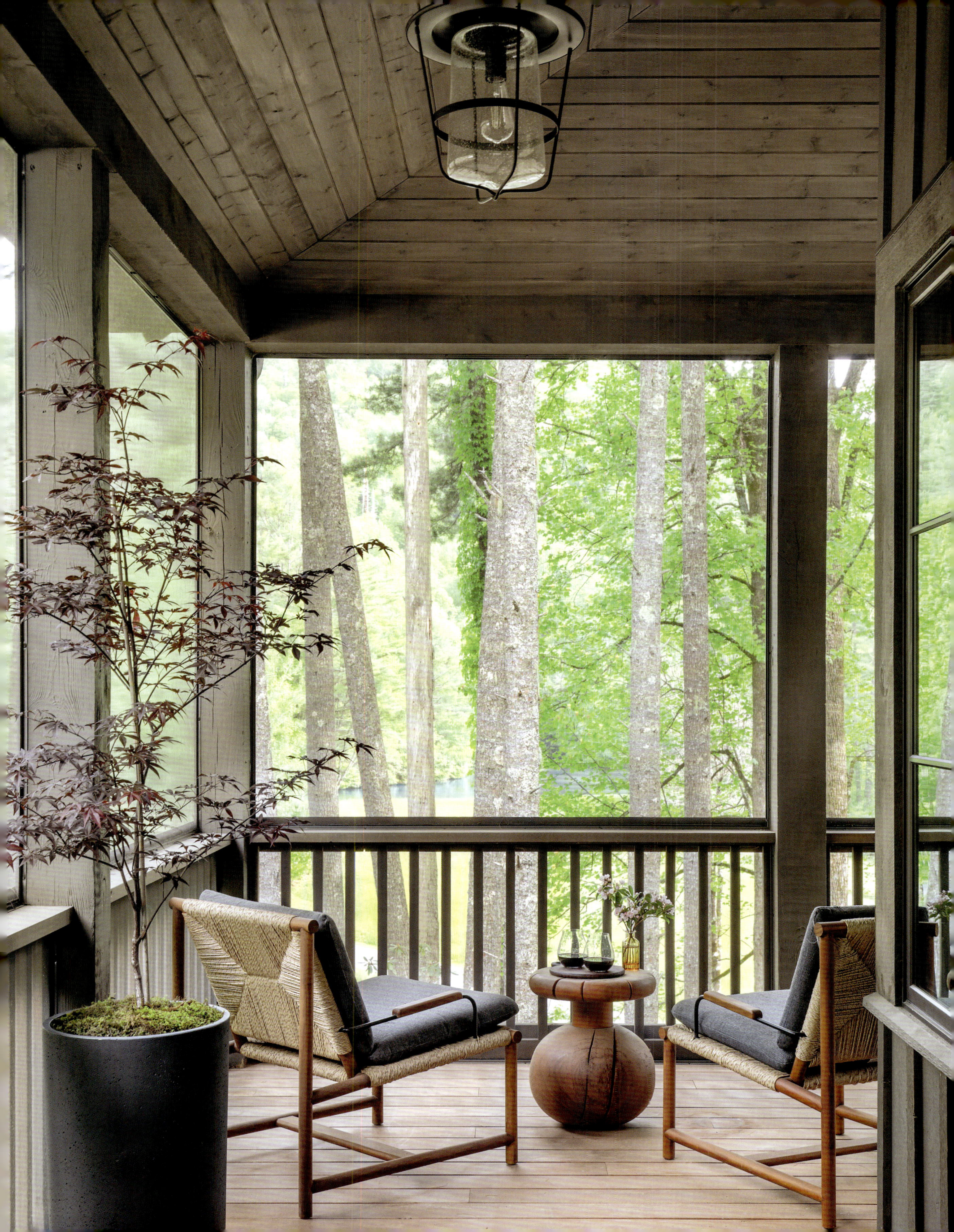

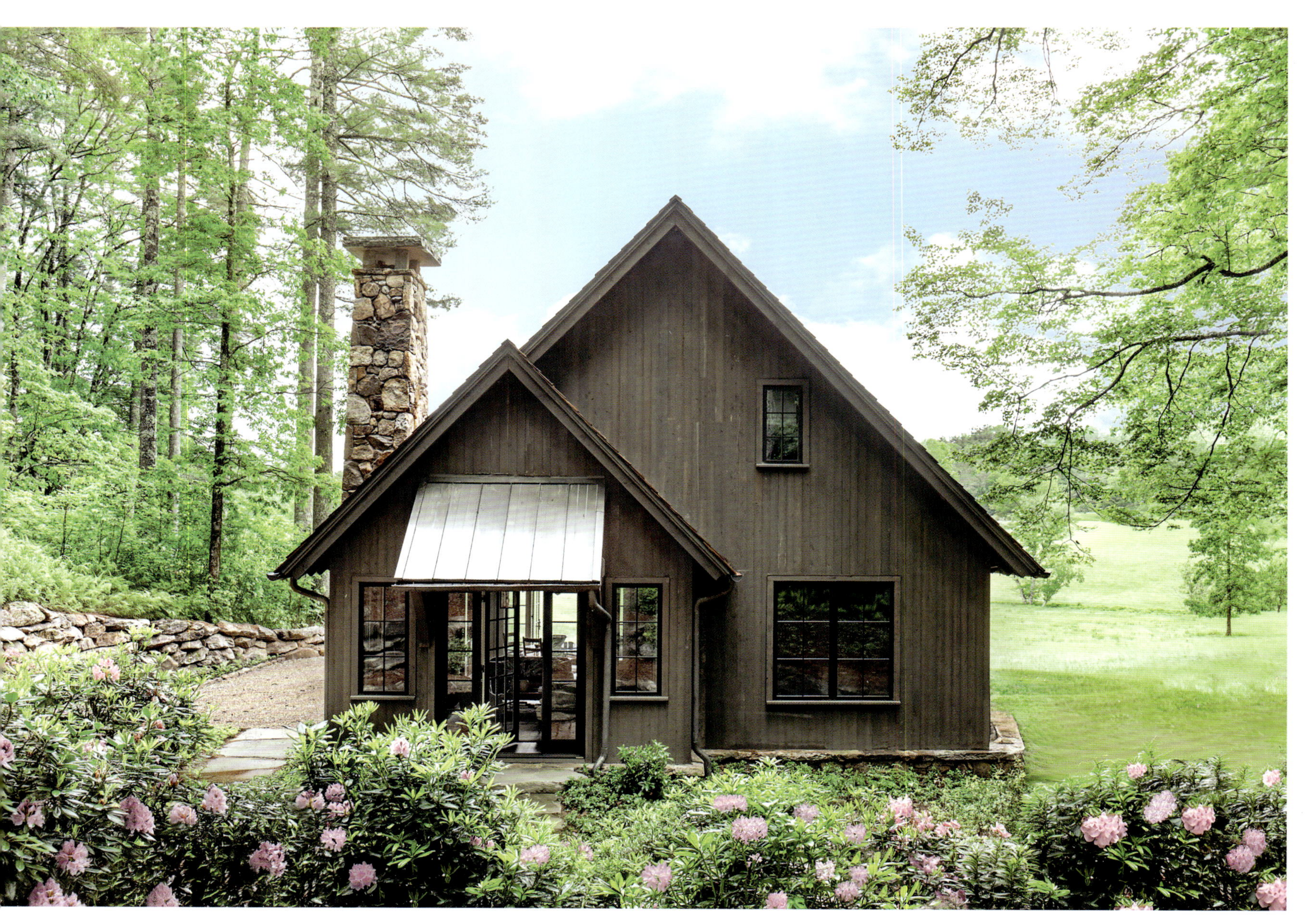

ABOVE: At the foot of the slope, just where the forest meets open grassland, stands the "meadow cabin." OPPOSITE: In keeping with its sunnier location, light tones define this cabin's interior style. FOLLOWING SPREAD: A grotto-like wine cave dug into the hillside is invisible from the main house and has to be discovered by walking down and around a stone retaining wall.

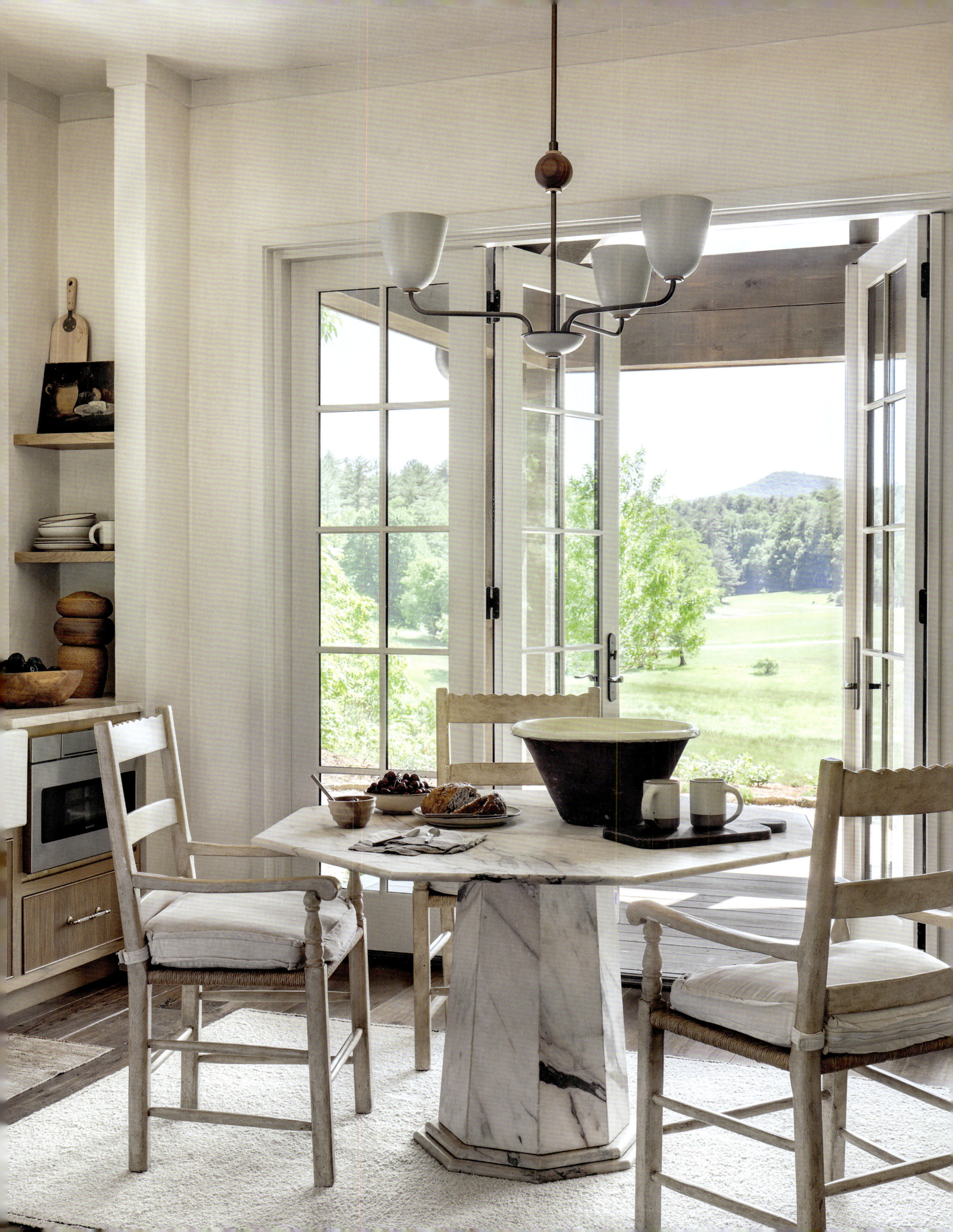

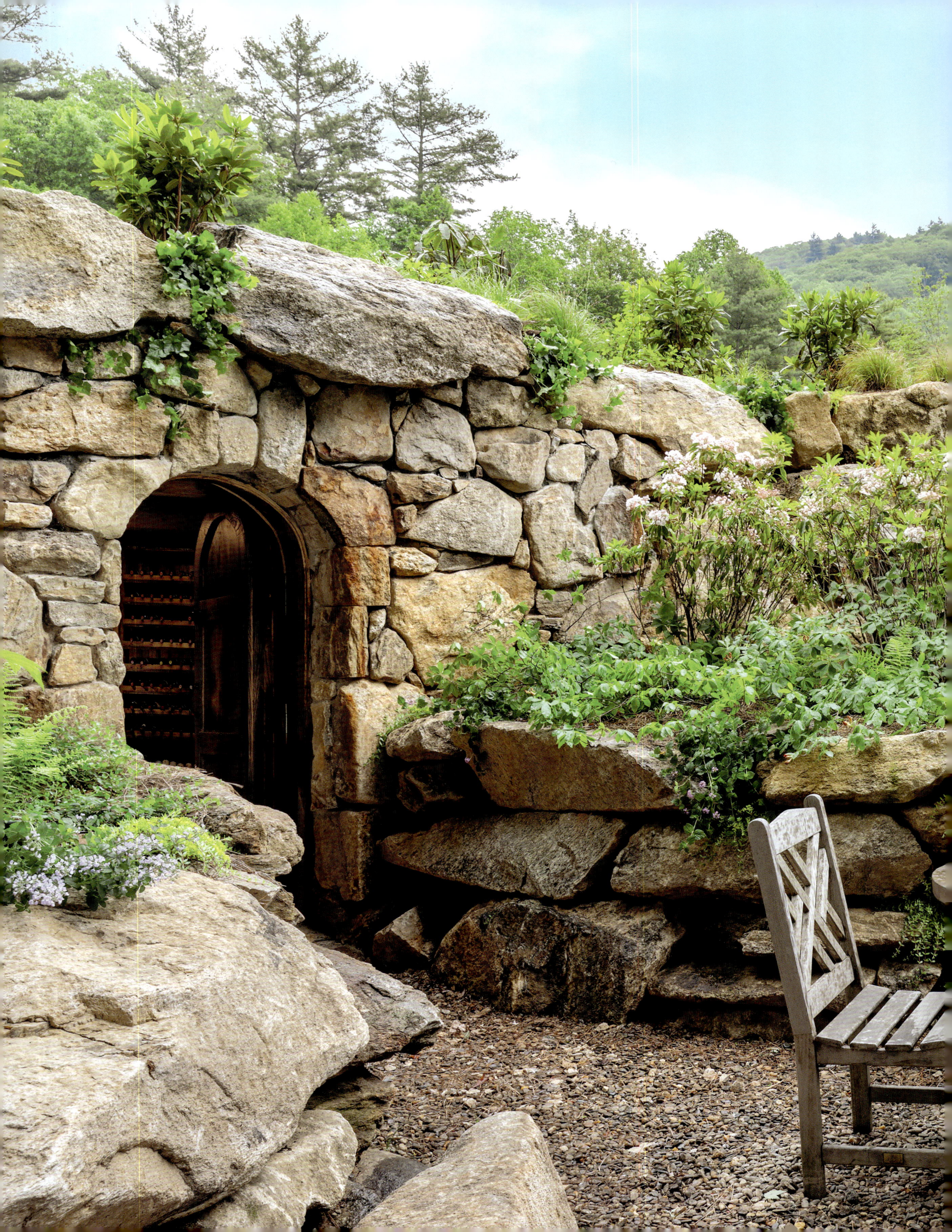

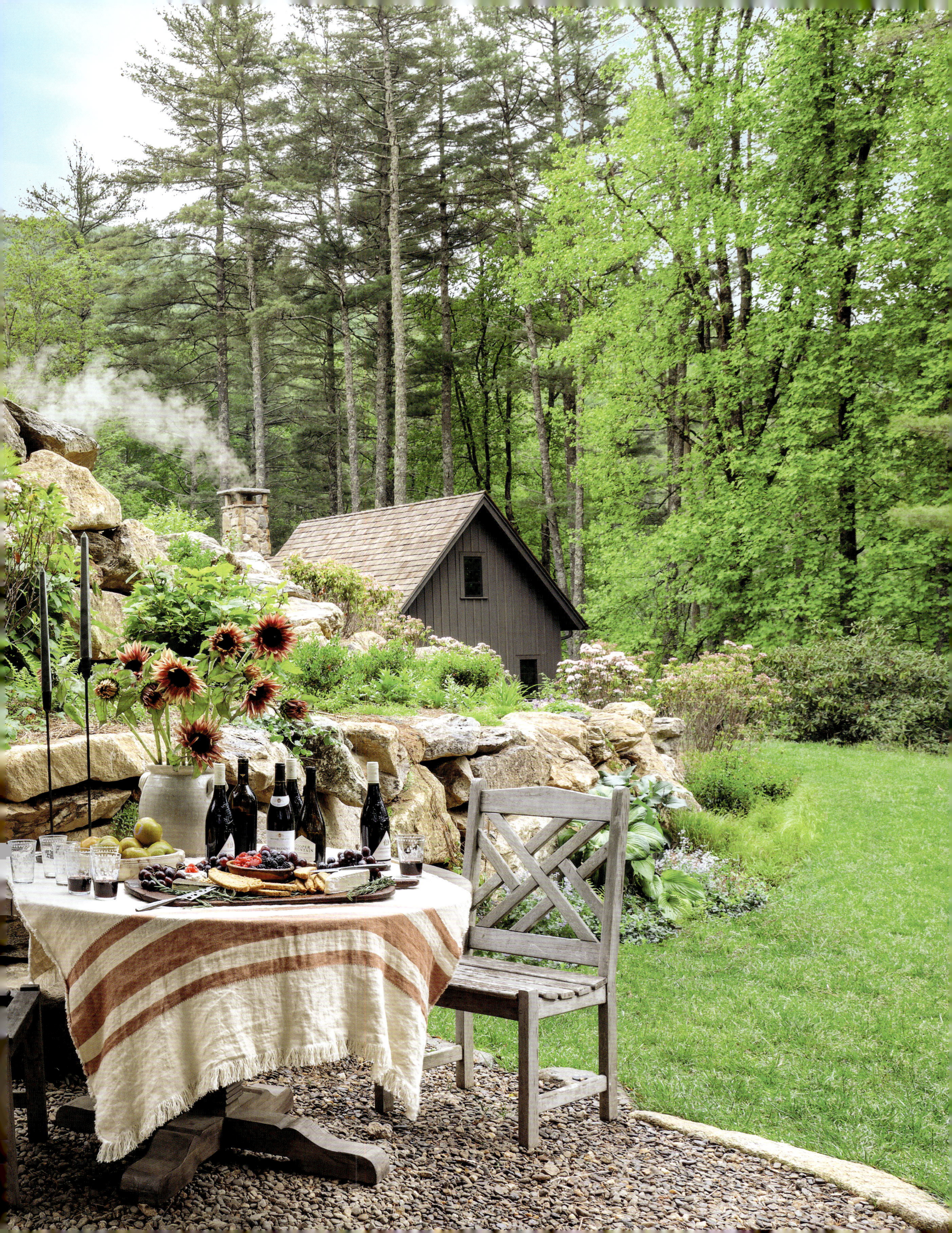

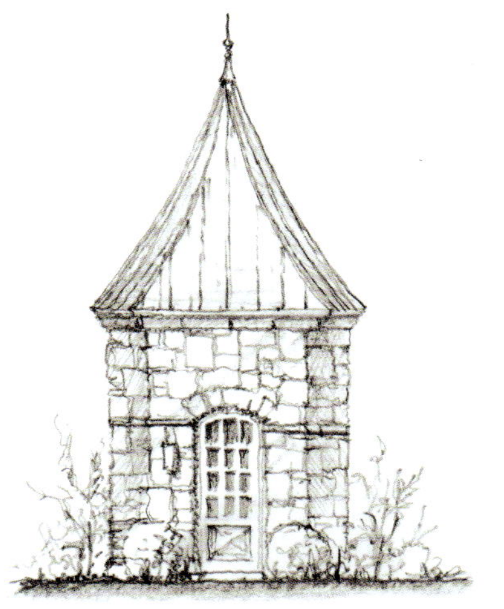

VILLA ON THE BLUFF

High above a bend in Louisiana's Vermilion River, you'll find a Provençal-style villa that gives every appearance of having stood there for hundreds of years. It hasn't, of course, but the sense of a long, eventful past is a quality that we worked very hard to infuse into the house.

The clients who commissioned this project travel extensively, and they have a special love for everything to do with France's southeastern corner: its landscape, its food and wine, and its culture, art, and architecture. They are also dedicated collectors, which I knew from collaborating with them on a previous home in Florida that incorporated some

OPPOSITE: This potting shed, with its zinc-coated copper roof, was a relatively late addition to plans for the property, but, of course, it was fully integrated into the architectural composition. FOLLOWING SPREAD: We designed the front door and its lovely transom window, and thoughtfully incorporated antique flanking sconces and an antique iron railing on the balcony above. Large terra-cotta urns, known as "Vases d'Anduze," are from the owners' private collection and lend authenticity to the overall design.

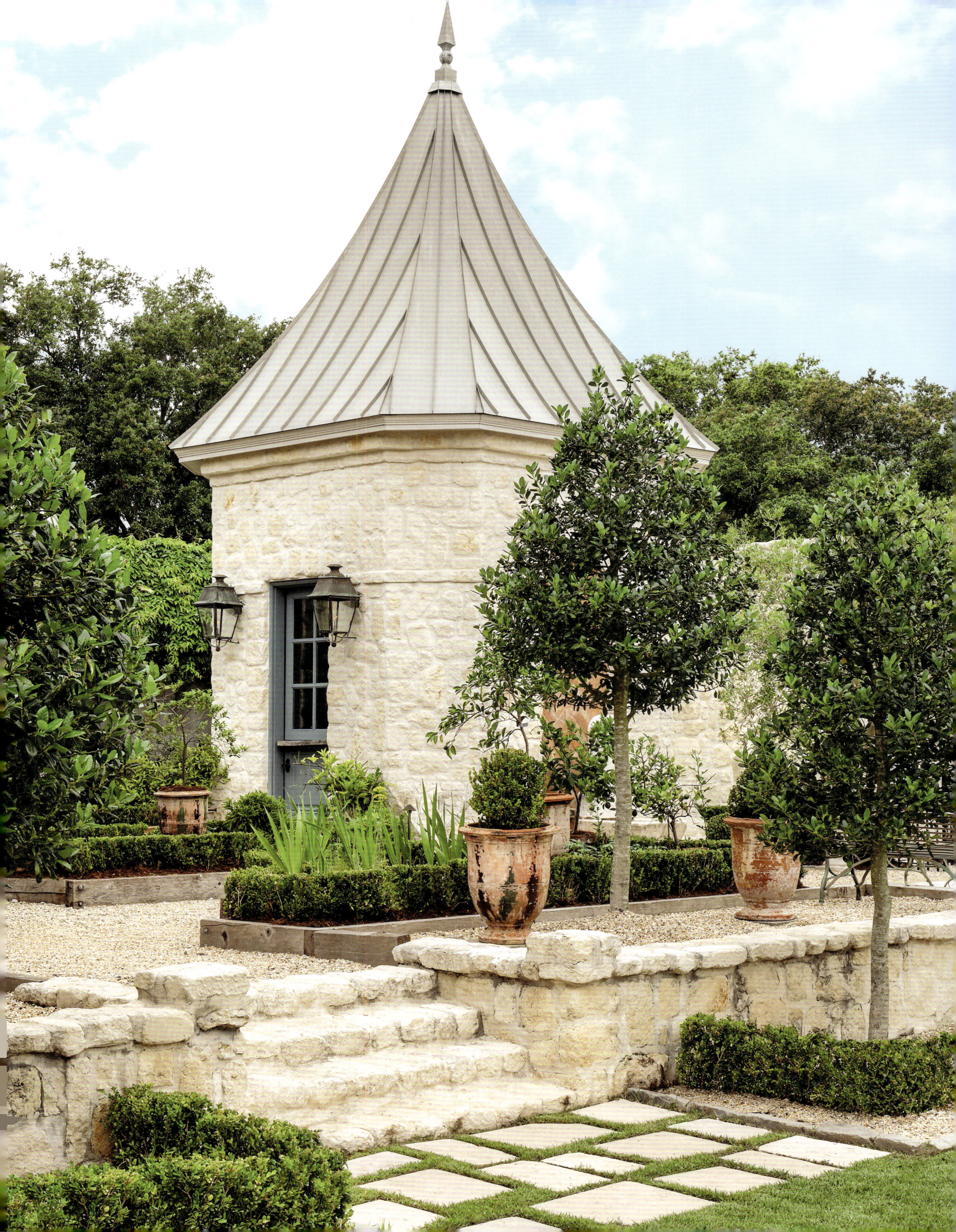

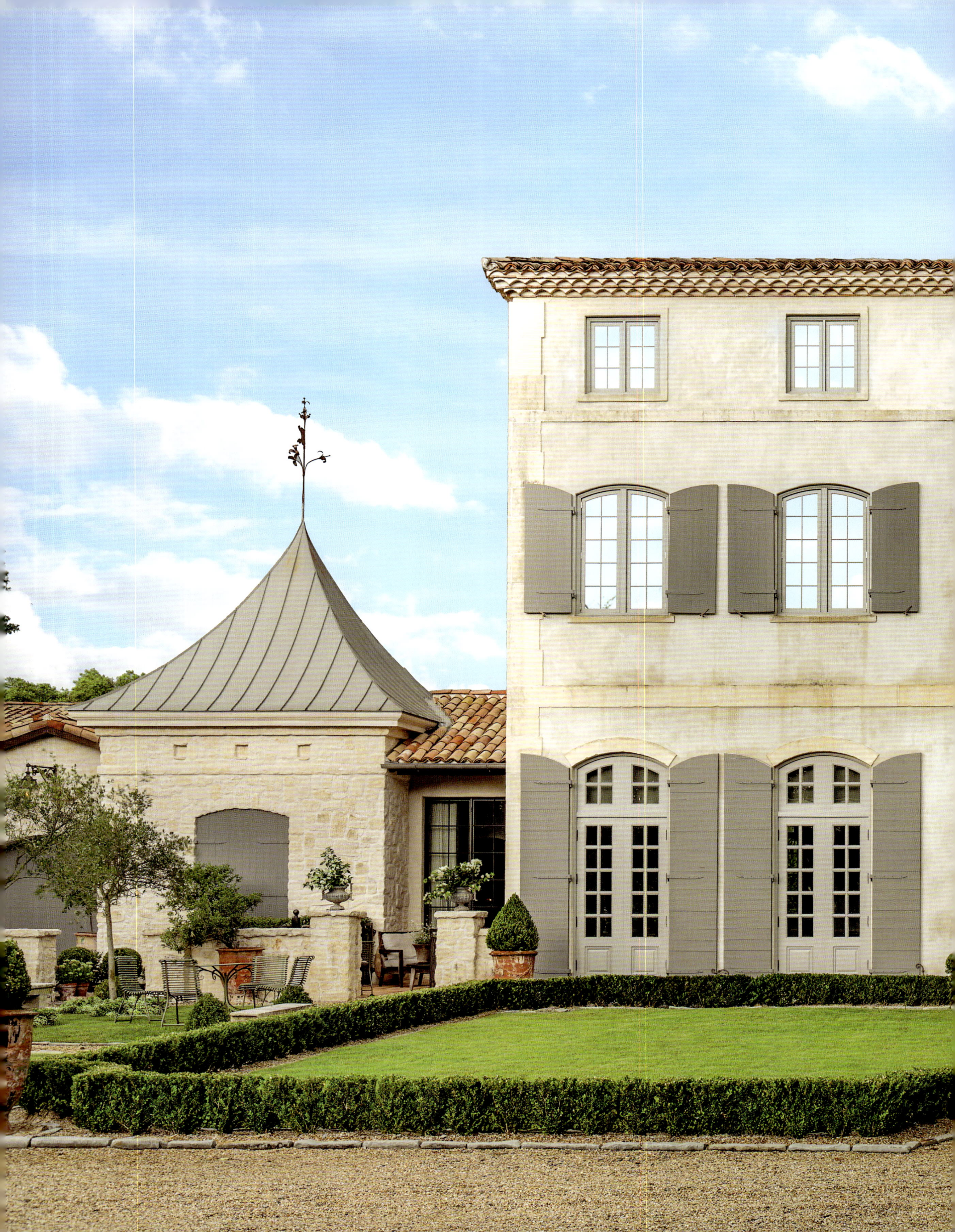

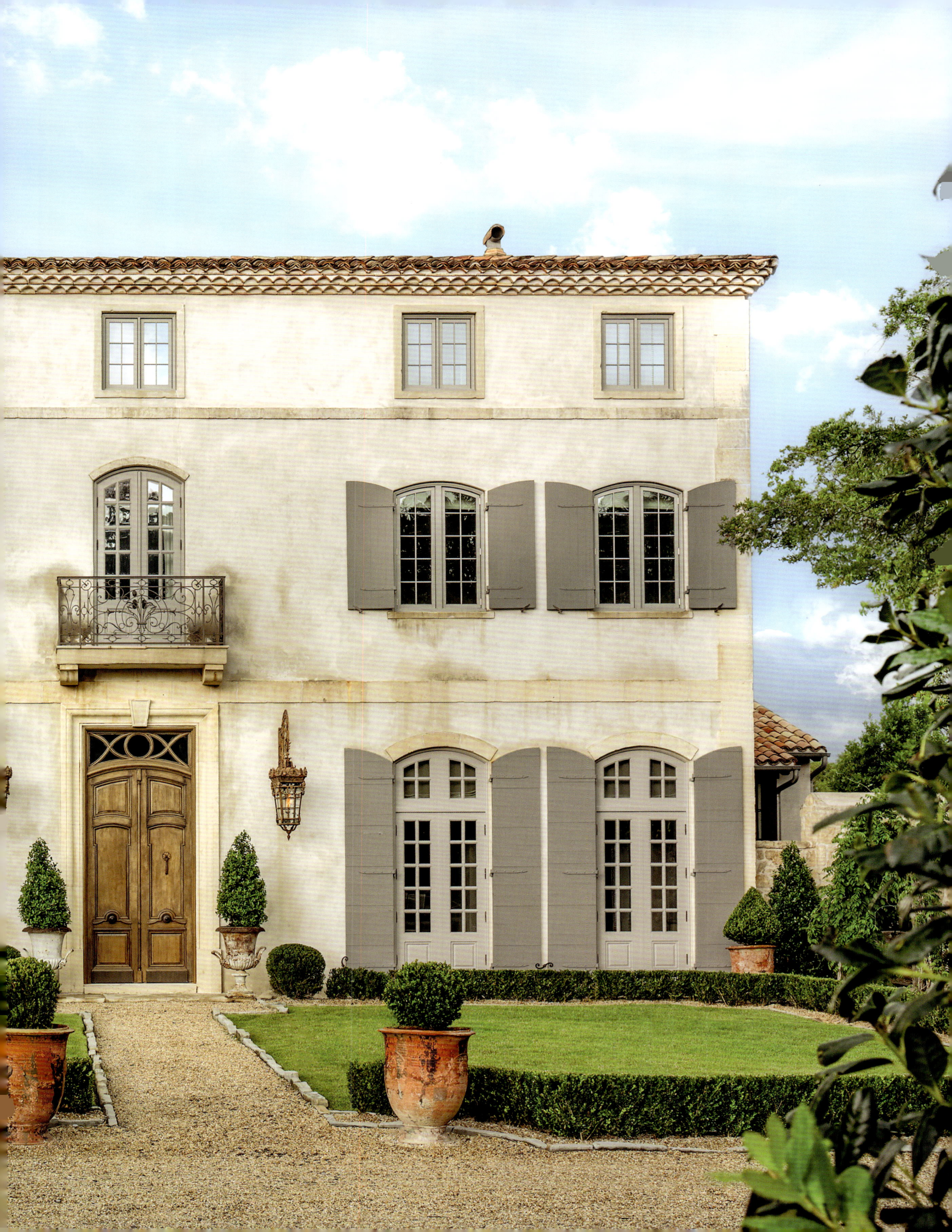

of their finds. This time, however, the trove of architectural elements they had amassed became one of the driving forces behind the new property's design.

For inspiration, the couple shared a photograph of their favorite inn in Provence—then the research began. When I undertake a project that references a particular region, I'll pull out the relevant books from my library and immerse myself, studying the characteristic architectural style, proportions, materials, and detailing—refreshing my memory in order to appropriately inform my creative decisions.

Subtle features can make a tremendous difference. The front elevation that we conceived for the main body of the house reflects a three-part vertical delineation of the floors that is typical for Provence: the ground floor, upper floor, and attic are all marked on the outside by horizontal courses of limestone that divide the stucco facade at each level. Even though the structure has a wood frame, we added a layer of eight-inch-thick concrete blocks to its exterior, then applied stucco over it, to give a substantial masonry feel to the residence. The thickness of the walls creates deep recesses around the windows and doors that cast beautiful shadows as the sun moves throughout the day. Finally, reclaimed barrel tiles make up the roof, with additional rows of them inset under the eaves in an application typical of southern France, known as *génoise*.

On a larger scale, we often like to come up with a narrative or backstory for our projects to help guide the overall vision. Here, we imagined the three-story central volume as the oldest, most formal part of the house. Then the lower, asymmetrical wings were made to look as if they had been added on, perhaps in several stages, over the centuries. The left wing is punctuated by a small *pigeonnier*, capped with a swooping metal roof, which houses the clients' extensive wine collection. Opposite, on the right side, is the couple's private domain, which looks out into a tranquil walled courtyard. Both wings are set back from the main house and are more relaxed in their visual vocabulary: windows

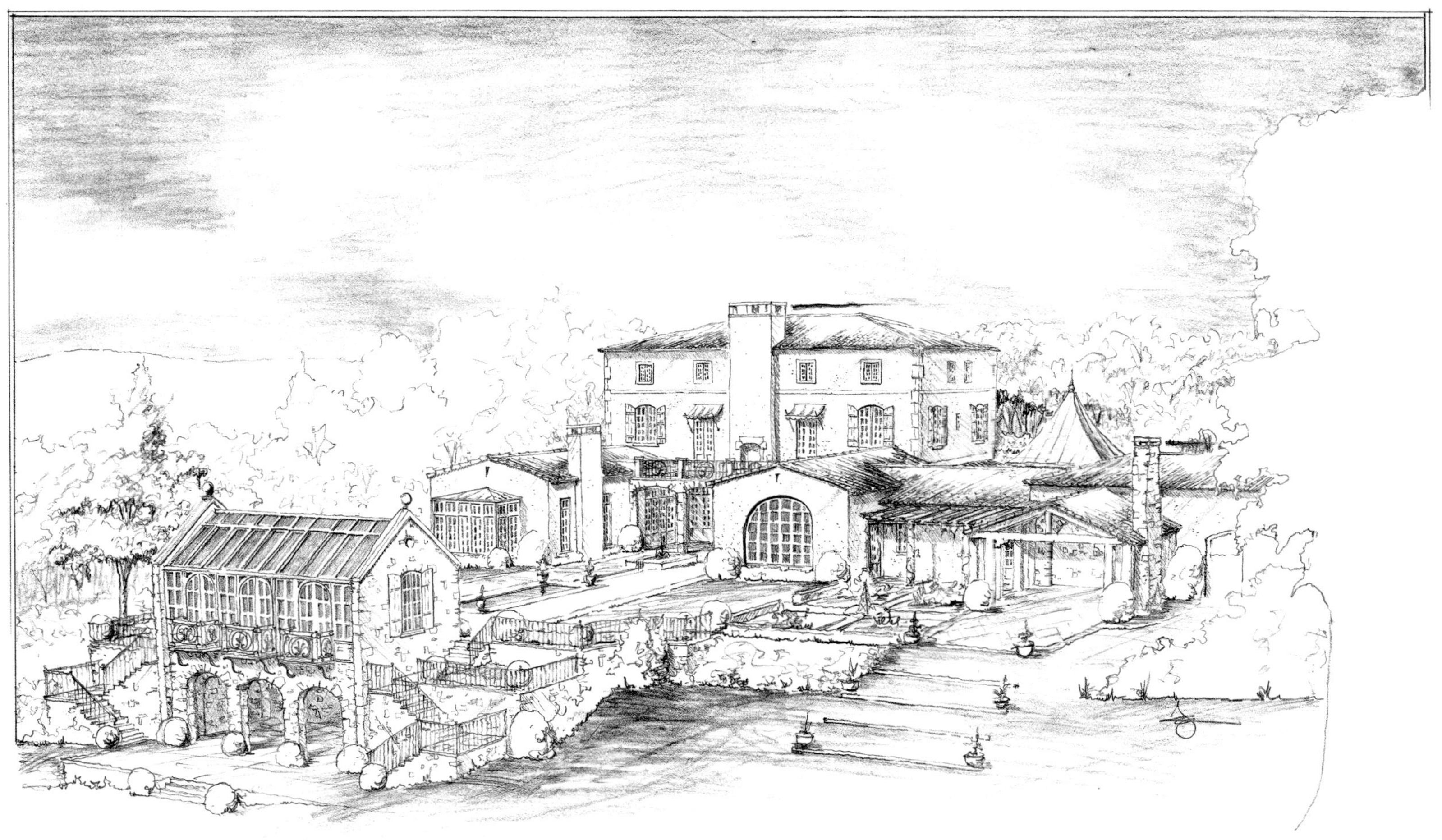

are larger, some walls are faced in mortared limestone, and exposed timbers make an appearance. Lastly, a glazed orangery for entertaining anchors the back of the site, while a potting shed echoes the hipped roof of the *pigeonnier* from the opposite corner of the plan.

The same hierarchy of greater versus lesser formality holds true inside the residence as well—made evident, for example, by ceiling finishes and details that range from the smooth plaster coves of the stateliest public areas to hand-hewn reclaimed beams and to round logs topped by butt-jointed wood in service spaces, such as the kitchen. Floors throughout are rendered in varied patterns of parquet or pierre de Bourgogne stone slabs—again supporting the story of different rooms having been built or renovated at different times—and wall surfaces with period-appropriate lime plaster and limewashed paneling contribute to the feeling of age.

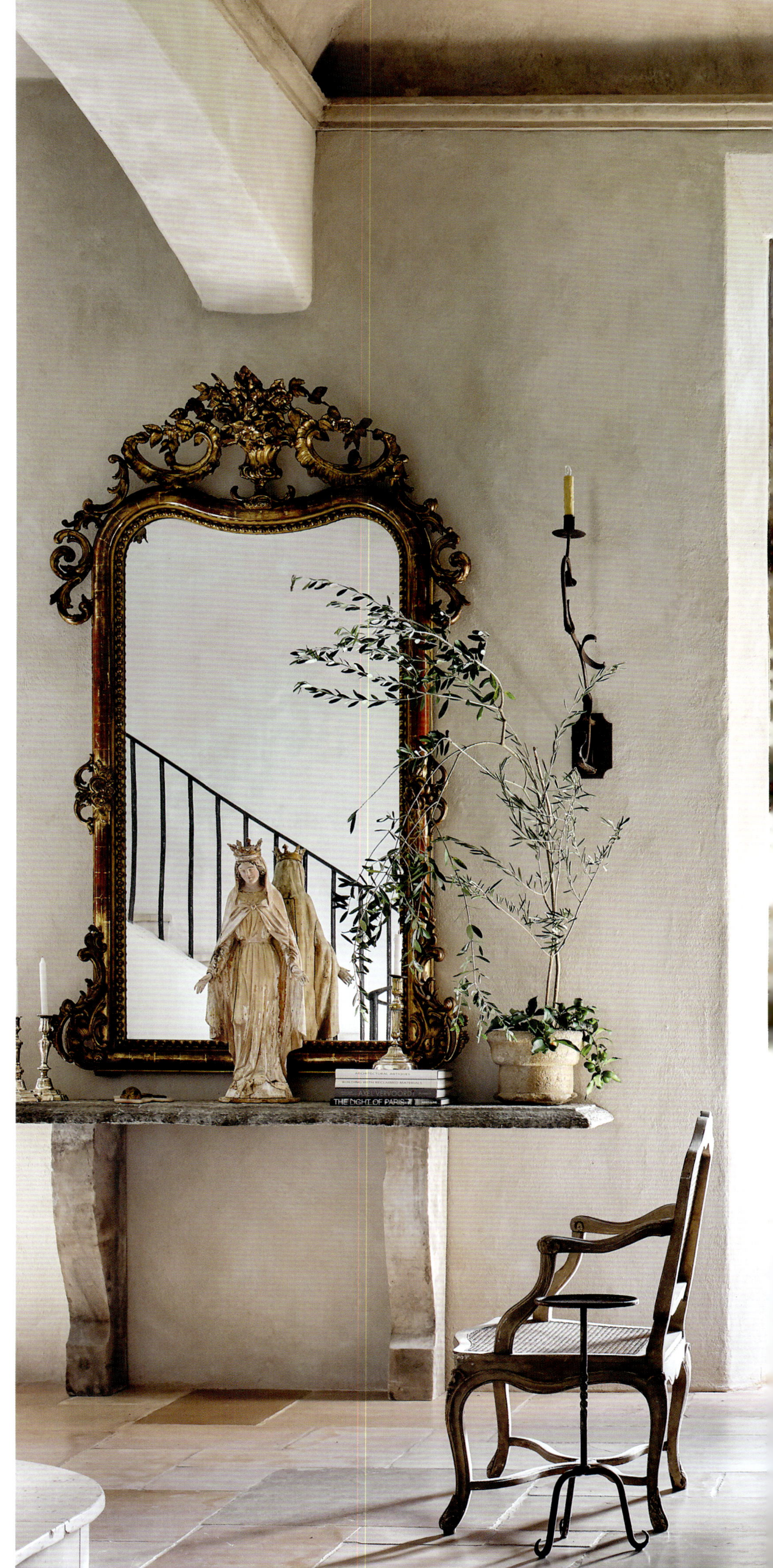

RIGHT: Minimalist stone and plaster details in the home's interior were inspired by the historic architectural precedents of Provence.

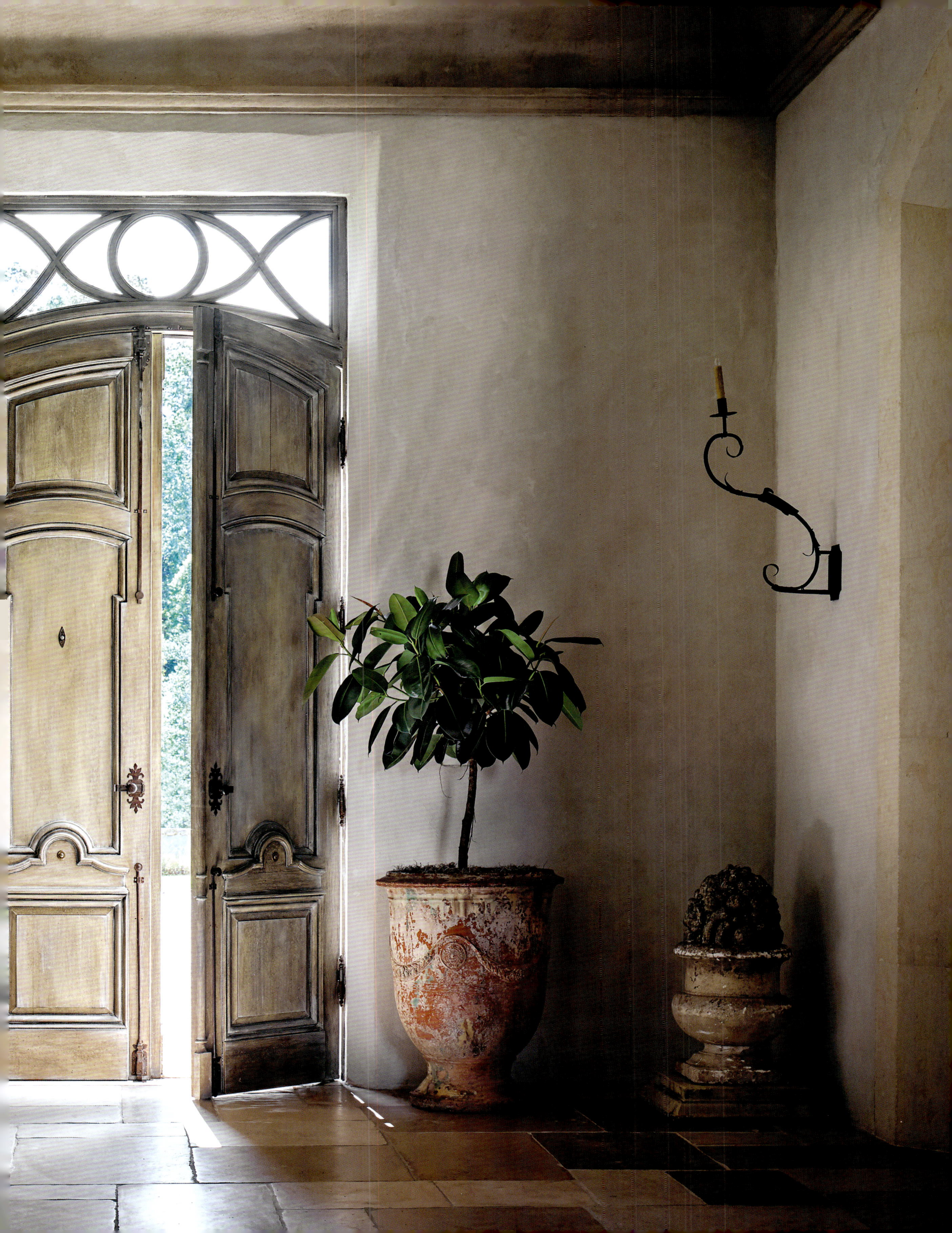

Perhaps the biggest challenge we faced—and one that was quite enjoyable—was how to integrate, in what seemed like an authentic way, the many building components that the clients had dedicatedly brought from France over the years and stored in a warehouse to await a new life. Mantels, iron railings, decorative light fixtures, boiseries, and more than twenty salvaged doors of different sizes and configurations had to be worked logically and seamlessly into our scheme. It couldn't be a process where you draw the house, start construction, and *then* begin inserting those pieces. Instead we added the various found artifacts into our initial floor plans, then adjusted the rooms, sometimes by a mere few inches, to make everything fit properly. In some cases, we embraced the quirkiness of, say, using two unmatched doors, one arched and one not, in the same hallway, because it furthered the idea that this house did indeed reach its present shape bit by bit over time. In the end, the new and the old were so well integrated that which parts are which is indistinguishable to the eye.

When building a house inspired by the past, it's important not to end up with a staid, museum-like replica. Yes, we were channeling a historic aesthetic; nevertheless, we still built a home with, for instance, all the functional kitchen amenities needed by a family living in the twenty-first century. Despite the invented narrative that went into its design, this house comes across as eminently lived-in and comfortable. It's a substantial home, yet it's very approachable—and its owners absolutely love being there.

OPPOSITE: An enclosed loggia is centered at the back of the house, on axis with a linear fountain and orangery outside. Interior design for this project was a collaborative effort among the clients, Cynthia Nunez of Antiques de Provence in New Orleans, and my staff.

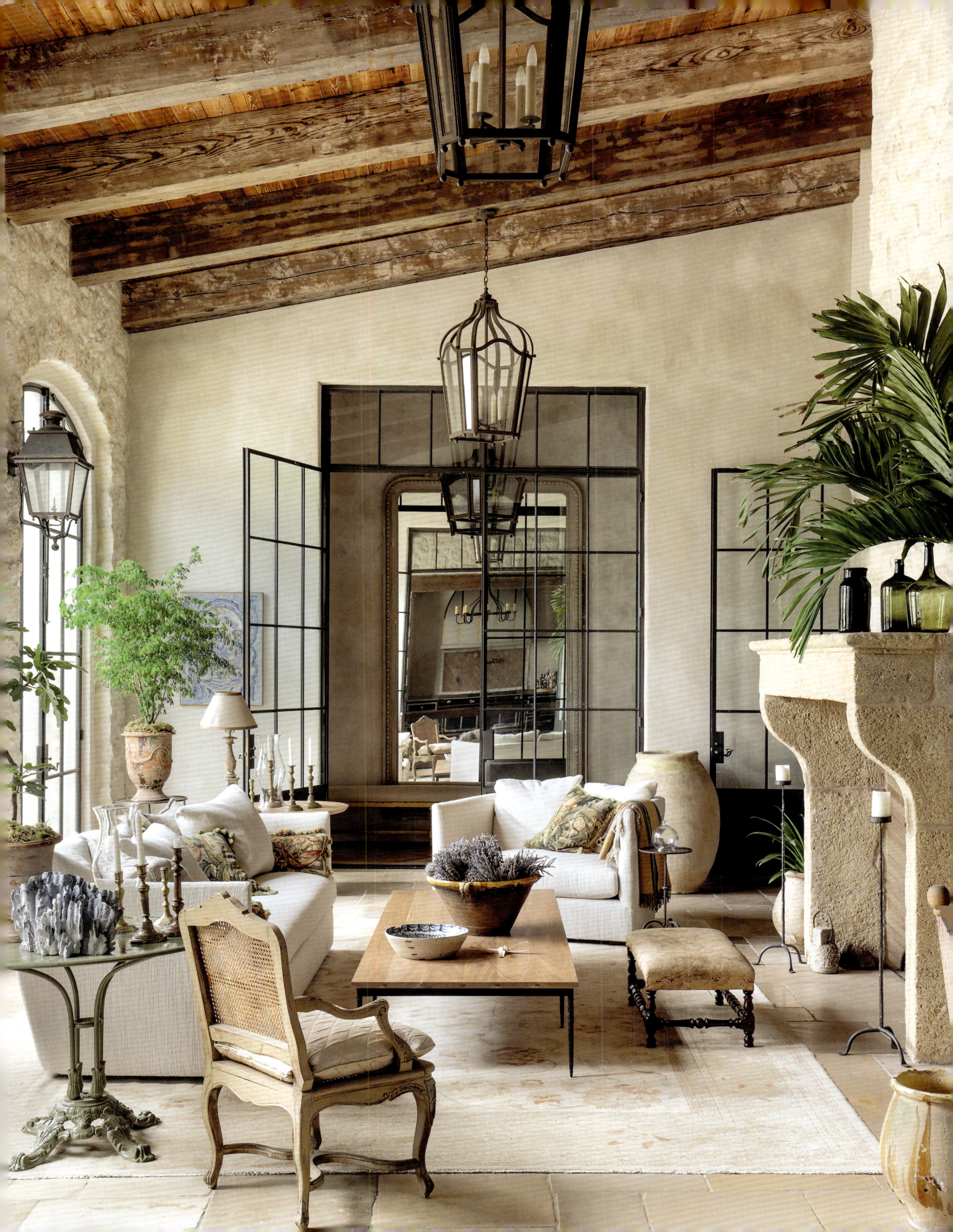

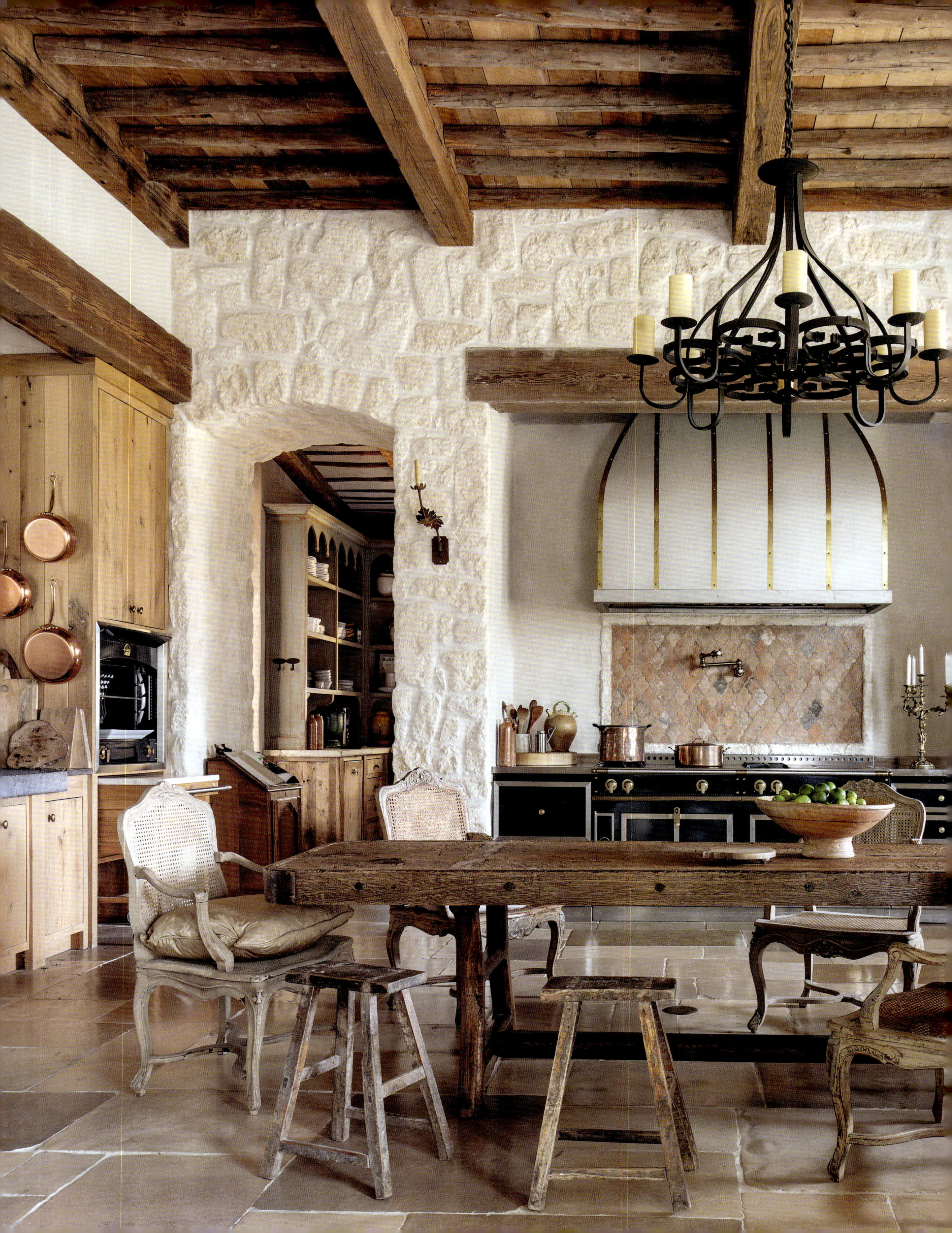

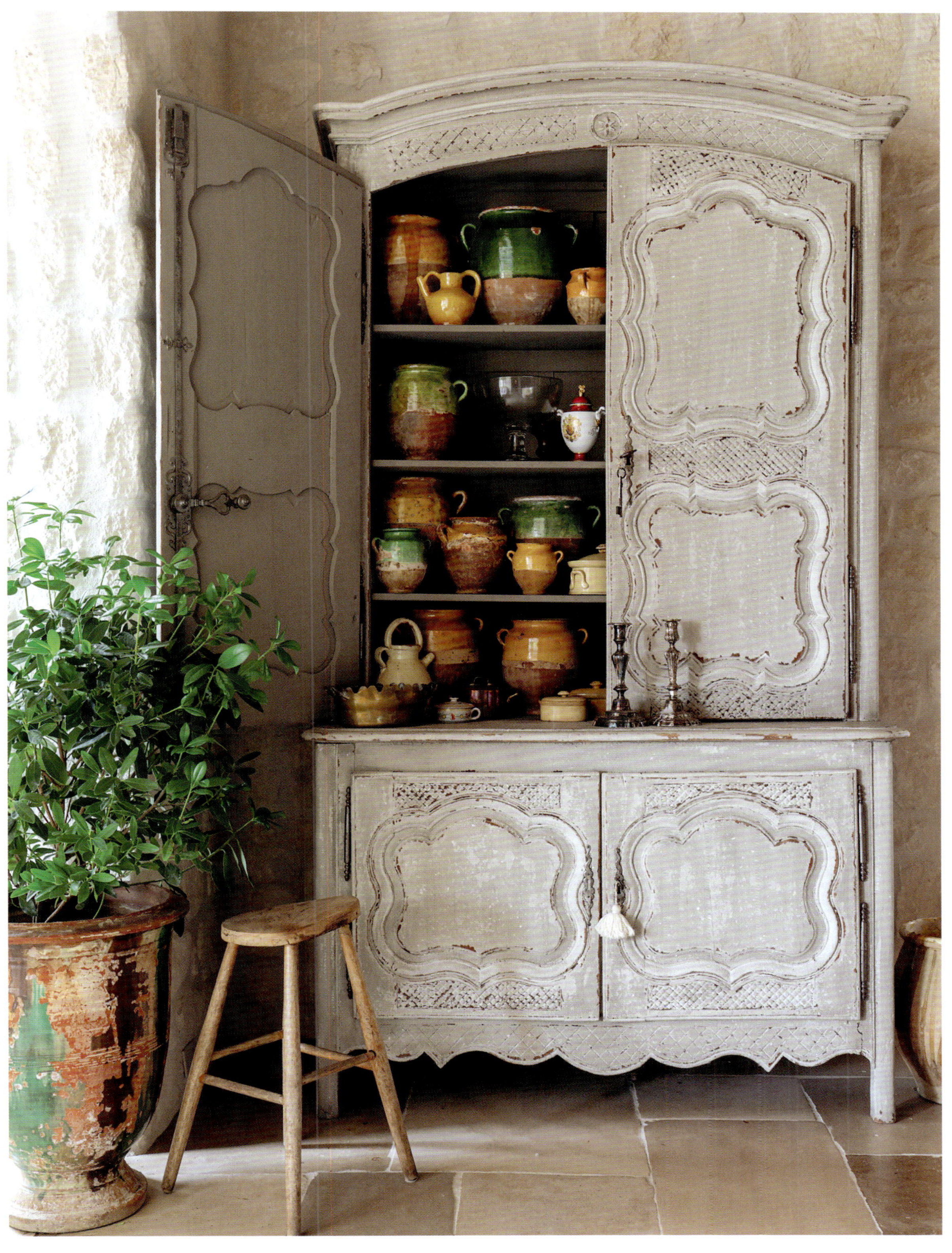

OPPOSITE AND ABOVE: Cooking and gathering blend effortlessly in the kitchen, whose layout, centered around a large antique farm table, is an homage to the past. A La Cornue range is recessed into what seemingly could have been an exterior wall, much of the prep space is relegated to an adjacent scullery, and further storage is provided by freestanding antique cabinets.

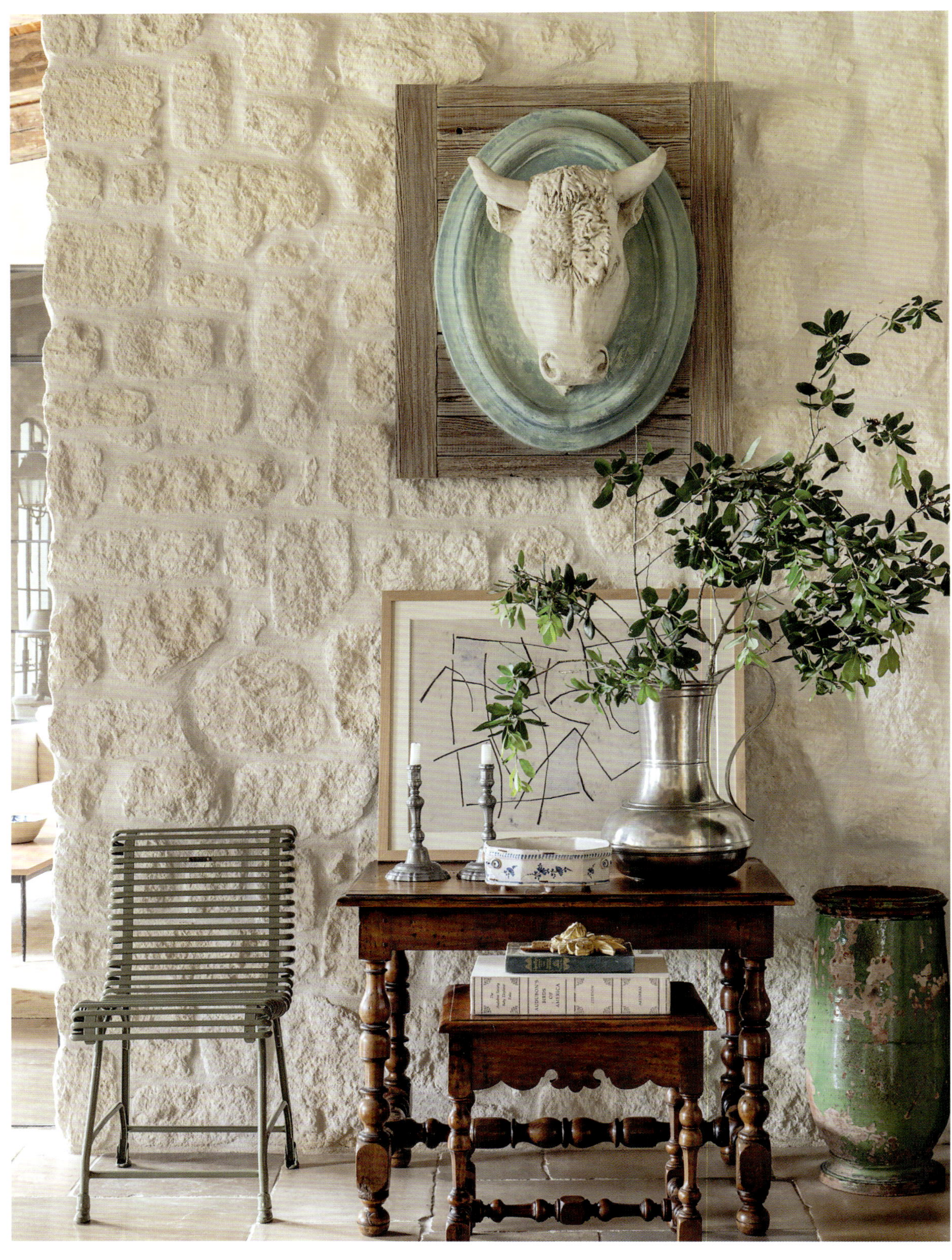

ABOVE: The house is full of evocative vignettes featuring items collected during the clients' extensive travels. OPPOSITE: An expansive arched window in the family room overlooks the orangery and the Vermilion River beyond.

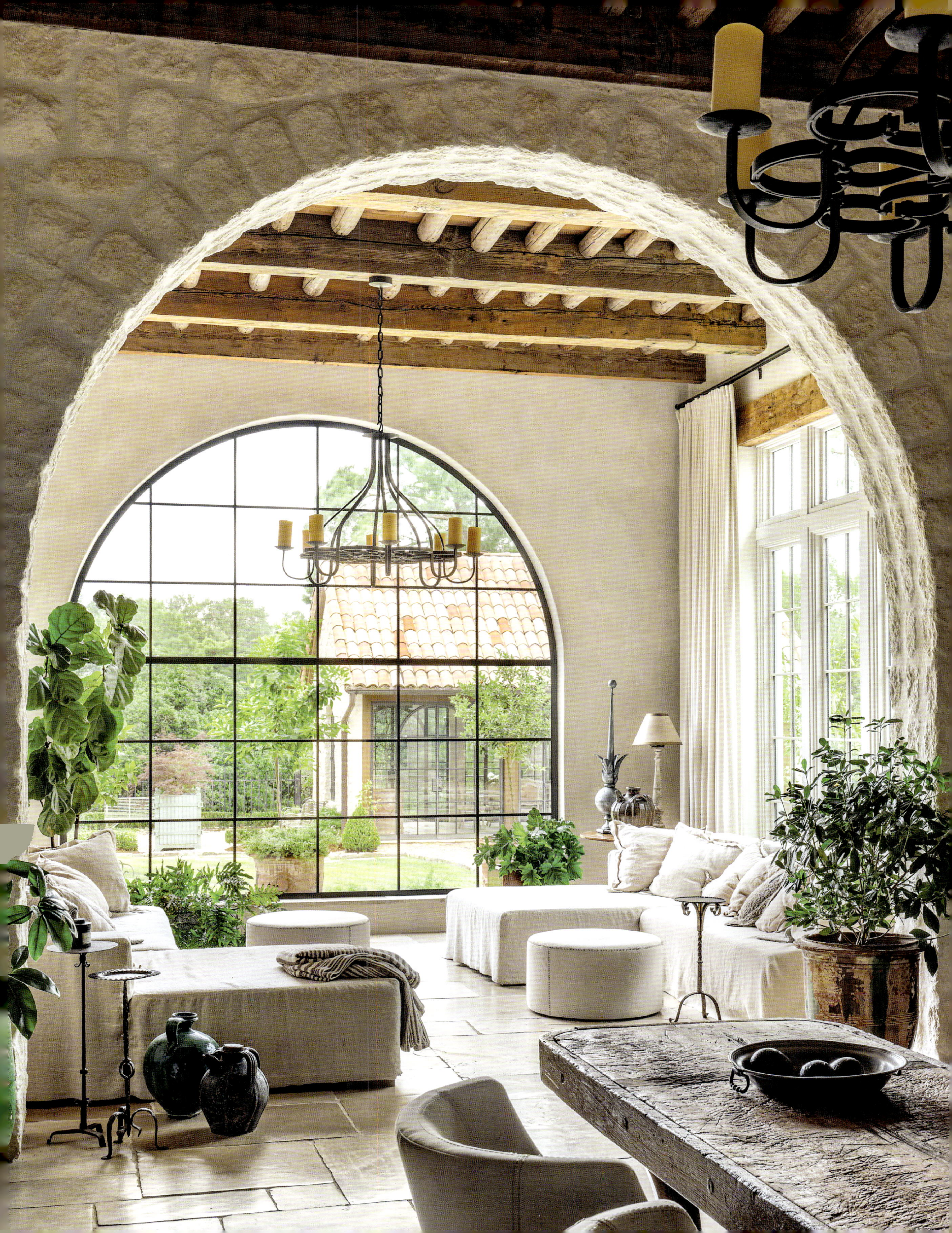

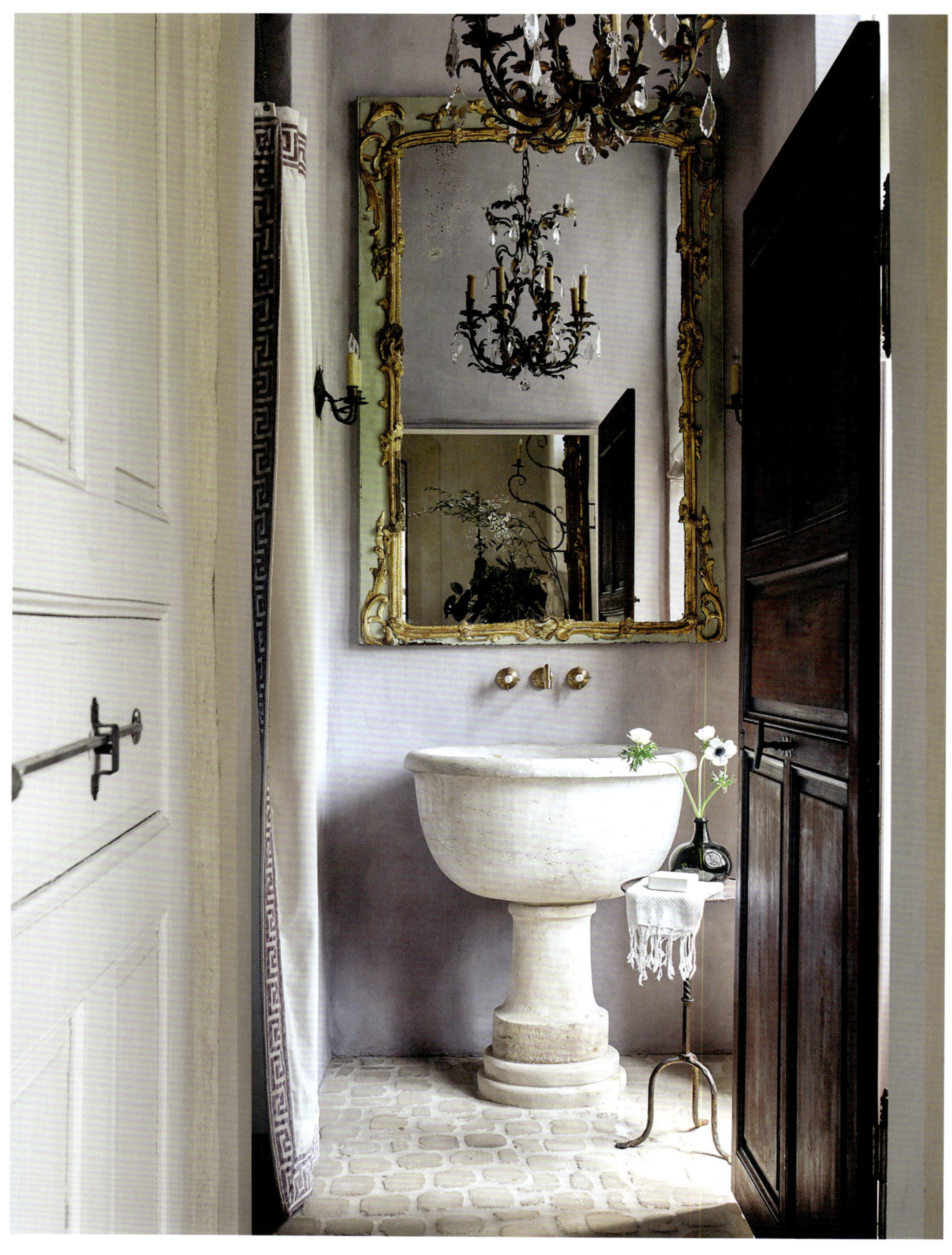

ABOVE: A repurposed baptismal font from the owners' collection serves as a sink in the powder room, which is located under the stairs in the home's entry hall. OPPOSITE: The boiserie paneling in the library was designed around four tall, narrow antique doors of varying sizes that we incorporated into cabinets at the room's four corners.

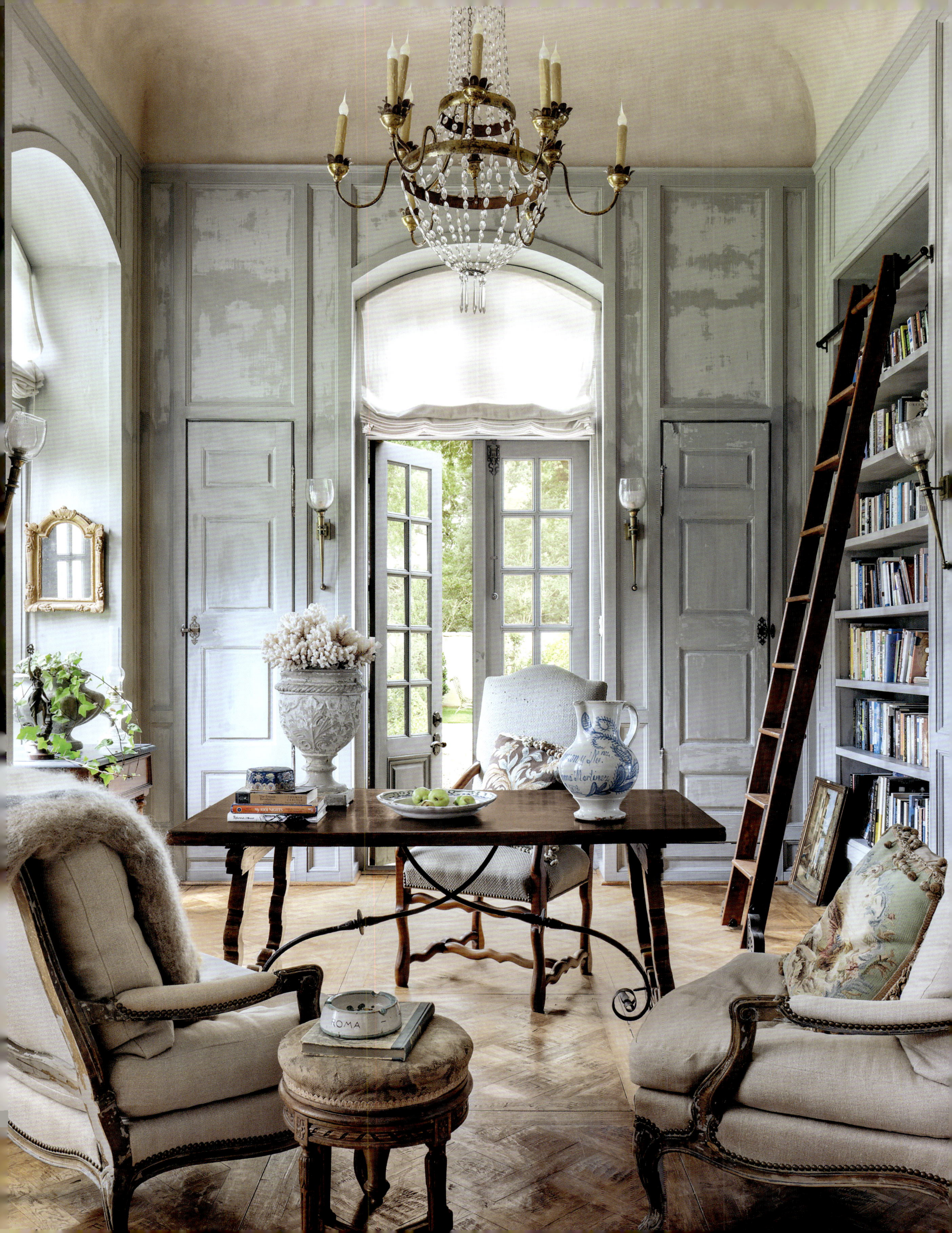
ROMA

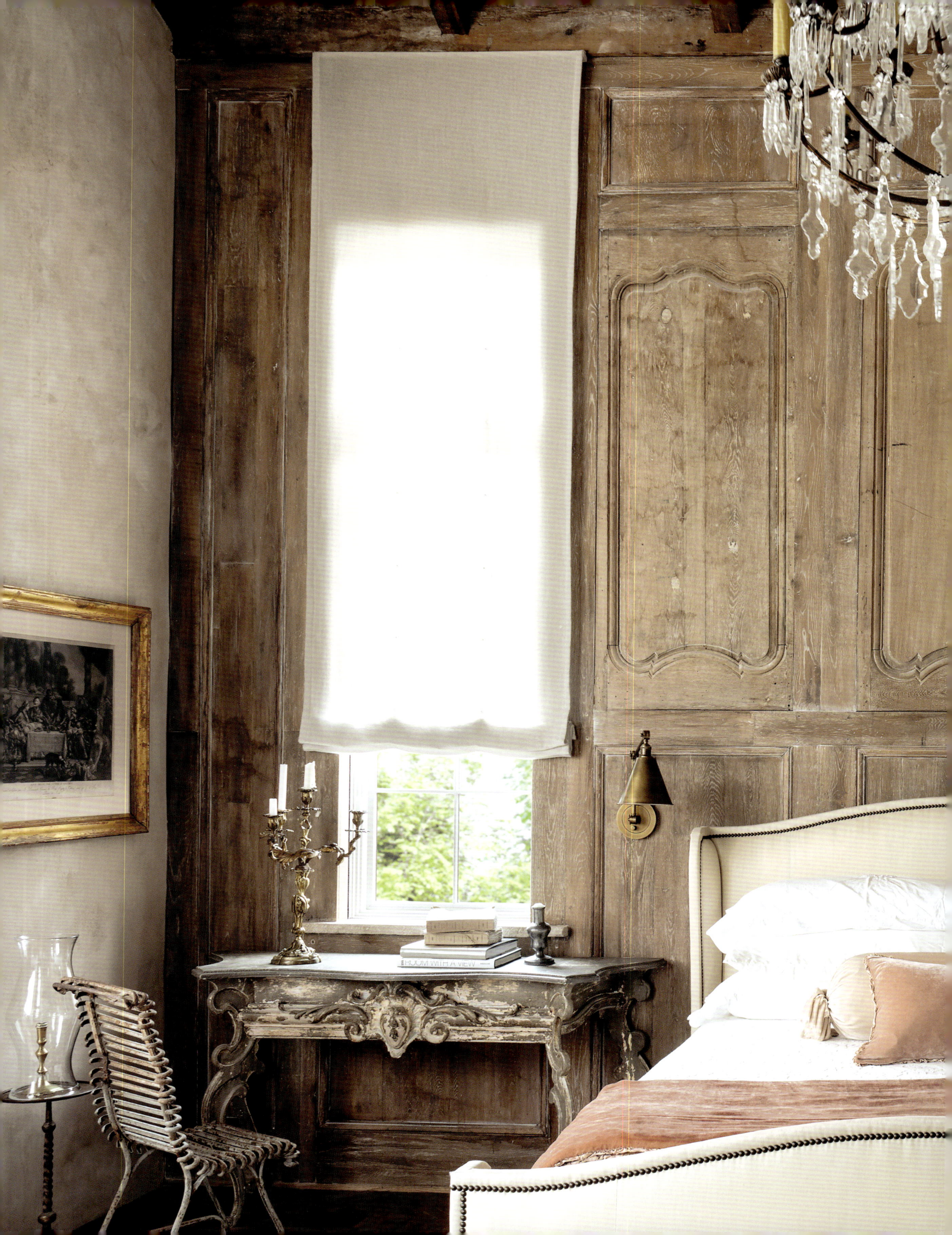
ROOM WITH A VIEW

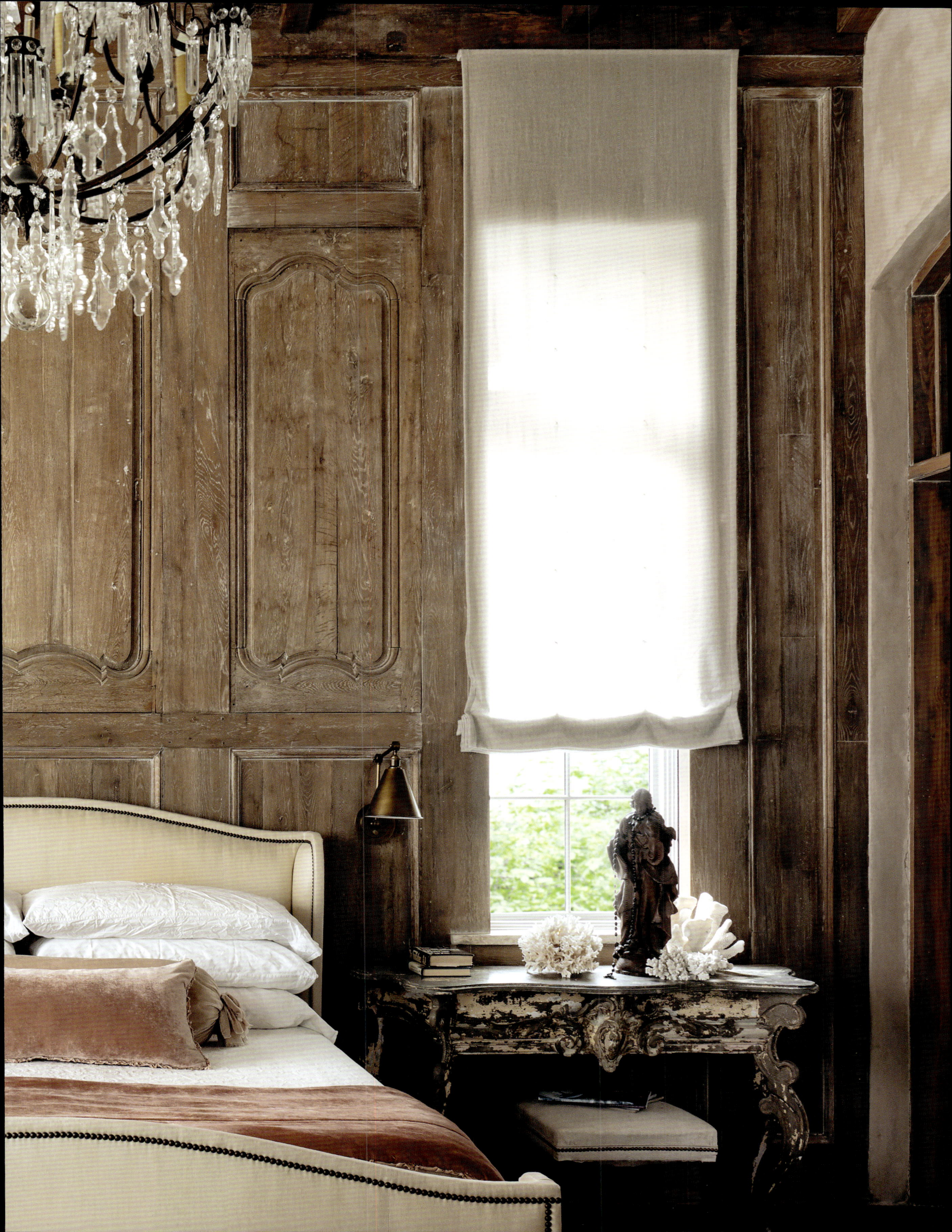

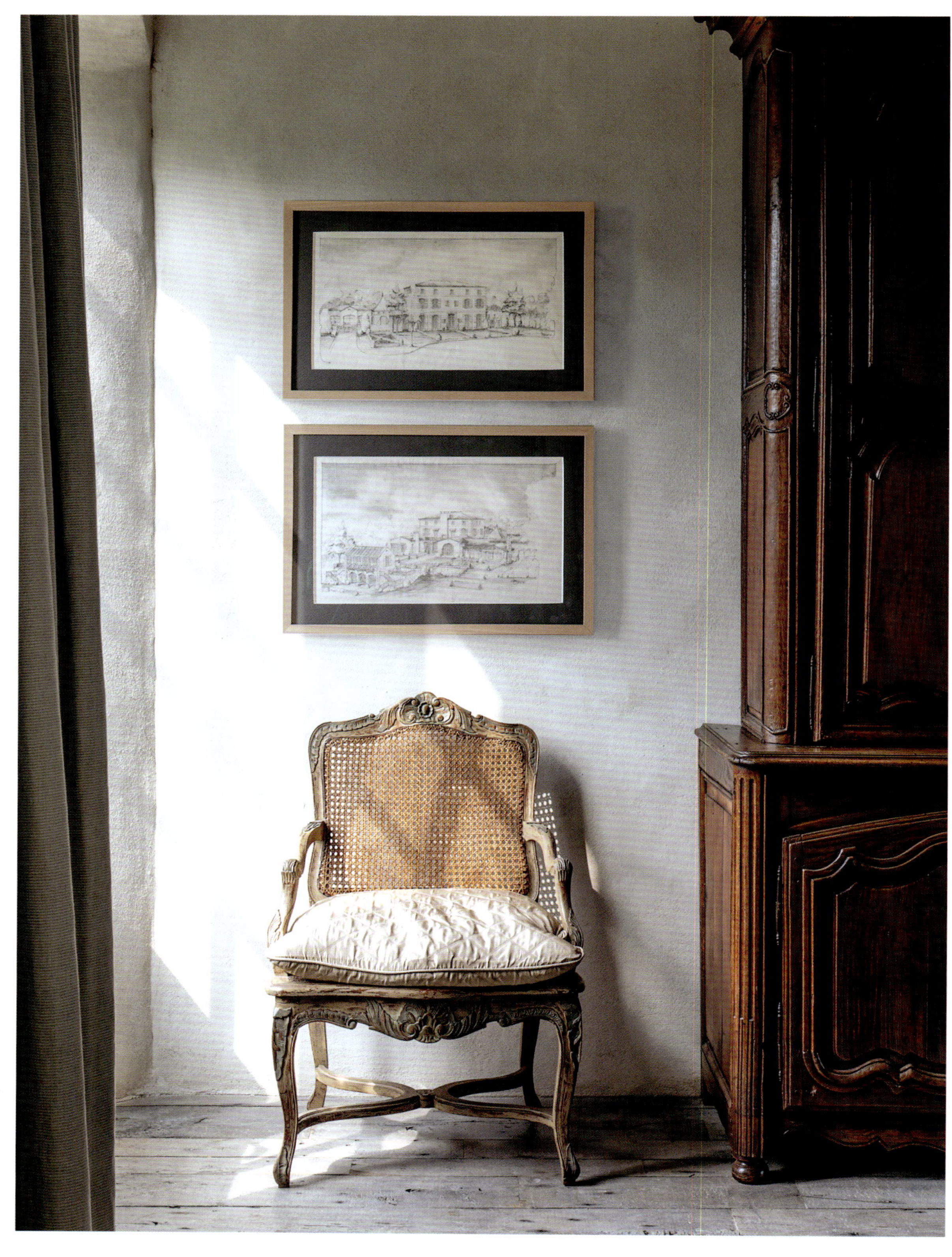

PRECEDING SPREAD: Reclaimed boiserie panels embellish the primary bedroom, where ornate antique consoles serve as nightstands. ABOVE: Two of my pencil sketches for the project hang in a quiet corner. OPPOSITE: The primary bath feels as if it's part of the small, private walled courtyard beyond the windows.

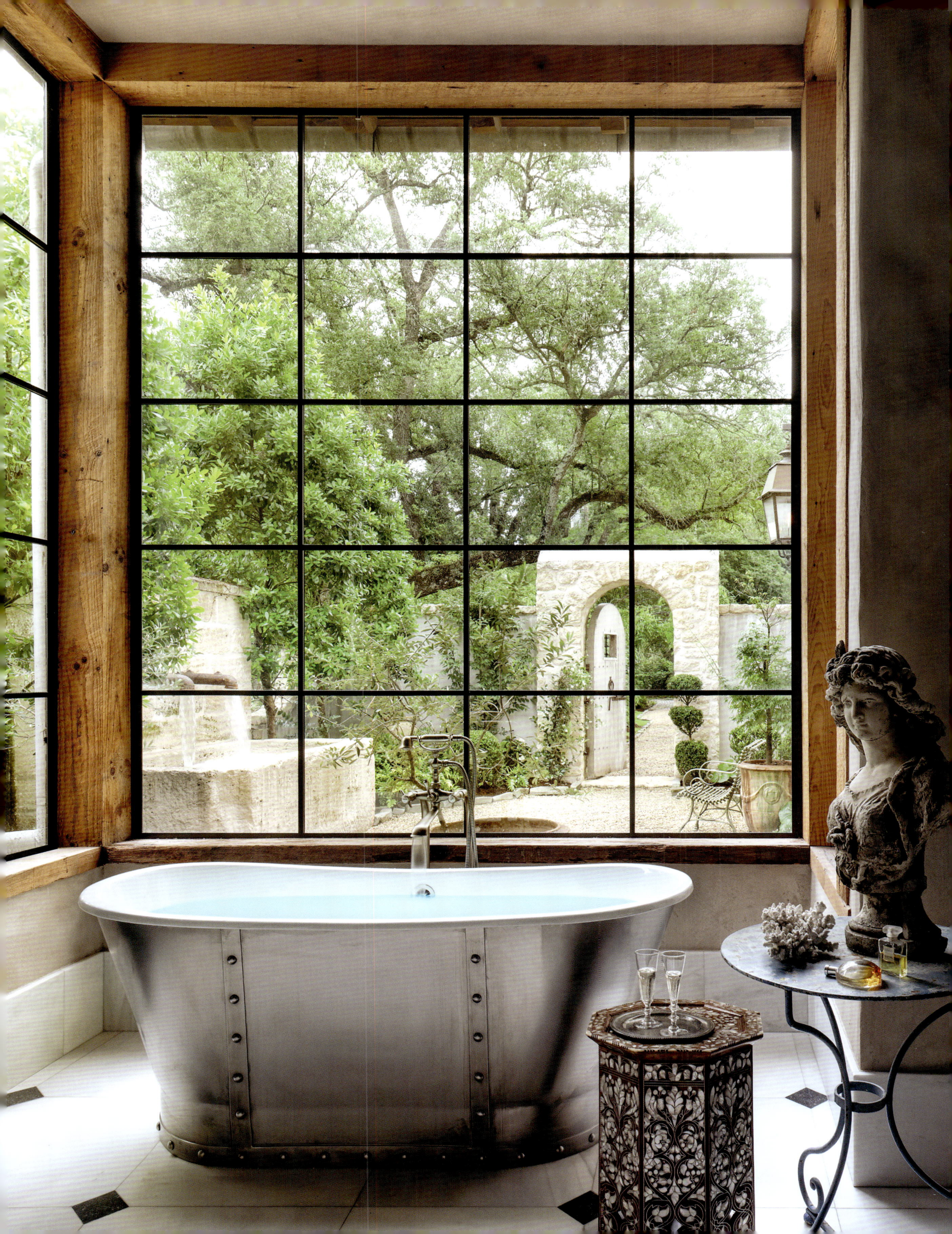

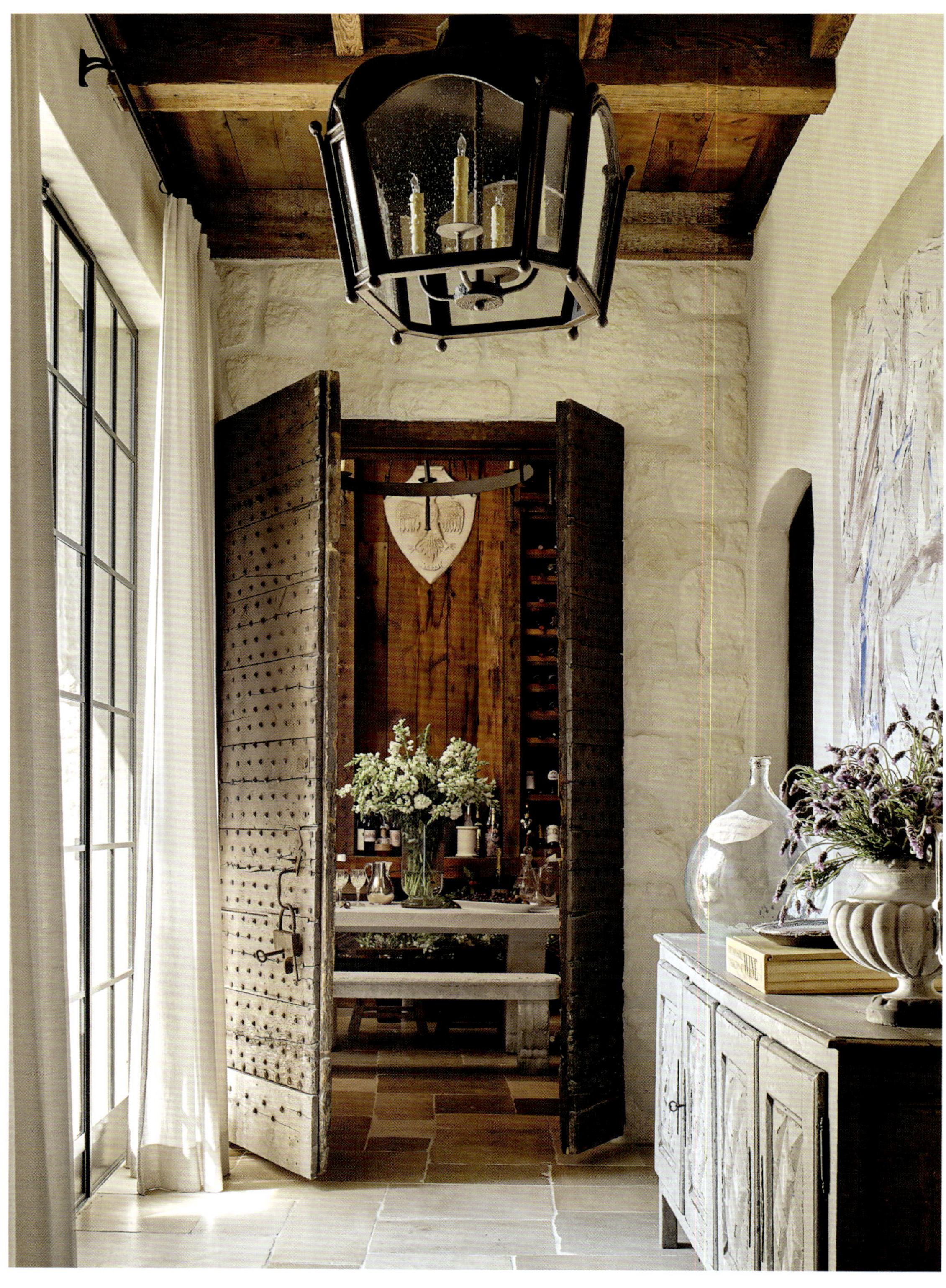

ABOVE AND OPPOSITE: A magnificent seventeenth-century door studded with decorative nails opens to the client's wine cellar inside the *pigeonnier*. A sliding glass door for climate control is concealed behind it. FOLLOWING SPREAD: A row of potted citrus trees marches across the rear of the home, which is notably less formal than the front. The axial reflecting pool at left points toward the orangery.

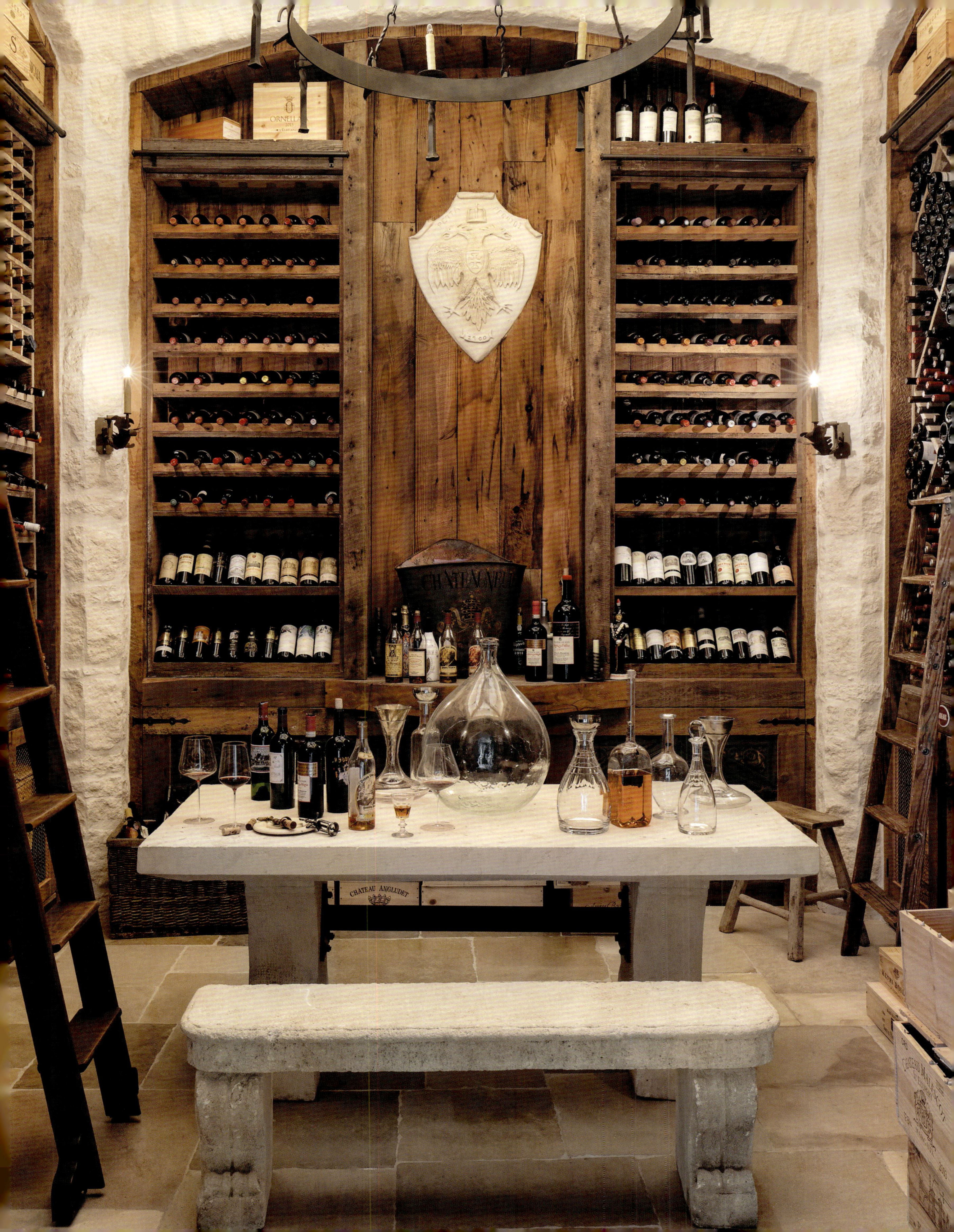
CHATEAU ANGLUDET

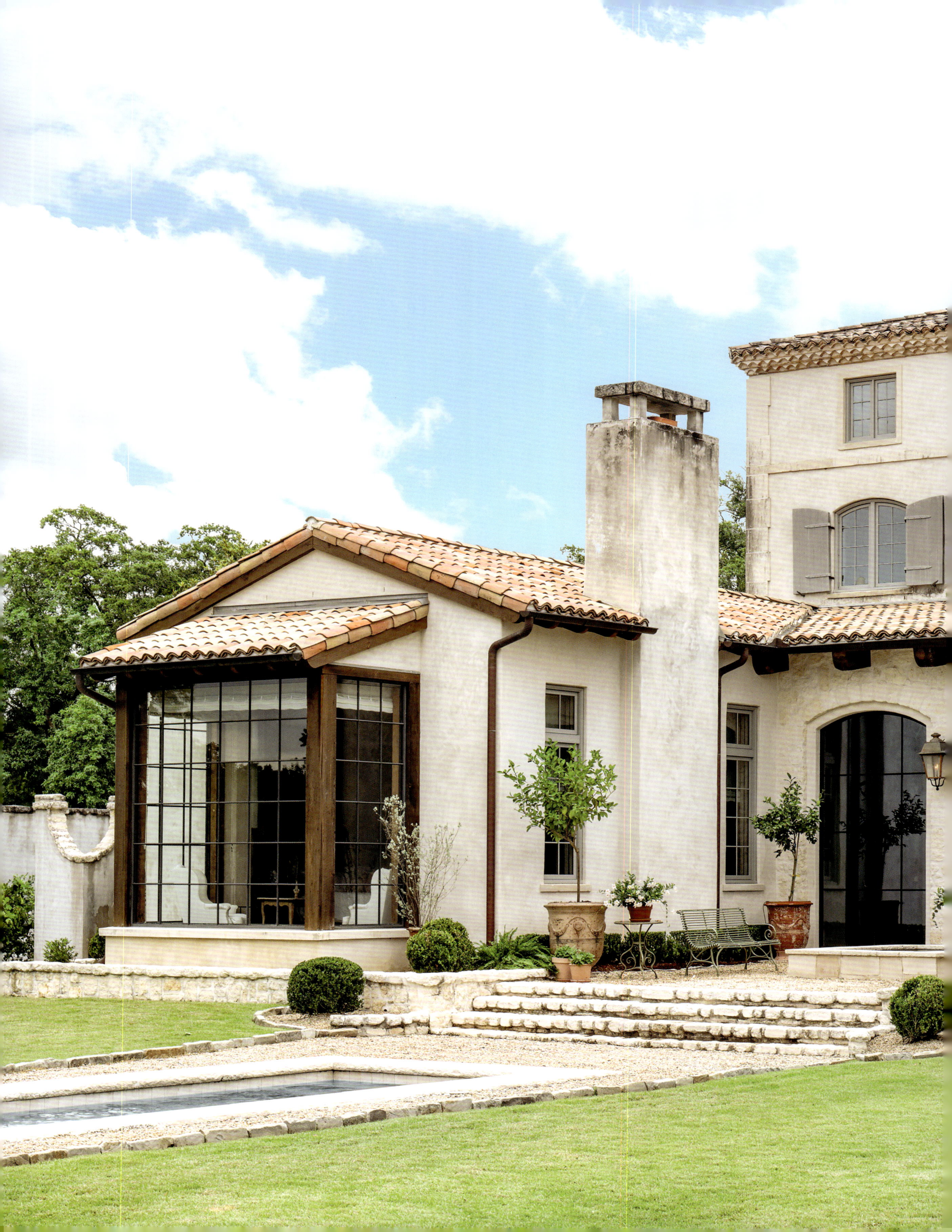

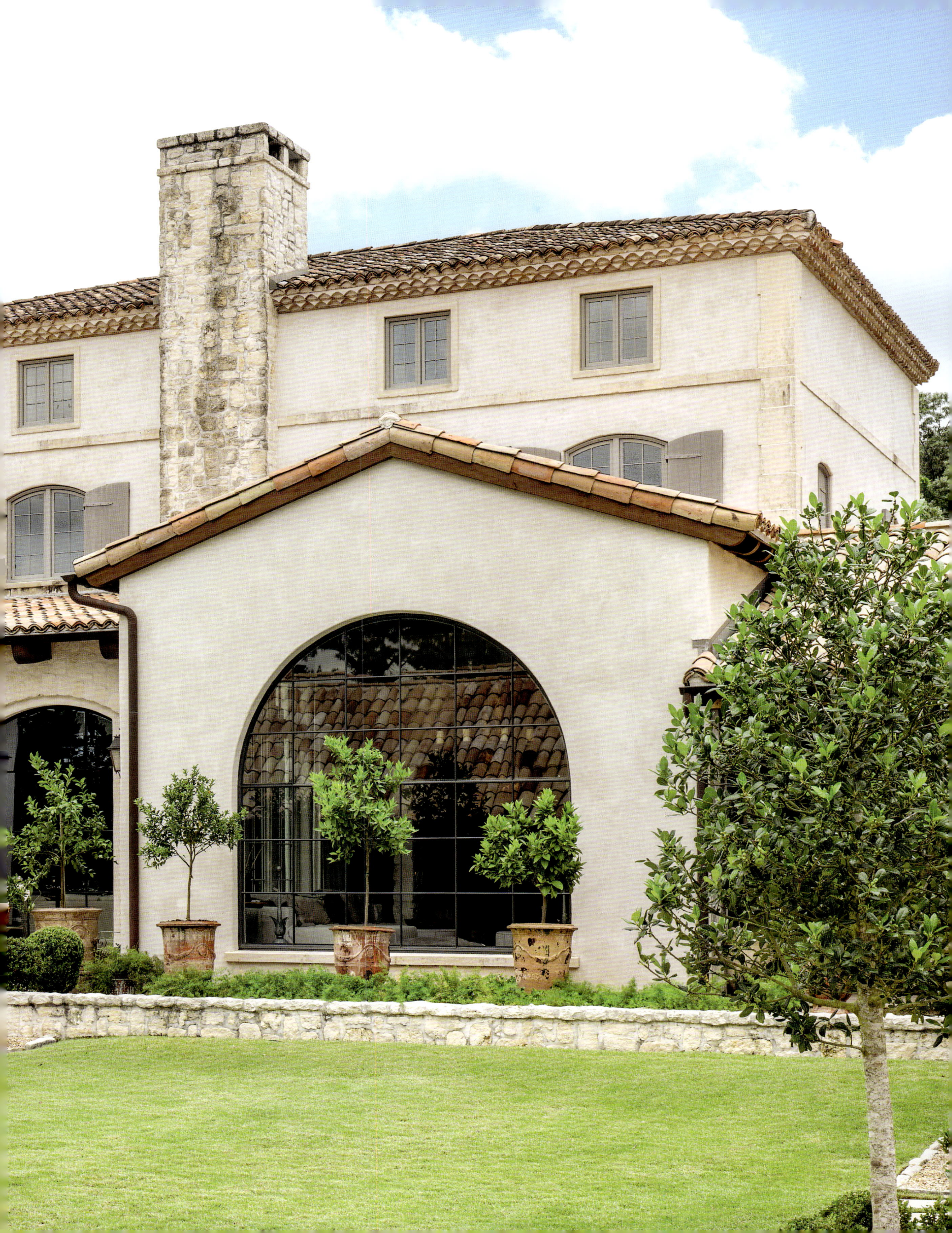

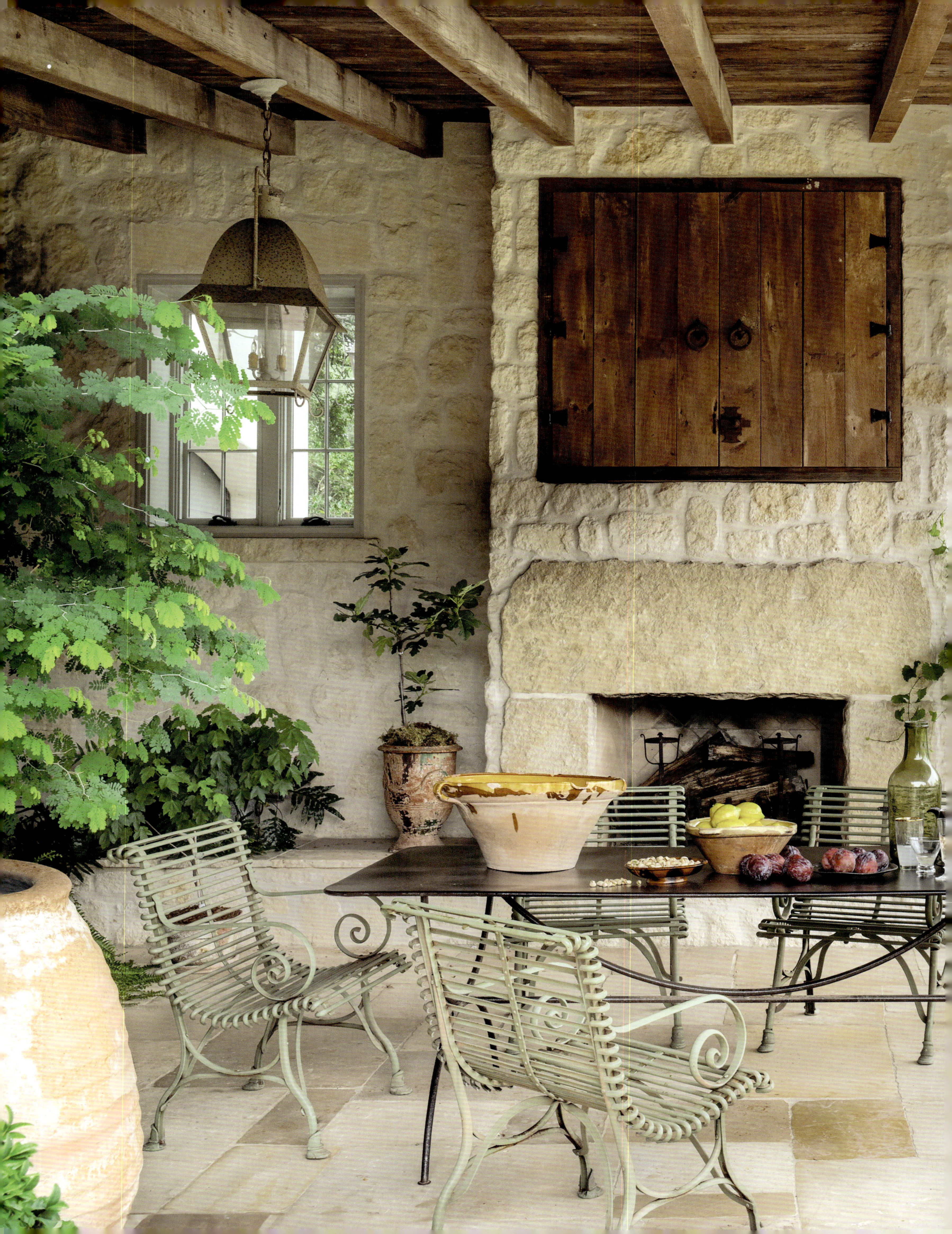

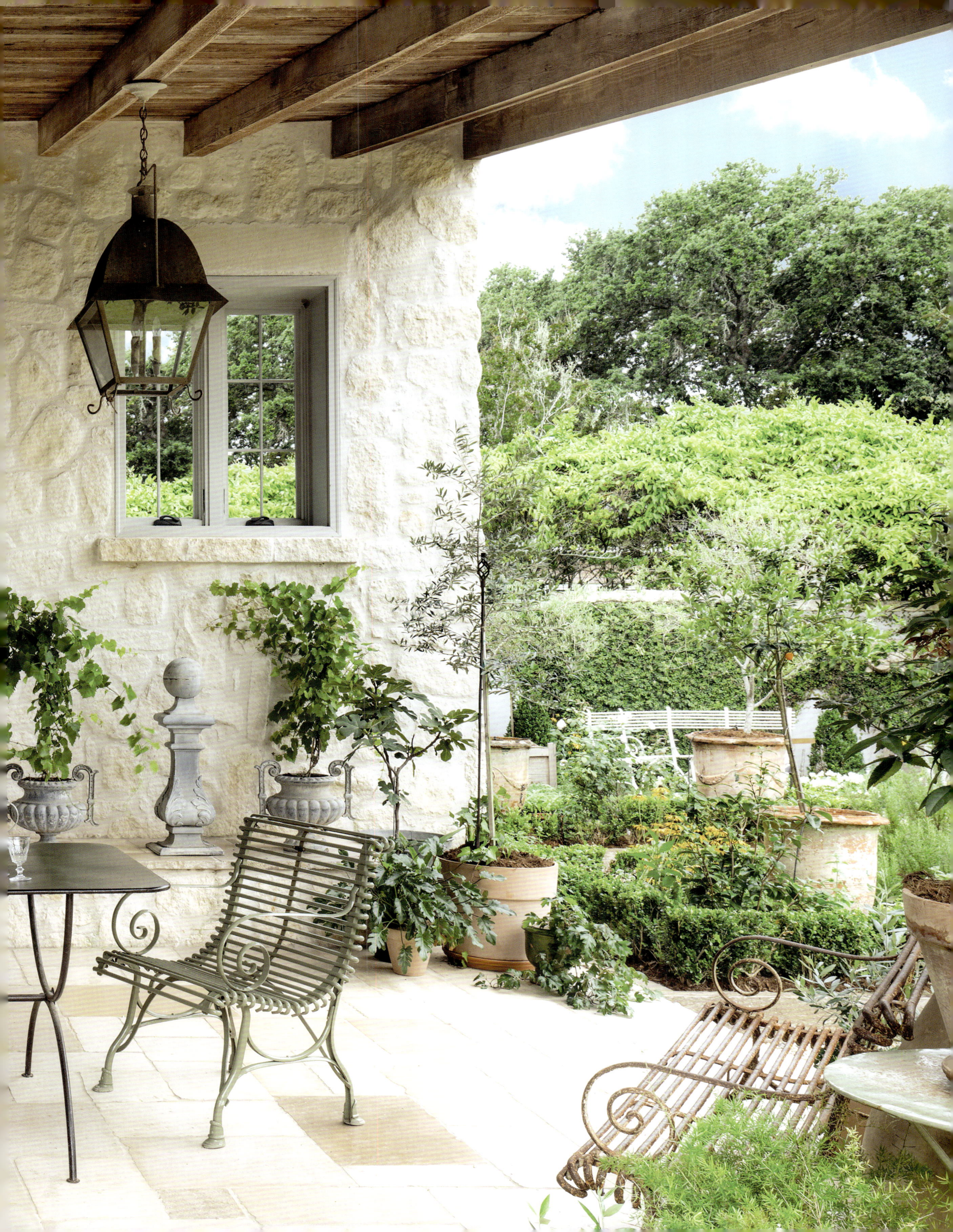

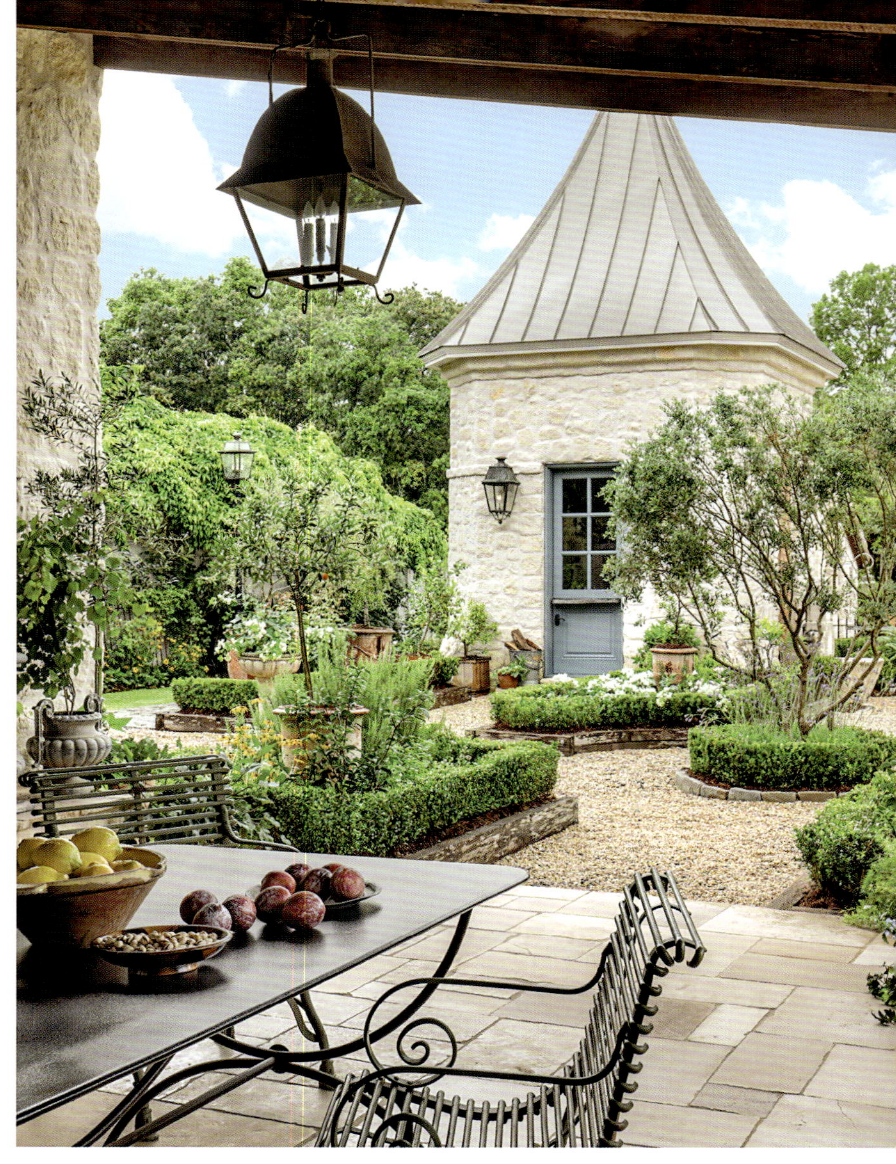

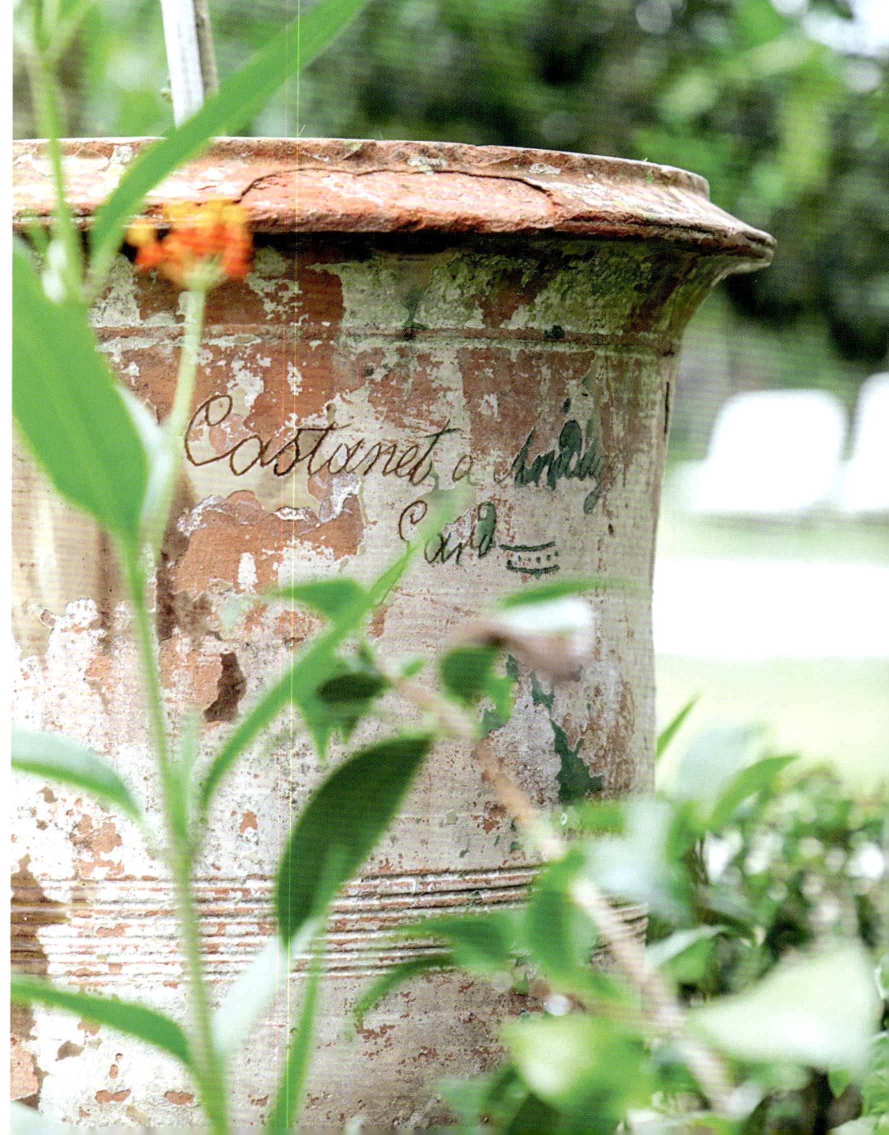

PRECEDING SPREAD: An outdoor loggia adjoining a garden full of herbs, flowers, and vegetables is warmed by a fireplace crafted of natural limestone. Windows pierce the exterior wall, which was constructed to appear as if it is a remnant from an earlier structure that has been put to new use. RIGHT: The ensemble of gardens (which were planned in association with landscape architect Ted Viator), outbuildings, fountains, koi pond, and various sheltered nooks for relaxing leaves an impression of having accumulated gradually over a great length of time.

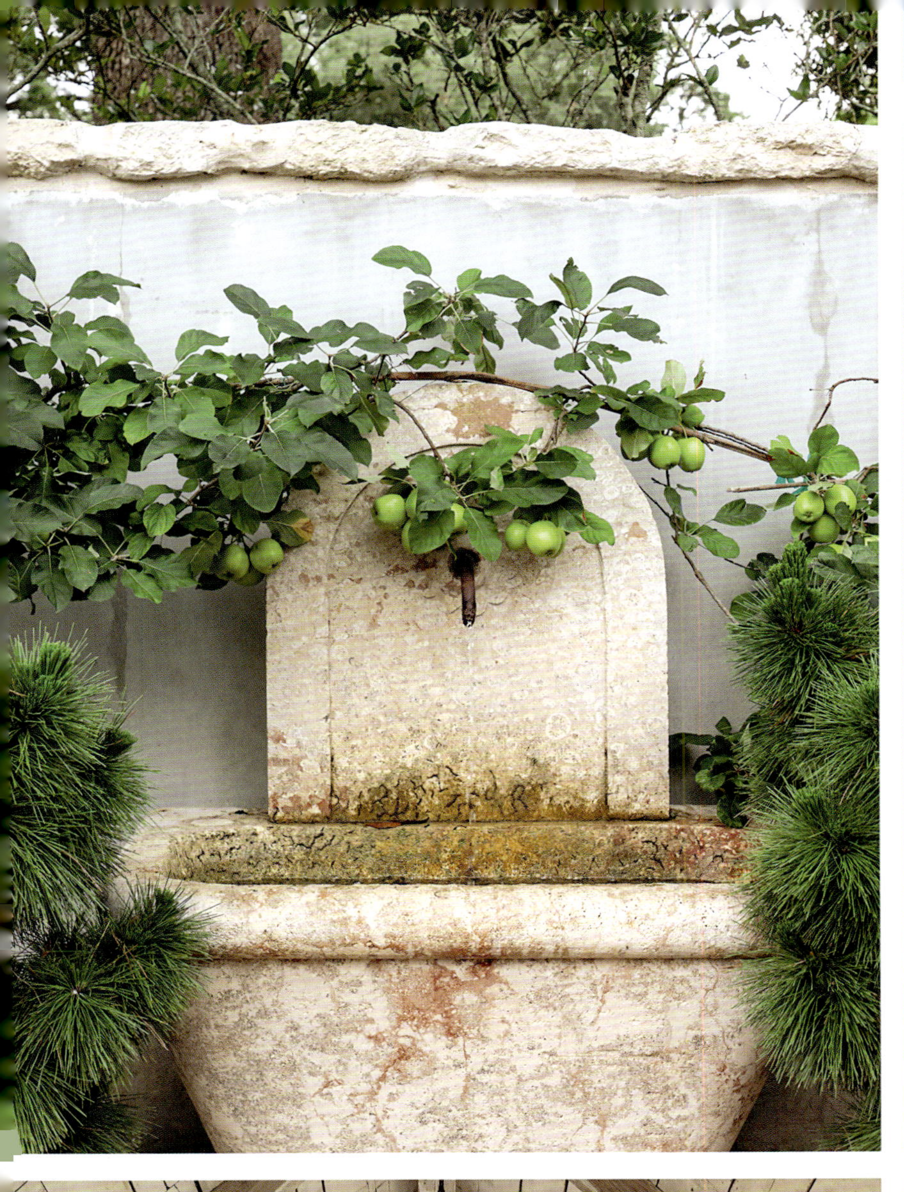
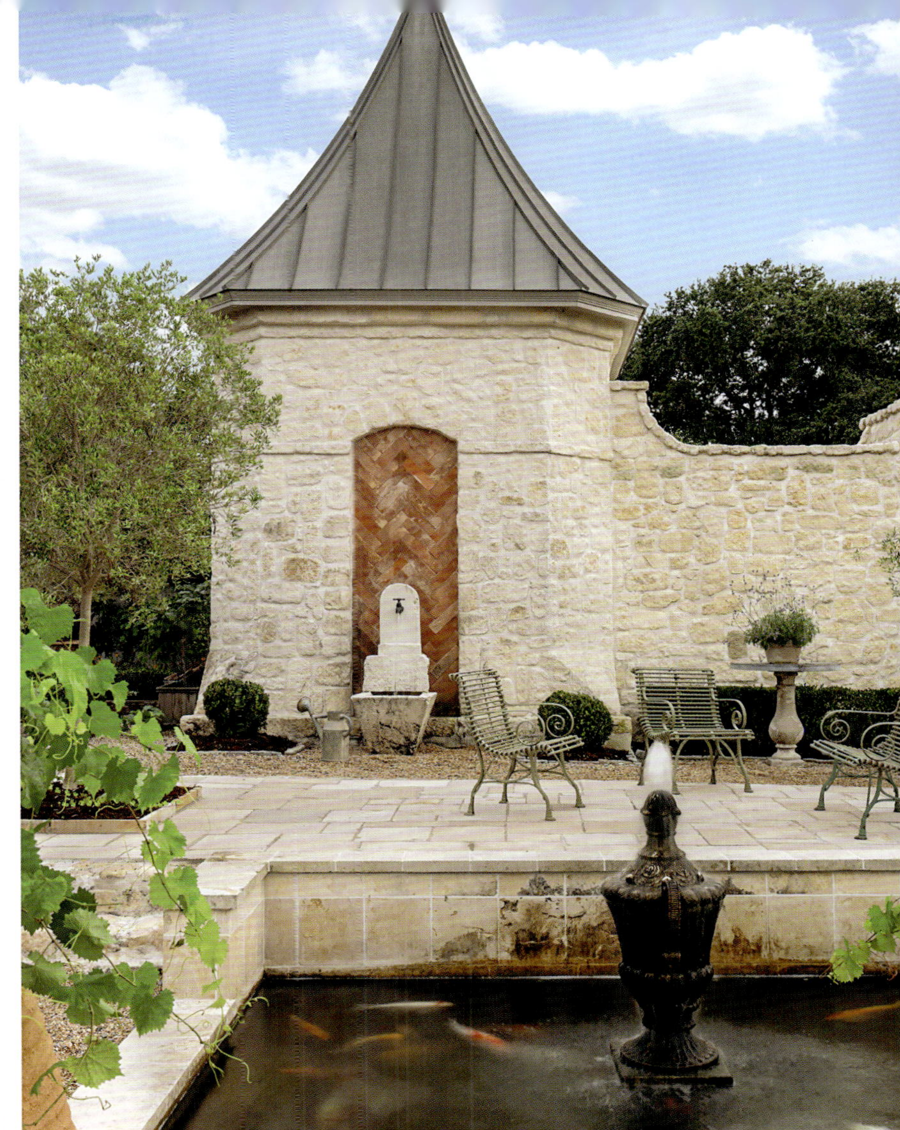
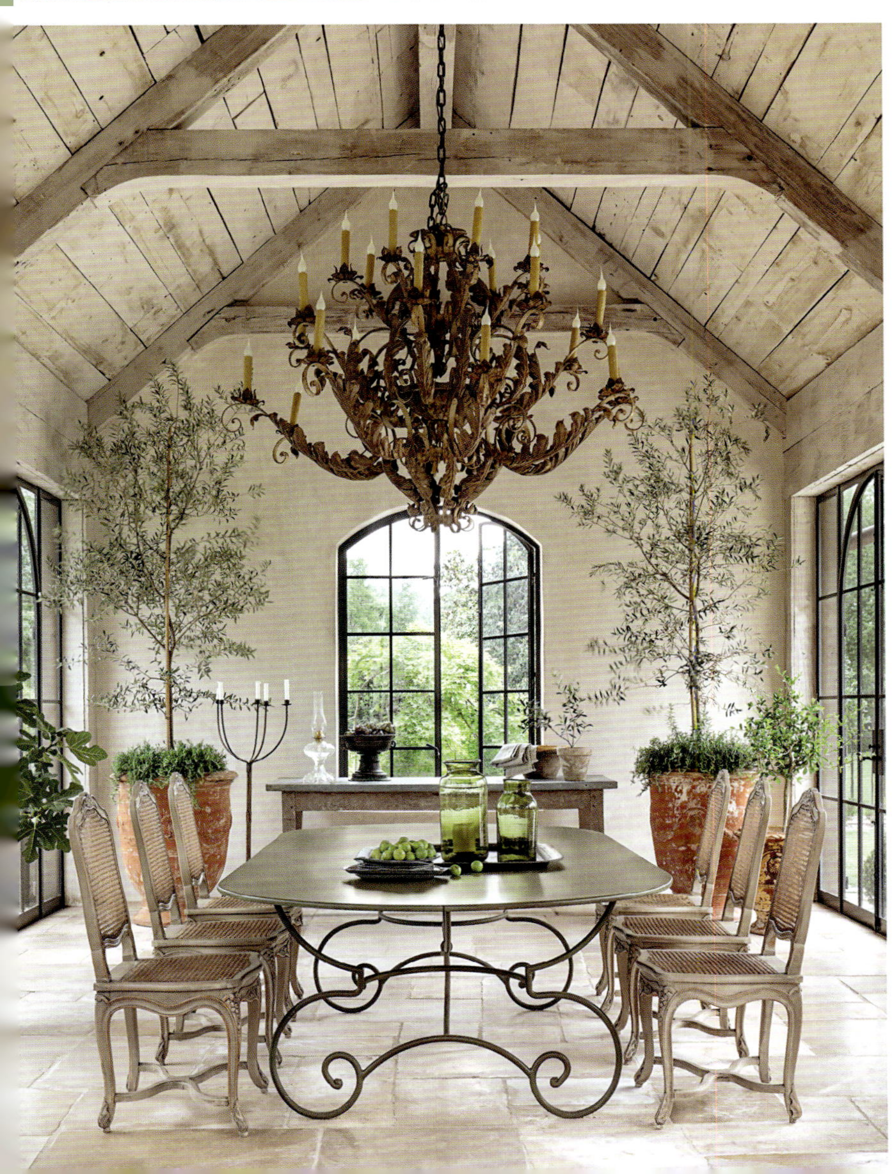
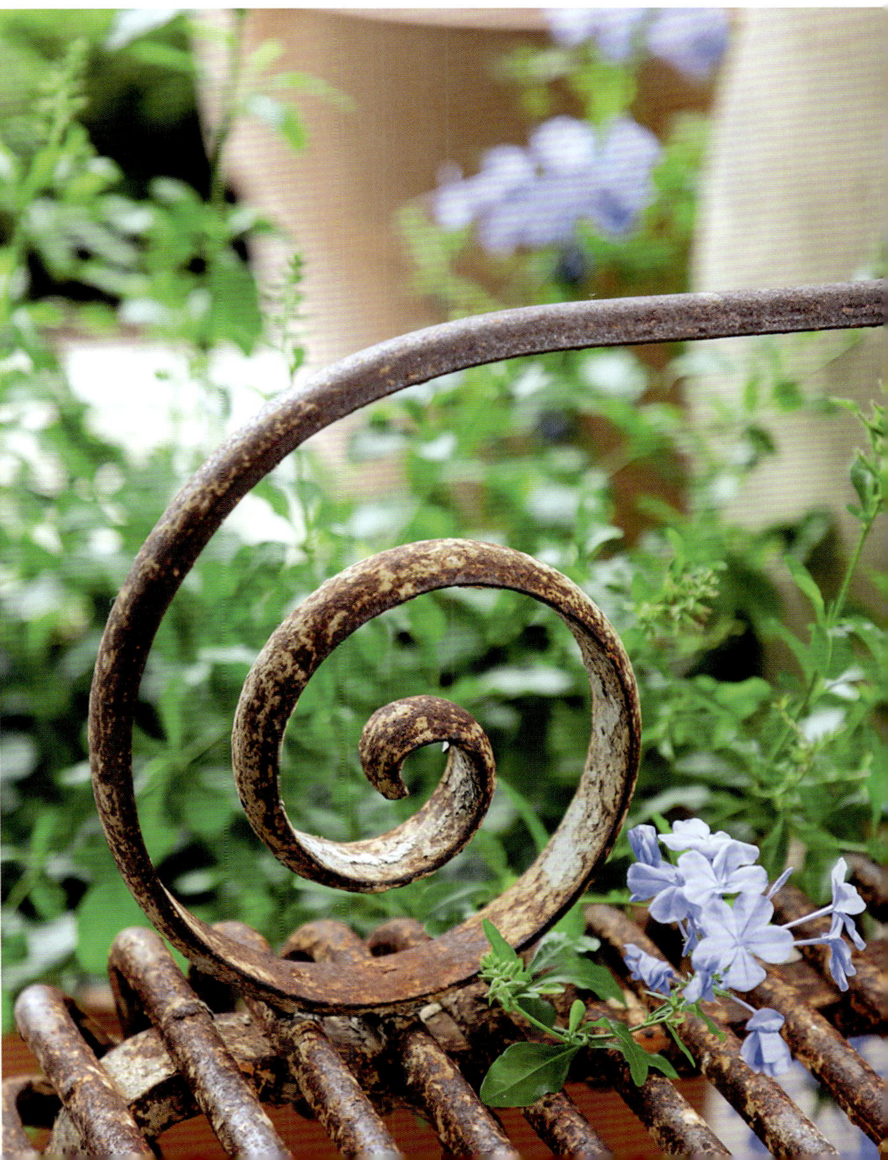

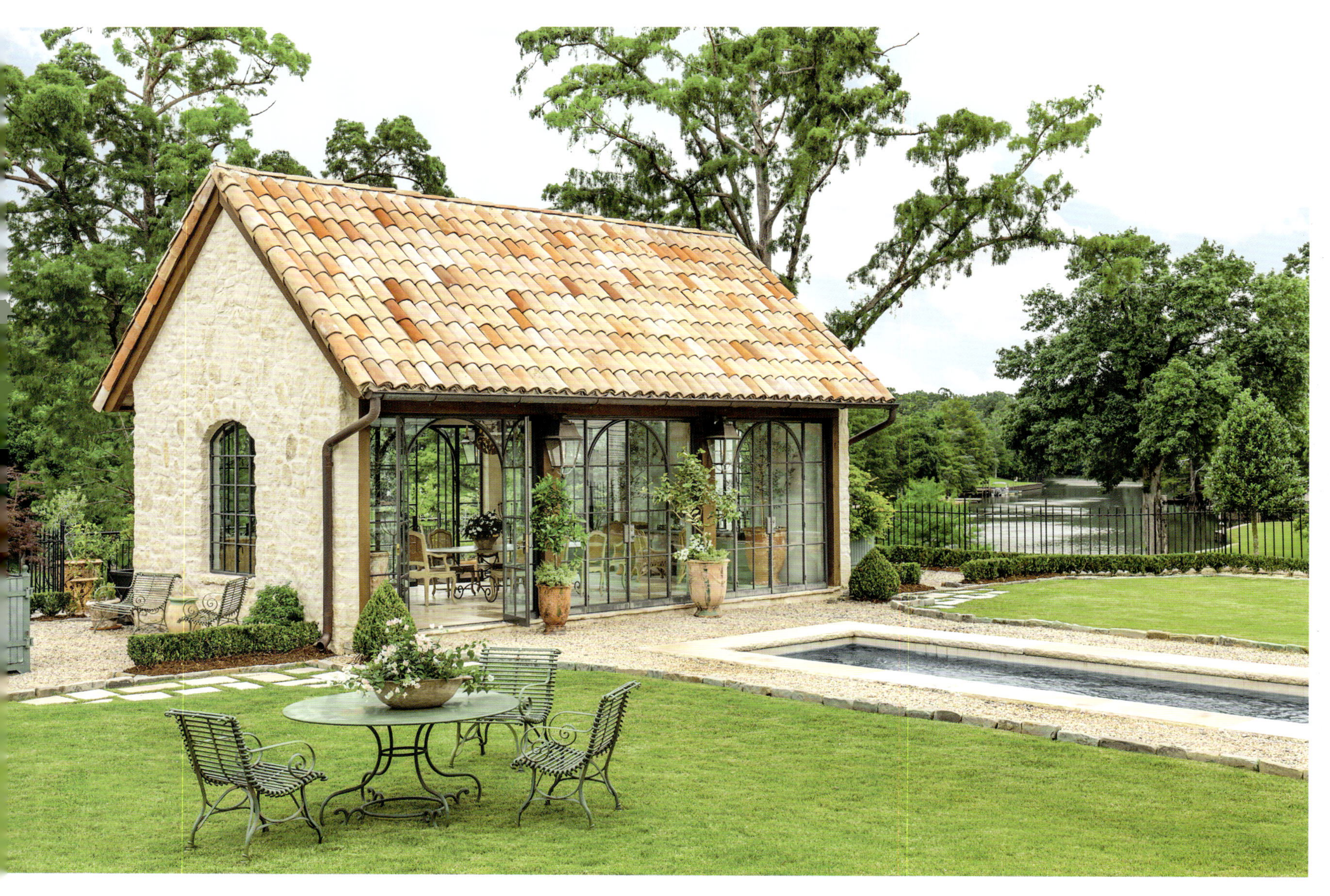

ABOVE: A central focal point behind the house, the orangery serves as a festive destination for dinners and entertaining. OPPOSITE: Some of the best views can be seen from a pea-gravel terrace at the very back of the grounds, looking up- and downstream on the river.

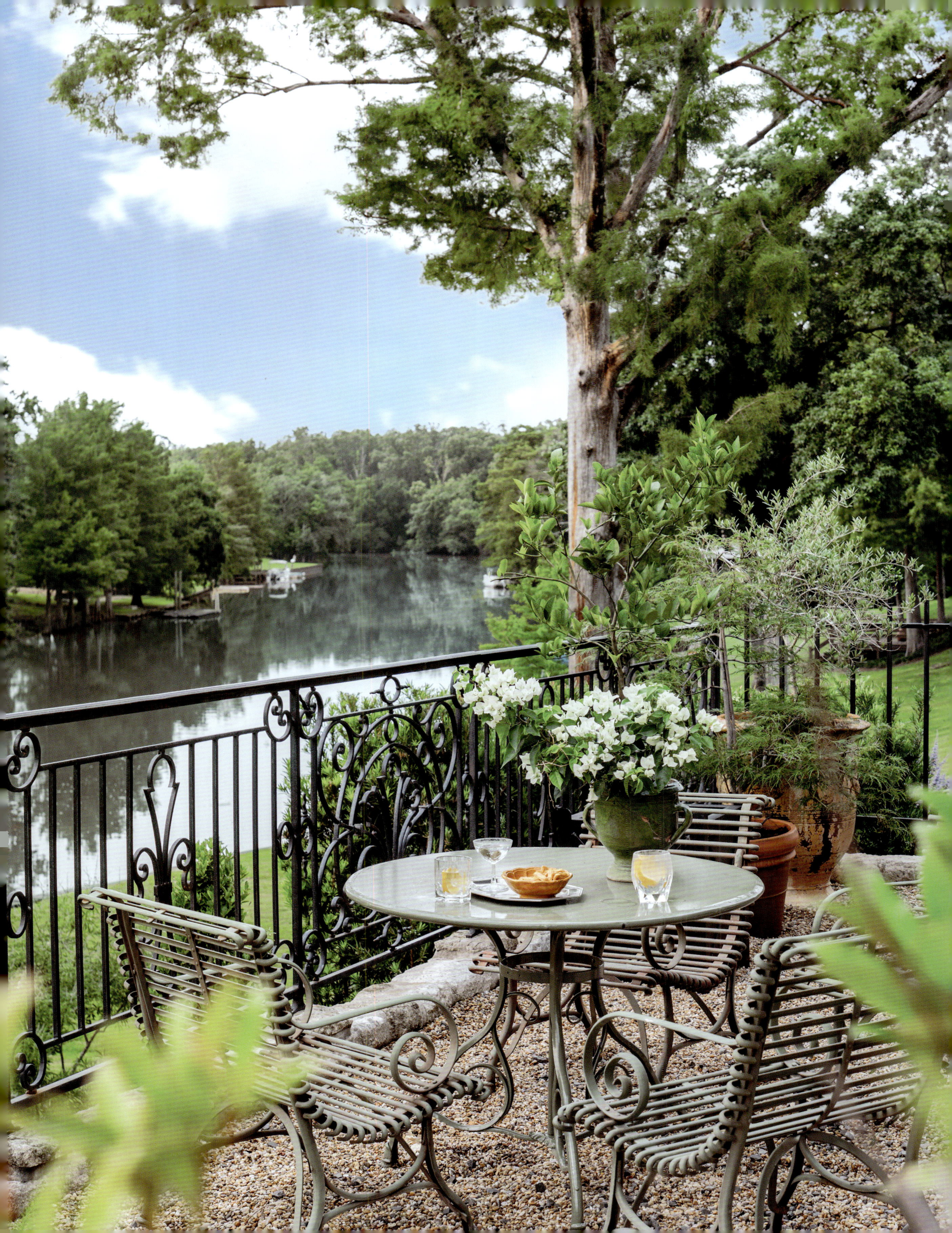

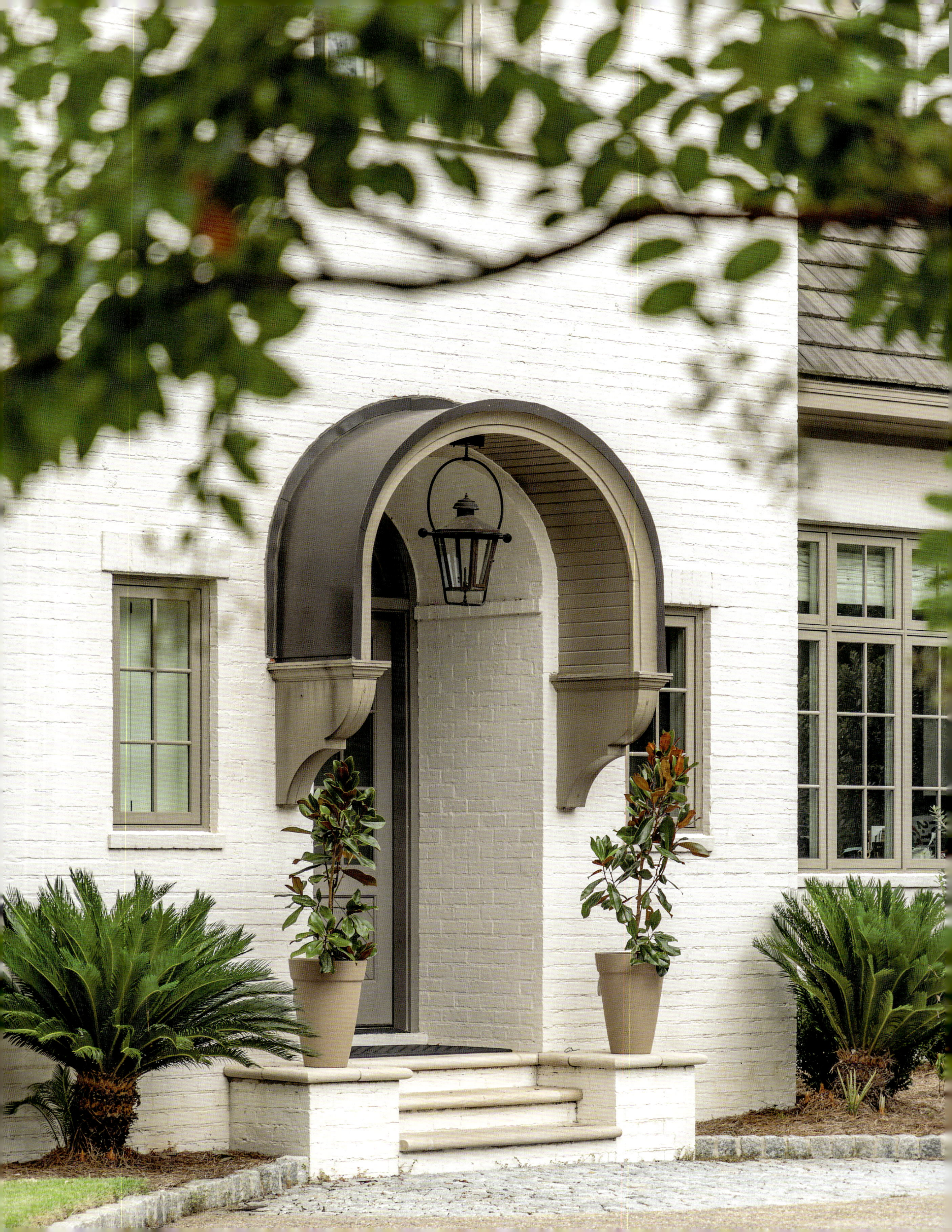

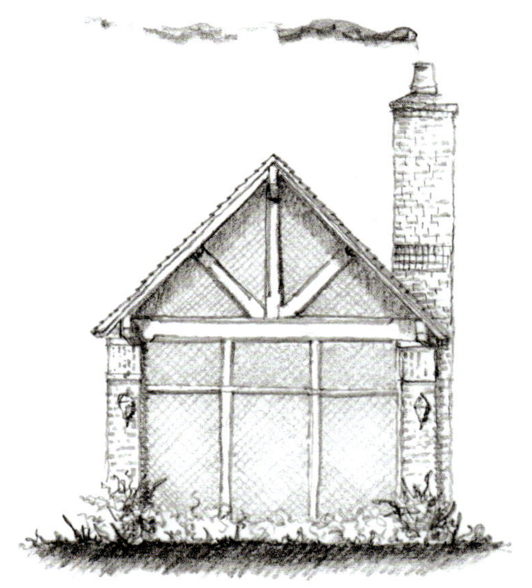

UNDER THE OAKS

Over the course of my career, I've had the pleasure of designing several homes in the gorgeous environment of St. Simons Island, the largest of the Golden Isles along Georgia's Atlantic coast. In this case, I was brought in to work on a project in a relatively new community called Frederica. In addition to the obligatory golf course and clubhouse, the neighborhood boasts another particularly attractive feature: a substantial man-made lake whose margins are dotted with gnarled live oak trees trailing banners of Spanish moss, forming an idyllic background for the numerous homesites and winding roads.

OPPOSITE: At the front entrance, a pair of substantial wooden corbels supports a curved sheltering canopy. The doorway itself is recessed by several feet to extend and enhance the progression from outside to inside. FOLLOWING SPREAD: A road winds through the live oaks on Georgia's St. Simons Island. PAGES 78–79: The approach to the house ends with a manicured circular driveway.

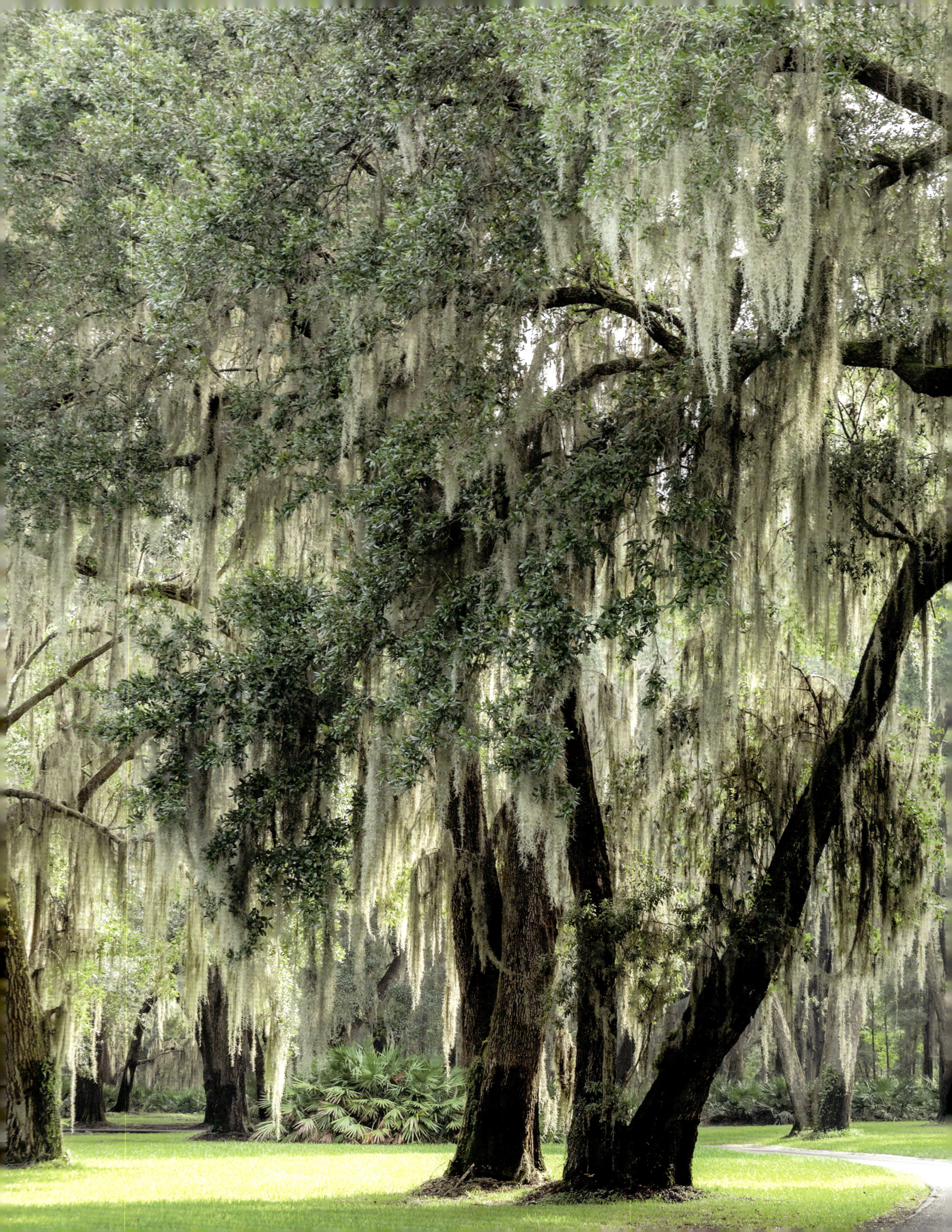

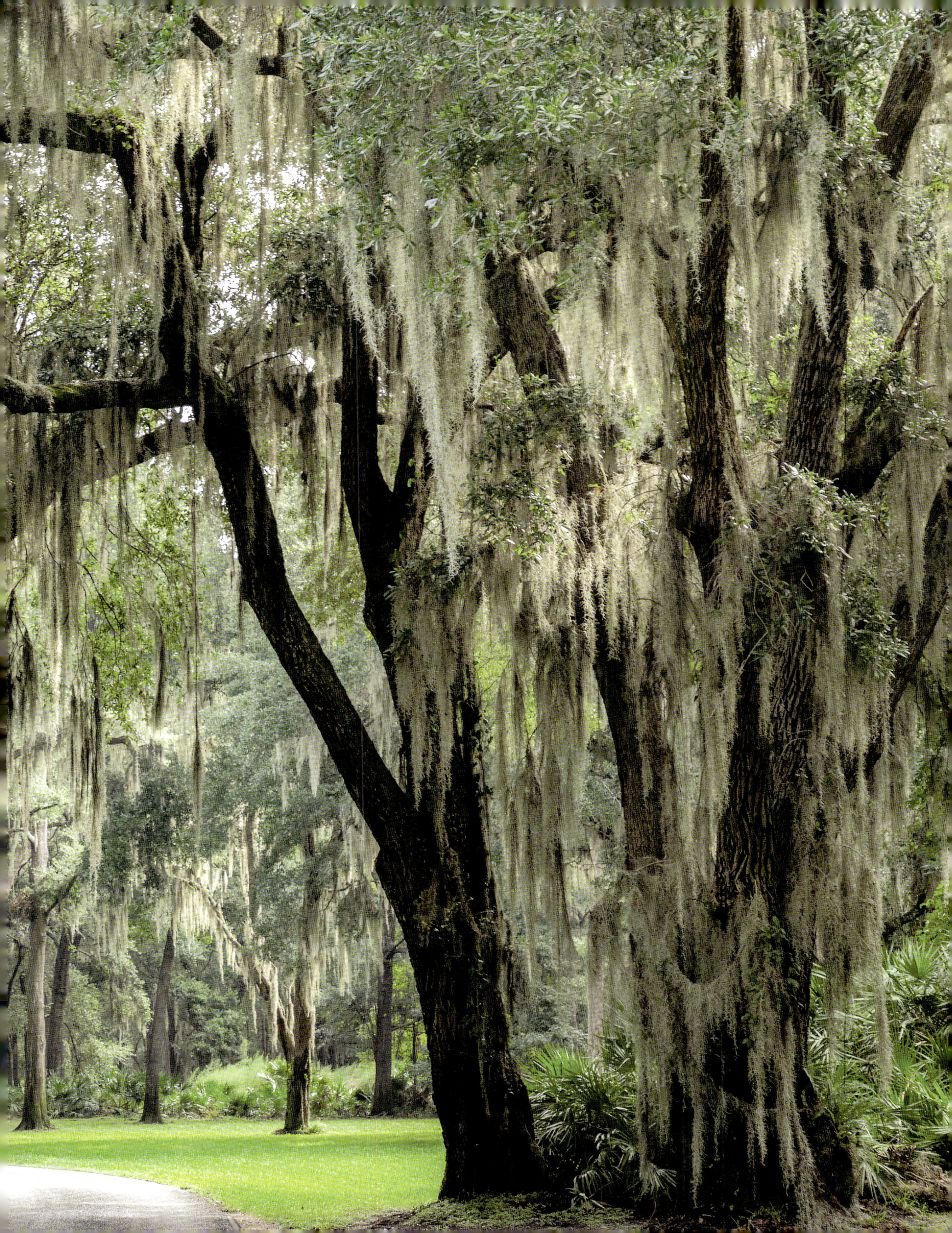

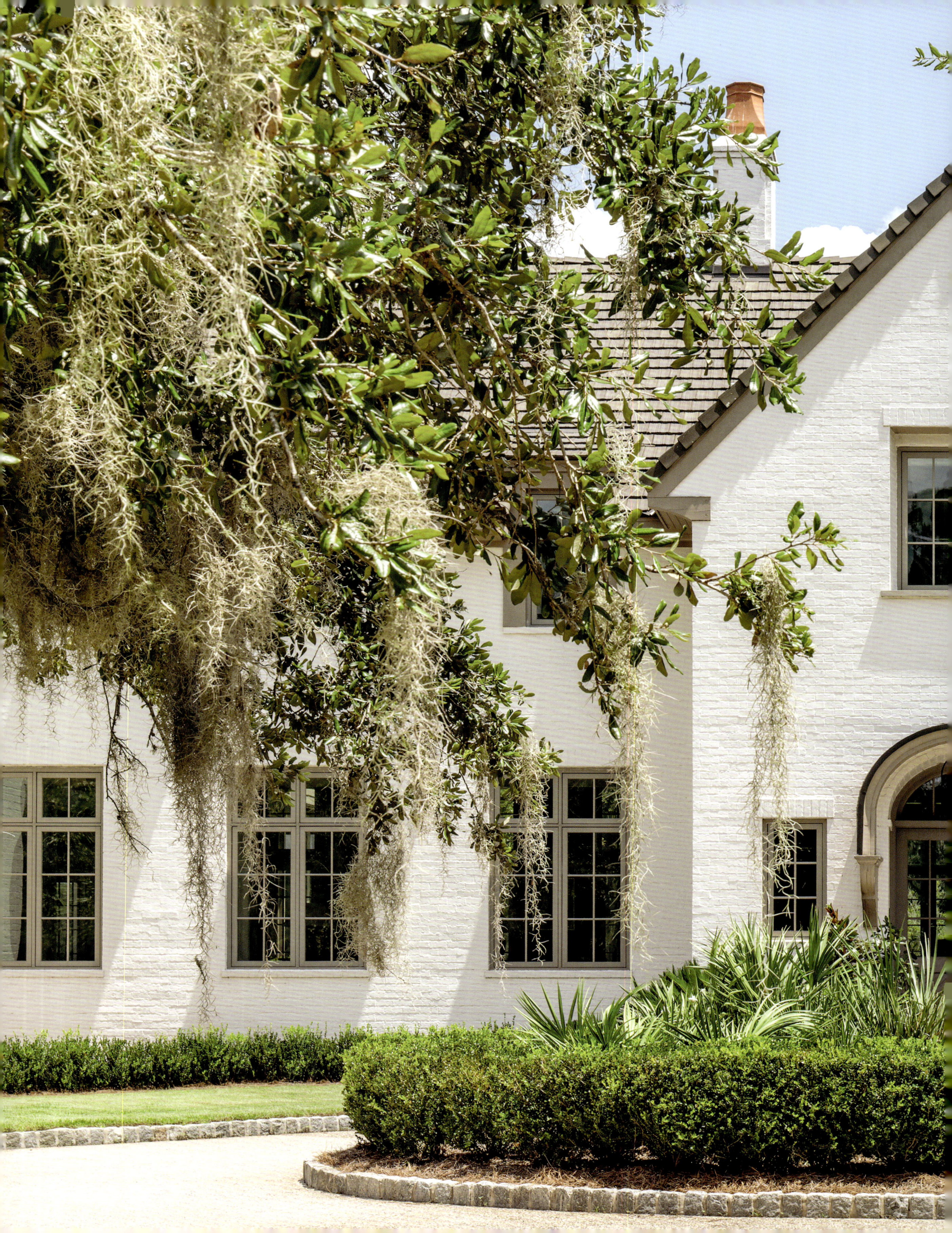

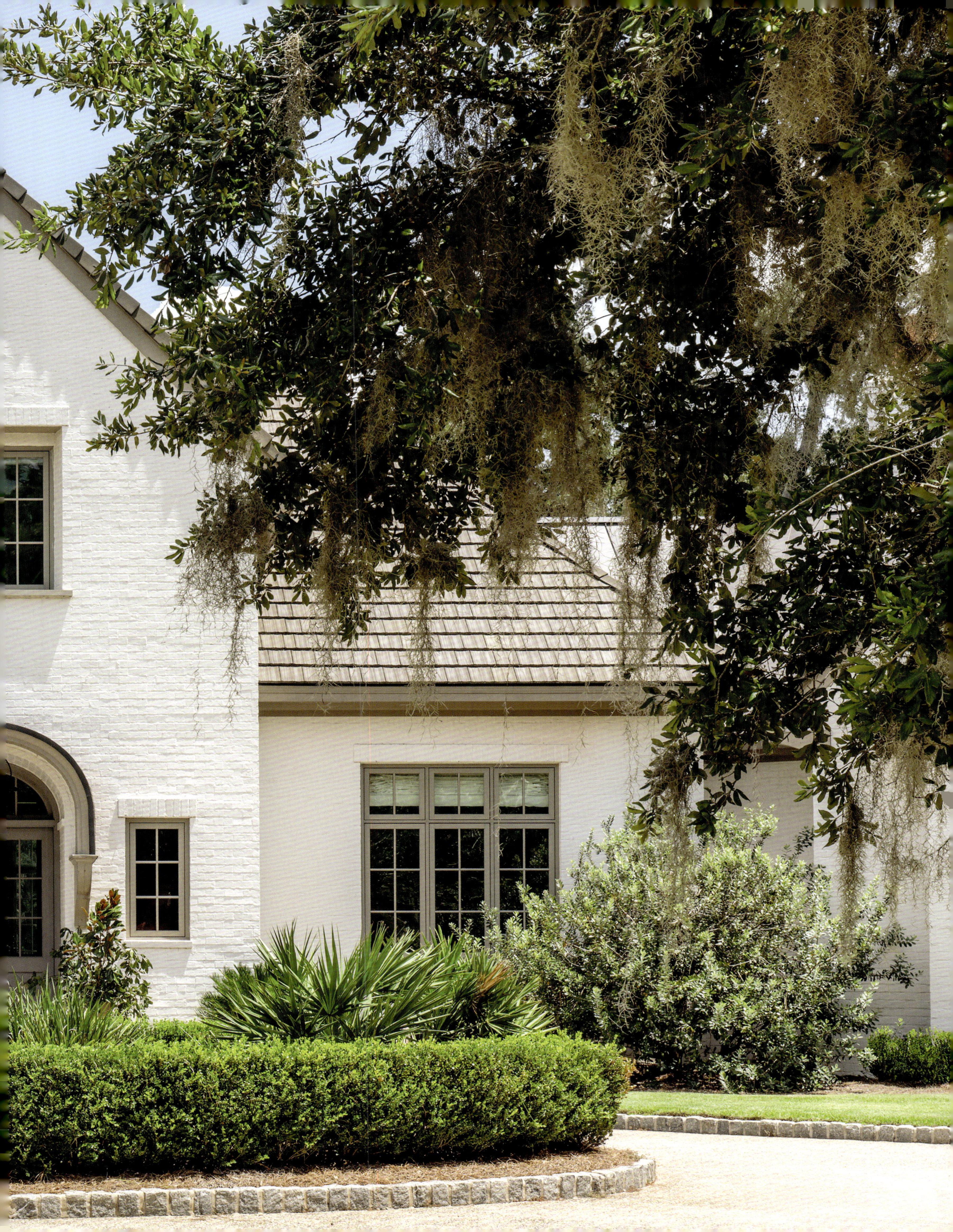

A young couple already living in the area were looking for larger residential quarters to serve as an expanded home base for a brood of young ones who were entering their teen years. They wanted it to be a place with plenty of play and hangout amenities to tempt both family members and friends—a media room, a pool and cabana, a screened porch complete with a fireplace and swings, a summer kitchen, a gym, and facilities for both indoor and outdoor basketball—along with, of course, a good-size bunk room for overnight stays.

The pair realized that such an ambitious program, which also ended up including multiple garages and outdoor parking for guests, would result in quite a large house—and they also hoped to preserve enough undeveloped waterfront to function as a buffer between them and the neighbors. Combining two lakeside lots furnished an ample canvas for their plans, and ensured that the residence and the property would be suitably balanced in scale.

The main challenge I faced as their architect, however, proved not to be the dimensions of the home's footprint, but instead a county-mandated maximum height restriction of thirty-five feet. How could we fit so many rooms beneath a roof without exceeding that limit? My approach was to divide the home into a series of additive volumes, creating a structure that meanders organically, following the shoreline of the lake. Each segment is essentially one room deep, and all are given separate pitched roofs, which keep them from becoming too tall. Single-story sections alternate with higher ones, and dormers allow second-floor spaces to be tucked behind cornices that appear lower. This gives the house a lot of movement, and the roofline becomes one of the most important animating elements of the architecture. Best of all, this kind of layout results in most rooms having windows on at least two sides, for an open, airy feeling, and you get a constant succession of new experiences as you navigate from space to space through the home.

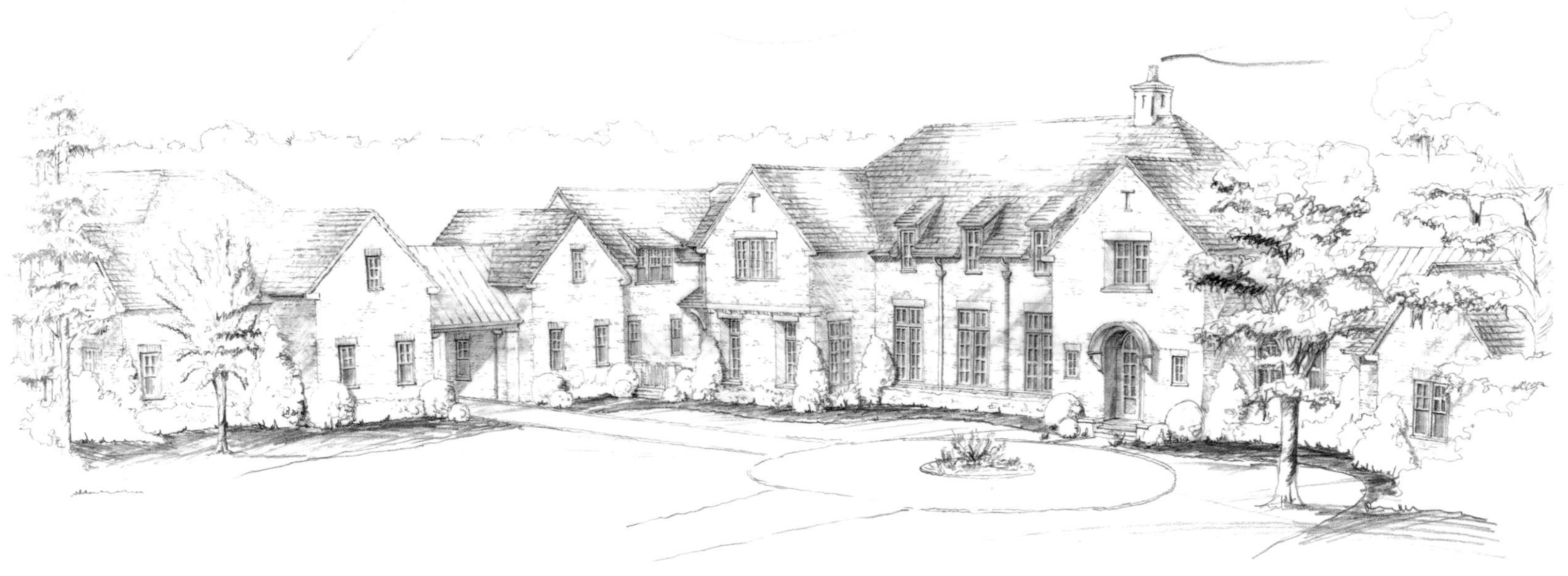

The layout's benefits are not just indoors. I love when buildings engage their natural surroundings with pocket gardens and courtyards—varied and intimate settings for people to spend time in. We have several of them here. A sheltered, plant-filled nook sits behind formal fencing next to the dining room, accessible via a set of French doors. (It simultaneously provides a beautiful view to be enjoyed from the wife's office.) An auto court off to one side is reached by passing under a porte cochere, defining a separate domain for vehicles and services. In the rear, the pool slots in between the cabana, a summer kitchen, an outdoor dining area, and a screened porch, with sight lines across the water carefully framed by two of the picturesque oaks.

In terms of style, the couple wanted the home to be bright, with a painted brick exterior. Otherwise, they allowed me the latitude to craft a structure that would be appropriate for the character of the site. As with many of my projects, you see echoes of Sir Edwin Lutyens here, bending toward a simplified, slightly stripped-down interpretation. Hefty oak corbels at the corners of the roof, a stepped-brick cantilever above the dining room's front windows, exposed rounded rafter tails

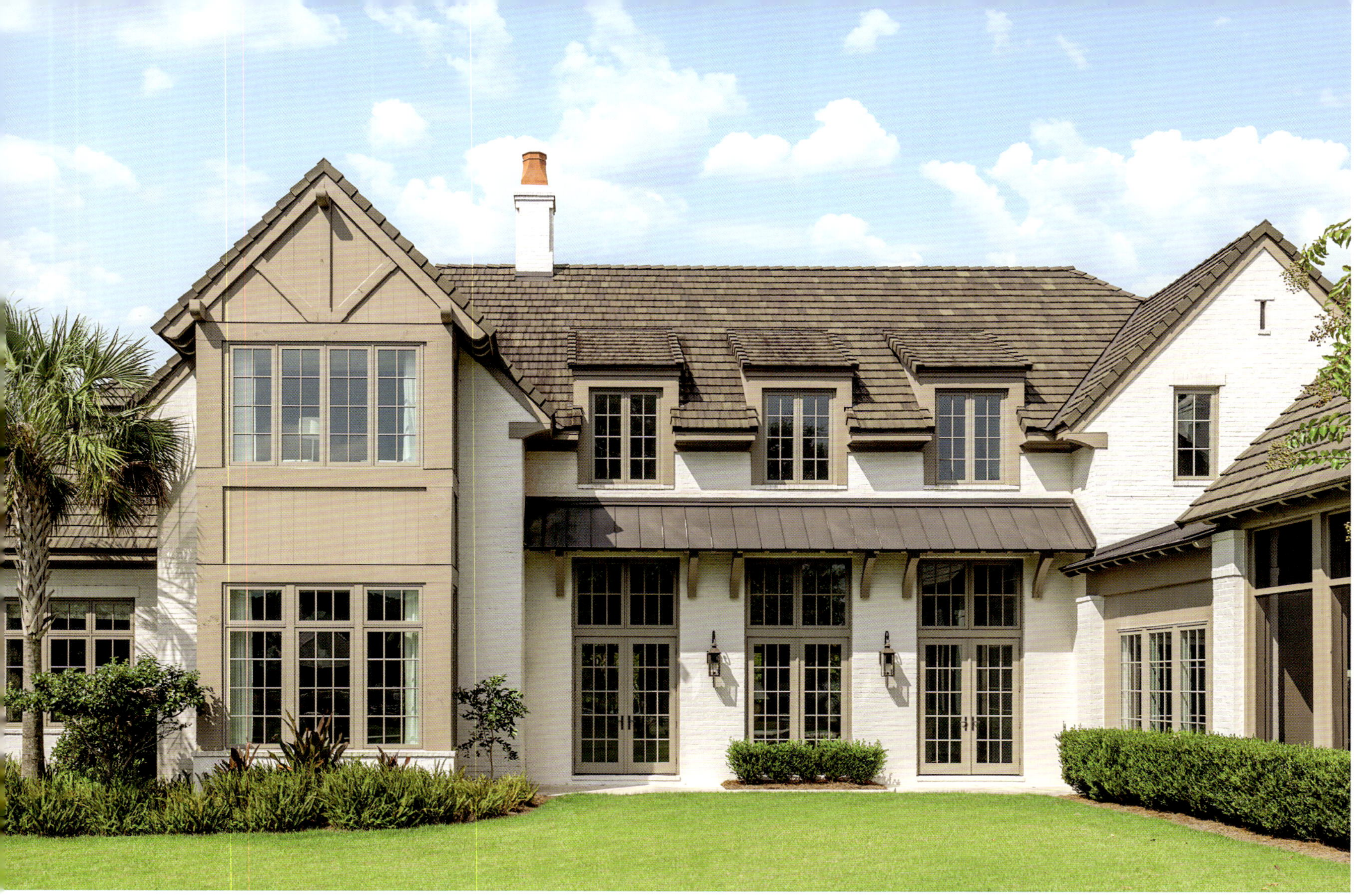

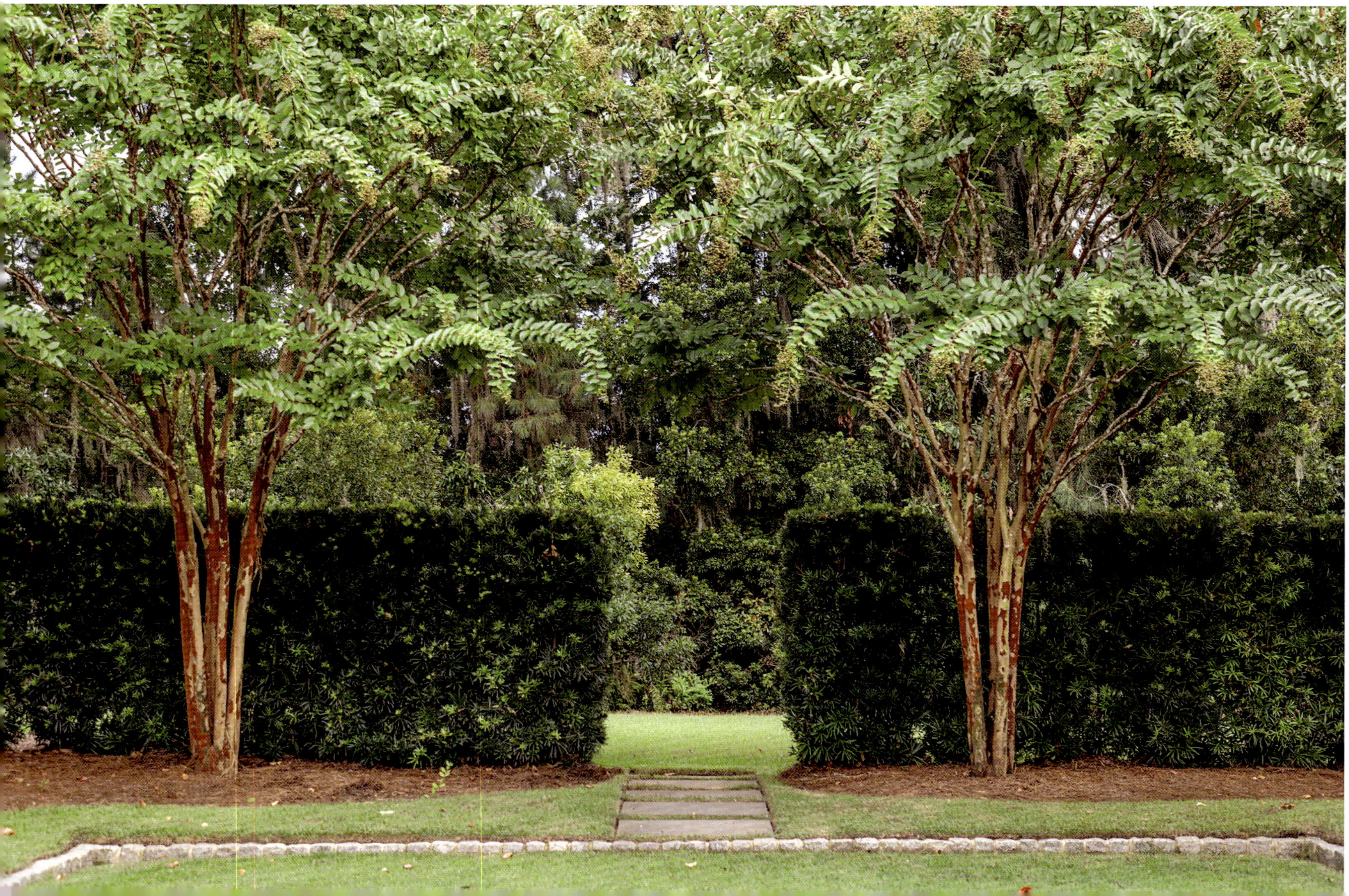

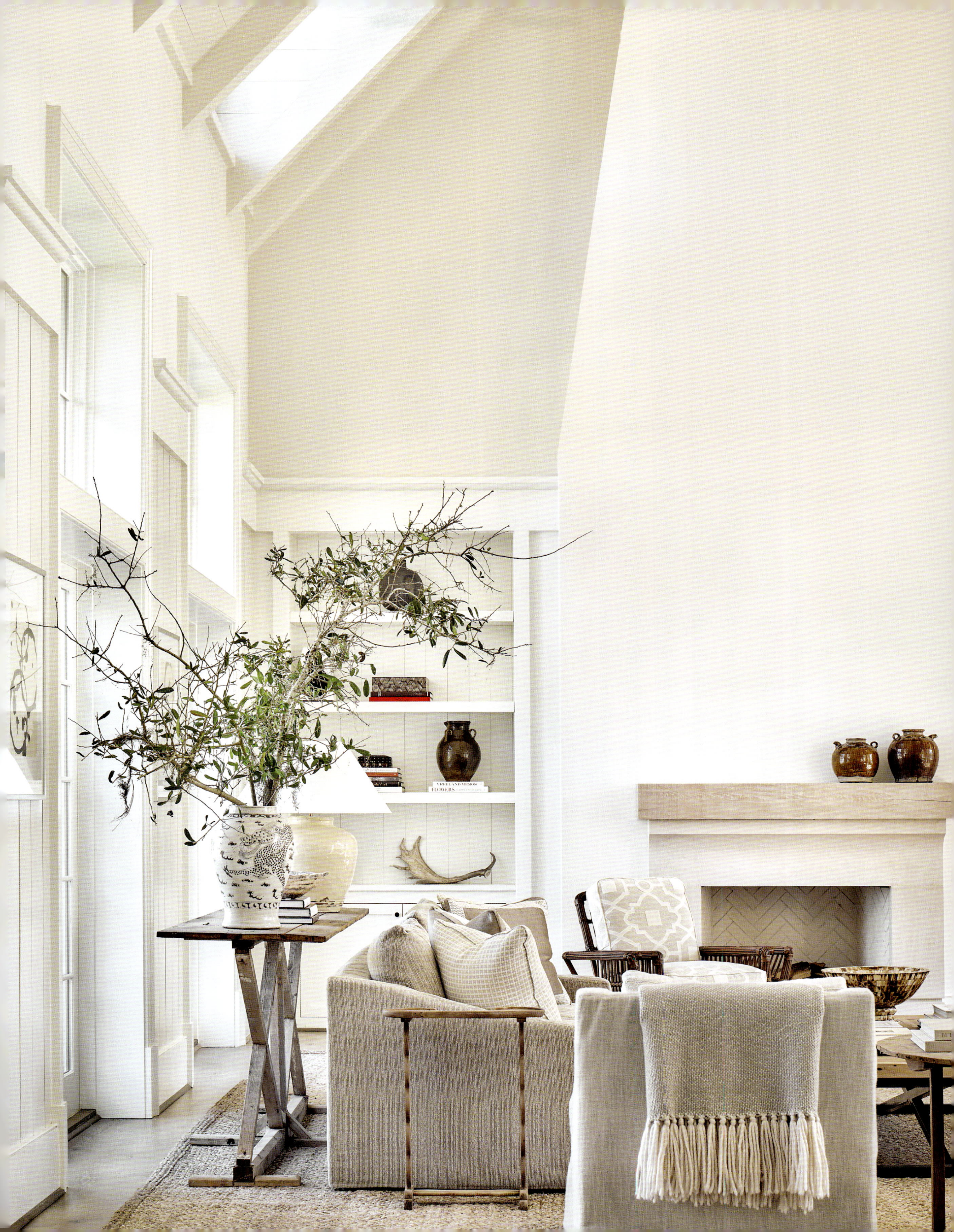

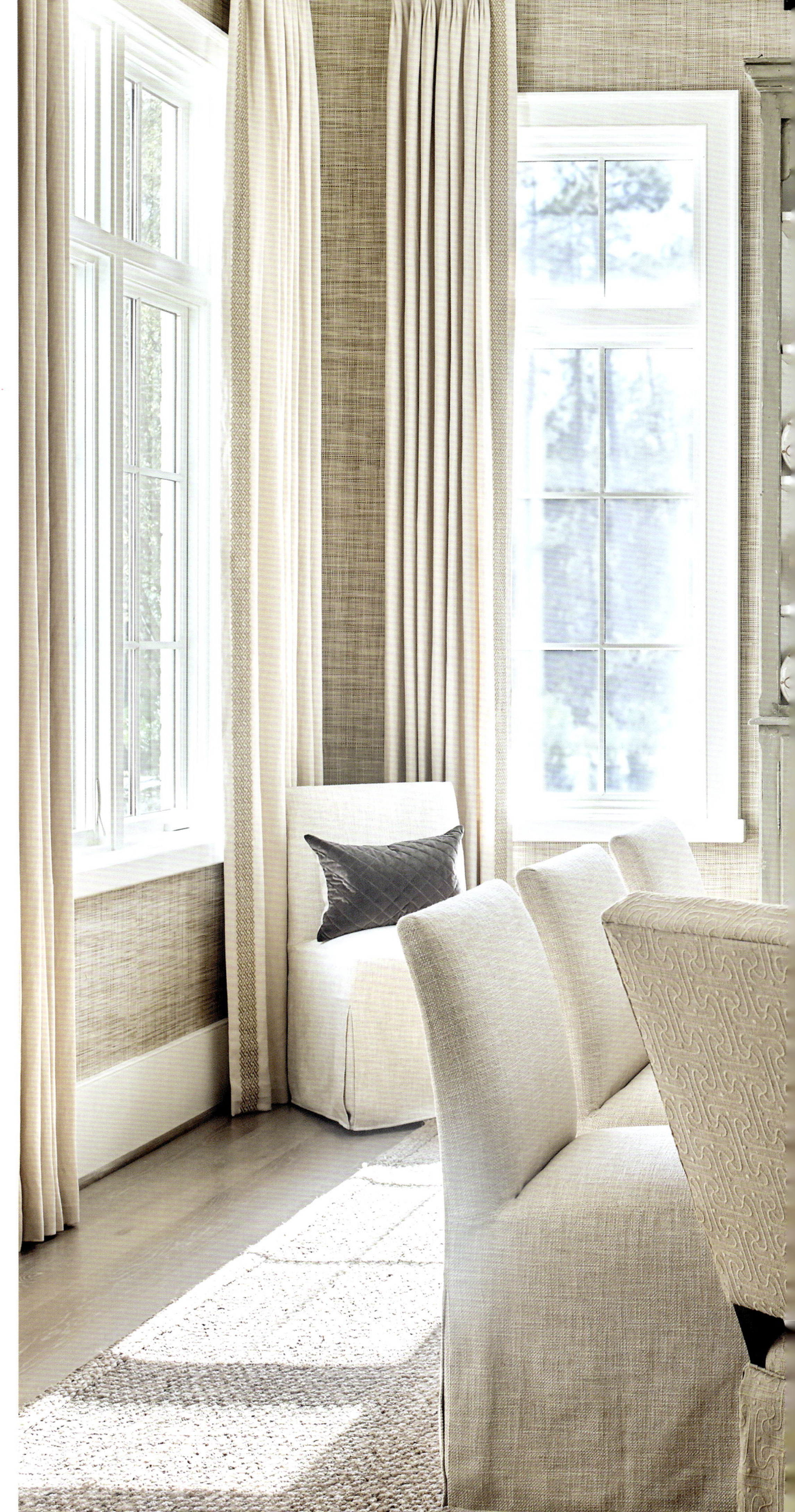

PRECEDING SPREAD, LEFT: In the front gallery, a trio of windows is mirrored by three corresponding openings into the great room. PRECEDING SPREAD, RIGHT: The great room has ten-foot wainscoting and bookshelves flanking a simple plaster fireplace. Transom windows and dormers above add natural light. RIGHT: The dining room's china hutch is built into the front wall. Interior designer Beth Webb furnished the home with pieces that have a suitably clean, transitional aesthetic. Colors are muted, bringing textures to the fore.

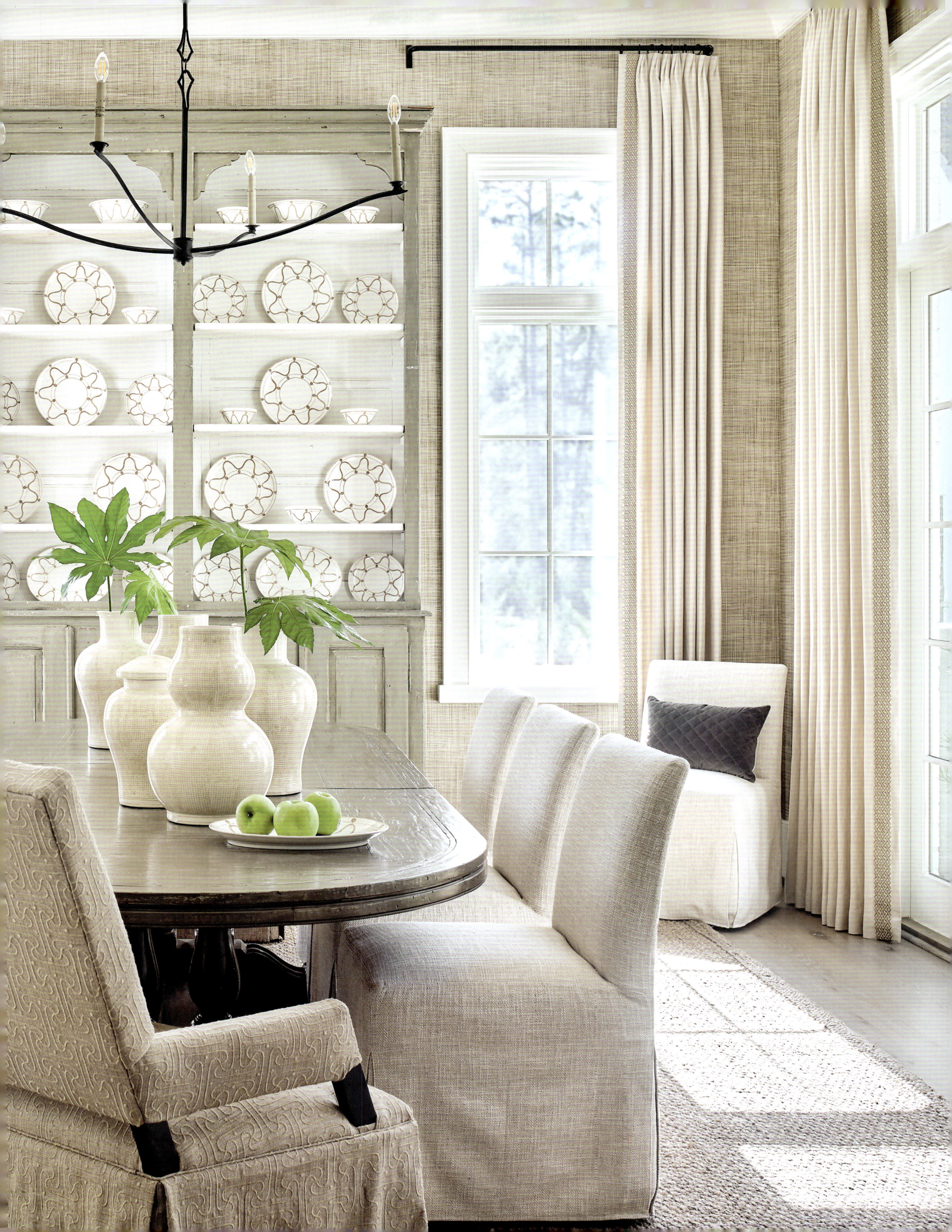

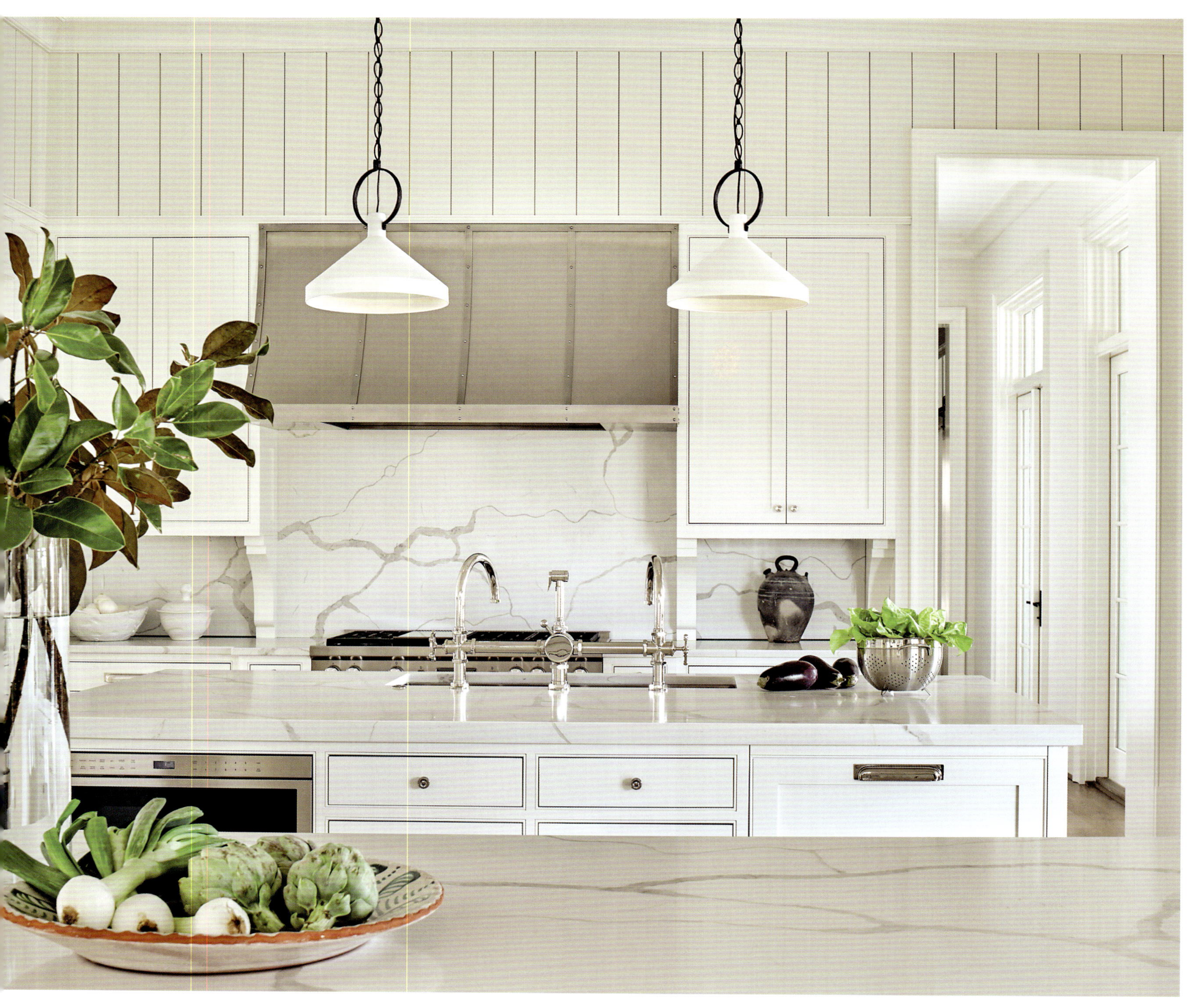

ABOVE: We designed the kitchen's Shaker-style cabinetry and millwork with upper cabinets supported by elegantly curved corbels. Underneath the upper cabinets, marble panels slide open to reveal storage for spices and oils. OPPOSITE: The countertops and backsplash in the adjoining working pantry are made of highly practical stainless steel.

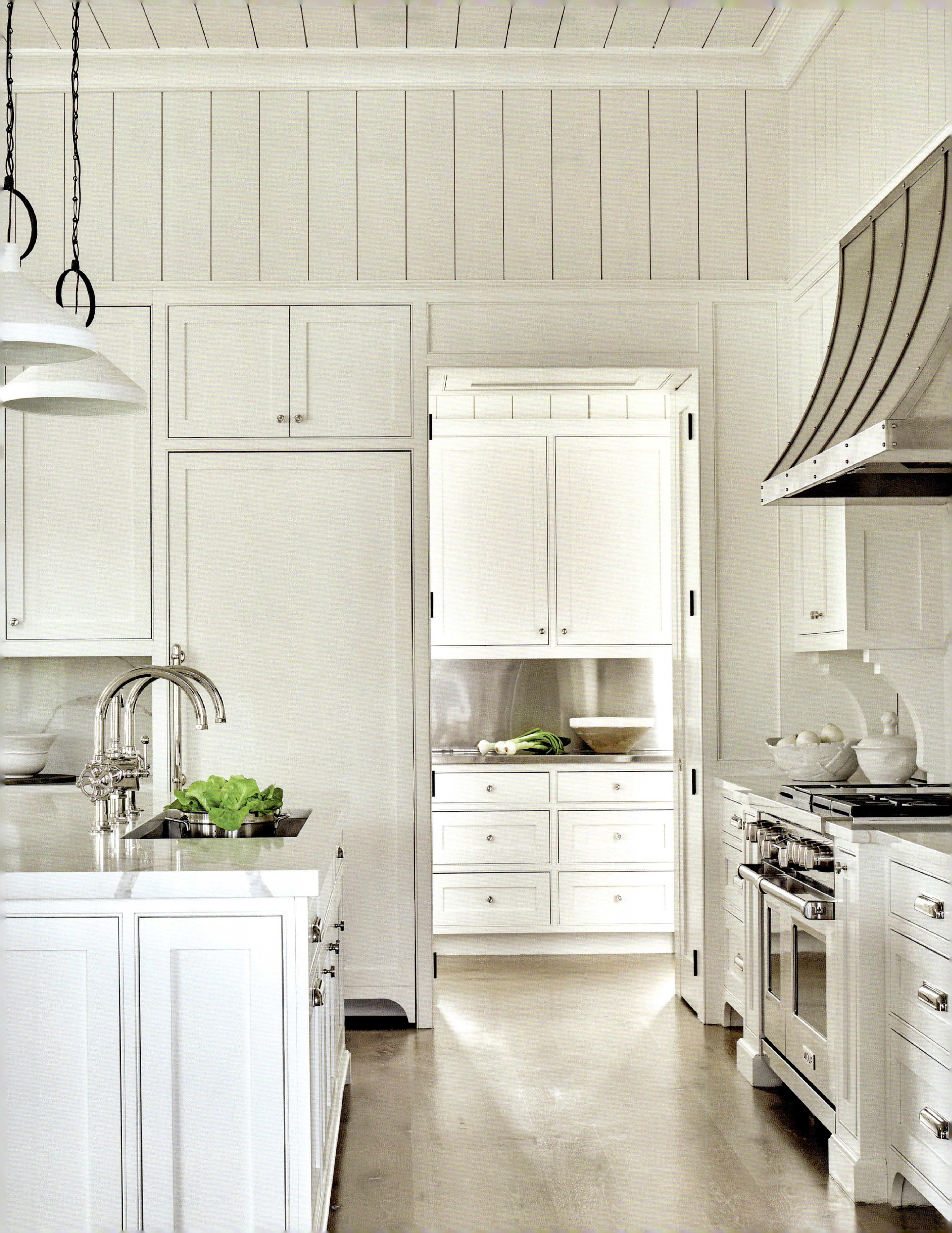

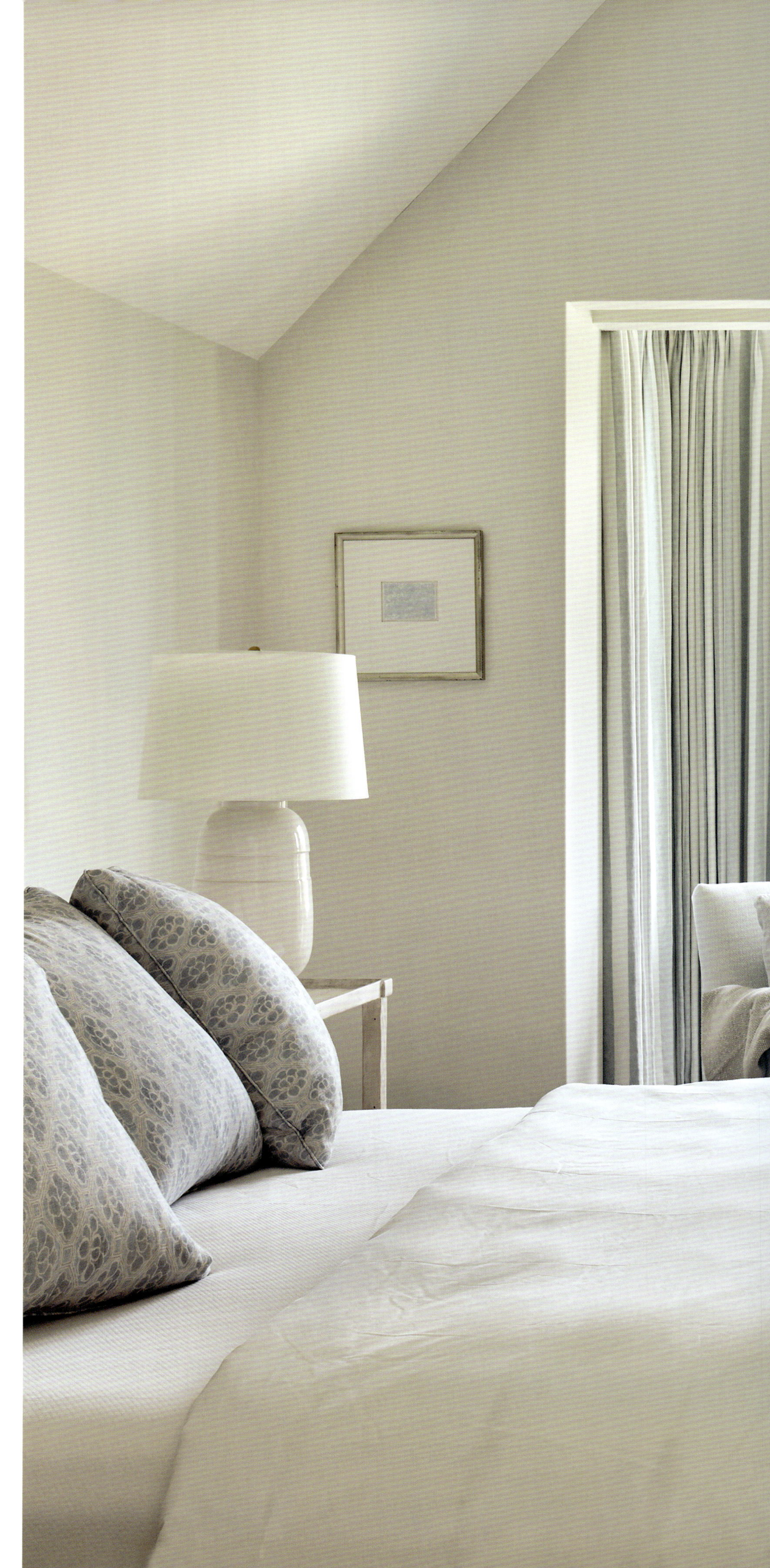

RIGHT: An upstairs guest bedroom, spacious as it is, has a cozy feeling of being tucked within the roof, while the window bay accommodates comfortable seating.

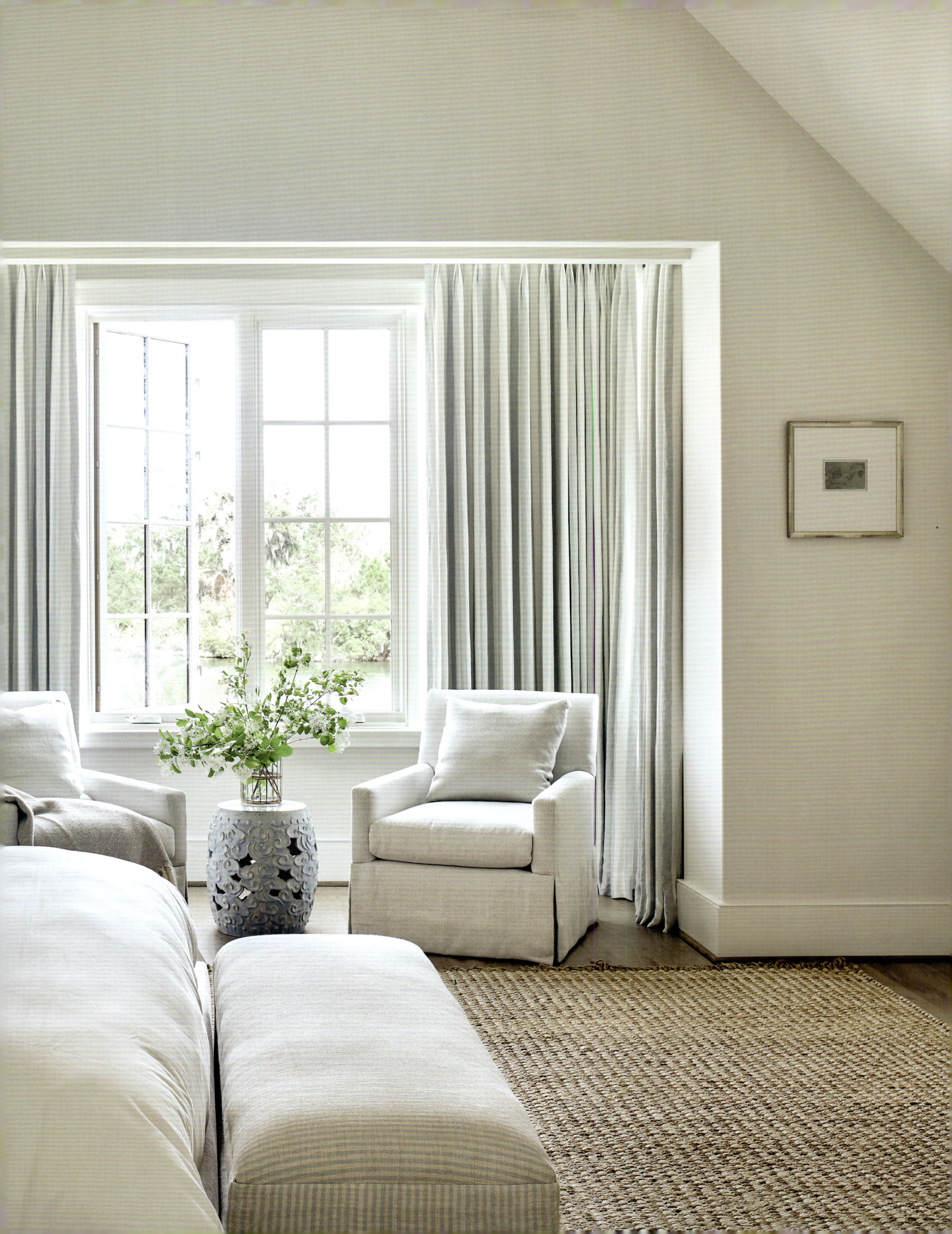

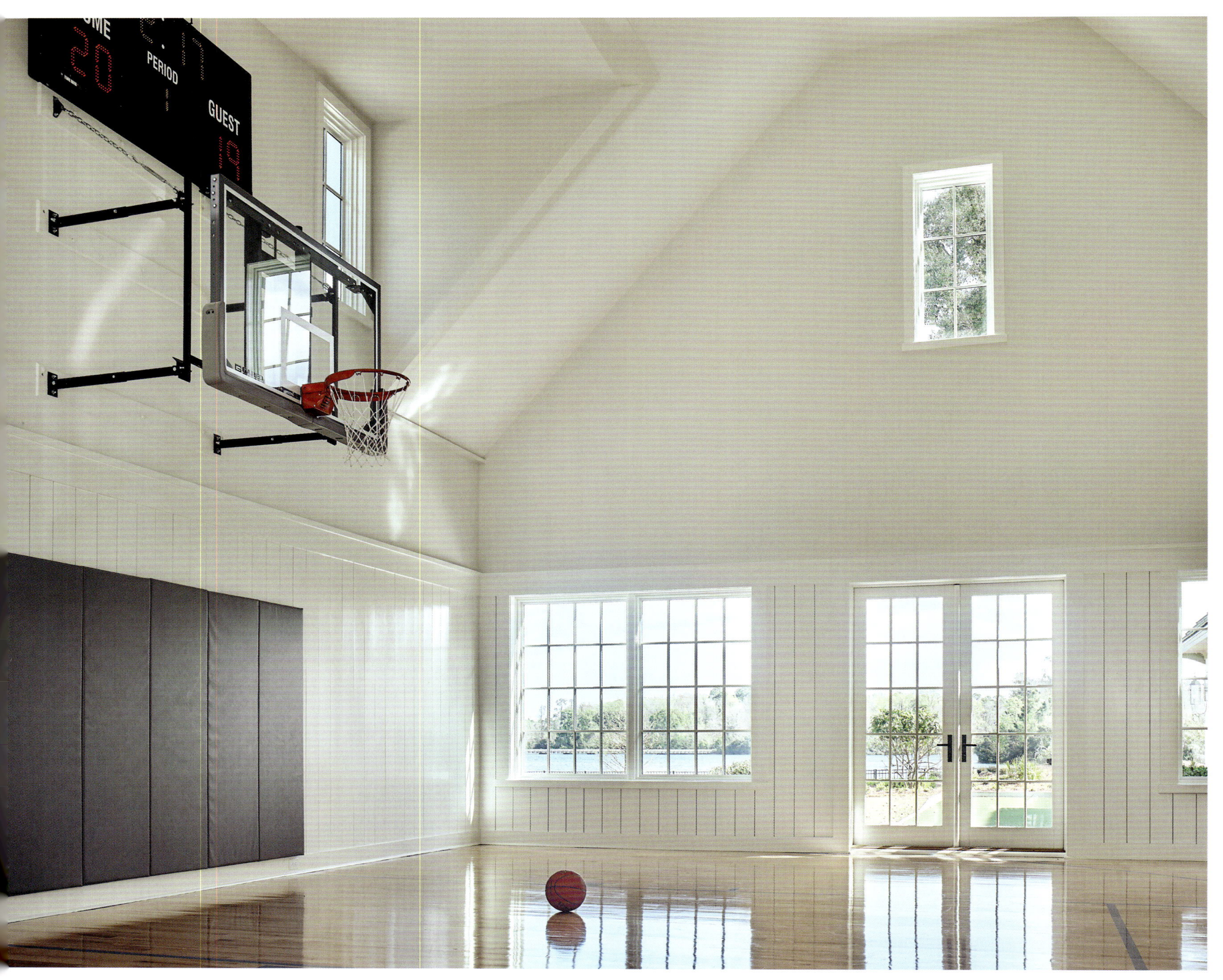

ABOVE: Having an indoor basketball court, complete with a scoreboard and buzzer, was a high priority for this client. OPPOSITE: The pool cabana is liberally equipped for lounging and game playing, and its arched window affords yet another water view. FOLLOWING SPREAD: Seen from across the lake, the house sprawls comfortably along the shore, varied in profile and never completely visible from any single perspective.

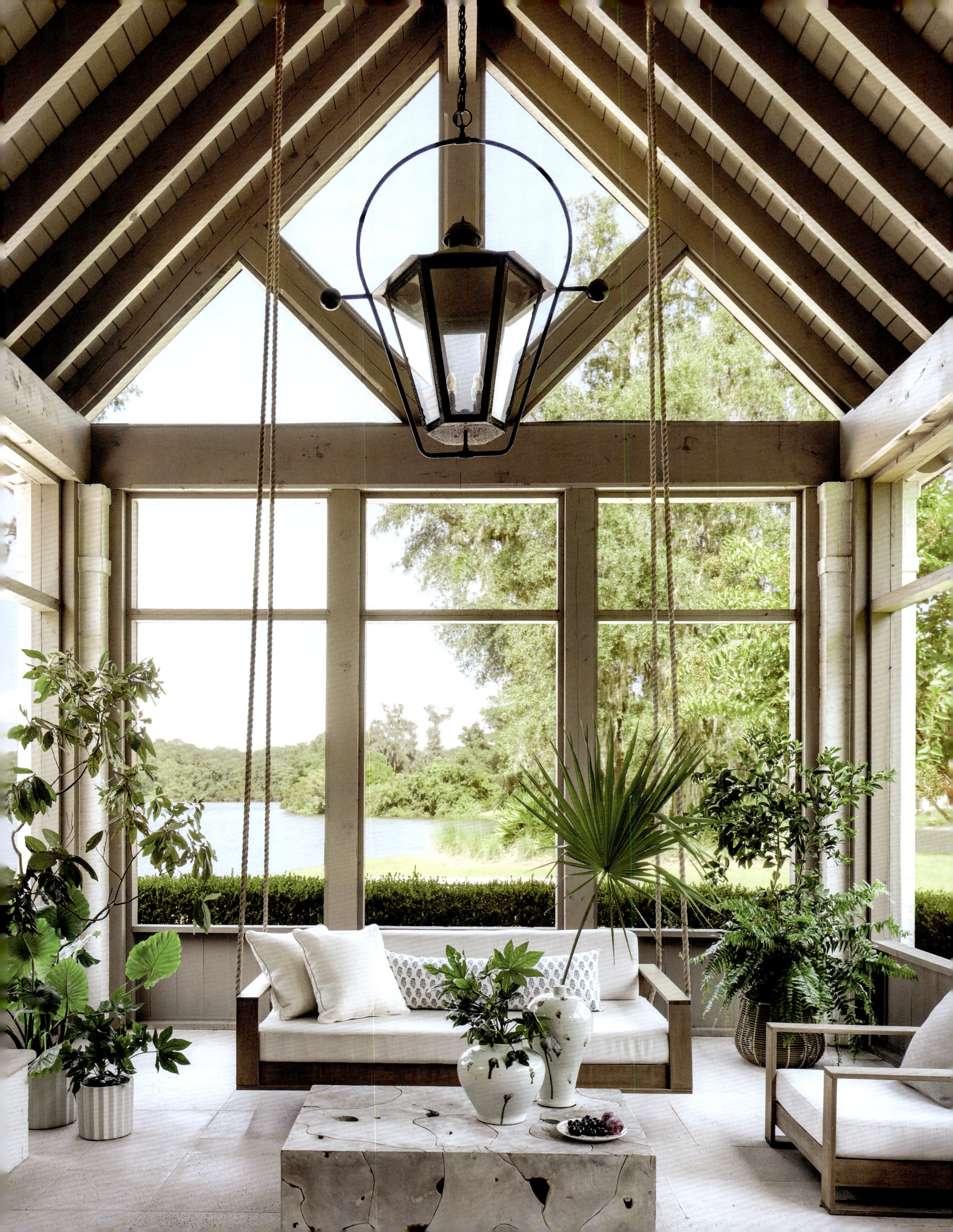

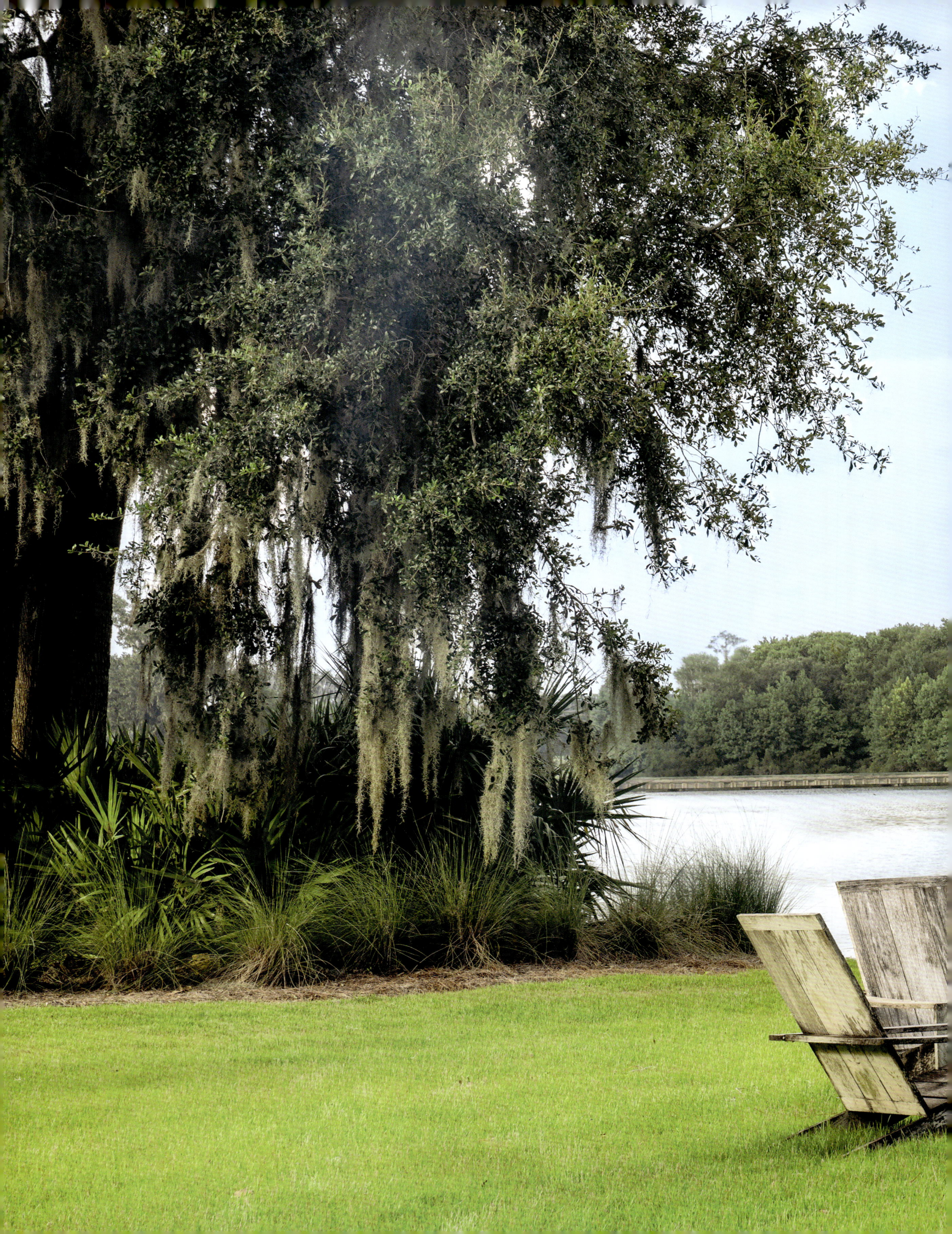

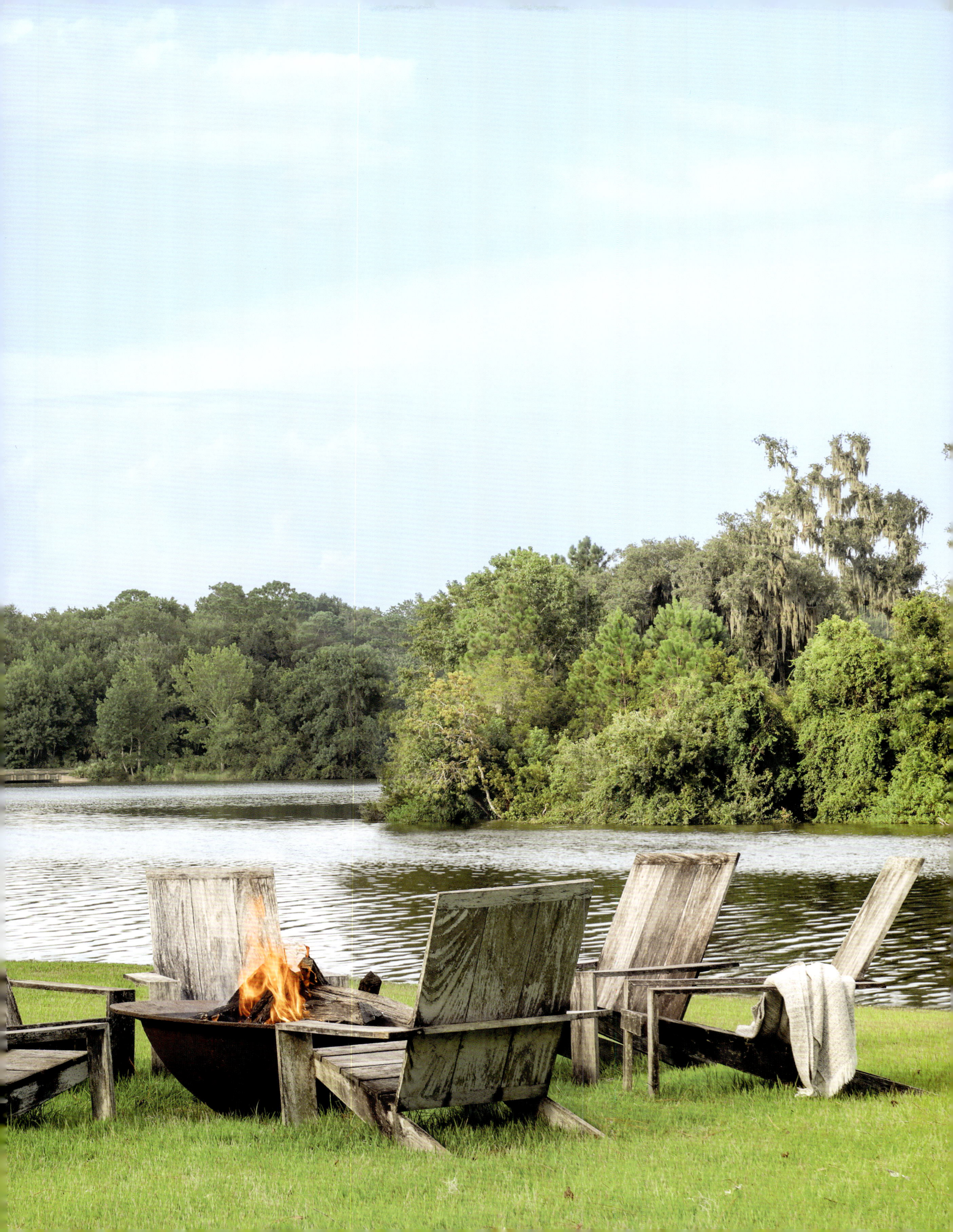

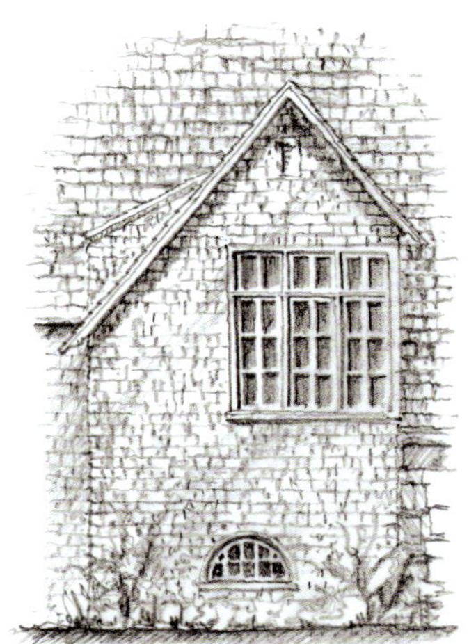

THE OVERLOOK

It's unusual to find much in the way of level space on a mountainside site in Cashiers, North Carolina. So I was surprised and pleased, when I first walked this piece of land, to discover a small clearing bordered by a beautiful, cliff-like outcropping of granite. The sheltered pocket struck me as a perfect location for an outdoor terrace and garden, and from there I was almost immediately able to picture an entire residence that would spread to the side of it. Tucking the house into the curve of the terrain and leading the driveway in at an angle from one corner of the property would allow me to center my scheme on a protected central courtyard, embraced on three sides by architecture and on the fourth by the natural wall of a rocky scarp that rises steeply to the adjacent road.

OPPOSITE: A favorite technique of mine to drop light into a lower level is to tuck an arched window under the stairs. The open treads here cast gorgeous shadows. FOLLOWING SPREAD: A small cupola tops the porte cochere that passes into the home's entry court.

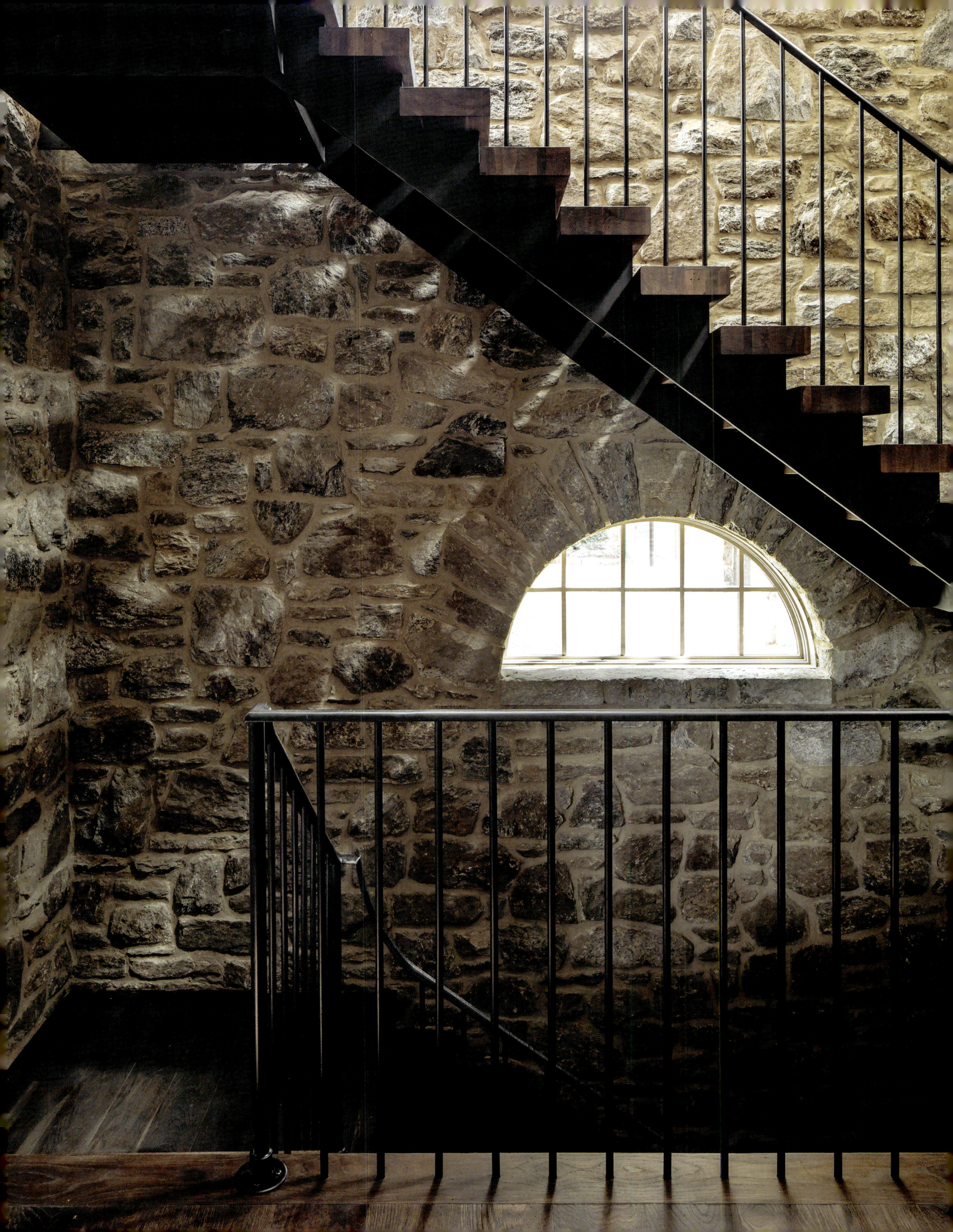

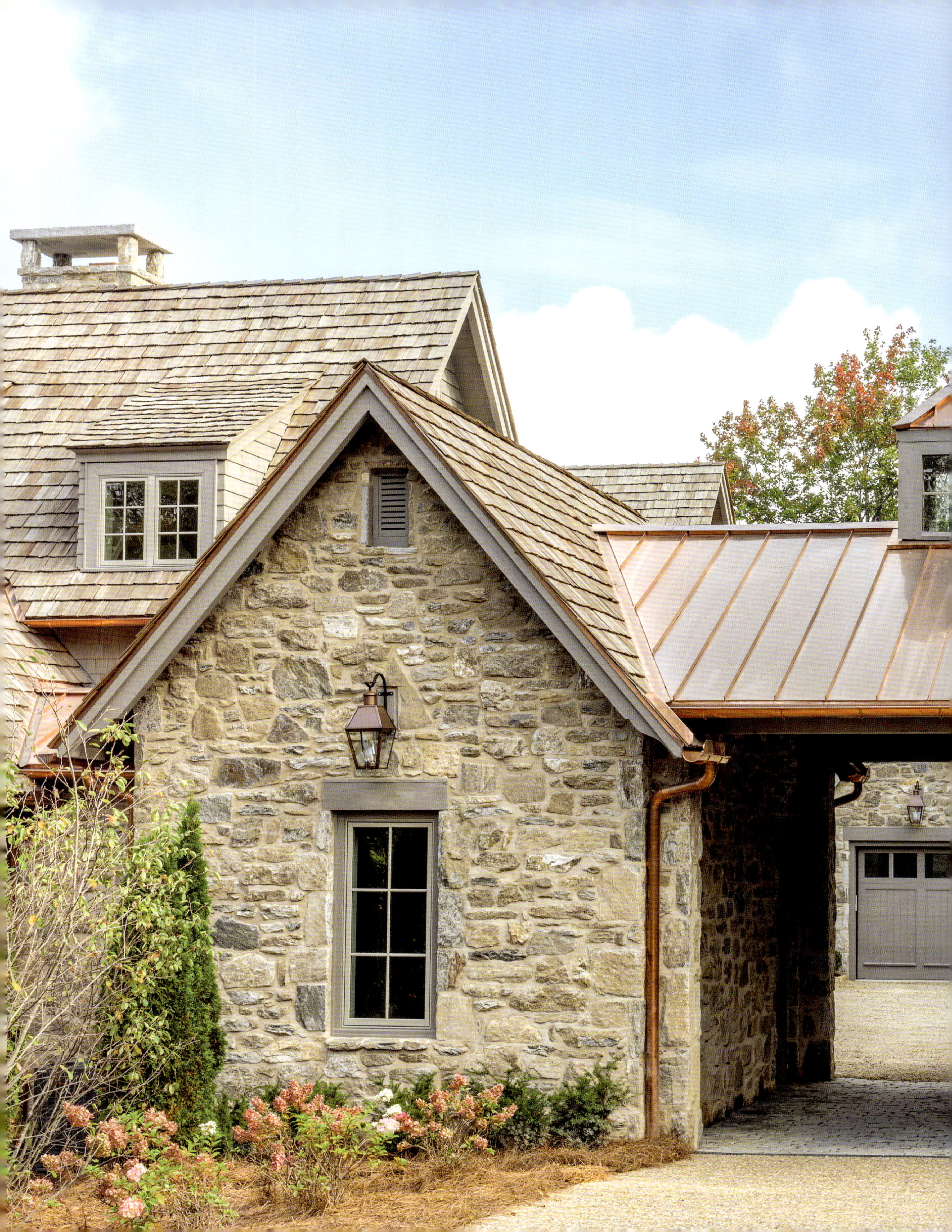

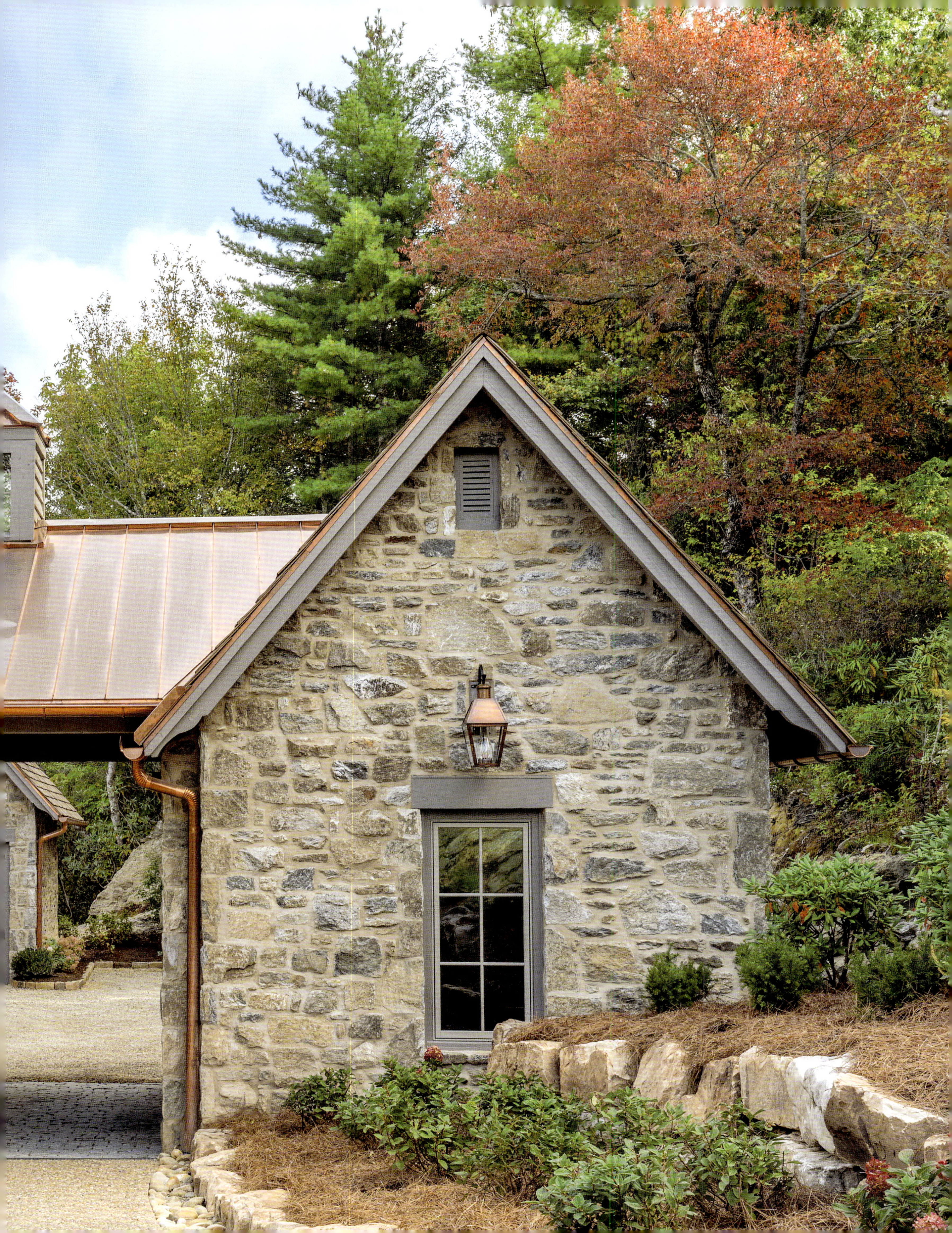

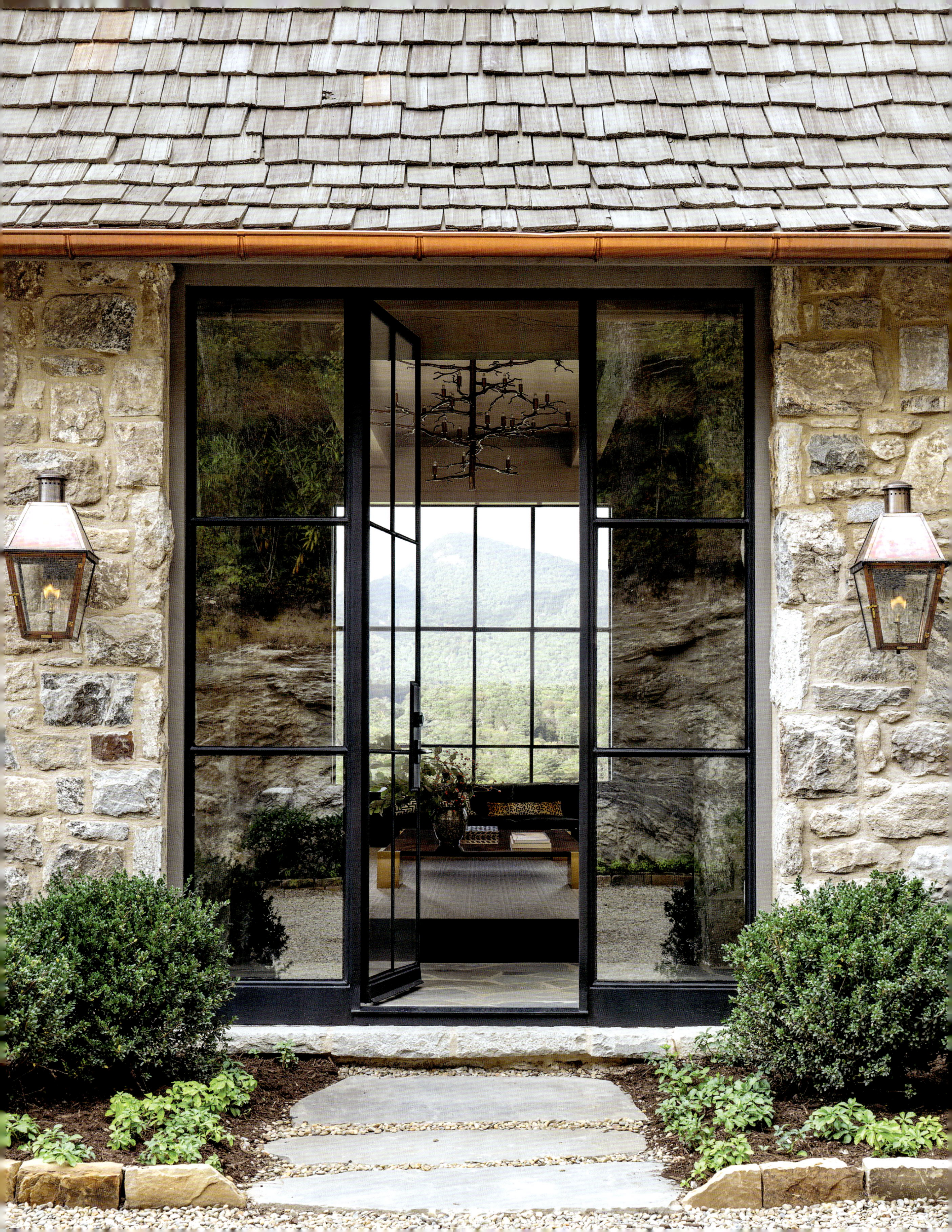

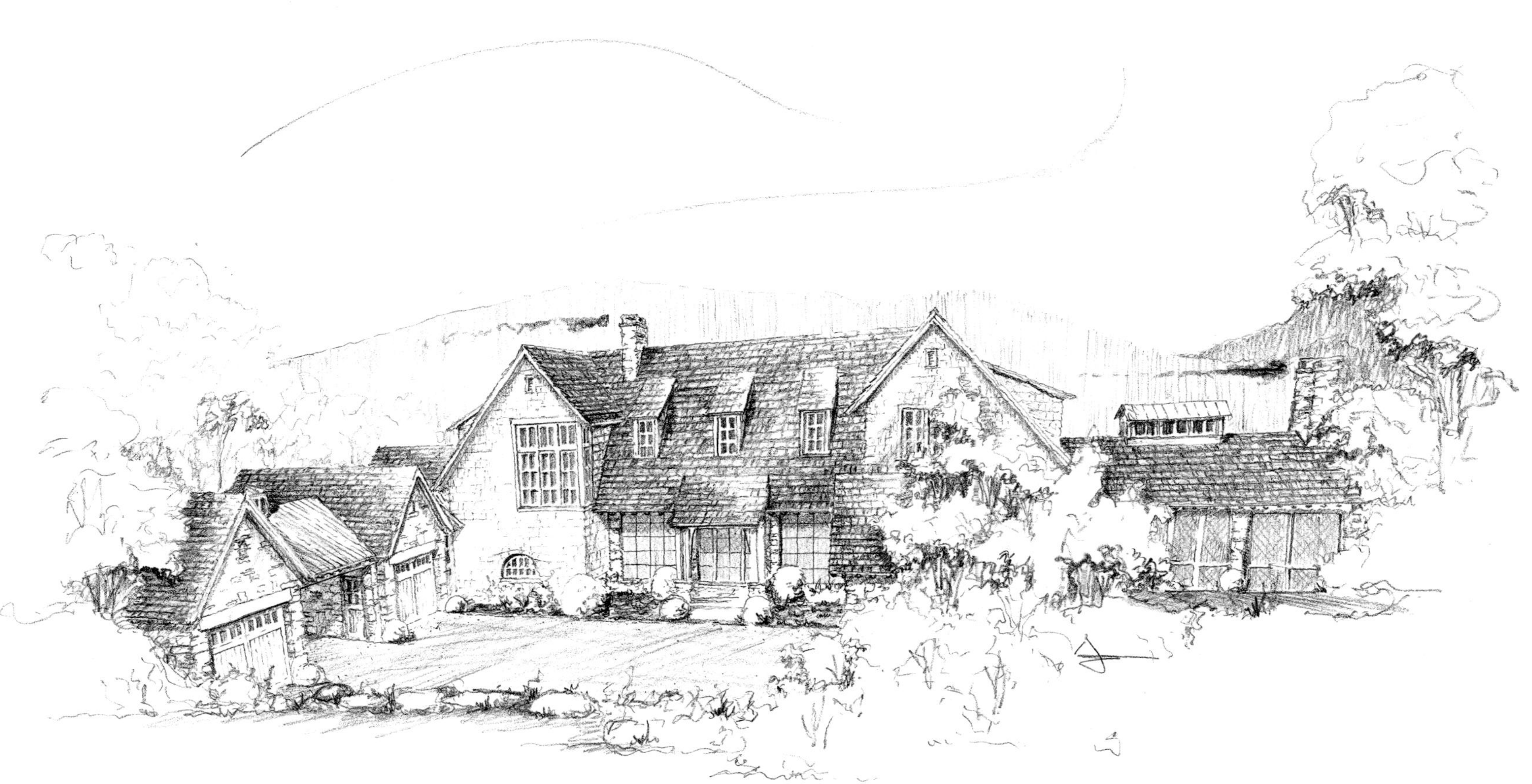

You reach the court by passing under a porte cochere between two freestanding single-car garages. Without realizing it, you've effectively already entered the family's private domain. A third garage blocks off the far end of the parking area, and a glance to the left suddenly reveals an unobstructed view into the front of the home via three broad expanses of steel windows, continuing straight out the back toward a spectacular panorama of the Blue Ridge Mountains. Stepping through the steel-and-glass front door, the lines between interior and exterior are blurred: brawny granite piers between the windows of a stone-paved entry hall are repeated on the opposite side, pulling the rhythms and materials of the exterior architecture into the interior realm. Only after you've progressed through the hall and into the spaces beyond does the ambience become completely "indoor." It's a unique experience that prolongs the atypical arrival sequence.

My clients, a couple with college-age children, wanted their vacation home to speak the language of its mountain environment without being

OPPOSITE: A steel-and-glass front door affords a perfect sight line to the forested ridges and valleys in the distance.

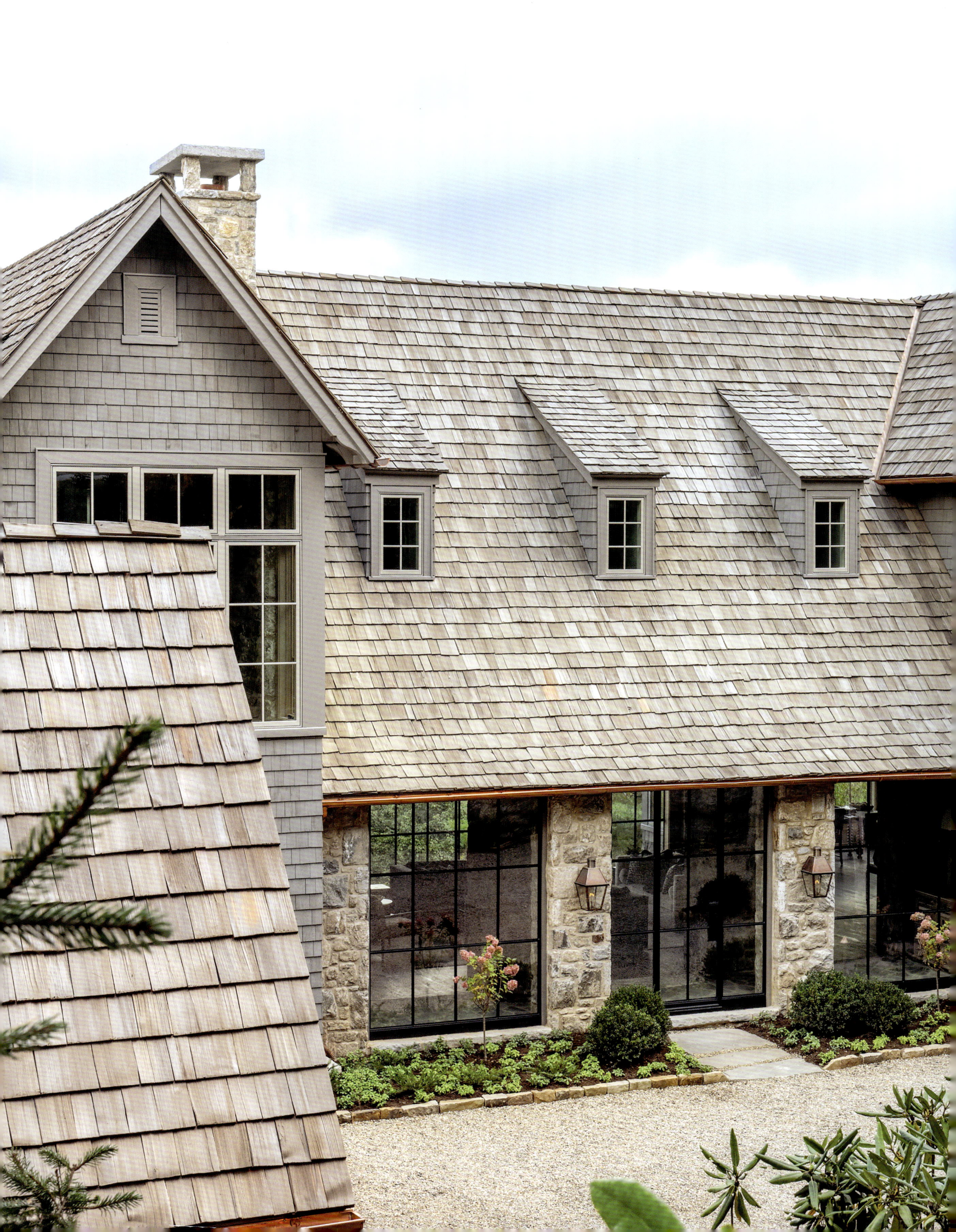

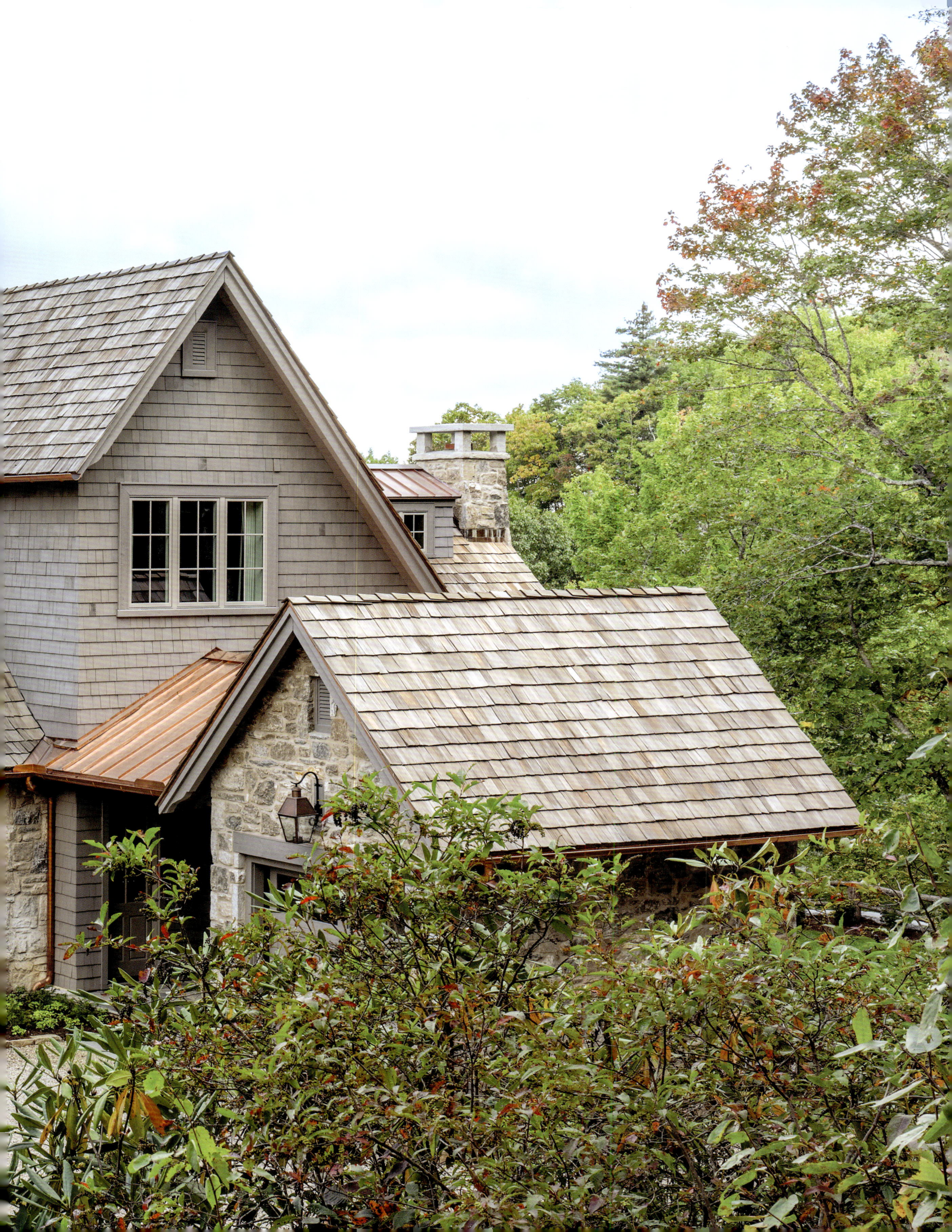

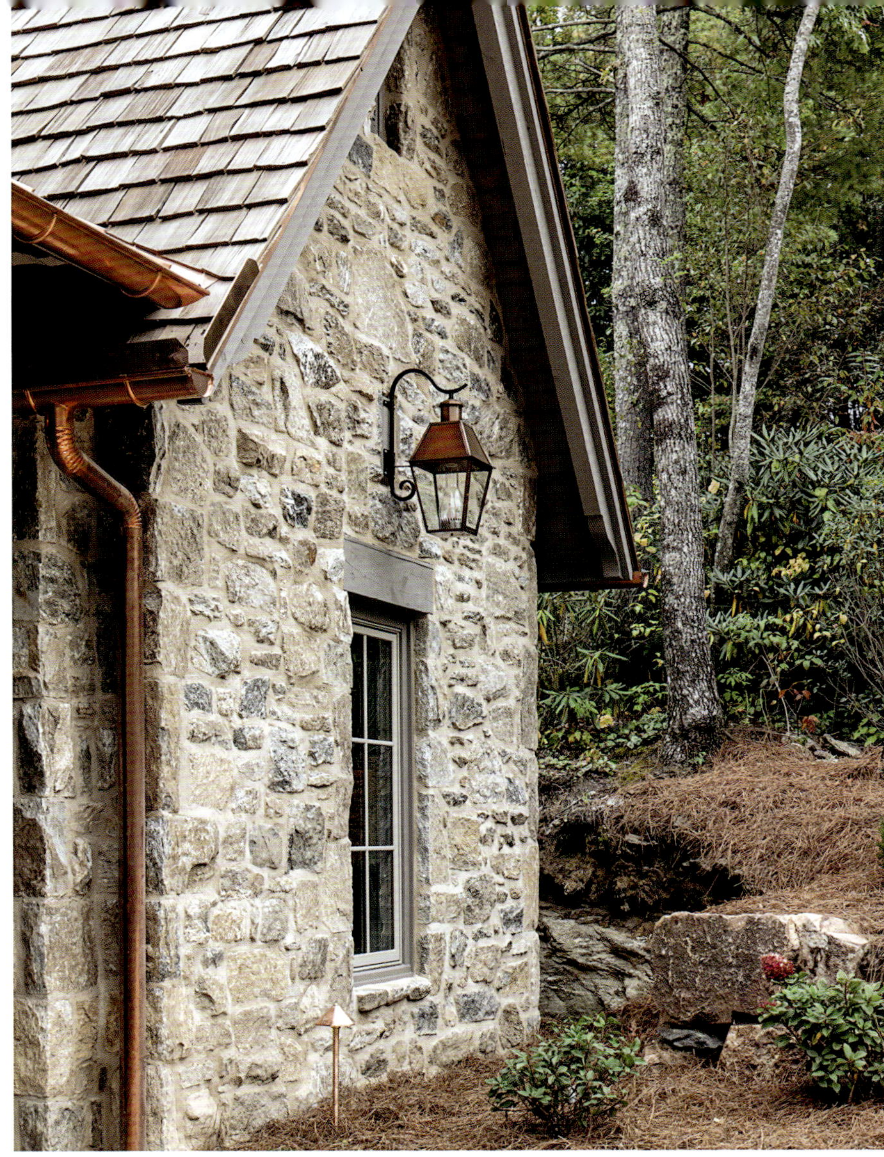

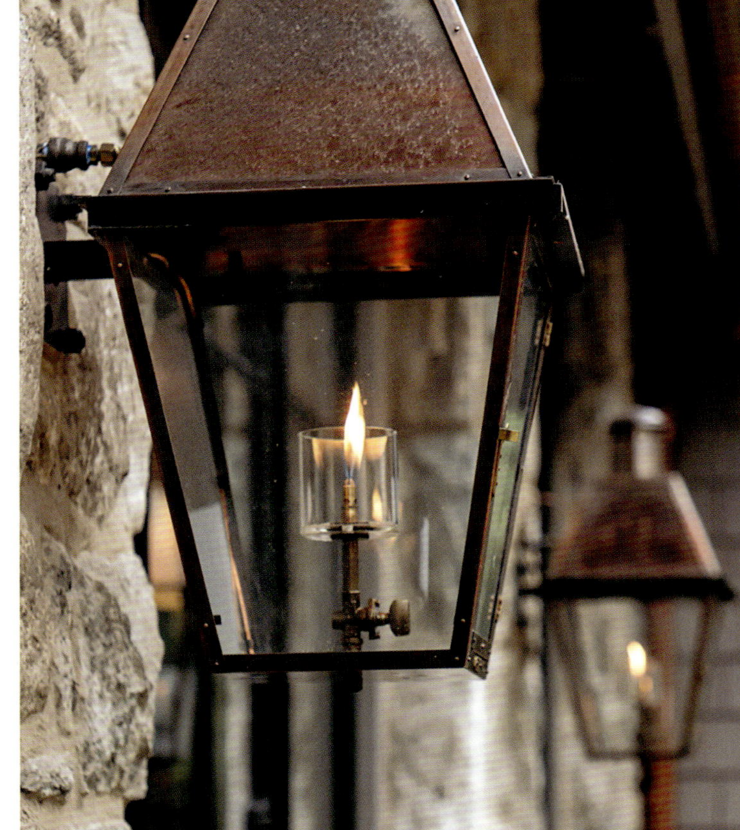

PRECEDING SPREAD: Seen from the adjacent road, the home's roofscape attracts the lion's share of attention. The whole property feels embraced by the land, nestled into the hillside and screened by mountain laurels and other indigenous vegetation. RIGHT: Architectural details—from a row of dormers to thick window lintels to a petite awning balanced on hefty timber brackets—add character at every turn. The many copper roofs, gutters, downspouts, and outdoor lanterns will acquire a beautiful patina over time.

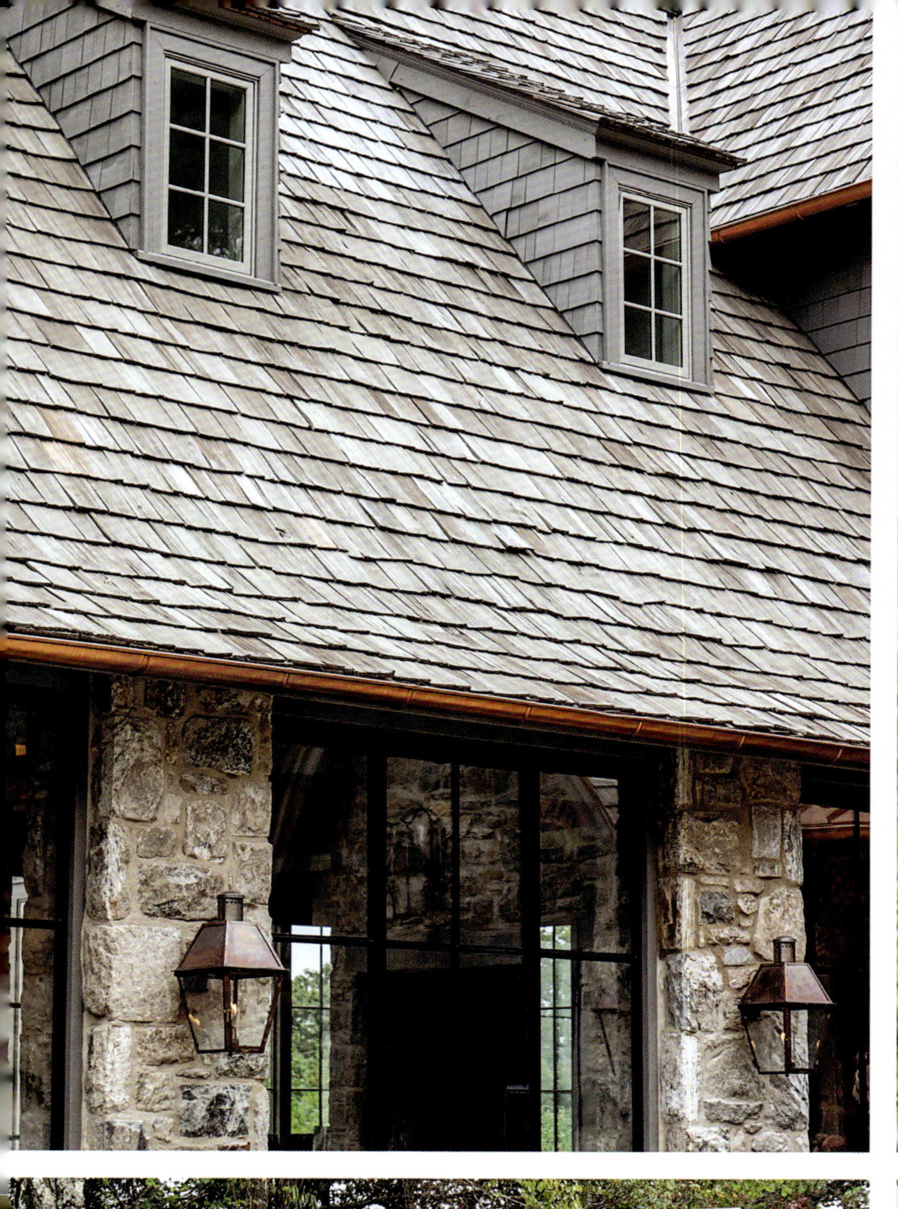
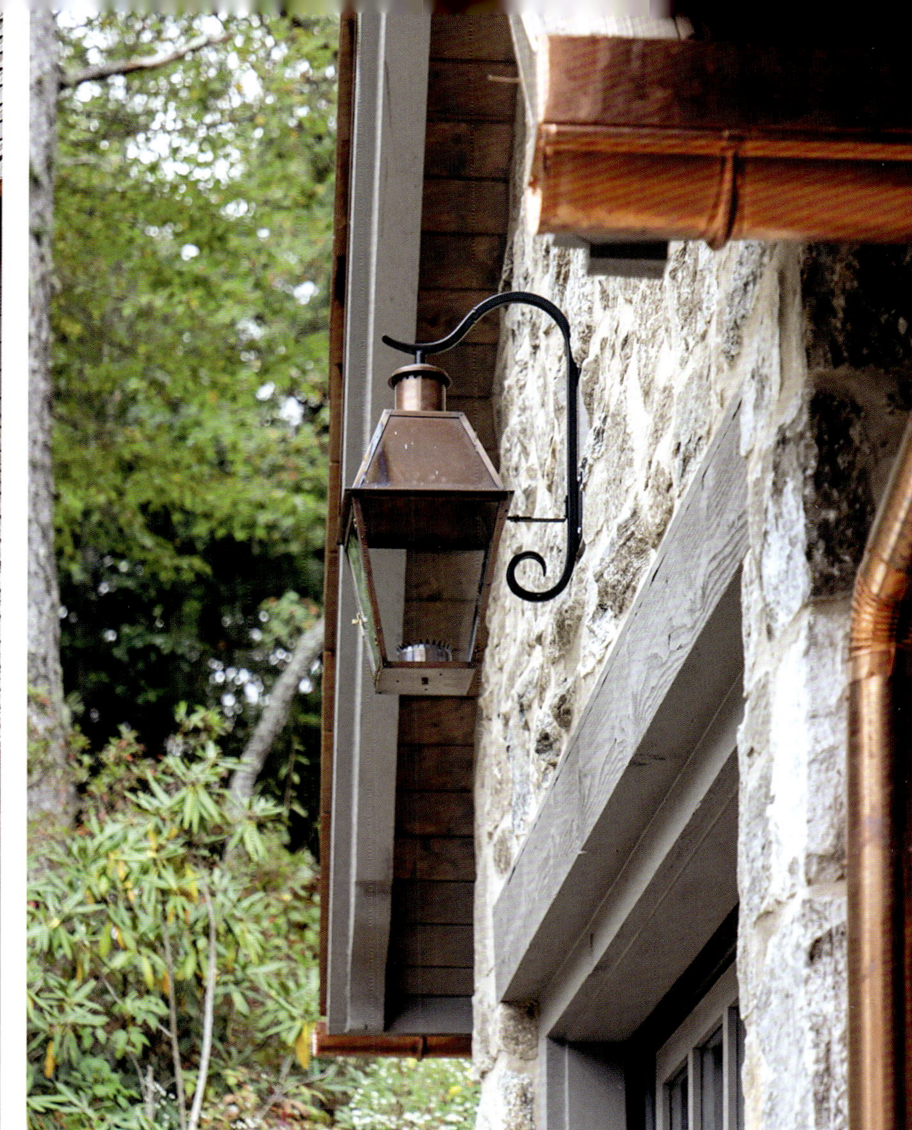
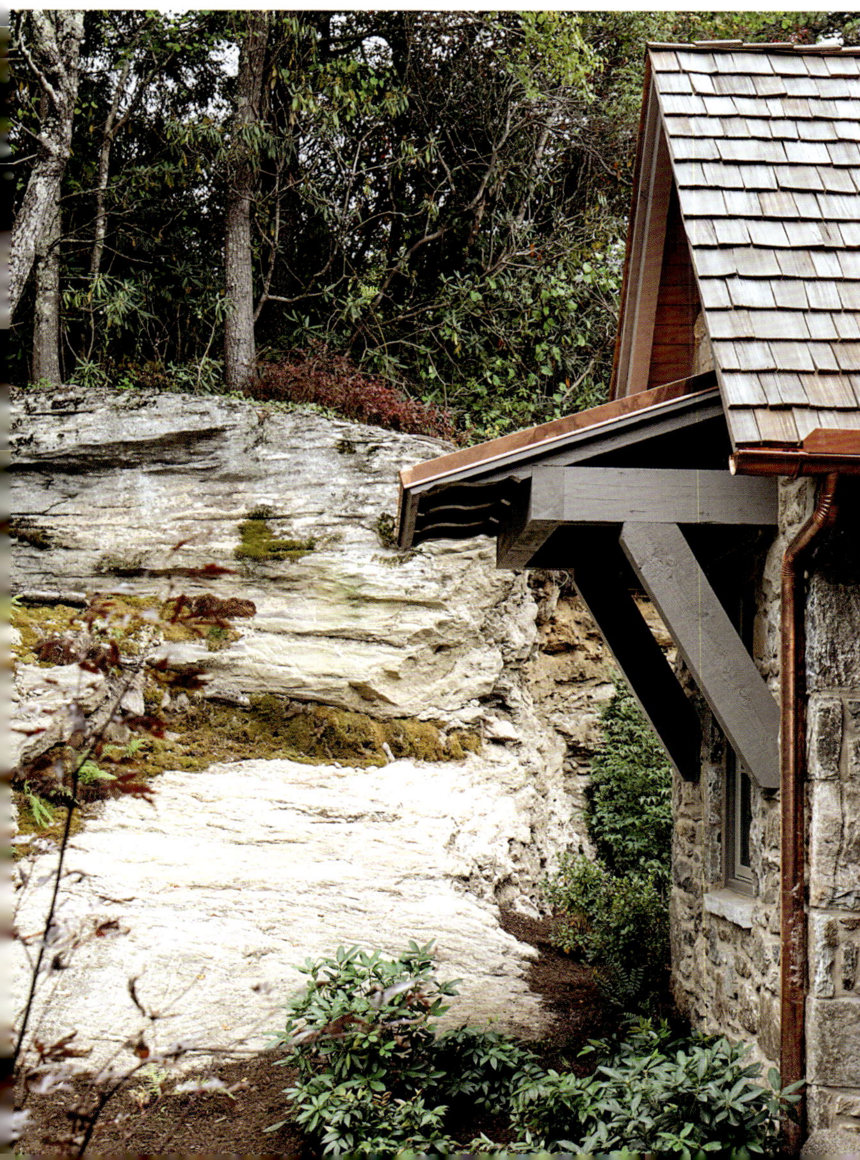
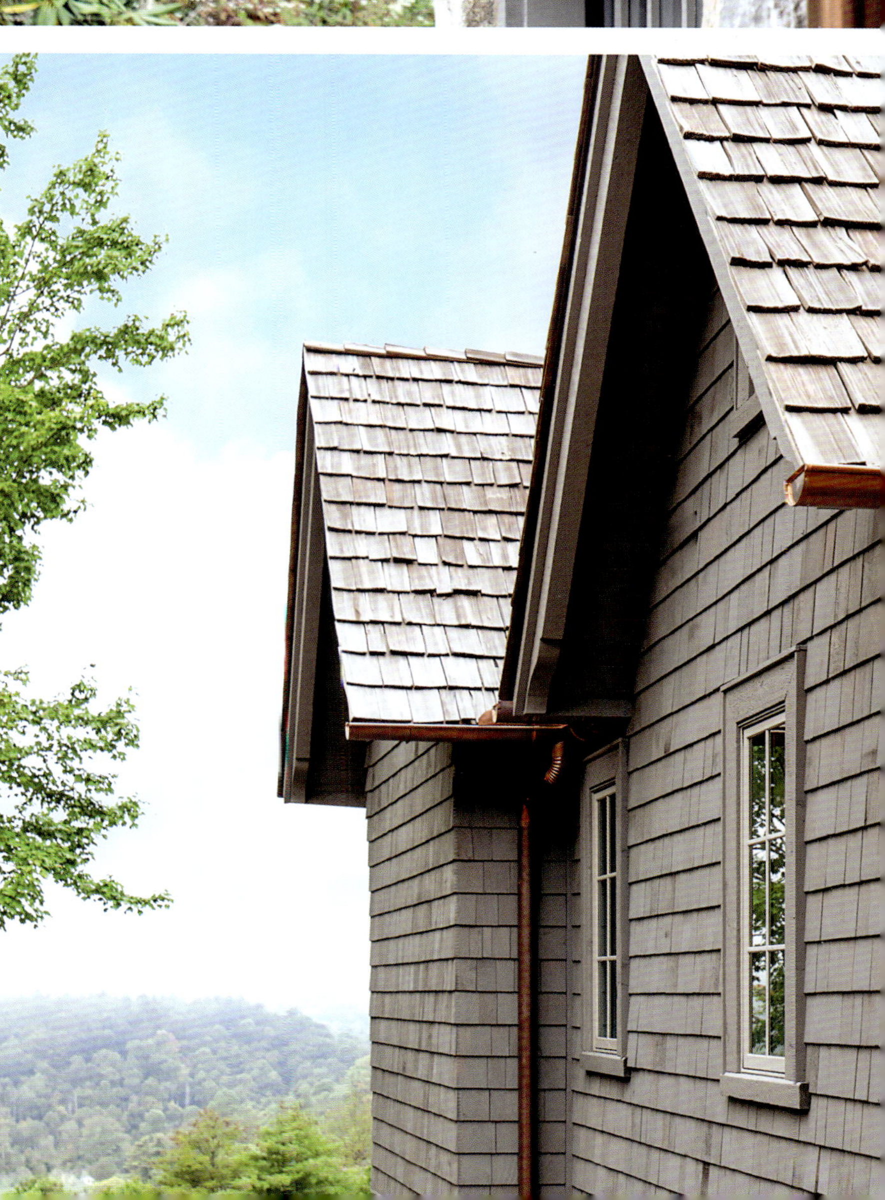

too dark or overtly rustic. So we used native stone and painted shingle siding for the walls and cedar shakes for the roof—all choices that are typical in the region—then tightened and simplified the lines of the structure to produce a cleaner, more formal vibe. It's a two-story house when seen from the front, though it appears lower because I brought the flared edge of the main roof down to nestle on top of the first-floor windows. Since the ground falls away quickly in the rear, there's an additional lower level on that side. As a result, the main-floor entertaining spaces feel lofty, as if they're perched in the trees, looking out across the rolling expanse of the valley below.

The same "make it rustic but not too rustic" rule holds true inside. While many walls and ceilings are rendered in stained oak, their surfaces are smooth and their detailing is refined, elevating the effect without shading over into anything fully contemporary. The crispness of the rooms' envelopes makes them the perfect backdrop for the occasional ornate piece of furniture or bold light fixture, included to indulge the owners' liking of color and a little bit of edge. Still, the scenery outside is breathtaking enough that we really wanted to let it shine, not compete with it.

The main floor is set up for entertaining, with spaces that are well-defined yet flow together for easy circulation. The kitchen acts as a hub, and the great room, a dining area, and a magnificent double-height outdoor porch are set around it. A blue painted bar with brass-framed open shelves sits next to the great room fireplace, contributing to the warm

OPPOSITE: The front entry hall acts as an architectural transition between the outdoor entry court and the "true" interior spaces of the home. FOLLOWING SPREAD AND PAGES 116–117: Interior designer Catherine Brown Paterson played to the homeowners' love of color and sophisticated style in her choices for the living room. Scattered notes of brass and gilding contribute an extra layer of shine within the stone and oak environment. Meanwhile, the expansive views speak for themselves.

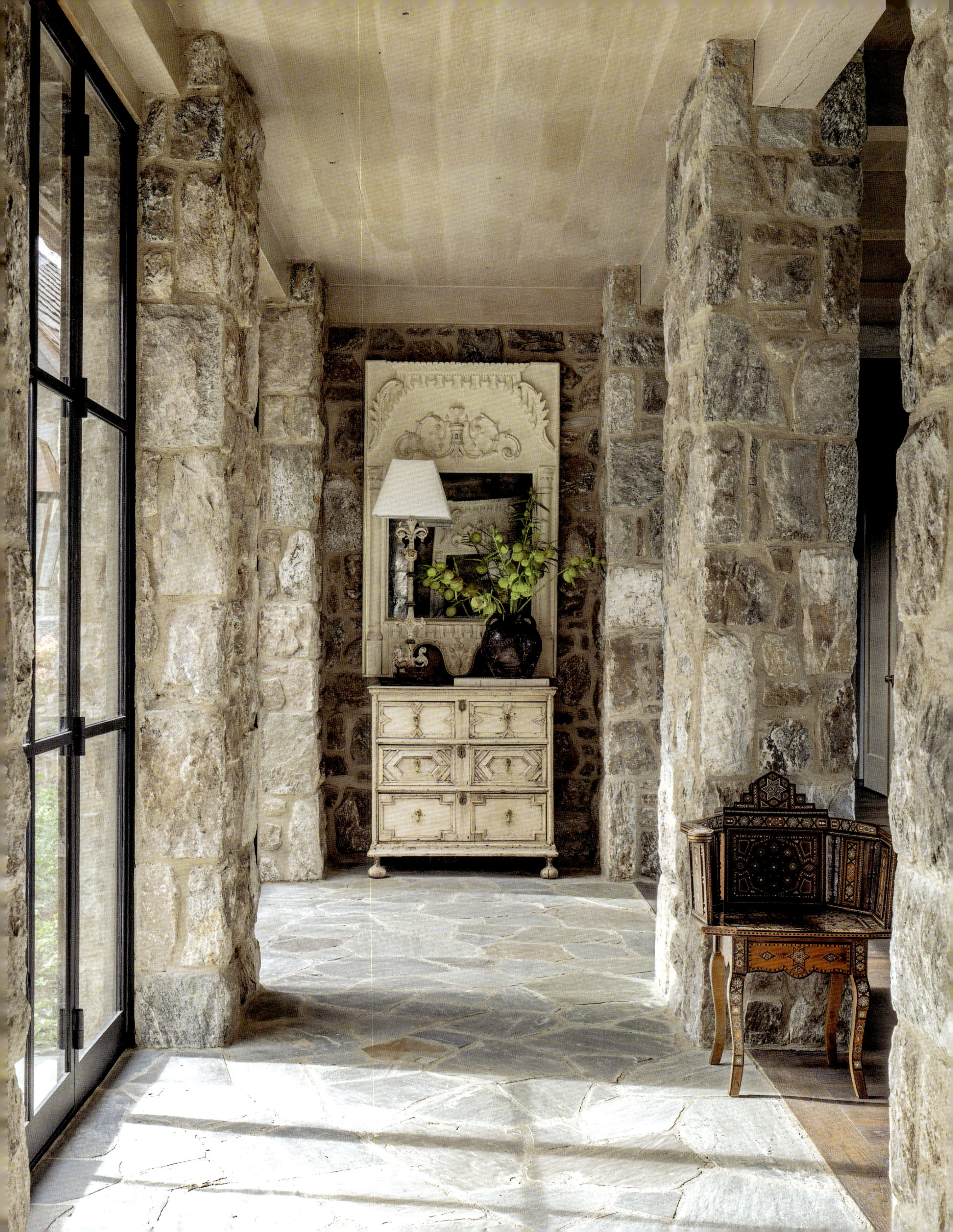

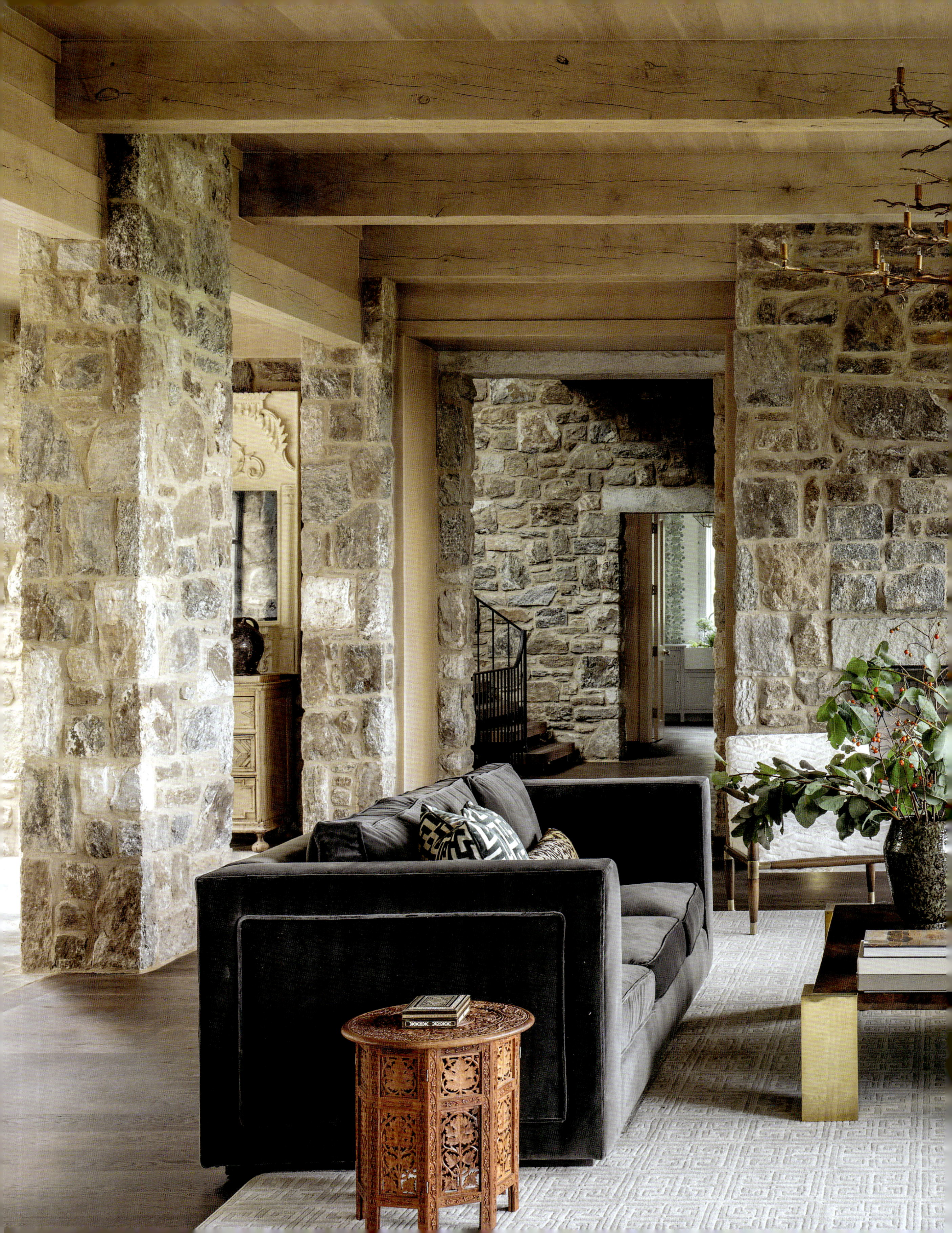

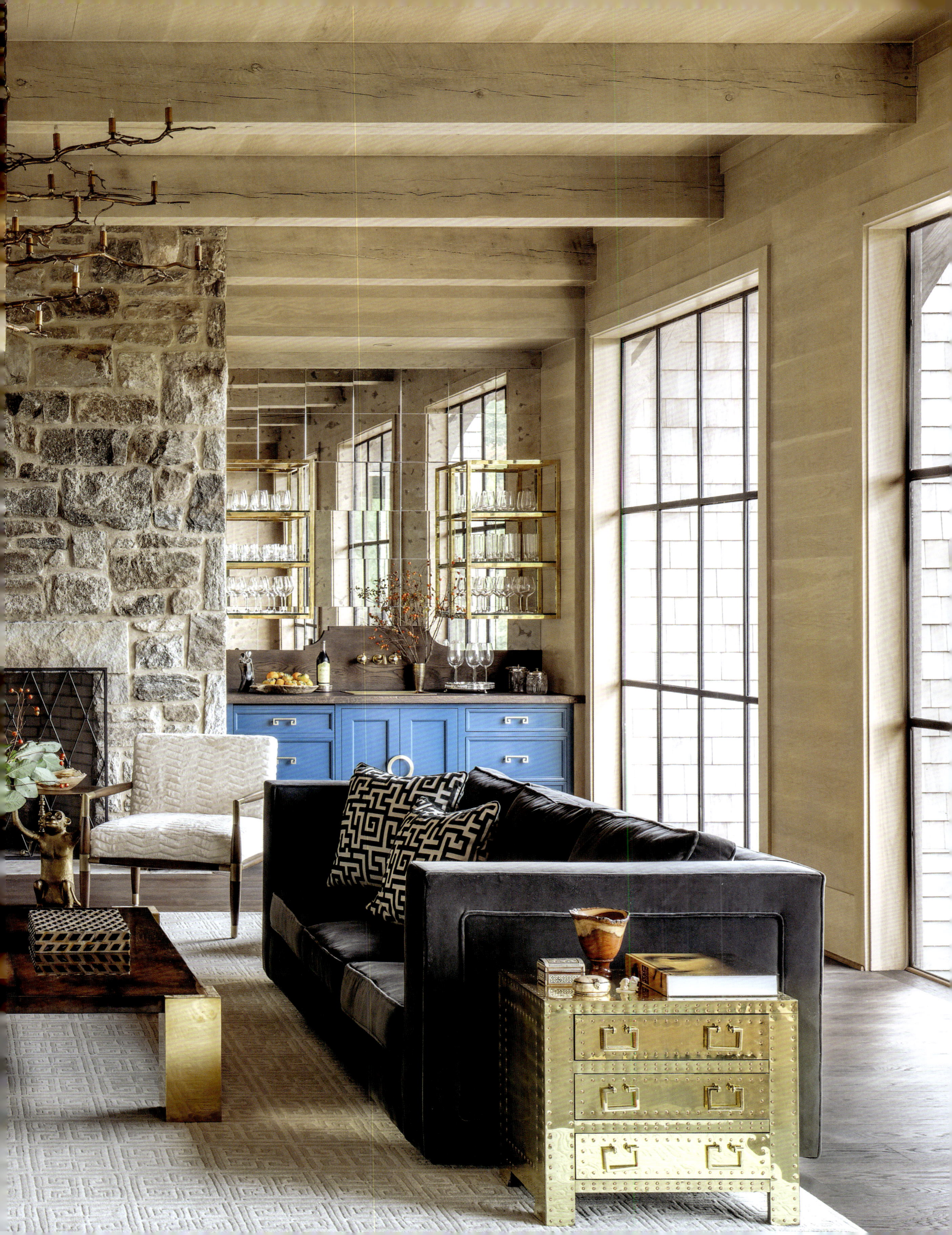

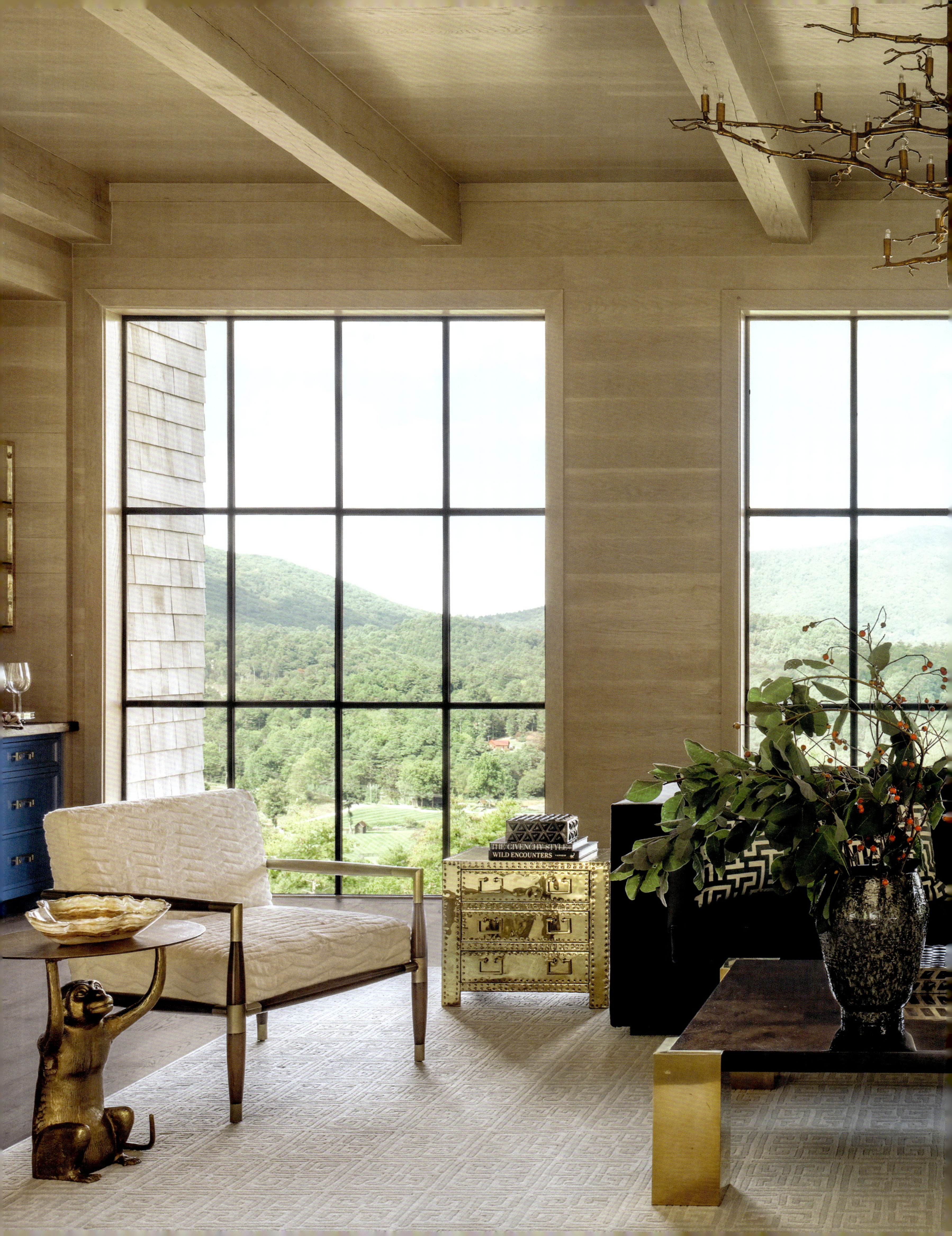
THE GIVENCHY STYLE
WILD ENCOUNTERS

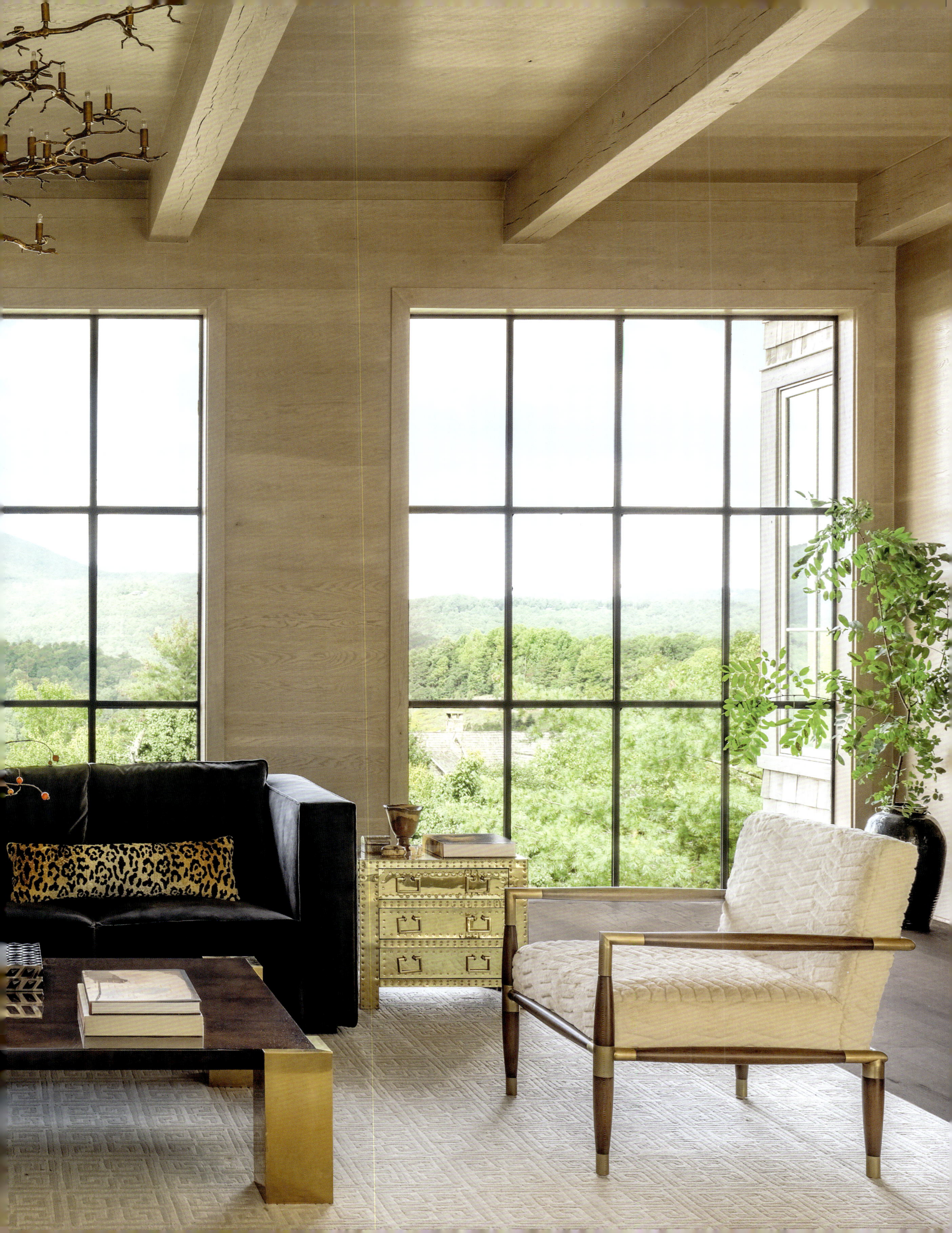

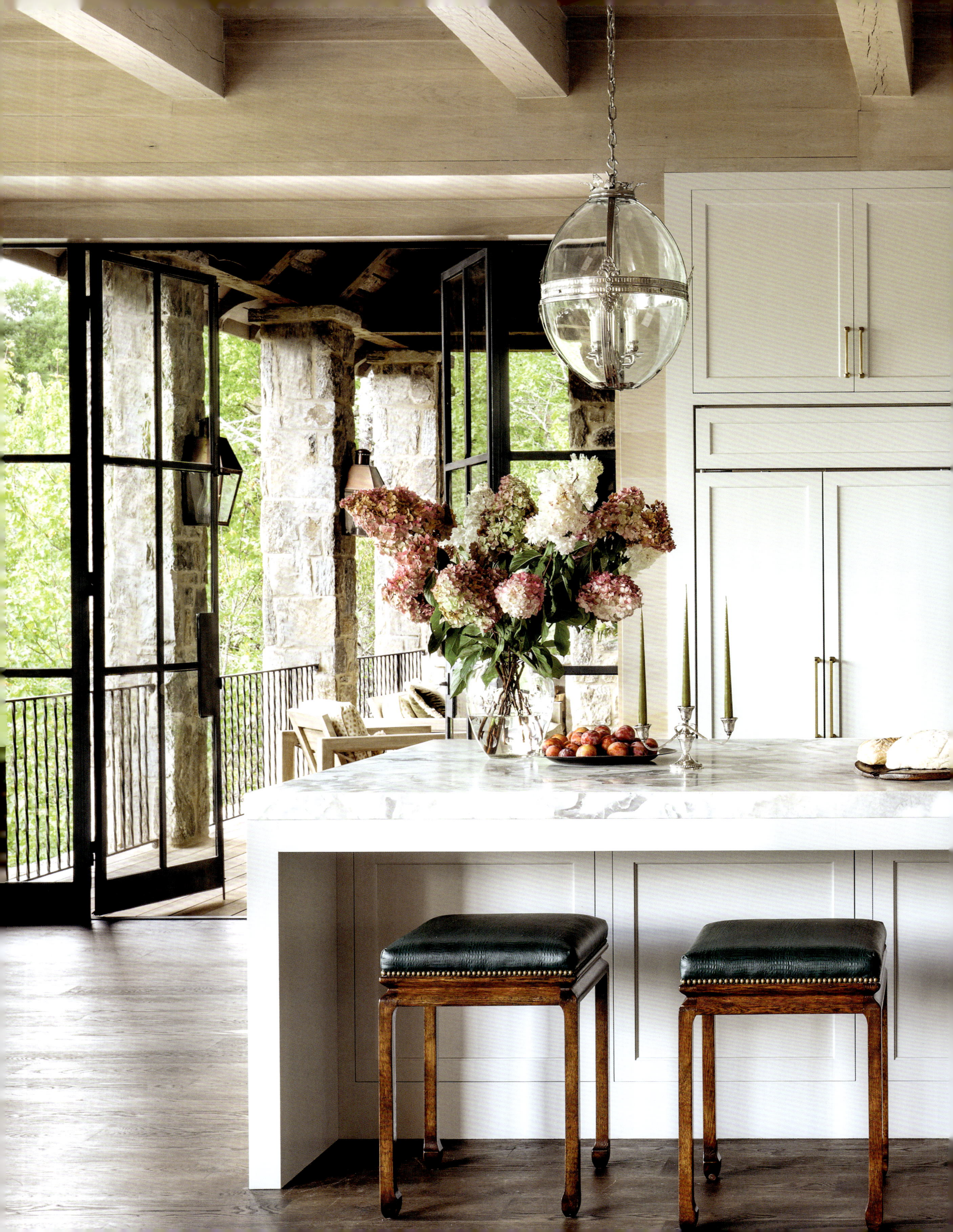

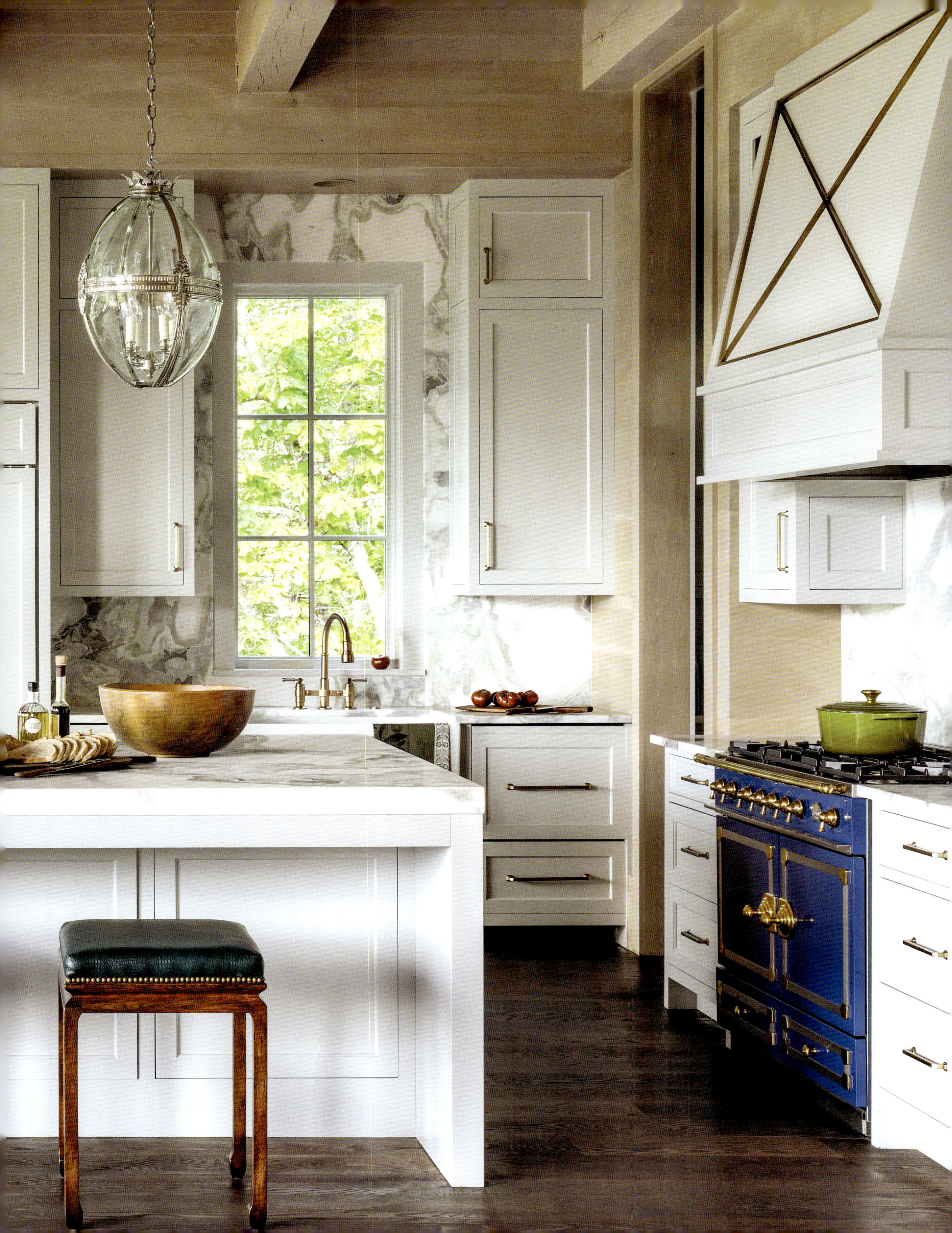

welcome. The porch, possibly my favorite part of the house, is dramatic, with its vaulted beam-and-barnboard ceiling and the brightness that floods in from clerestory windows far overhead. It also provides walk-out access to the pocket garden that was my original inspiration for the layout of the home.

I wanted the main stairway to be a special spot—stairs are a prime opportunity for a sculptural moment in any home because they're so three-dimensional and span multiple levels. The treads here are thick wooden slabs that float slightly away from the stone walls, rising from the lowest floor all the way to the top of one of the home's front gables, supported by thin steel stringers and lined with an intentionally simple iron railing. Light filters through the open risers to wash and reflect off the stone, enhancing the sense of its texture. Steel doors at the very bottom lead to a romantic wine cellar that could almost have been carved directly from the bedrock.

In architecture, it's vitally important that you don't shoehorn a building into its site. This house was constructed in a challenging place, and we approached it in a carefully considered way that responds to and capitalizes on the qualities of the landscape. Reacting to the topography made the design better, more interesting. My impressions during that initial amble across the land turned out to be spot-on: even in sight of the road, the house ended up feeling far removed from day-to-day concerns, enfolded and kept safe by the hillside it stands on. And the little garden now ensconced in the granite-bounded clearing that first caught my eye and sparked my creativity? It's every bit as magical as I imagined it would be.

PRECEDING SPREAD: The kitchen is designed for entertaining, with an open dining bay (not shown) to the left and a direct connection to the covered porch. The prep space on the far right allows for work to continue while guests gather around the island. OPPOSITE: A distinctly romantic air permeates the lower-level wine cellar, with its stepped stone floor and natural oak racks. The configuration of the ceiling beams echoes the X-shaped lower storage bins.

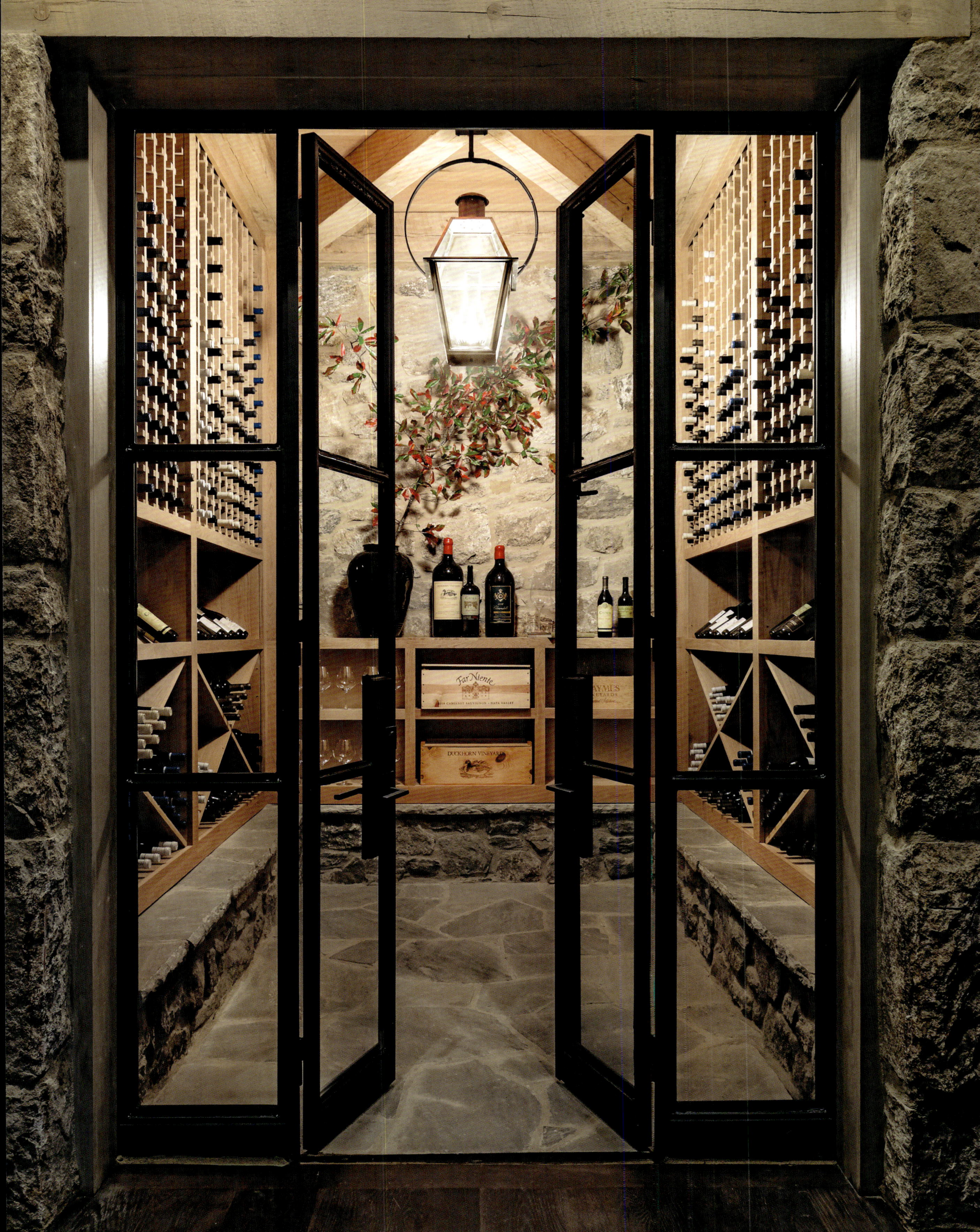
Far Niente
CABERNET SAUVIGNON · NAPA VALLEY
DUCKHORN VINEYARDS

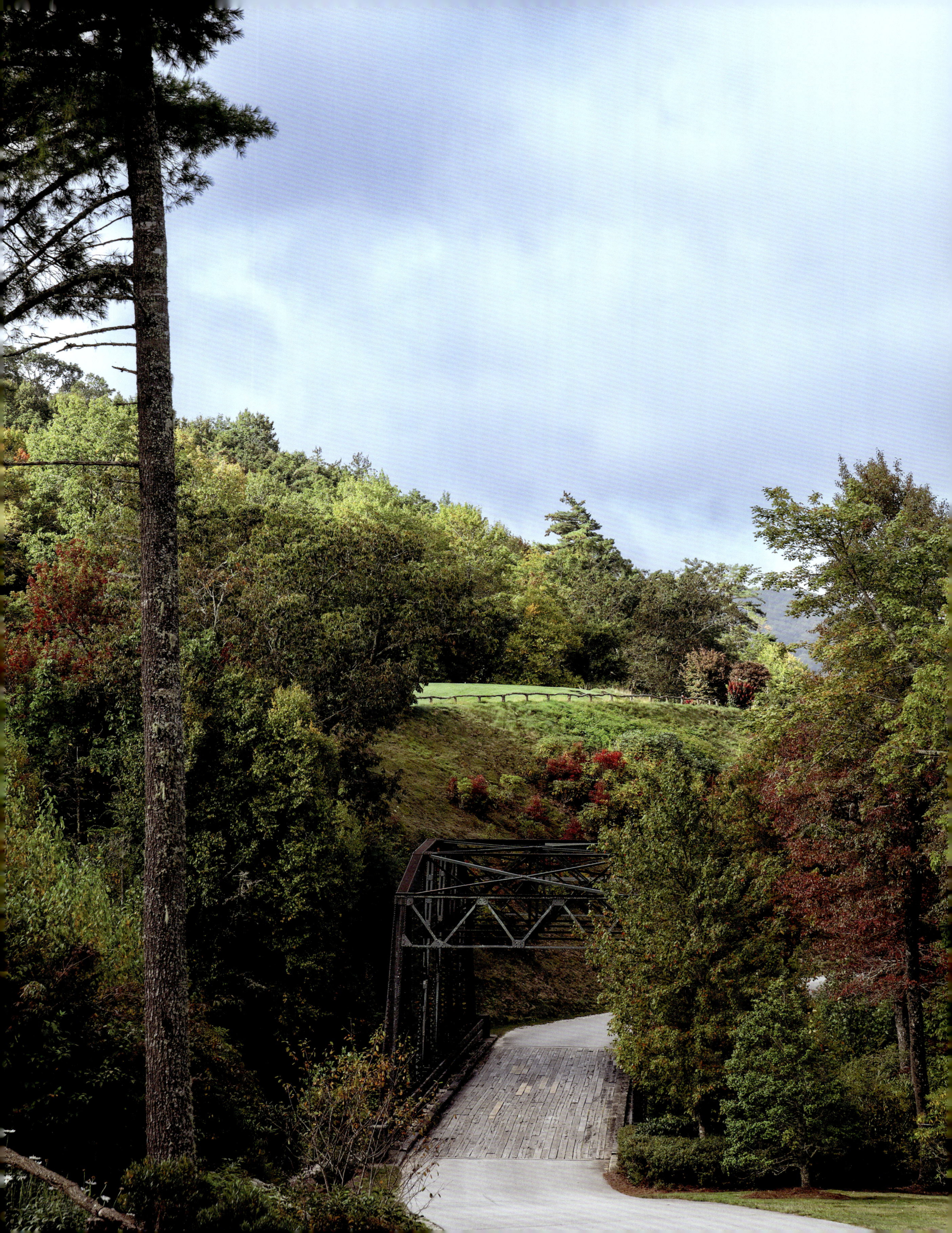

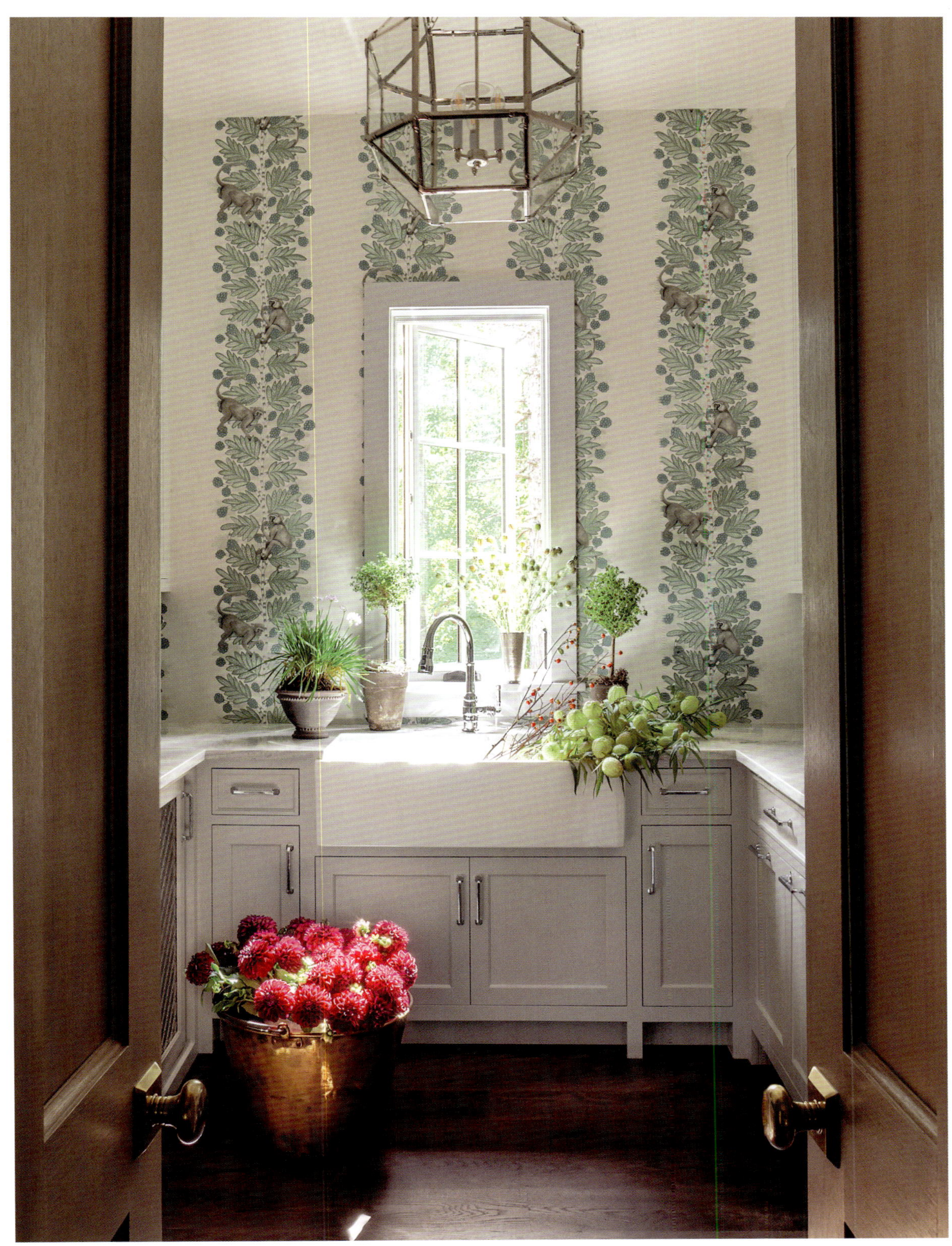

OPPOSITE: This picturesque old bridge, with its steel trusses and wooden deck, is a well-known landmark in the neighborhood. ABOVE: Monkeys hiding in the laundry room wallpaper are a whimsical touch. There's no reason a functional space shouldn't be enjoyable as well. FOLLOWING SPREAD: A downstairs porch is defined by arched openings on both sides. The blind inner arches are clad in poplar bark shingles for rich, organic texture.

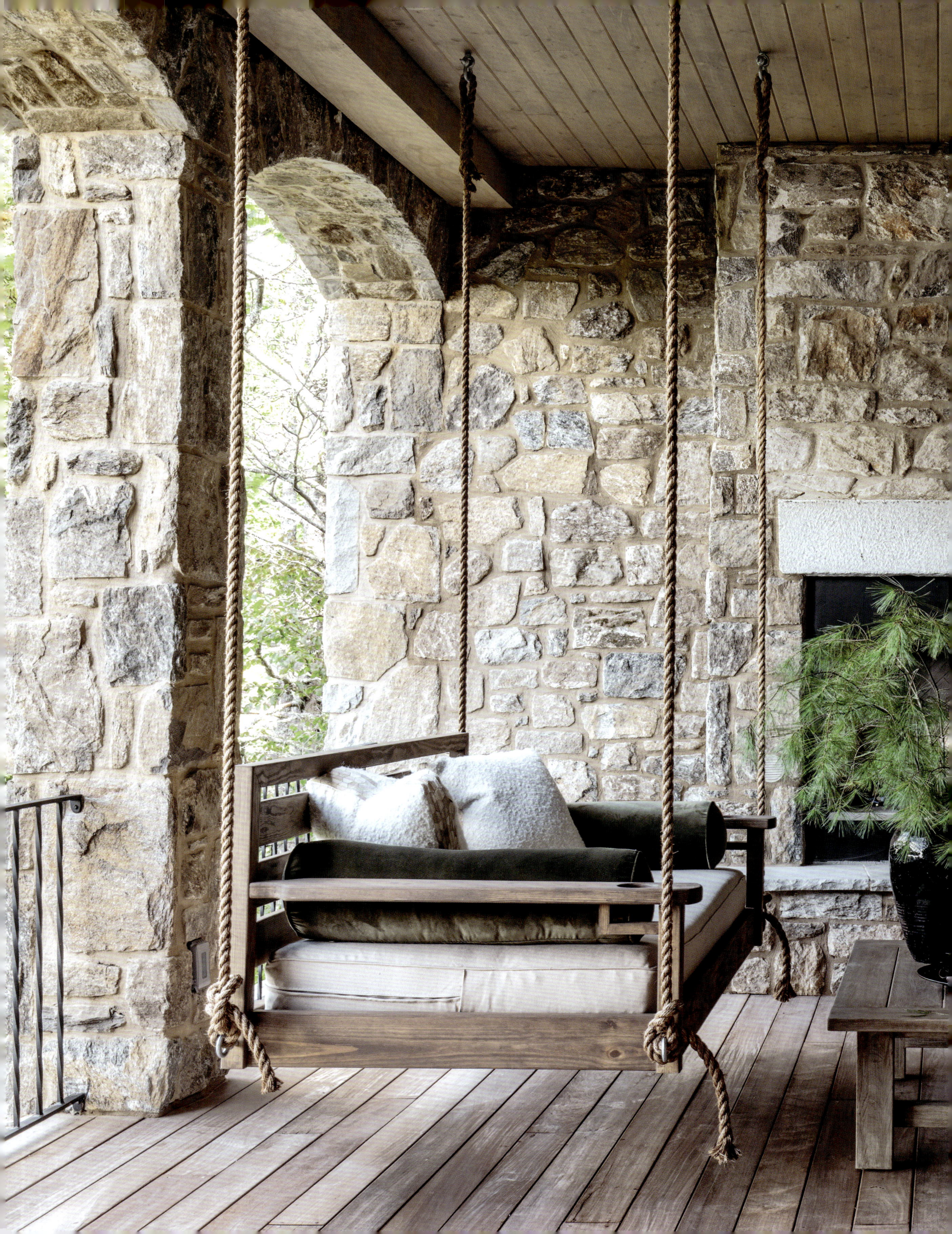

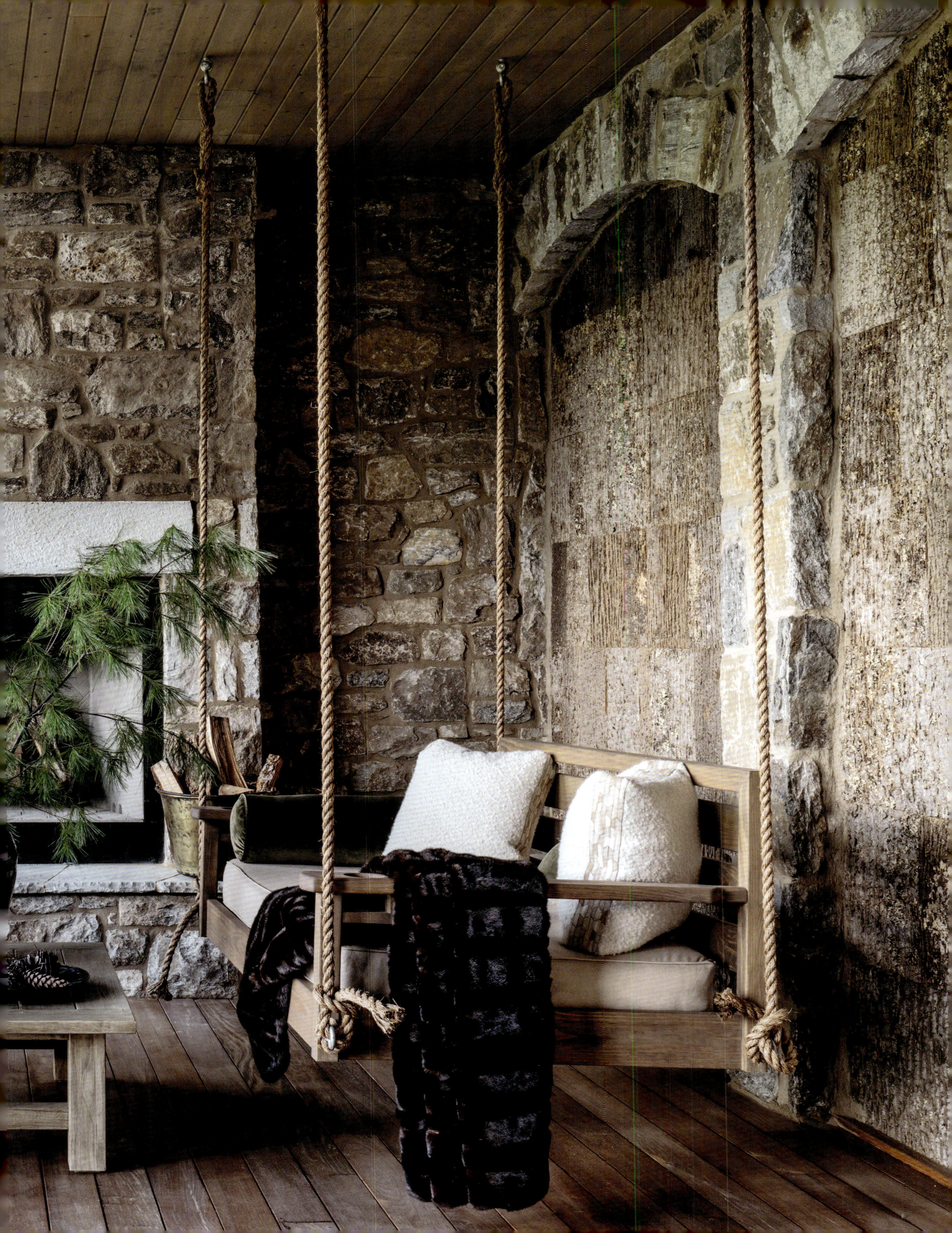

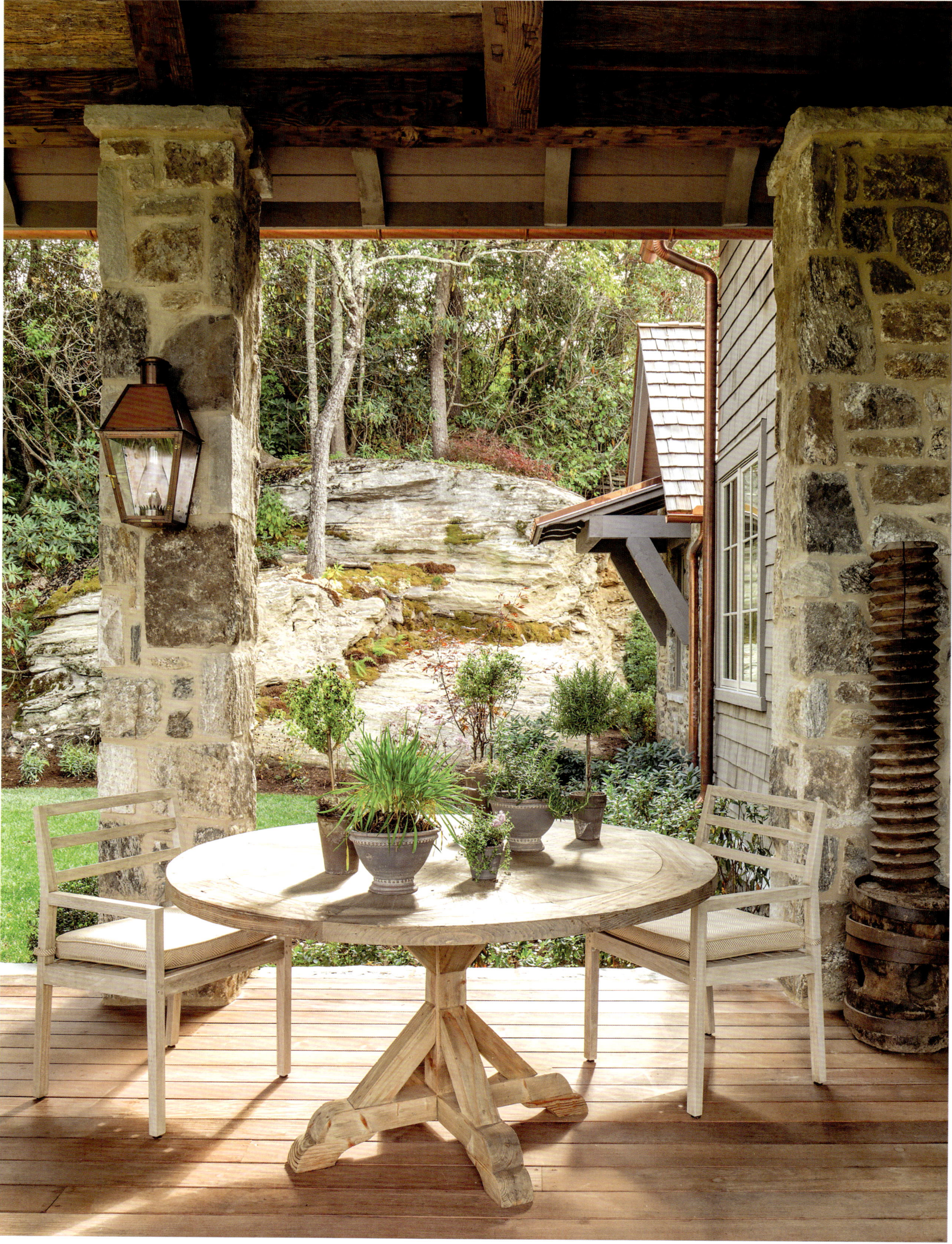

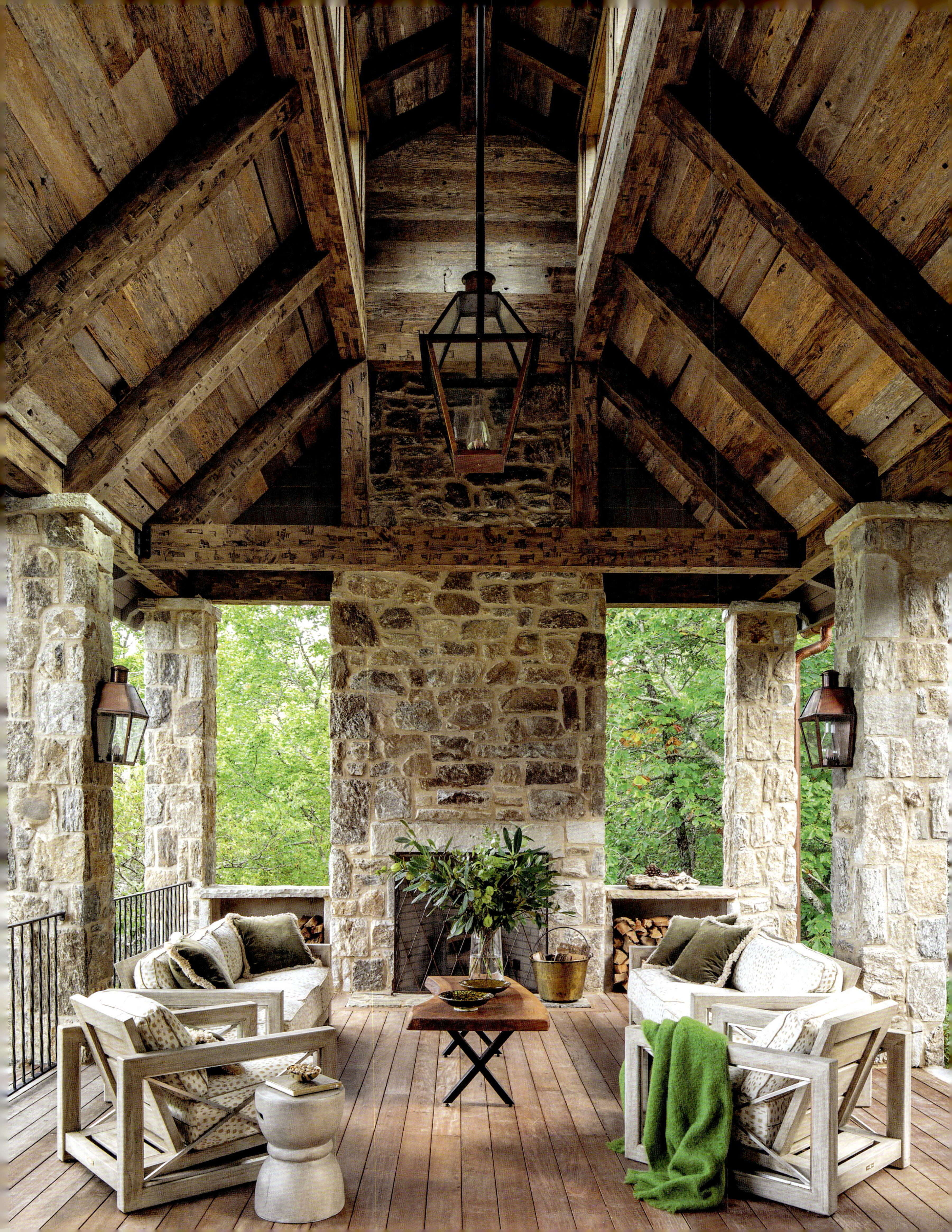

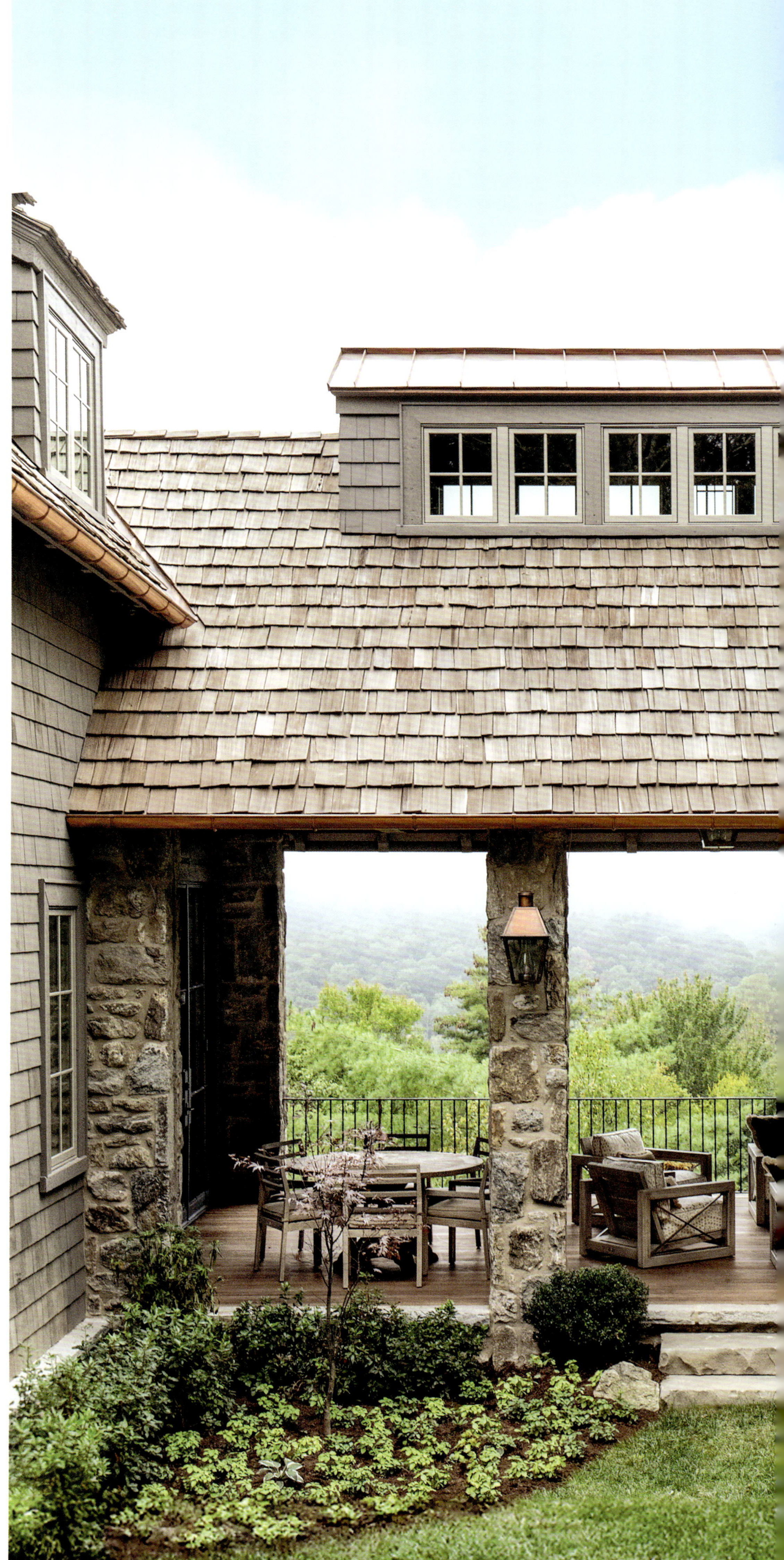

PRECEDING SPREAD, LEFT: An old, eroded granite cliff covered in moss and ferns makes a fine backdrop for outdoor dining. PRECEDING SPREAD, RIGHT: Stone supports and a cap of reclaimed timbers and barnboard ensure a dramatic experience in the main-floor porch. One side connects to ground level, while the other side sits above the treetops. RIGHT: On mountain properties you don't always find a lot of flat ground, so having this space where you can step out on grass and enjoy a pocket garden is a luxury.

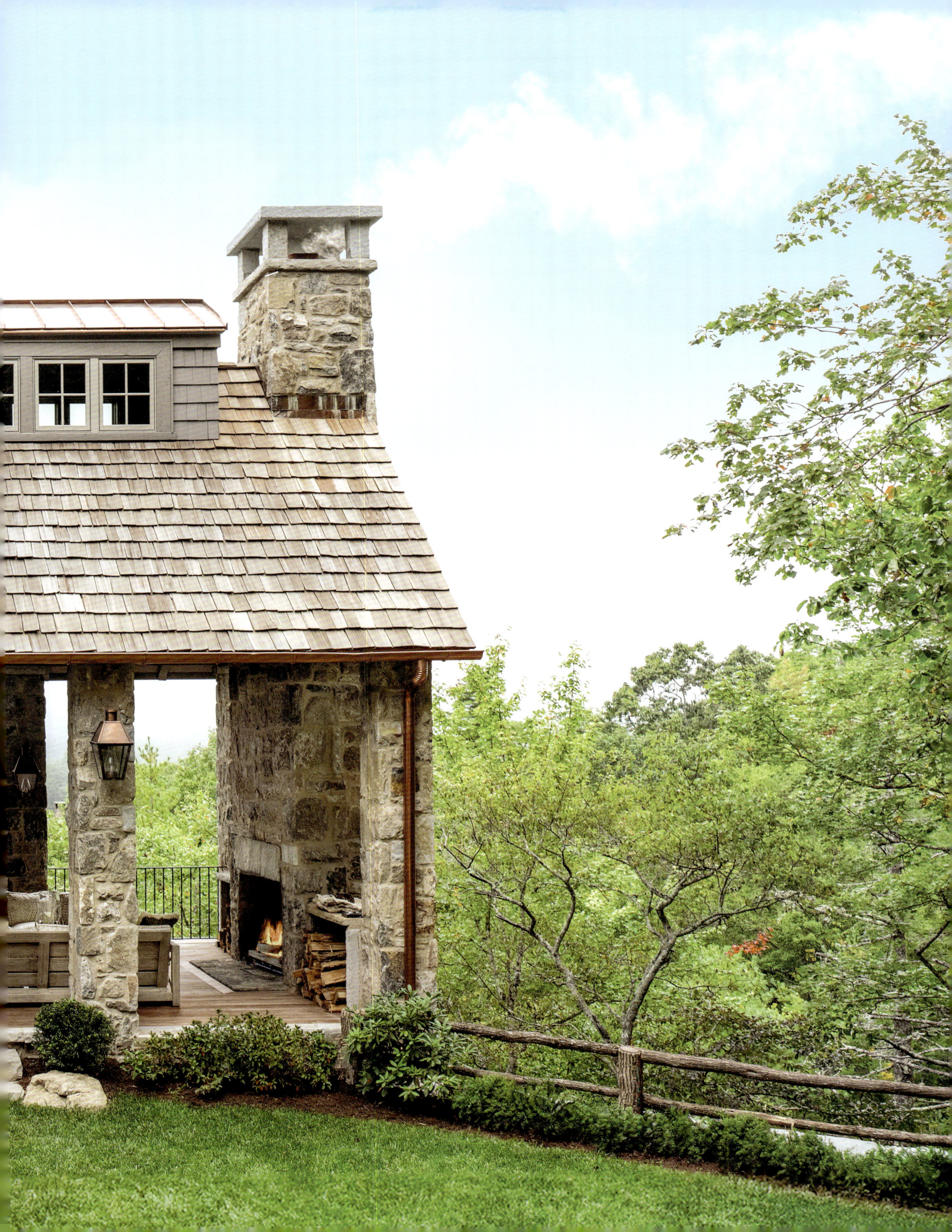

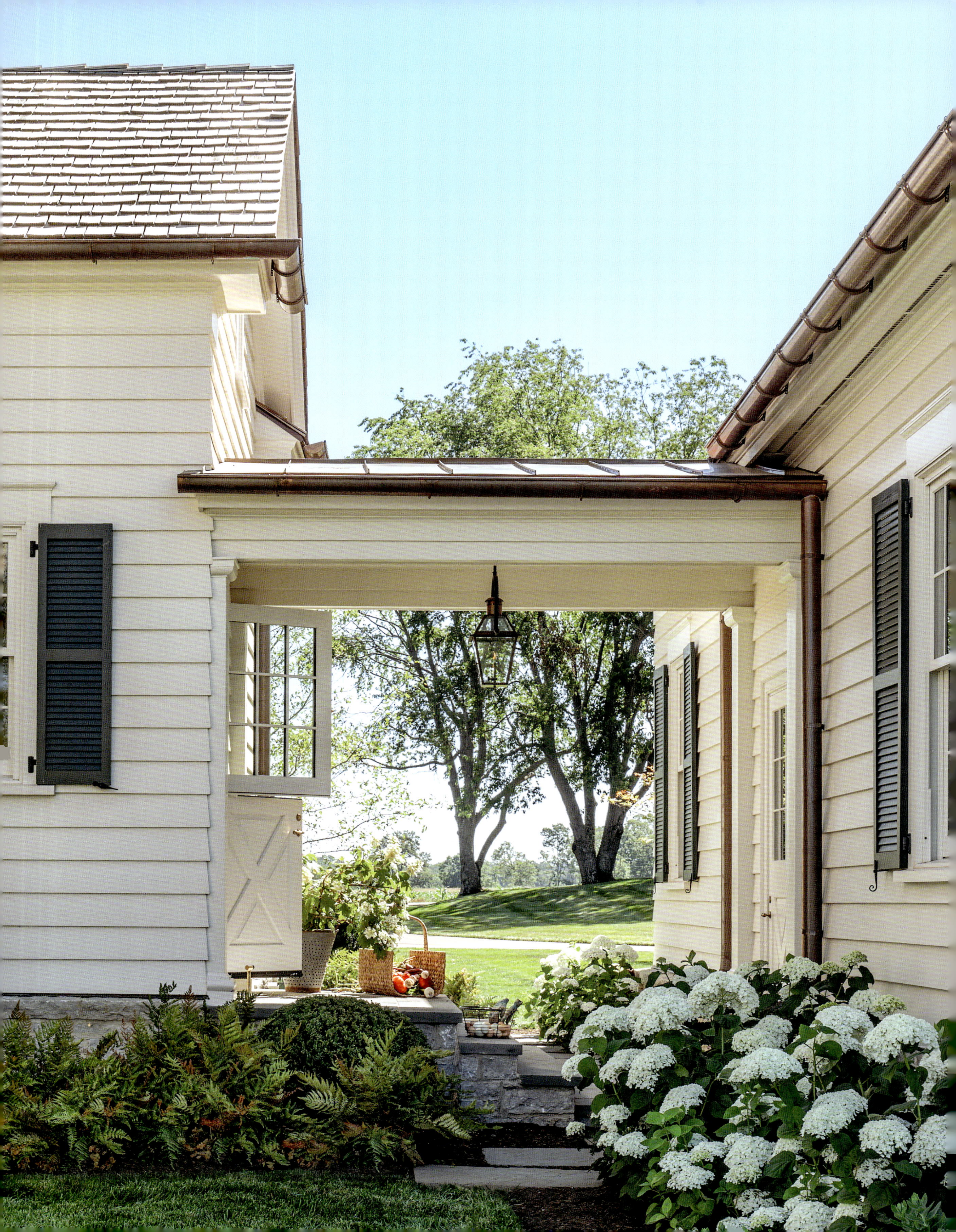

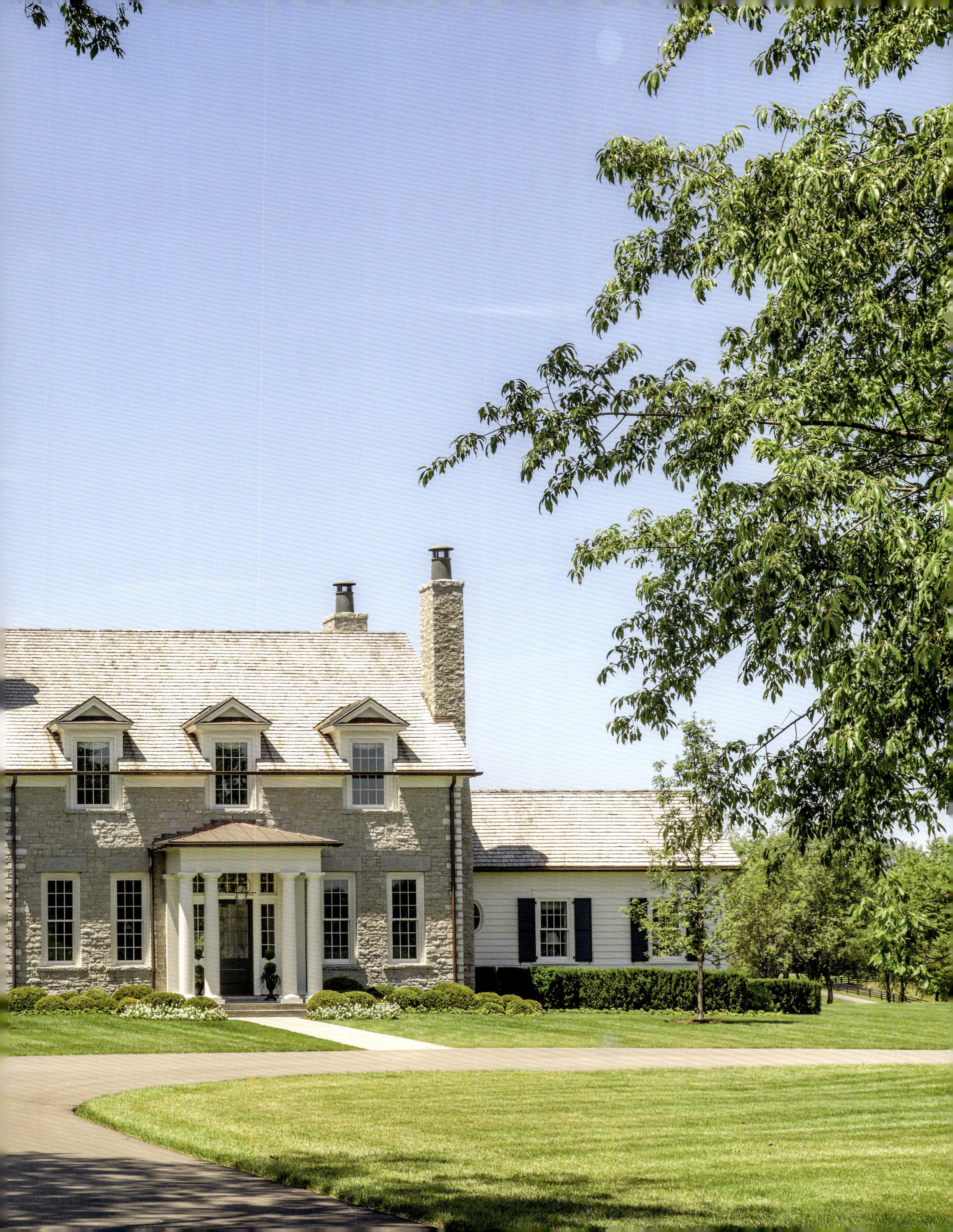

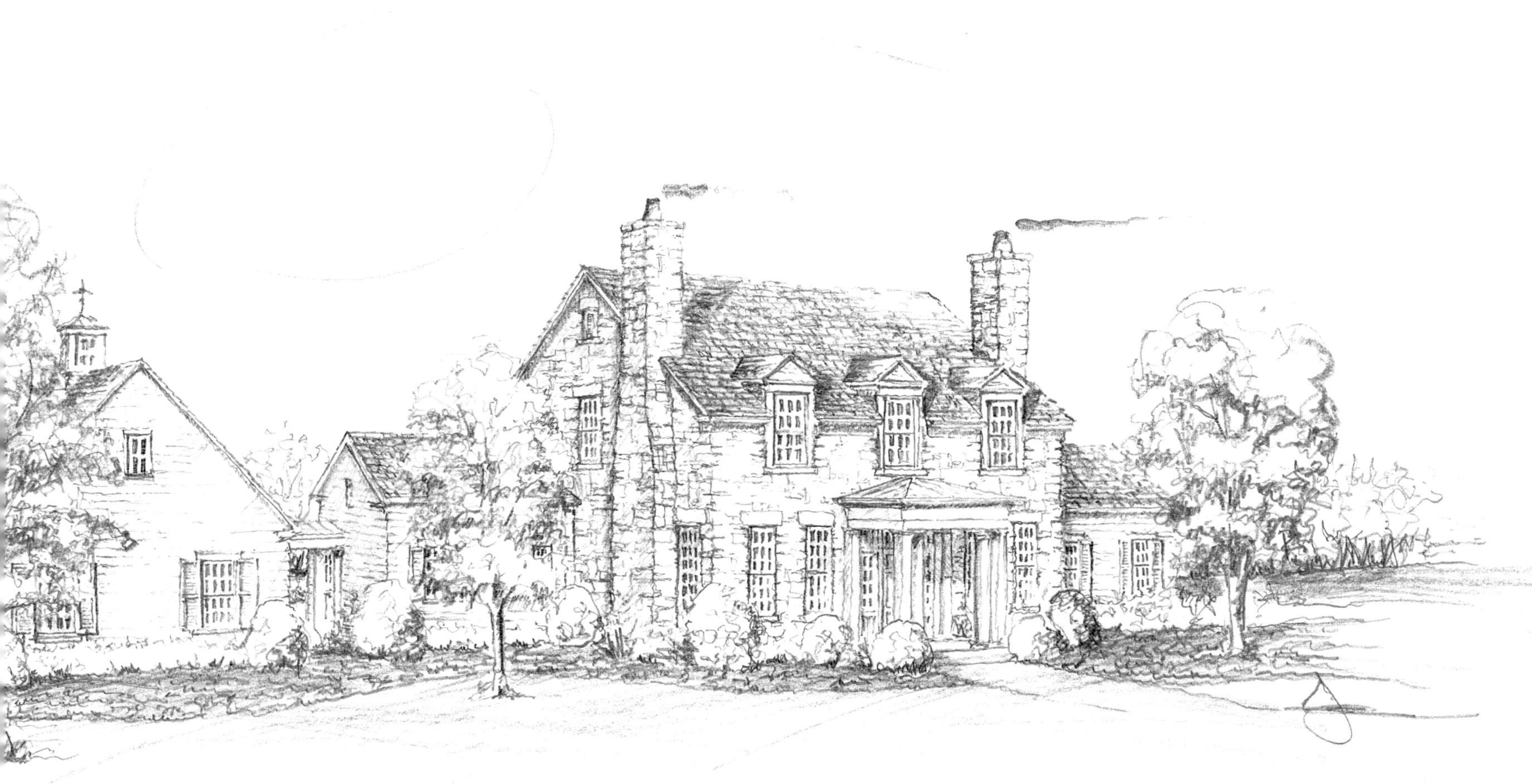

When I first laid eyes on what is now Seven Stones Farm, a spread of about three hundred rolling acres located in horse country just outside of Lexington, Kentucky, it was in deplorable shape: roads and fences were missing or in disrepair, the fencerows were all overgrown, and three antique tobacco and cattle barns located on the property were dilapidated and needed restoration. Initially, my clients were looking to create a "gentleman's farm," with horses and perhaps some cows and chickens. As we got deeper into the process of development, however, the scheme grew more ambitious. Often I'm constrained by unchangeable aspects of a project, but in this case, the lack of preexisting conditions was a distinct advantage; we had the freedom to conceptualize the whole sequence and flow of the farm literally from the ground up.

OPPOSITE: The front door, sheltered beneath a classical portico, opens to a view straight through to the back of the house. FOLLOWING SPREAD: I love how this home stands proud in the middle of the land, seemingly pinned to the earth by its three chimneys and with a wonderful sense of receding space on all sides.

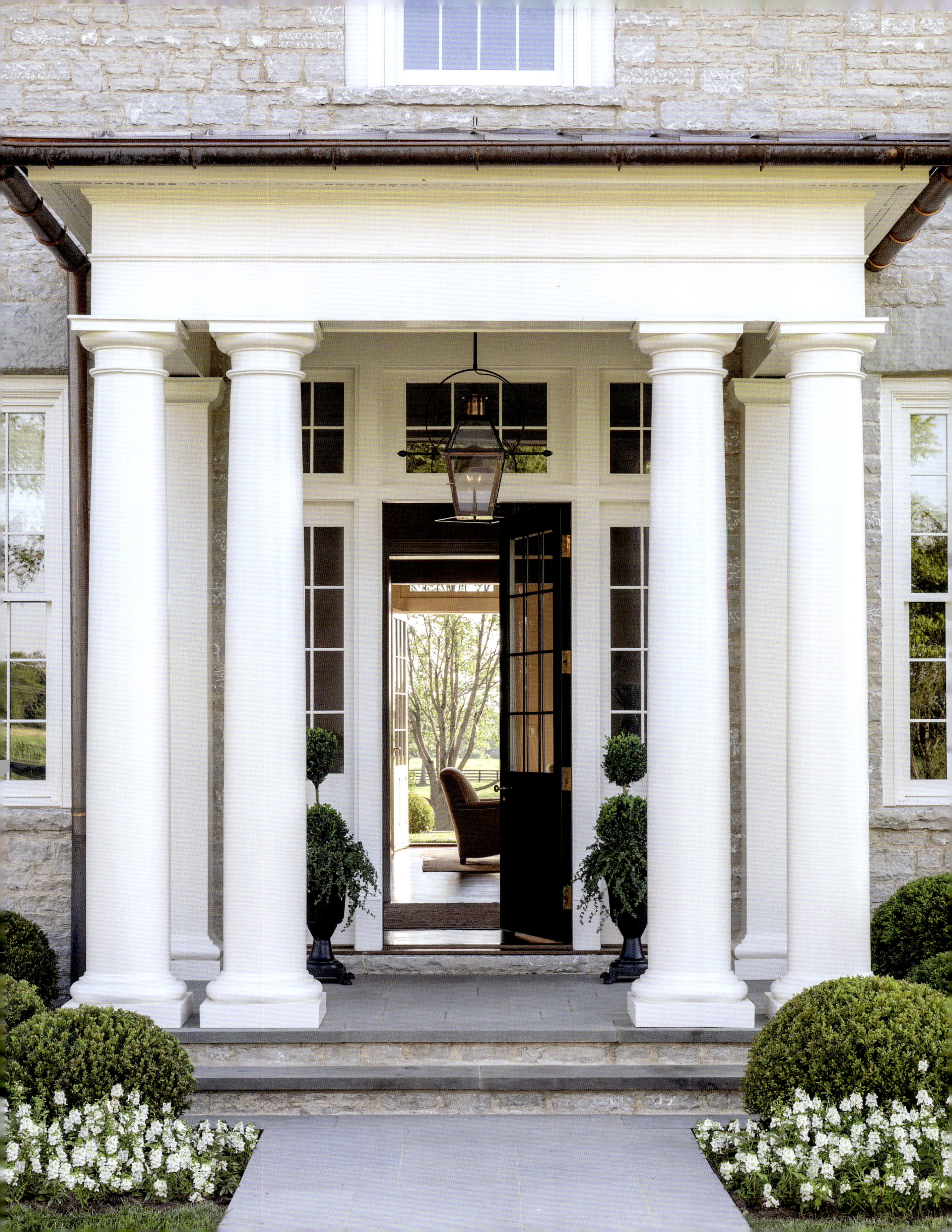

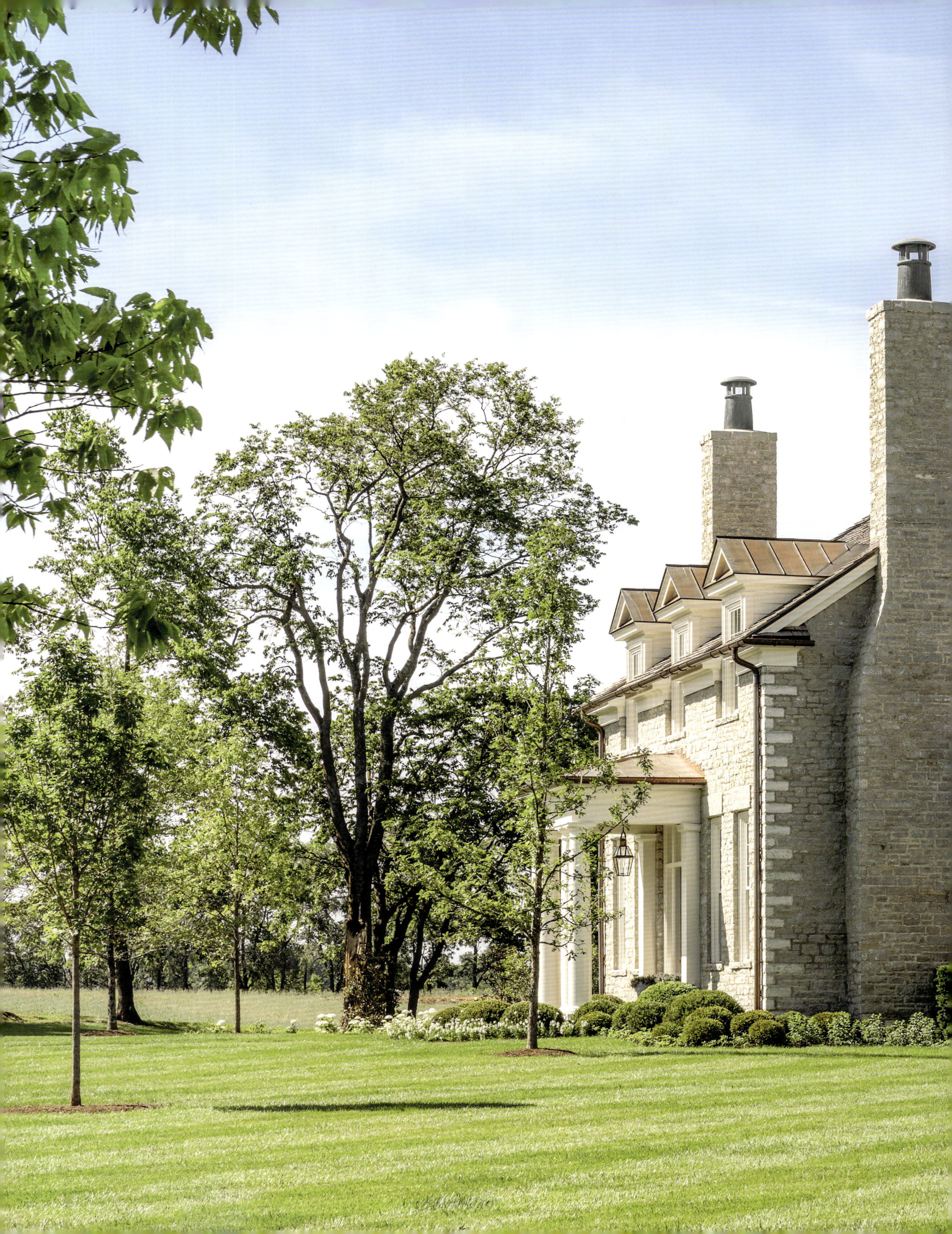

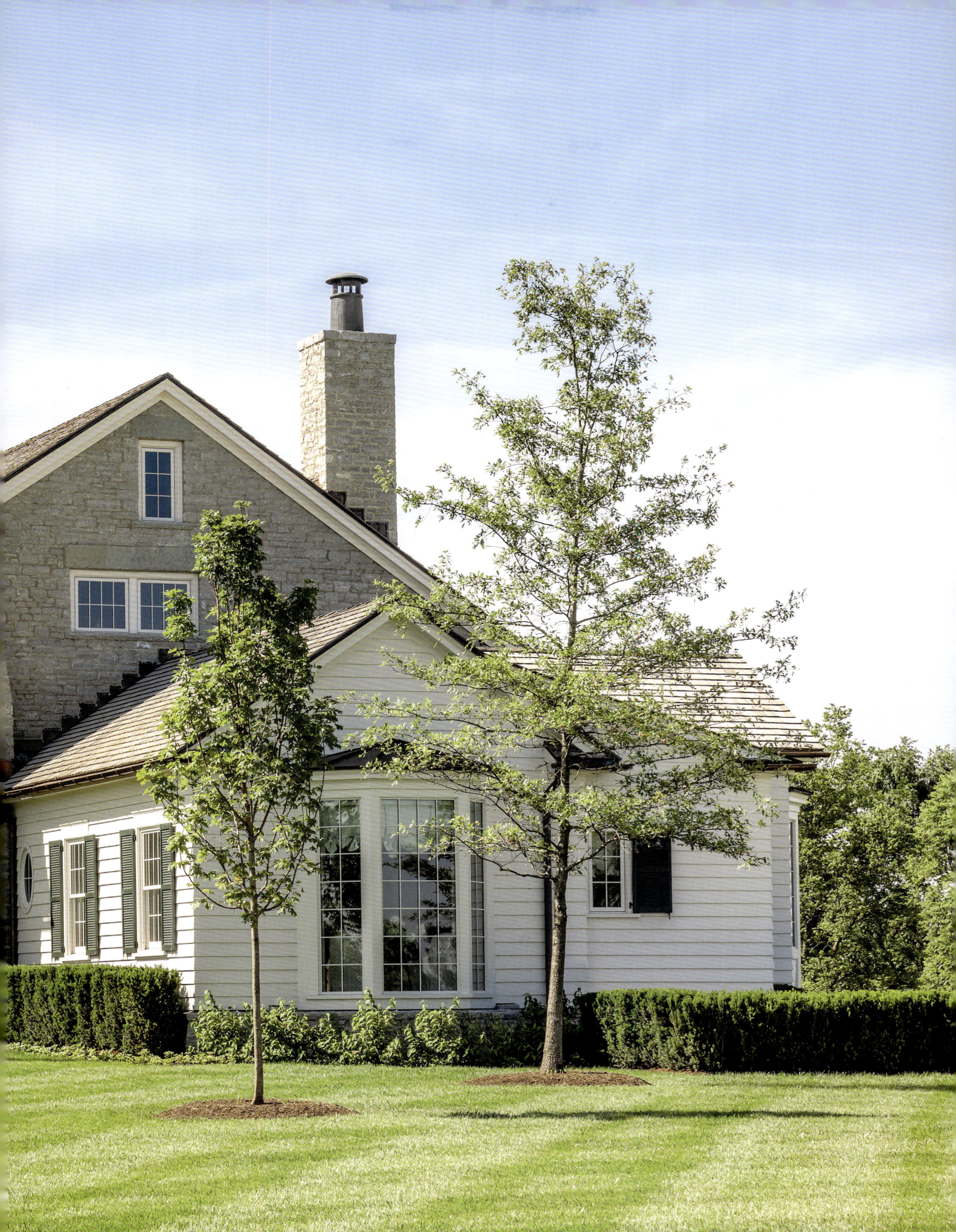

Eventually, in addition to a main house, we artfully arranged a chicken coop, potting shed, vegetable garden, dove field for hunting, and newly constructed pond among pastures and cornfields that are planted for livestock feed. Roads and footpaths—many now lined with picturesque four-board fences—provide access to the various destinations, which were spread across the site in order to promote engagement with the land. The formerly impenetrable fencerows were thinned out, removed, or strategically opened up to frame scenic views of the countryside and the various outbuildings.

For the main house itself, we settled on a refined colonial style, alluding to—but not specifically copying—historical building traditions that moved west through Kentucky during the eighteenth and nineteenth centuries. One of the first things I did when I started this project was buy every book that I could find on the state's architecture. Although I already knew well the basics of the look, I really wanted to reimmerse myself in its proportions and details. The form I gave the home here is very balanced but intentionally asymmetrical. A tall central core that's all stone is flanked by lower, siding-clad wings, and there's also a freestanding carriage house attached by a breezeway. The differentiation between parts gives the impression that the outlying sections were added on at a later date.

The entire region around Lexington sits on limestone bedrock, so we felt that this stone should be used for the veneer of the house. Deciding how it should be laid, though, required deliberation. One day, as the client and I were driving back from lunch, we passed an early-nineteenth-century church in the nearby community of Pisgah and saw exactly the inspiration we needed for the stone pattern. The way the horizontal courses were run; the way the long-ago masons had dressed the building's corners with thin,

OPPOSITE: Sidelights and transom windows around the front door brighten the oak-floored foyer. FOLLOWING SPREAD, LEFT: Traditional raised paneling accents the walls of the stair hall. Even though it's an internal space, a window on the upper landing allows light to filter in. FOLLOWING SPREAD, RIGHT: The home's interior furnishings, as seen here in the living room, were selected by the clients' daughter and serve as a delightful formal counterpoint to the rural setting.

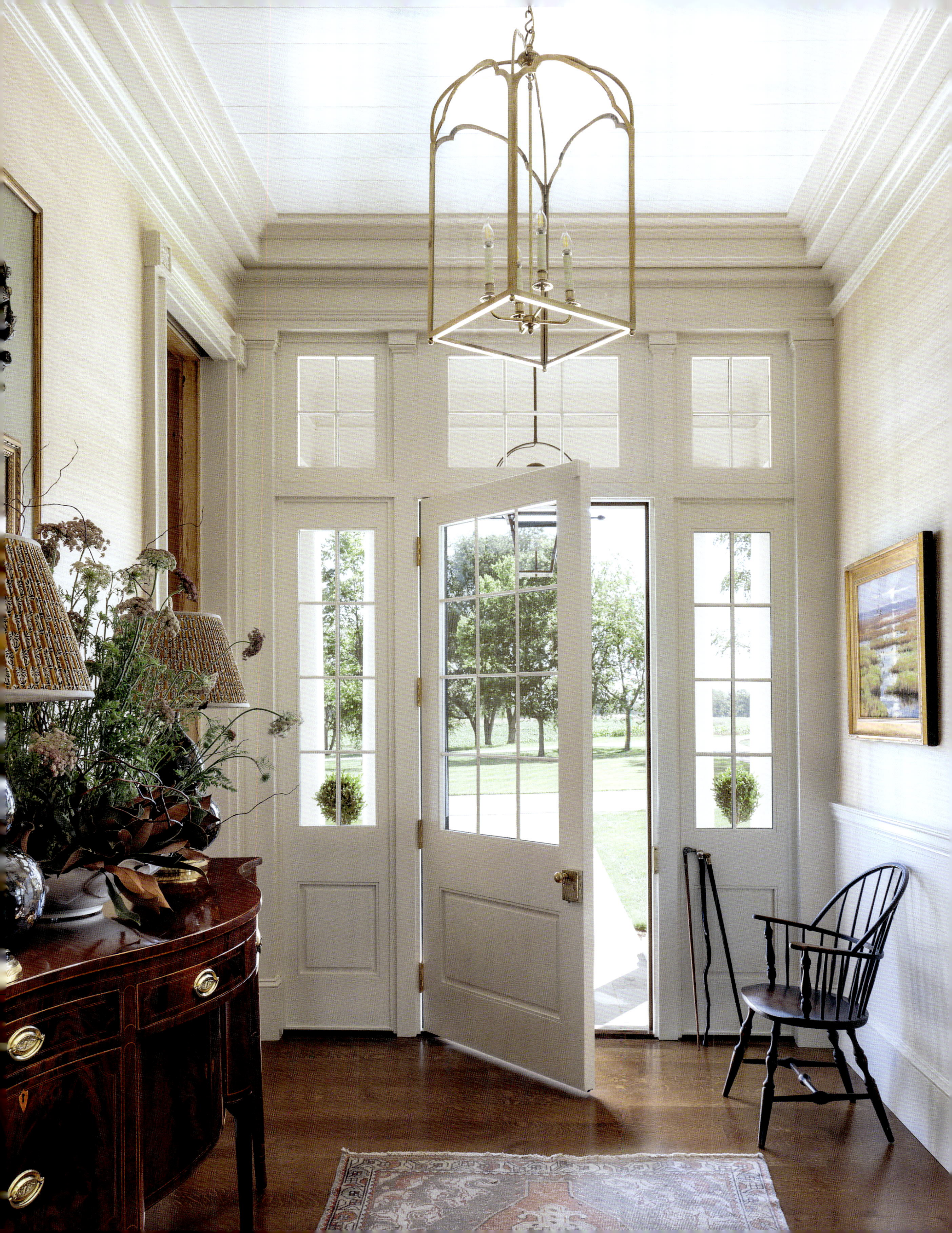

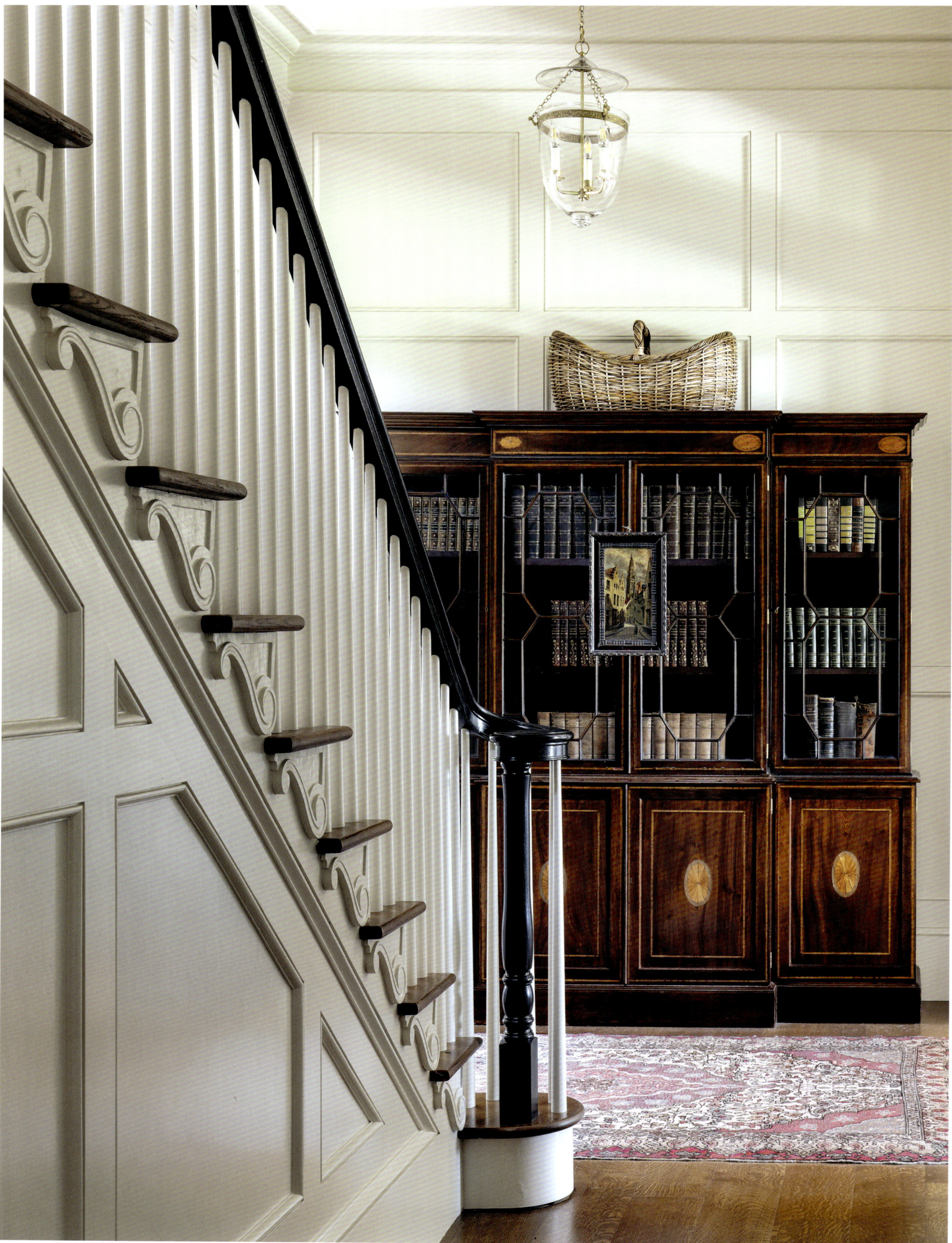

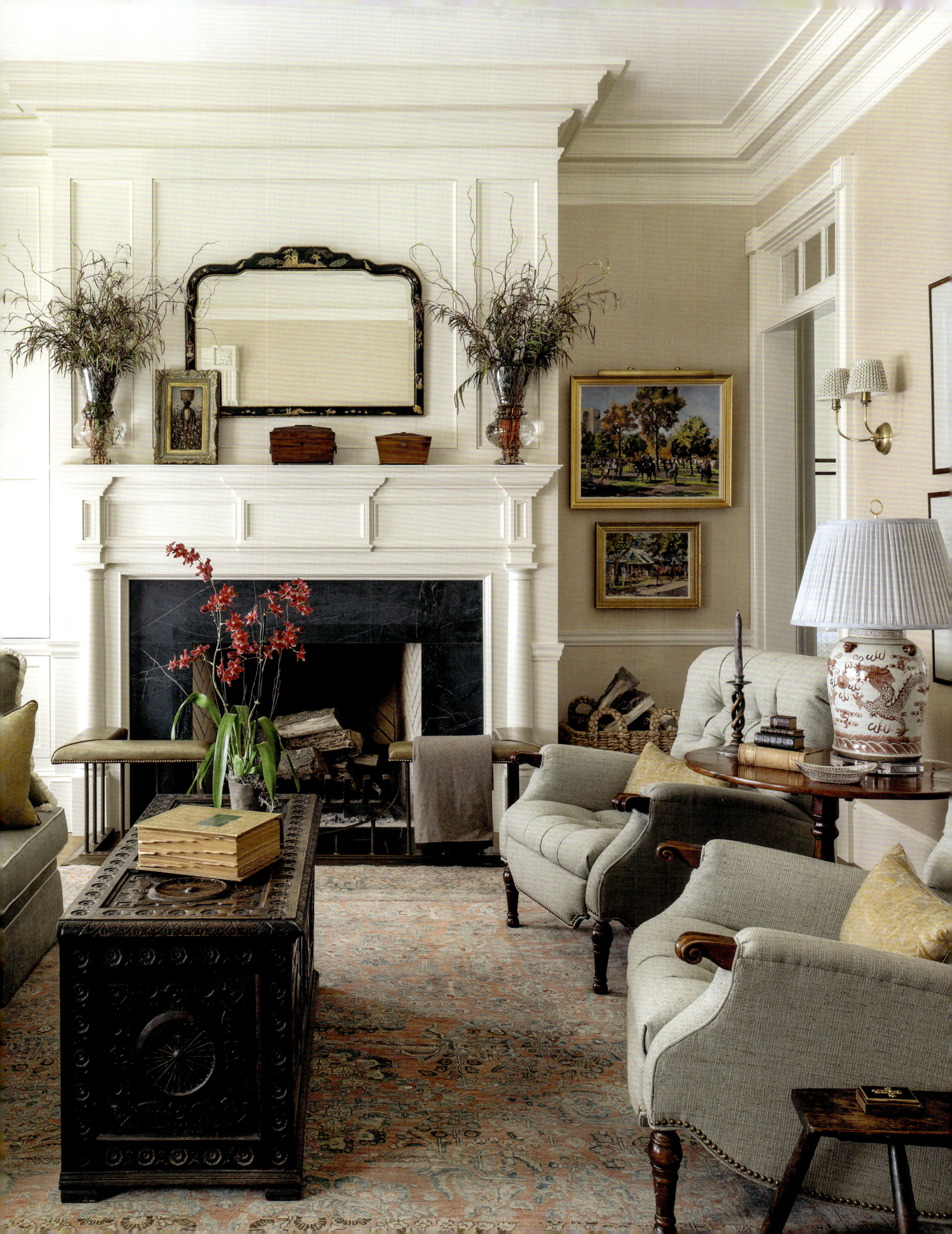

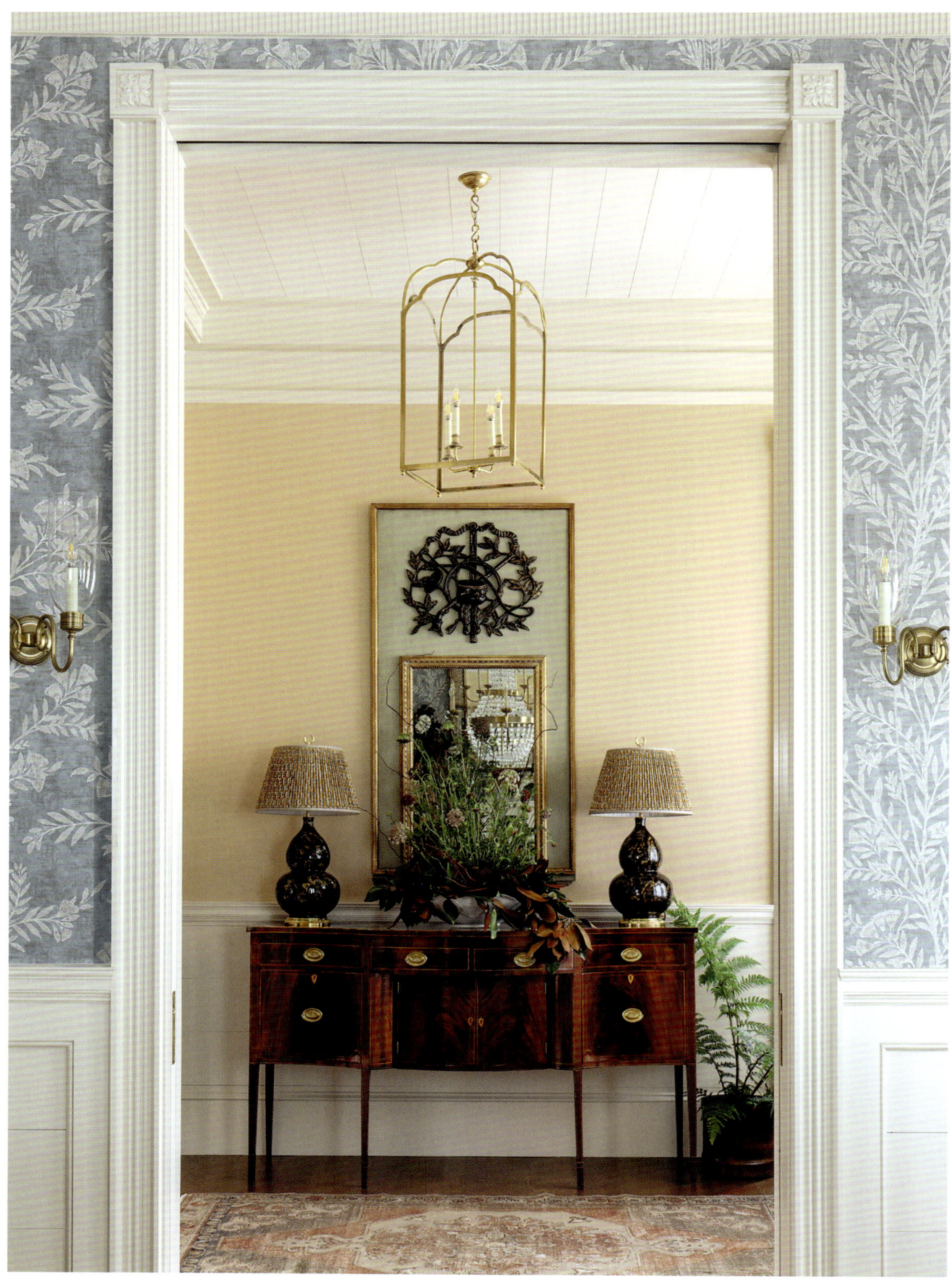

ABOVE: Wainscoting and paneled ceilings of butt-jointed boards were constructed using time-honored methods. OPPOSITE: The dining room is symmetrical and balanced; a plaster ceiling medallion adds elegance. Like most of the home's first-floor spaces, the room offers multiple connections to the outdoors.

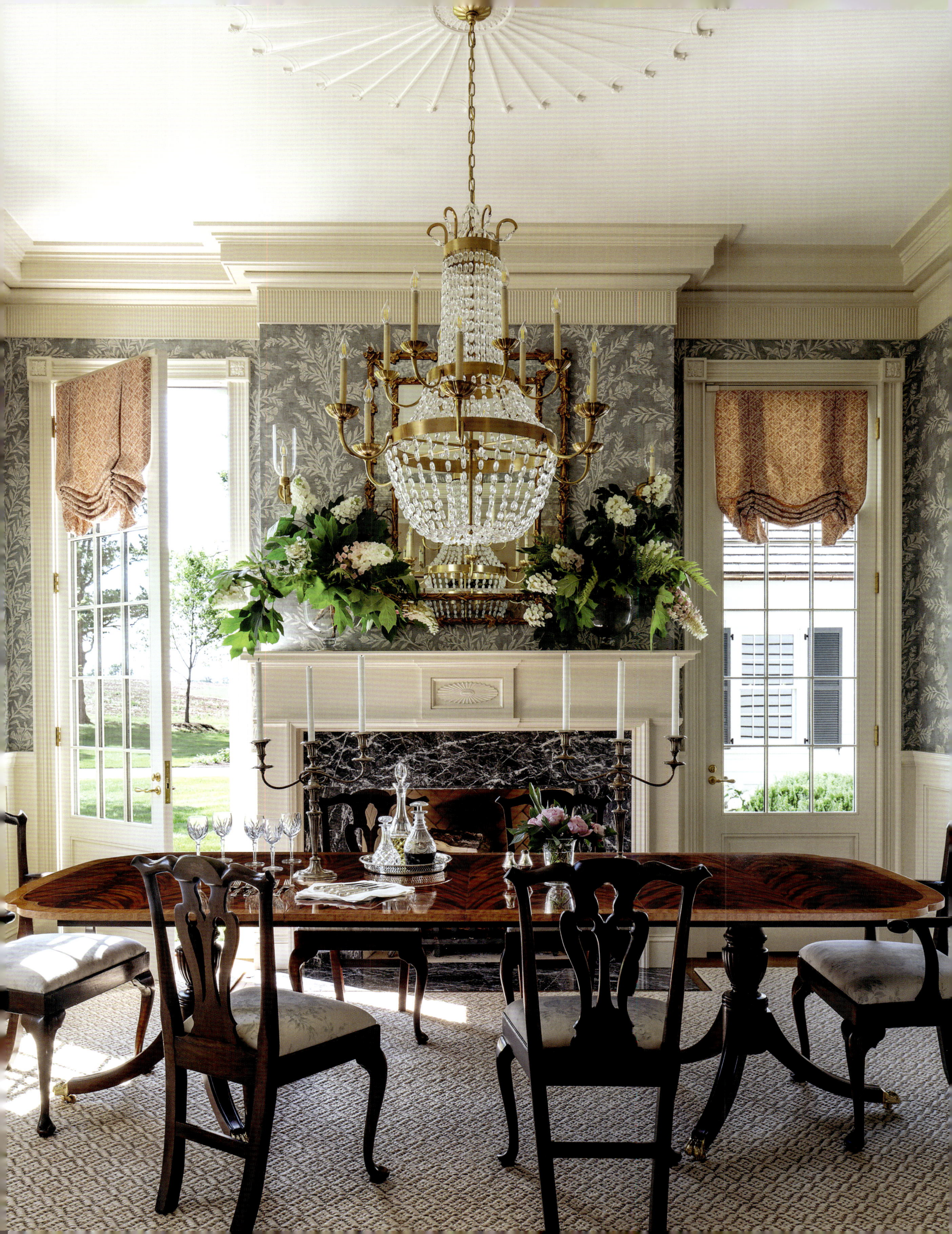

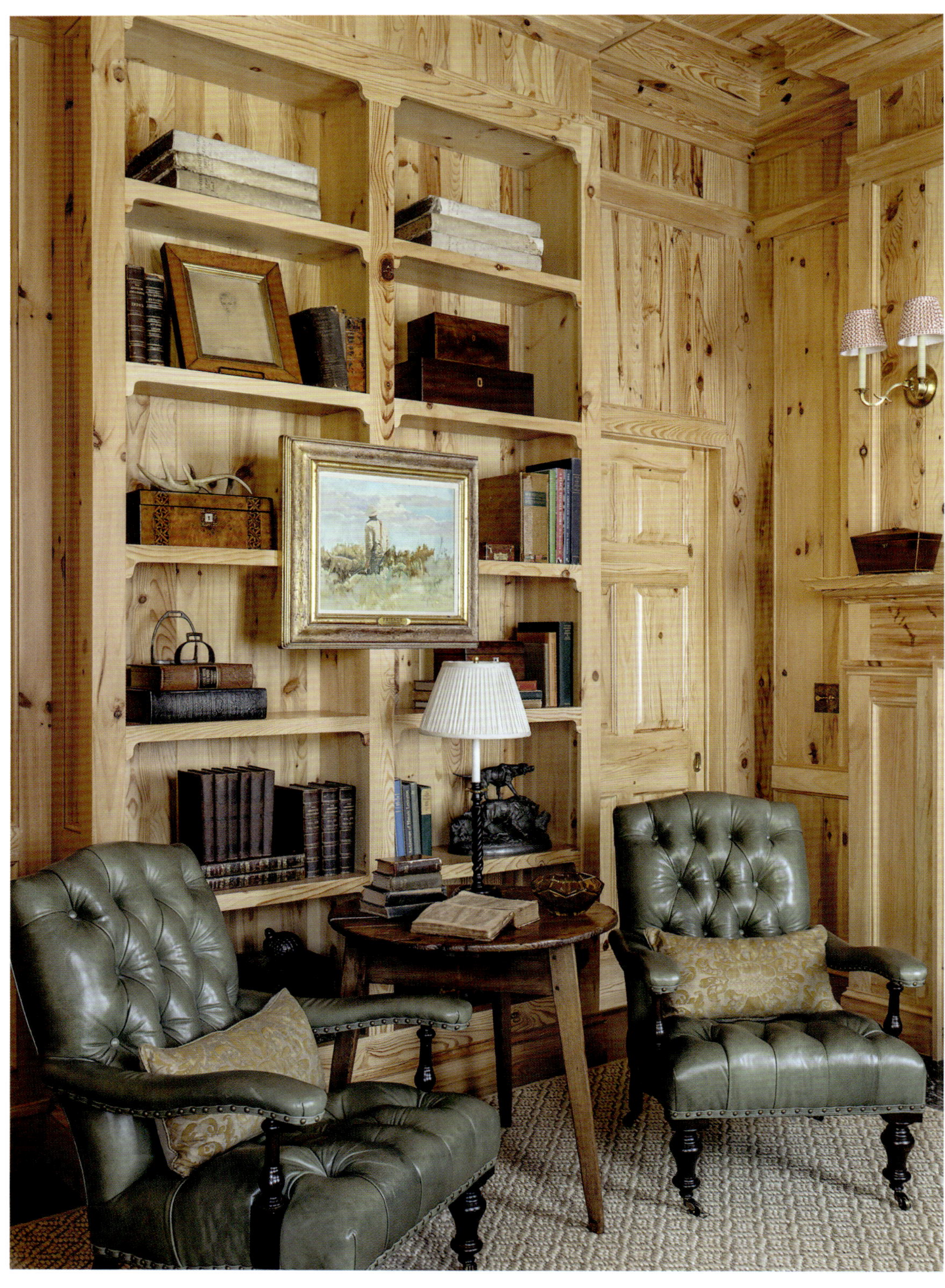

ABOVE AND OPPOSITE: An envelope of warm knotty pine adds texture and a distinct character to the husband's study. We left the wood natural so that it will acquire a soft brown patina over time. Simplified millwork details fit the room's relaxed character, and an old musket and powder horn feel right at home.

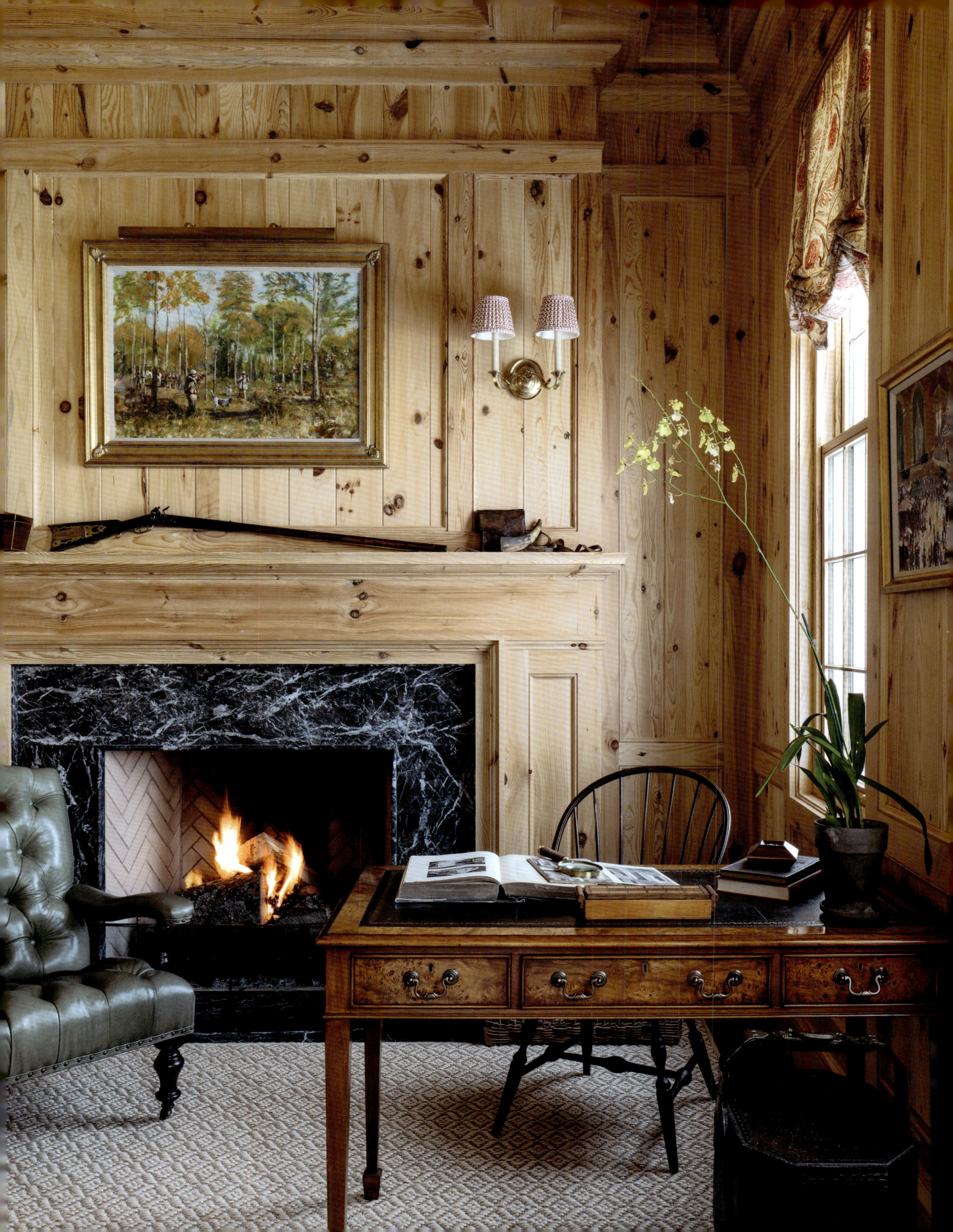

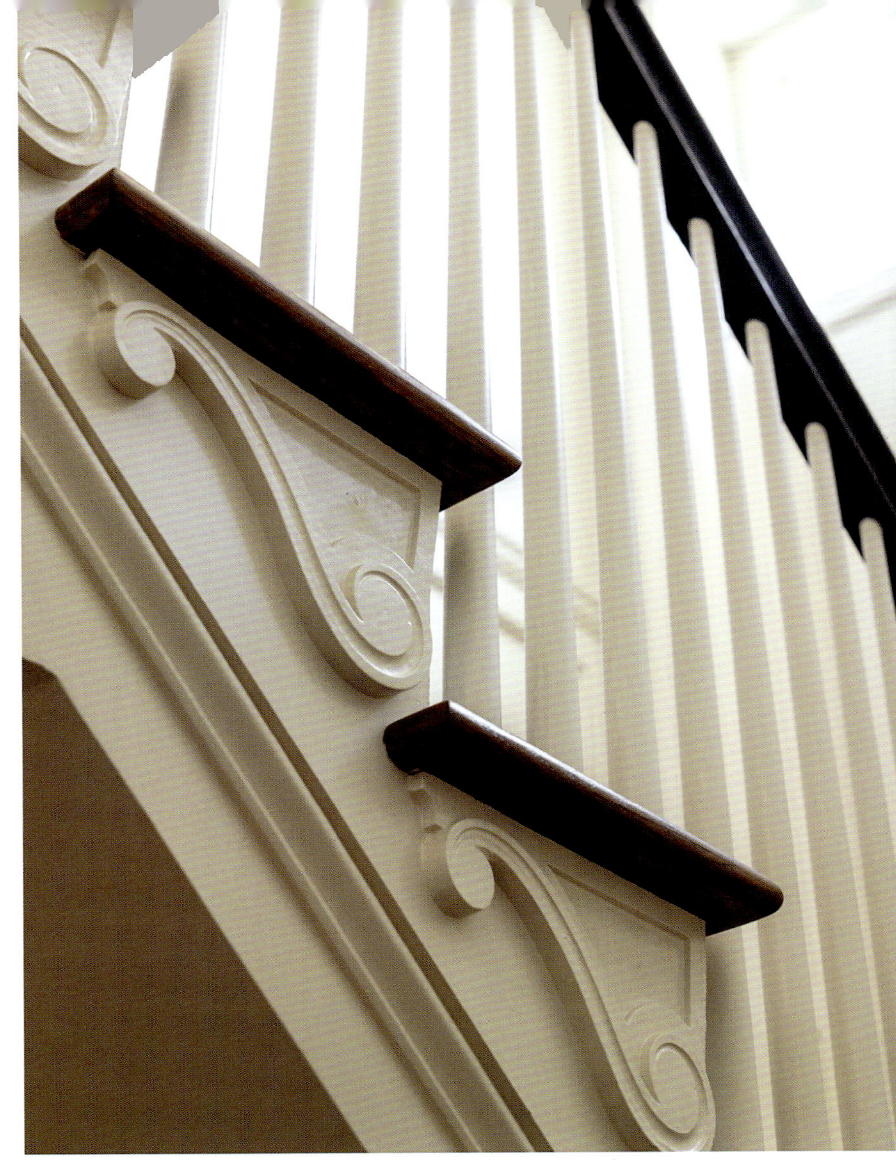

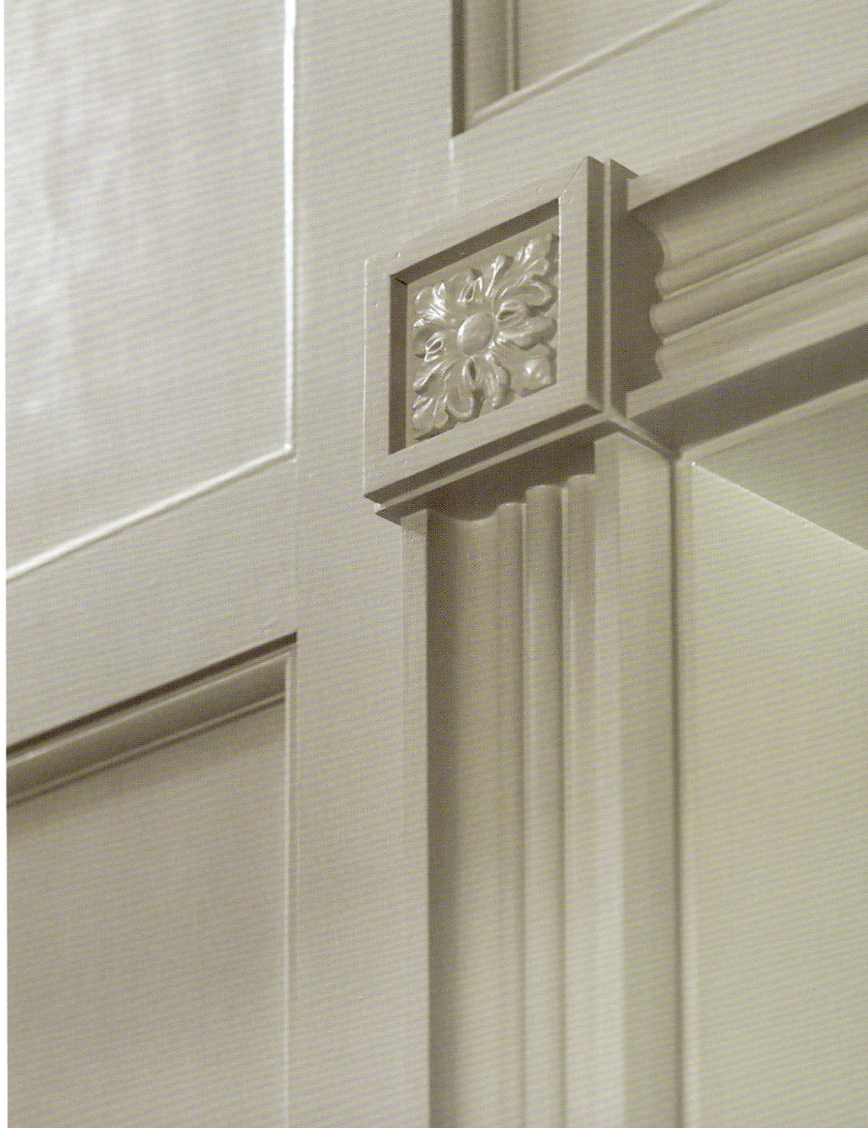

RIGHT: A suitable collection of interior and exterior details imbues the home with colonial style. Adornments such as rosettes, scrolls, reeding, and elaborate crown moldings and casings for doors and windows were thoughtfully applied throughout. The cupola and weather vane on the carriage house add an agrarian touch appropriate to the site.

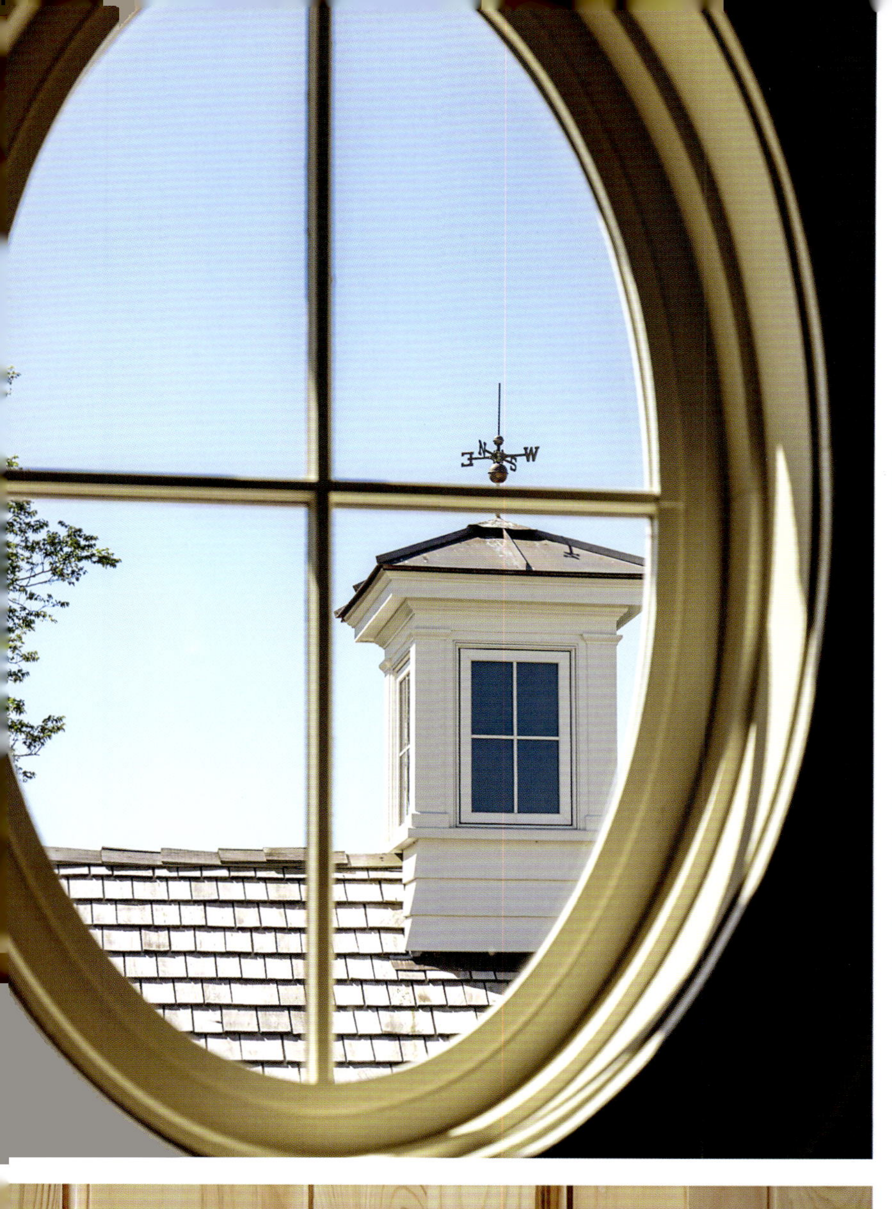
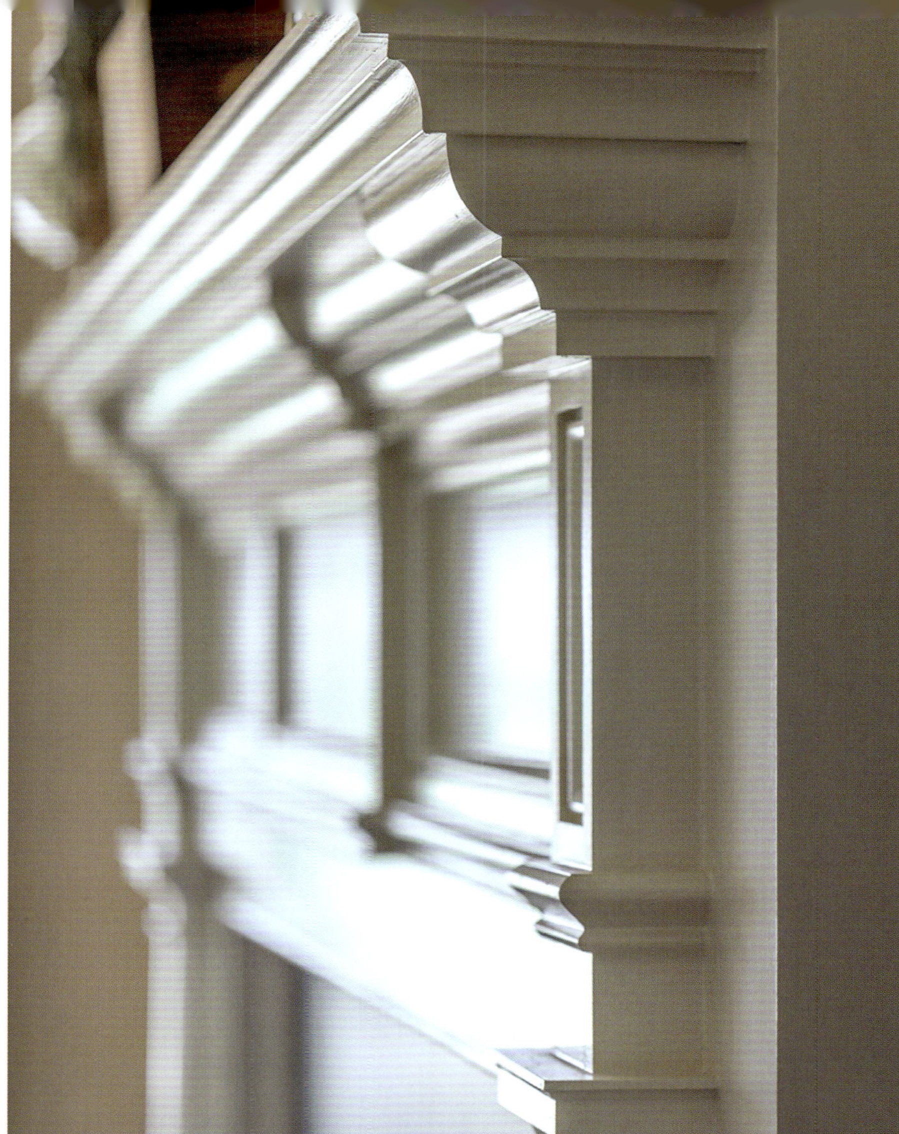
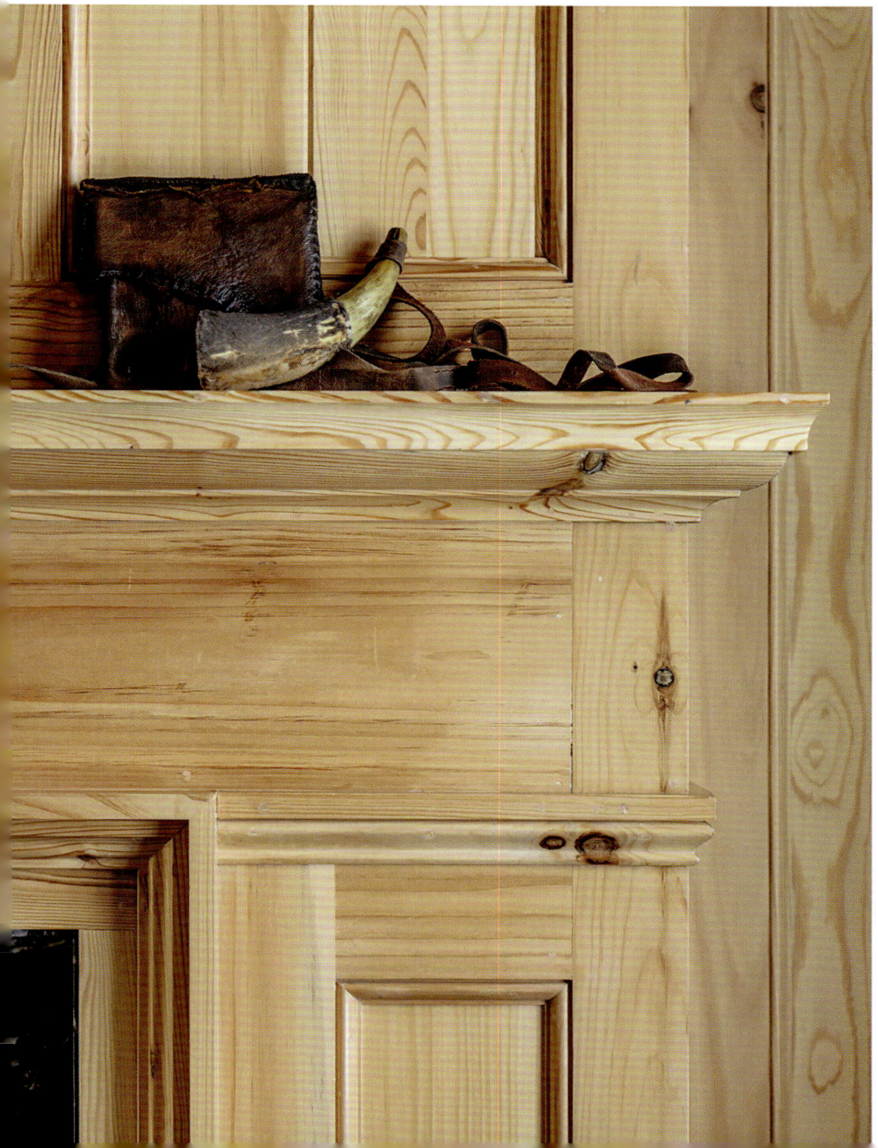
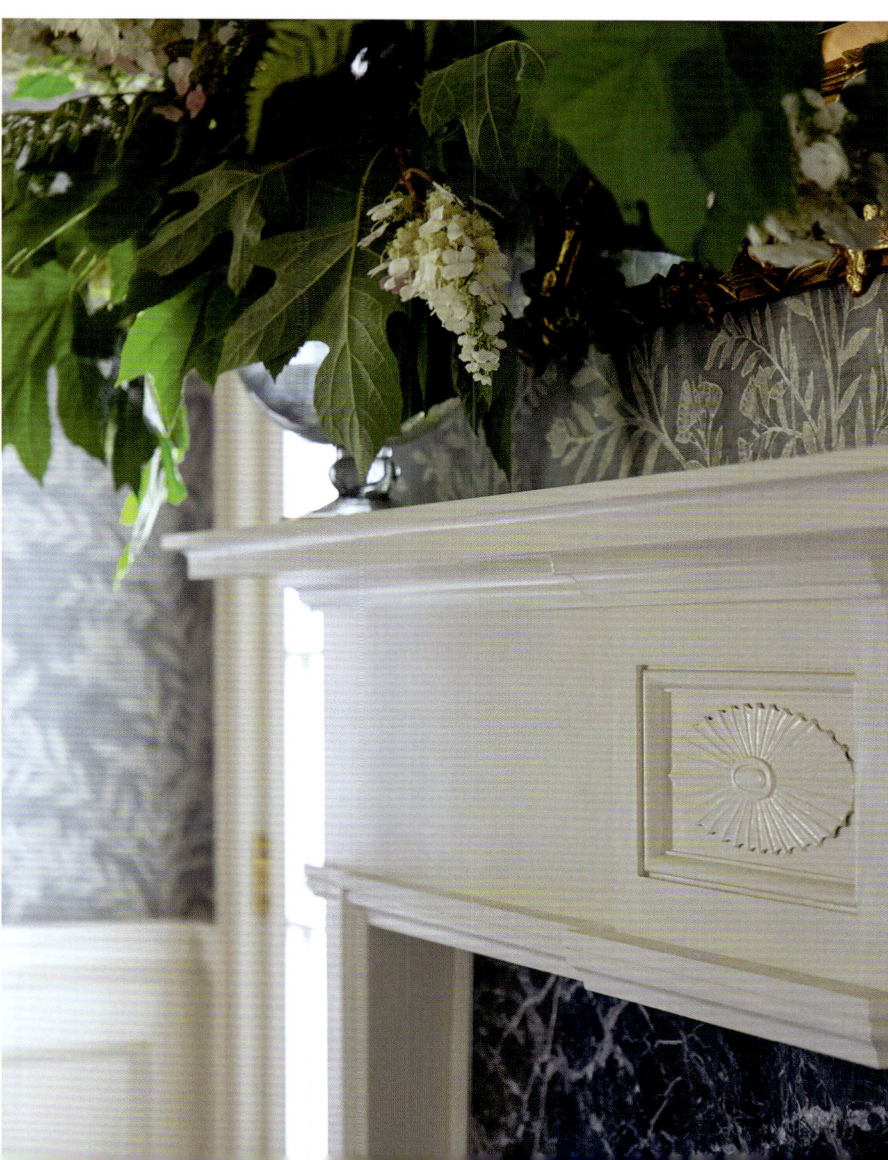

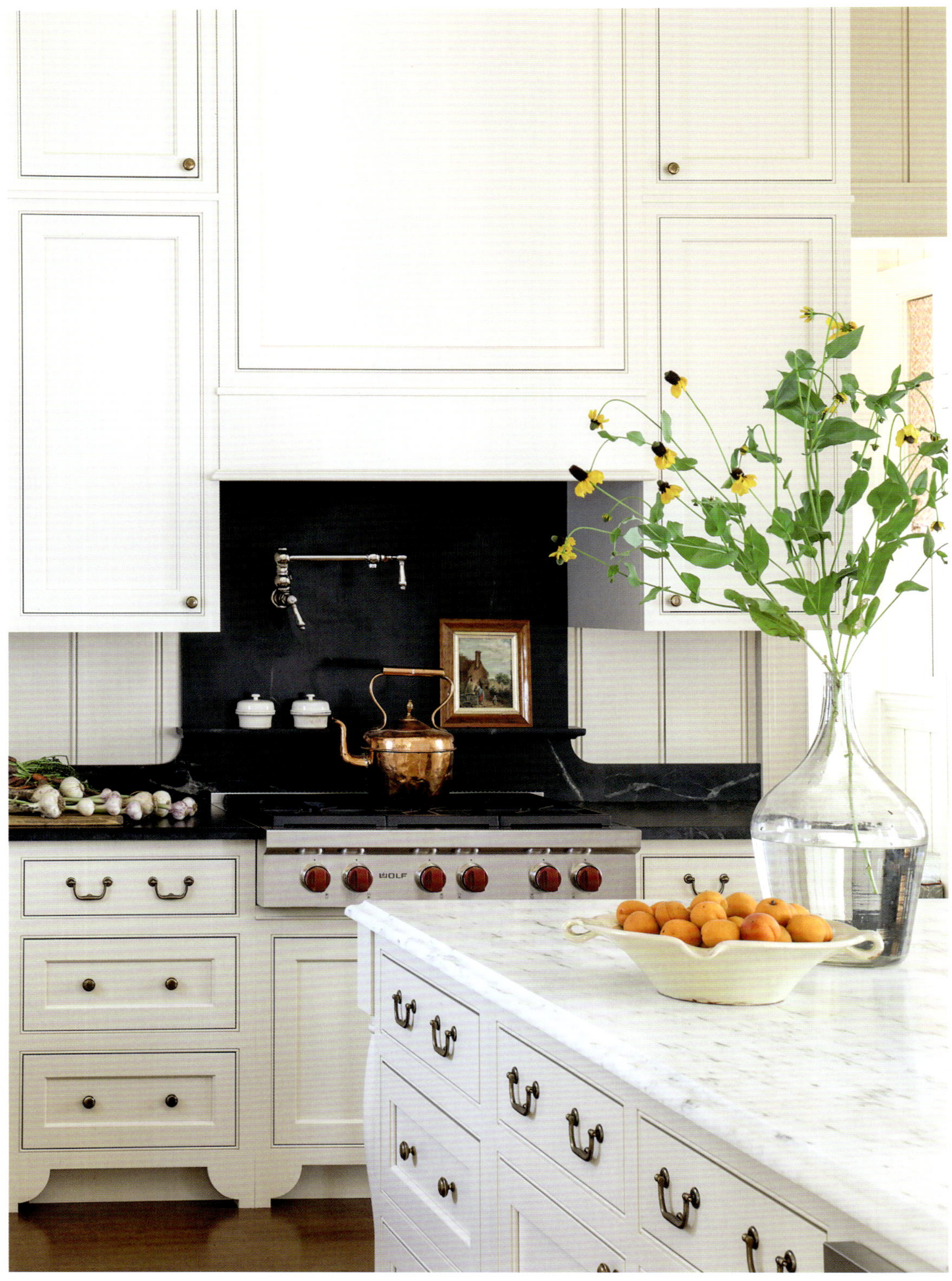

ABOVE AND OPPOSITE: The kitchen is very traditional, with high Shaker-style cabinets. Soapstone countertops on the perimeter make a pleasant contrast with the white marble used on the island; the island itself was designed to feel more like a piece of furniture than like a modern built-in fixture. The quarter-round toe-kicks are a subtle inversion of the curves on the backsplash.

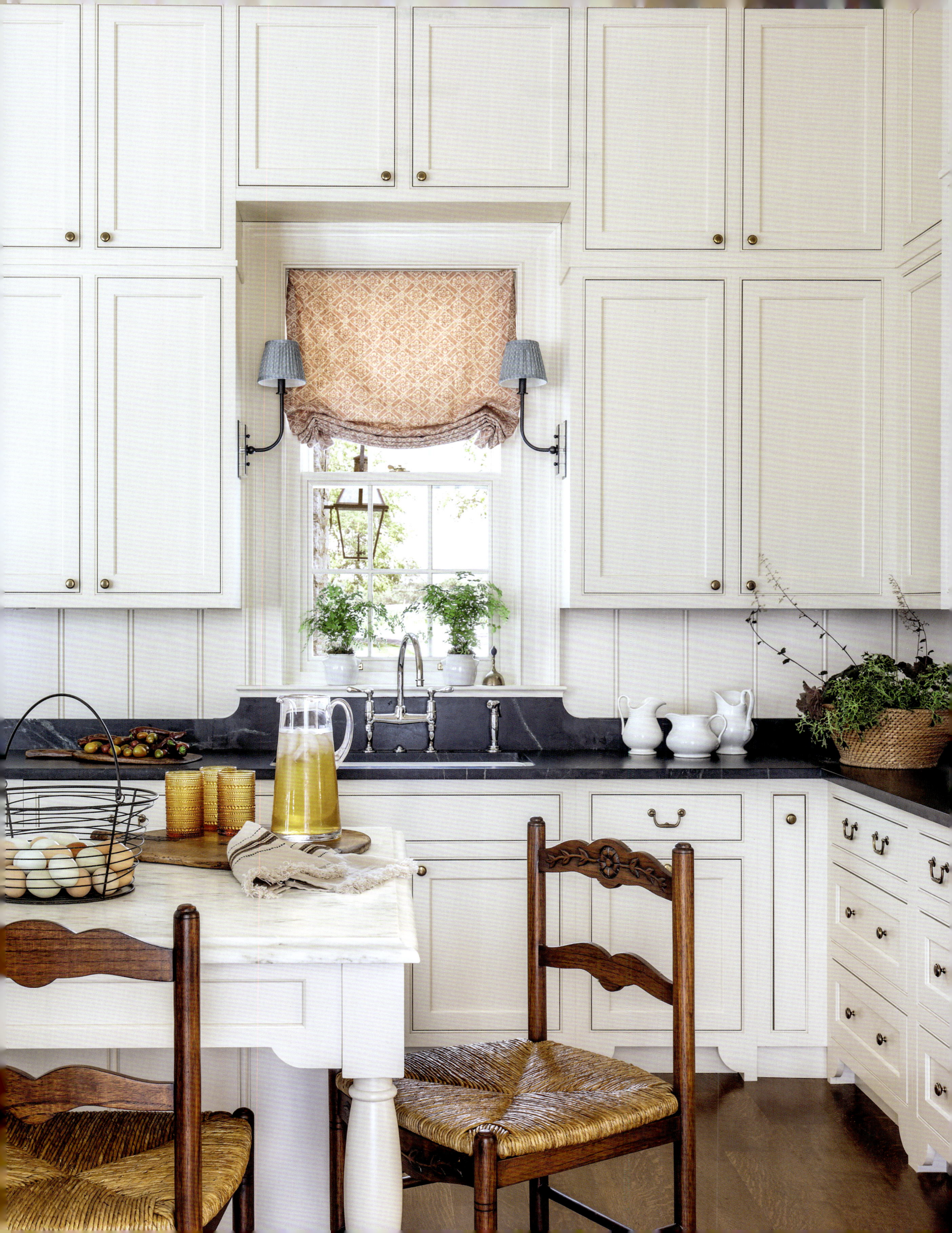

somewhat irregular quoining; and the variations in the depth of the trowel work—all would look stunning on the new house while tying it even more firmly to its locale.

In spite of the agrarian milieu, this is an undeniably elevated dwelling, with a classic layout of clearly defined spaces for the living room, kitchen, dining room, study, and stair hall. Interior elements such as wood walls, traditional wainscoting, and millwork flourishes are characteristic of the architectural language. Beneath three stately dormers on the exterior, a Tuscan order entablature and columns (formal but relatively clean-lined) constitute the entry porch that shelters the front door. In other respects, the home includes down-to-earth gestures toward pure practicality: for example, there's a boot wash station next to the breezeway that ensures easy cleanup when you're headed back in from the fields or garden.

I love designing in opportunities—both physical and visual—for effortless movement between a house and its natural setting. When a home is encircled by the kind of landscape we have here, it becomes especially critical. Pairs of doors in the living and dining rooms lead to pleasant open-air gathering spots, bay windows in the primary bedroom and bath frame choice portions of the scenery, and a big sitting porch faces the sunset for late-afternoon lounging.

In the end, Seven Stones beautifully combines a variety of purposes: as a central locus for the family (a second house is in the works for the clients' daughter and her family, and there is plenty of room for more homes if other relatives choose to follow suit), as a hunting preserve, and as a productive cattle farm. It's not just a pretty place and it's not just a place for utility. It's all of the above, as well as romantically infused with the history and character of old Kentucky—and that, to me, is the heart of its story.

OPPOSITE: This fireplace warms a small seating area attached to the kitchen—a comfortable spot to have morning coffee or sit and chat during meal prep. FOLLOWING SPREAD: The broad, west-facing porch has grand views of the farm and lake beyond. L-shaped stone piers define the porch's corners, their strength and solidity softened by inset Tuscan columns.

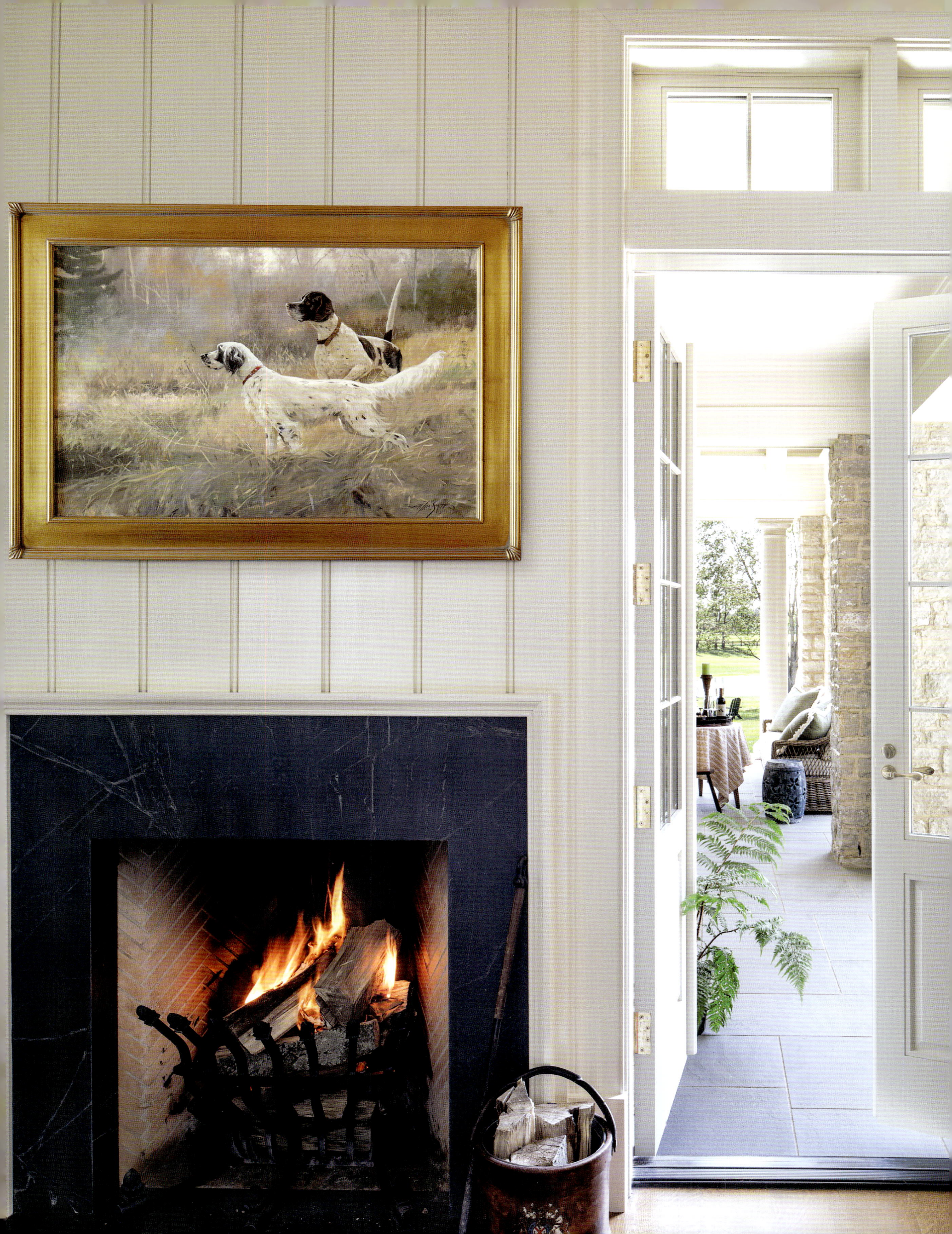

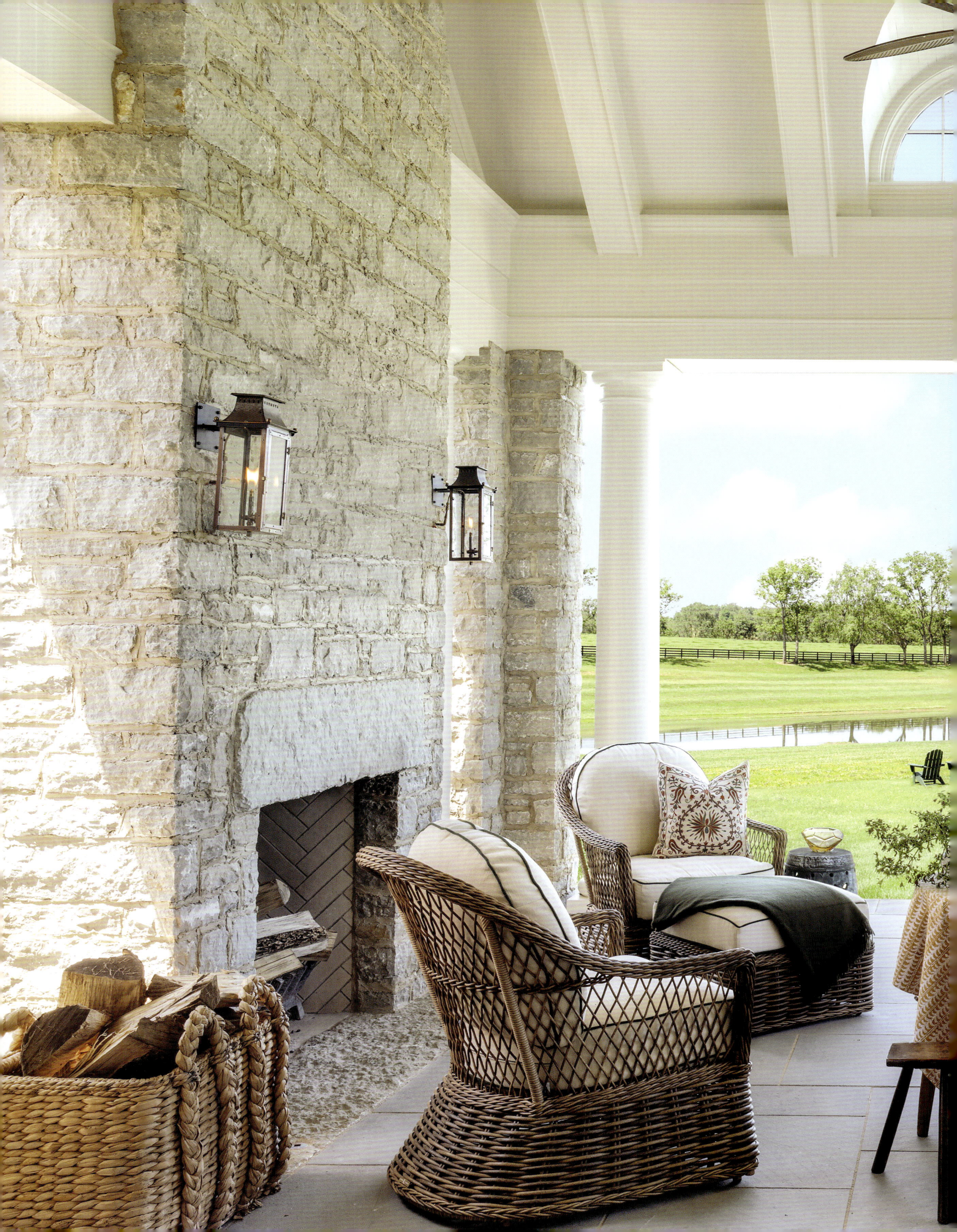

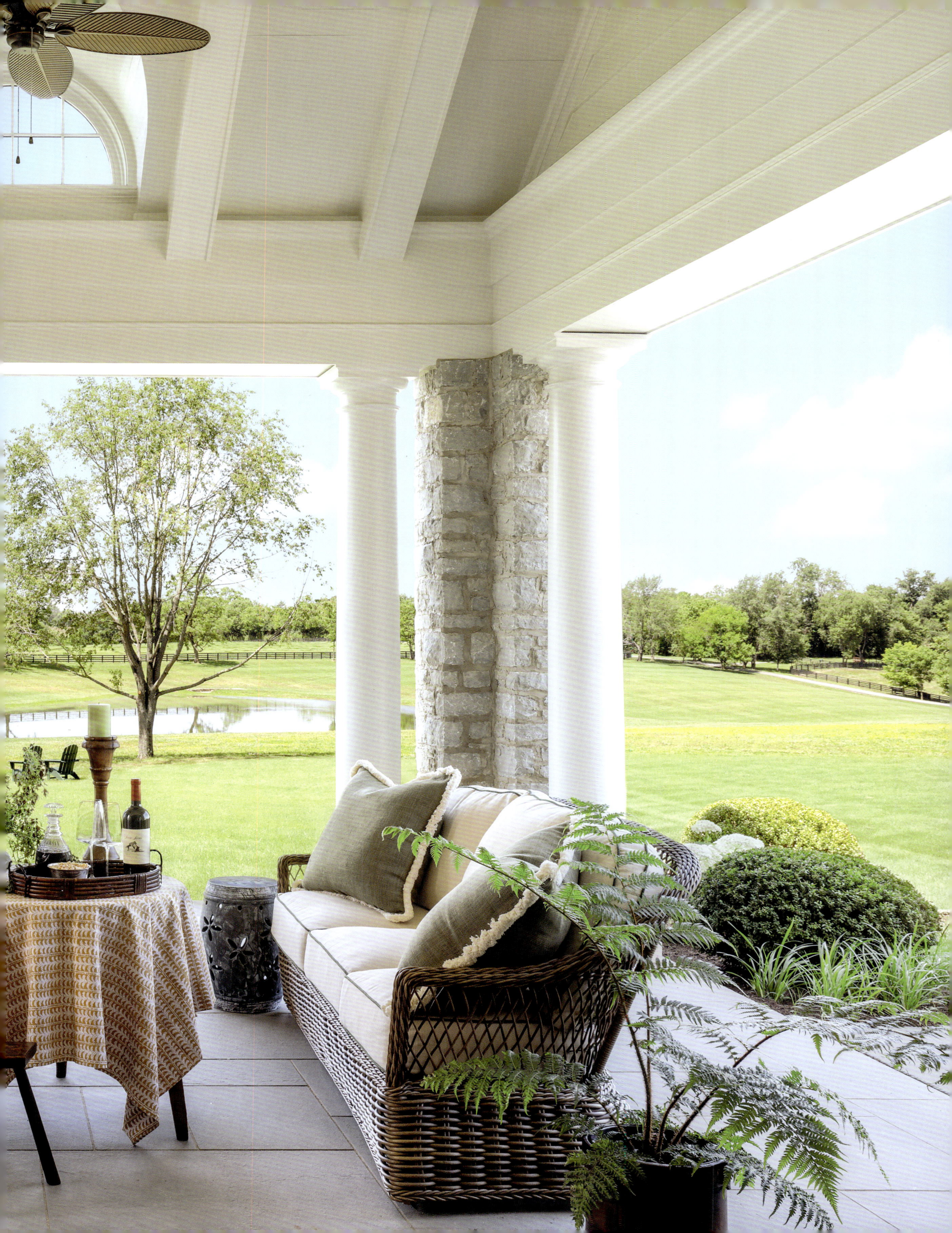

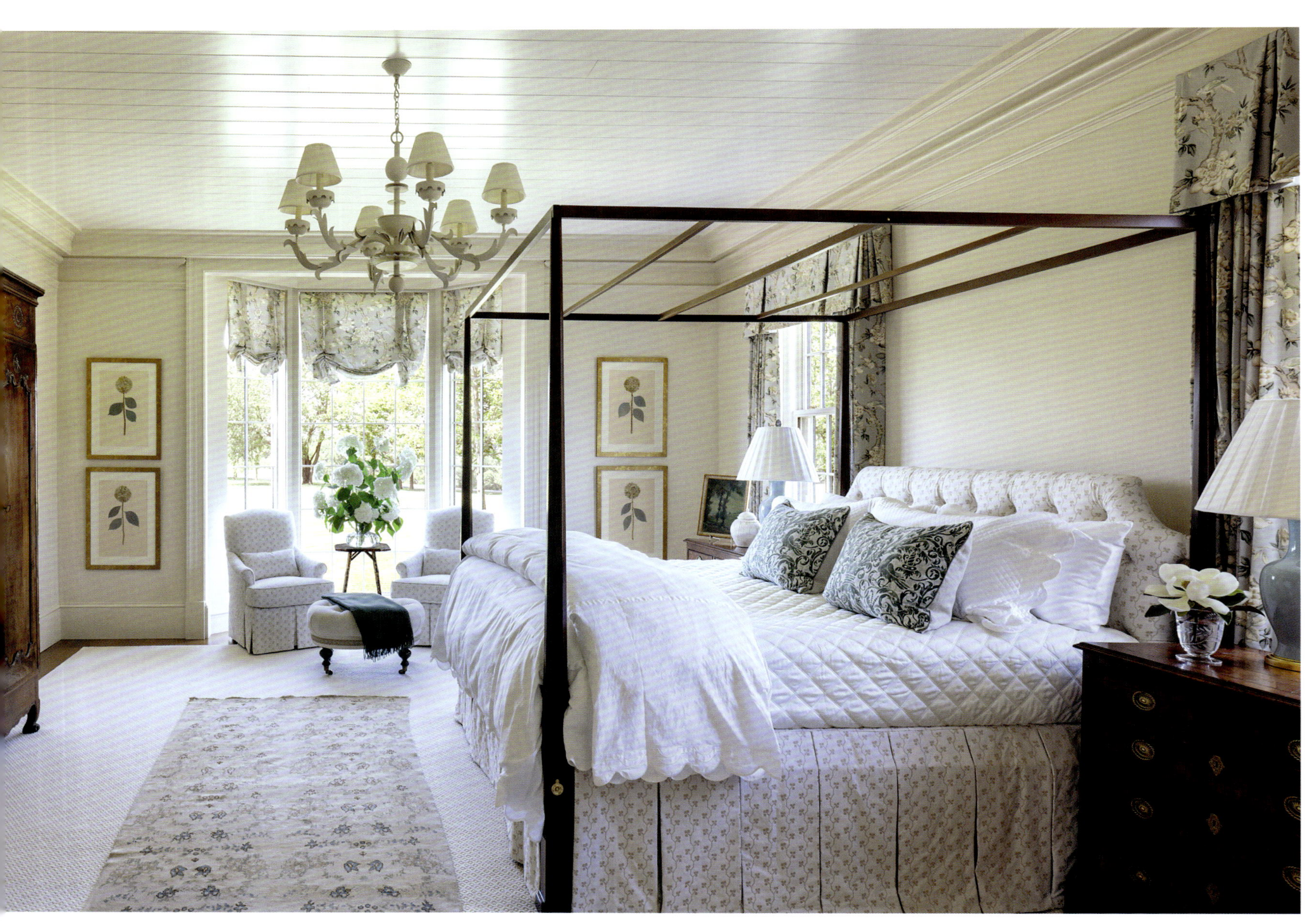

ABOVE AND OPPOSITE: The principal bedroom and bath occupy their own wing, making them an oasis of calm for the homeowners. Both spaces include bay windows that, figuratively speaking, reach out to embrace the scenery beyond. FOLLOWING SPREAD: Visiting grandchildren can stay in the bunk room, although it's equally comfortable for adult guests. Beadboard walls make it cozy, and two sets of casework steps, rather than simple ladders, provide access to the upper beds.

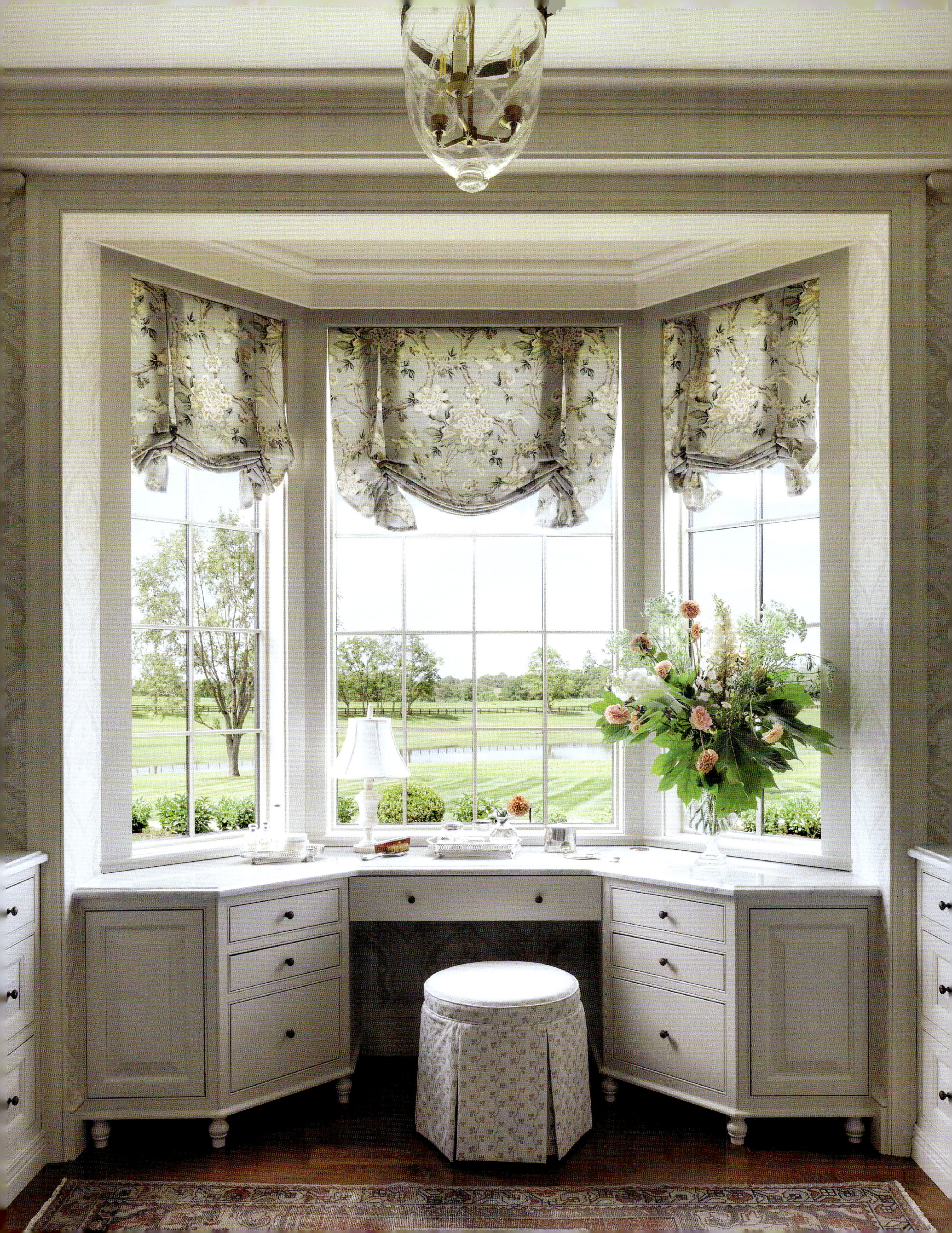

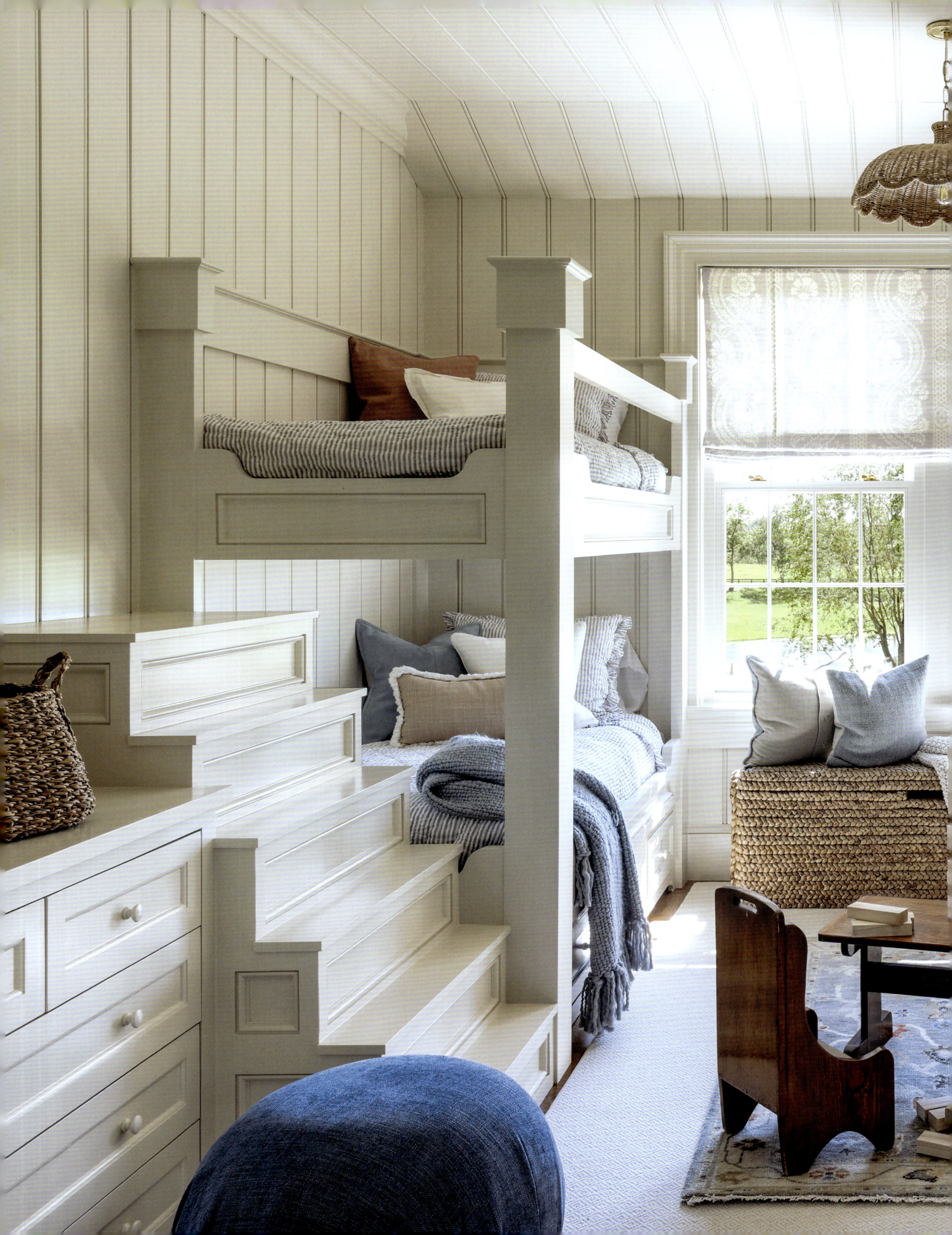

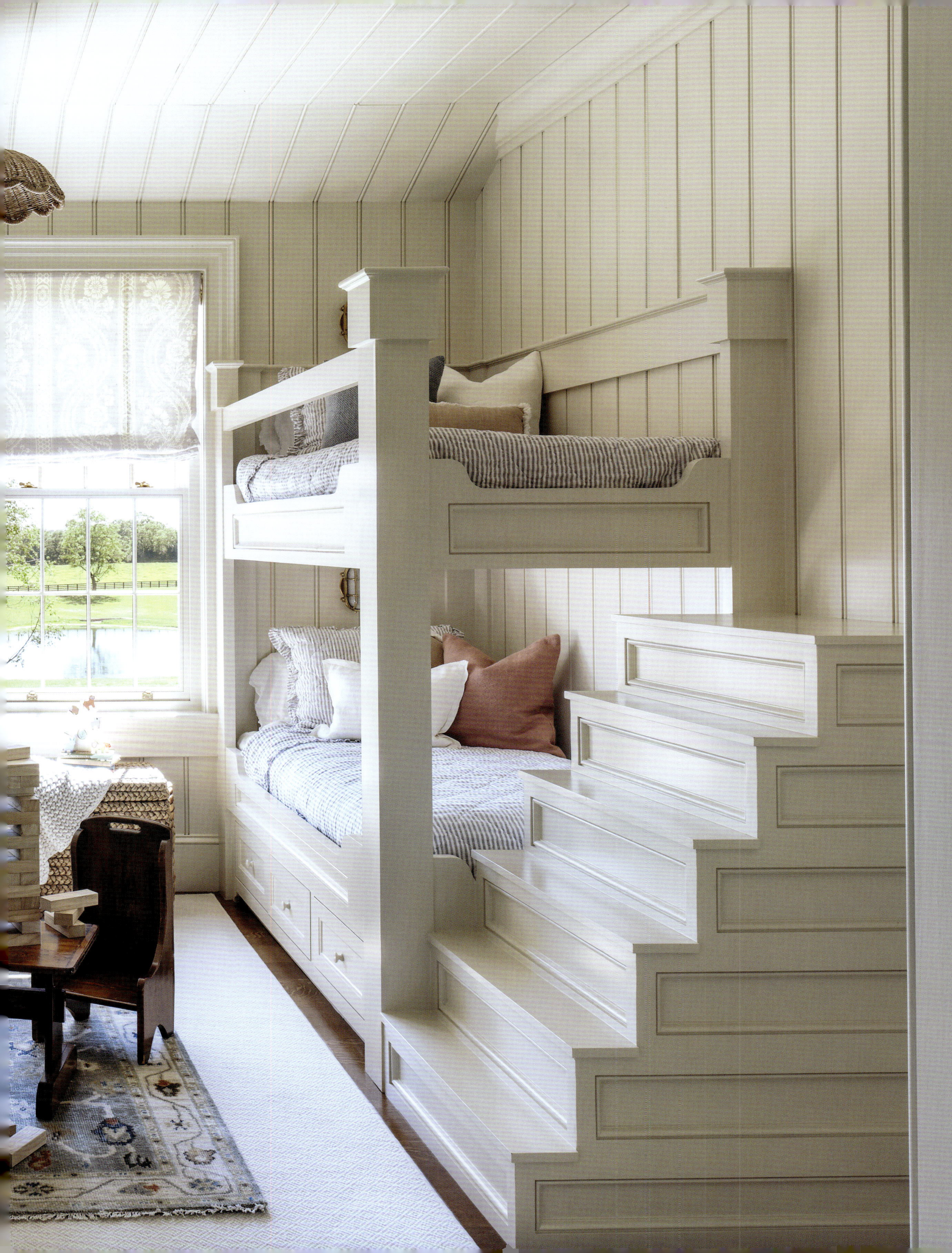

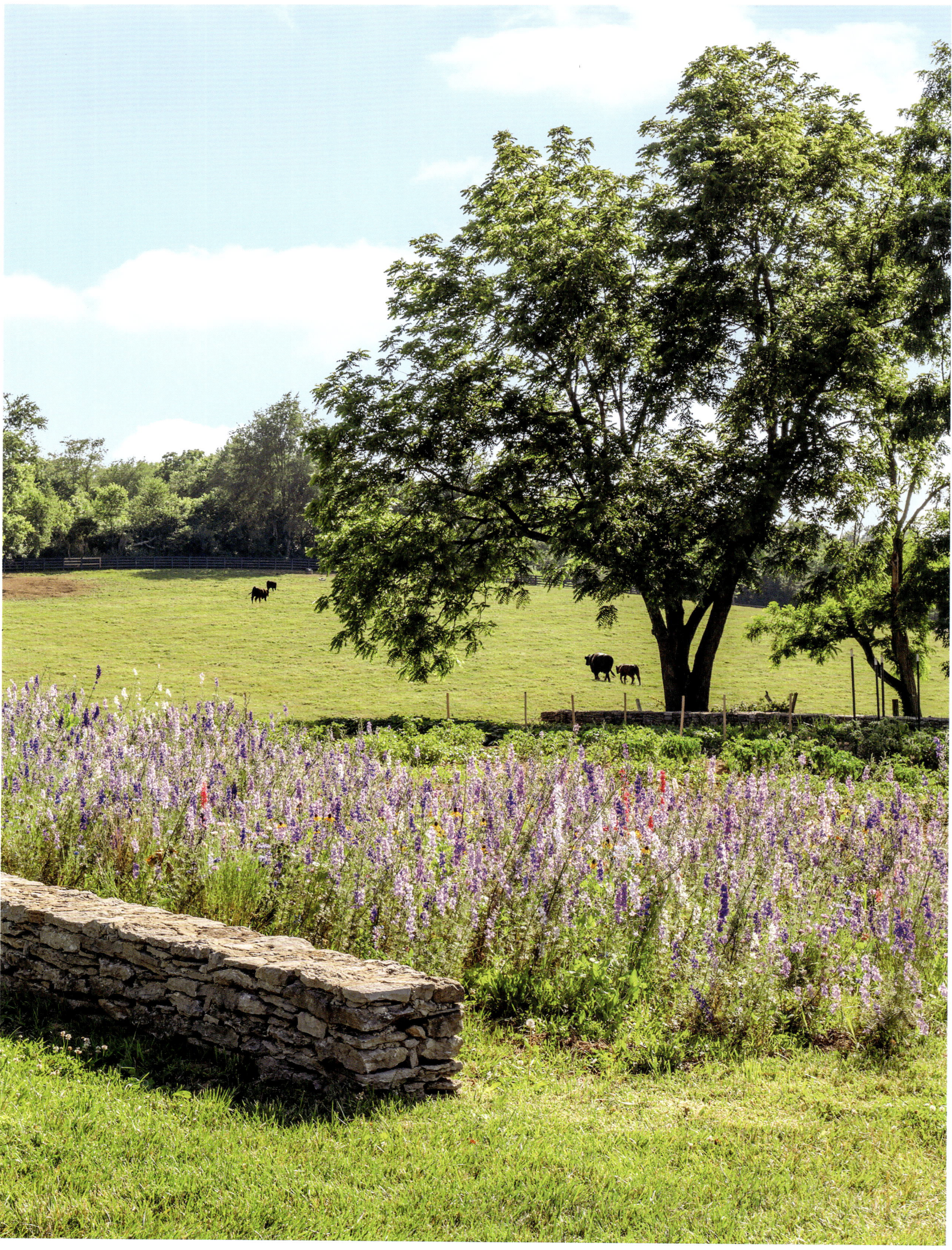

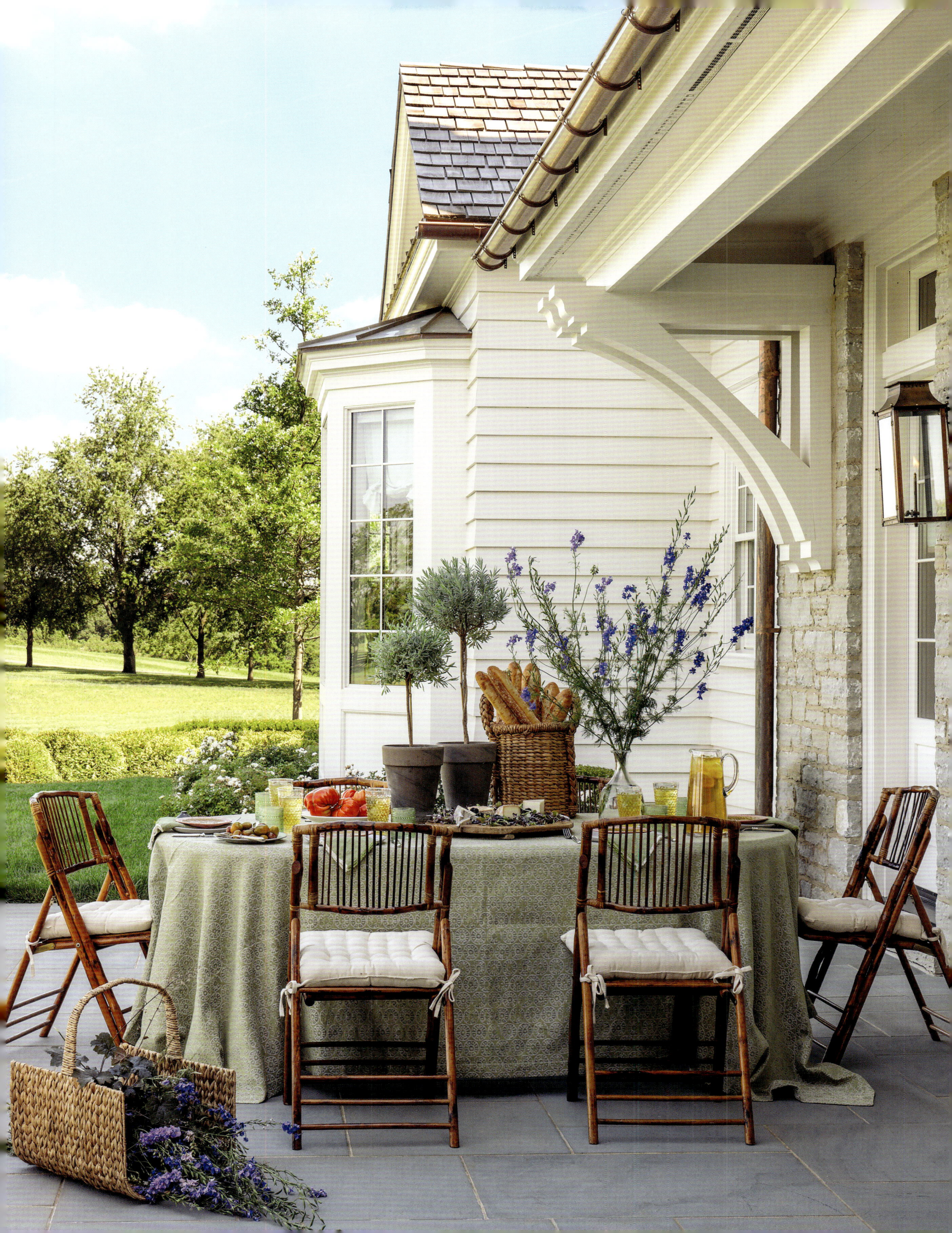

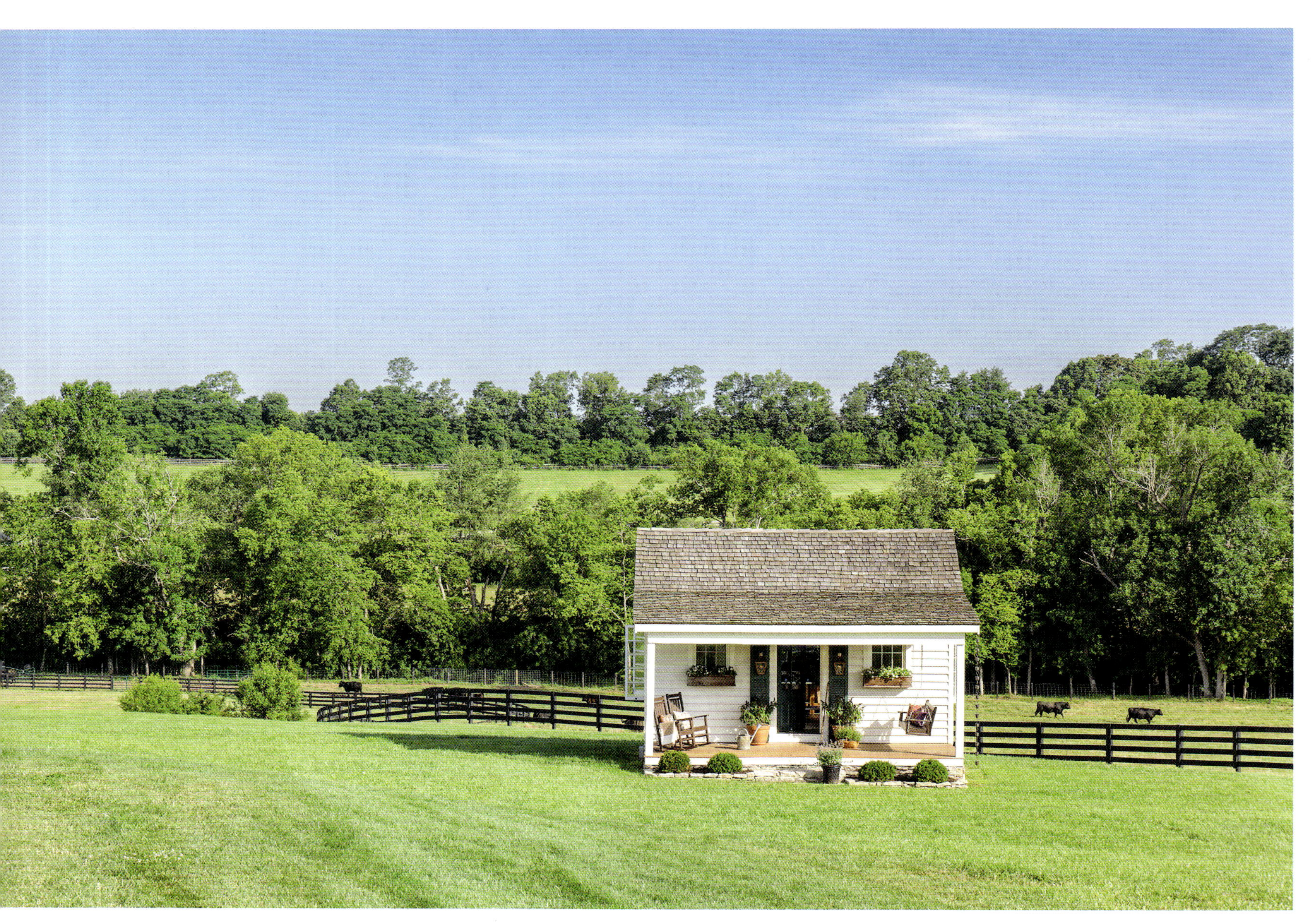

PRECEDING SPREAD: The house is surrounded by carefully planned vistas and outdoor destinations, such as a vegetable and cutting garden (left) and an alfresco dining terrace off the living room (right). ABOVE AND OPPOSITE: The charming potting shed features a covered porch and doubles as a site for enjoying the occasional cigar and glass of bourbon. FOLLOWING SPREAD: The clients' chicken coop serves as a reminder that this gentleman's farm is very much a working agricultural property.

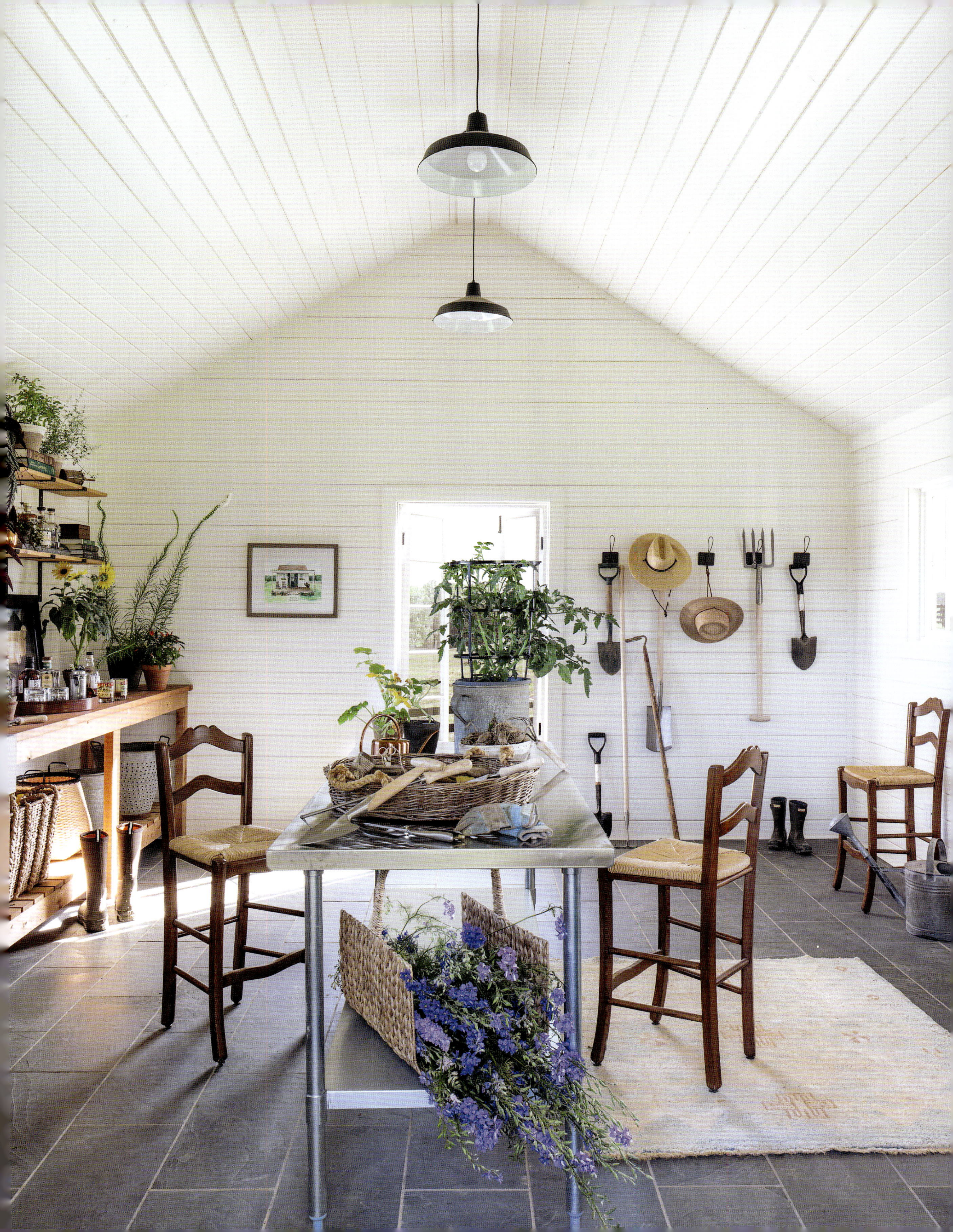

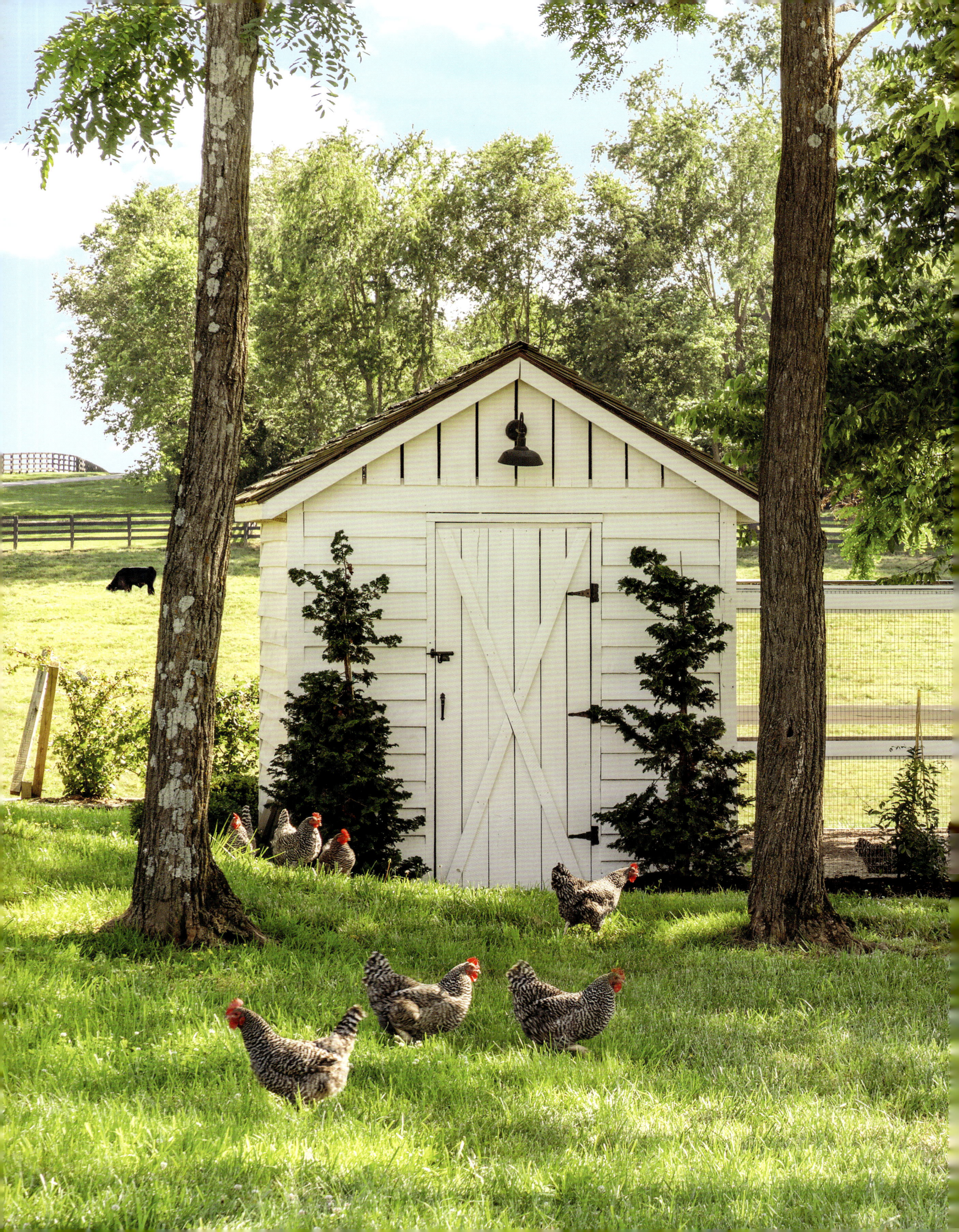

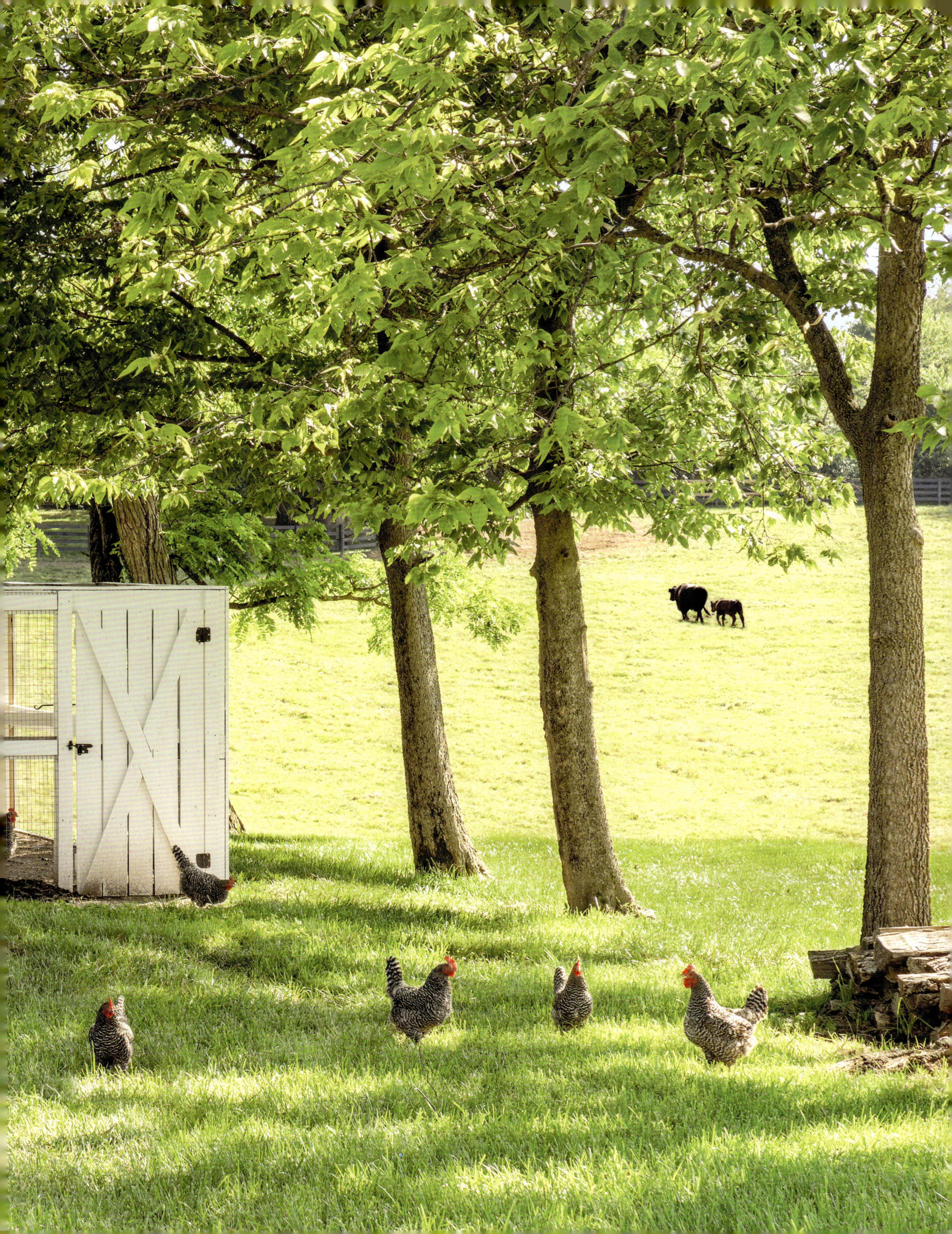

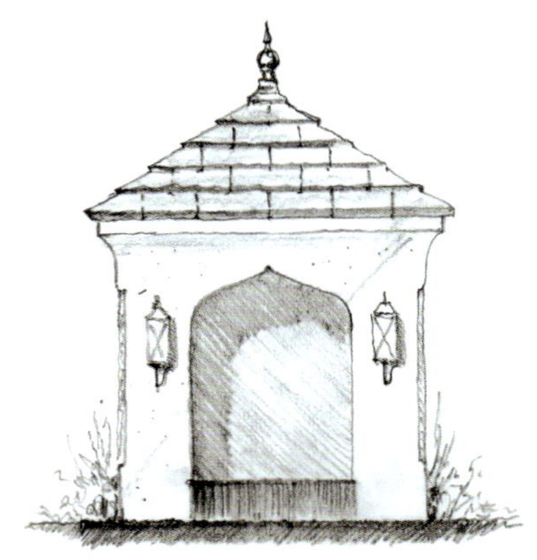

OASIS HOUSE

Alys Beach, a thriving, upscale vacation community located on Florida's Emerald Coast, stands as a particularly successful example of town planning. Curated materials and rigorous architectural guidelines rooted in Caribbean colonial, Moroccan, and Mediterranean styles harmoniously unite every structure within its borders, beautifully capturing a breezy seaside vibe. Brilliant white stucco cladding, stepped roofs, and curving Flemish gables lend consistency to the close-packed neighborhoods, with individual combinations of specific details giving a distinct character to each home. As a result, designing a house in Alys Beach is a bit like creating a sculpture: you work in from the edges, carving out voids for porches, adding deep roof overhangs to mitigate the harsh subtropical sun, and arranging chimneys and bays

OPPOSITE: The home's front facade exhibits many of the architectural features that characterize the Alys Beach community, such as the distinctive Flemish gables and pierced balcony and terrace railings. PAGES 168–169: A palm tree–shaded internal courtyard, known as "the Oasis," is the home's heart, with all the living spaces arranged around it. Recessed planters in the rear wall contain additional greenery, and water trickles gently from a row of spouts into the central pool.

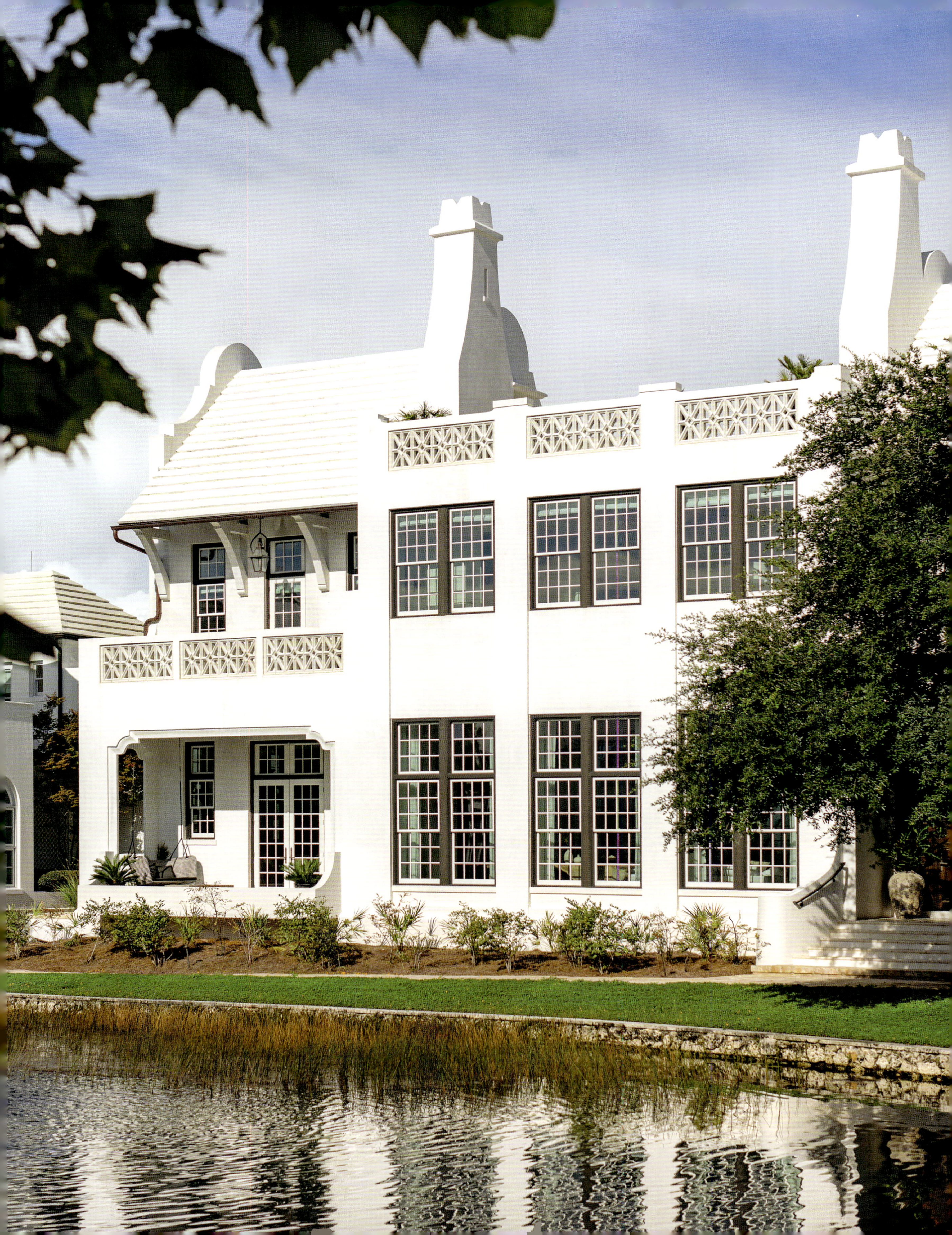

to vary the profile, with the goal of fashioning an artful composition that fits sympathetically into its context.

When a longtime client of mine purchased an unusually expansive corner lot facing a local landmark called Lake Marilyn, he immediately commissioned me to design a house that would have a strong presence from the street while functioning as a private retreat within. The size of the property and the fact that it has street frontage on two sides allowed us to make the home a freestanding structure, which is relatively rare for the immediate area. To balance both aspects of the client's wishes, I developed a U-shaped plan that shelters an internal courtyard with a pool, lanai, and sauna—which we dubbed "the Oasis."

The home's front facade faces the lake and is organized as three distinct volumes, with large panels of windows in the center and inset porches and doors adding depth to a pair of gabled flanking sections. Two wings in the rear reach out like arms to embrace the internal court; one wing contains a covered loggia and combined garage-guesthouse, and the other holds the principal bedroom and bathroom suite. A quartet of palm trees provides shade for the Oasis and softens the atmosphere. An elevated spa pavilion, accented with Moroccan tiles, serves as a strong focal point when viewed from the main living room.

Embracing the owner's love of tall spaces, we incorporated fourteen-foot ceilings on the ground floor and twelve-foot ceilings on the second floor for soaring, light-filled rooms. Stairs ascend to an additional story under the Flemish gable at one end of the house, mirrored on the opposite end by a third-floor bar. Nestled in between you'll find a rooftop terrace—complete with comfortable seating and an outdoor fireplace—

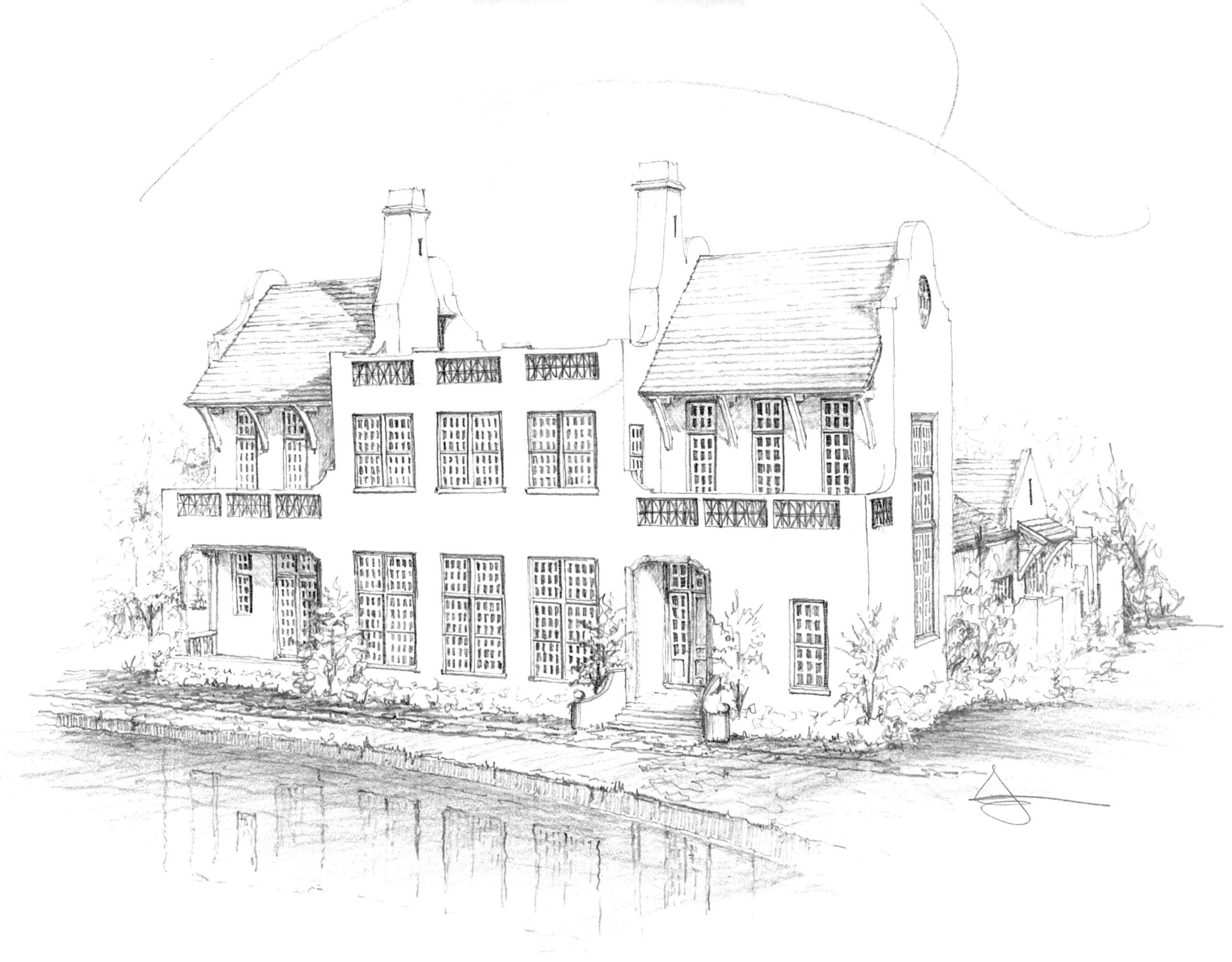

that offers unparalleled views of the neighboring lake, the Oasis, and the surrounding houses receding into the distance.

I think second homes should be an opportunity to be a little bit whimsical, to try playful and one-of-a-kind designs, and to invent a place you want to go that feels distinct from your main residence. Here, we had fun with the style possibilities and with the materials and finishes. Inside we embraced North African flourishes like pointed arches, geometric cutouts, and filigreed screens. This house is quite different from much of my work because the interior trim is deceptively simple: rounded coves and corners rather than traditional moldings, for instance. Openings between rooms are frequently decorative in outline but devoid of casings. The interior walls are rendered in a rich, glossy Venetian plaster; contrast is supplied by elaborately detailed ceilings and doors made of textured reclaimed oak. Barring the occasional touch

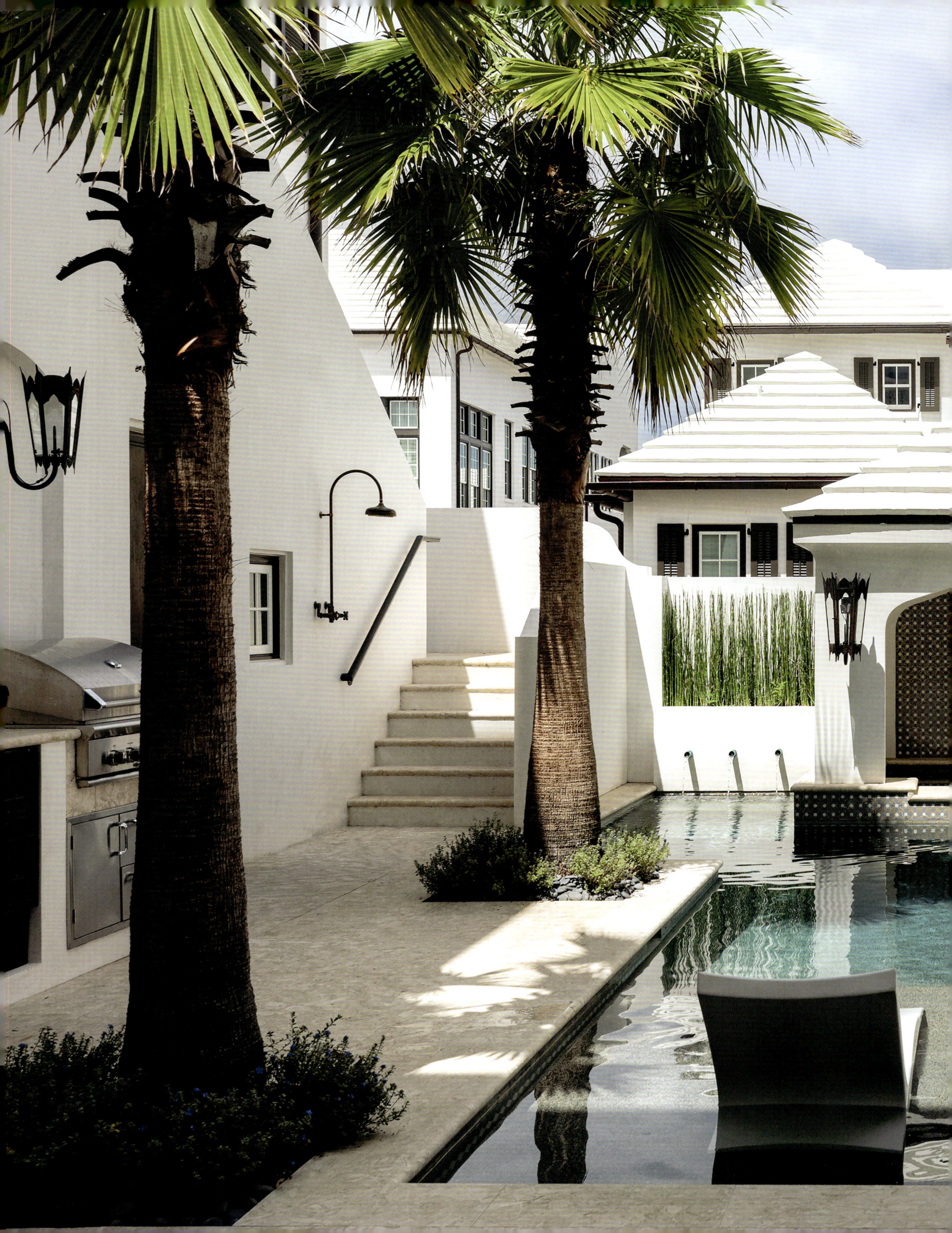

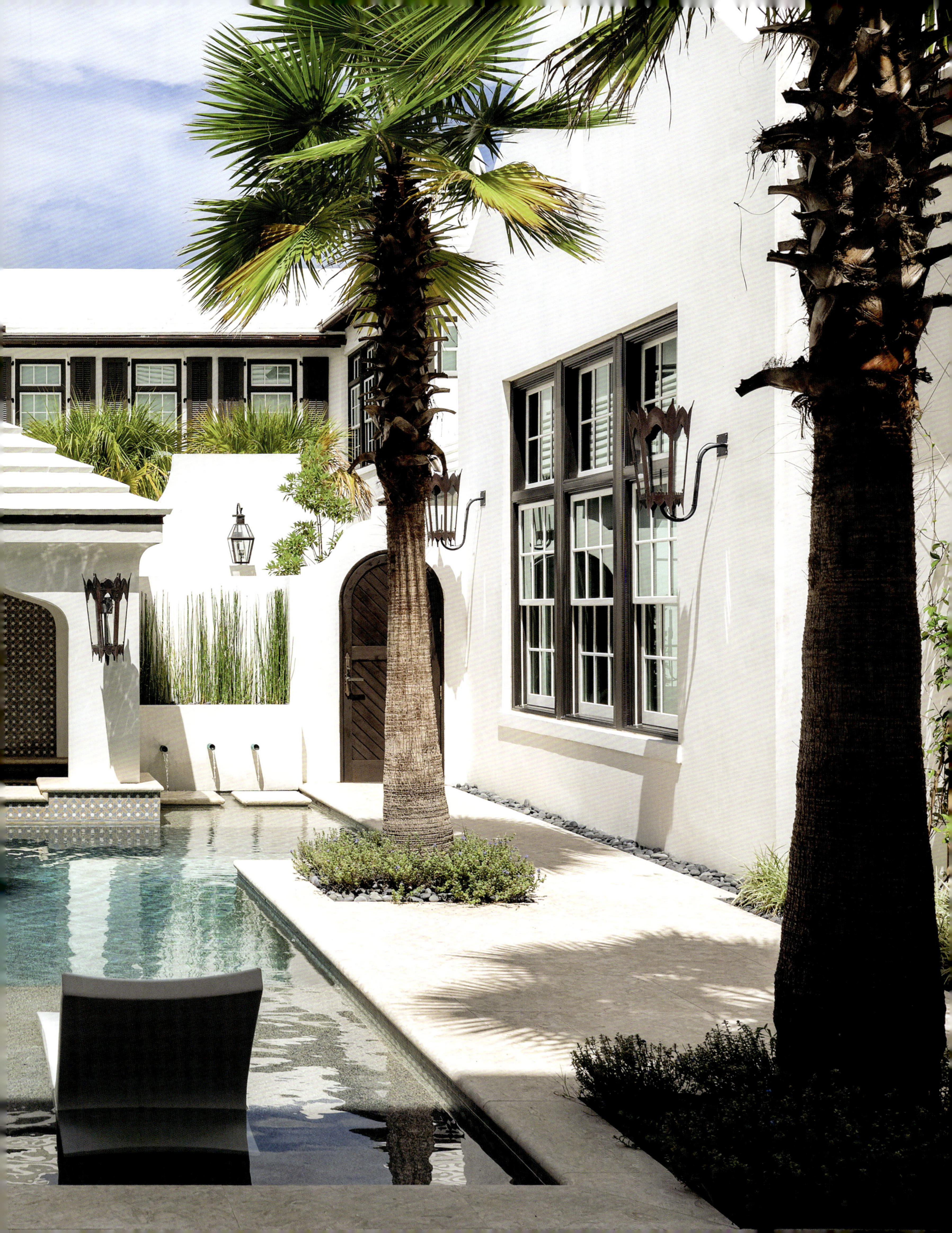

of black, we limited the palette to just white and variations on gold, brown, and red orange—all closely related hues. The radiance from the tall windows, the sensuous surface qualities of the materials, and the overarching sense of shaped space combine to striking effect.

In a house that has no shortage of drama—consider the almost Gothic bar tracery that crowns the great room or the flared vaulting in the primary bath—perhaps the most spectacular feature is the elliptical main staircase, which sweeps up from ground to roof, flooded by light coming in on three sides. From the first floor to the second, the stair has traditional closed treads, but as the climb continues toward the third floor, the spaces between the oak treads open up so that each step seems to float. Meanwhile, a huge pierced-brass lantern hangs in the center of the spiral. At the base of the stairs, a cozy speakeasy bar and wine cellar are tucked away behind a draped opening—yet another setting for enjoying those special moments that a vacation getaway ought to provide.

All in all, this house was both challenging and satisfying to conceptualize. The community's strict regulations required us to be innovative, and the client was an enthusiastic partner, always pushing us to consider options that would further elevate the design. The result speaks for itself: controlled, atmospheric, and a jewel of layered interest and detail.

OPPOSITE: Oak treads spiral up three floors around a monumental Moroccan lantern in the stair tower, illuminated by tall banks of windows. FOLLOWING SPREAD: An iron chandelier is suspended from the great room's ornate wooden ceiling, and a dramatic limestone fireplace anchors a pair of plaster arches. Nashville-based interior designer Chelsea Robinson introduced spare yet weighty furnishings that stand up to the power of the architecture.

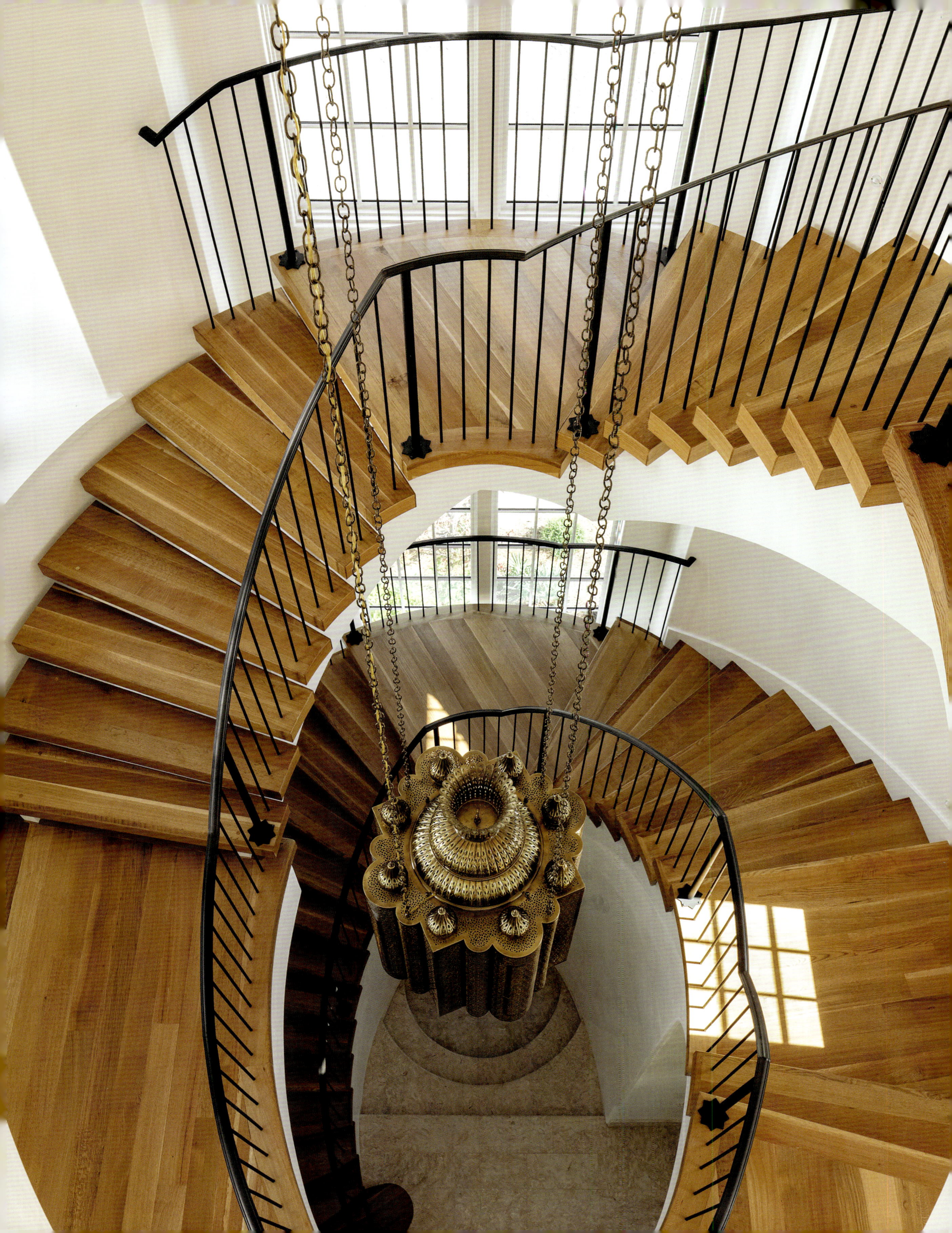

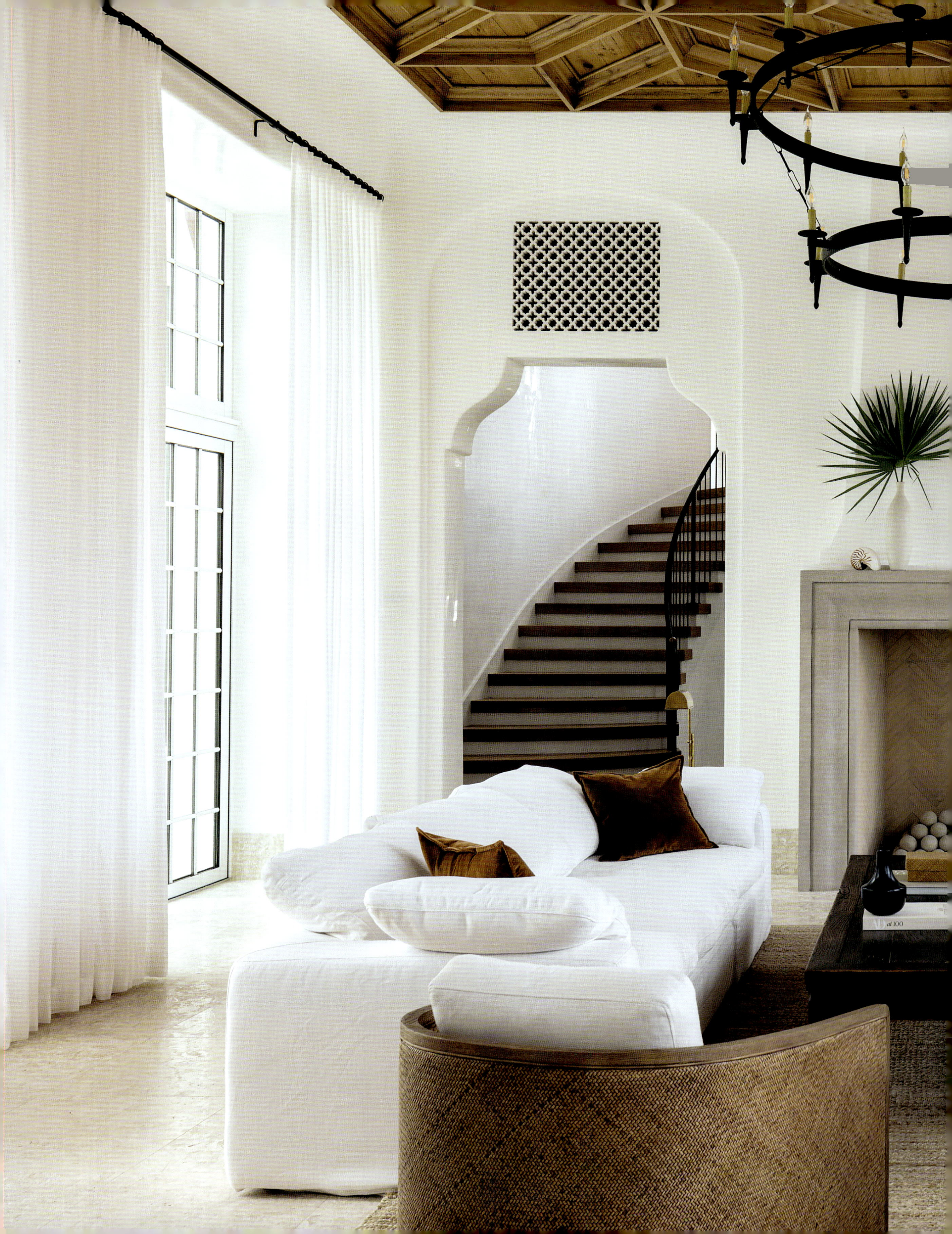
AD at 100

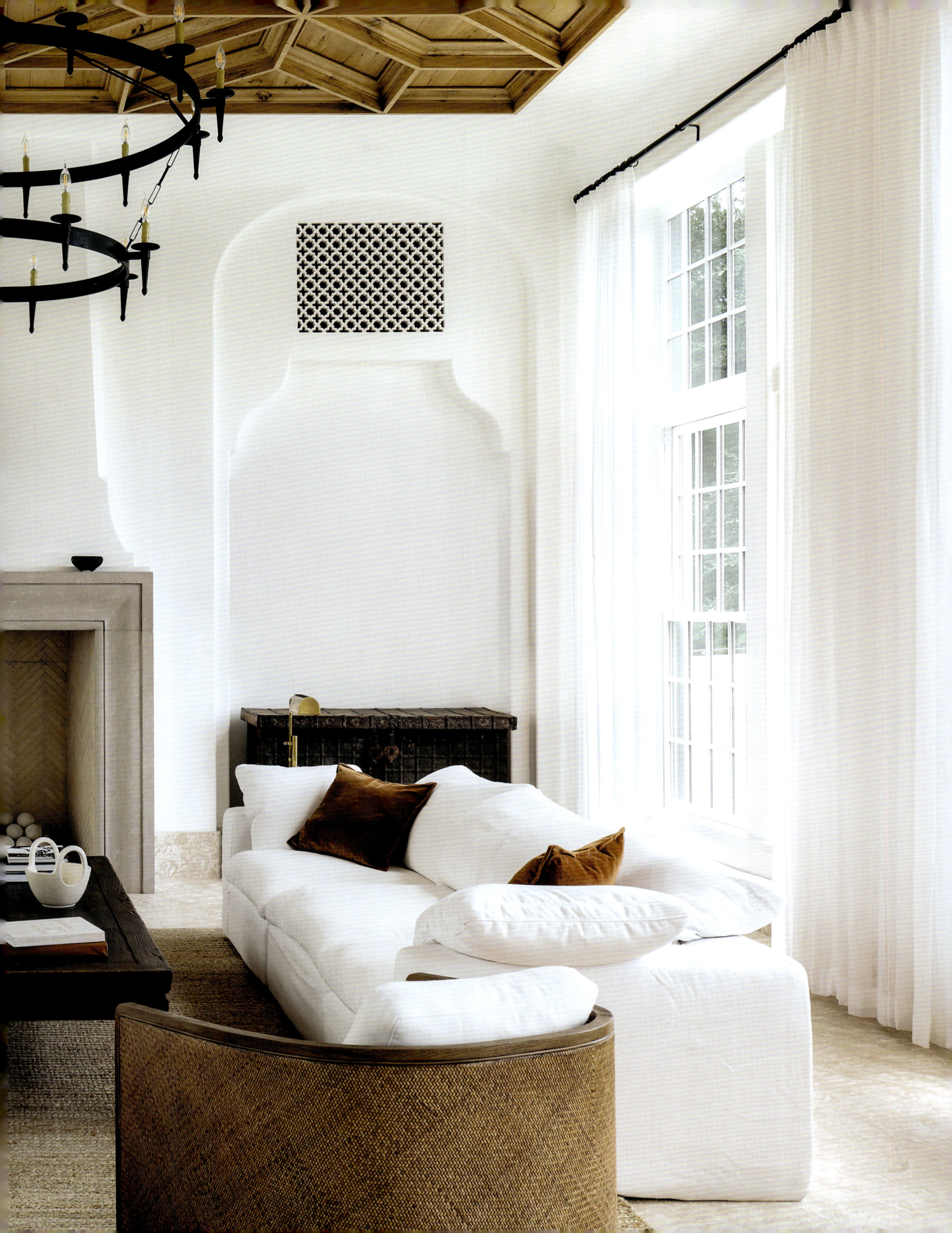

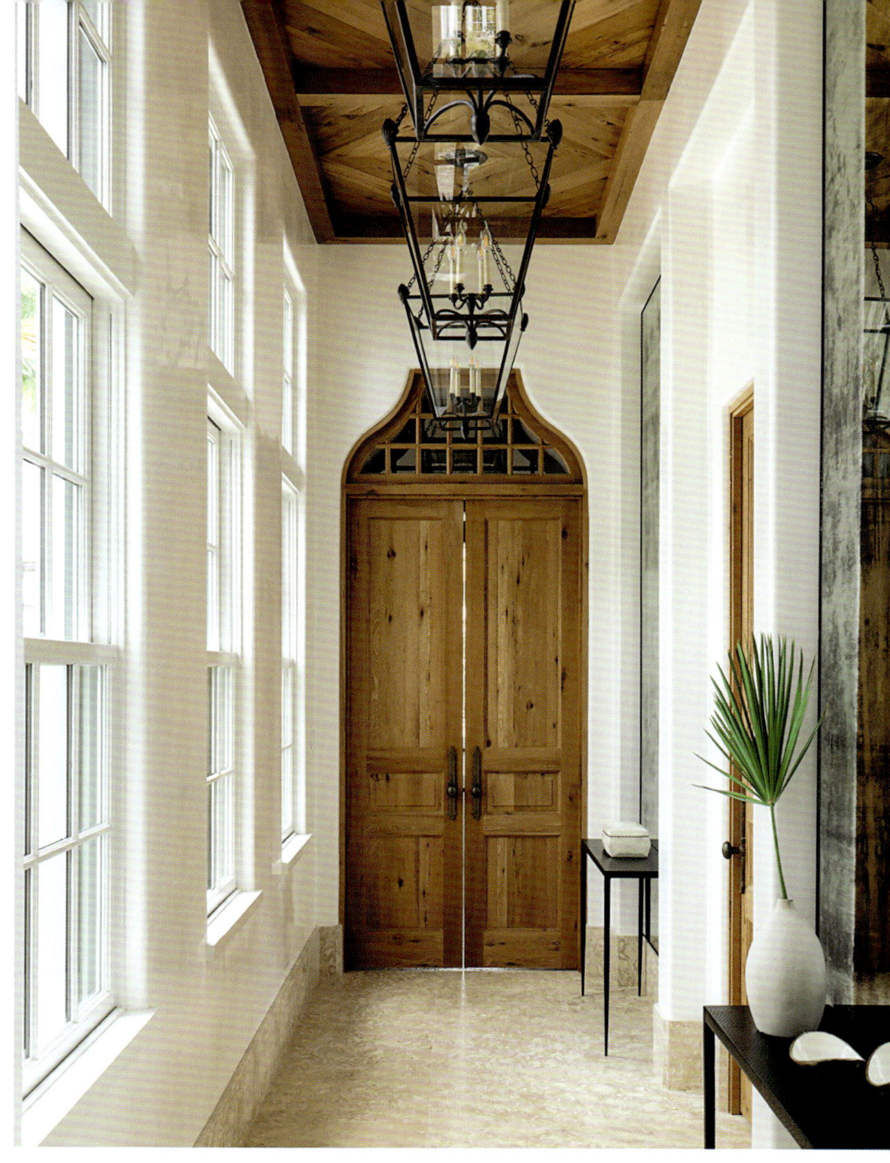

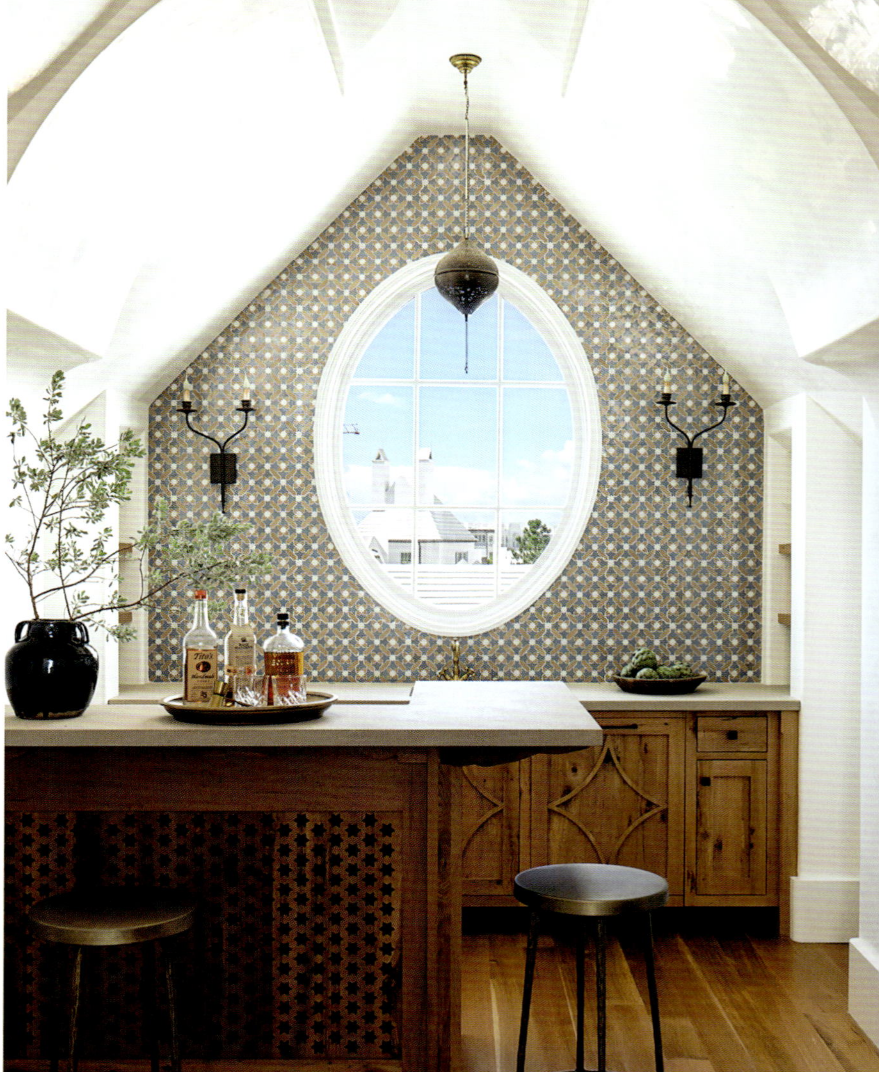

RIGHT: In this residence, a relatively simple collection of materials, colors, motifs, and profiles is implemented consistently but with a great variety of expression. FOLLOWING SPREAD: Within the kitchen's plaster envelope, the oak cabinets are treated as a suite of furniture to fill the space. Geometric cutouts and a pair of hanging lanterns continue the Moroccan theme.

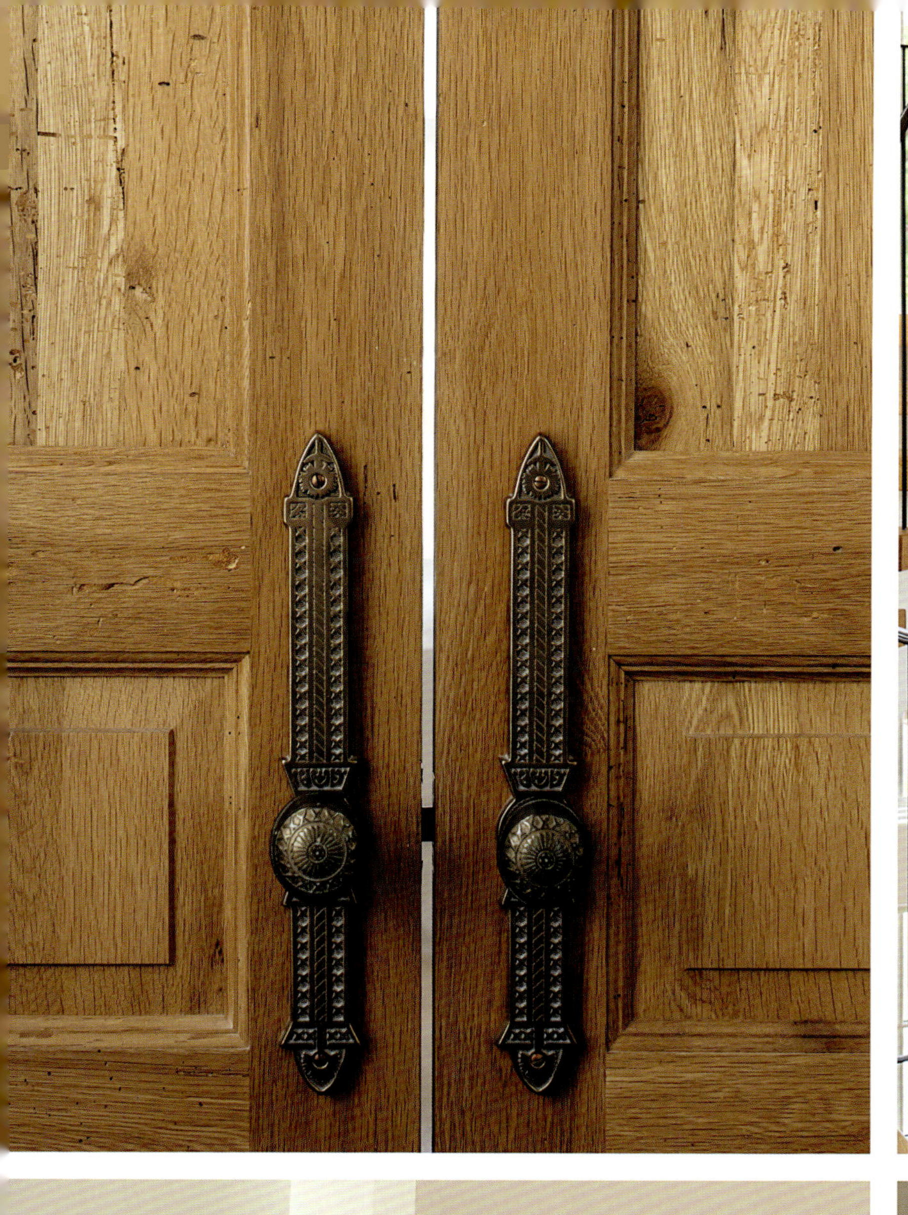
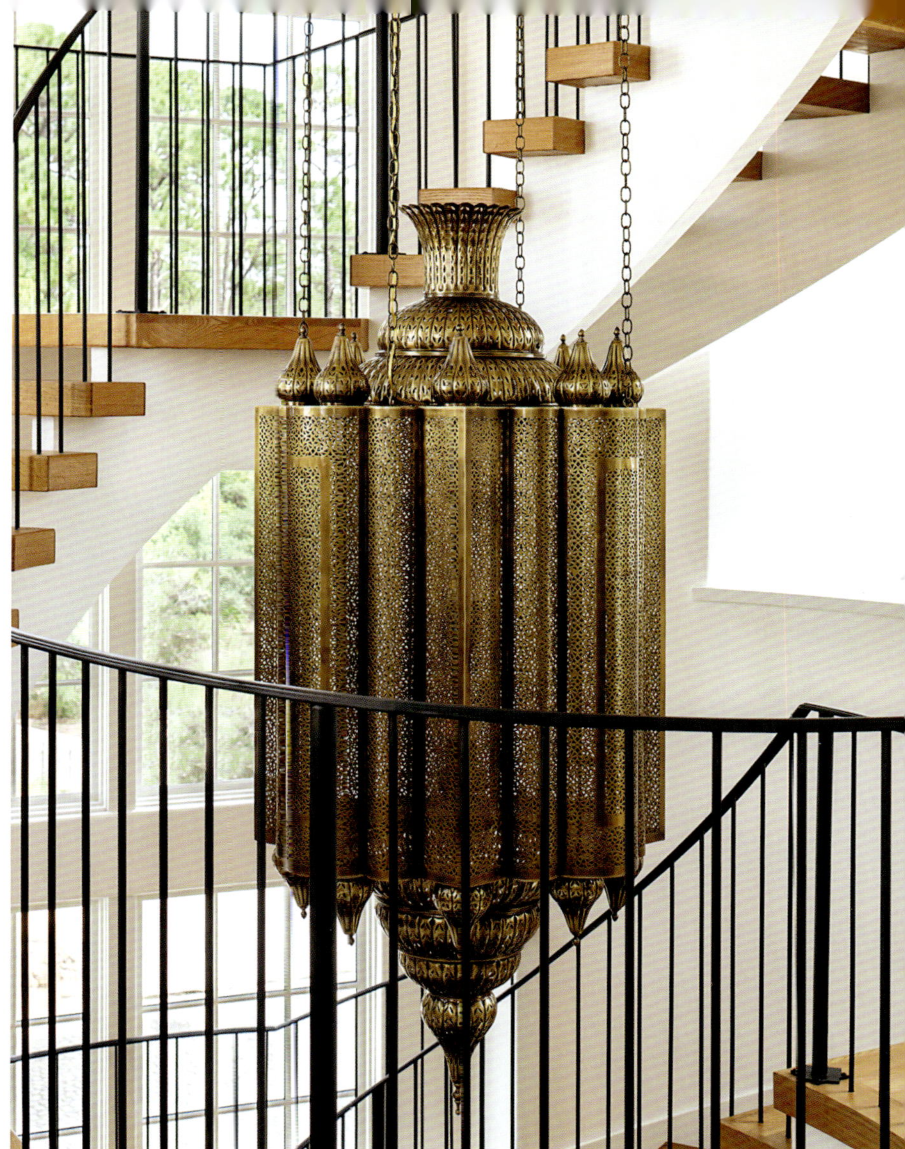
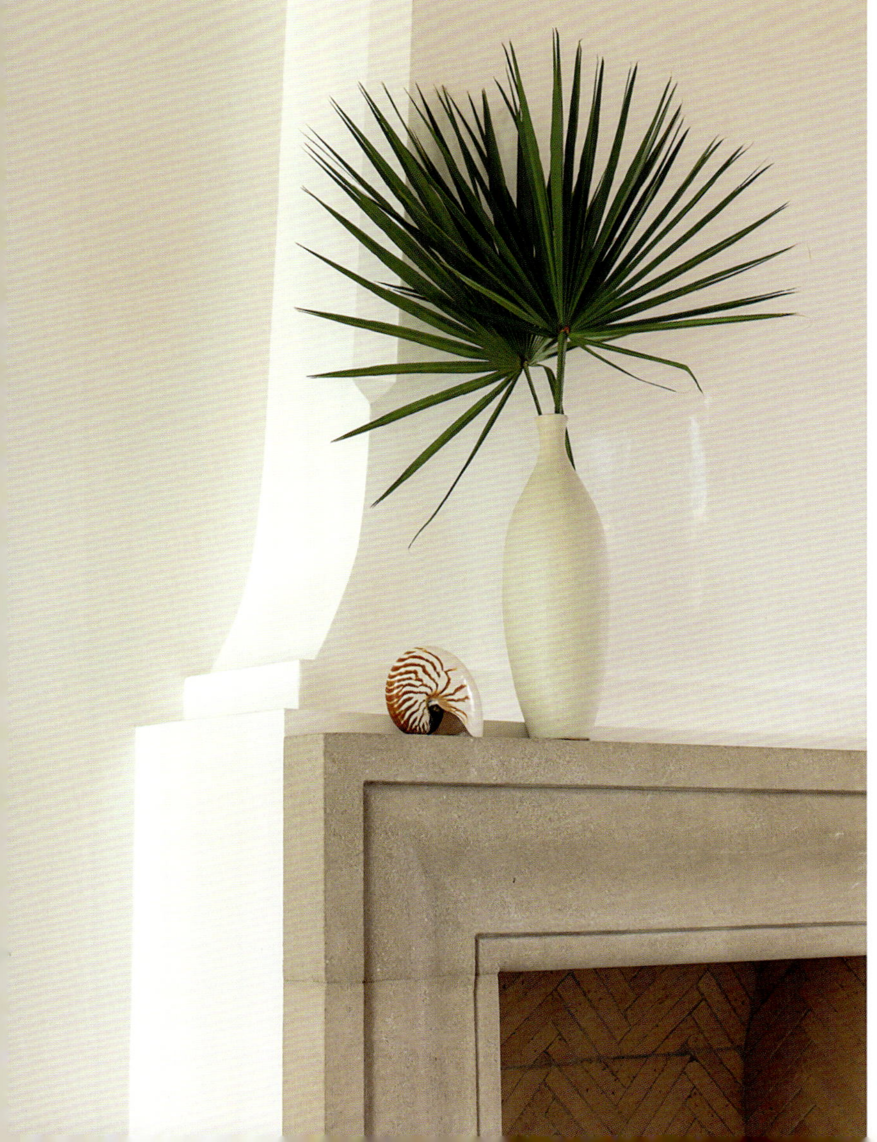
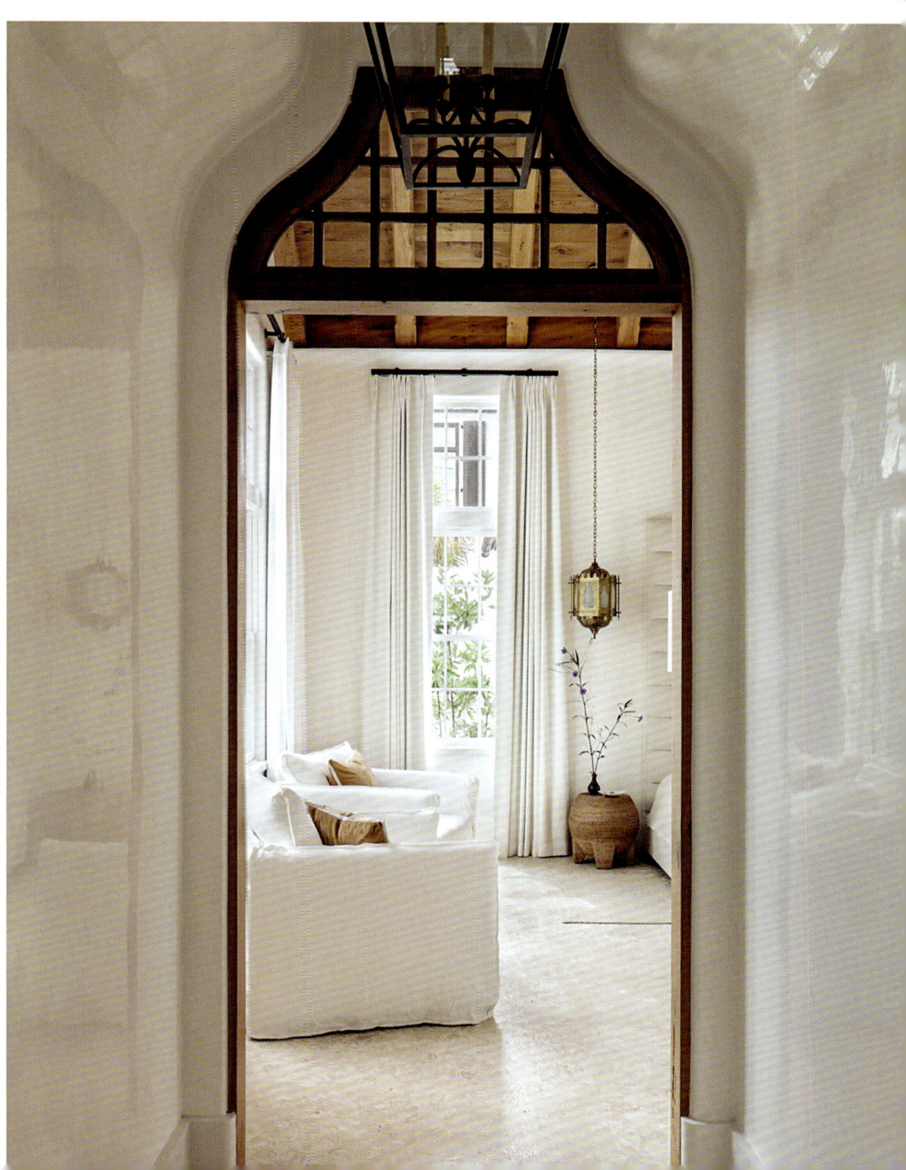

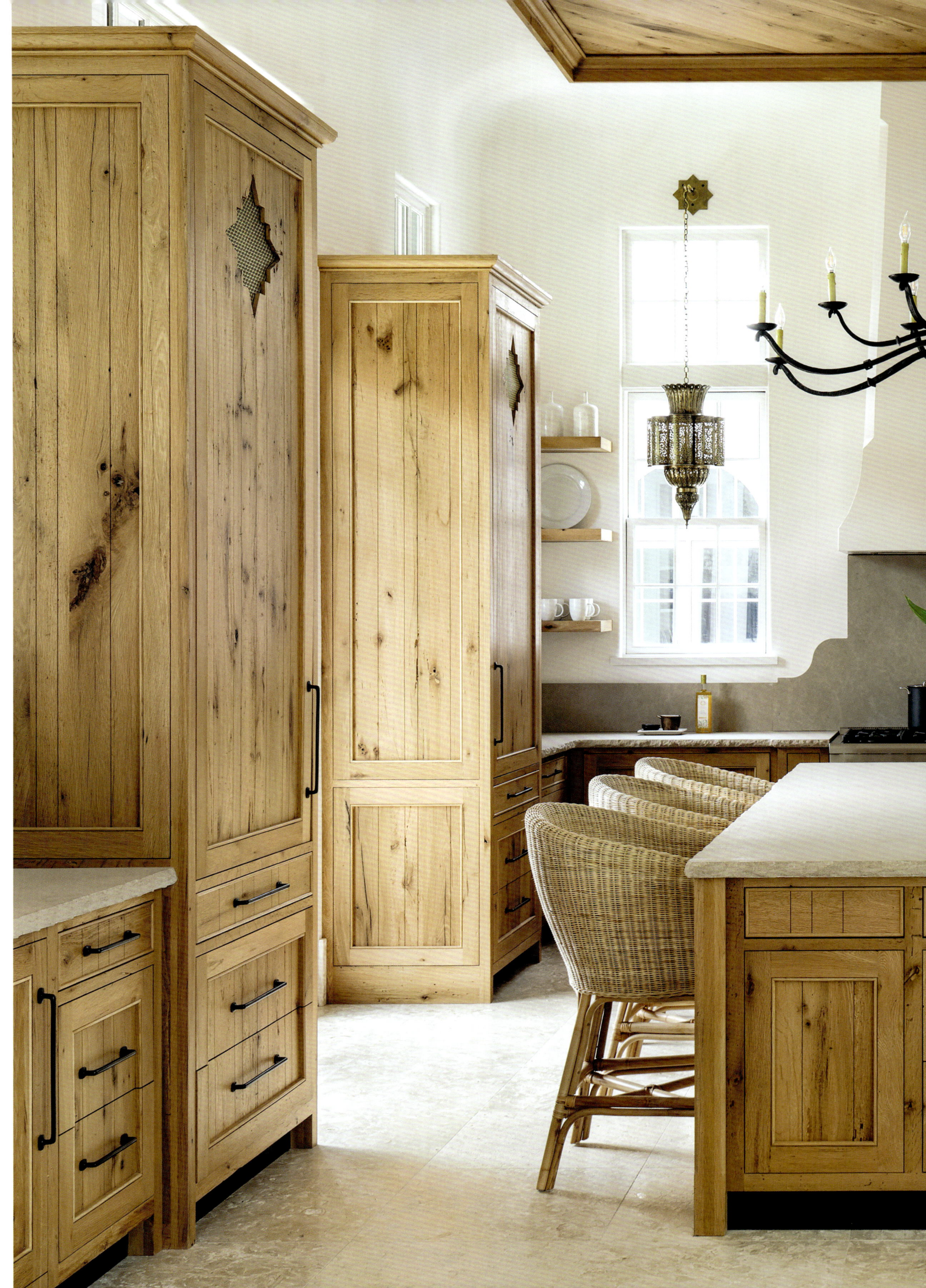

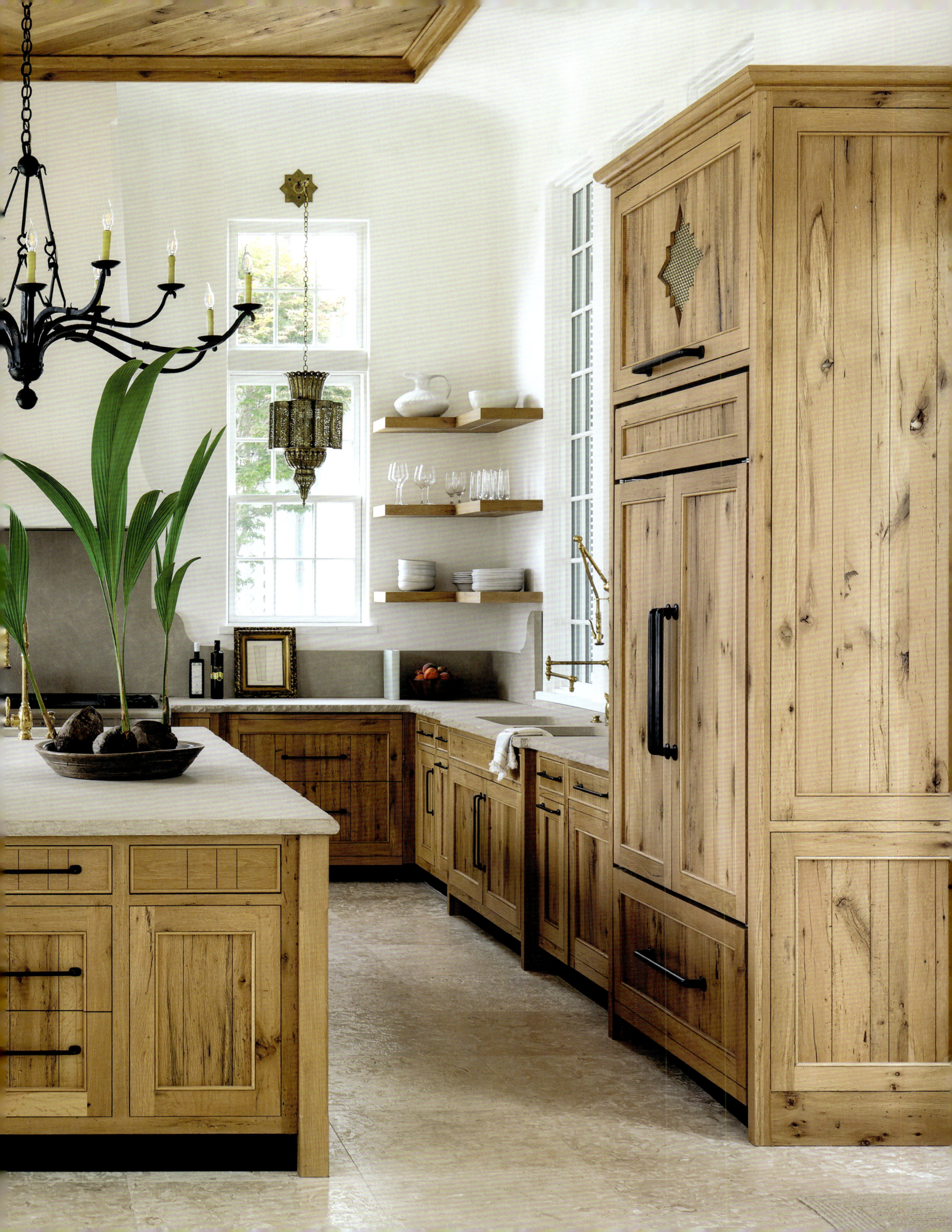

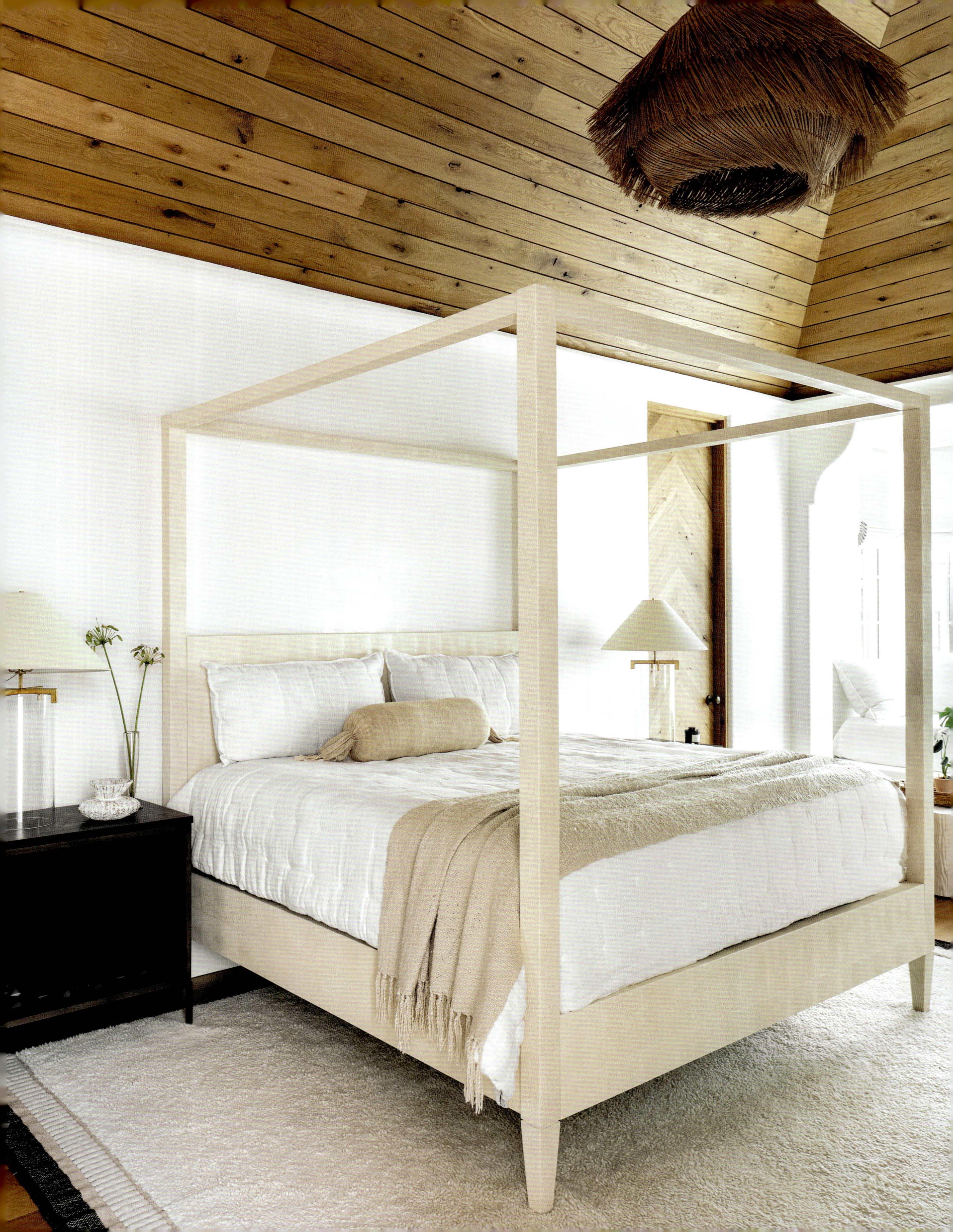

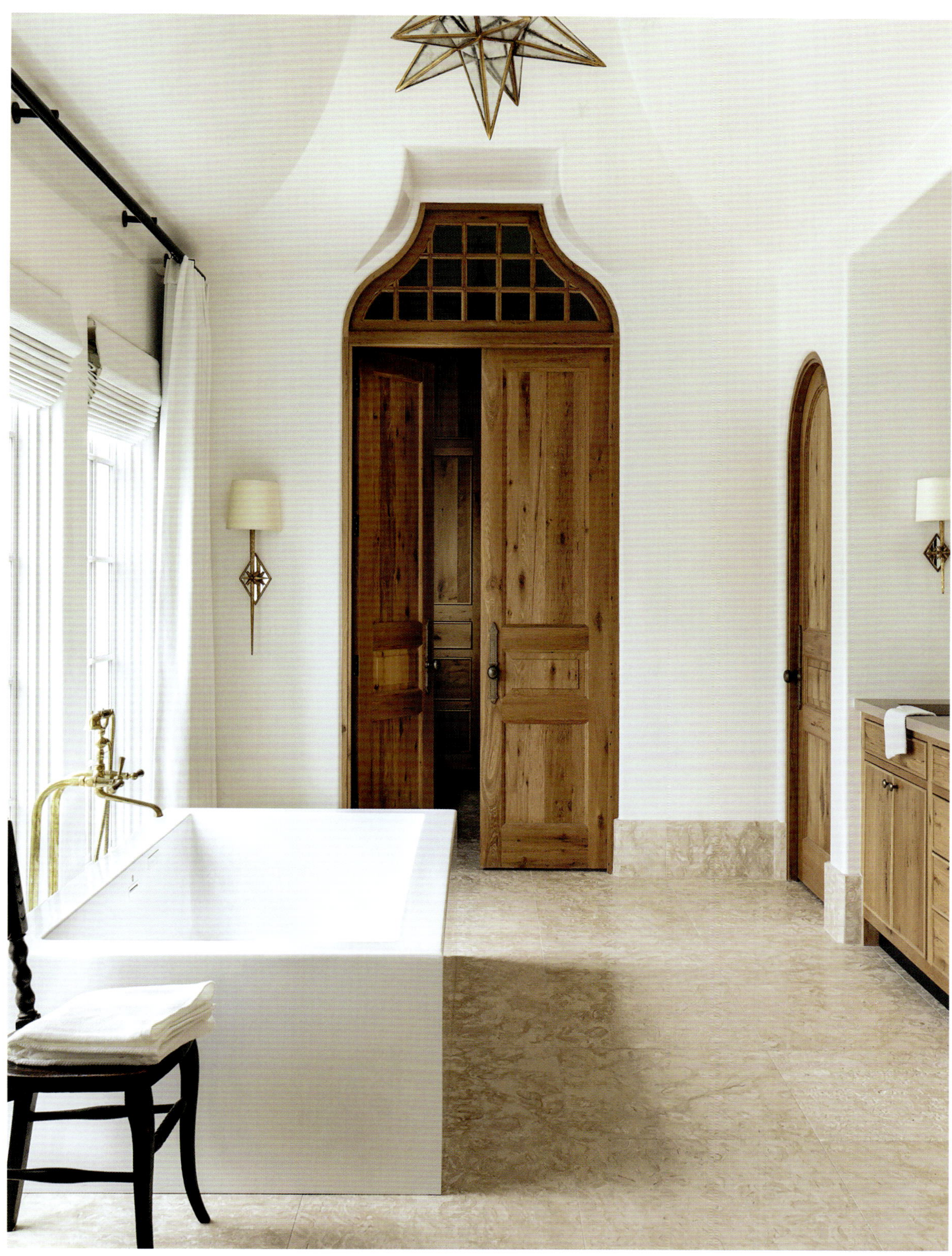

OPPOSITE: In a guest bedroom, a V-groove paneled ceiling echoes the curved plaster ceilings found elsewhere in the home. ABOVE: The soaking tub in the principal bath sits in front of windows that overlook a small private courtyard. FOLLOWING SPREAD: The rooftop terrace invites lounging, with its sectional sofas, fireplace, and unparalleled view. The door leads to a top-floor bar cleverly tucked into the roofline.

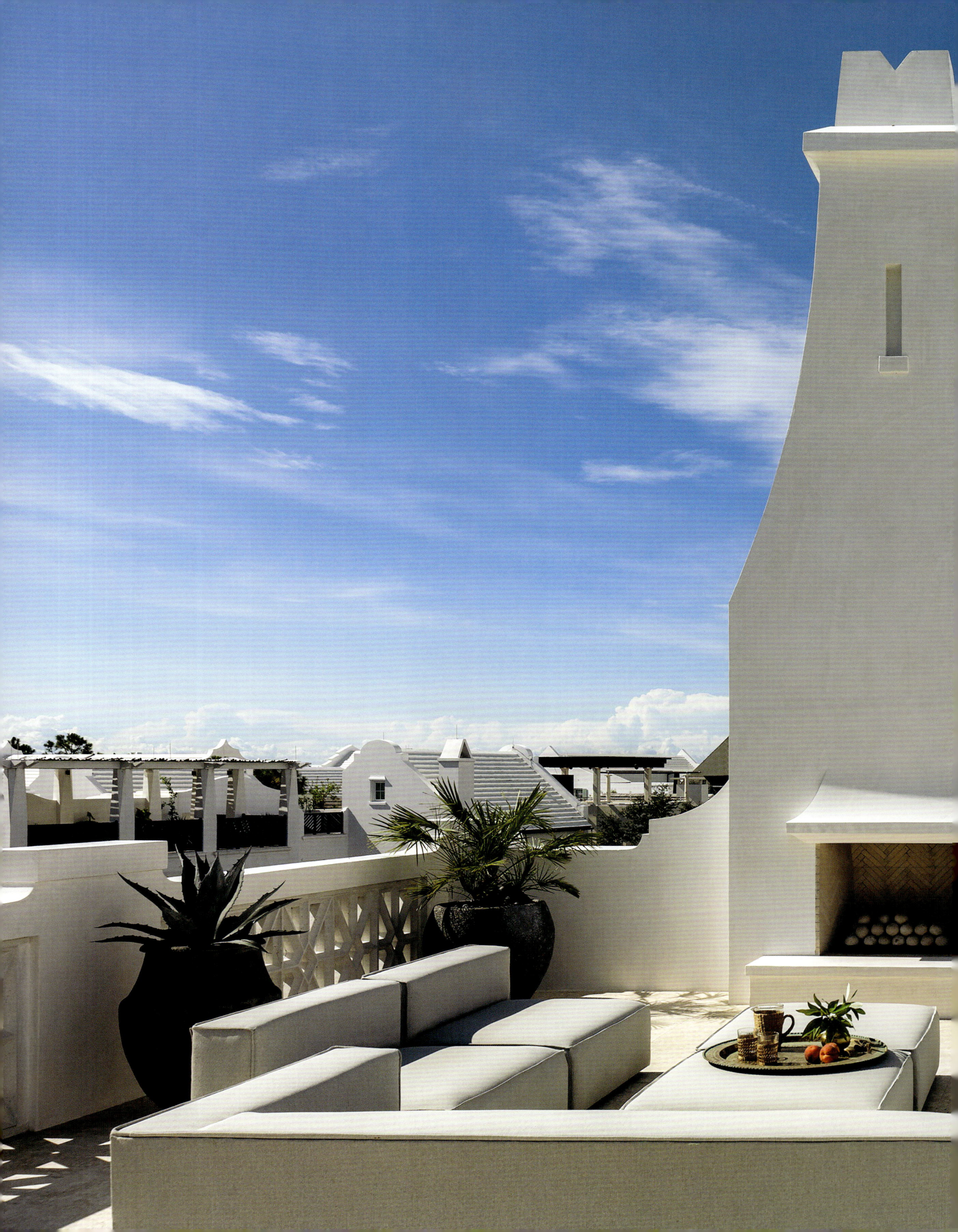

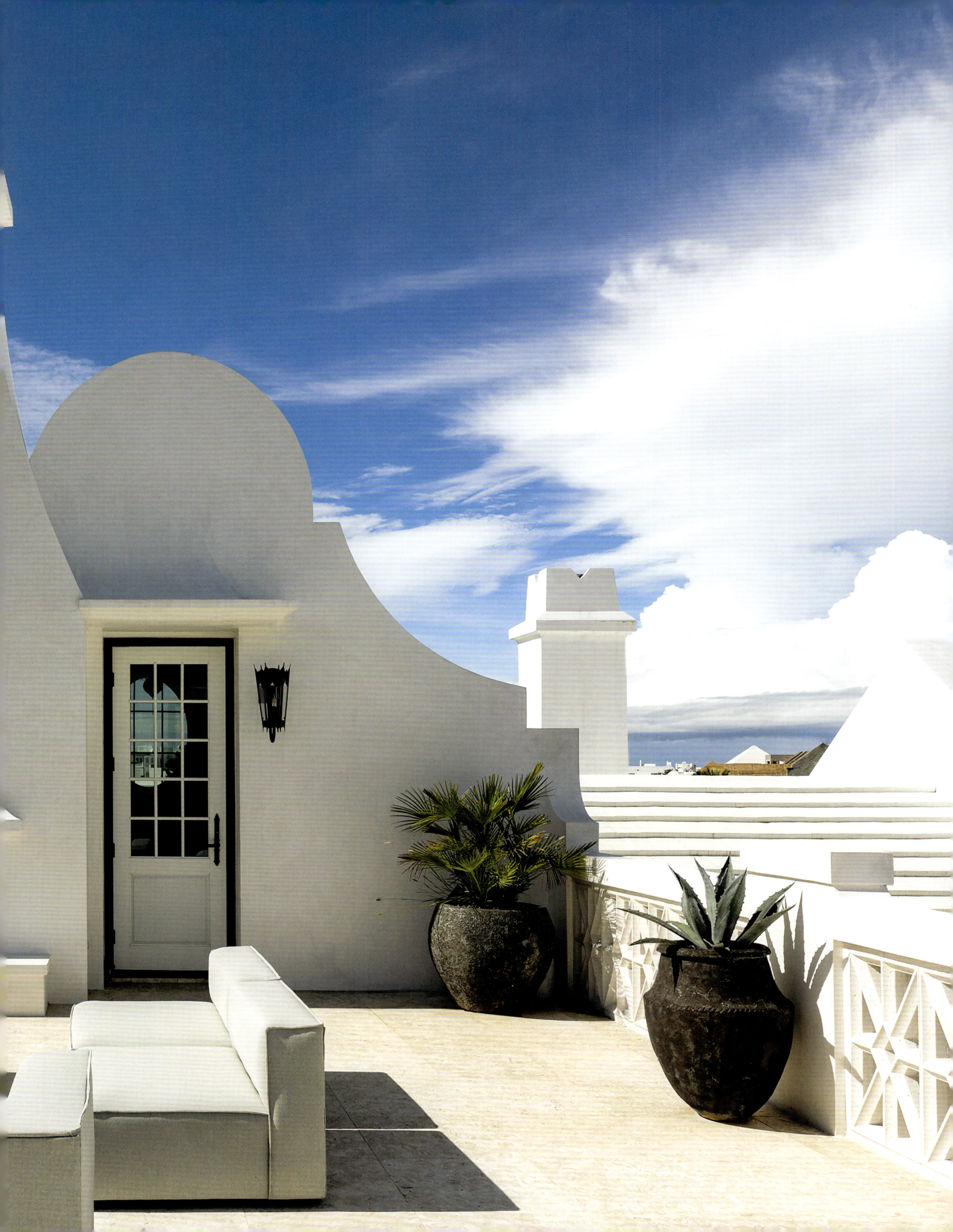

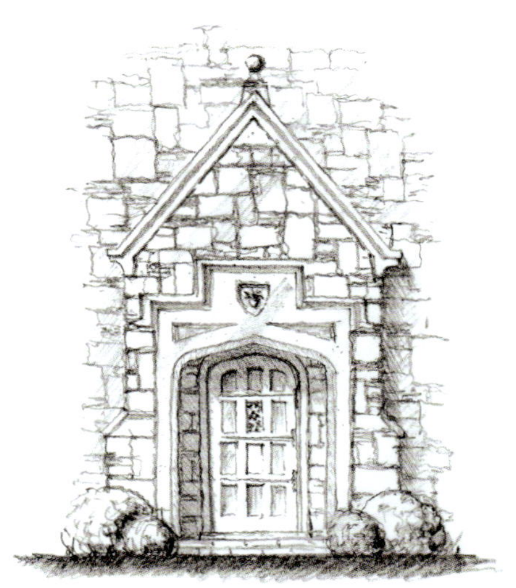

STONECOURT MANOR

The commission for this magnificent house gave me the opportunity for a truly deep dive into one of my favorite architectural styles. Early on in my discussions with the clients, it became clear that they embraced the idea of creating a true English manor home and were entirely on board for the intensive thought, layering, and complex details that would go into doing the job right. So, out came the relevant books from my library, and we began researching historic properties in the Cotswolds and elsewhere in England to use as models and inspiration.

OPPOSITE: Many aspects of the grand stair, which stands opposite the living room, are inspired by historic English manor houses. FOLLOWING SPREAD: The front facade incorporates characteristic Tudor attributes, such as limestone hood moldings over many windows, parapet walls on the gable ends, and crenellations. The wing on the right contains the primary bed and bath suite.

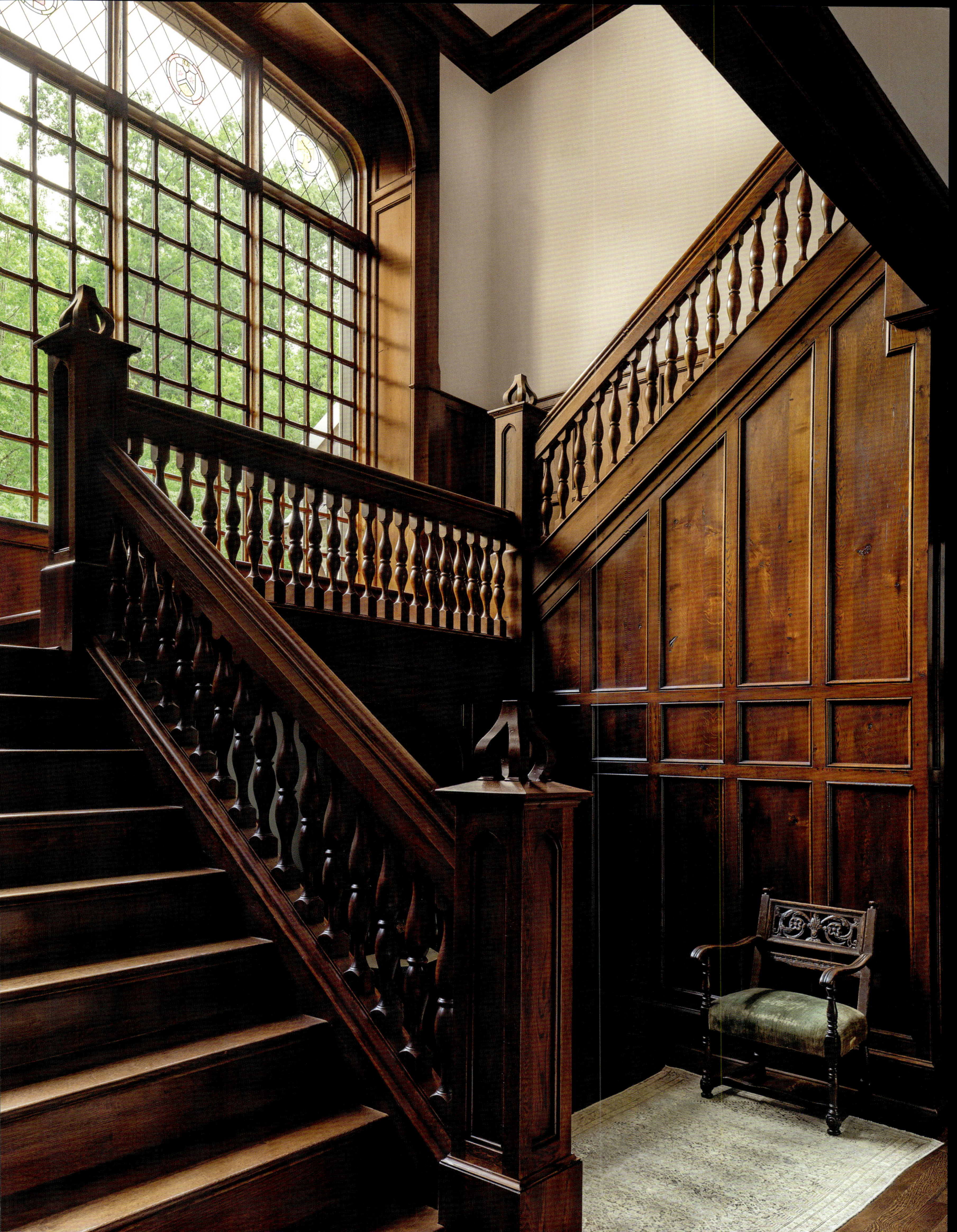

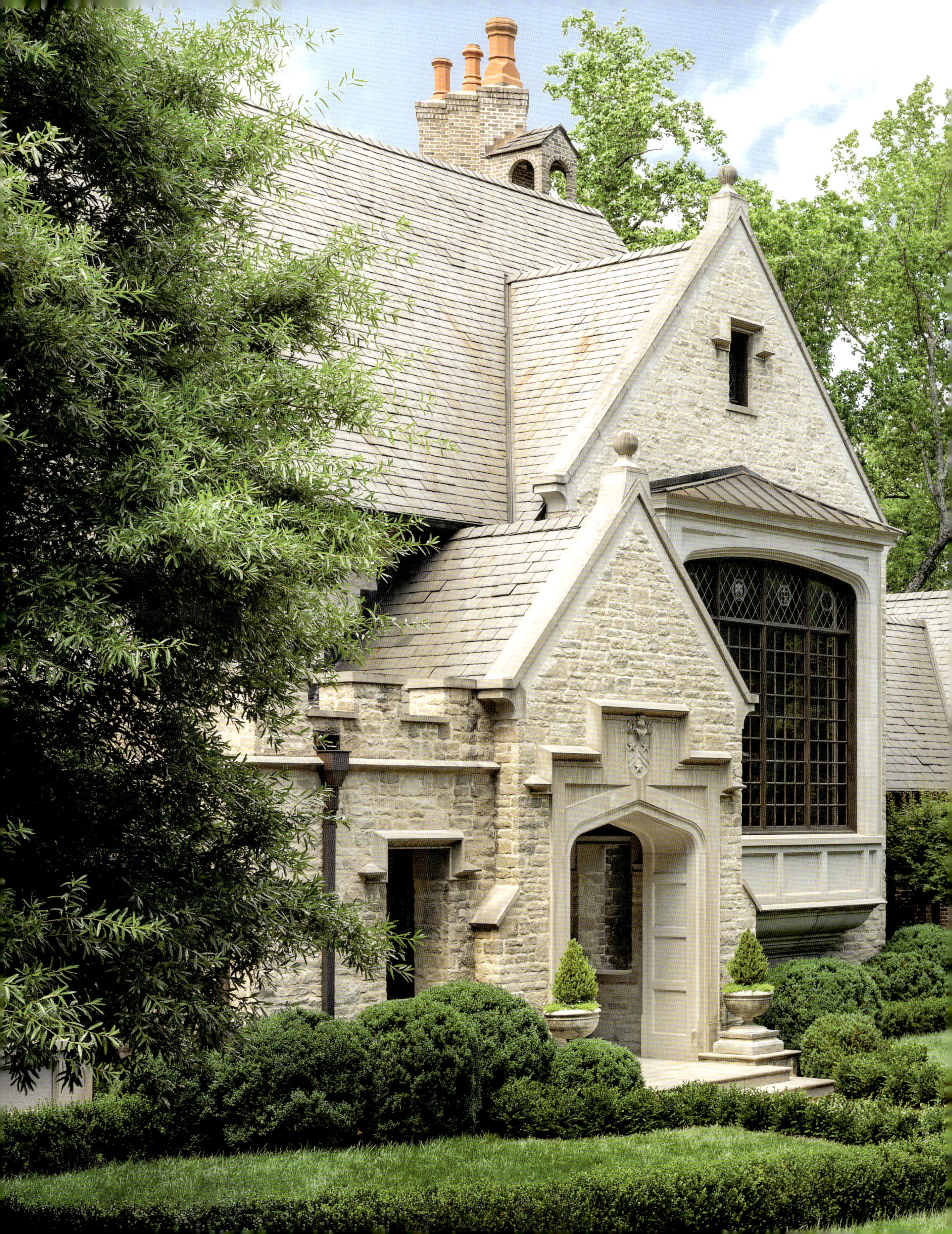

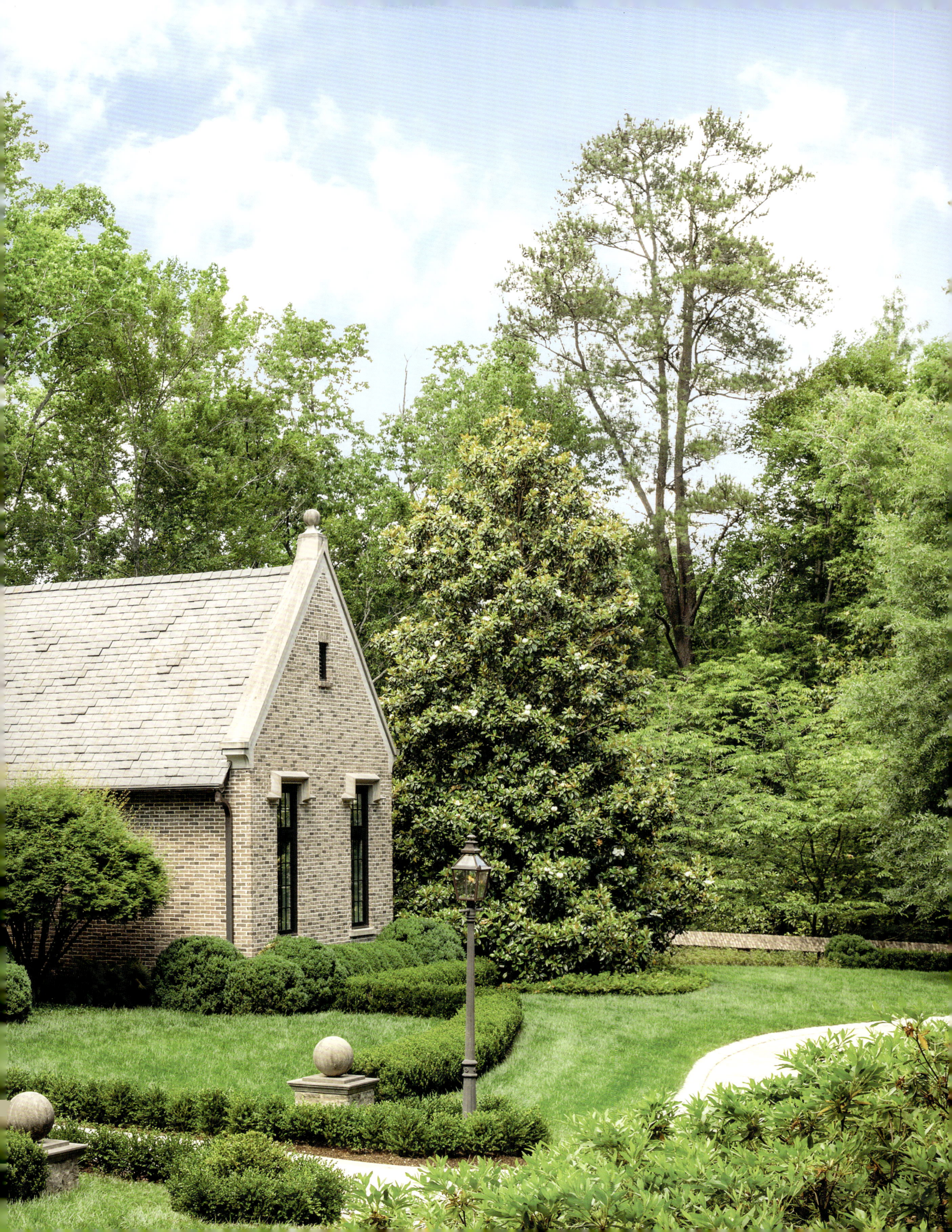

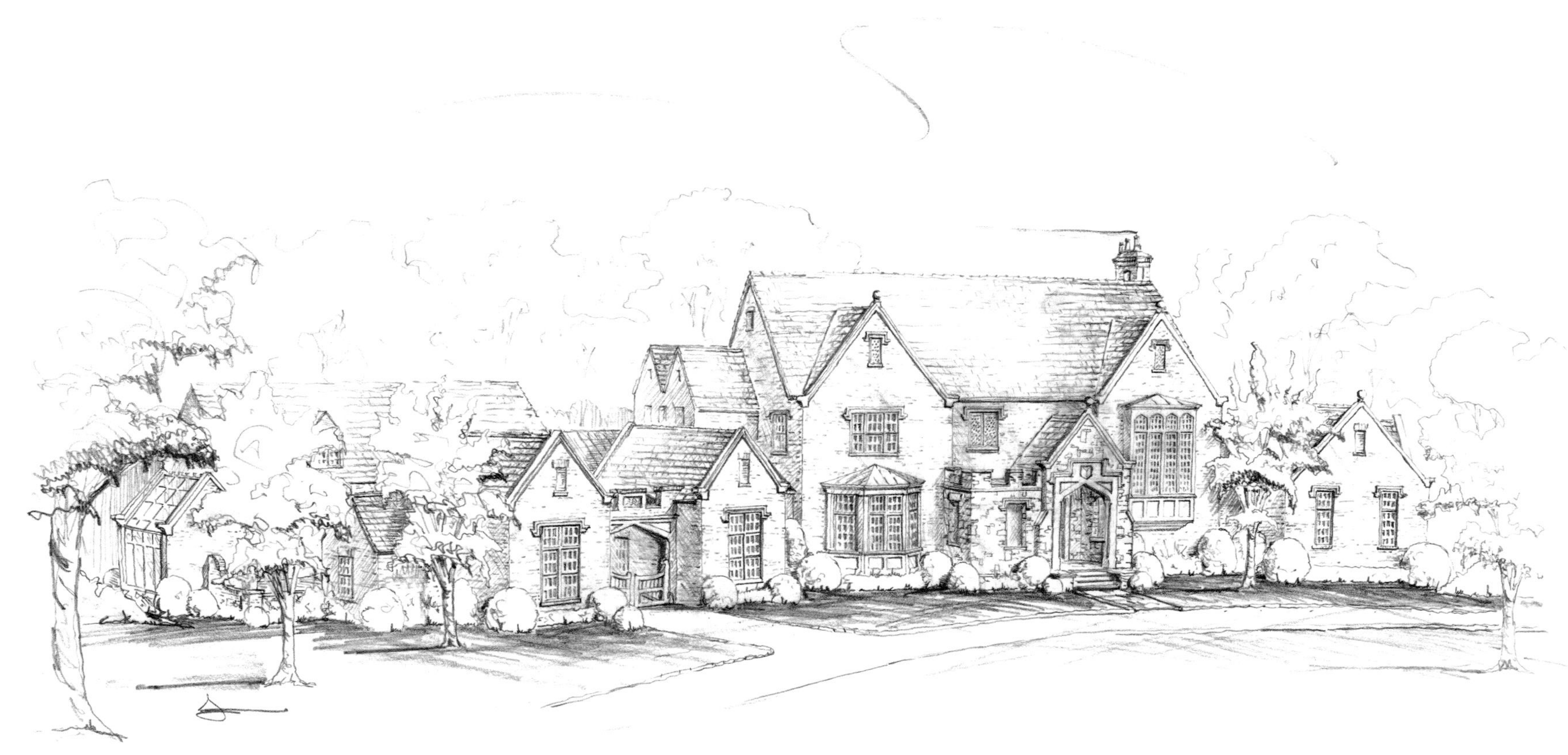

As it happened, I was watching *Downton Abbey* when this project started, meaning that my immersion in British country house aesthetics wasn't limited to office hours only. The show's influence on the building taking shape in my head wasn't direct—we didn't copy anything exactly from Highclere Castle, where the show was filmed—but an overall atmosphere and certain striking images, such as light pouring down into a grand staircase, definitely became part of the mix.

My clients had purchased a four-acre lot on Atlanta's north side that was already cleared, leveled, and waiting for a suitable home to be constructed. However, the lot also presented a challenge that would significantly shape the evolution of our design: it's bisected by a small creek, creating a buffer zone that can't be built on. Therefore, one large rectangle of land became, in practice, two long, narrow ones: the first a swath of civilization, where

OPPOSITE: The front entry loggia is recessed behind a deep Tudor arch and cut-limestone panels. A second arch with the same profile outlines the front door, flanked by two built-in stone planter boxes. FOLLOWING SPREAD: The wainscoting in the entry hall rises to eight feet, with lime plaster above it. The arched opening in the far wall lets light into the home's lower level.

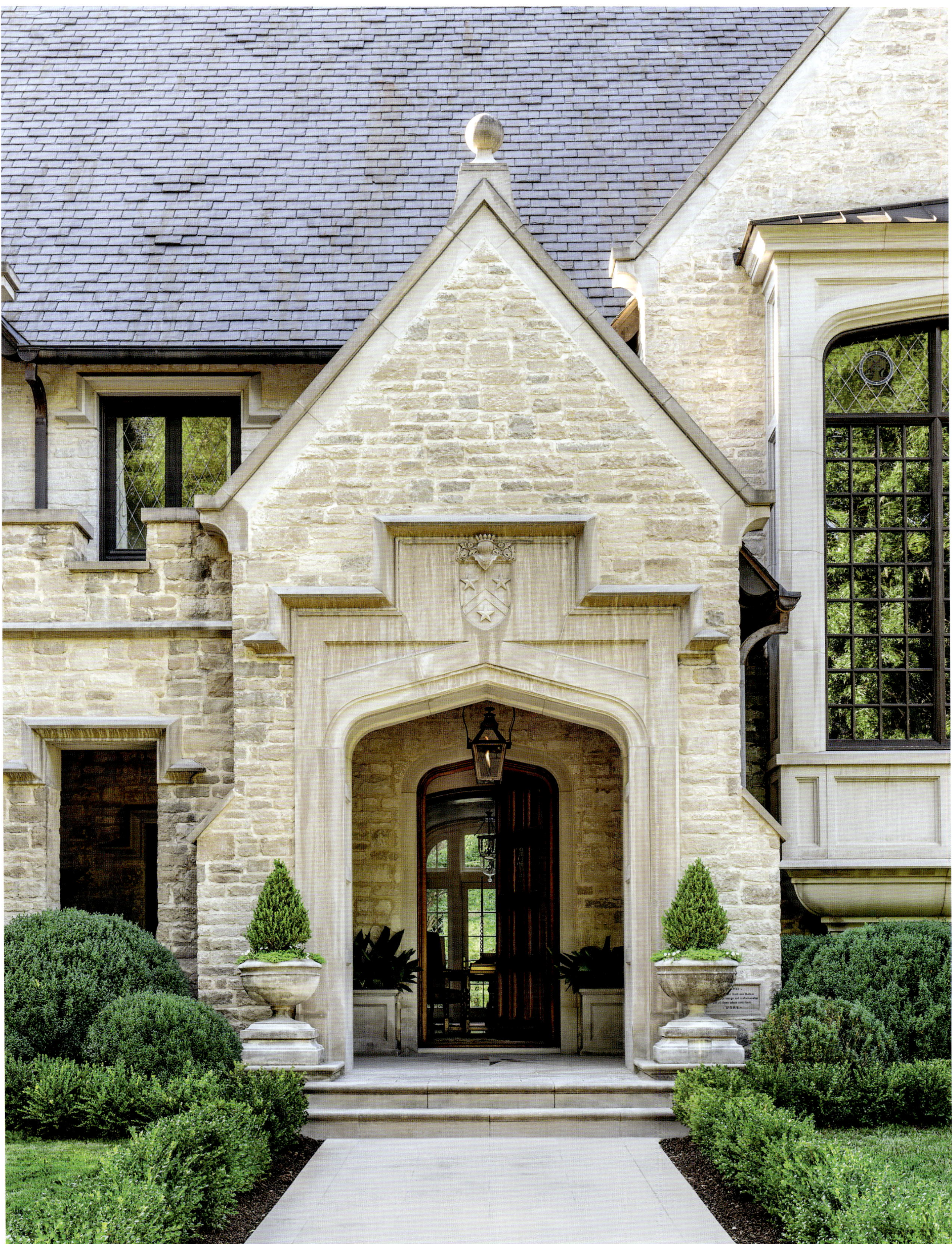

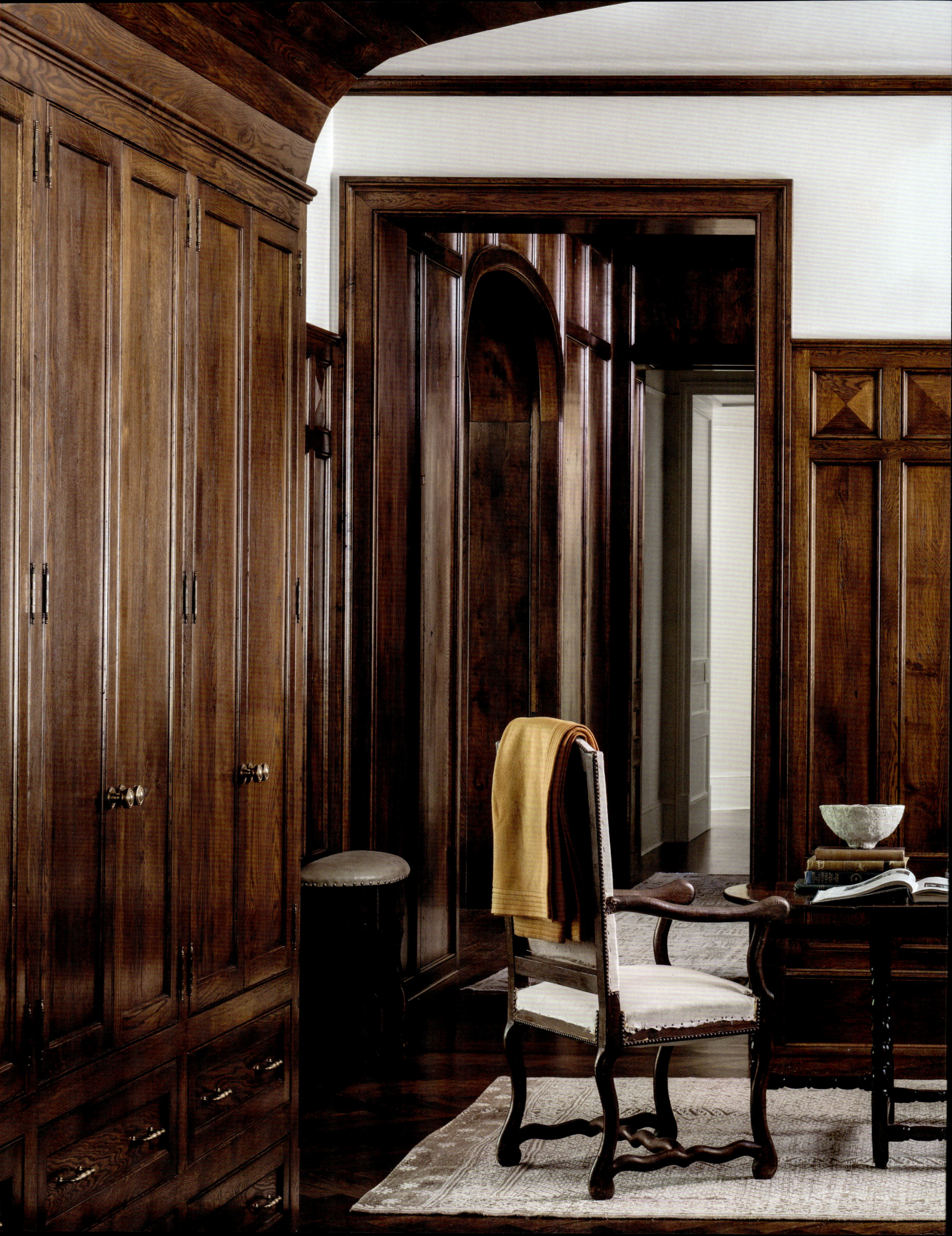

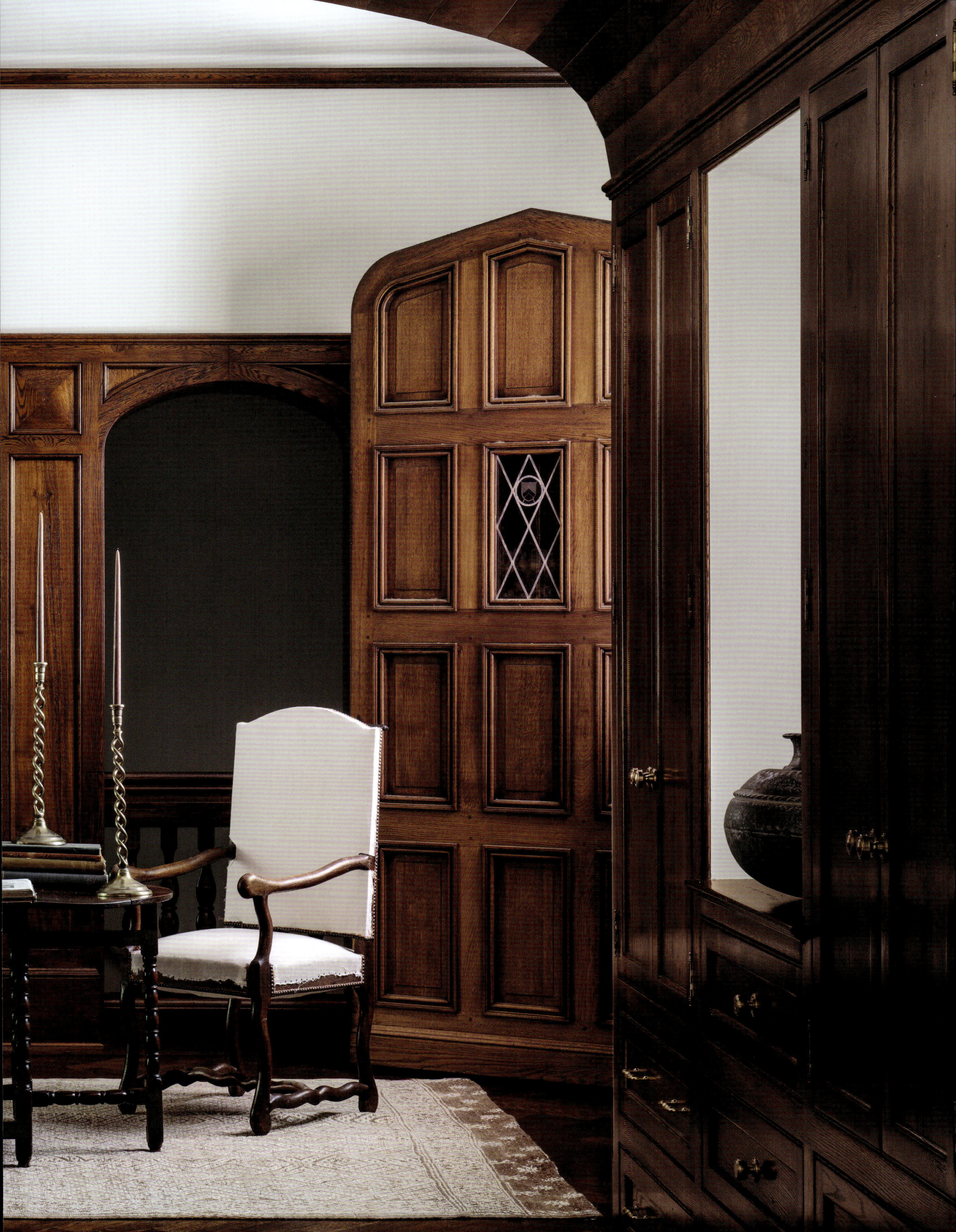

the house would stand, and the other a neighboring strip of nature, which we turned into a parklike setting complete with picturesque paths, decorative plantings, and the aforementioned rippling brook. The site's linear constraints called for an equally linear concept.

In addition, the home's layout and massing were governed by the kind of "imagined history" that I often dream up for our projects. A large central section, which represents the "earliest" portion of the structure, is clad in ashlar-pattern limestone and equipped with characteristic Tudor or Elizabethan features such as crenellations, pointed arches, diamond-pane windows, and carved stone detailing. Brick-covered wings on both sides are lower and somewhat less formal, as if they were added on later. On the left, a gated porte cochere leads to a parking and service court reminiscent of the carriage courts of days gone by, its far end closed off by a glass greenhouse (a common fixture on estates in Britain) set amid a lush cutting and vegetable garden.

Spaces indoors are lofty and are also full of appropriate period touches. The tall wainscoting of stained reclaimed oak that adorns most of the rooms has a furniture-grade finish, and textured lime plaster was used on the upper walls and ceilings. The ceilings themselves frequently get dramatic treatment: either beamed or groin vaulted or embellished by wood tracery. Certain motifs appear repeatedly as unifying devices, including elliptically arched door frames and timber trusses as well as rows of beveled squares incorporated into the paneling. Above the front door, and in several other locations in the house, we went so far as to place armorial crests that we devised for the couple, which combine elements from crests used informally by the wife's and husband's families.

As you may have guessed from the homes featured in this book, I love stairs—their sculptural nature and the opportunities they afford for creating

OPPOSITE: The crenellated archway leading from the auto court toward the kitchen captures the essence of service entries from a bygone era. FOLLOWING SPREAD: The rear terrace includes a lush parterre garden. Inside the central door, a barrel-vaulted passage extends through to the front entry hall.

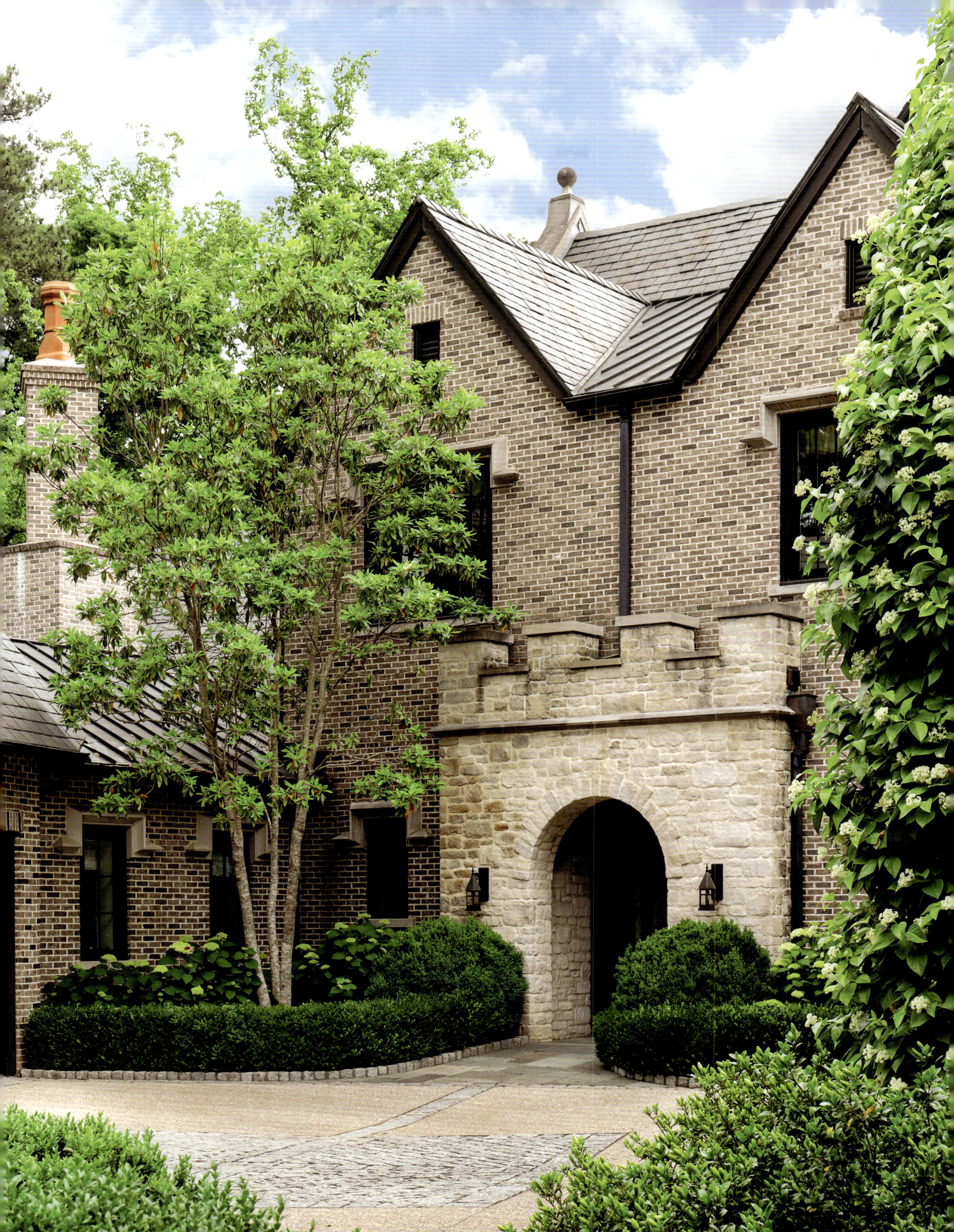

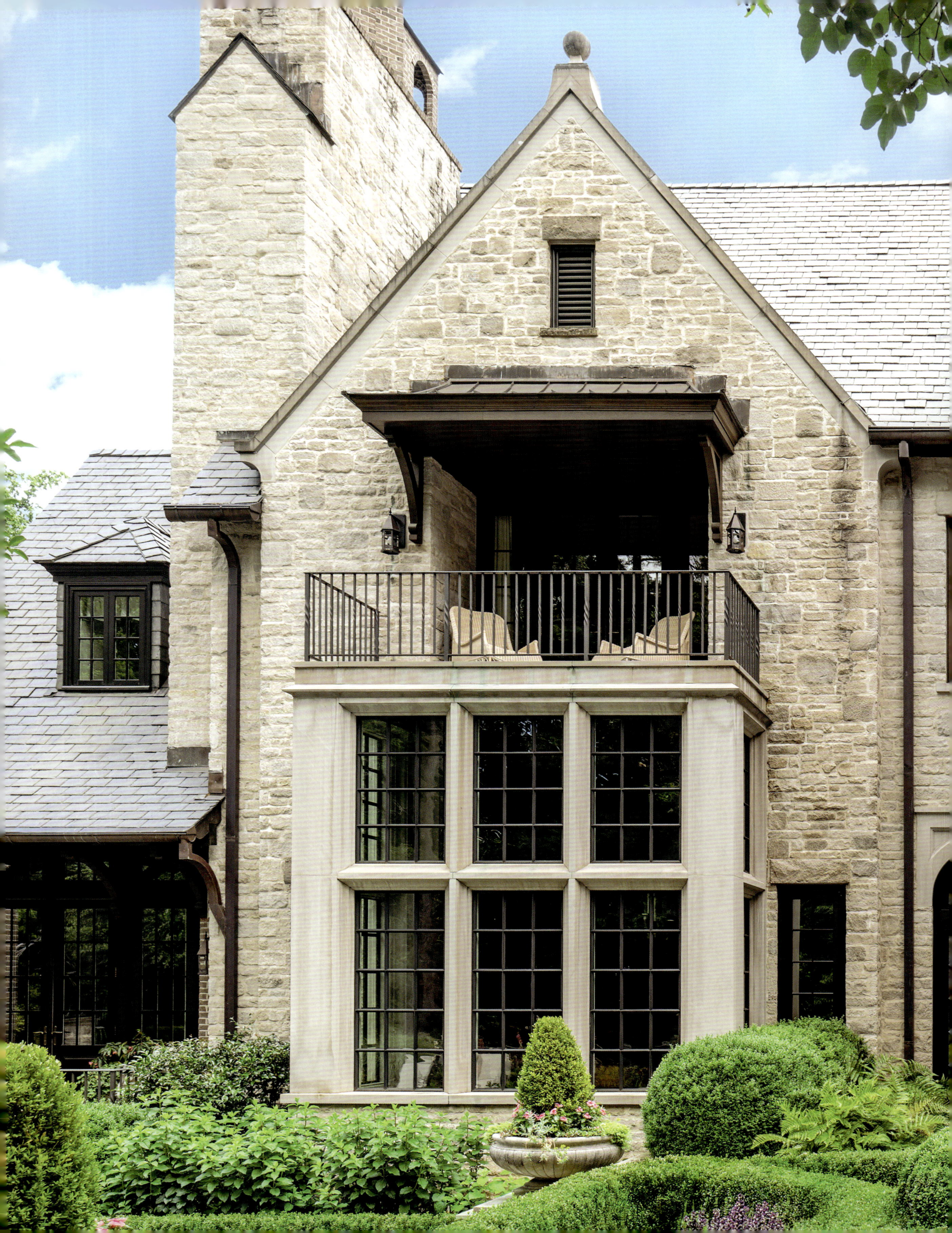

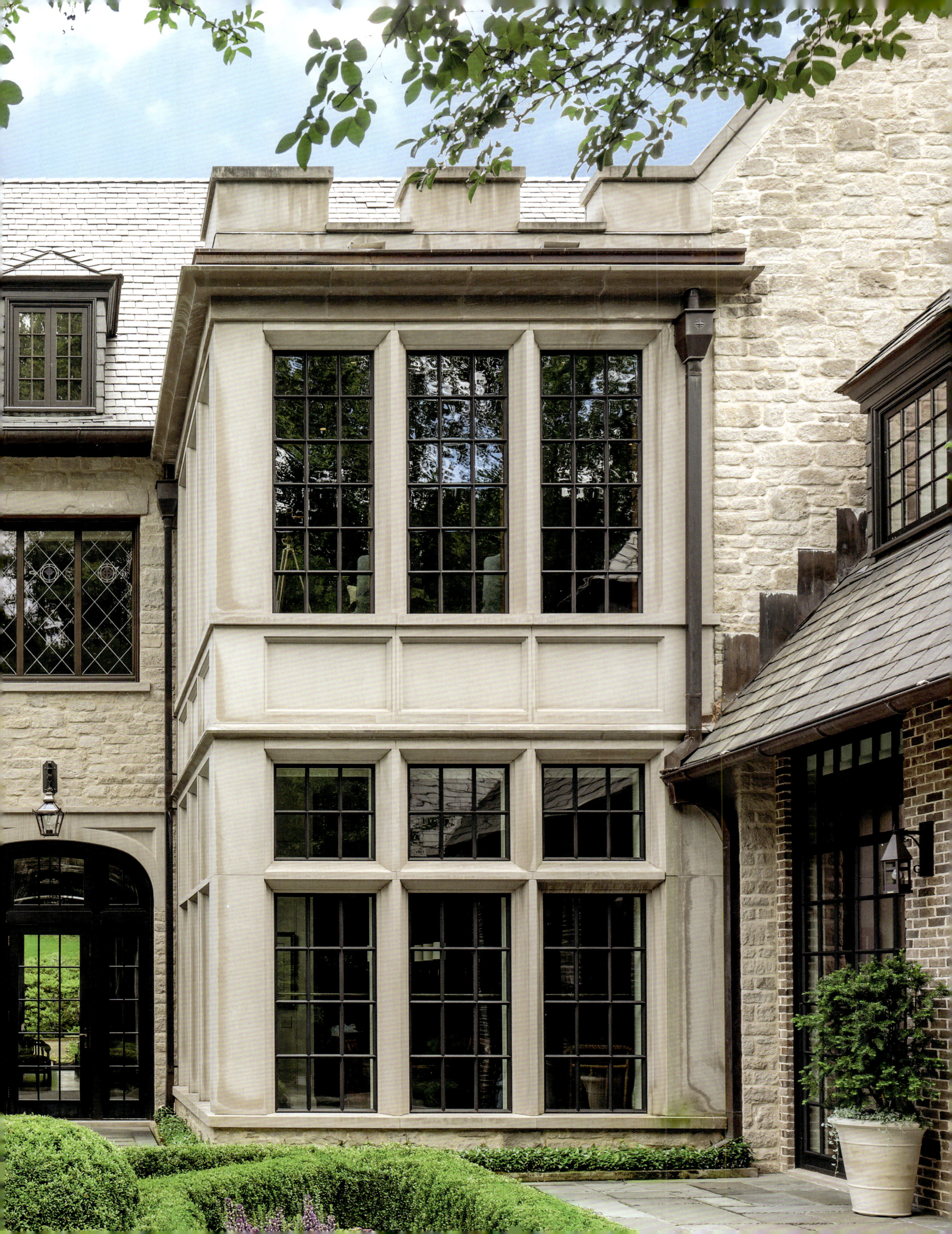

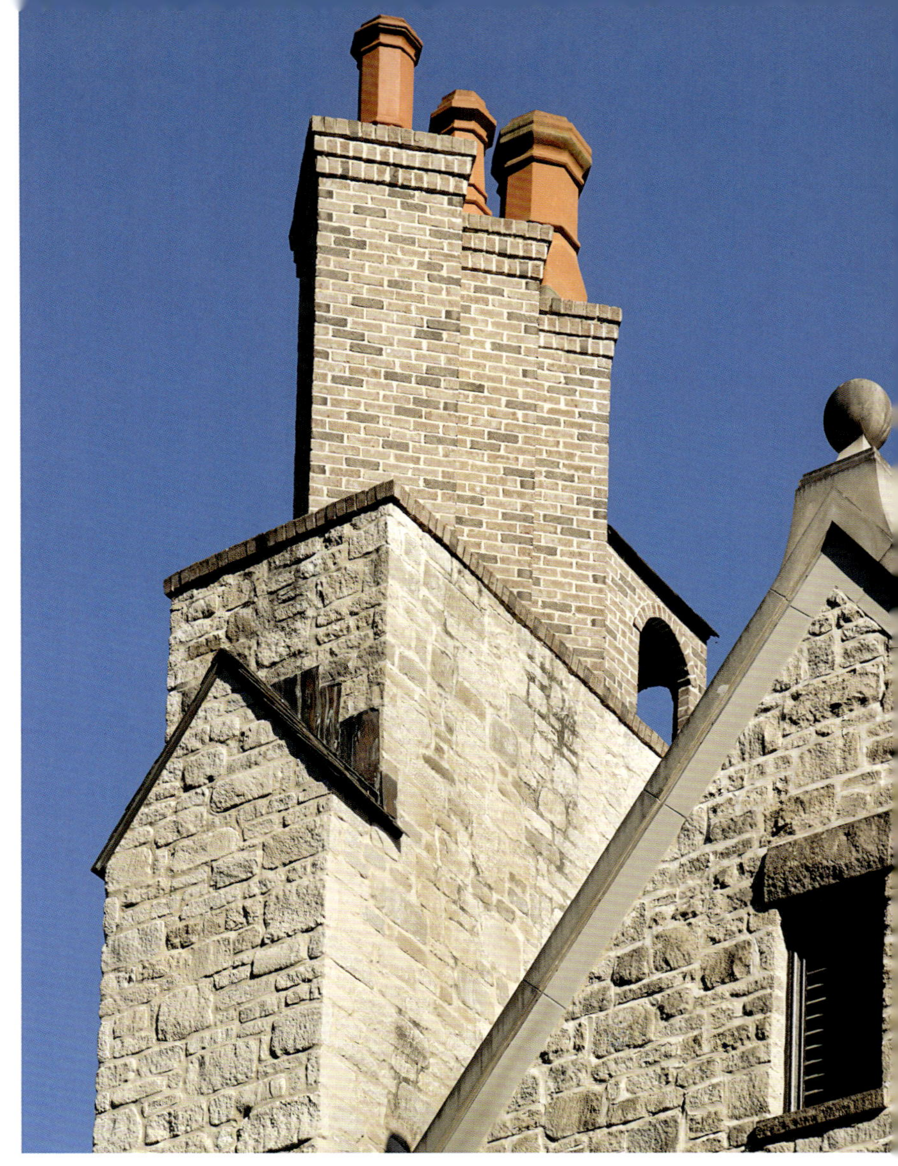

RIGHT: A restricted palette of materials—limestone and brick masonry; copper for awnings, gutters, and downspouts; slate for the roof; and leaded or steel windows—is employed to create a complex and highly imaginative architectural composition. There is constant variation in the building's constituent elements; nothing is done the same way twice. One example: every chimney is different, down to the chimney pots, which is a common quirk in English manor houses.

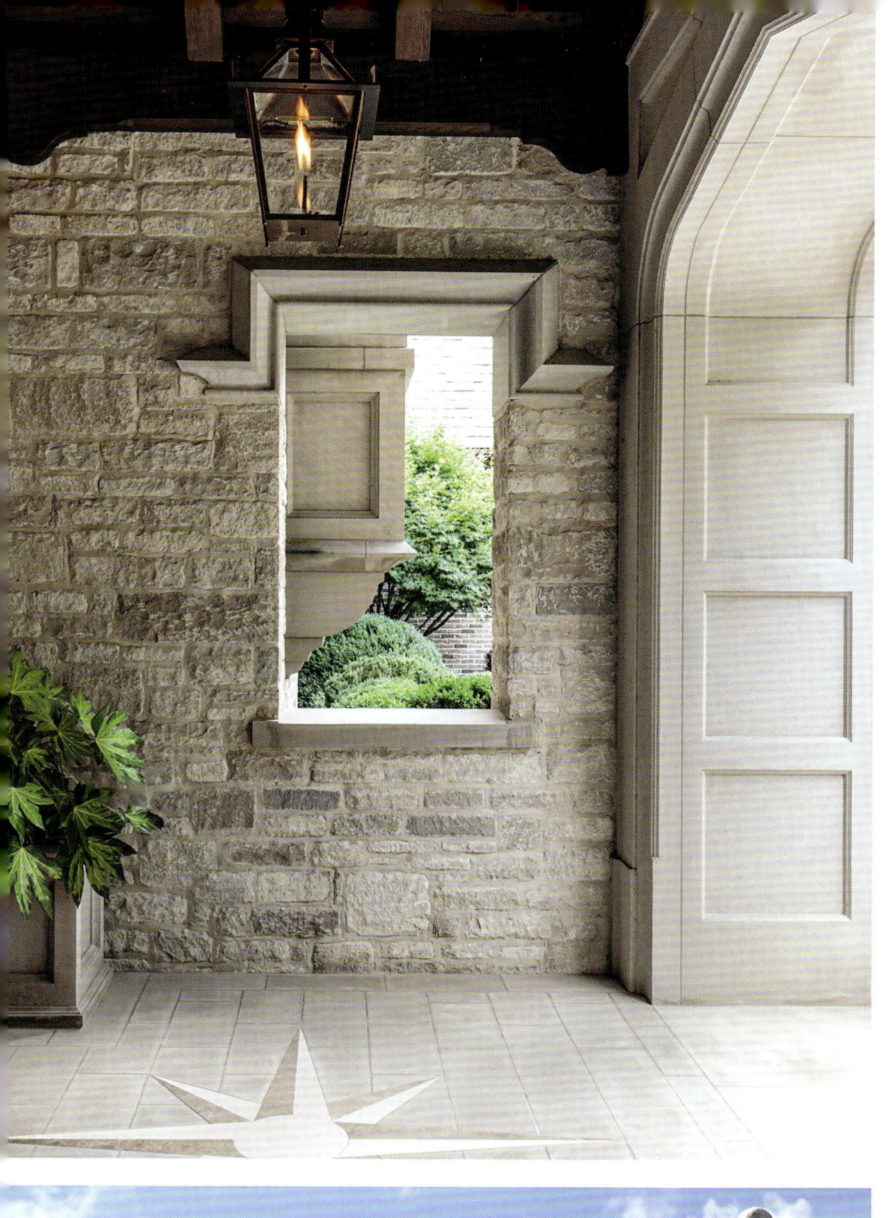
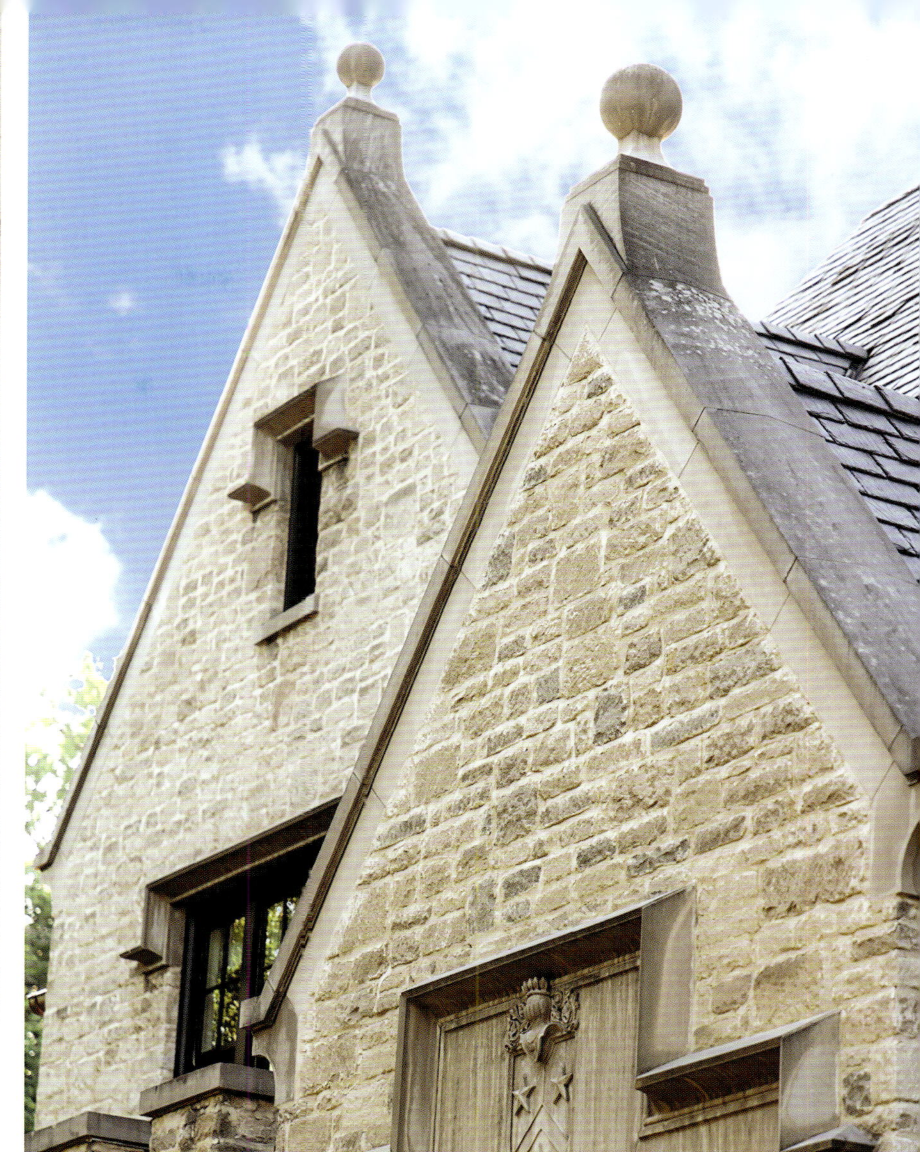
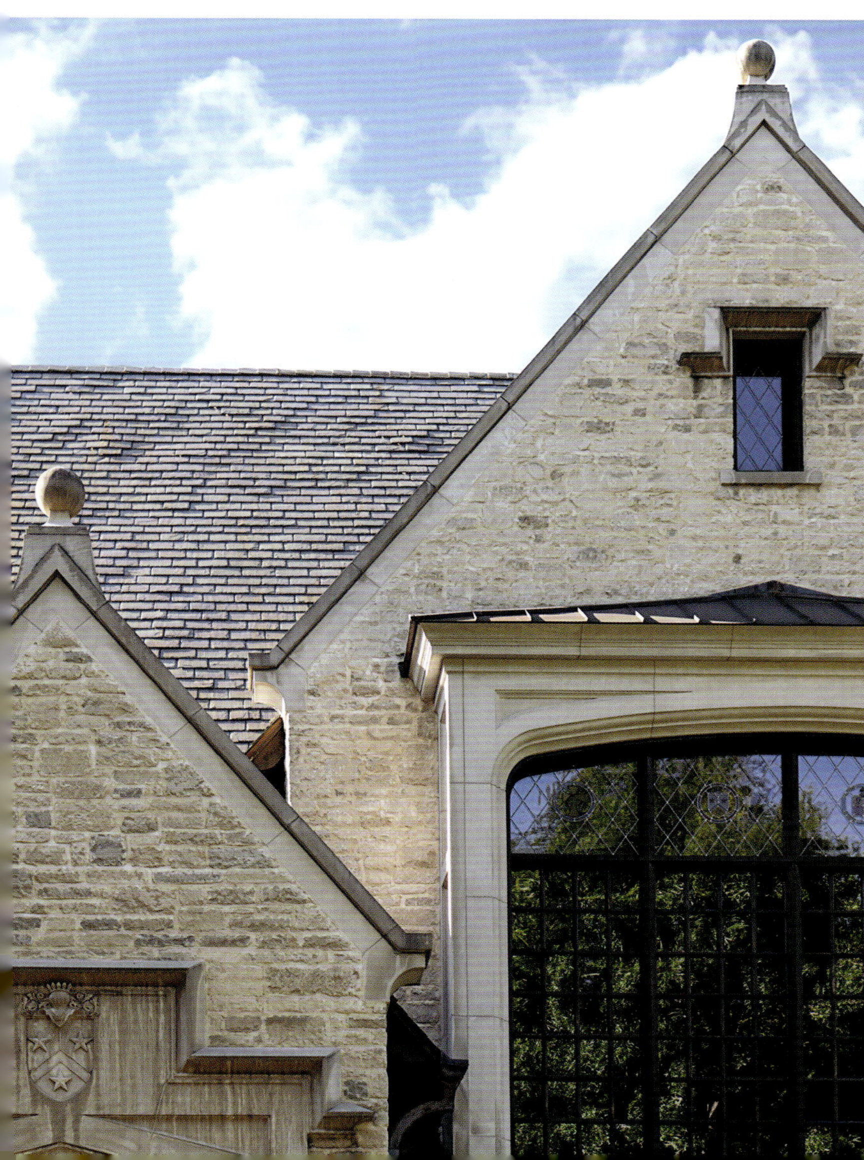
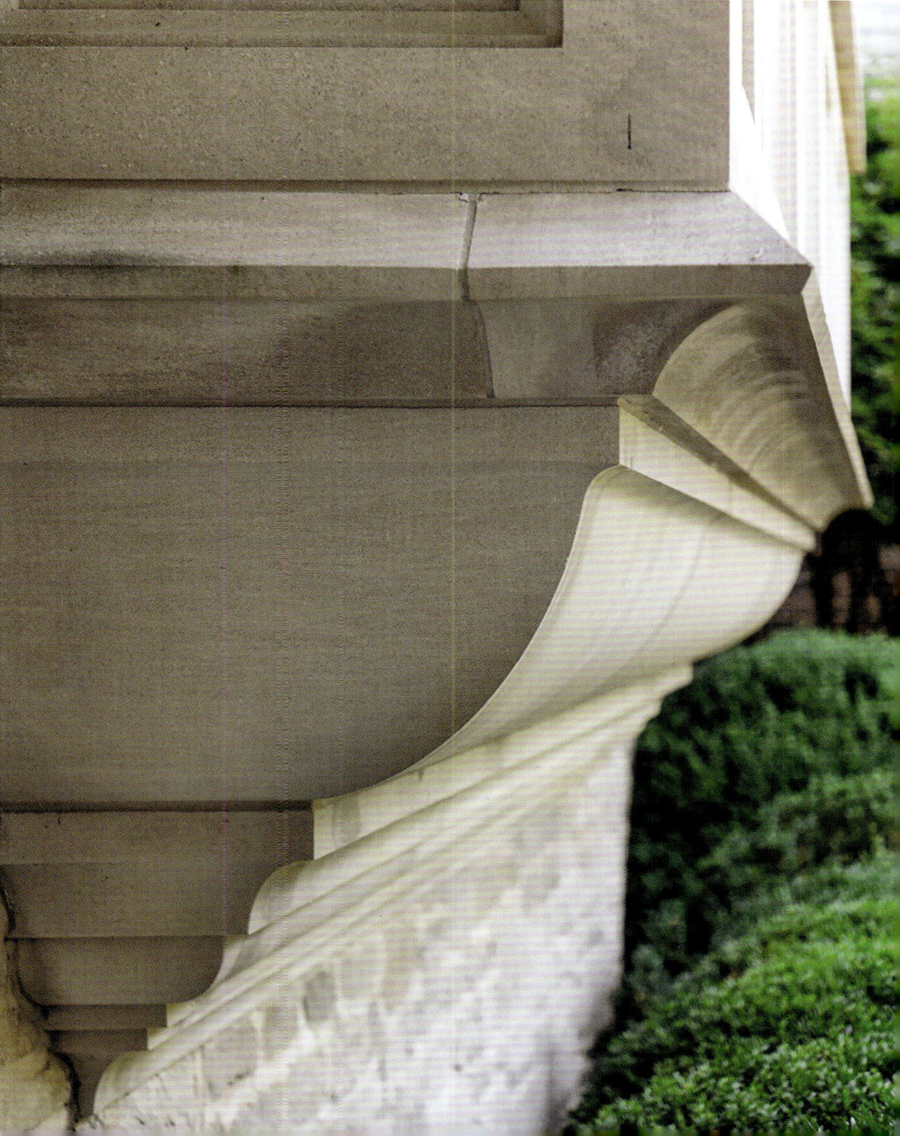

wonderful details. The grand stair in this house hugs three walls opposite the baronial living room; people crossing the massive arched window behind the stairway will be silhouetted against the glass (an aspect of the *Downton Abbey* inspiration I mentioned earlier). The heavy, carved balustrade and curved, open finials further reference specific English examples that came up in our studies. I hand drew everything in this space before we entered it into our drafting program, because it needed to be a totally organic whole.

Another of my favorite parts of the house has a narrative angle to it. The couple had an old, ornamental iron gate that they wanted to use in their new home, and an obvious place for it was the lower-level wine cellar and tasting room. Instead of simply installing it as a quaint entrance, though, I thought we'd try a more intriguing approach: passing through the gate itself is now just the beginning of a subterranean procession through a twisting stone-lined corridor with irregular sets of steps—a journey similar to the one described in Edgar Allan Poe's short story "The Cask of Amontillado," except much less creepy and without the unfortunate ending.

Behind the house, we built an elevated terrace with walk-out access to the pool and formal garden area. Steps then descend to the wooded park and stream in the back. In a nod to Atlanta's climate, a timber-framed porch extends out from the home's main body in order not to block the light in interior rooms and to maximize airflow on steamy Southern days.

Structural volumes and roofscapes are arranged so that this imposing dwelling is varied and beautiful when seen from any angle, with architectural components such as elaborate chimneys and brick-filled blind arches providing plenty of enchanting moments. All the stars aligned for our work here, allowing us to transfer an impeccably realized experience of British romance to twenty-first-century Georgia.

OPPOSITE: Even with all the dark oak woodwork we put into the house, interior spaces, like the living room, still feel bathed in light because of their lofty ceilings and stacked windows. (The higher the windows, the farther outside illumination will penetrate into an interior.) Arched trusses emphasize the effect of verticality, and I love the authenticity of using the pale limestone mullions both inside and out.

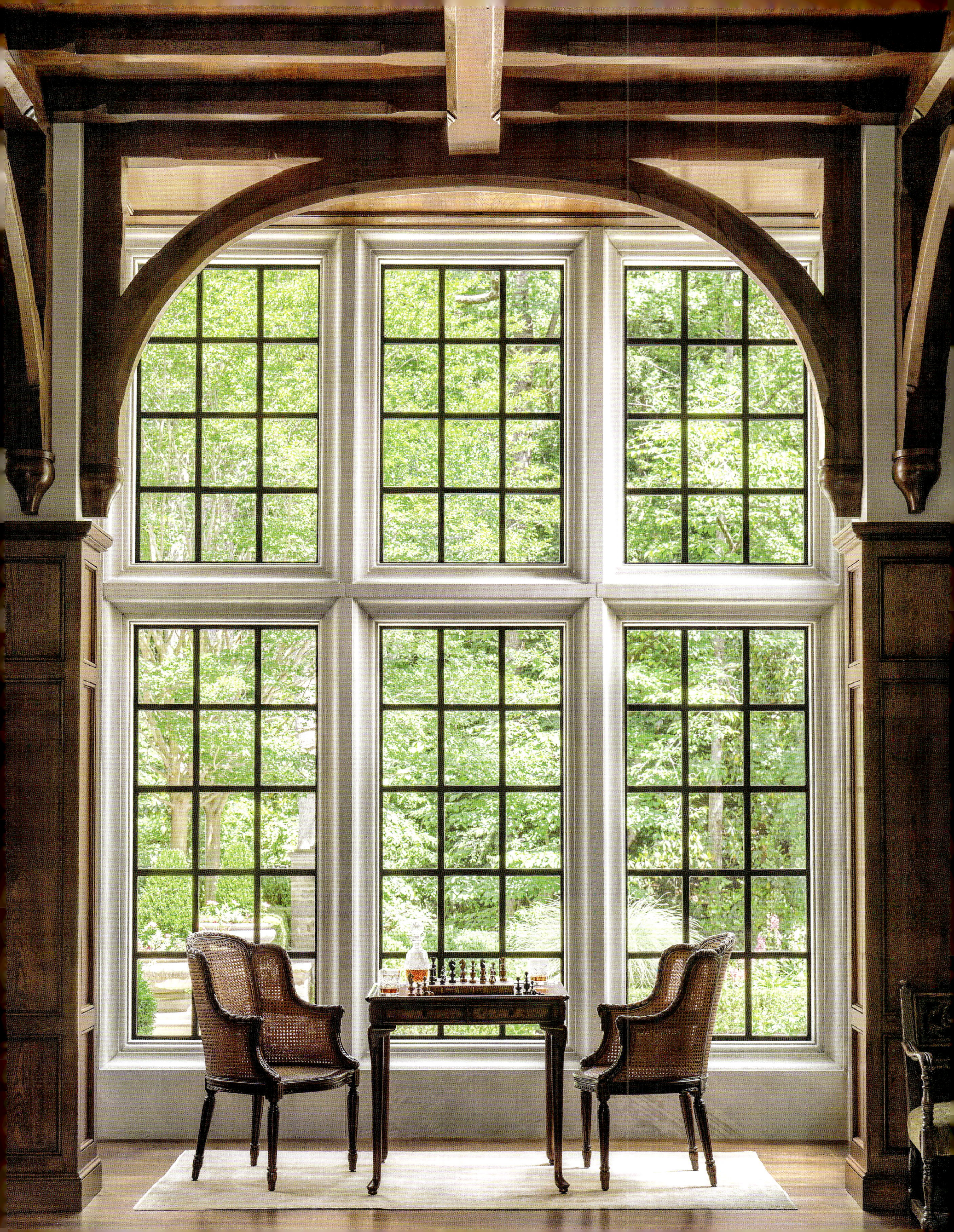

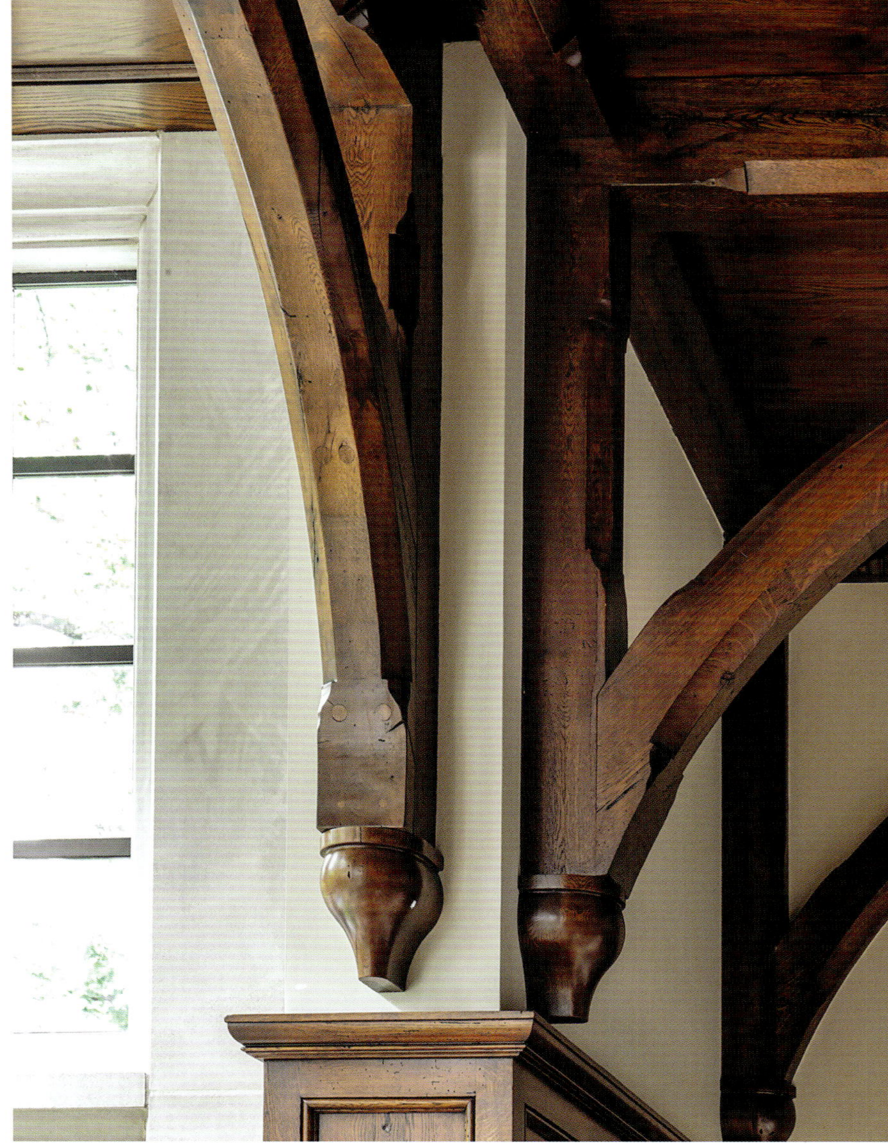

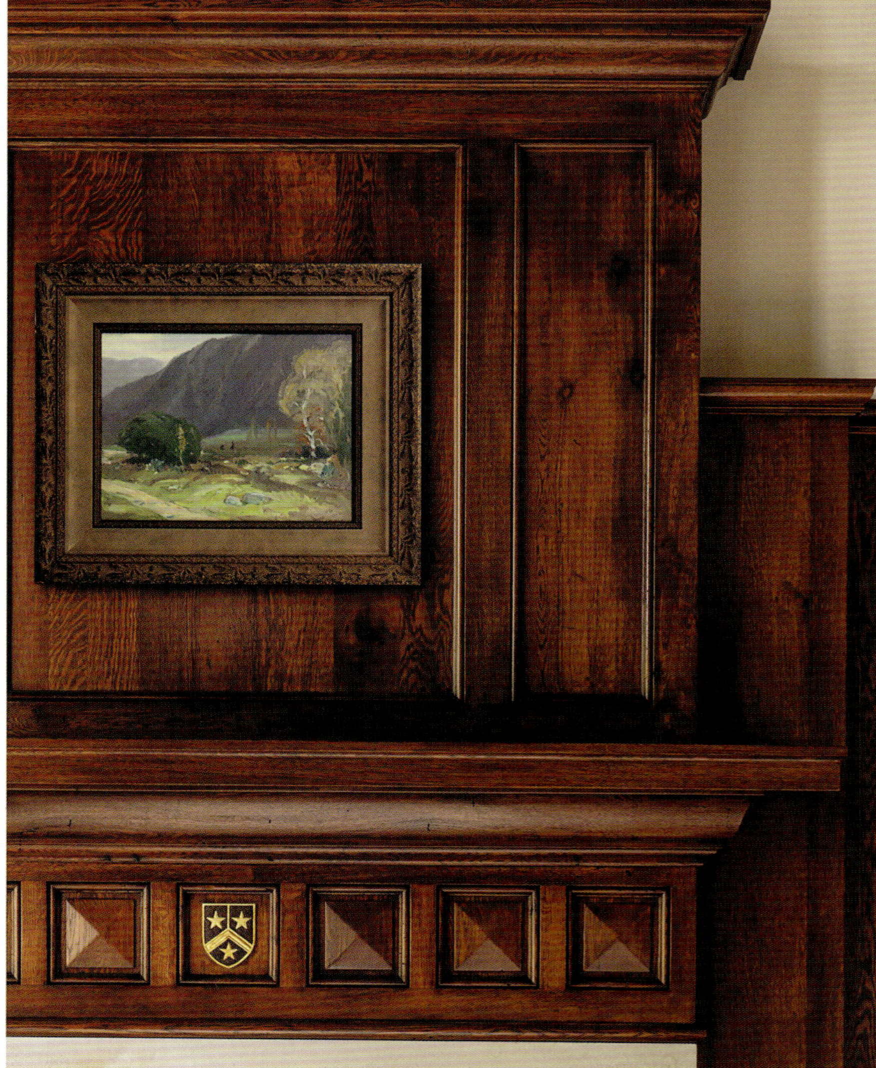

RIGHT: Interior spaces, as well, share an array of features that are constantly recast in inventive ways, to avoid too much sameness. Arches may be pointed, round, or elliptical, and appear in the form of doorways, vaulted ceilings, or trusses. Different rooms are composed of varying proportions of wood versus plaster, from the husband's all-walnut office to an almost entirely plaster-clad primary bathroom. Fidelity to an English country house aesthetic unites the design.

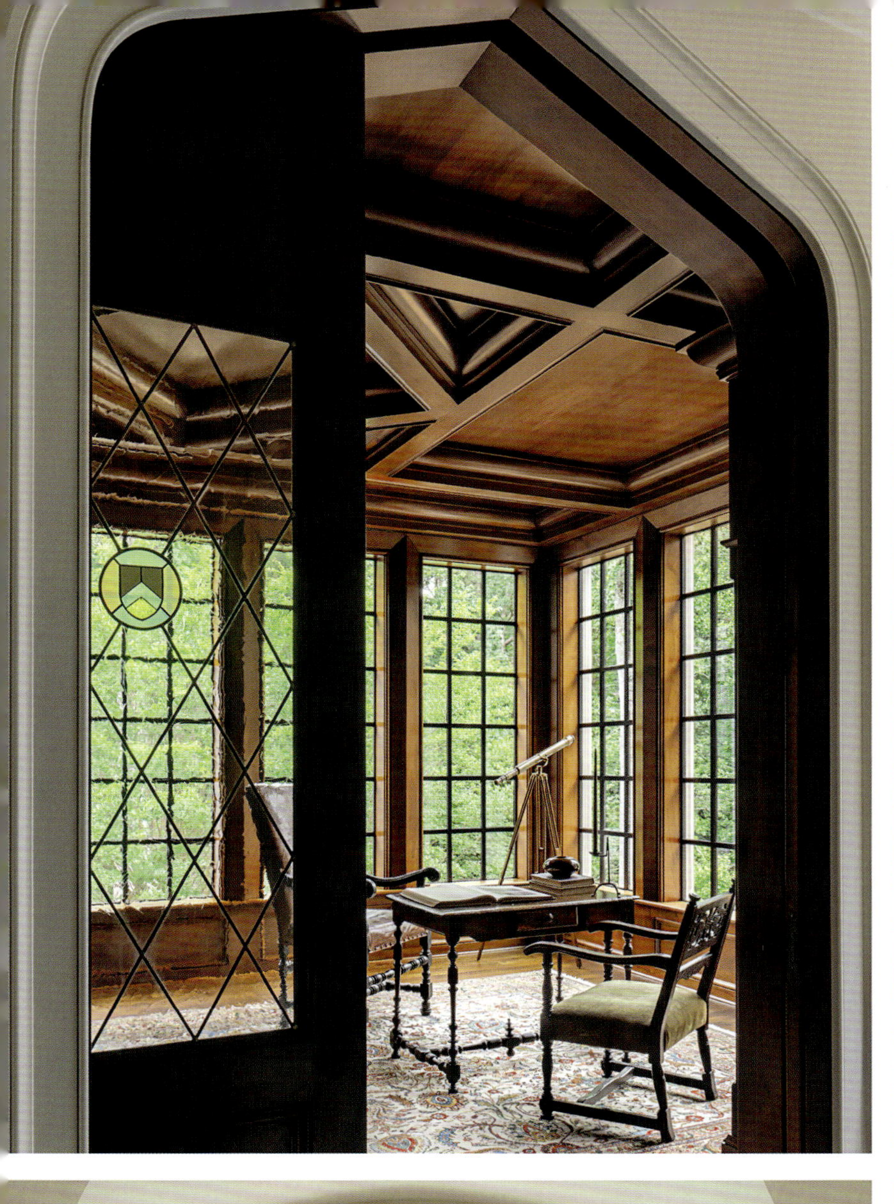
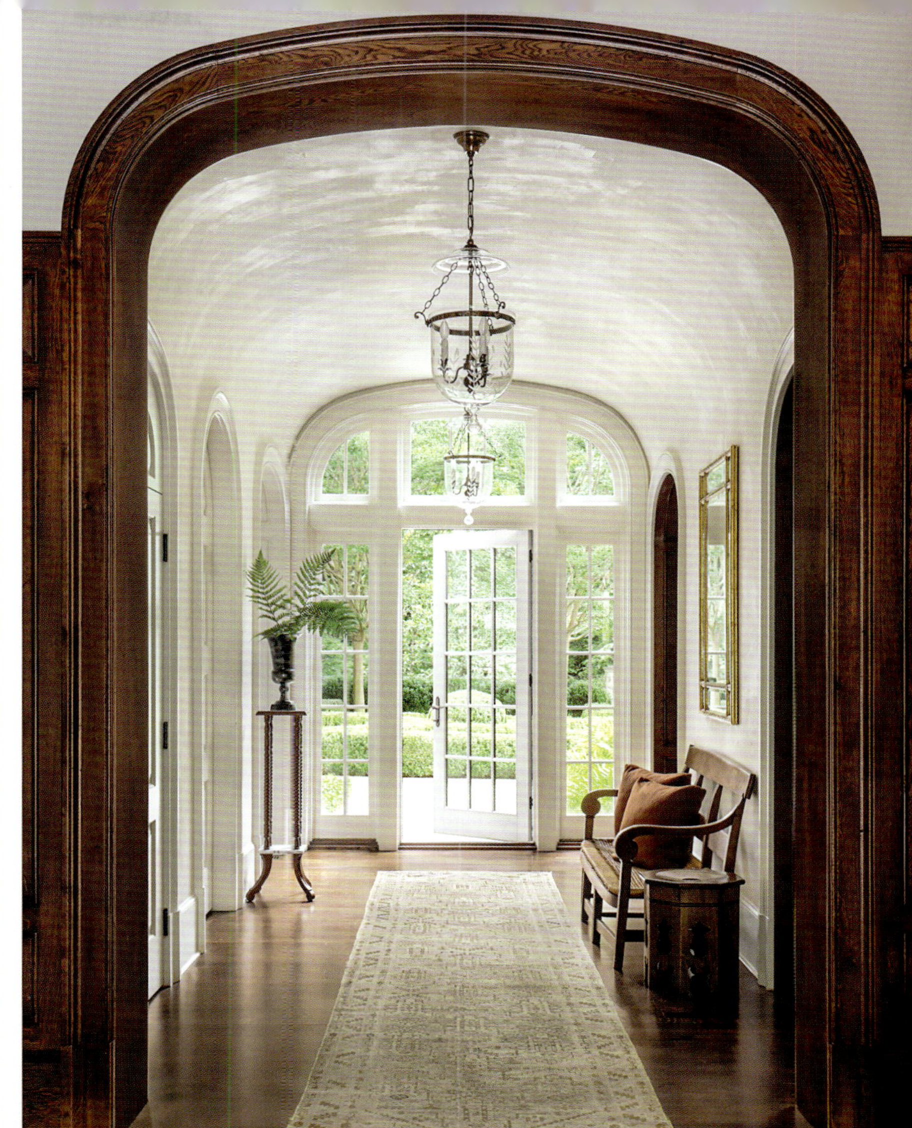
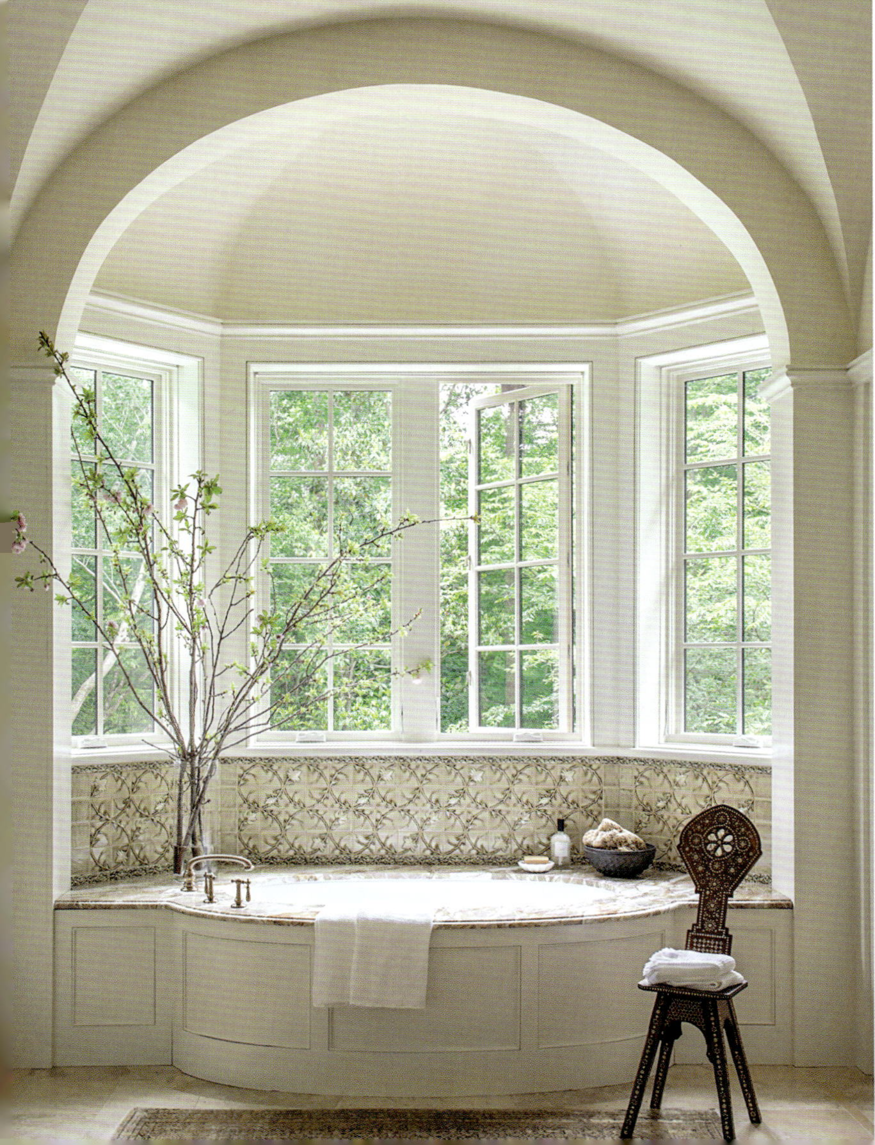
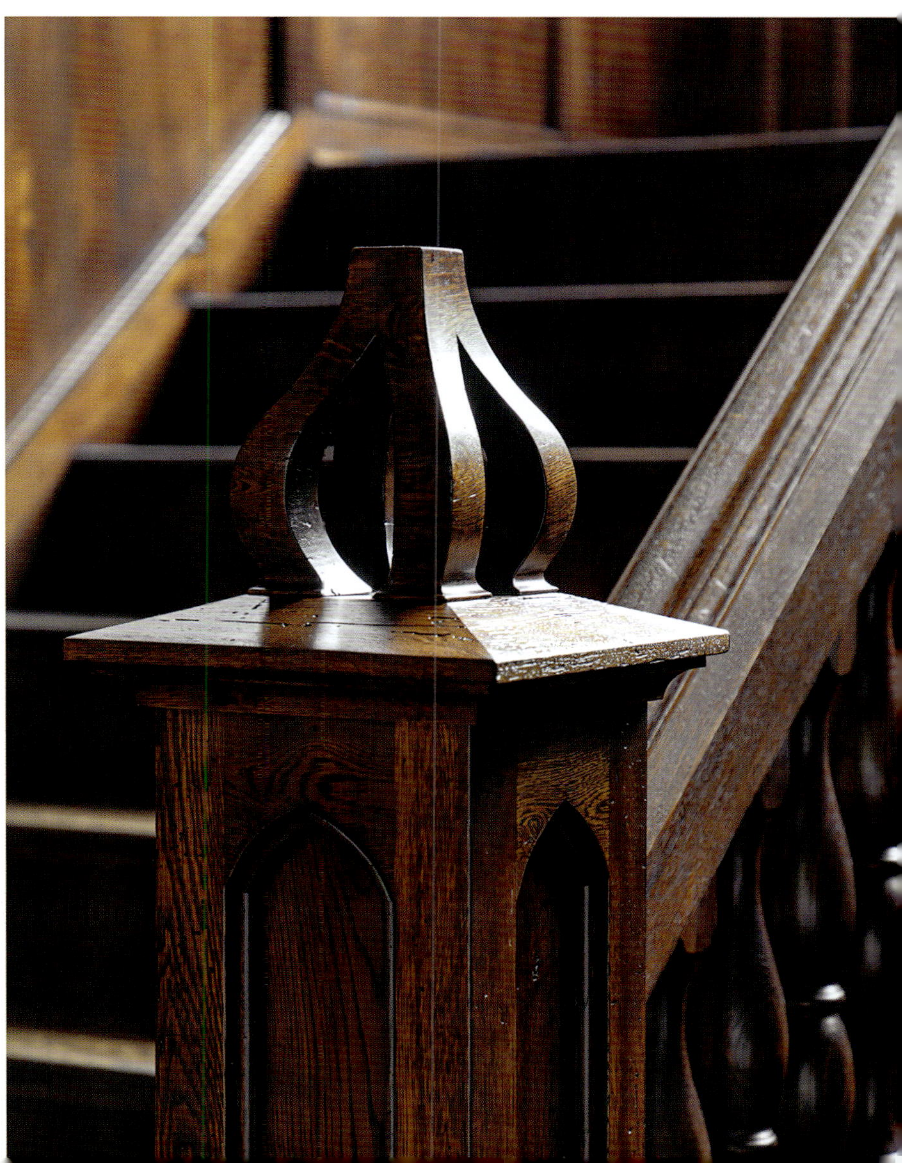

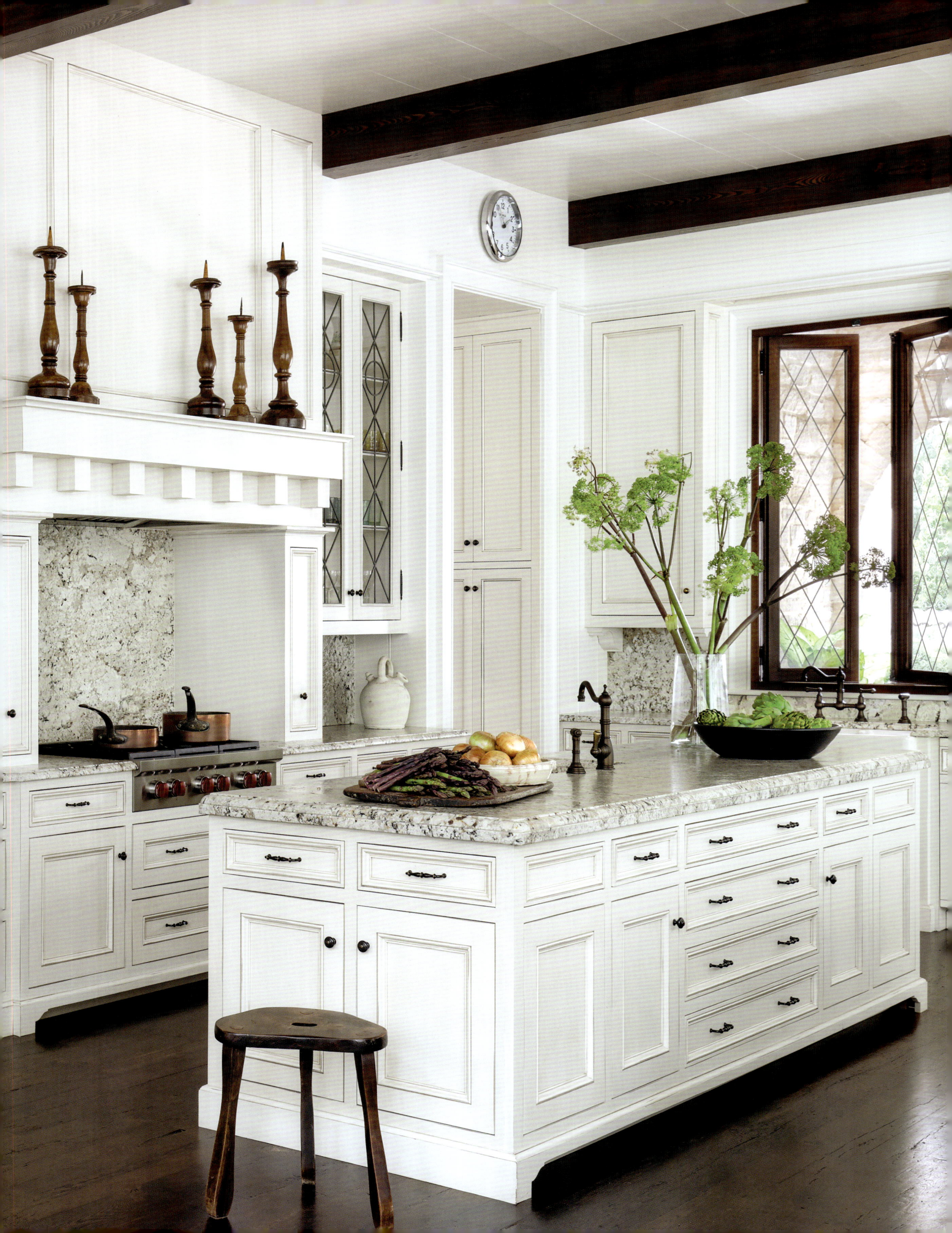

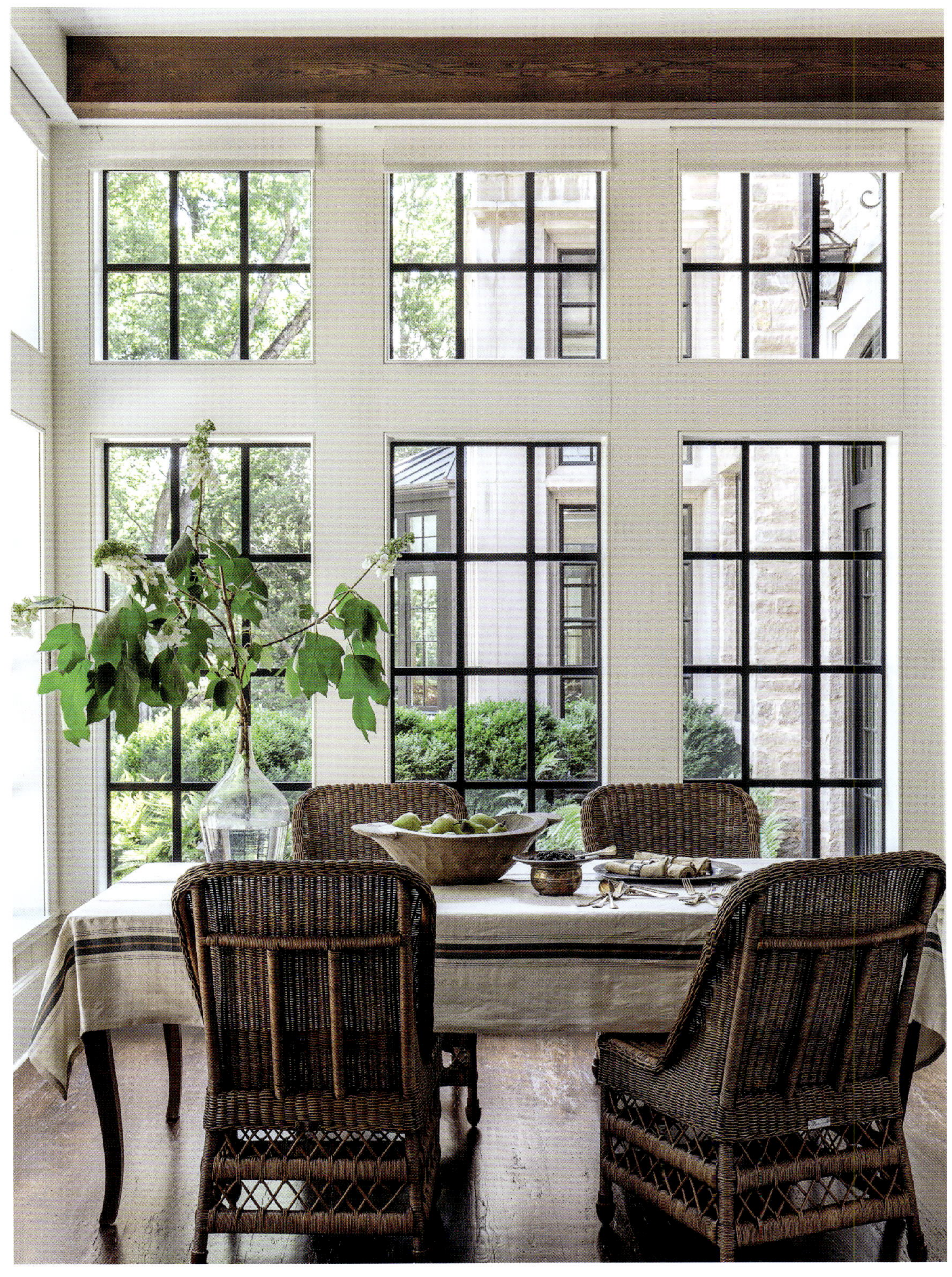

OPPOSITE: The walls and ceiling in the kitchen are covered in butt-jointed boards, while dentil corbels support the decorative cornice on the range hood. We incorporated diamond-patterned leaded glass in the cabinetry that recalls similar glass used in the room's casement windows as well as other windows throughout the home. ABOVE: The breakfast room, too, is tall, airy, and bright.

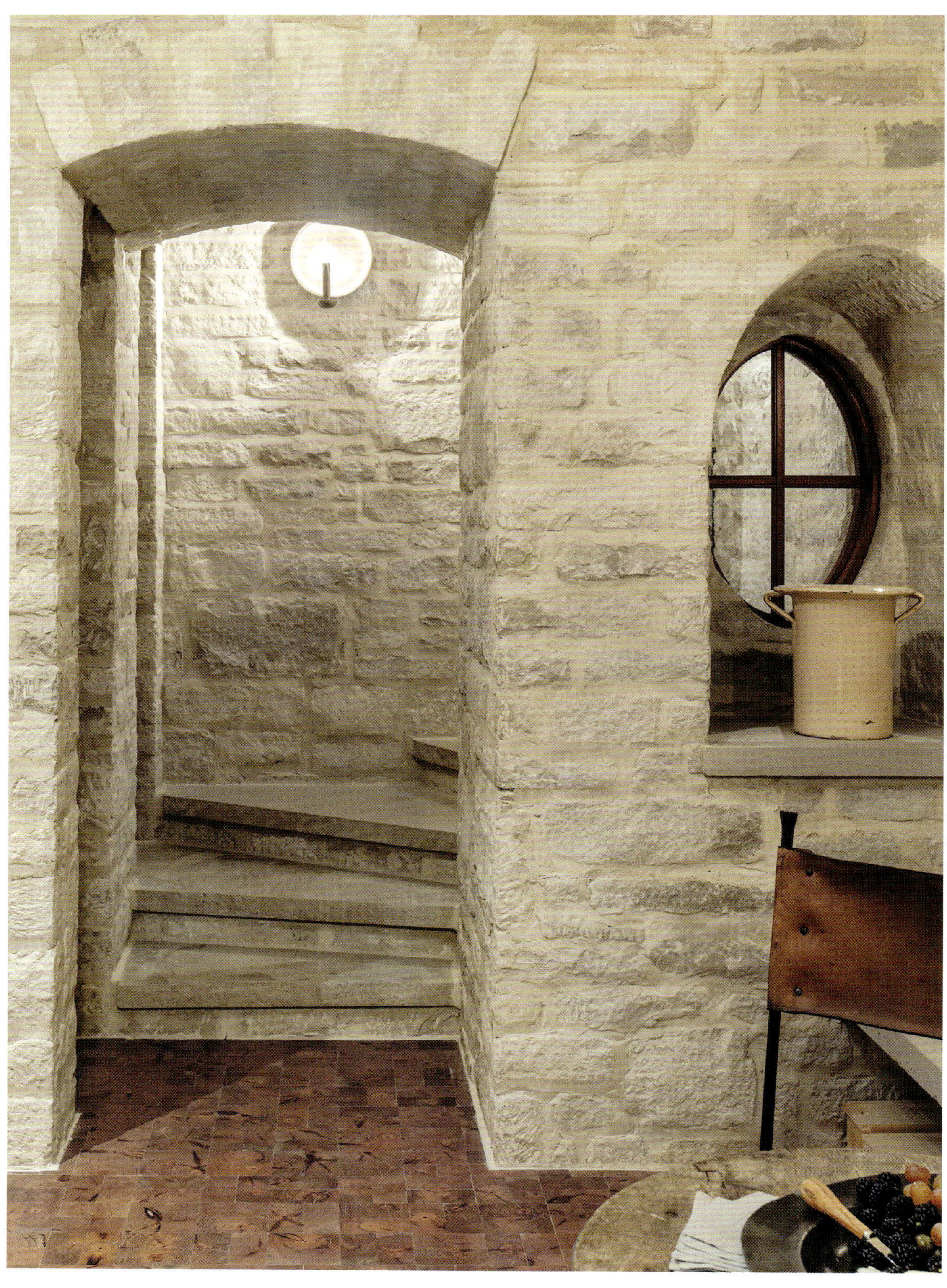

ABOVE: An oval window provides a glimpse into the wine tasting room as you descend the winding stone corridor that leads to it. OPPOSITE: Another arched doorway opens from the tasting room to the wine cellar. The tasting room floor is crafted from four-inch-square blocks of end-grain heart pine—like a giant butcher block—with a built-in stone bench on the left.

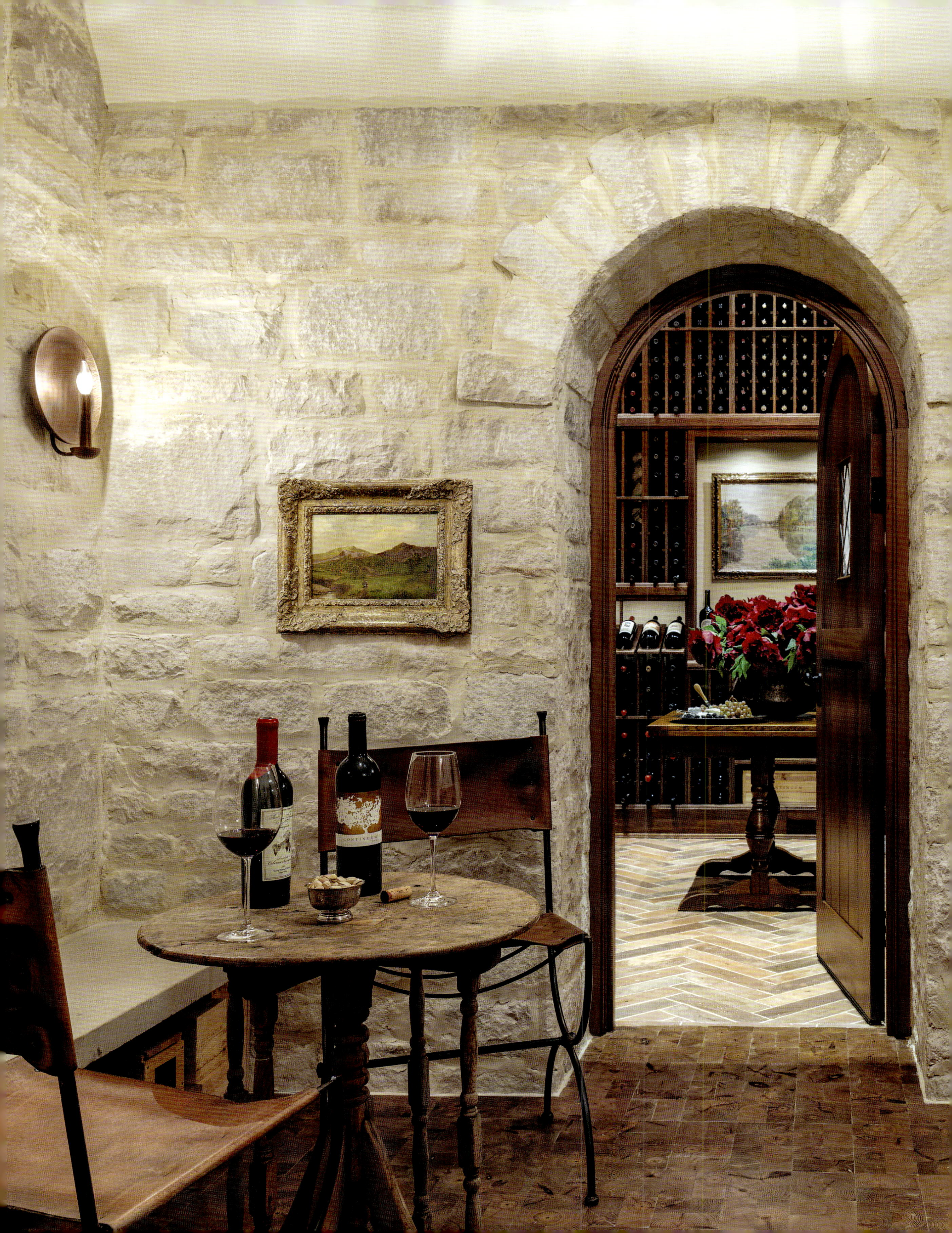
CONTINUUM

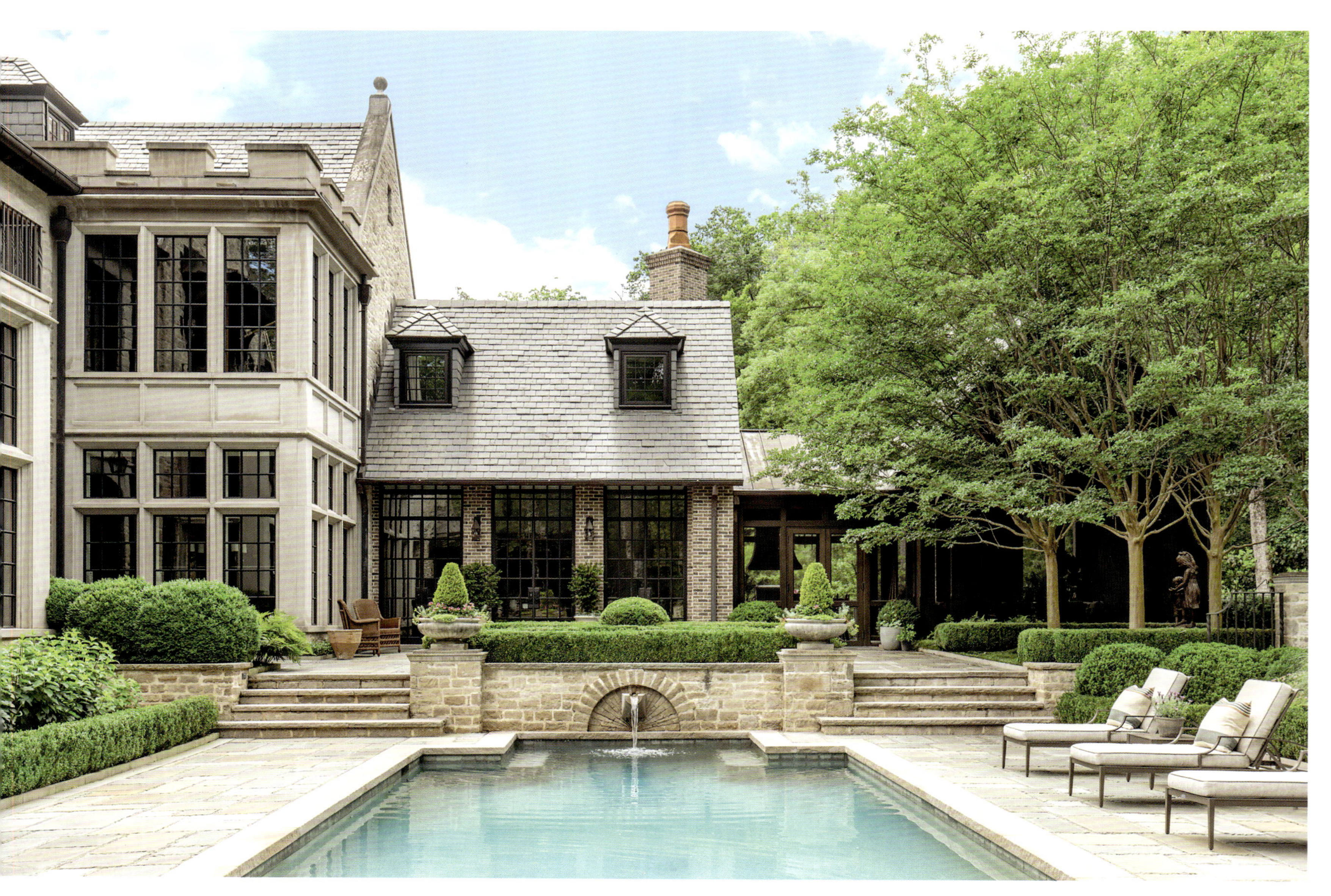

ABOVE: A pool occupies one section of the rear terrace, separated from the parterre garden by a low wall. The waterspout centered in its decorative arch is a nod to the work of English horticulturist and garden designer Gertrude Jekyll. OPPOSITE: The screened porch is framed in hefty timbers, with an open gable end for more light.

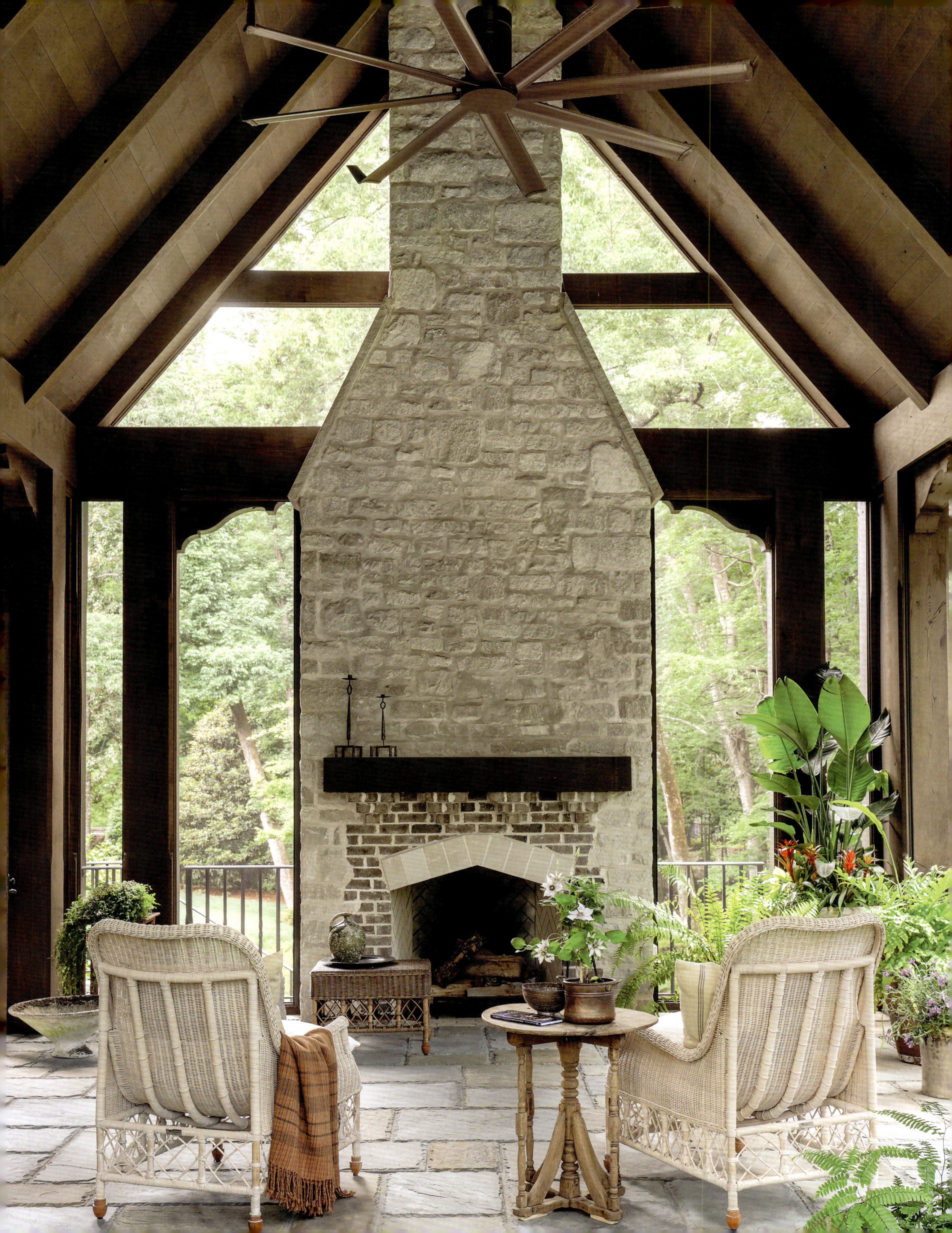

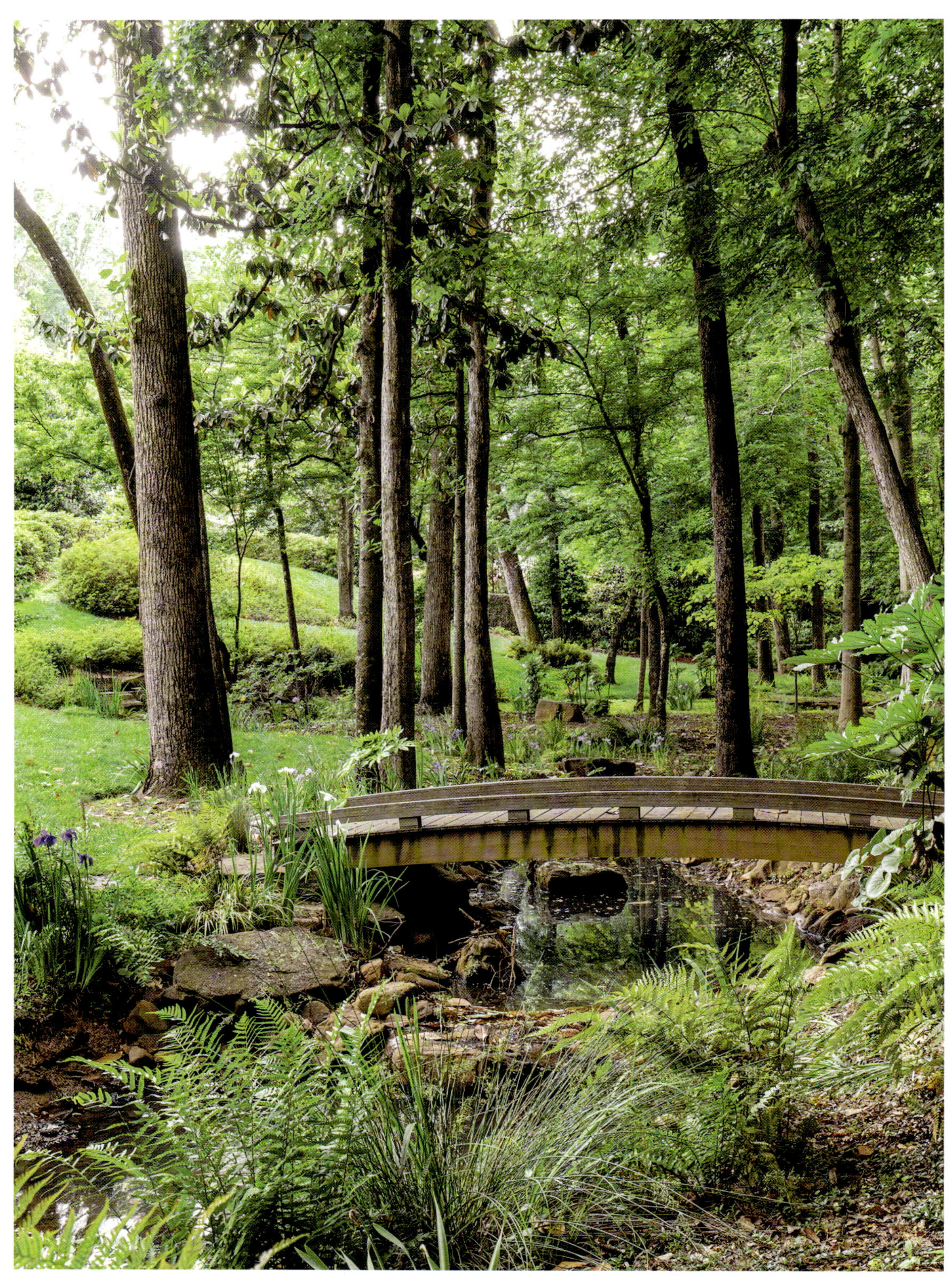

ABOVE: A gently arched bridge spans a brook in the parklike grounds. OPPOSITE: Pea gravel and raised beds define a small cutting and herb garden next to the greenhouse. FOLLOWING SPREAD: The greenhouse itself makes a beautifully scenic "fourth wall" for the far end of the auto court, where climbing hydrangeas soften the corners of the parking structures.

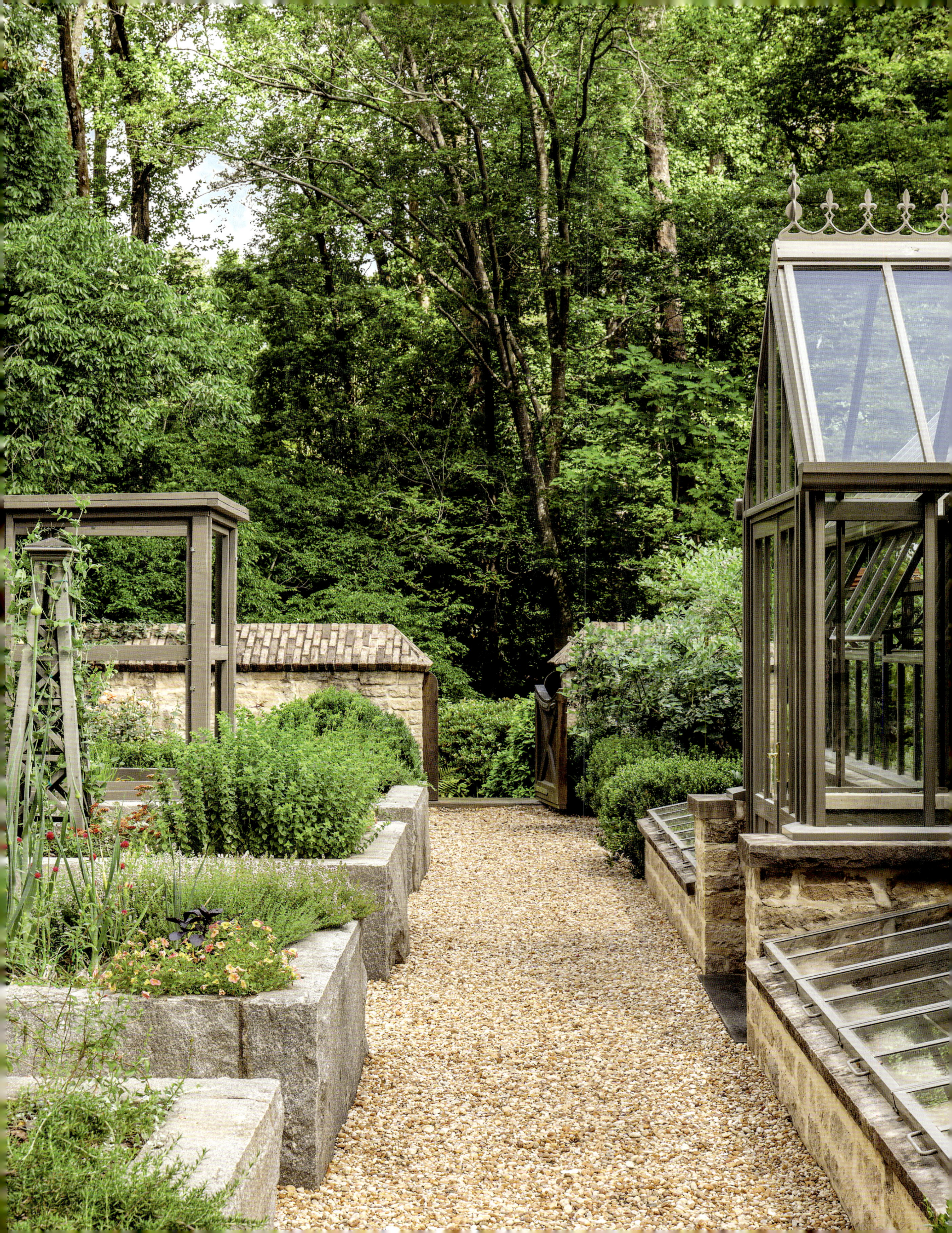

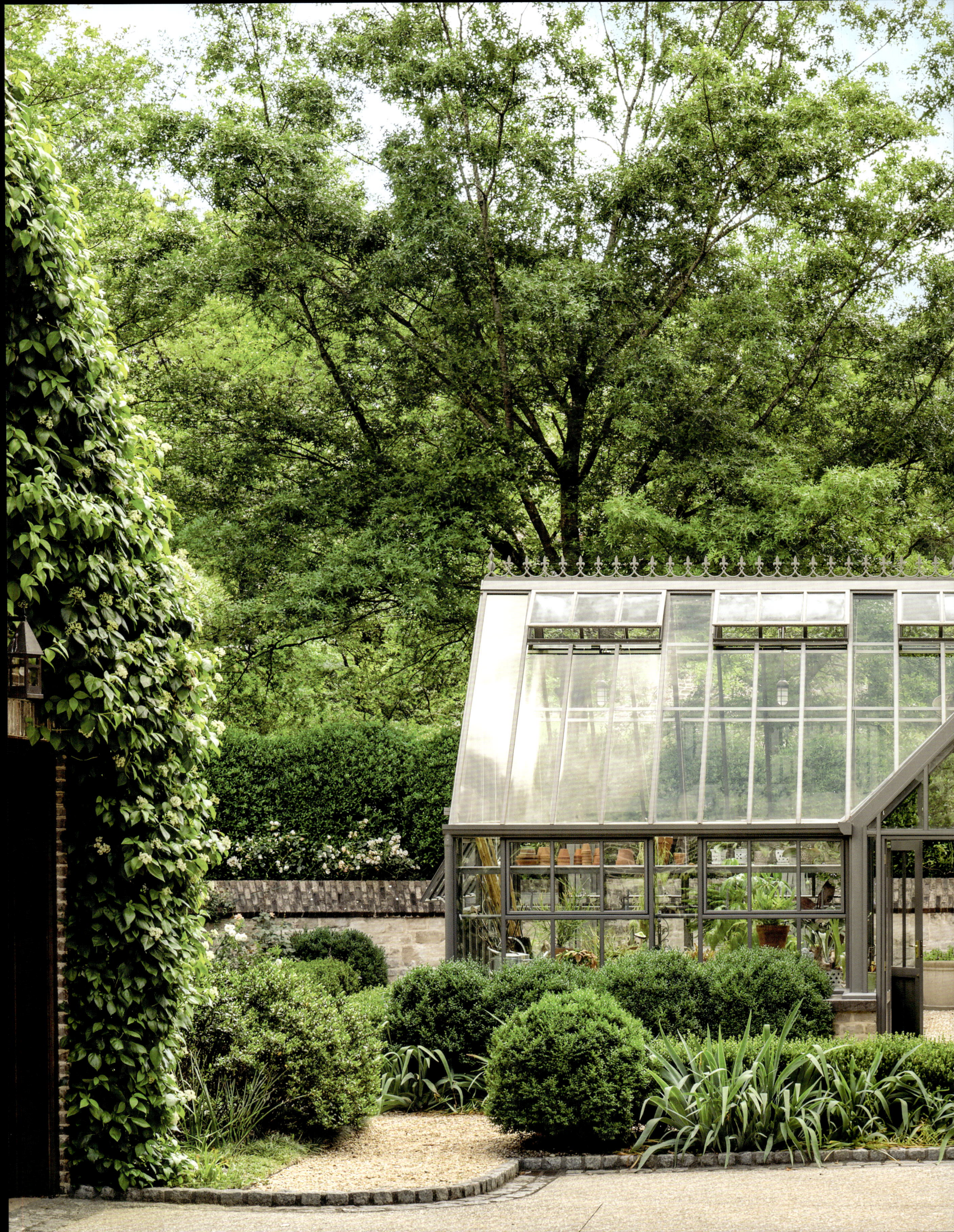

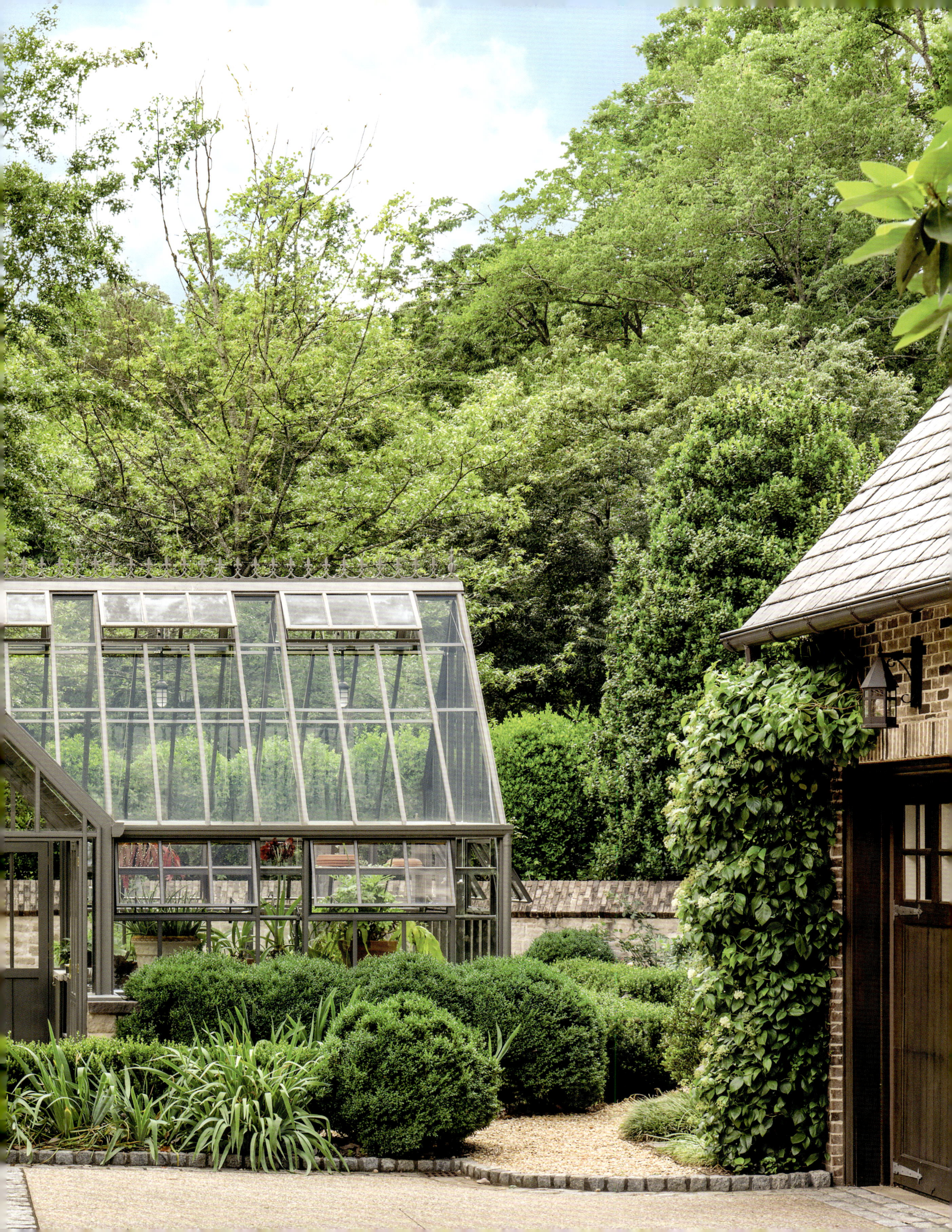

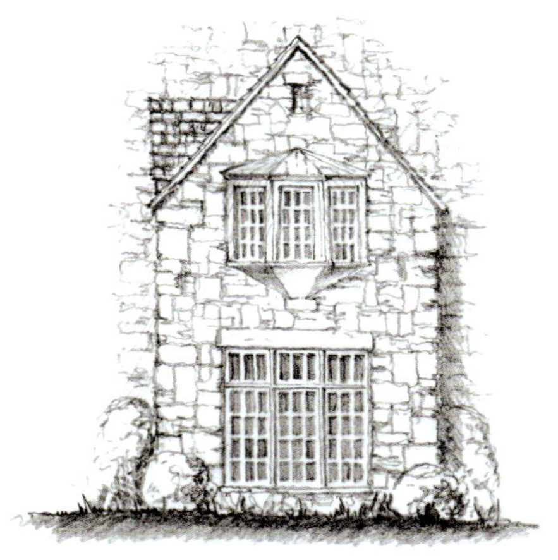

HARDWOOD RIDGE

As I've mentioned, an important part of my practice as an architect is to spend time walking a property prior to designing the home that will go on it. Almost always, the contours and feel of the land and its clothing of plant life will suggest what kind of house wants to exist there. Which natural features should we take advantage of? What will we need to design around? What characteristics do we want to enhance?

When clients I had worked with in the past purchased a new piece of property adjacent to their house in Athens, Georgia, we imagined a unique family compound. The two parcels share a boundary back-to-back in a wooded area with a little creek running through it. We devised a plan for the couple's existing home to go

OPPOSITE: This four-season room was originally designed as a porch, but we decided to enclose it for year-round use. The steel windows can be opened on temperate days, and concealed screens drop down from pockets in the beams above. FOLLOWING SPREAD: A flowing driveway and front walk foreshadow the curved arches of the home's asymmetrical entry loggia. This approach is intended to set an informal, romantic tone that carries through the overall design.

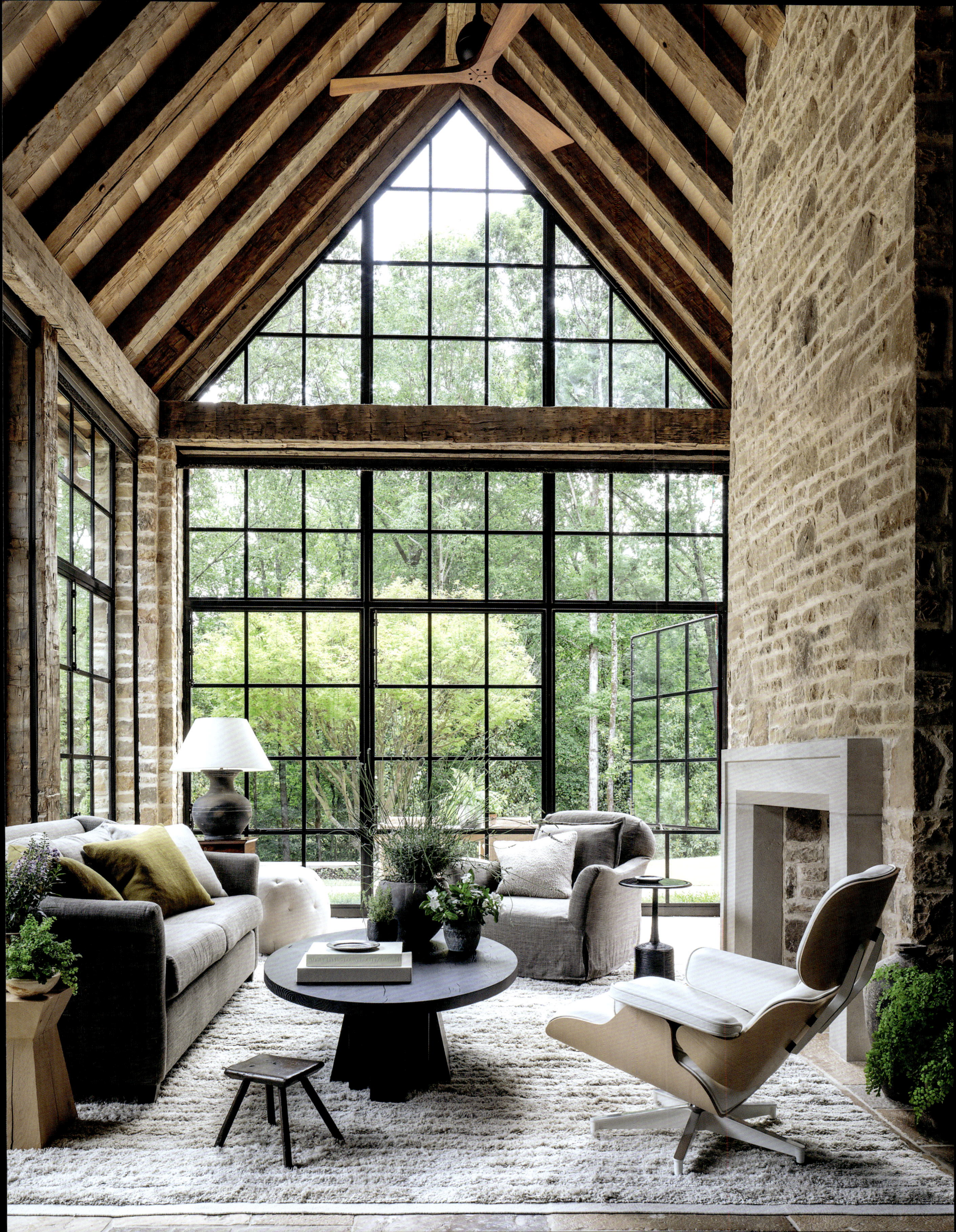

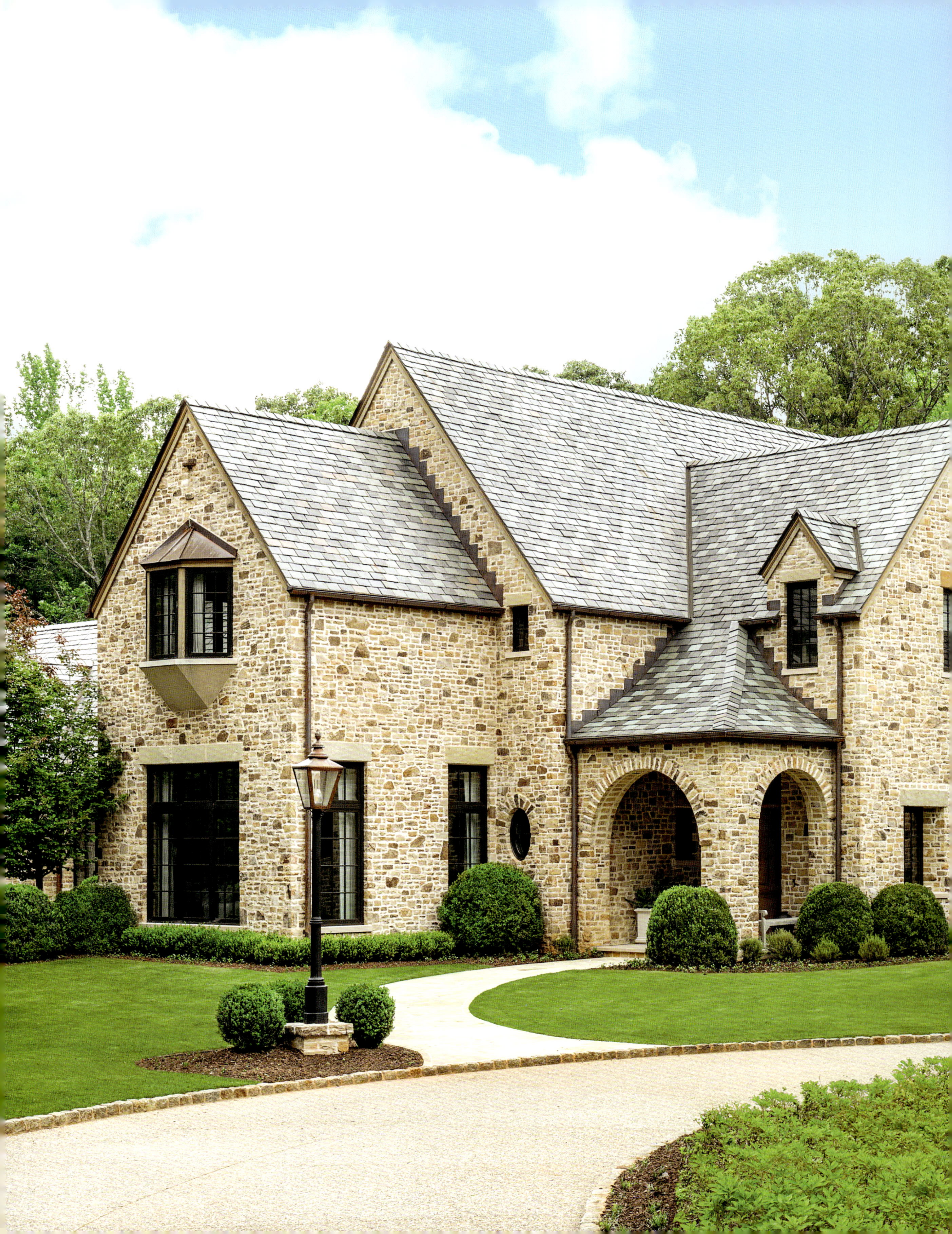

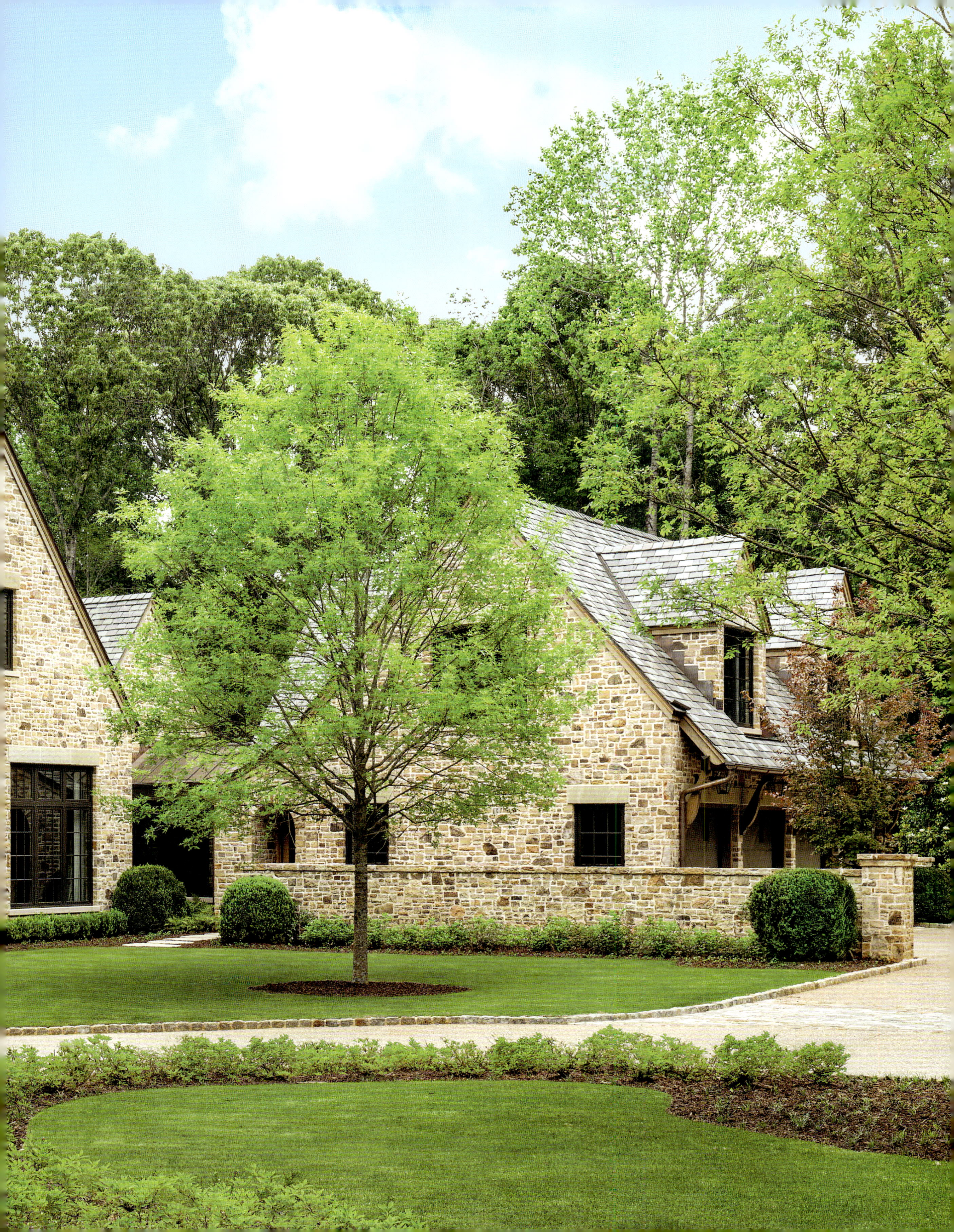

to their daughter, son-in-law, and grandkids, and then I'd design a new residence for them on the neighboring lot. Both households would have easy access to one another via a bridge to be built across the creek.

During our first tour of the recently acquired parcel, which covered a bit more than five acres and was heavily wooded, I noticed a low ridge meandering among the trees. It wasn't terribly wide, but given some grading work on one flank, I knew it would make a fine building site that overlooks the shallow valley holding the creek as well as a second scenic dip on the opposite side. In my mind, I began to assemble a series of rooms strung along the spine of the ridge, with additional volumes attached at left and right—a layout that would be rooted organically in the underlying terrain and capitalize on the picturesque surroundings in all directions.

As a result, the house as it evolved is very much about linking indoor space with the world beyond. The experience starts as you follow a stately, serpentine driveway that now comes in from the road, weaving among stands of white and red oaks and ending in a loop. To your right, discreetly screened off behind a low stone wall, lies a service and parking court. A multicar garage is treated as a separate carriage house, joined to the main body of the home by a lower, single-story corridor. This breaking-up of masses is characteristic of the dwelling as a whole; although it has a large footprint in total, it doesn't feel overwhelming because you only see pieces of it at any one time. In front of you is a small corner loggia with two arches and a curved roof sweeping down above it—an understated entrance to the house that nonetheless gives a clear sense of arrival while pointing toward further destinations inside.

The owners came to me with inspiration images drawn from English country houses and photos of spare, textured interiors by Axel Vervoordt and Vincent Van Duysen. The influence of the two Belgian minimalists is

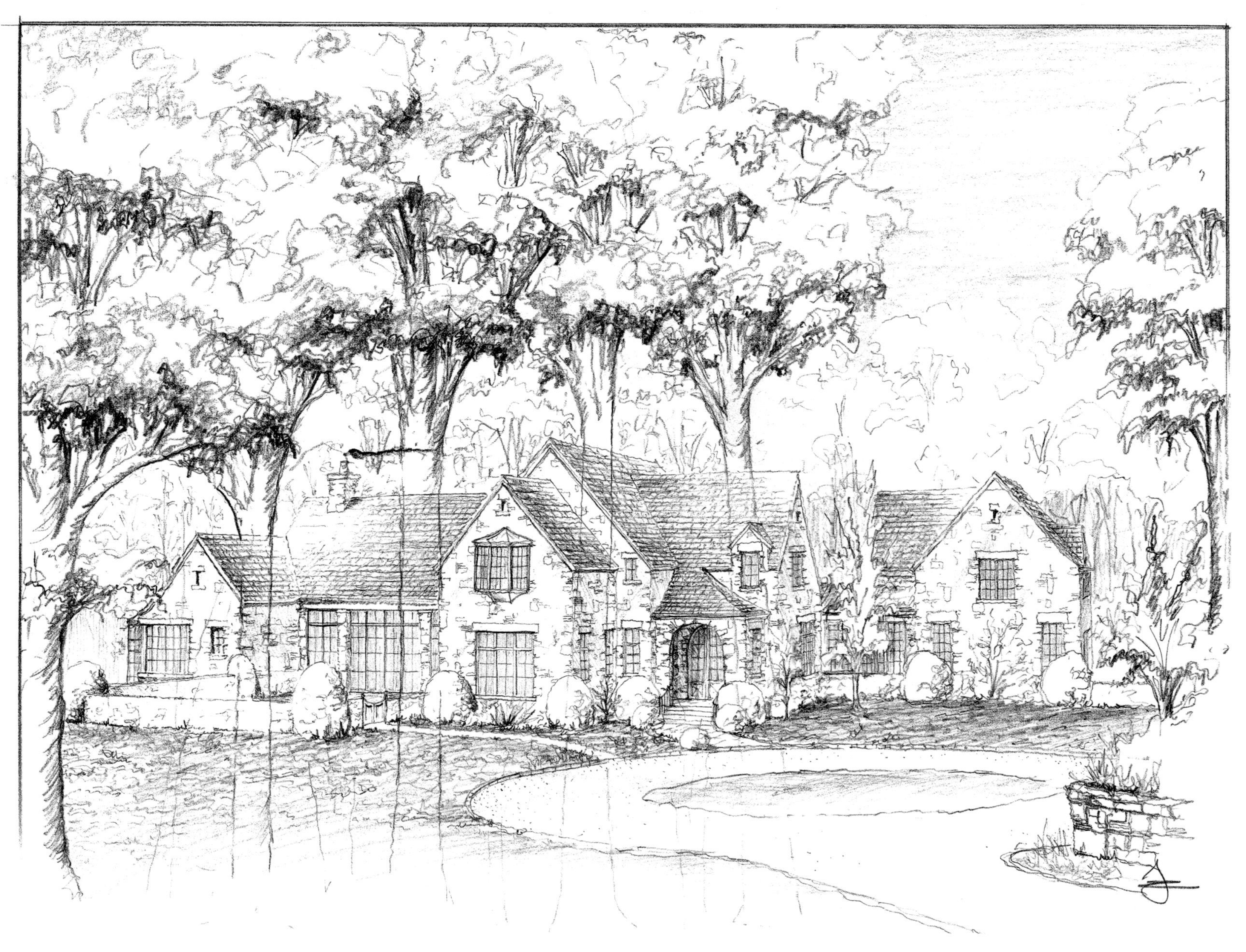

especially noticeable in the rough-hewn beams, wide-plank oak floors, and creamy plasterwork of the home's great room and main stair. Other elements of the structure are more reminiscent of M. H. Baillie Scott and the architecture of the Arts and Crafts movement—stacked-stone walls climbing up to the peaks of tall gables, narrow overhangs at the edges of the roof, and monolithic lintels and sills—but simplified. We employed a limited palette of materials—primarily fieldstone, slate, glass, and wood—to execute a similarly limited vocabulary of basic forms: rhythmically repeating gables, round arches, and an occasional swoop added to a roofline. Steel

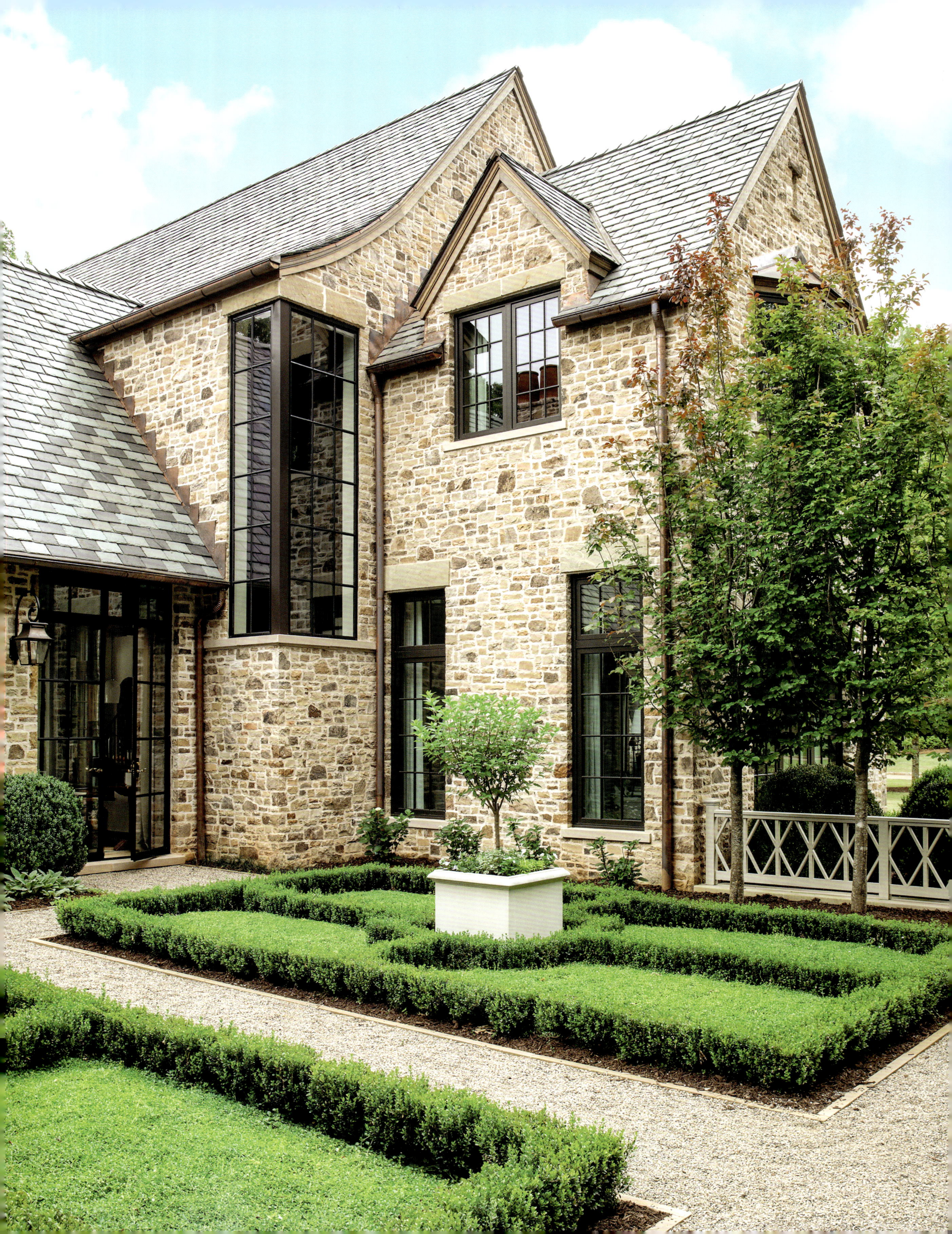

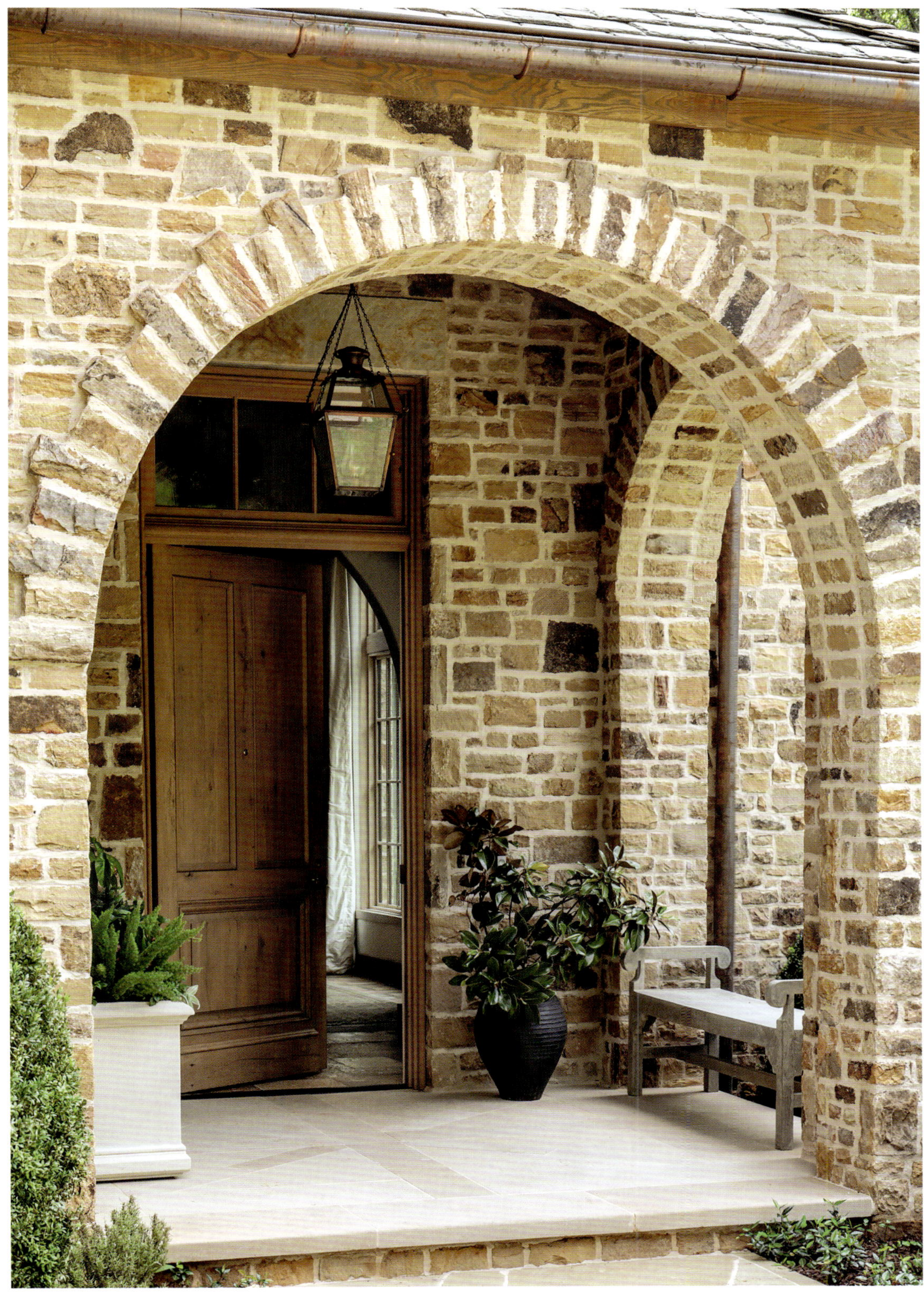

OPPOSITE: I enjoy creating homes that thoughtfully embrace—and enhance—beautiful gardens and outdoor living spaces. In this case, guest bedrooms and the great room surround a front garden that is enclosed by a stand of maple trees. The tall corner window illuminates the home's main staircase. ABOVE: The front door is protected from the elements by a cozy arched loggia.

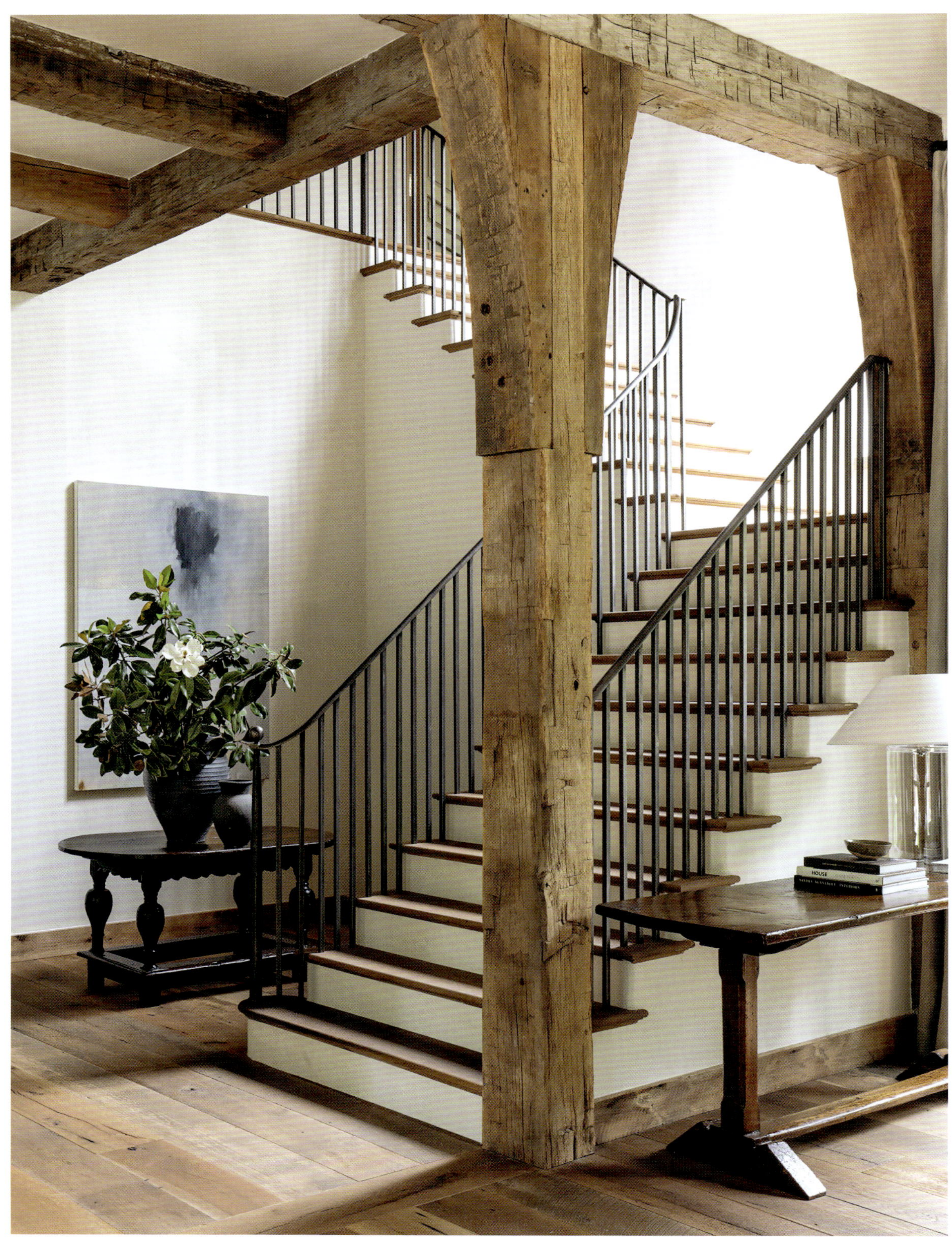

ABOVE: The home's main stairway adjoins the great room and features an elegantly slender hammered-iron railing that contrasts with the solidity of other architectural elements around it. OPPOSITE: The great room features hand-hewn reclaimed timbers that form a dynamic geometric design. Elongated corbels atop timber columns echo the curved rooflines of the exterior. In the background, arched openings lead to the front foyer and dining room.

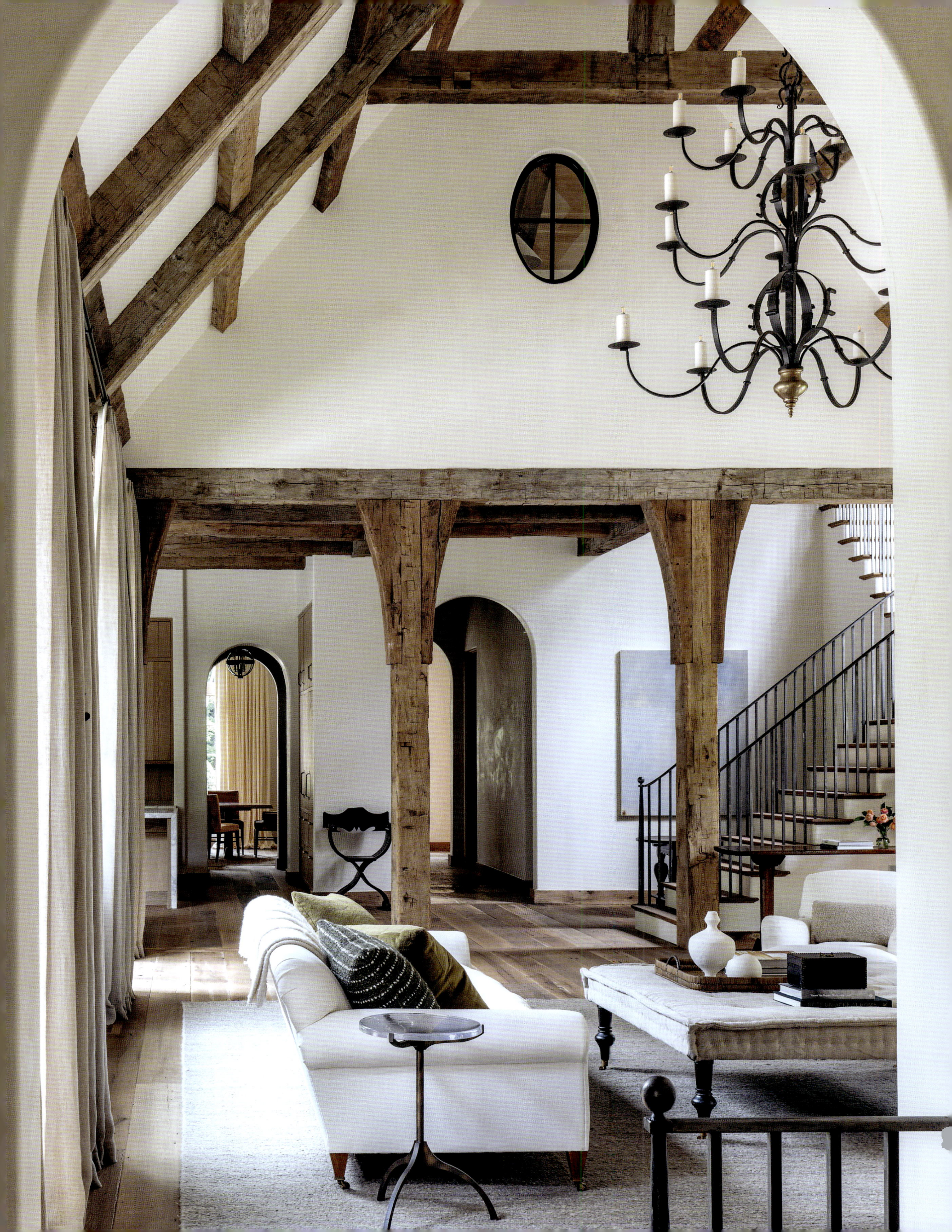

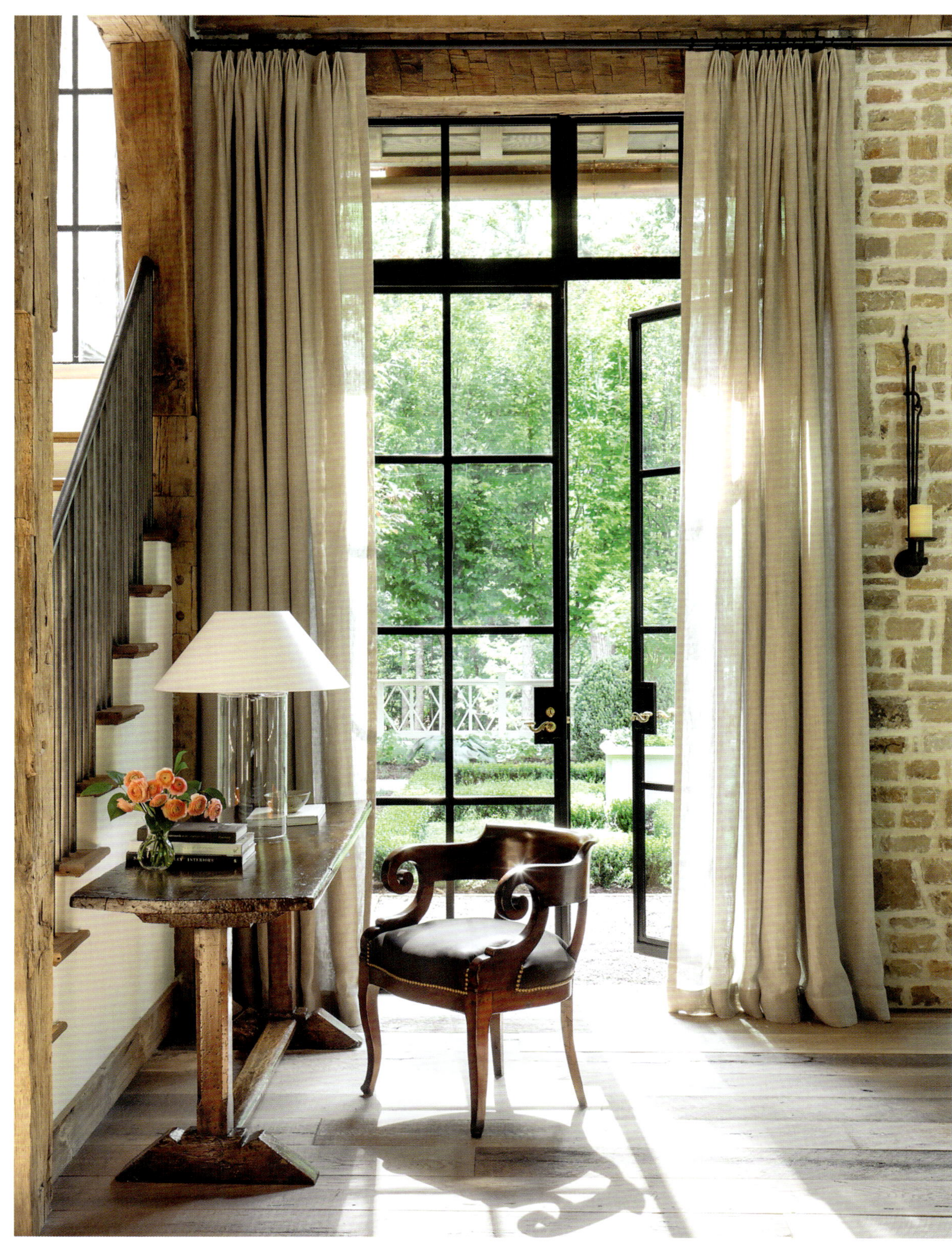

ABOVE: An antique trestle table in one corner can be used as a desk for correspondence. The door leads out to the hidden front pocket garden. OPPOSITE: The smooth plaster walls and fireplace lighten the room and balance the visual weight of the rough-hewn beams. Interior designer Barbara Westbrook masterfully embraced the architectural style by seamlessly integrating fabrics, furnishings, and decorative lighting into the aesthetic.

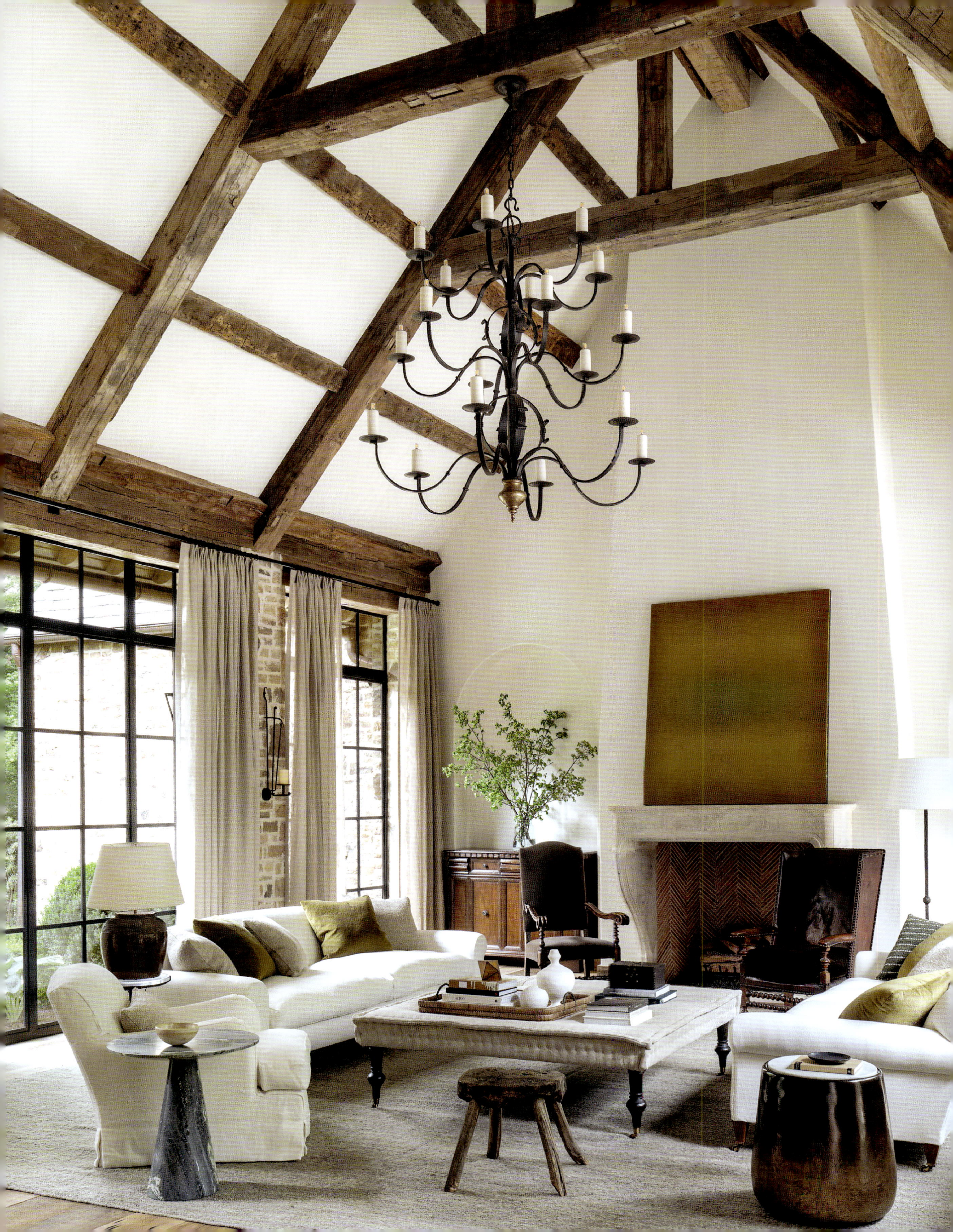

windows marry beautifully with the stone, their transparency making them nearly disappear, particularly when you're gazing out from the primary spaces of the house.

And gazing out is a signature experience here. Banks of windows on either side of the centrally located great room provide an incredible amount of daylight along with unobstructed views of a private parterre garden in the front and, in the rear, an outdoor living-dining terrace adjoining an infinity pool. A gabled four-season room timber-framed in oak projects from the back of the house; in good weather, its window walls can open wide, while a monumental fieldstone fireplace supplies warmth at other times of the year. The husband's almost completely glass-enclosed office, which lets him track the grandchildren's backyard activities as he works, is a smaller companion, sitting beneath a hipped copper roof. The owners' main-level bedroom also boasts a large bay window that offers a prospect down the continuing axis of the ridge that the house sits on. The feeling is one of being nestled within the treetops.

Grand yet low-key, intimately connected to its environment (as well as to the younger folks' place next door), this home is designed to have an interior life that extends far outside its physical walls. An organic process of creation has led to a handsomely organic result.

OPPOSITE: The restraint and subtlety of the home's lines and details are evident in the dining room; the baseboards, for instance, are an extension of the wood floors, and the cove ceiling, clad in plaster, flows downward onto the walls with no visual interruption. FOLLOWING SPREAD: The kitchen's tranquil design features an understated waterfall island, a simple backsplash of the same marble, and butt-jointed panels for the cabinetry. Traditional hardware adds a touch of ornamentation.

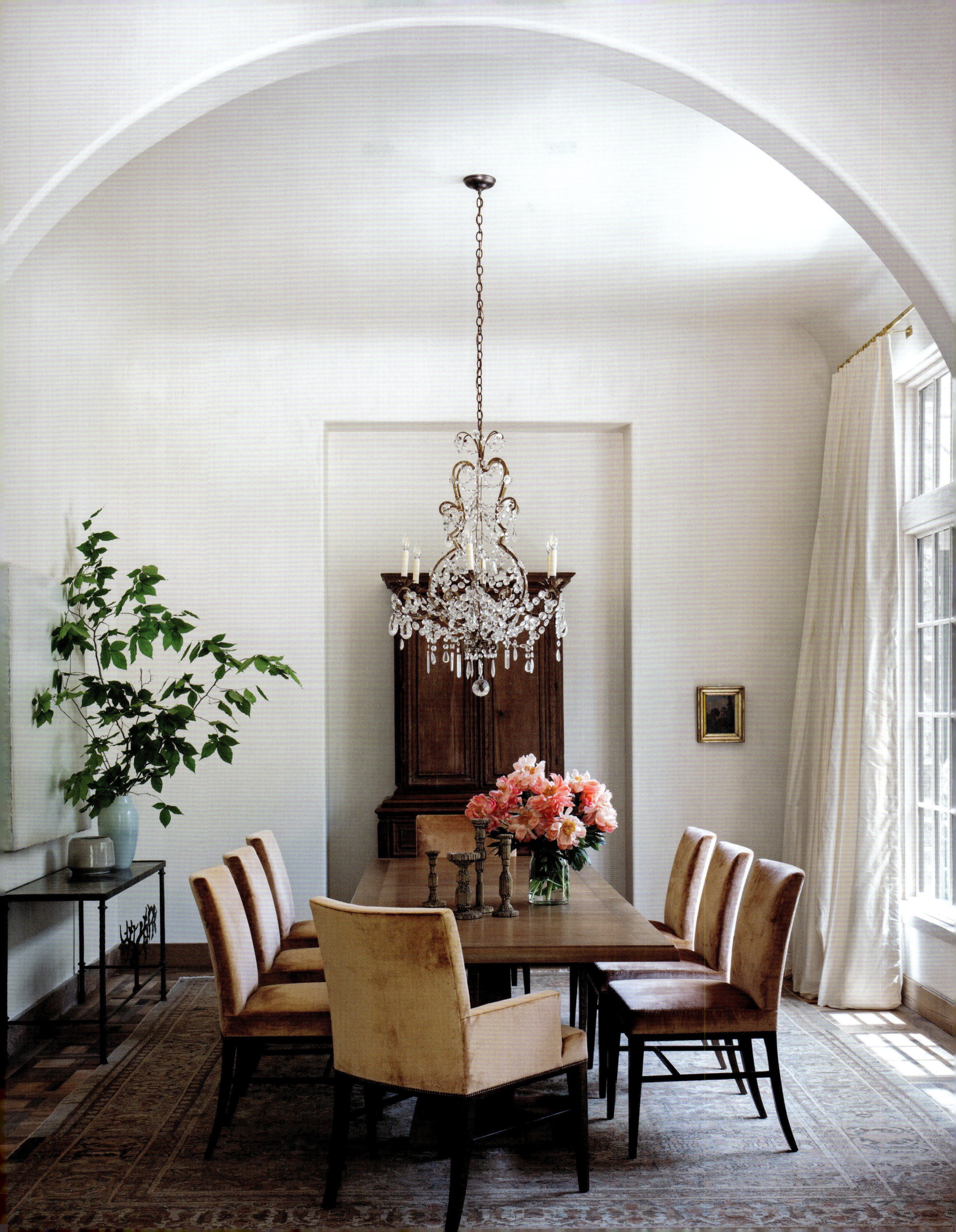

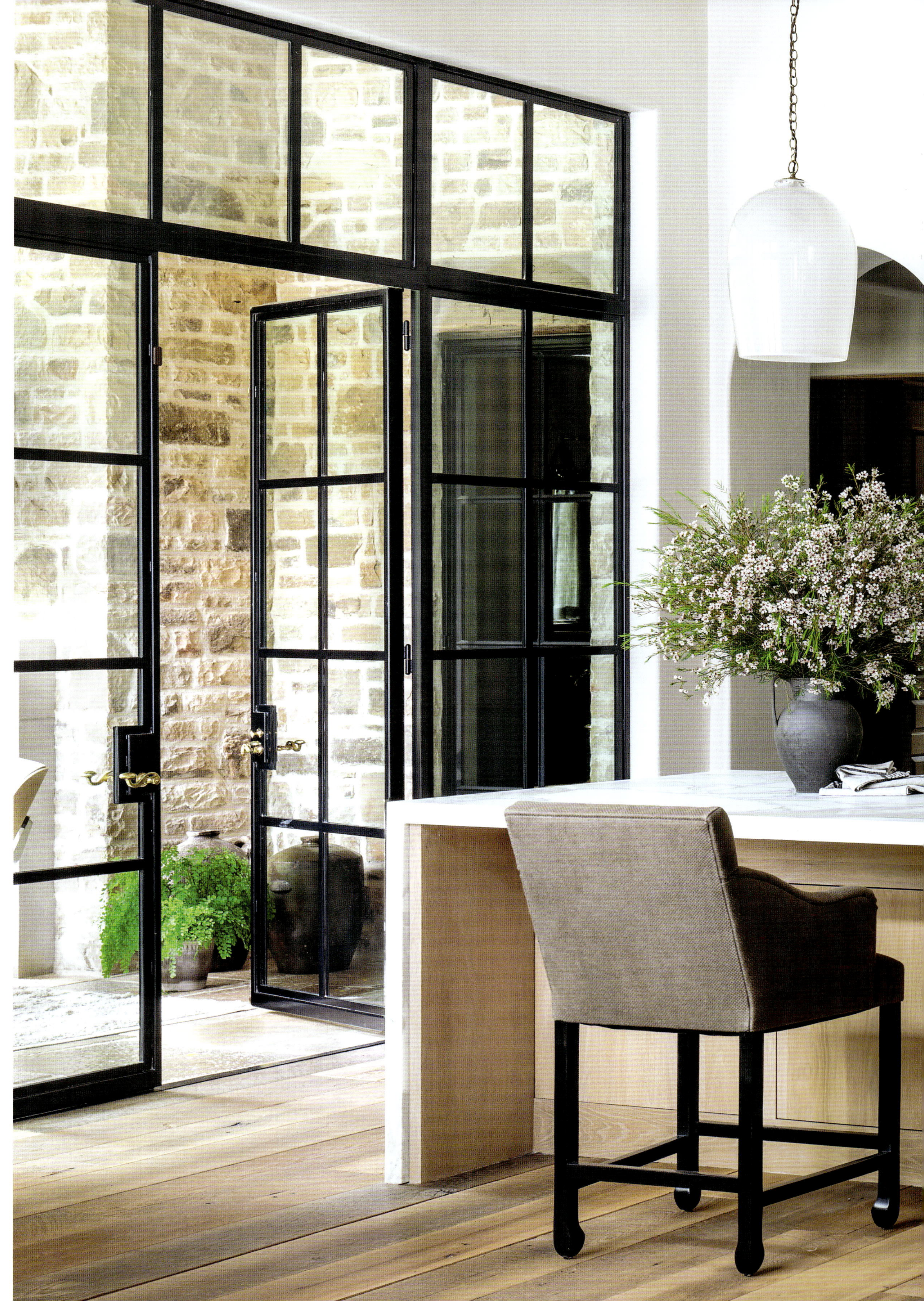

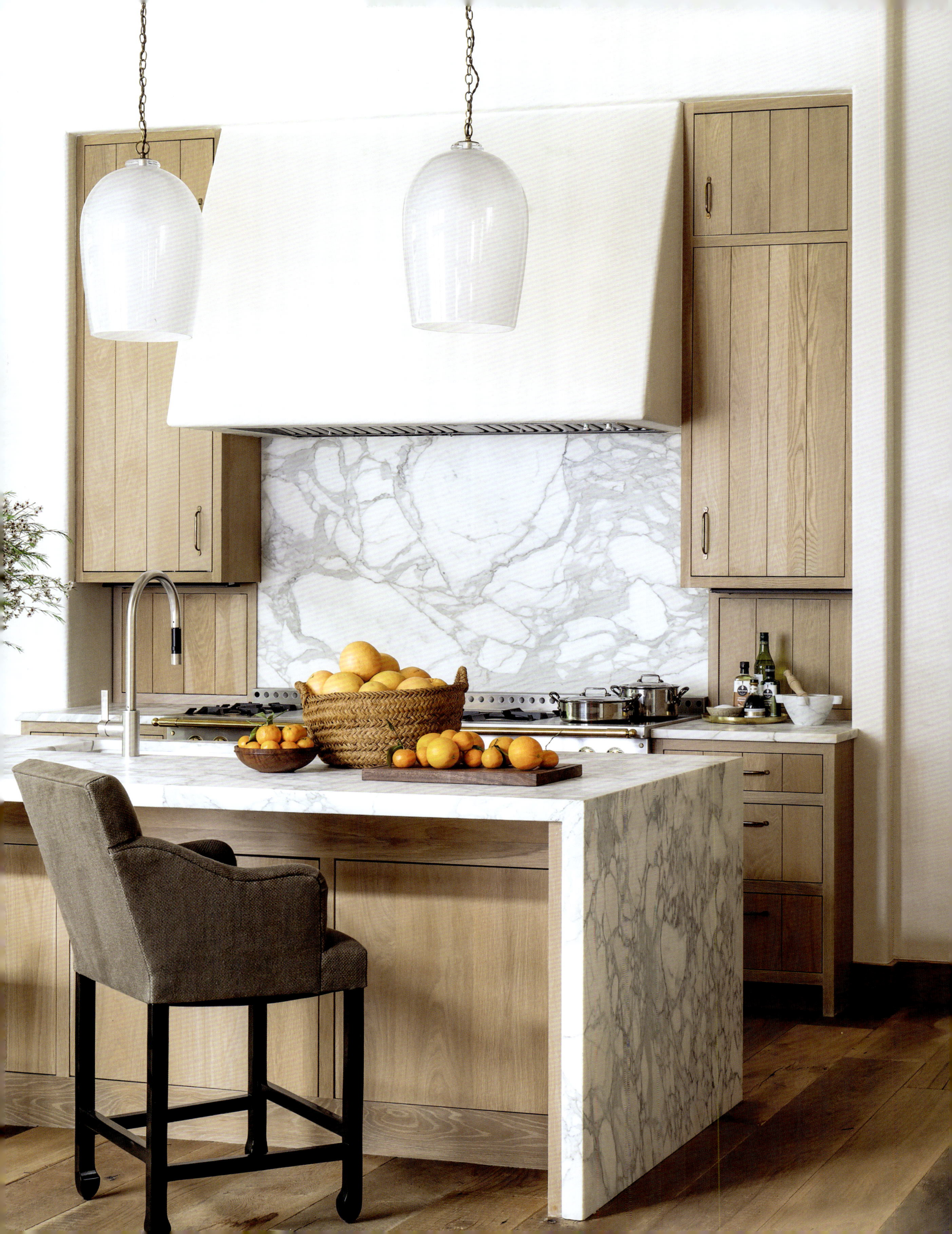

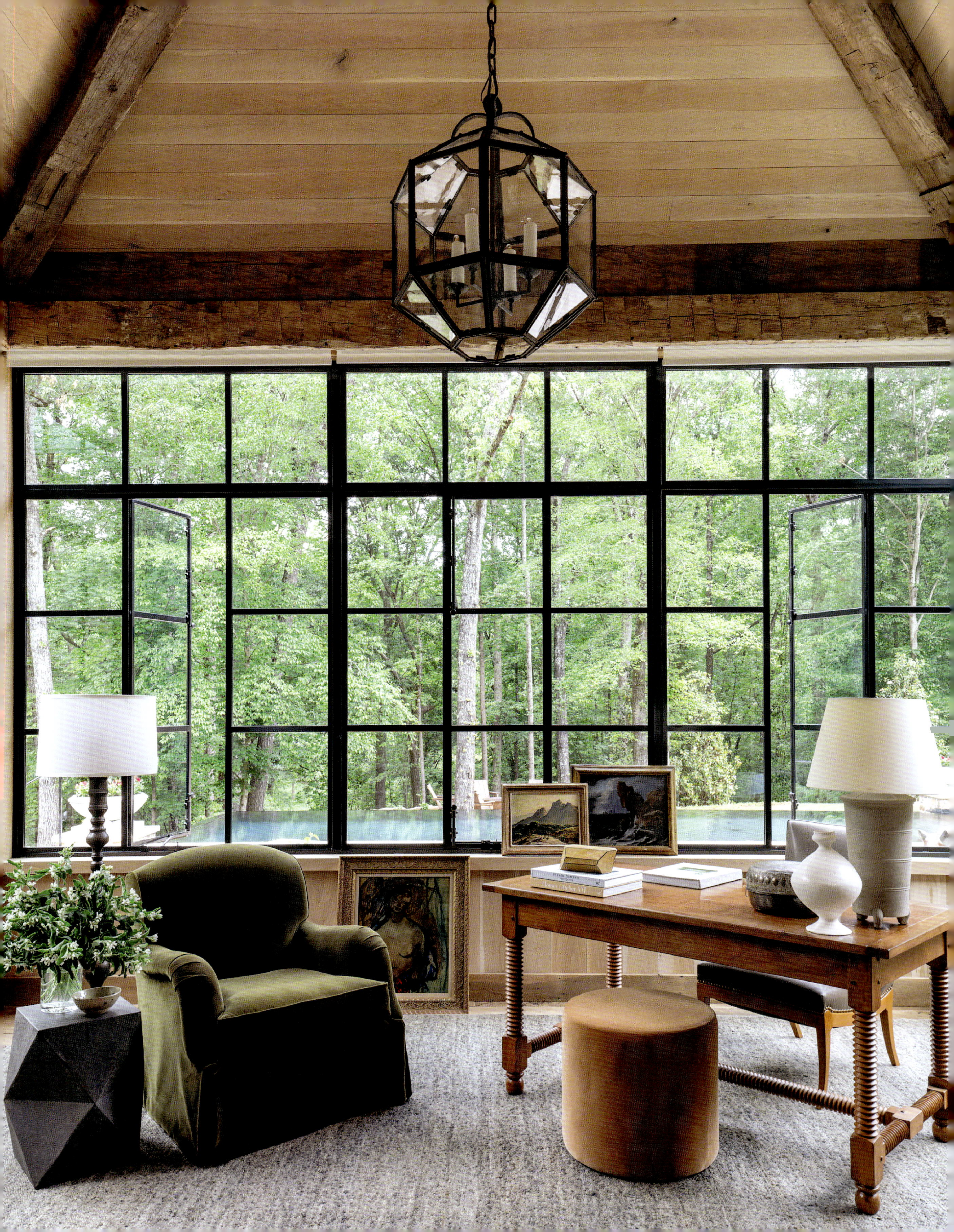
STEVEN GAMBREL
PERSPECTIVE
Houses | Atelier AM

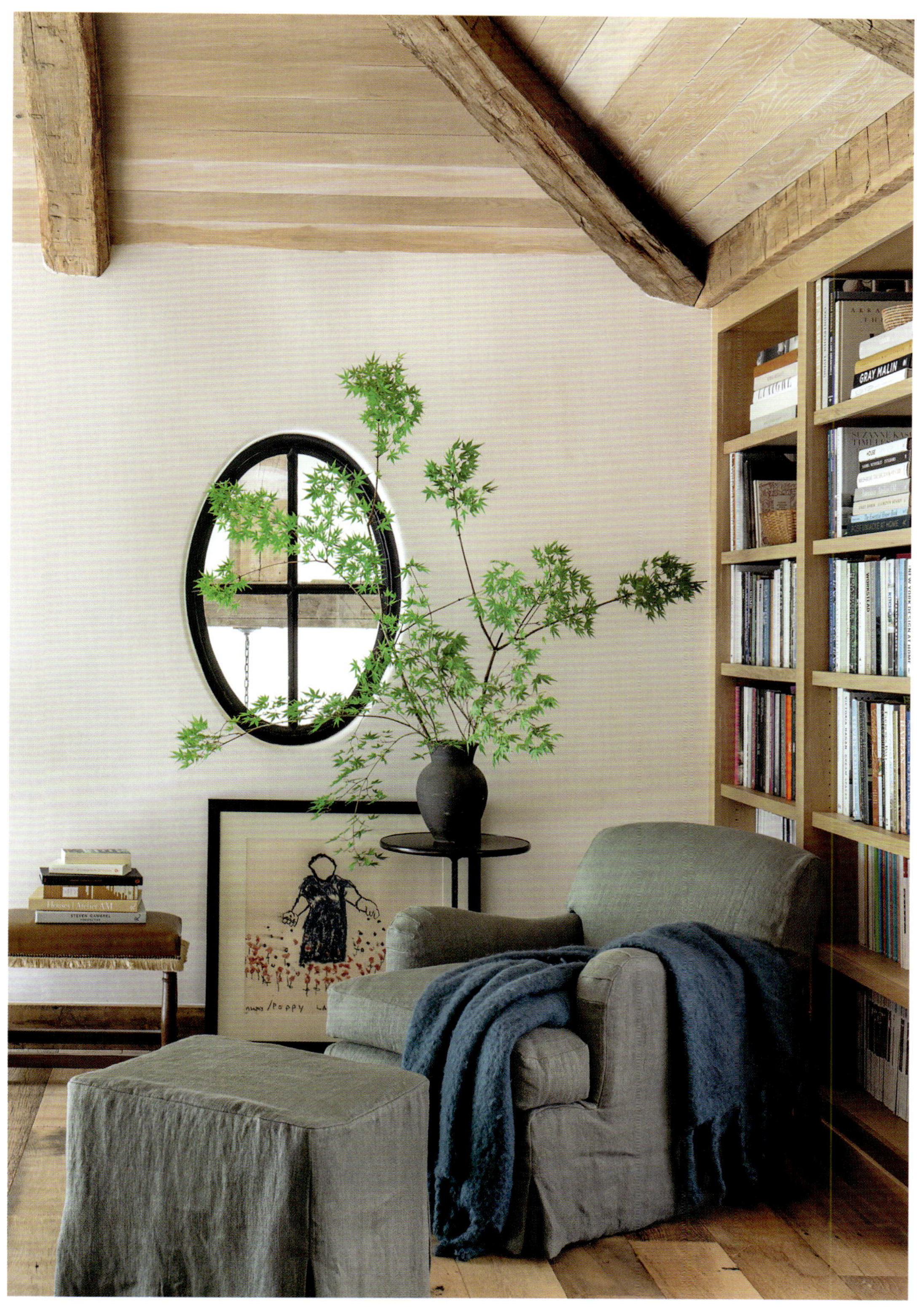

OPPOSITE: Connectivity with the outdoors was paramount for the husband's office. The oak-paneled ceiling and glass-and-steel hanging lantern give the room a more masculine ambience. ABOVE: The second-floor stair landing is a charming reading nook, illuminated by an oval window that overlooks the great room below.

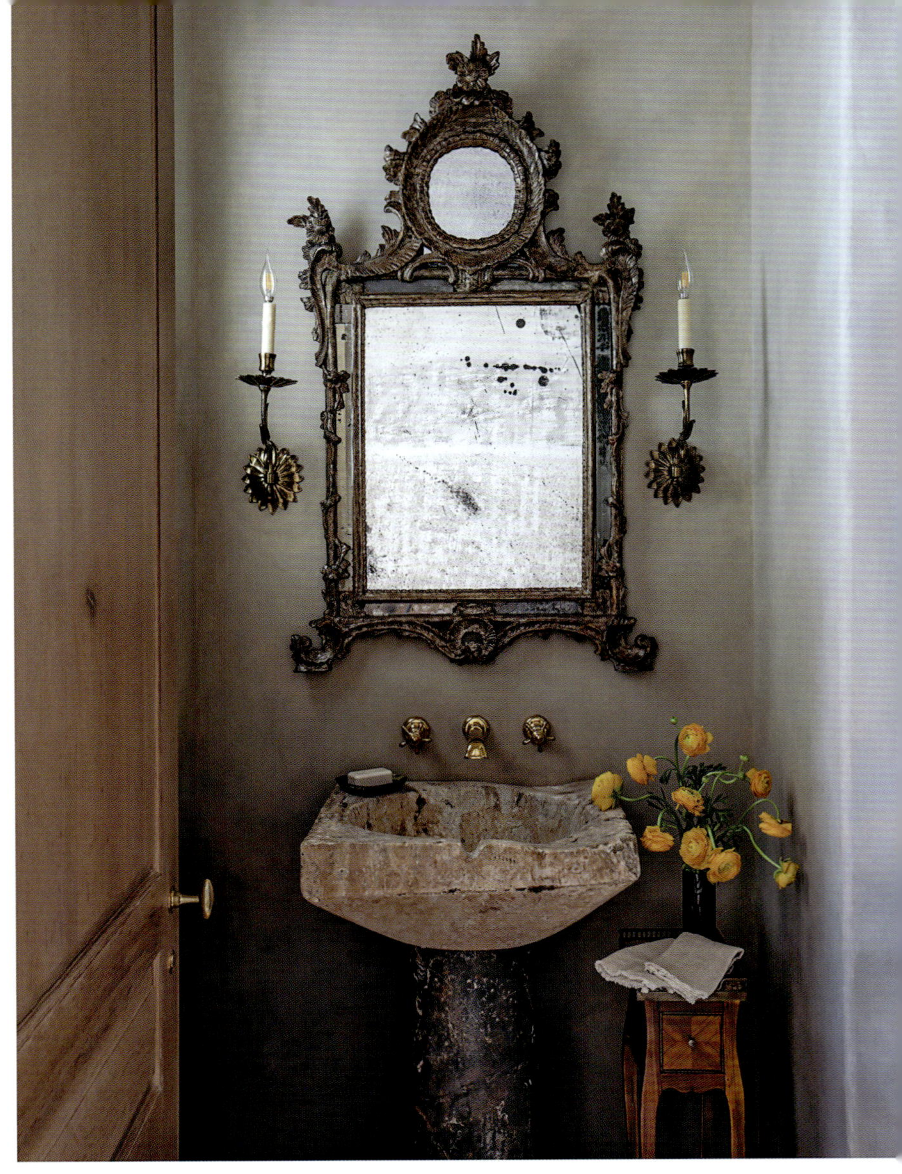

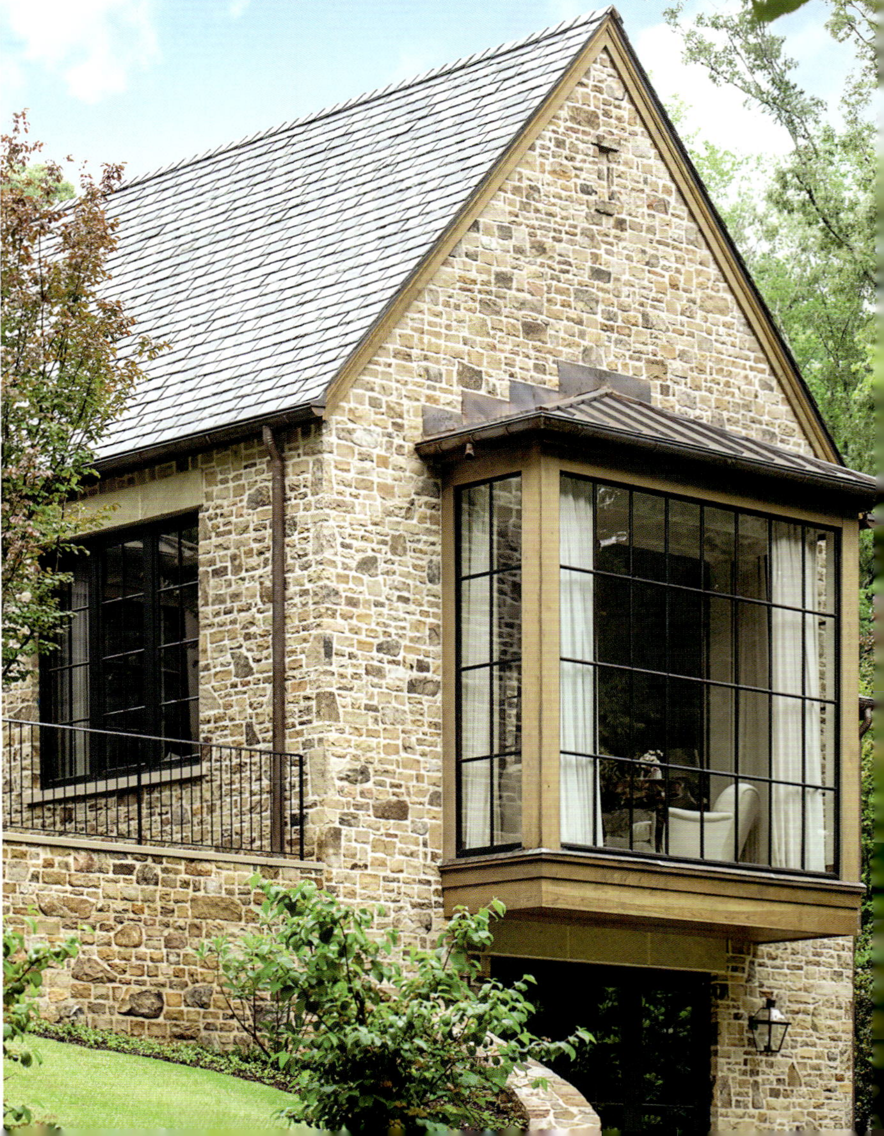

THIS SPREAD, CLOCKWISE FROM TOP LEFT: An antique sink and mirror add romance and texture to the powder room. Brass brackets make a glamorous contrast to marble shelves in the butler's pantry. A simple oak sill underlines the stairway's corner window. The guest bath vanity illustrates the repeating union of marble and oak found throughout the home. Understated furnishings in the principal bedroom don't compete with the view. A projecting glass bay connects the principal bedroom to the surrounding woodlands. FOLLOWING SPREAD: Inside, the principal bedroom has the feel of a sumptuously appointed tree house.

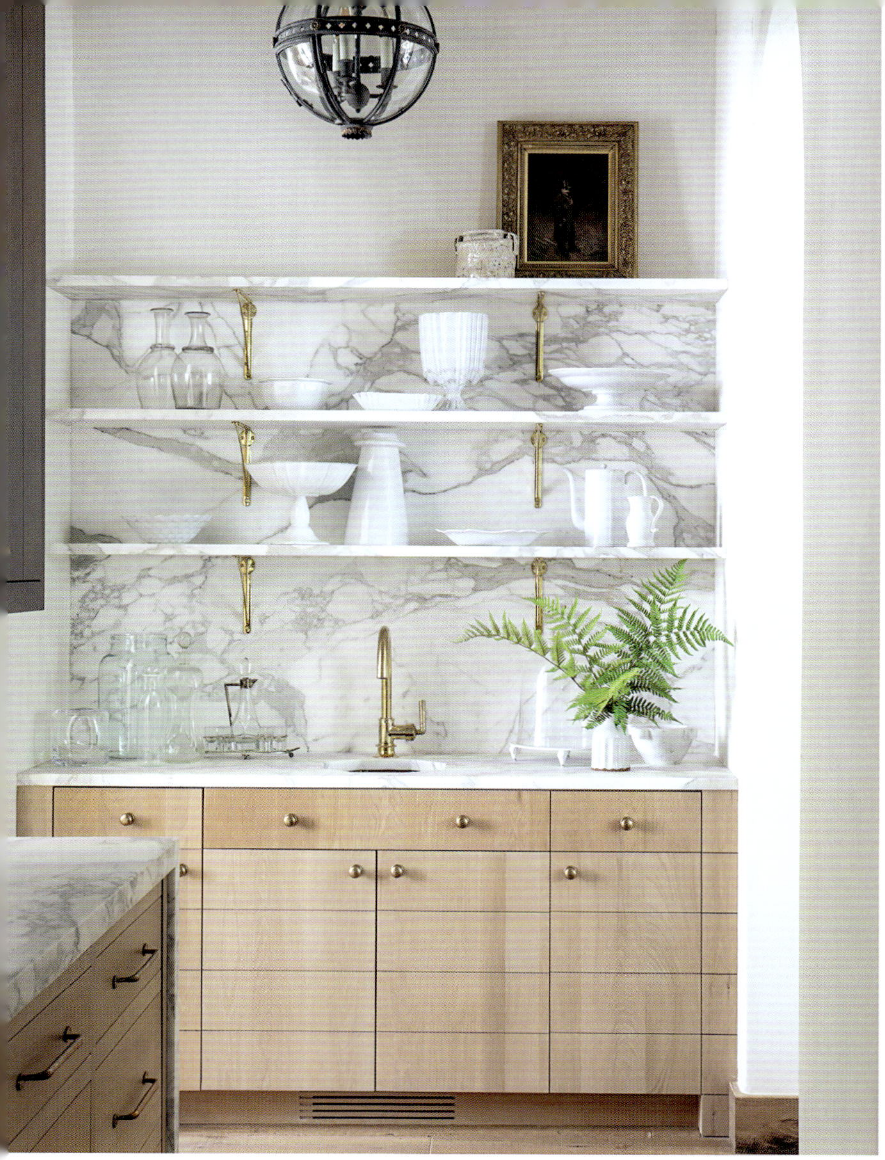

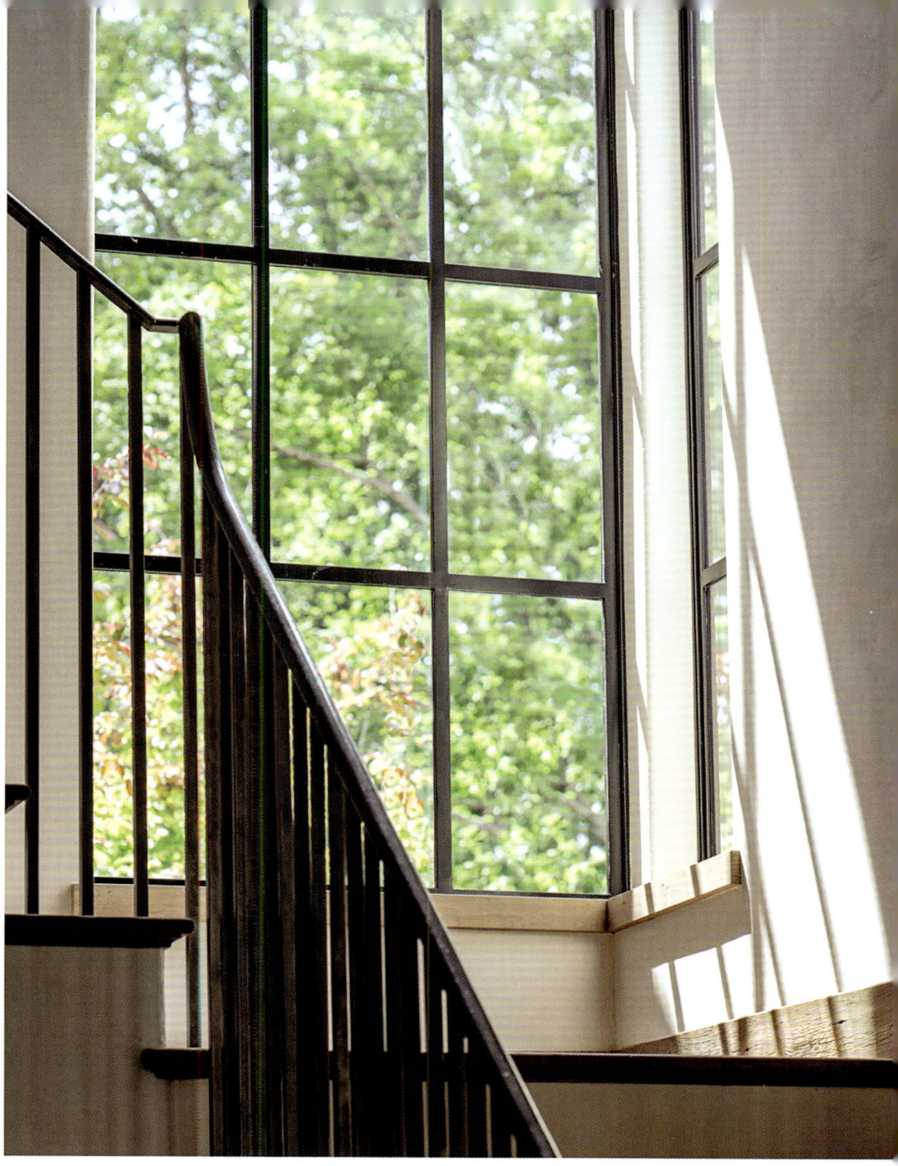

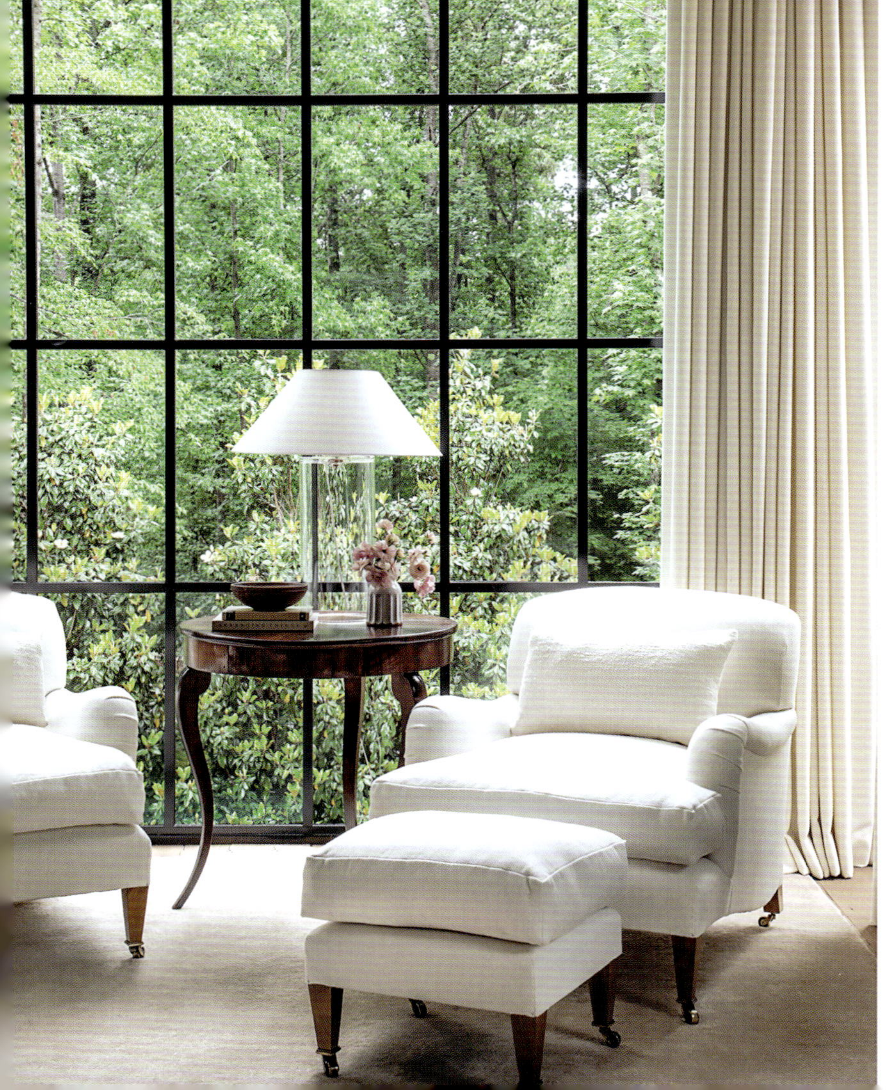

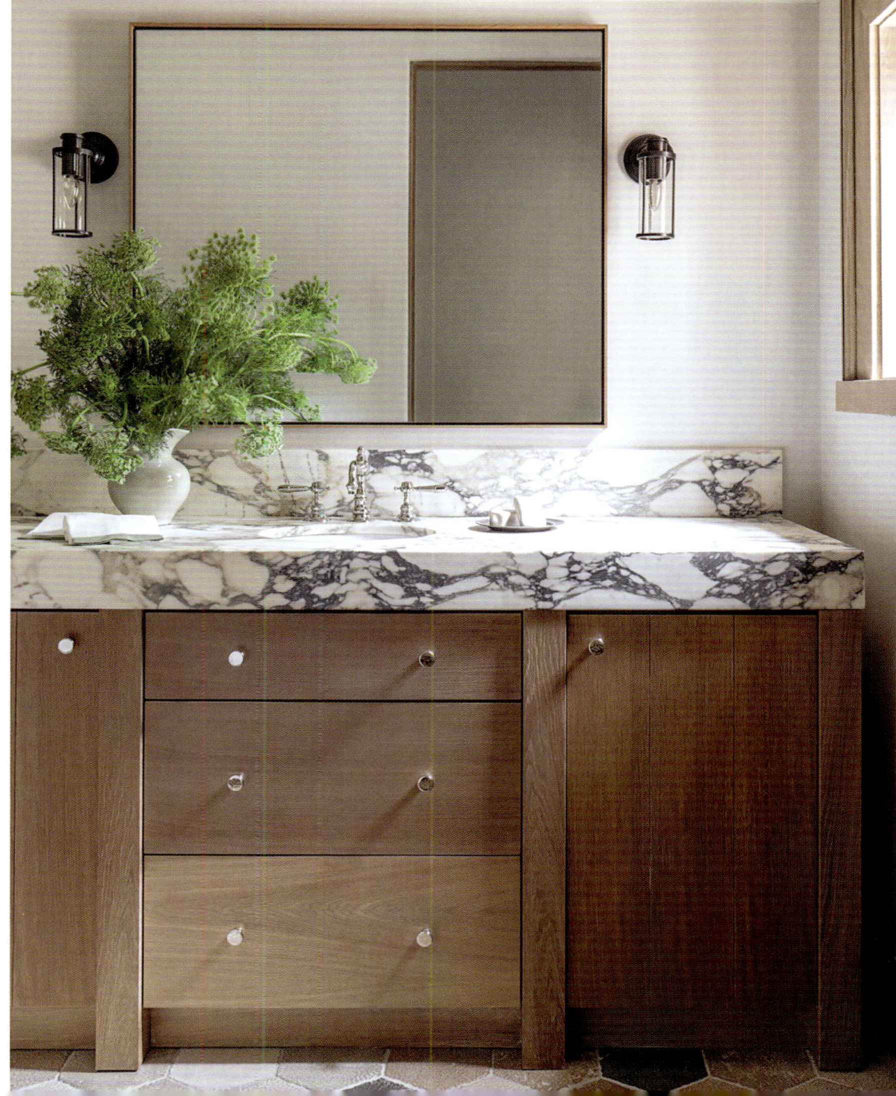

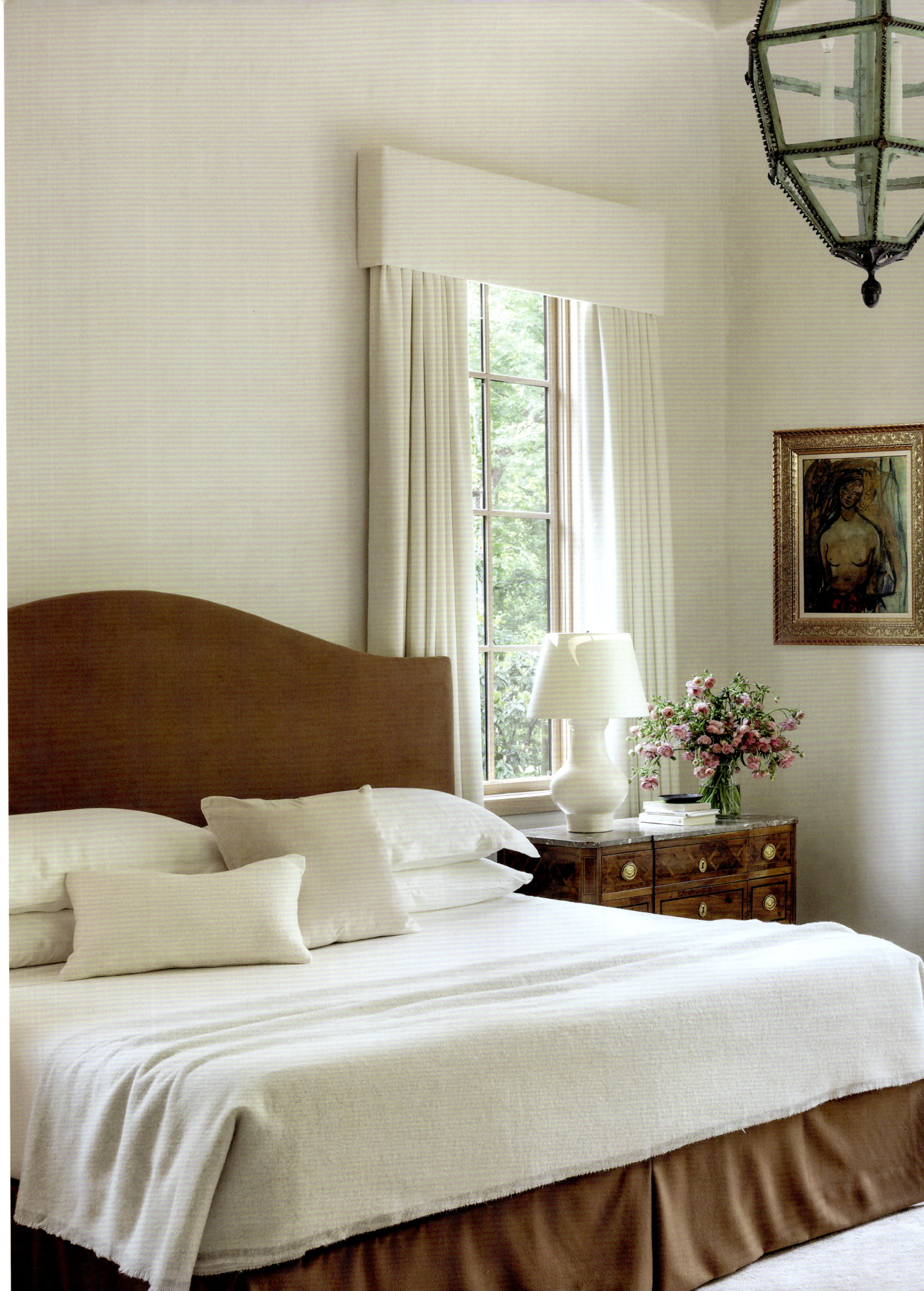

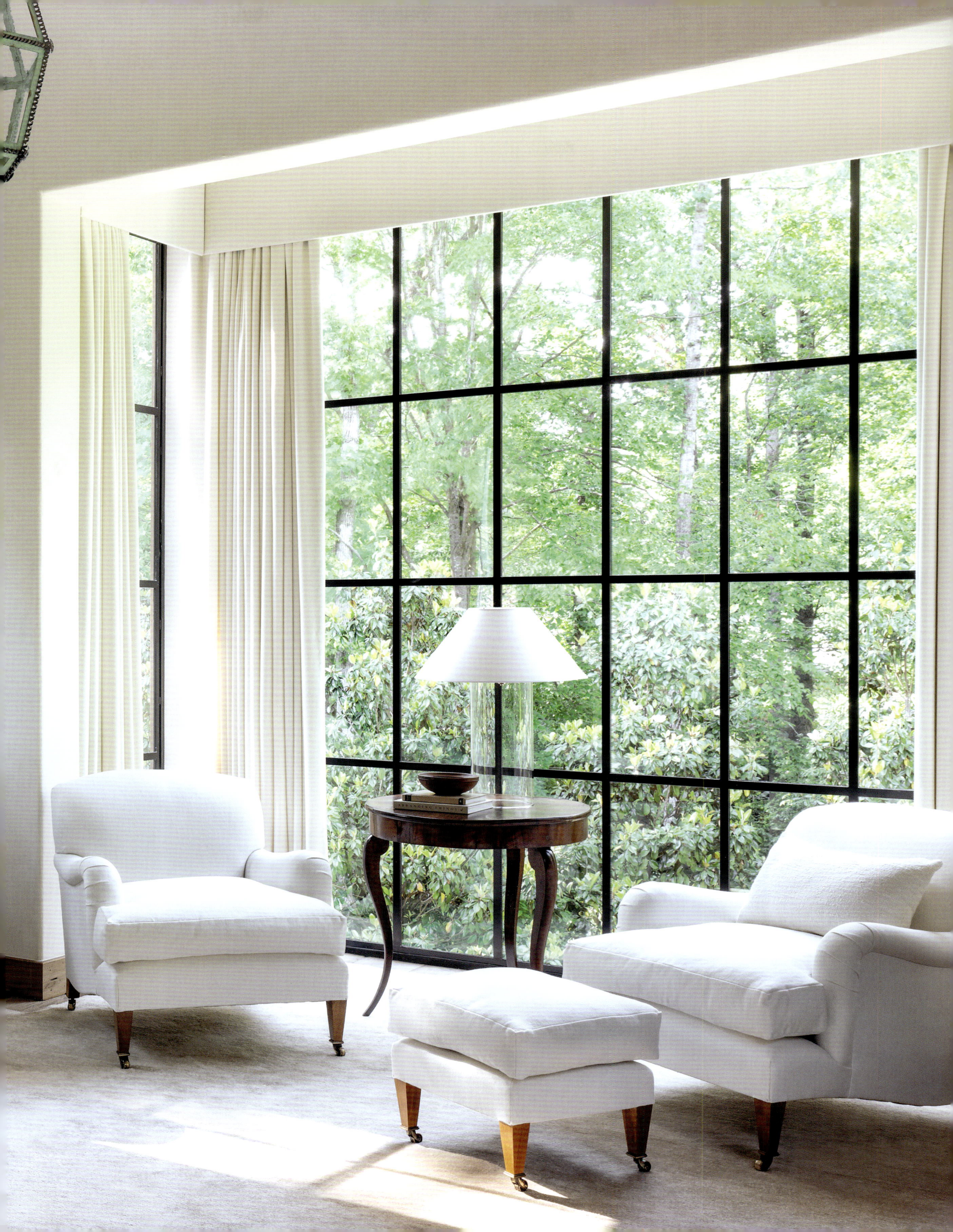
ARRANGING THINGS

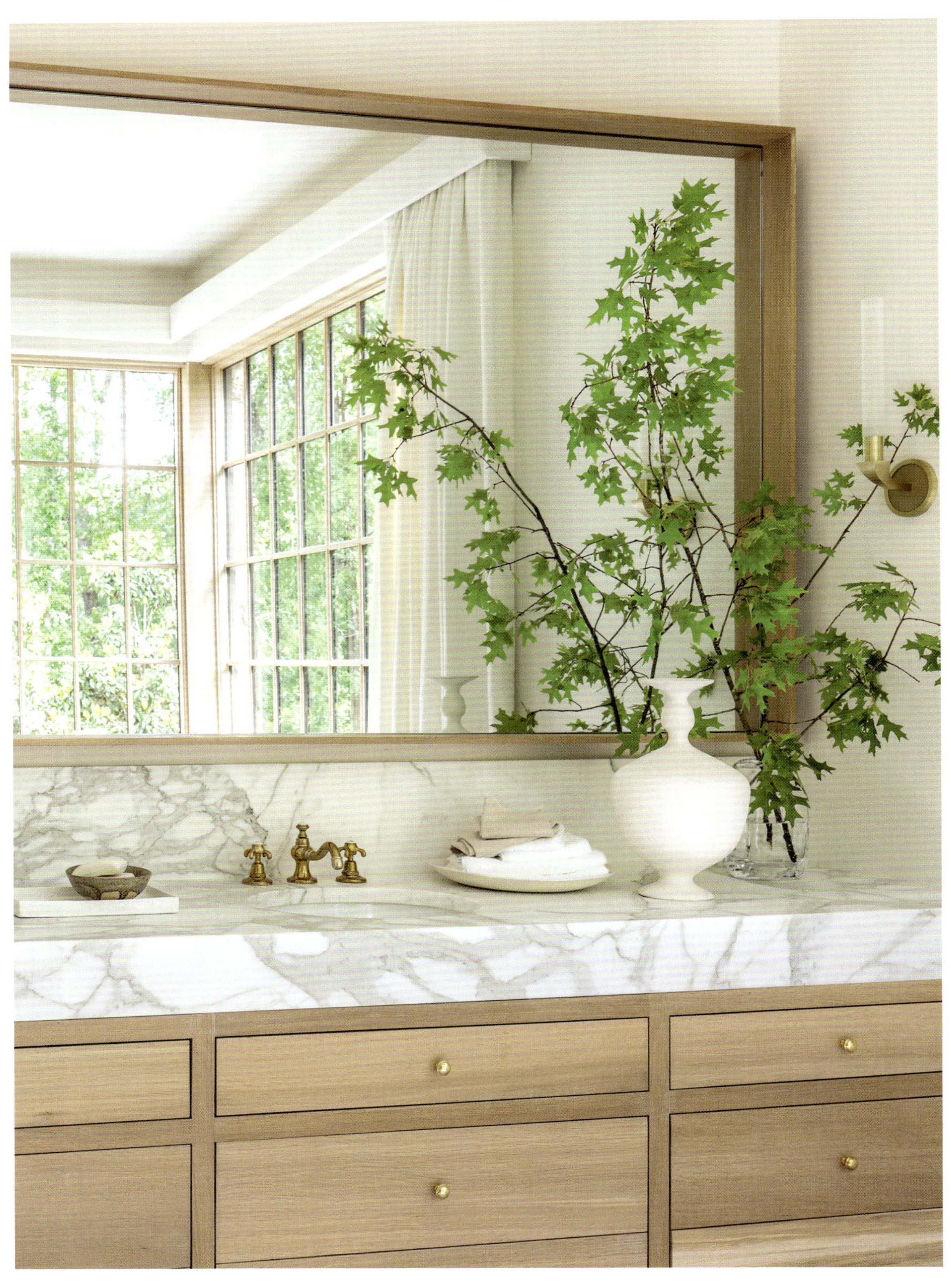

ABOVE: The clean lines of the principal bath's oak and marble vanity are punctuated by simple brass hardware. OPPOSITE: Sitting atop a matte-finish marble tile floor, the glossy soaking tub offers another relaxing prospect of trees and sky.

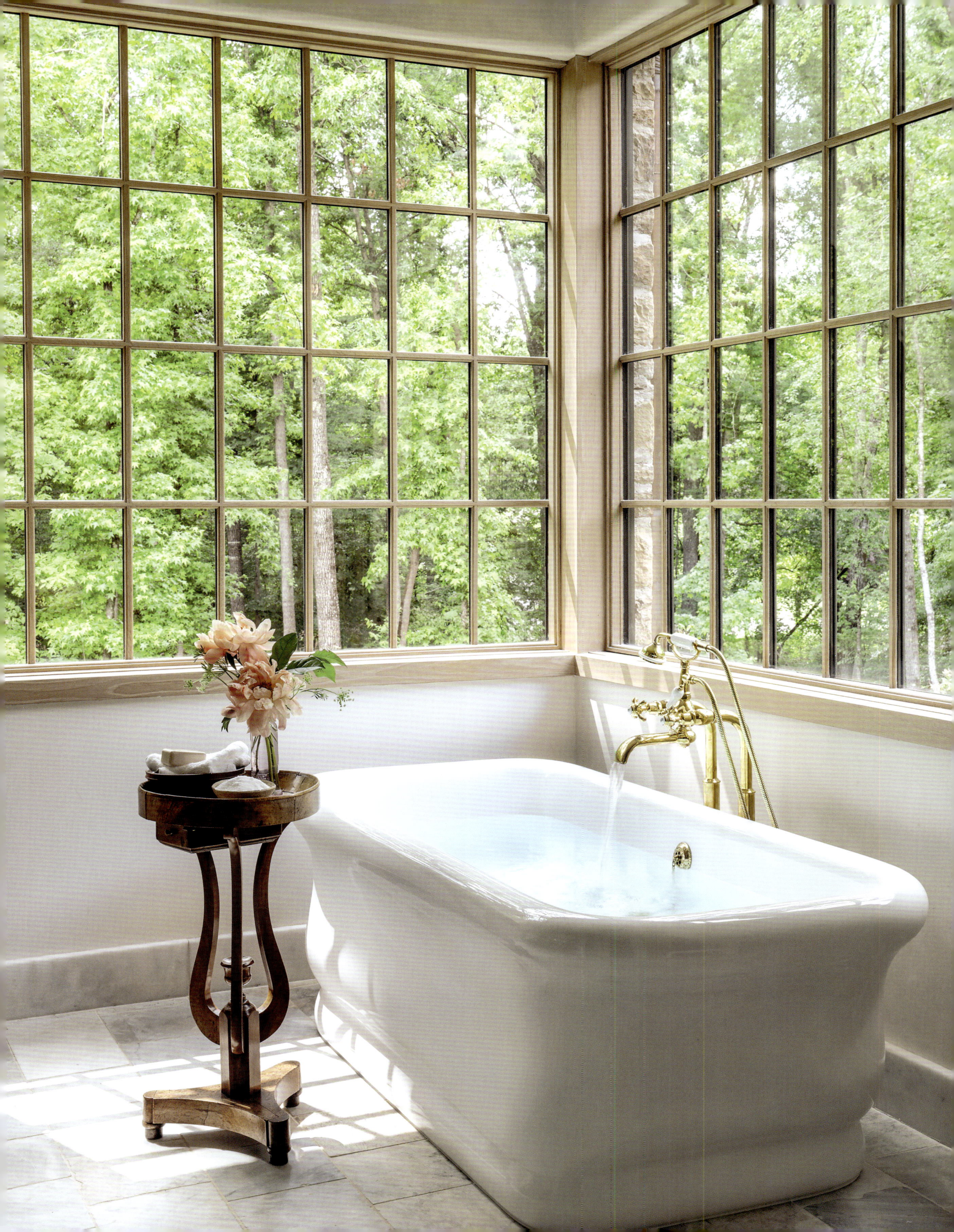

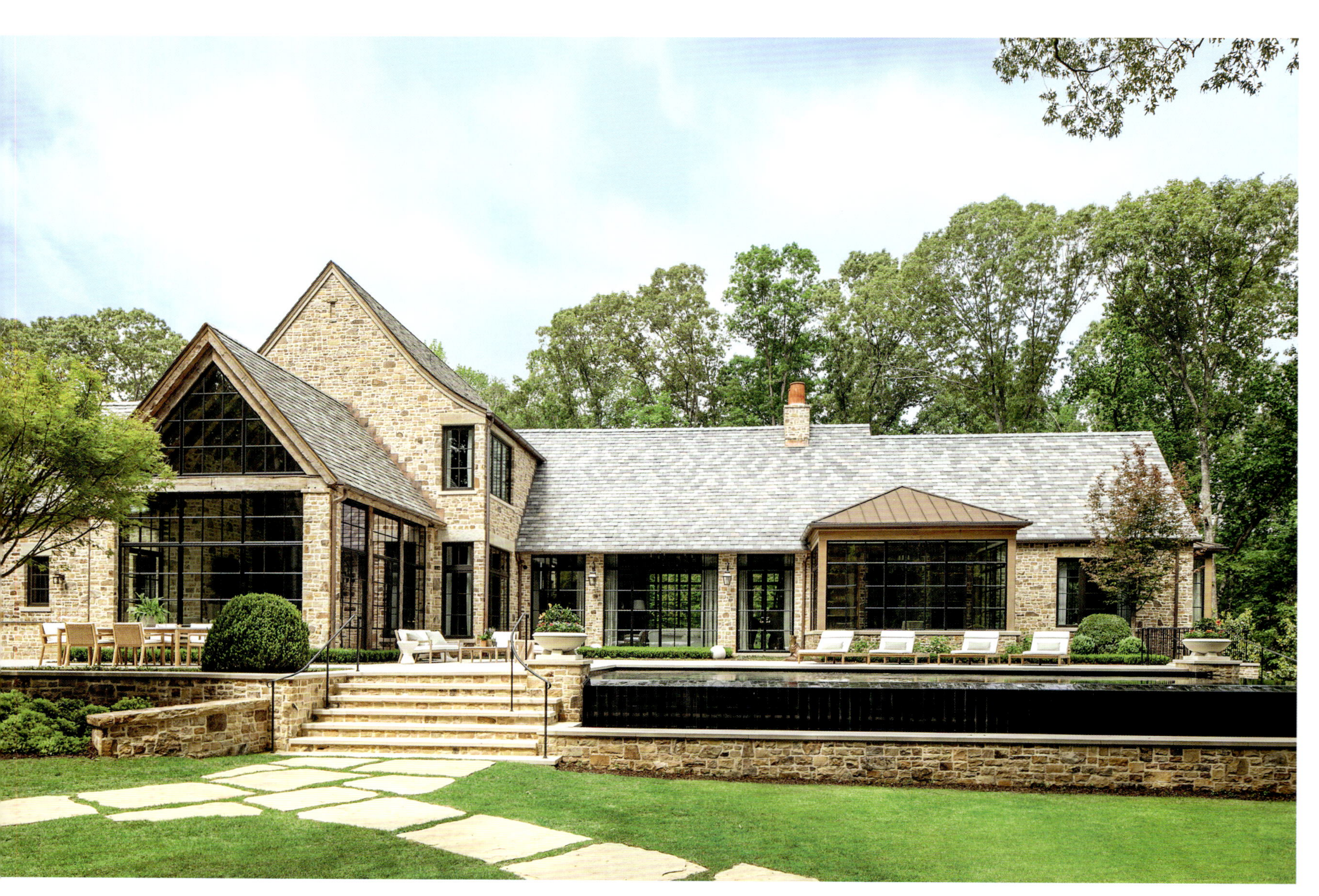

ABOVE: The pool terrace serves as an inviting outdoor living space, visible from many of the main rooms indoors. The pool's infinity edge extends along two sides, creating the illusion that its water merges seamlessly into the oak forest beyond. OPPOSITE: A smaller dining terrace outside the four-season room is adjacent to the pool area.

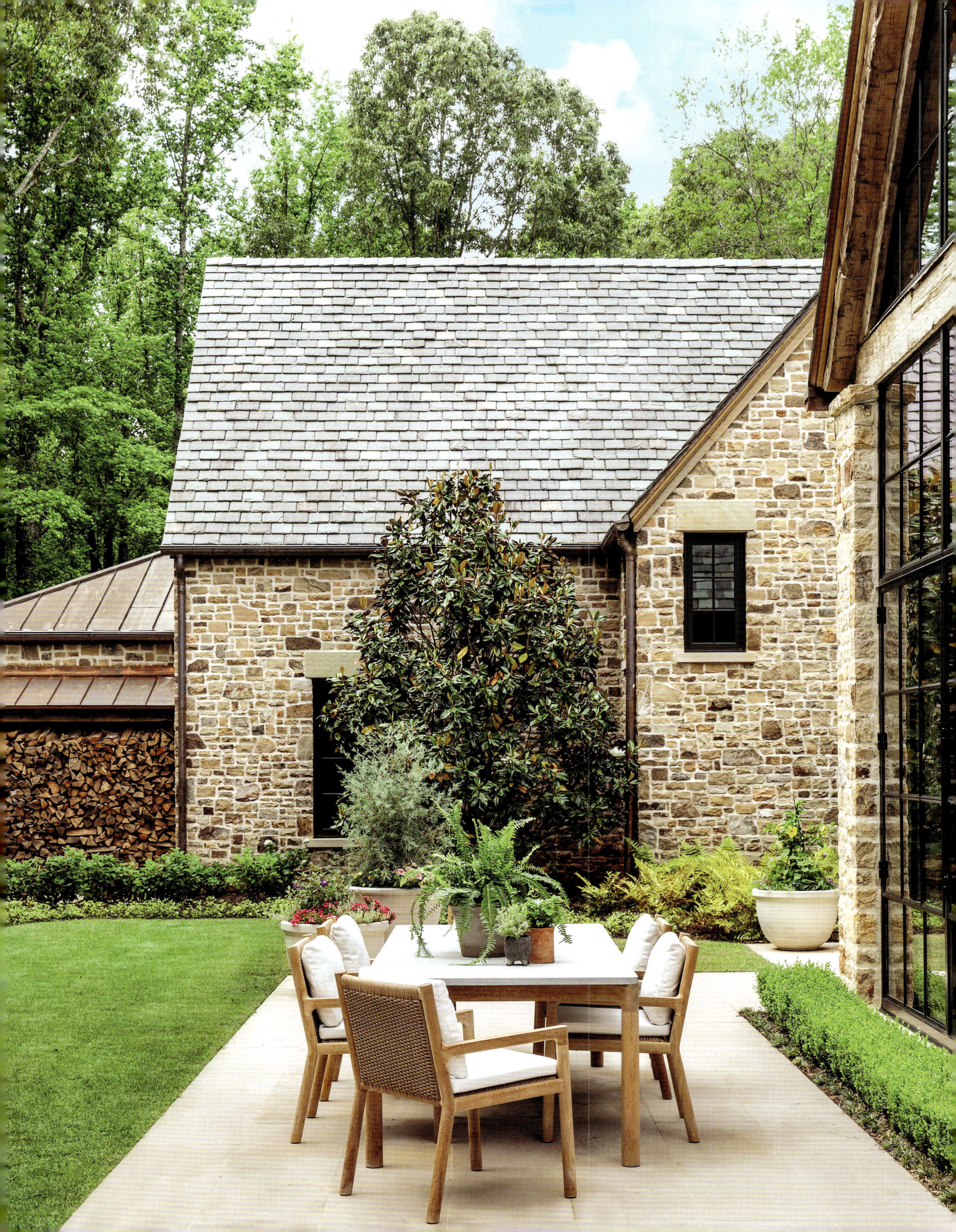

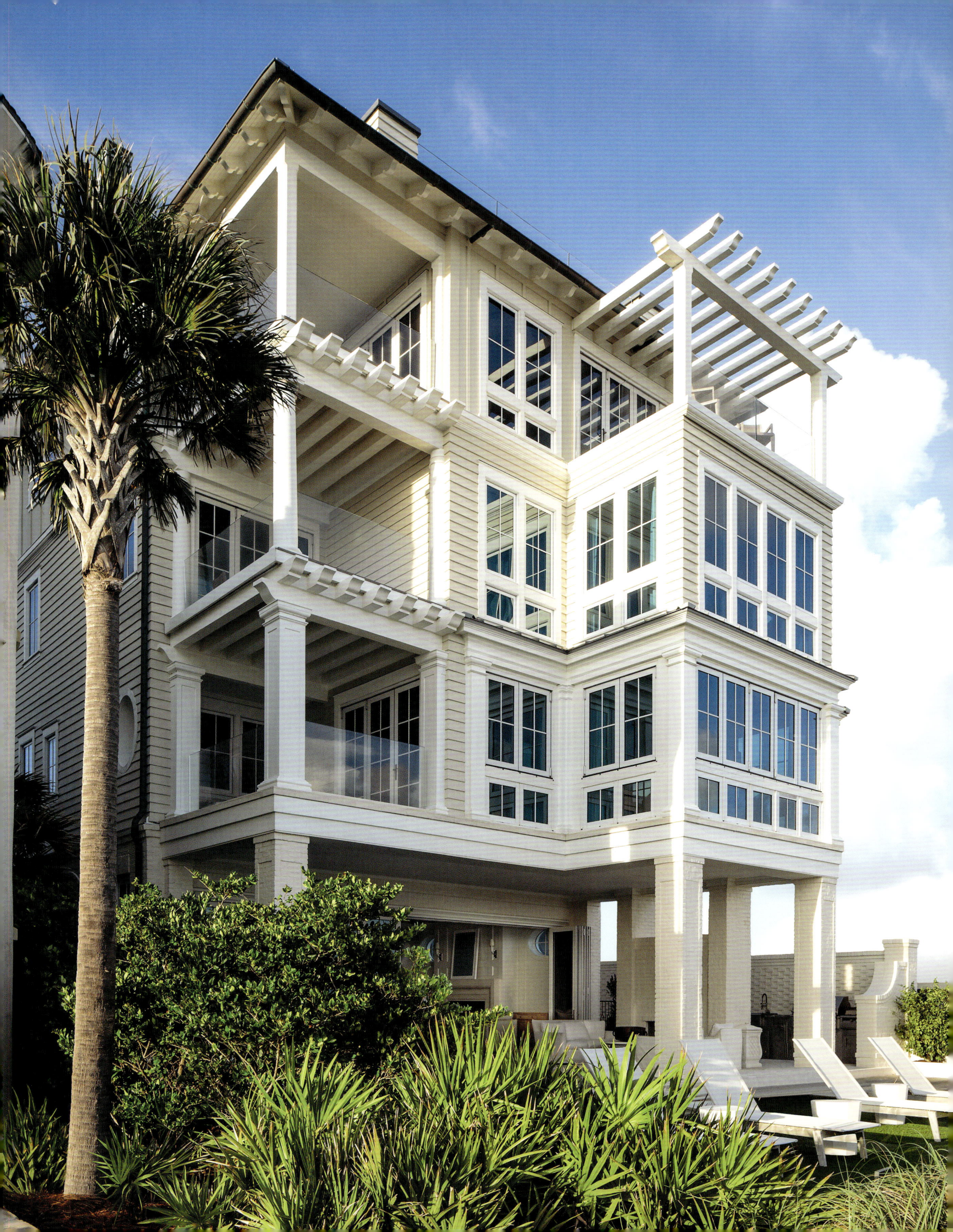

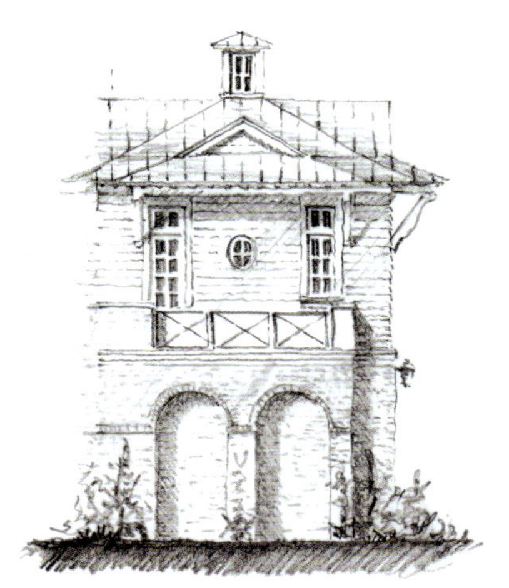

BEACHVIEW RETREAT

The feature that makes oceanfront lots in this part of Seaside, Florida, so fiercely sought-after only becomes apparent when you approach from the rear: a panoramic south-facing view of powder-sand beach, rolling breakers, and the emerald–turquoise–deep blue waters of the Gulf of Mexico. In most other respects, the properties present a special challenge for an architect because of their layout. They're long from front to back but narrow in width, with houses crowded close on each side. What would traditionally be the public face of a residence nearly butts up against County Highway 30A (from which the whole area derives its commonly used nickname, "30A"), meaning that the "front yard" has to double, in an almost urban fashion, as driveway and parking accommodations. Creating a cohesive home design that responds to all of these conditions requires serious thought and care.

OPPOSITE: The waterfront side of the house is designed to establish the most direct visual link possible to the Gulf of Mexico. Three of the four floors feature bifold windows or doors, allowing large sections of the wall to open up.

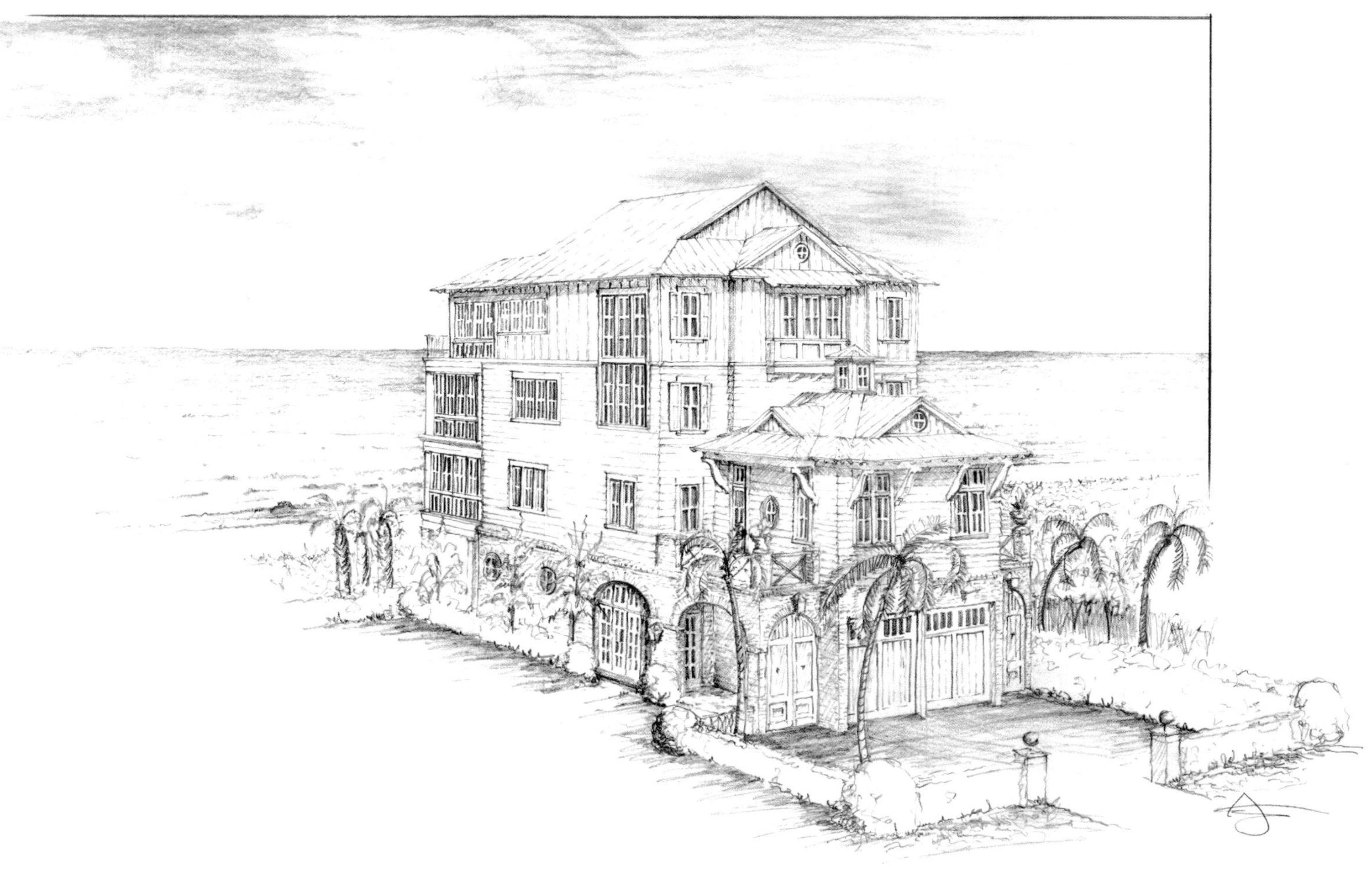

Maximizing a homeowner's experience within the constraints of the setting is key, and in the case of this house, it meant building up. The result is a four-story structure that presents a symmetrical, balanced facade to the street and then opens up behind to take in every bit of sunlight, ocean breeze, and spectacular coastal scenery it can.

Northern Florida's residential vernacular, which Seaside's founders drew on when they planned the community in the 1980s, has roots in what architectural historians call the Florida Cracker house of the nineteenth century. It's a style based on simple elements: mostly wood construction, exposed rafter tails, and deep roof overhangs and porches to provide shade and shelter from the weather. Diagonal brackets often support the eaves, seeming as if they're intended to hold the roof down during hurricanes. My intention here was to produce an elevated version of that regional archetype for clients who wanted more than your typical beach retreat.

OPPOSITE: A pair of custom metal doors leads to a secluded entry court, guiding you to the front door of the house. A charming garden inside the courtyard adds to the romantic atmosphere.

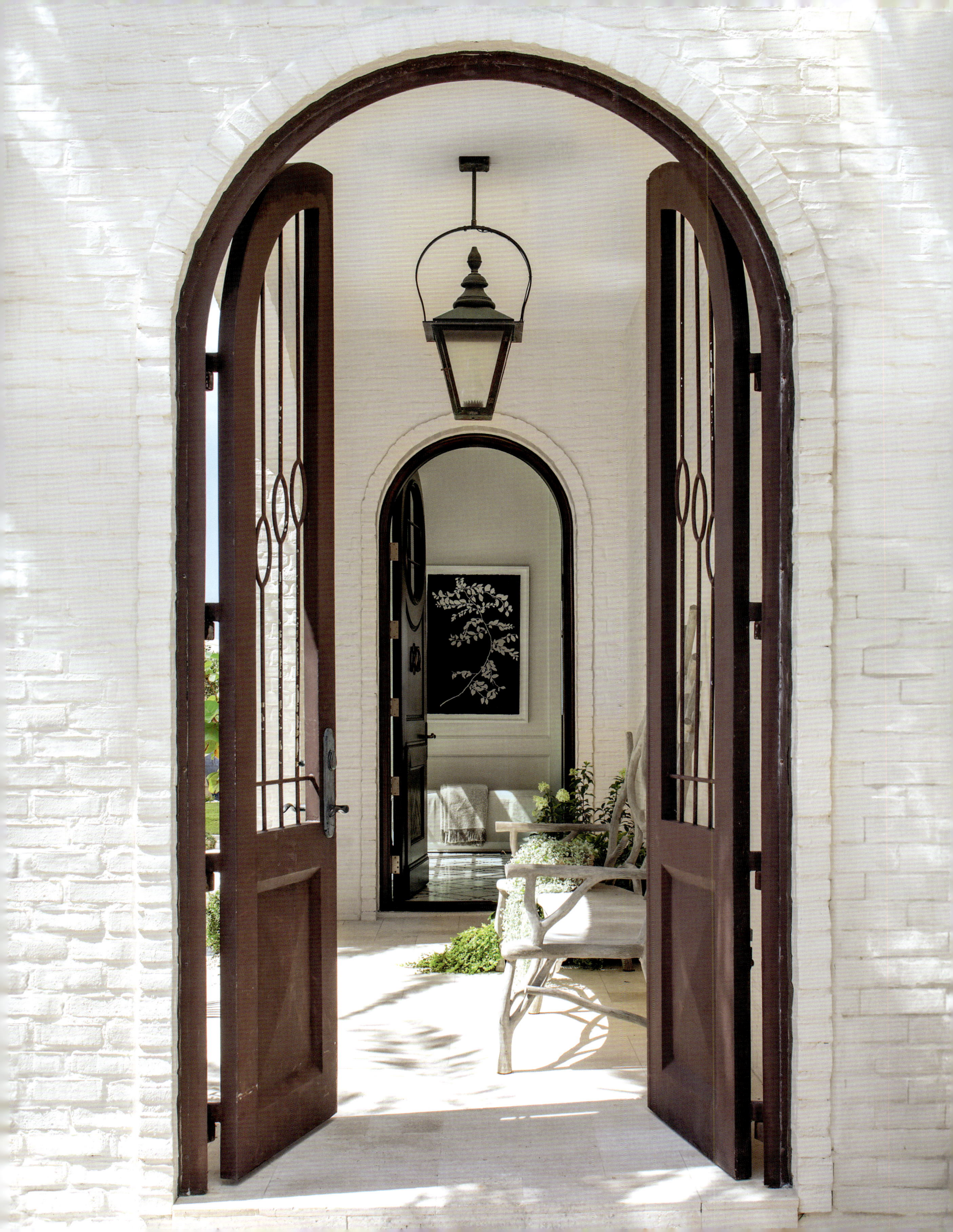

Since the house would be so tall, it was important to break down its verticality, visually speaking. We achieved this goal by varying the materials used to clad the different floors. Many older farmhouses sit on a two- or three-foot brick foundation; for this house, the brick extends upward to enclose the whole first level, almost like the rusticated basement story of a Renaissance palazzo. The next two levels are covered in lap siding, and board-and-batten is used for the topmost floor. Adding gables pierced by small, circular windows brings an extra dash of formality to a scheme derived from what was originally a very basic, utilitarian building tradition.

Seen from the road, the main house sits behind a lower "carriage house" section that contains a garage on the bottom and a bedroom suite above. Twin arched doors on either flank are modeled on the side porches characteristic of Charleston, South Carolina. The door on the left opens to a hidden courtyard and leads to the home's actual front entrance beyond.

On the beach-facing side, the exterior cladding materials disappear almost completely in favor of tall, rhythmic ranks of casement windows looking out across the water. My clients were especially enthusiastic about including a unique feature: awning-style windows installed at floor level, beneath the main windows, that give a direct sight line down to the neighboring sand and surf. Covered porches on every floor, surrounded by frame-free glass railings that obstruct none of the incredible views, let the family make the most of their outdoor living opportunities. Again, little touches of elegance—ogee curves carved into the ends of beams and rafters and support columns with a unique shape and profile on each story—raise the level of sophistication.

OPPOSITE: A paneled archway allows arriving visitors their first glimpse of the ocean.
FOLLOWING SPREAD: The clients were looking for a blend of contemporary and traditional styles, so interior designer Beth Webb and I put our energy into achieving that balance. As the living room shows, our approach was to combine relatively restrained overall lines with a significant amount of thoughtful detail.

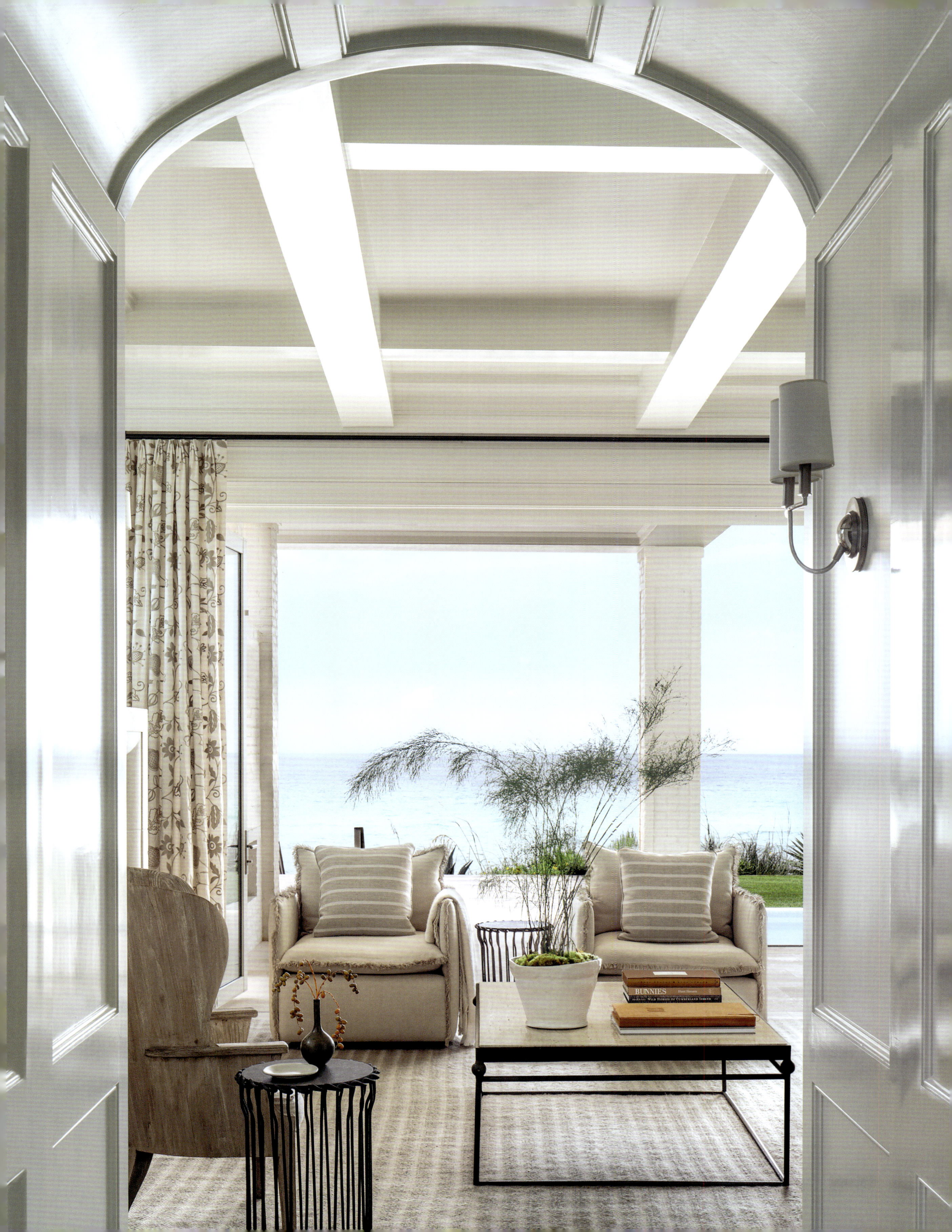
BUNNIES
Hunt Slonem
WILD HORSES OF CUMBERLAND ISLAND

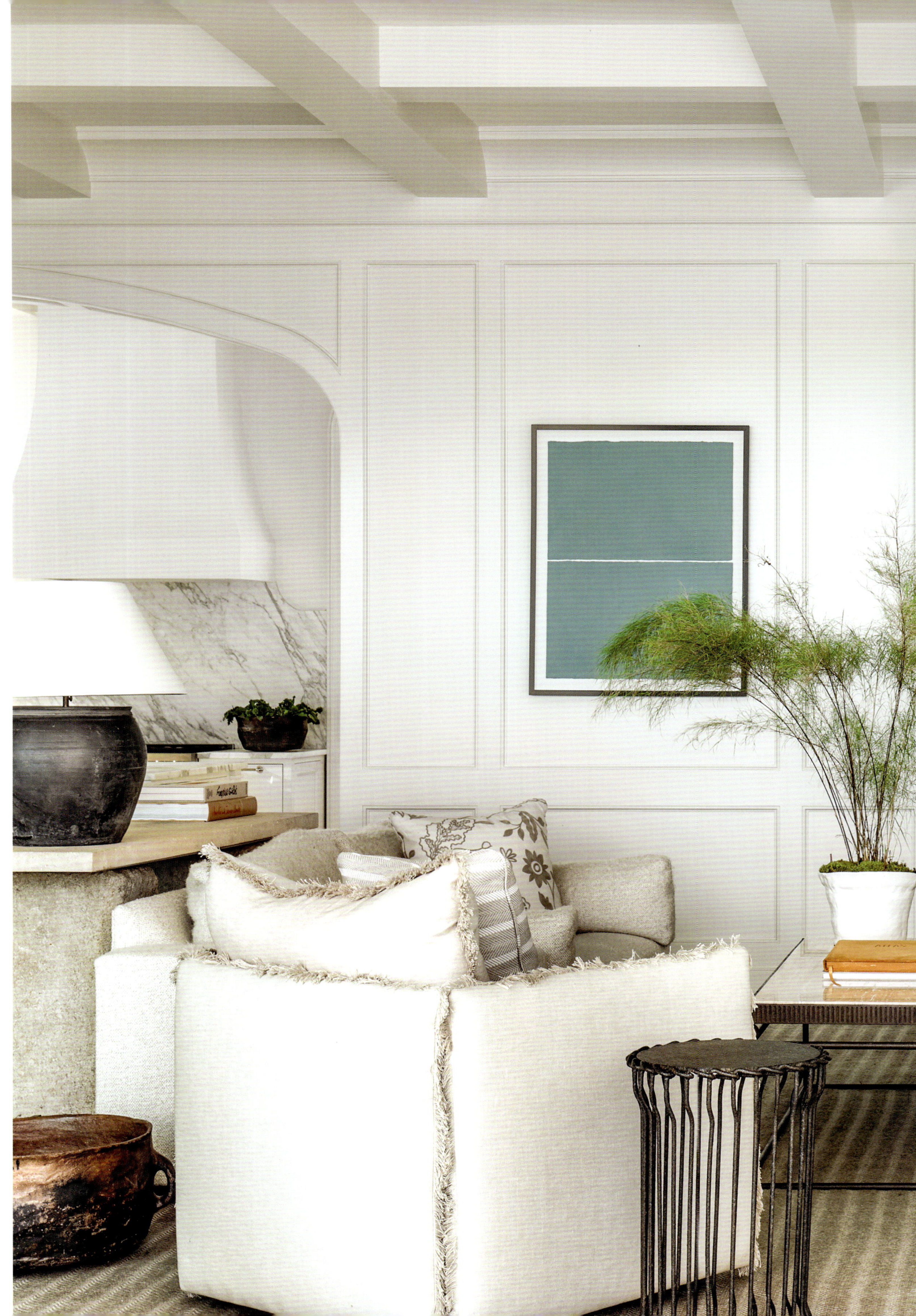

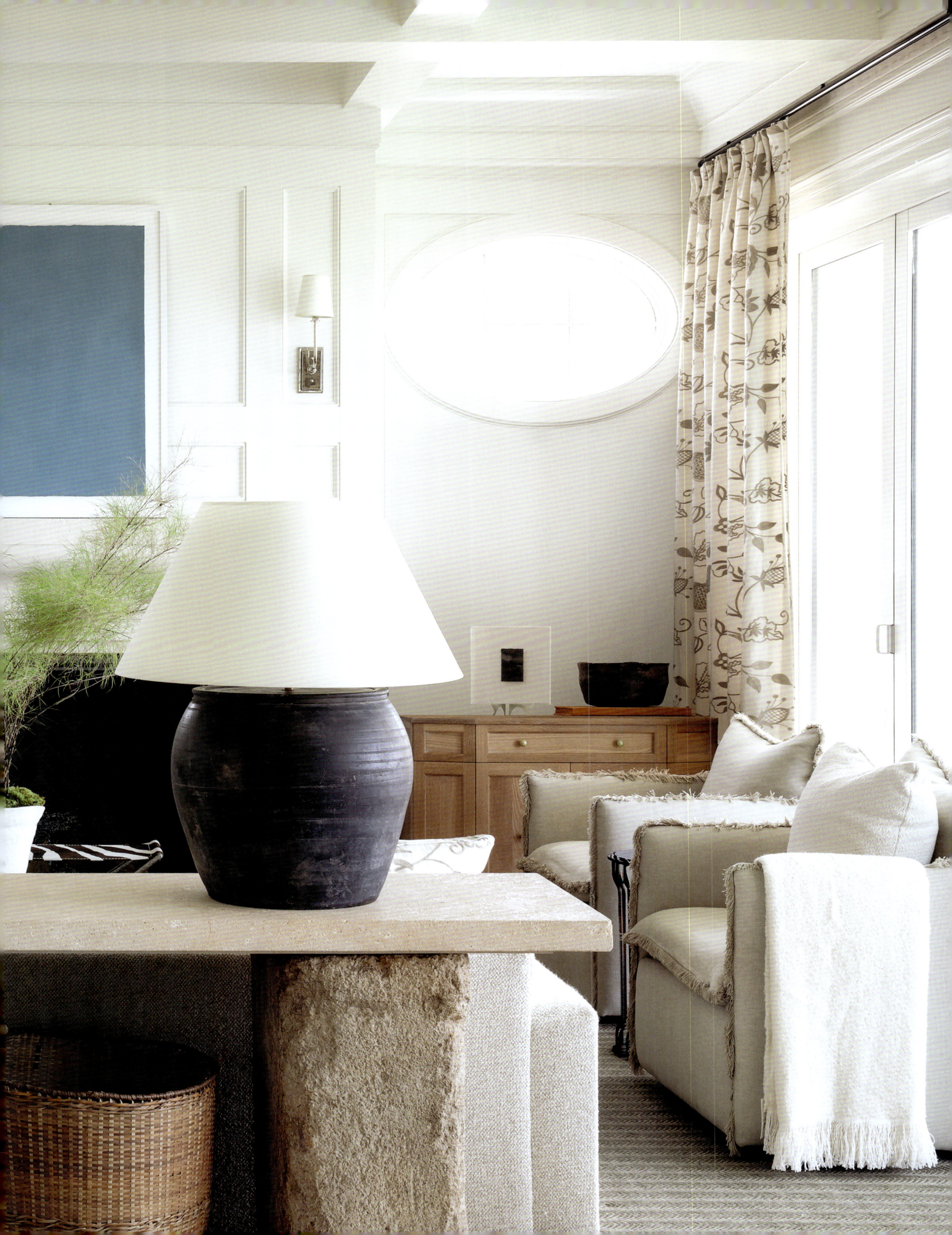

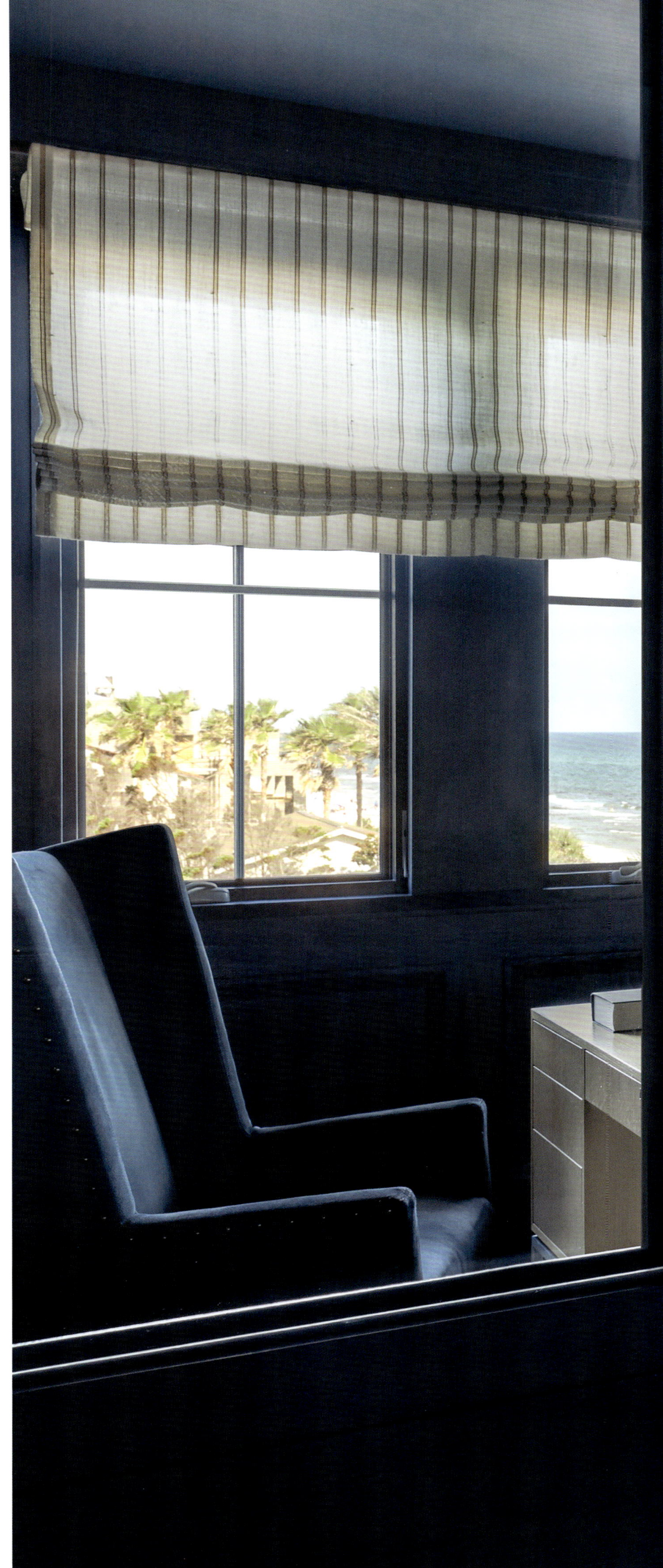

RIGHT: The office was a top priority for the clients, as the husband required a dedicated space for work when visiting their vacation home. The room is a moody, personal retreat, in contrast to the airy atmosphere of the rest of the house. Sliding doors offer privacy while still allowing natural light to filter through.

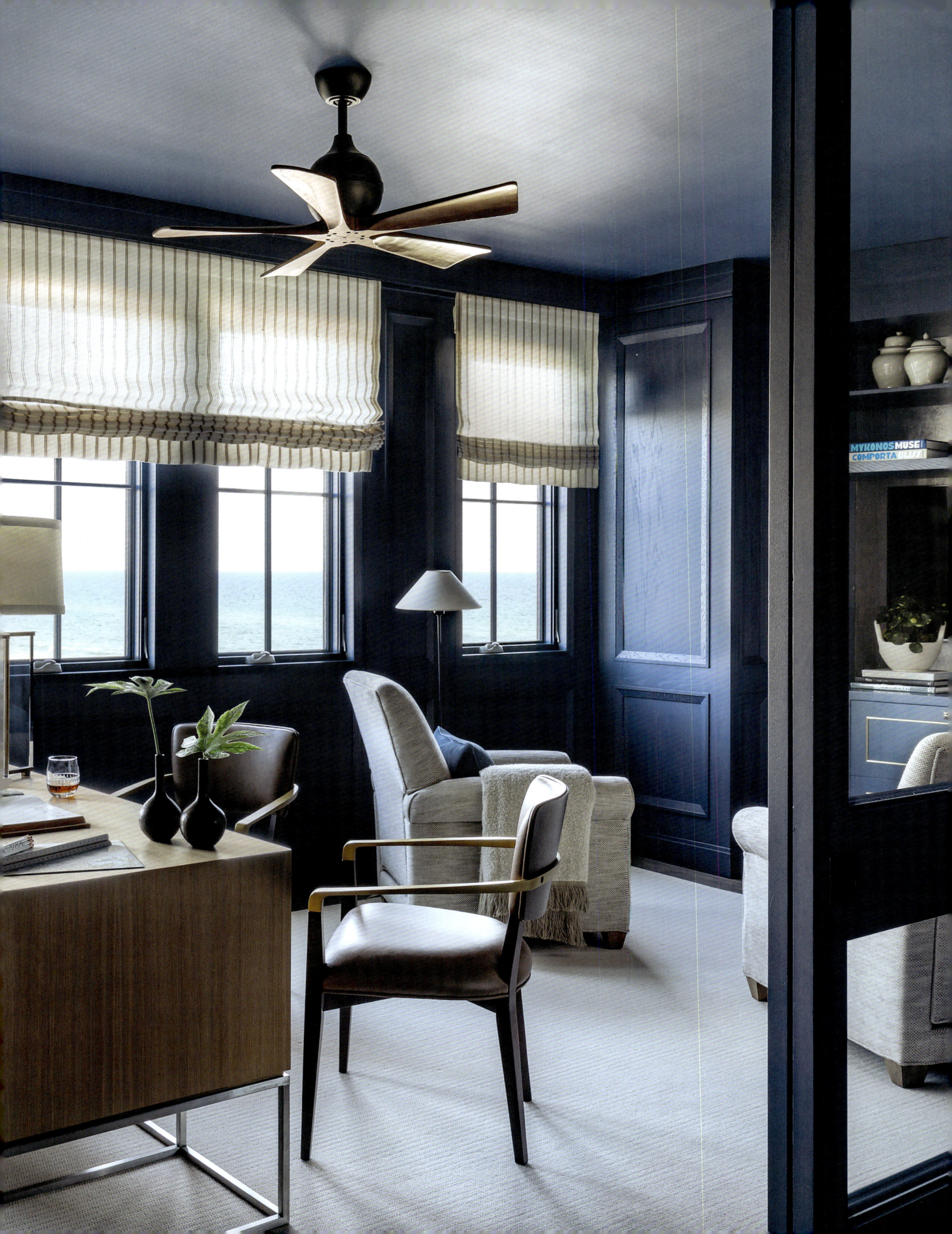
MYKONOS MUSE
COMPORTA

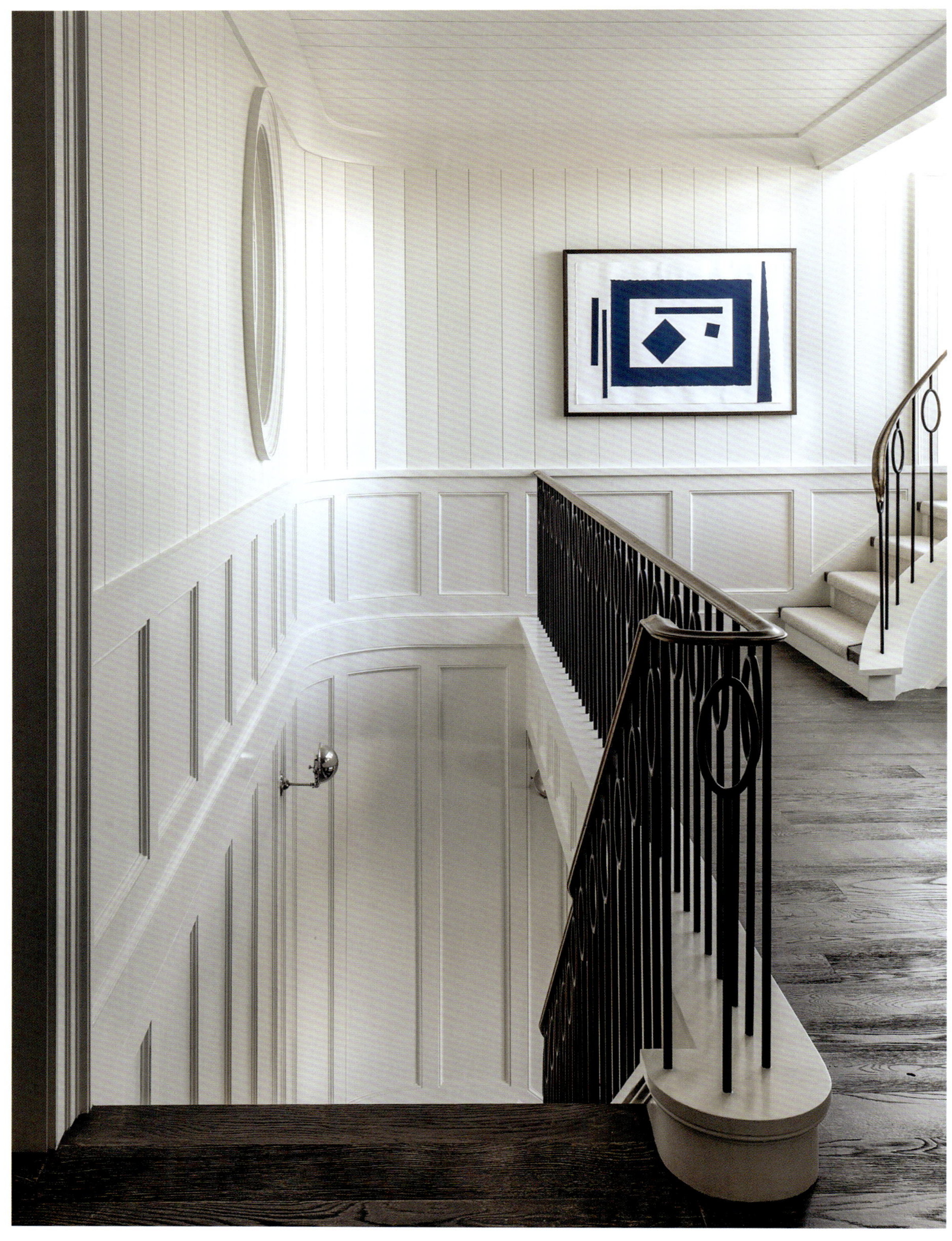

ABOVE AND OPPOSITE: The home's stairway splits at the third level, where formal wall paneling ends and the feeling of the interiors becomes more laid-back. The upper stair floats in front of tall windows, providing a dynamic view. FOLLOWING SPREAD: Bifold windows atop a row of awning windows give the impression that a seating area in the couple's bedroom is suspended above the beach.

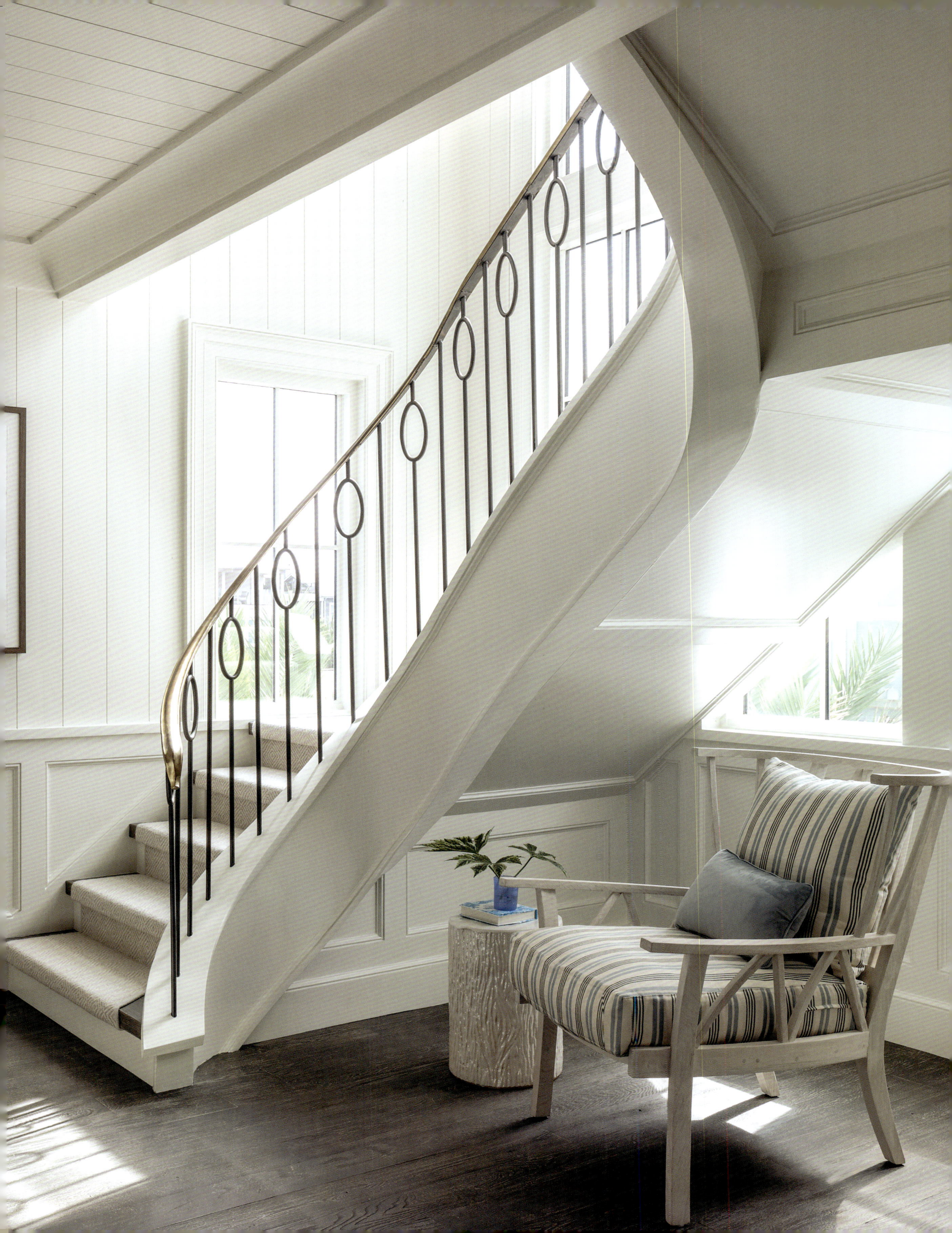

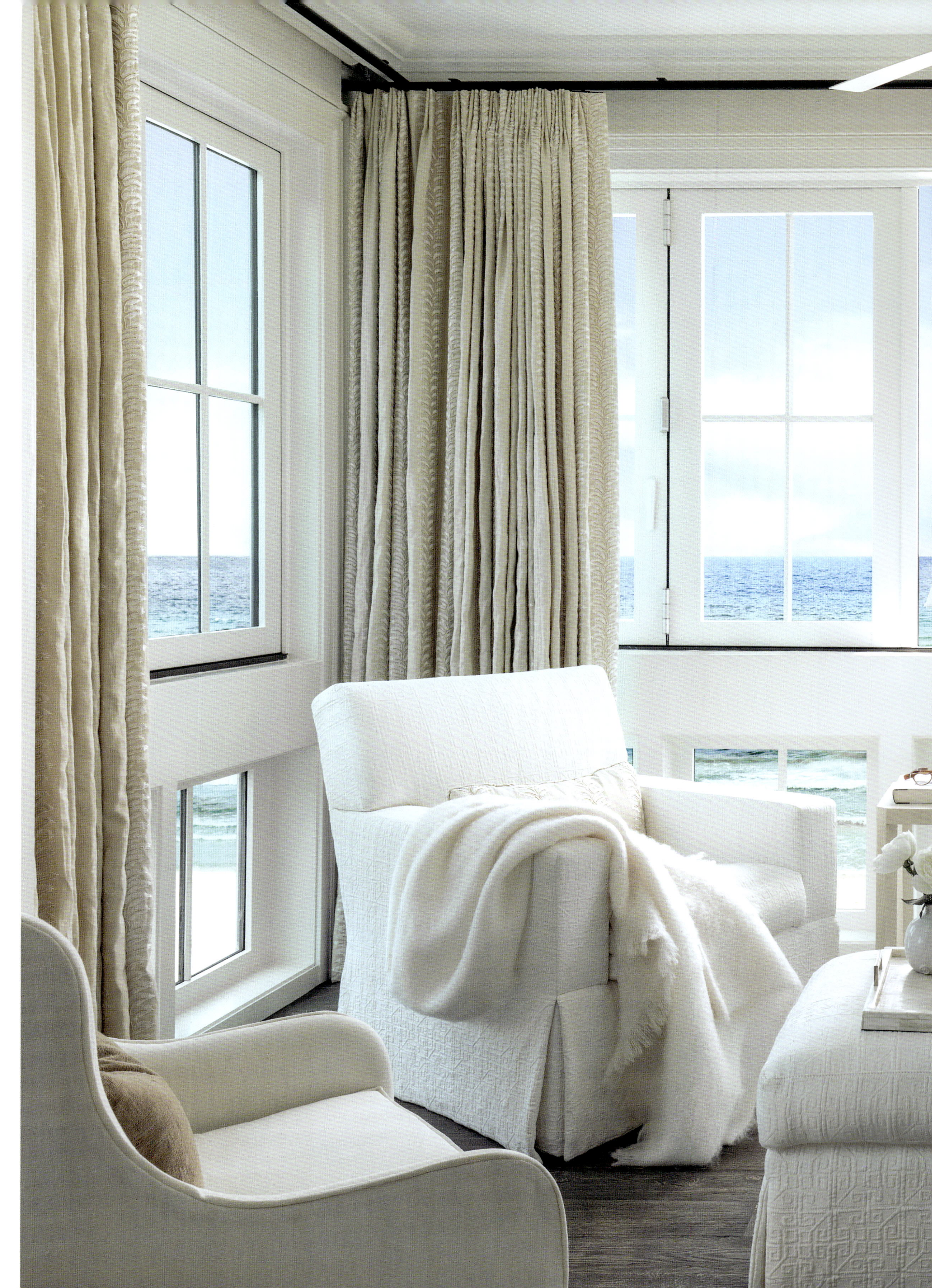

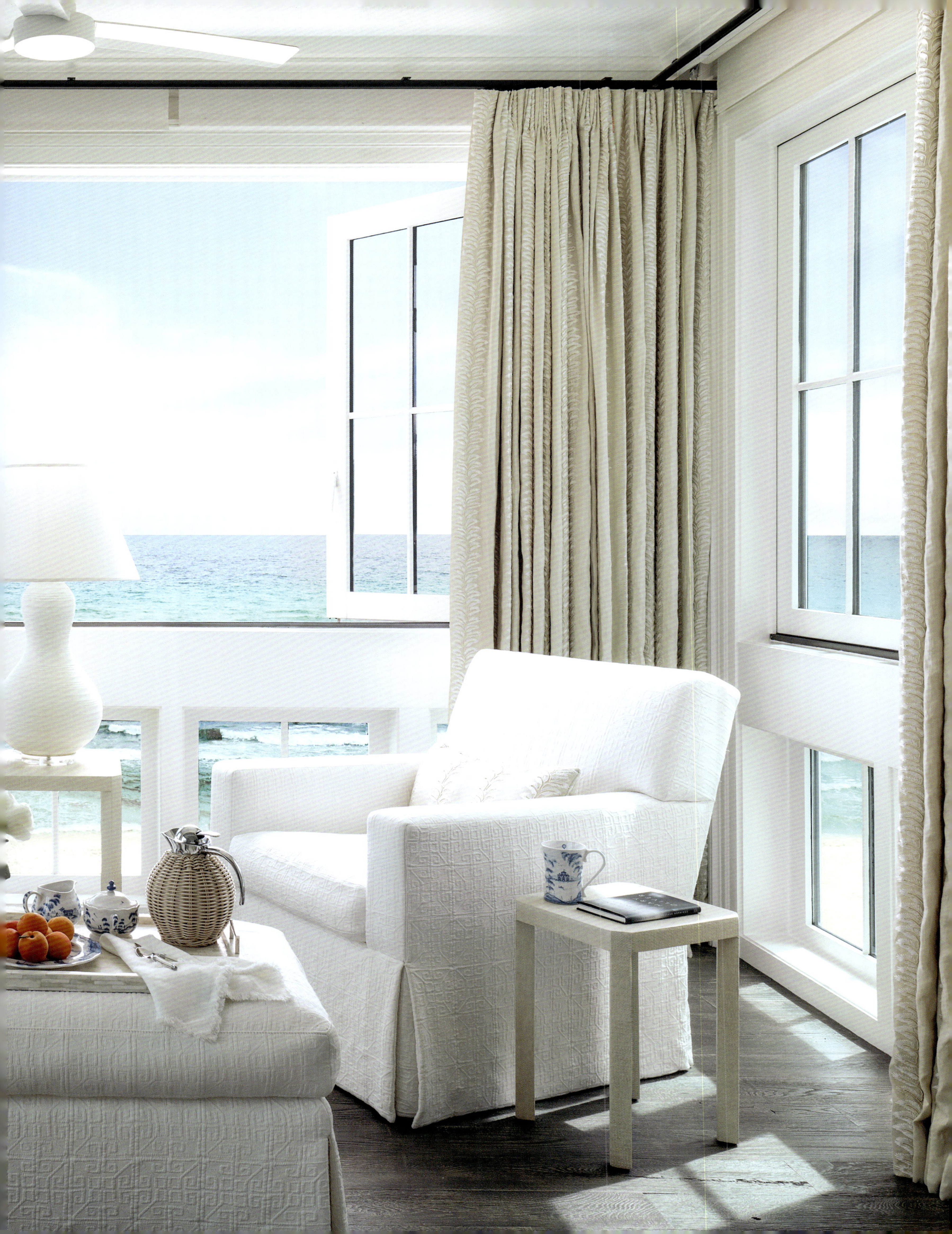

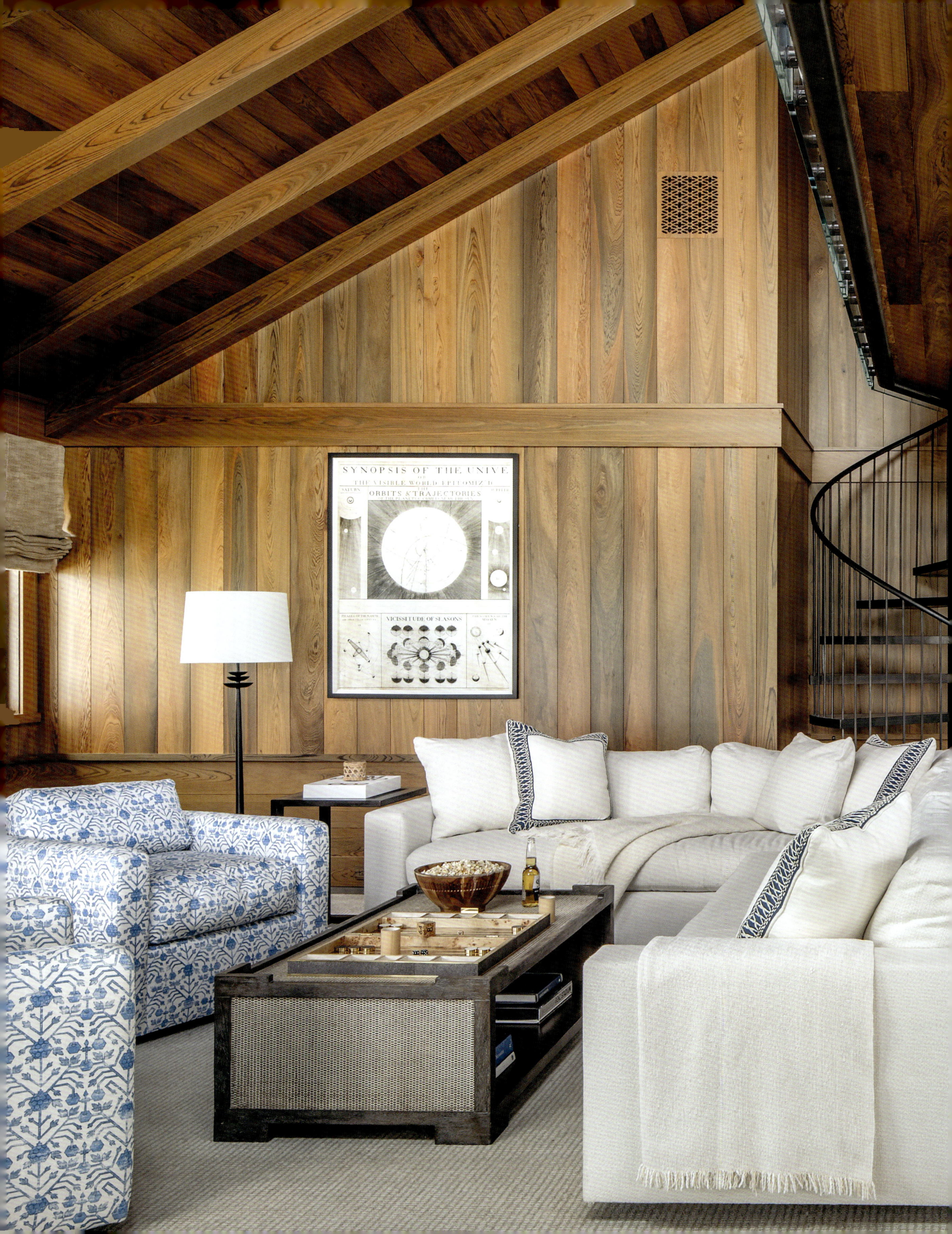
SYNOPSIS OF THE UNIVE
ORBITS & TRAJECTORIES
VICISSITUDE OF SEASONS

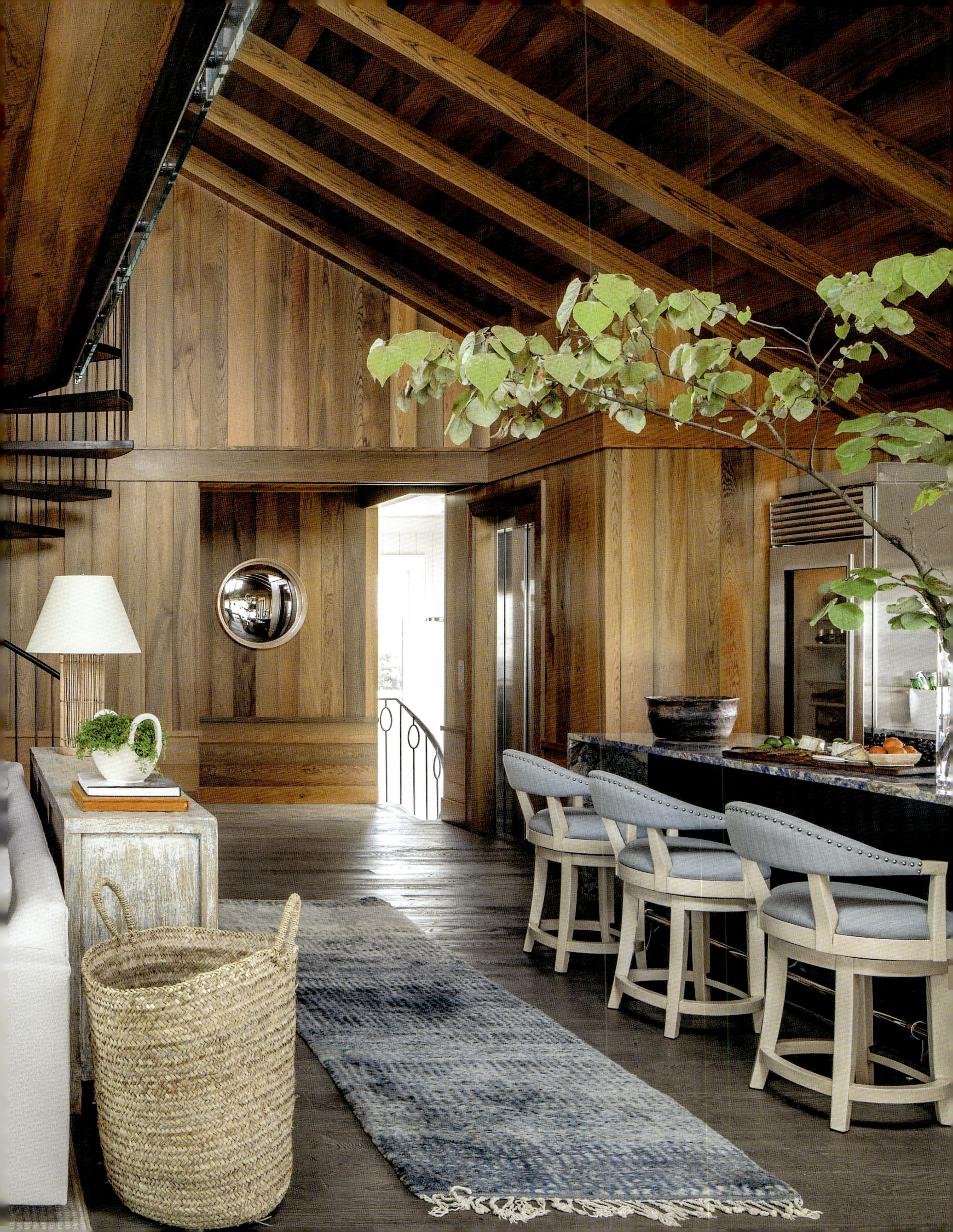

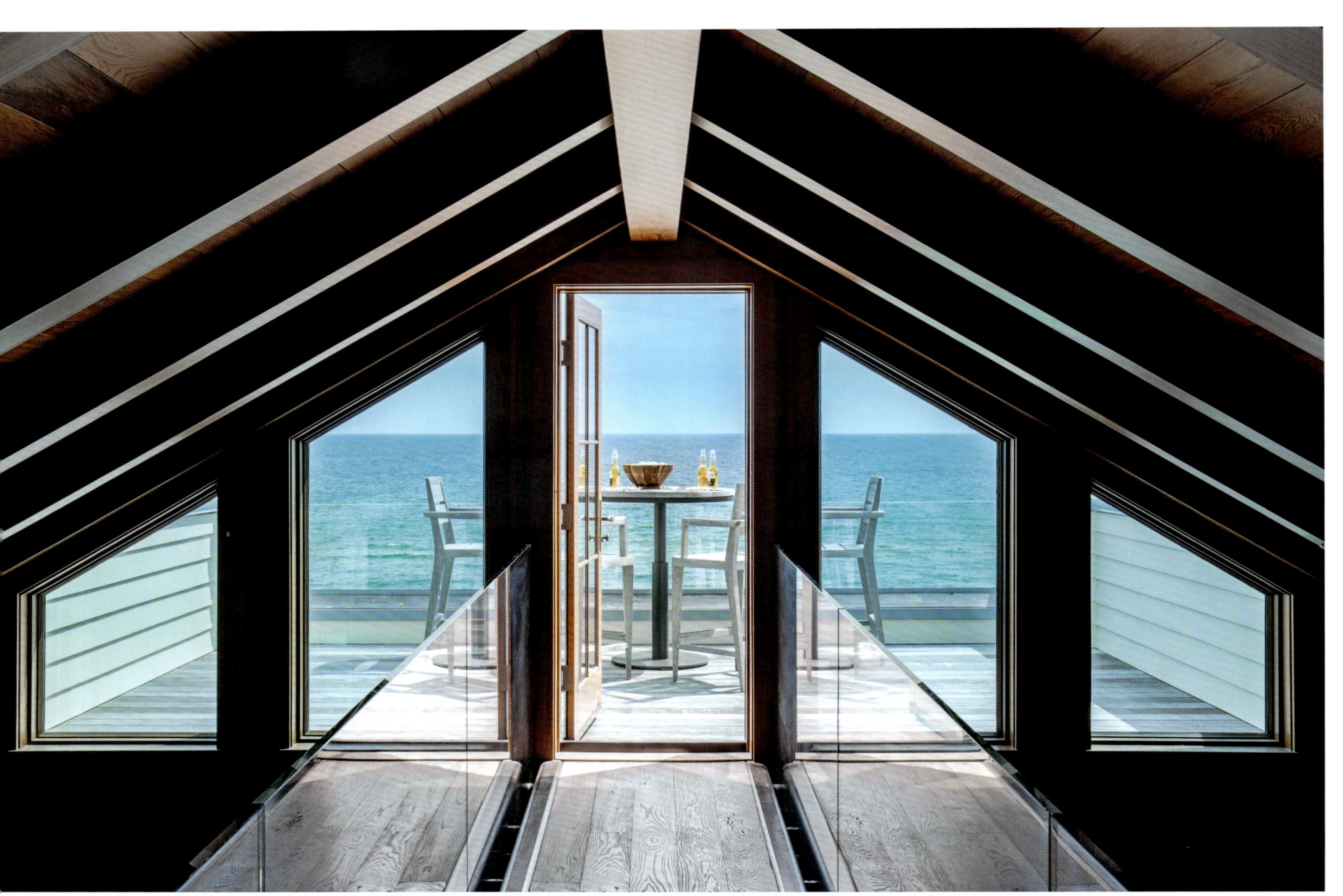

PRECEDING SPREAD: The top level of the house is completely open, with plenty of square footage for a substantial bar and lounging area. ABOVE AND OPPOSITE: The space features access to three different outdoor terraces for immersion in the seaside experience, one of which is reached via an overhead catwalk. Pulling aside a set of folding doors turns the terrace adjacent to the pool table into an extension of the room.

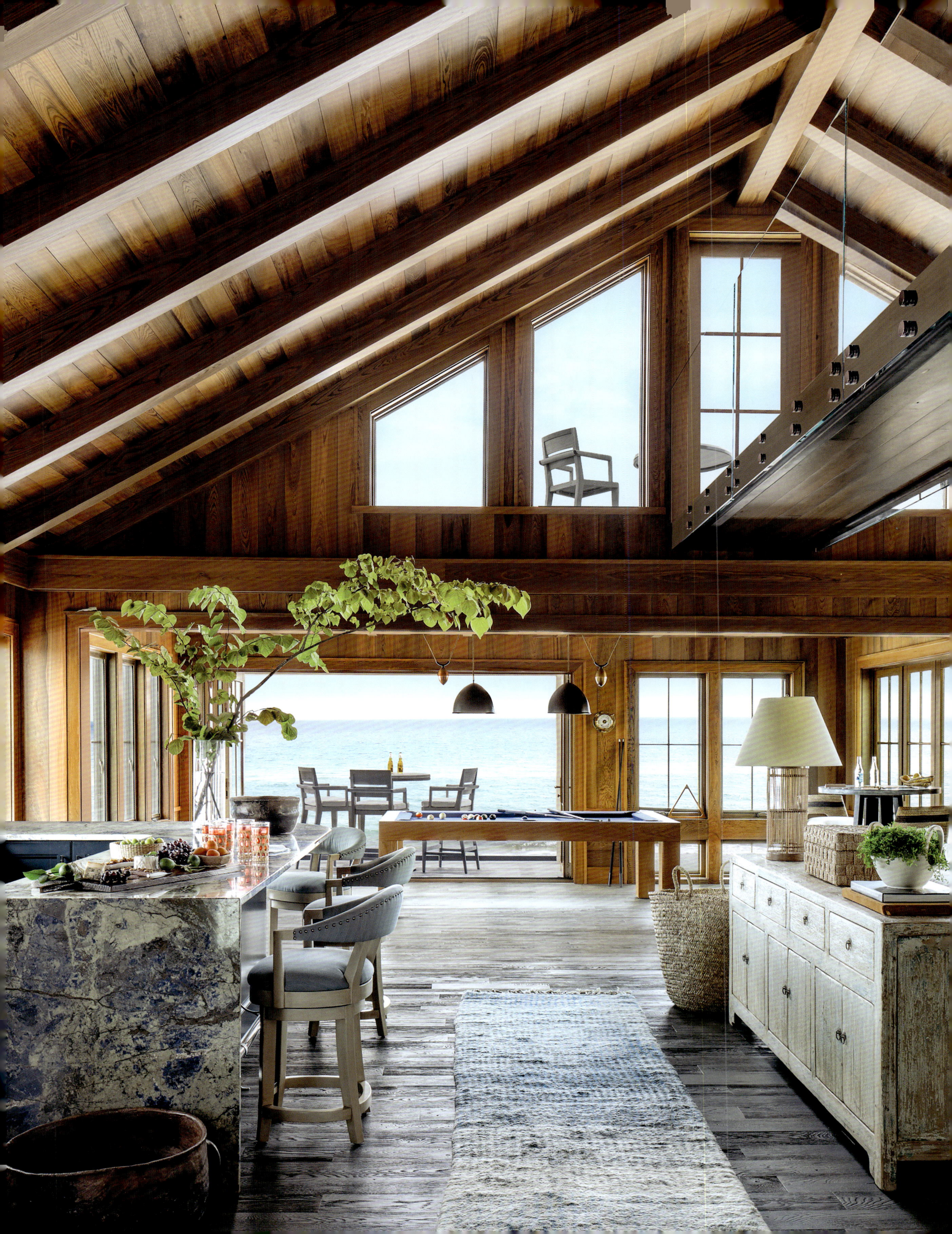

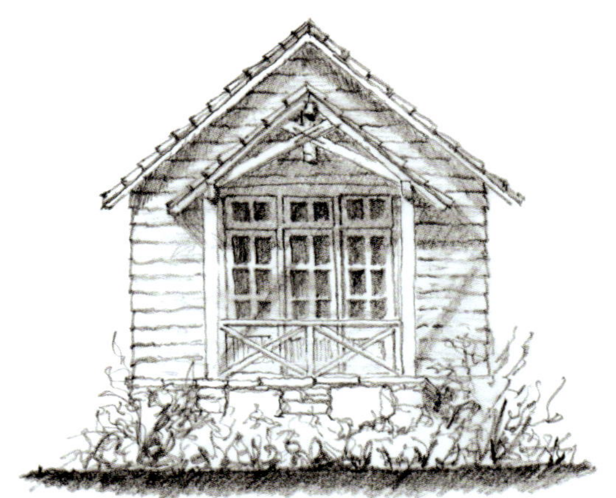

HICKORY BANK

When I'm designing houses, I try hard to make sure that each one has a central focal point. By "central," I don't mean literally in the center; even in an asymmetrical plan, there will be a specific feature or set of features intended to draw you in. Once you reach that spot, another point of interest will be in view beyond it, enticing you farther into the space. The home becomes an ongoing sequence of experiences you navigate from one goal to the next.

OPPOSITE: A breezeway provides walk-through access to the back side of the house. Rather than giving it a simple low-pitched roof, we decided to add character via a raised eyebrow. FOLLOWING SPREAD: The front of the house displays a trio of stone arches: one opening into the entry loggia, one surrounding a window that drops light into the home's lower level, and one that leads to the breezeway.

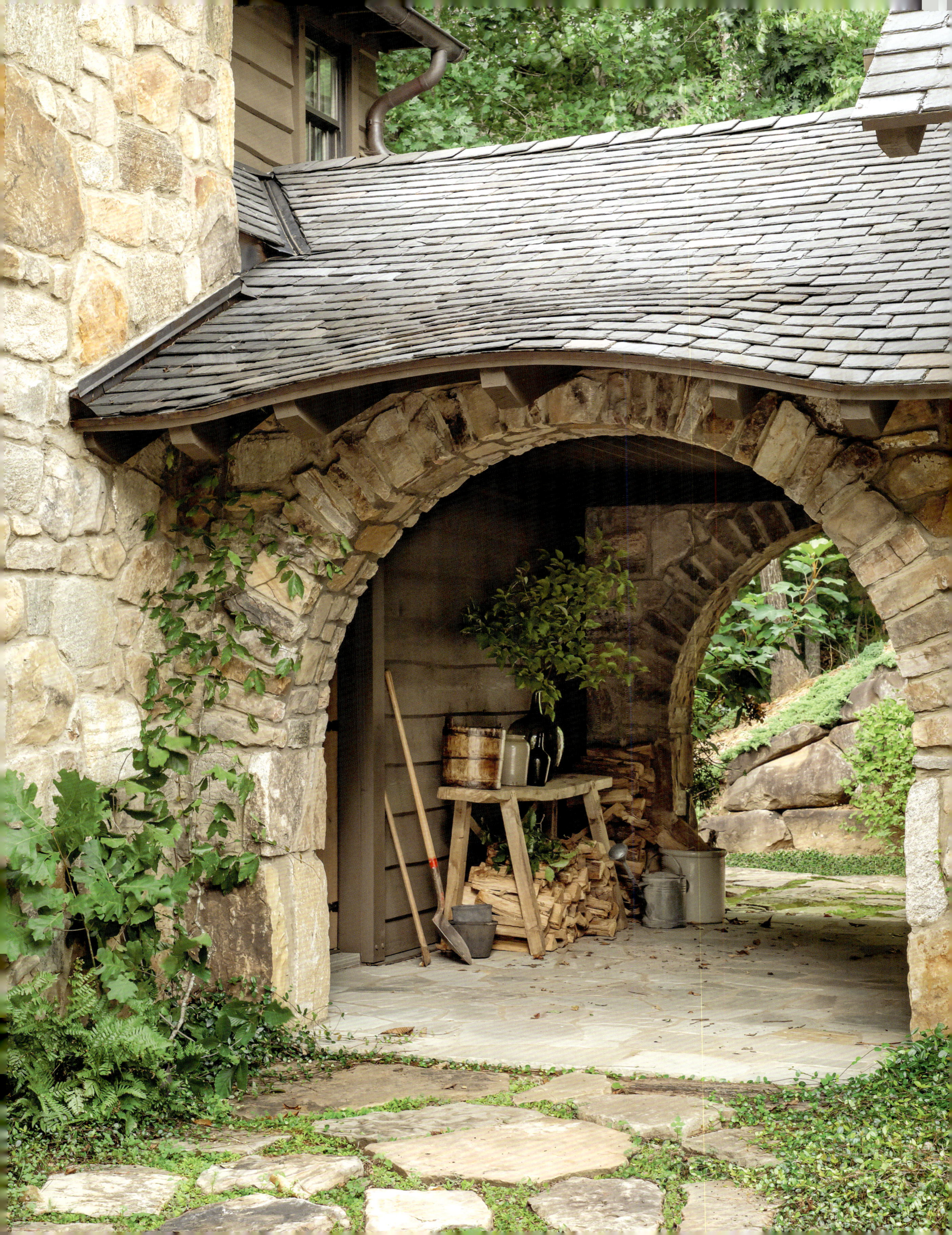

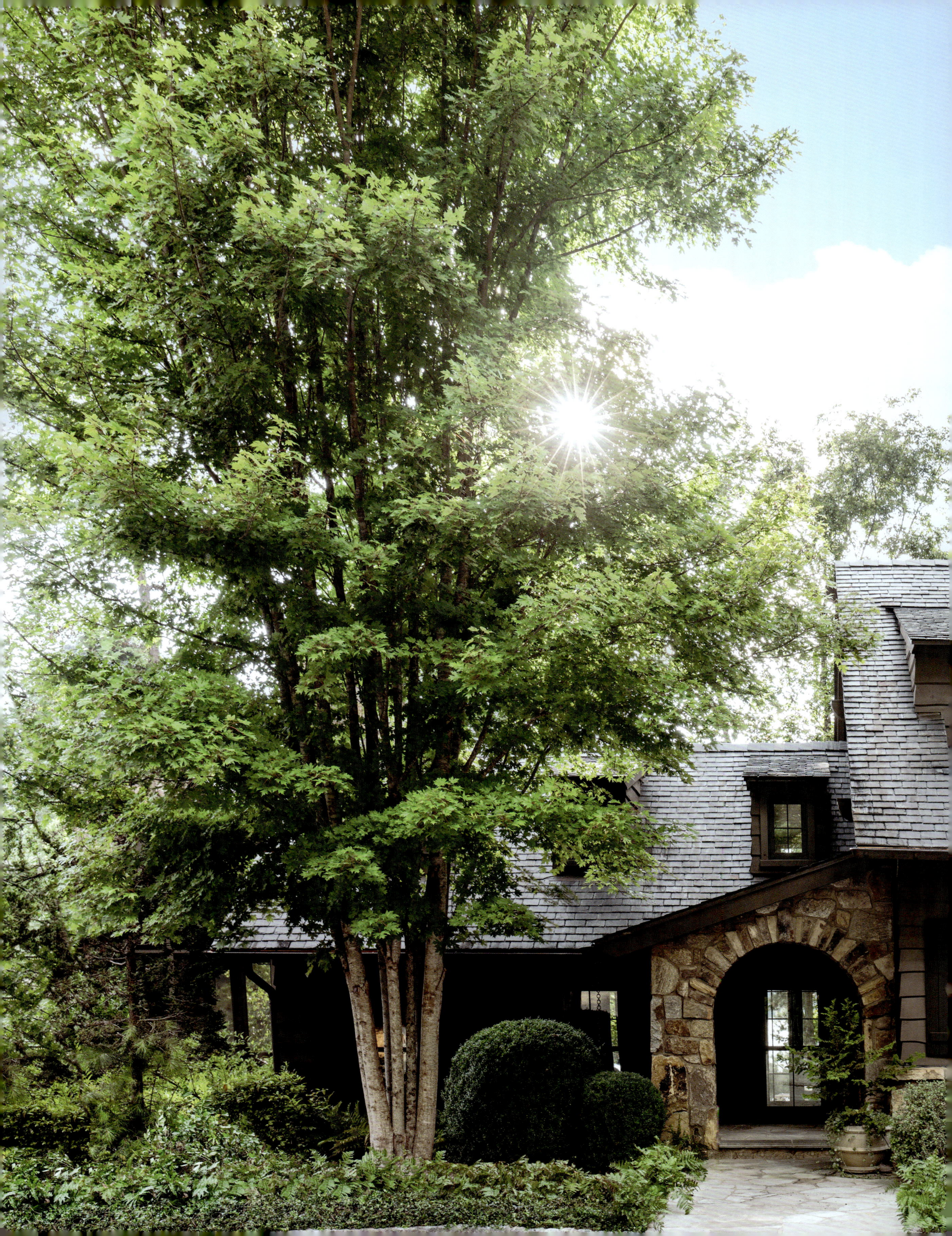

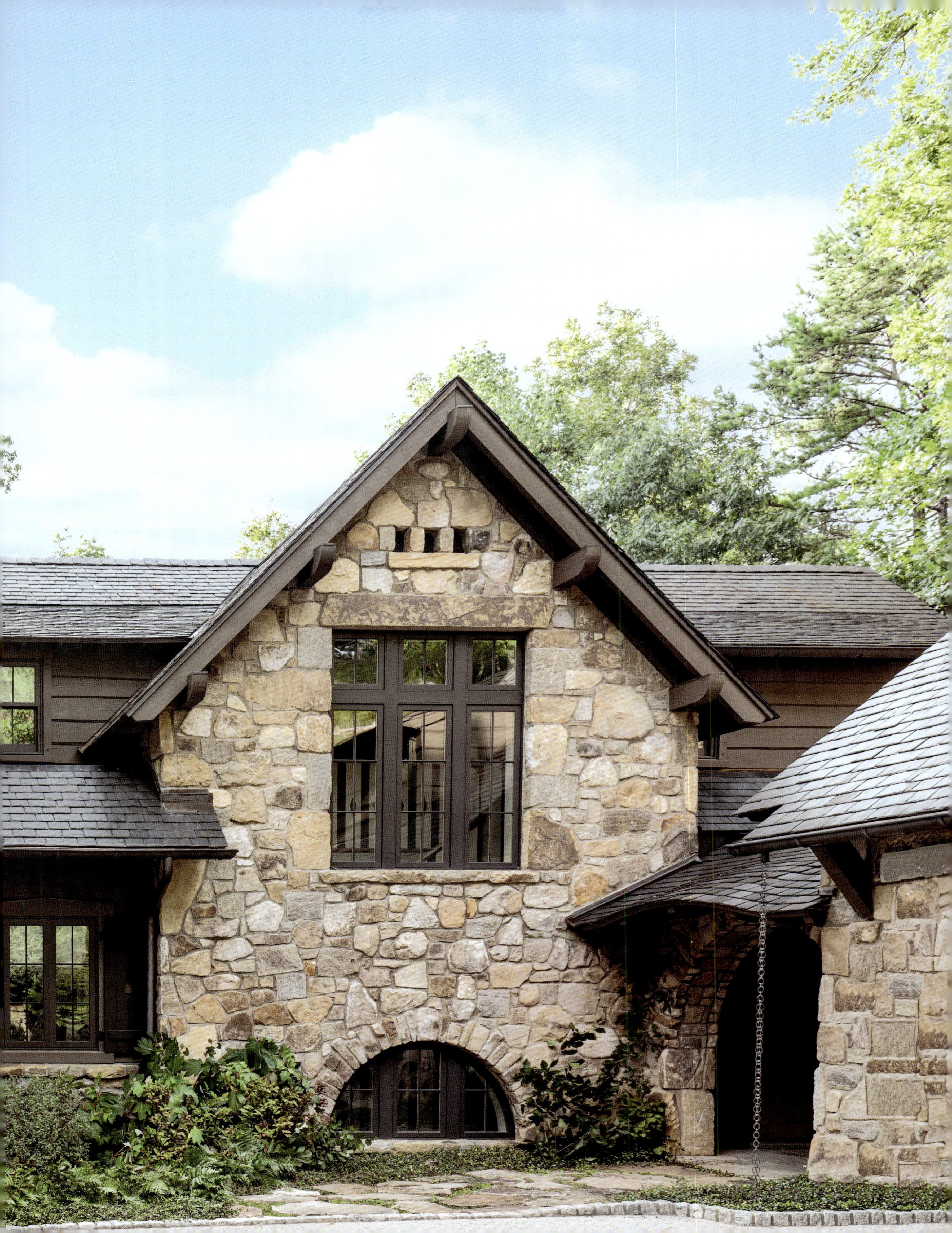

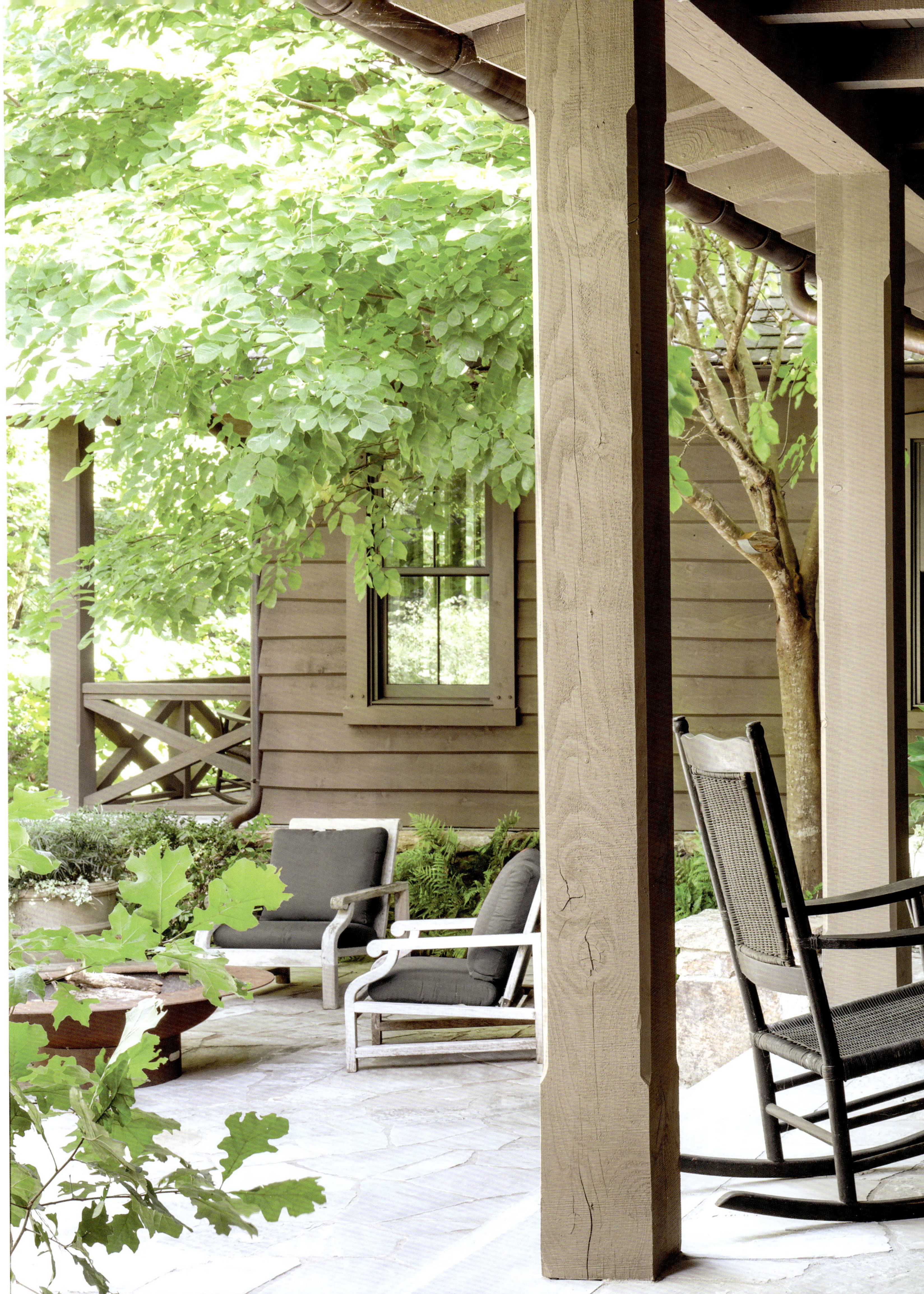

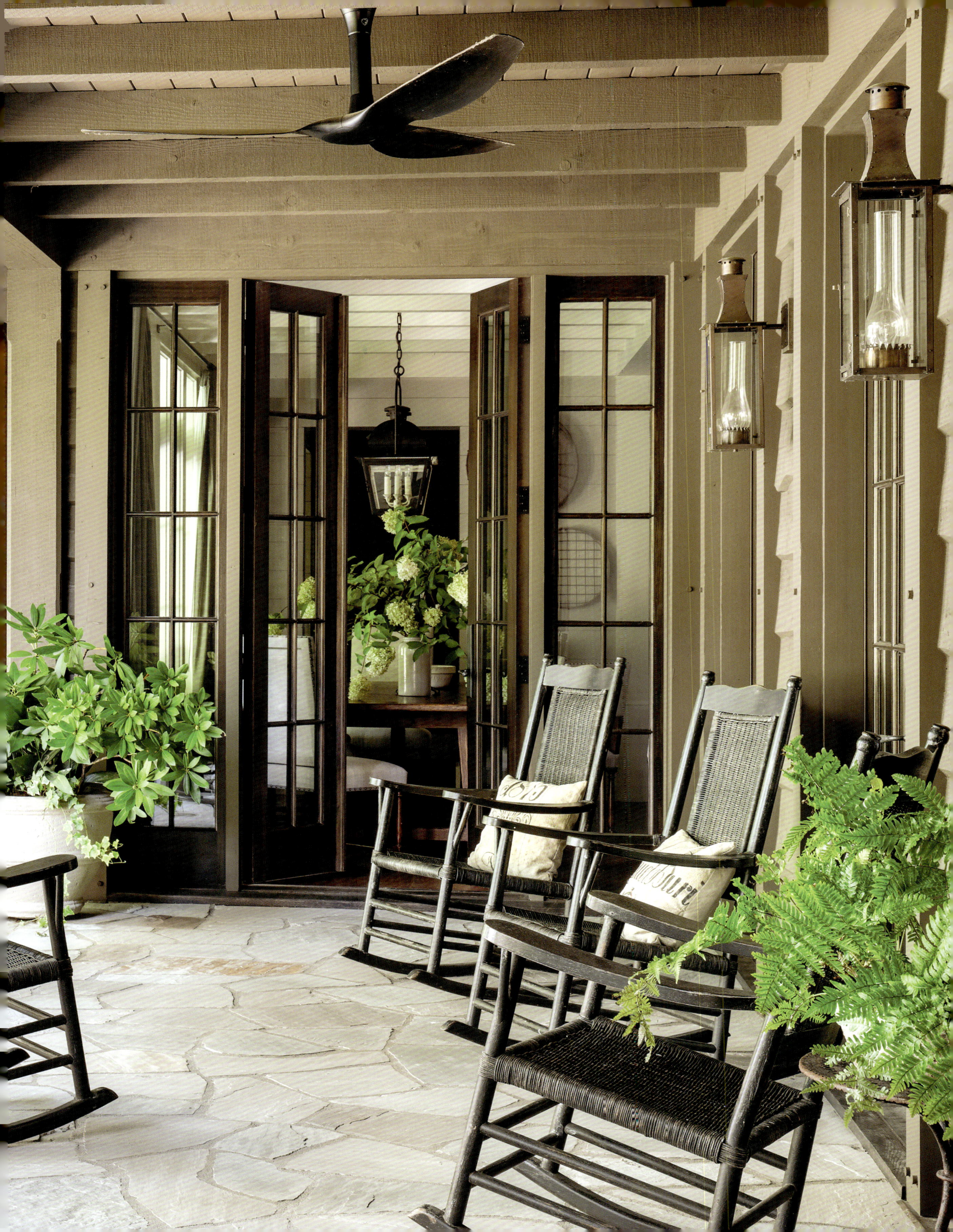

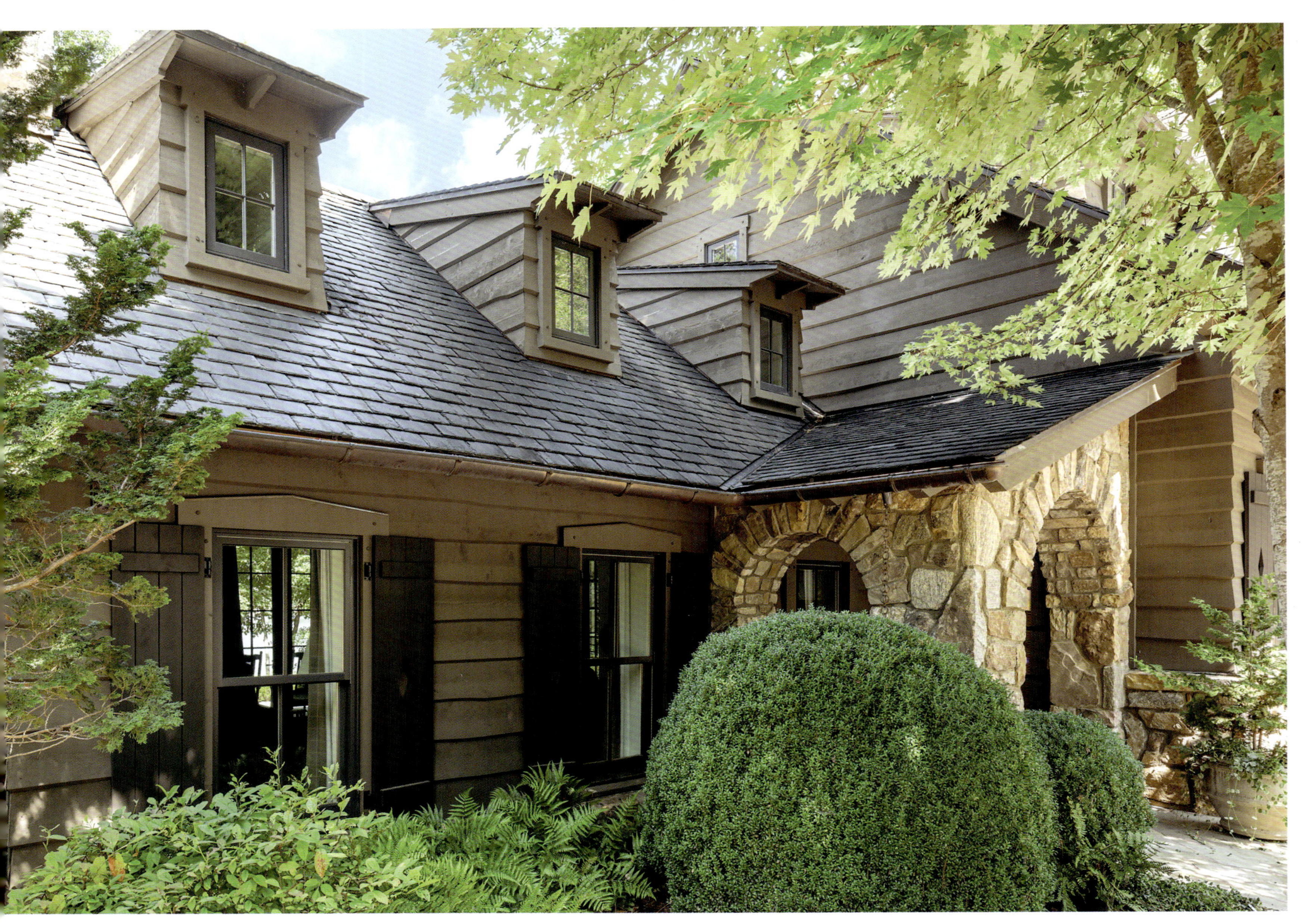

PRECEDING SPREAD: Rocking chairs on the rear veranda invite casual conversation. Flagstone pavers underfoot unite the veranda and the terrace beyond. ABOVE: The stone entry loggia has the charm of a thoughtful addition, nestled at the junction of two sections of the house as if it were added during the home's evolution over time. OPPOSITE: The loggia's arches are mirrored in the design of the front door, where iron hardware adds a touch of timeless elegance.

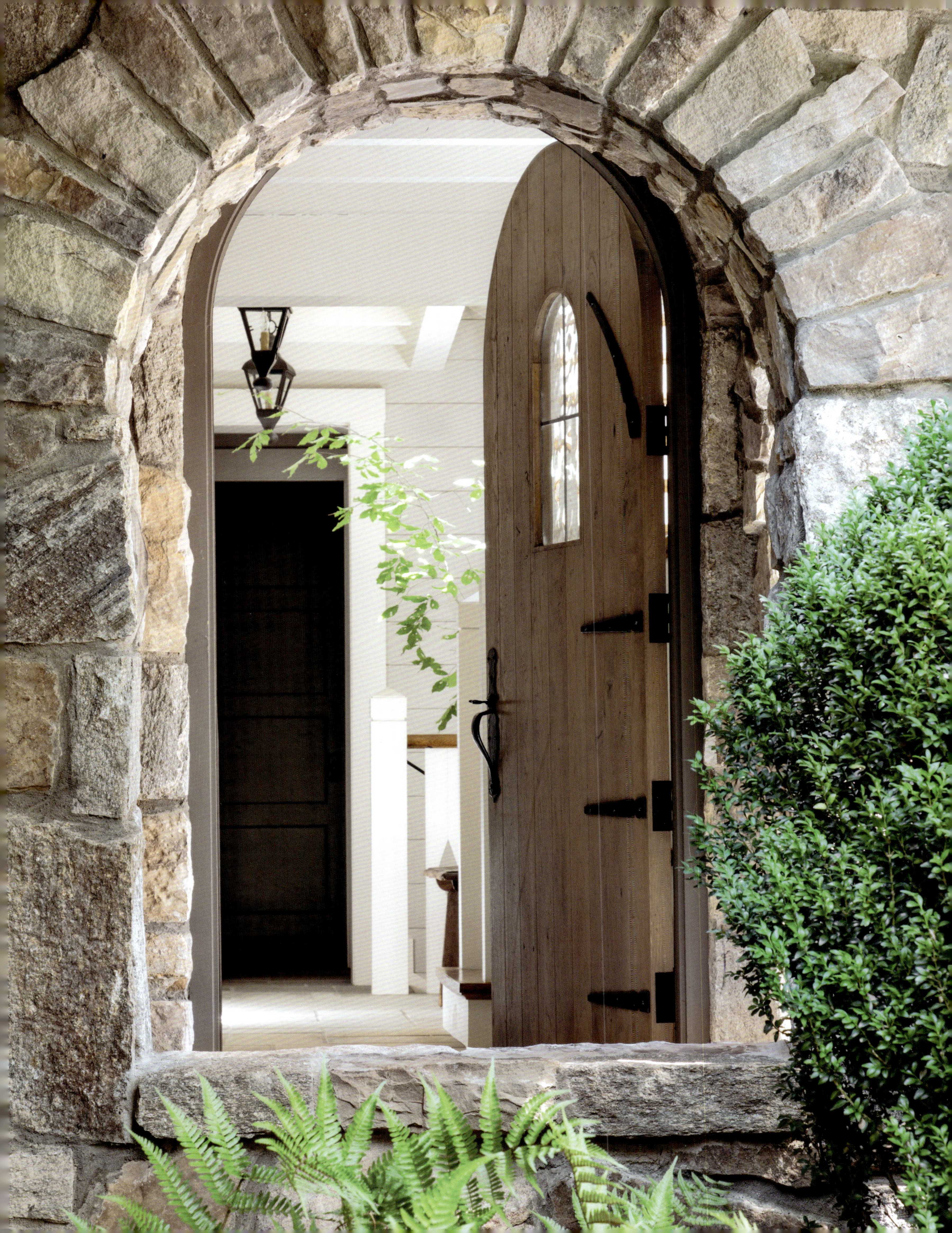

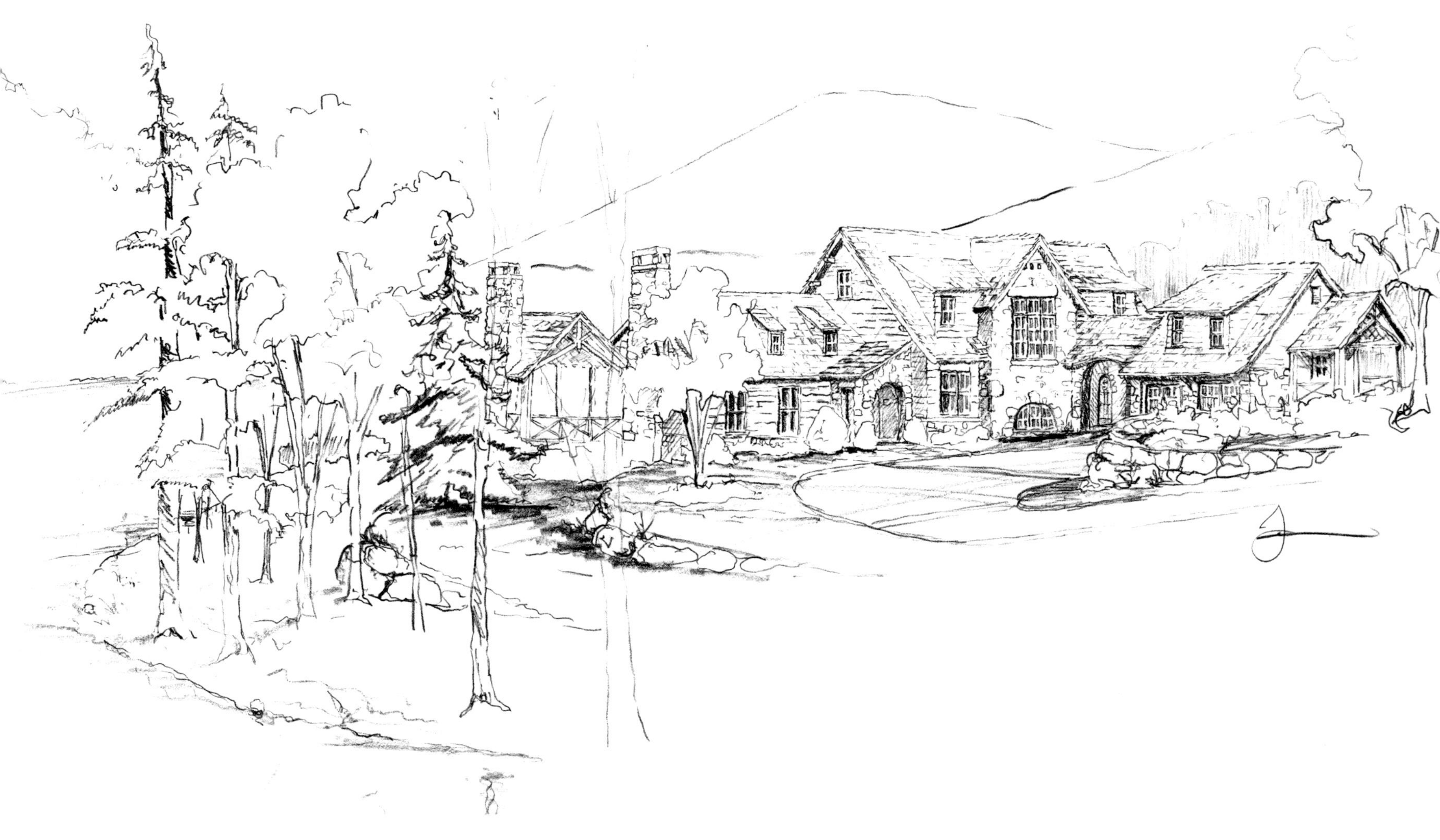

That's very much the story of this cottage on South Carolina's Lake Keowee. You approach the home from above, via a lengthy driveway that winds down a steep hillside toward the water. Initially, your viewpoint is above the house, looking out across the lake. Then, rounding a curve reveals a small plateau where the structure—an informal assembly of gables, shed dormers, stone walls, and slate shingles—actually stands, and a covered loggia with a graceful, arched opening invites you inside. The journey won't be over, however, until you've completely traversed the building (including its internal destinations) and a rugged stone stairway has led you the rest of the distance to a private boat dock on the water below.

We wanted the house to feel comfortably grown into the landscape, as if it had long been there and evolved gradually to its current layout.

OPPOSITE: The home's rich, earth-toned exterior contains a bright, neutral interior. The stone-floored stair hall, located within the front gable, is wrapped in clean-lined nickel-gap paneling. FOLLOWING SPREAD: So-called scissor trusses, designed without a horizontal bottom beam, give the living room an enhanced sense of height. Shed dormers on both sides introduce additional natural light from above, further emphasizing the feeling of openness.

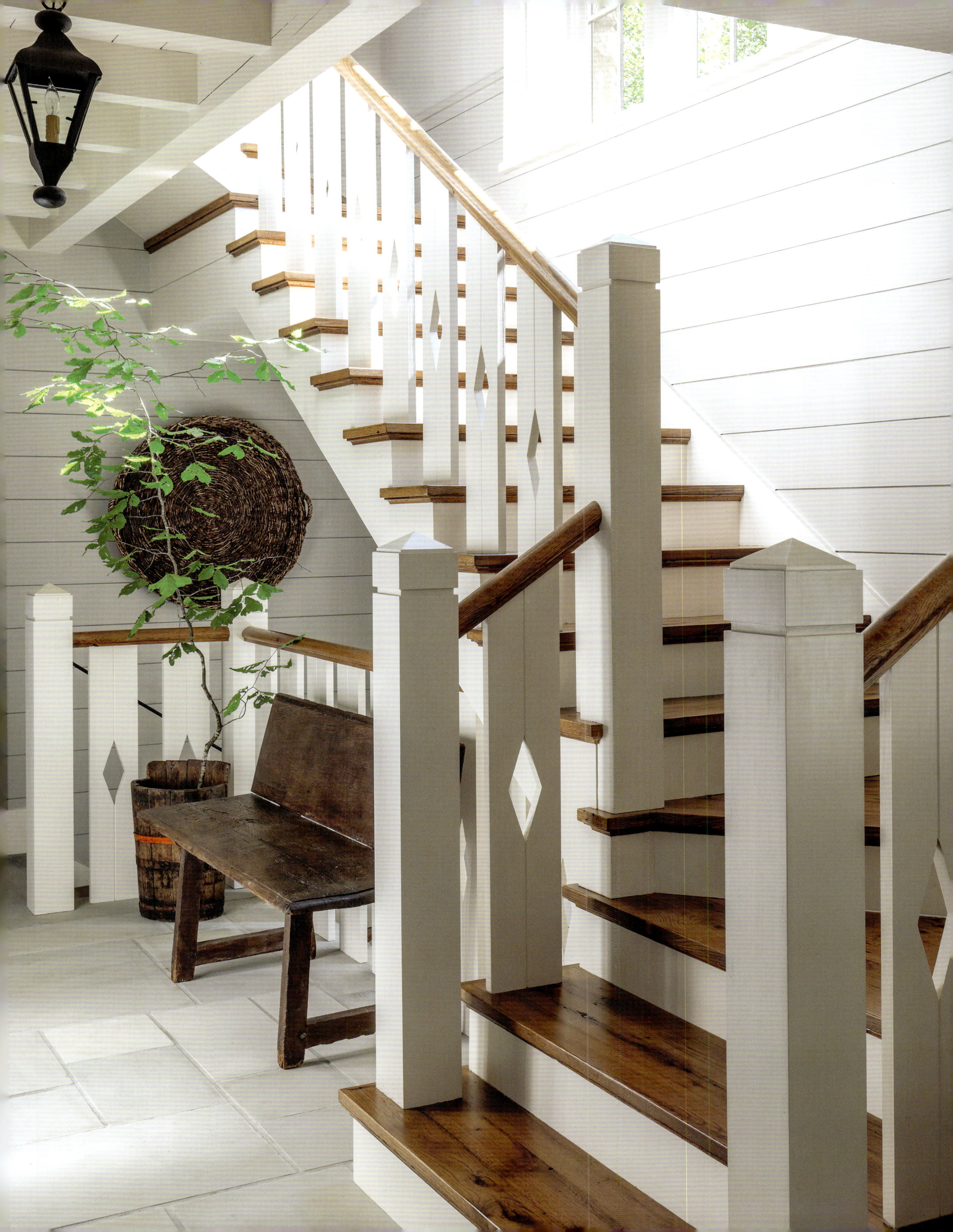

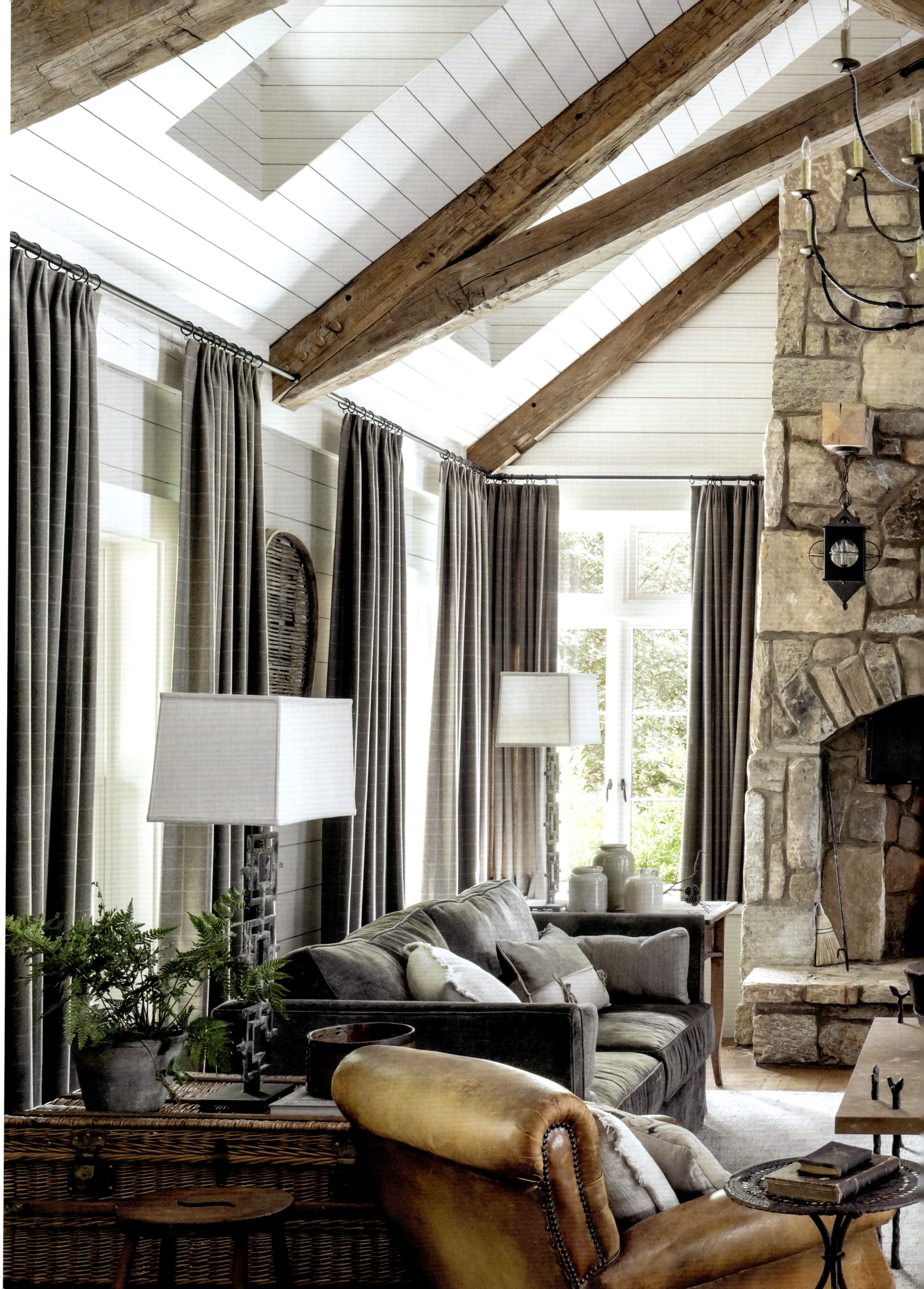

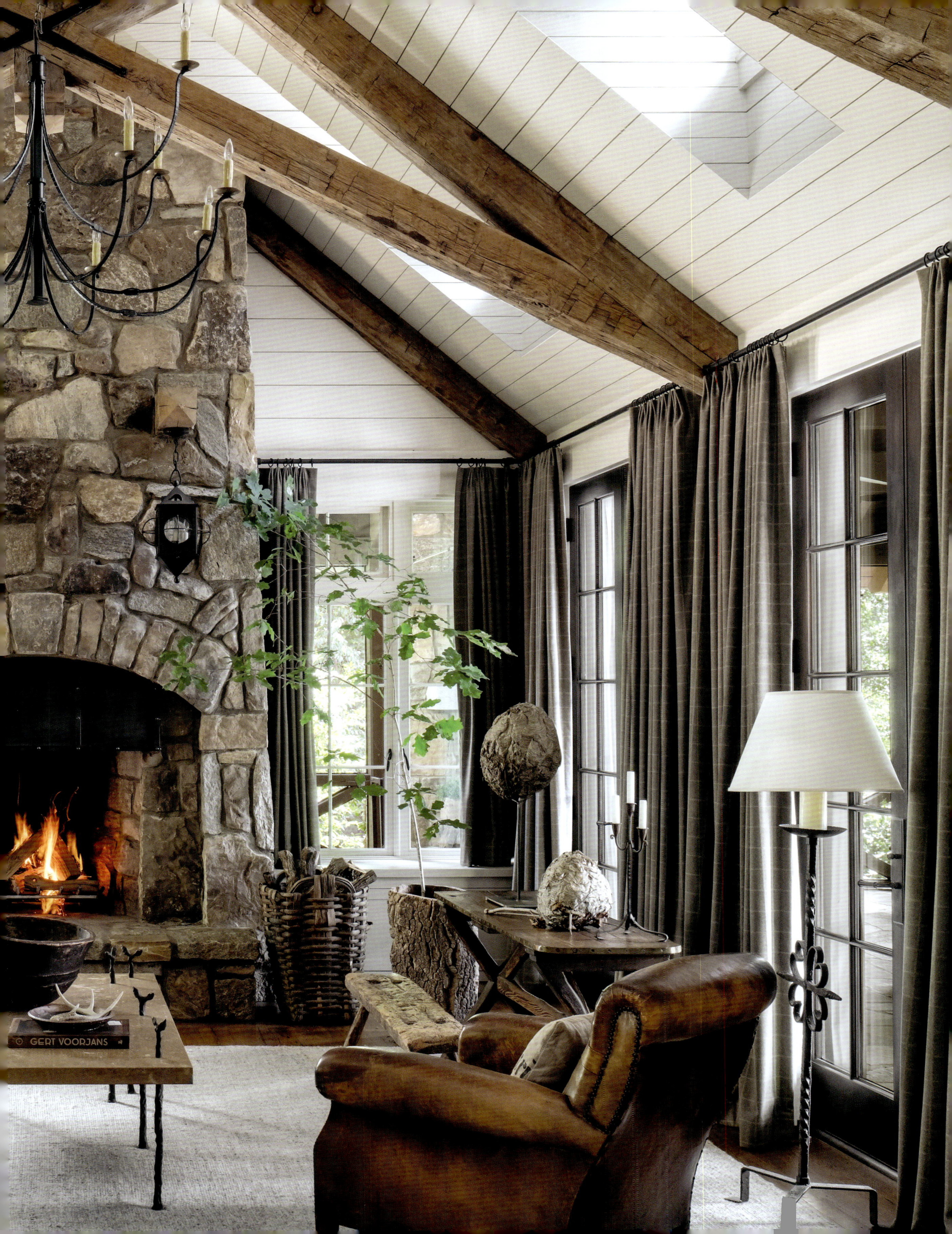
GERT VOORJANS

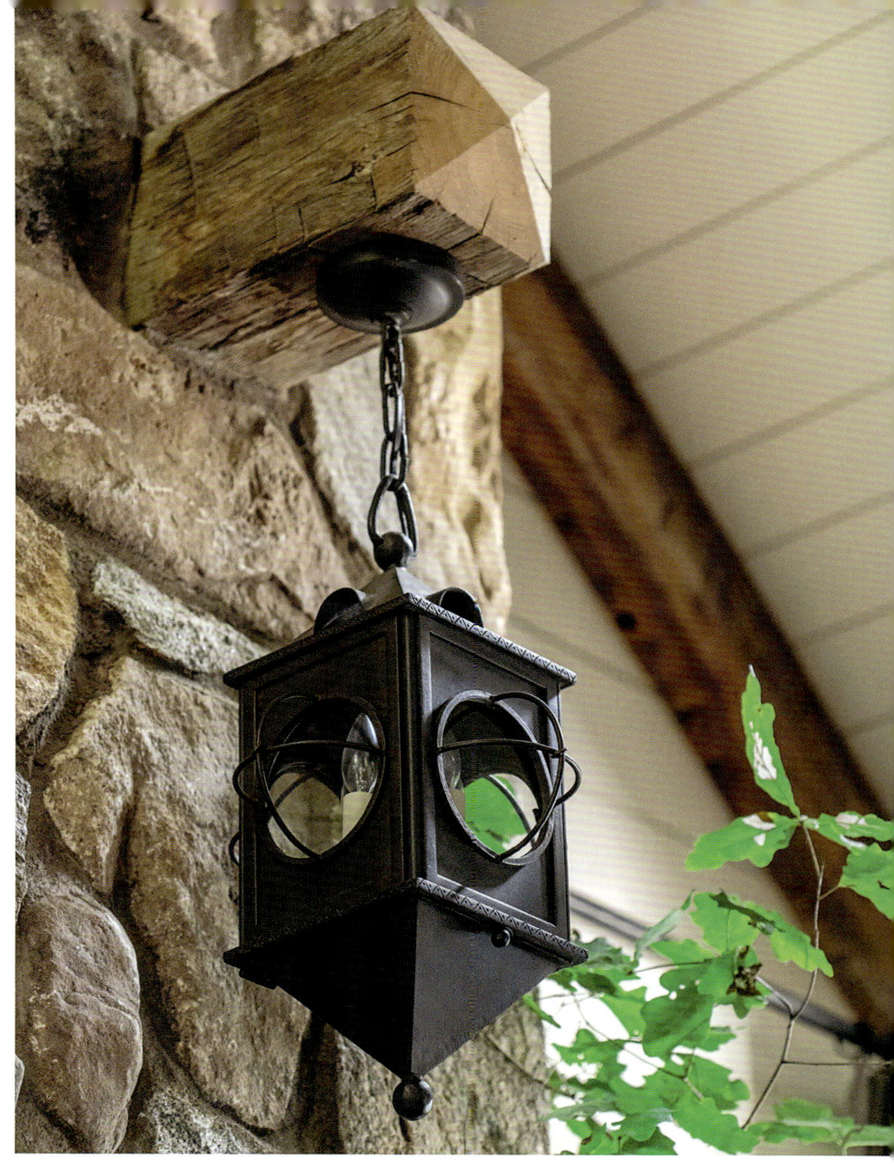

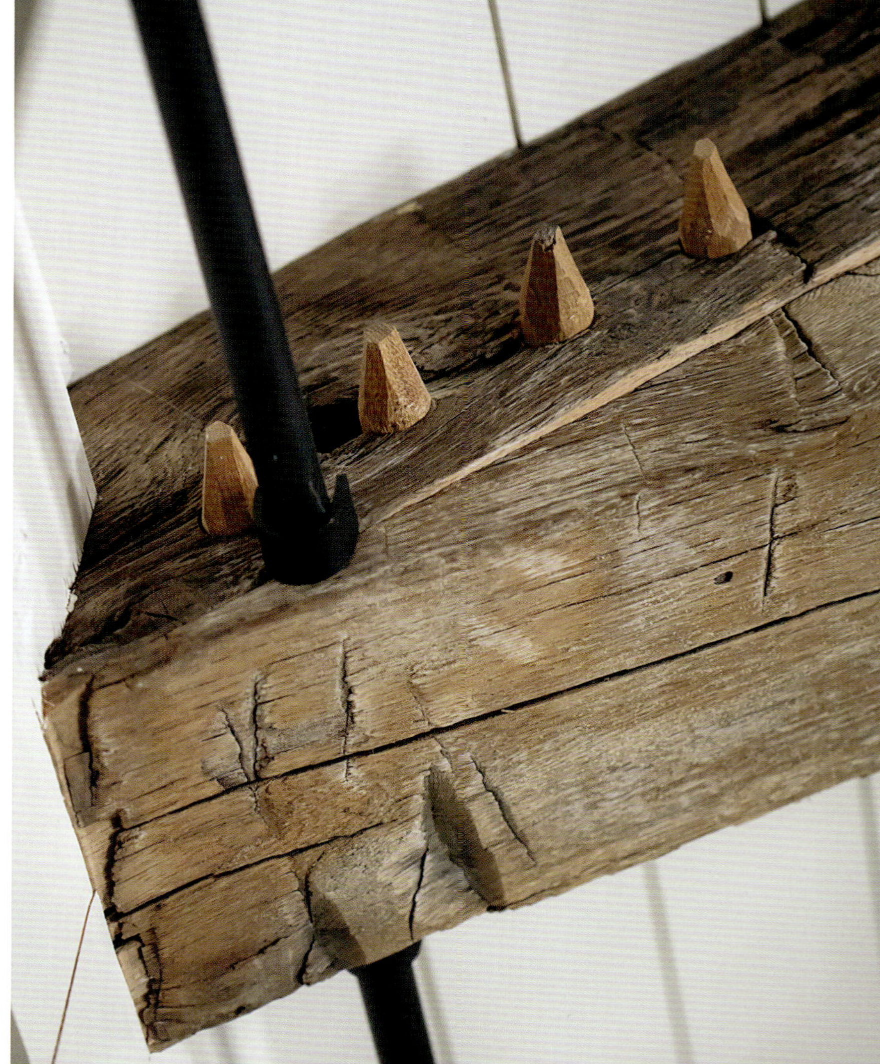

RIGHT: Details throughout the residence, such as hand-carved pegs, decorative cutouts, iron straps on the trusses, and interior windows that hint at a possible past life as exterior openings, evoke a narrative of gradual construction over time. Interior designer Barbara Westbrook's choices of rustic and relaxed furniture and decorative lighting perfectly complement the sense of history.

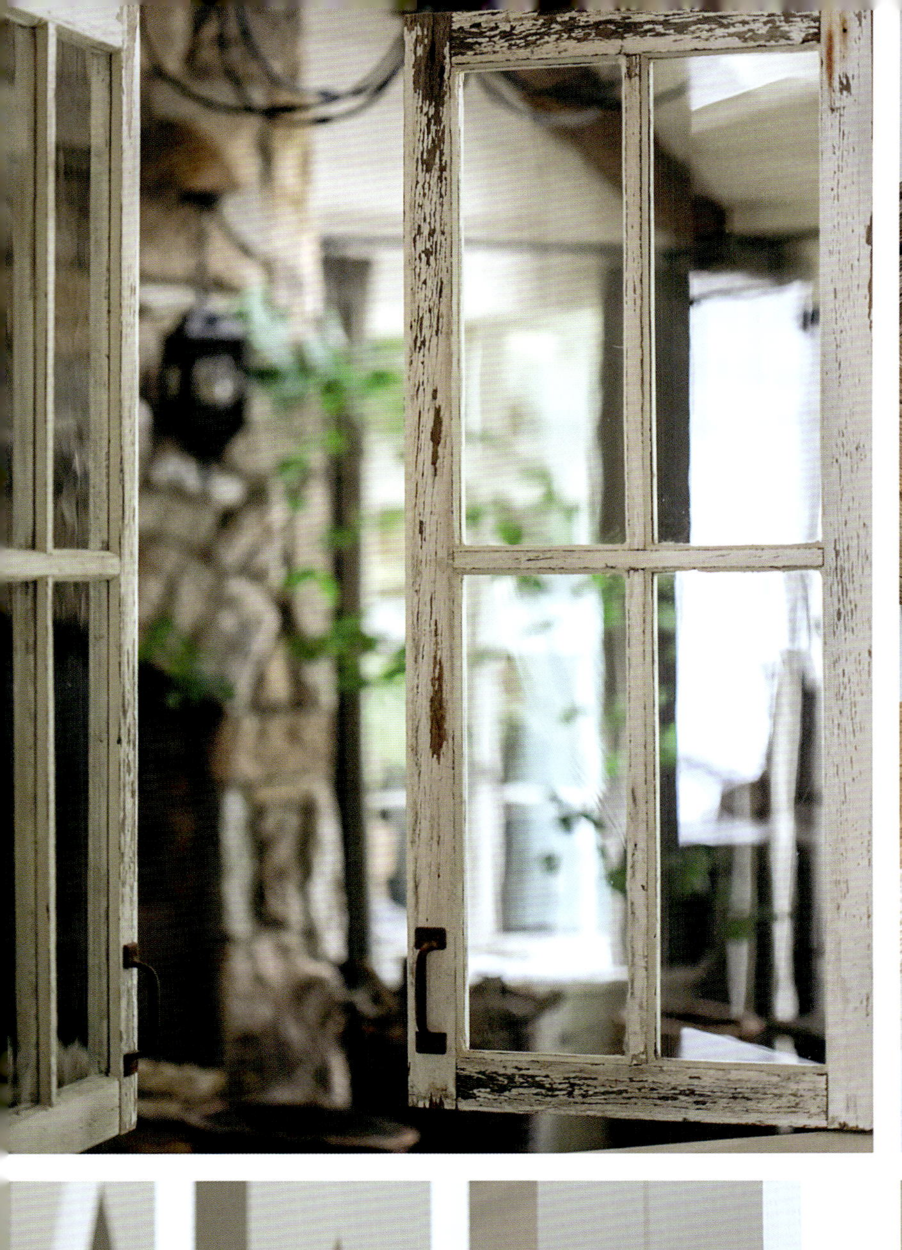

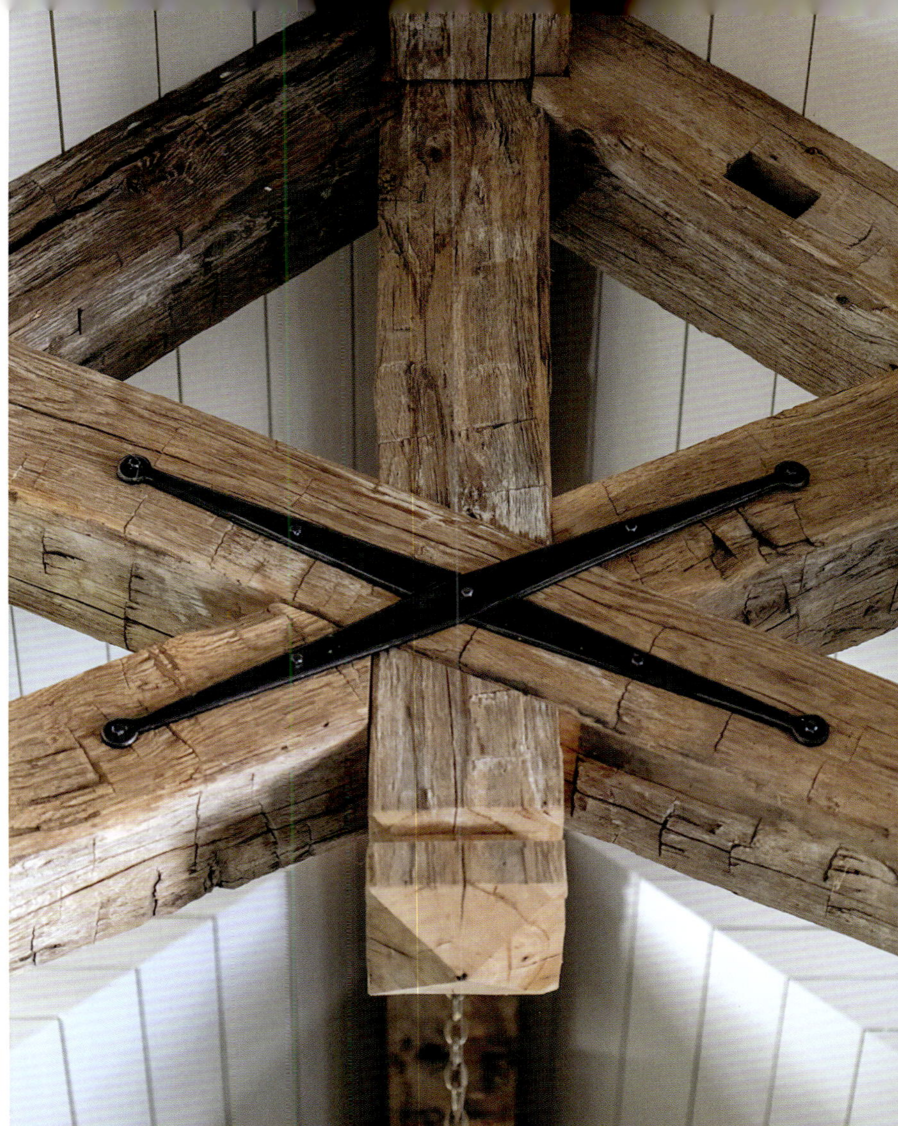

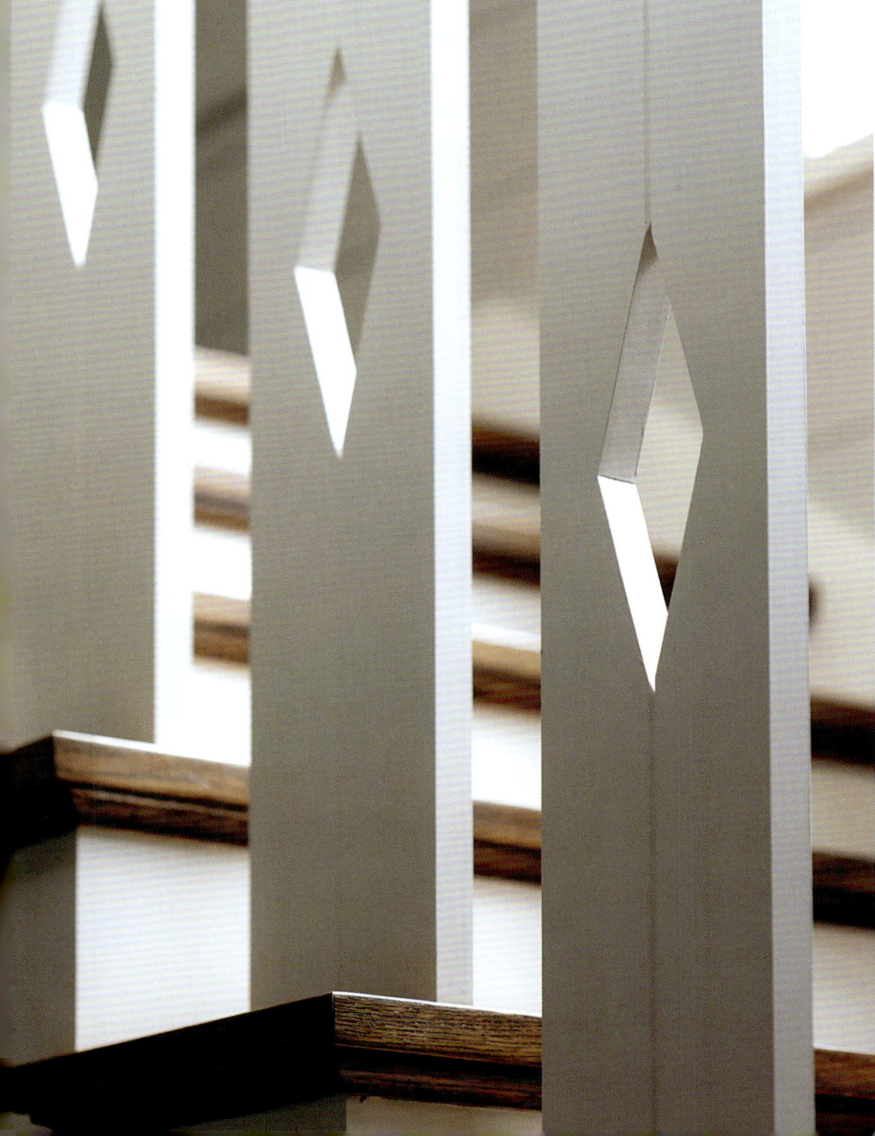

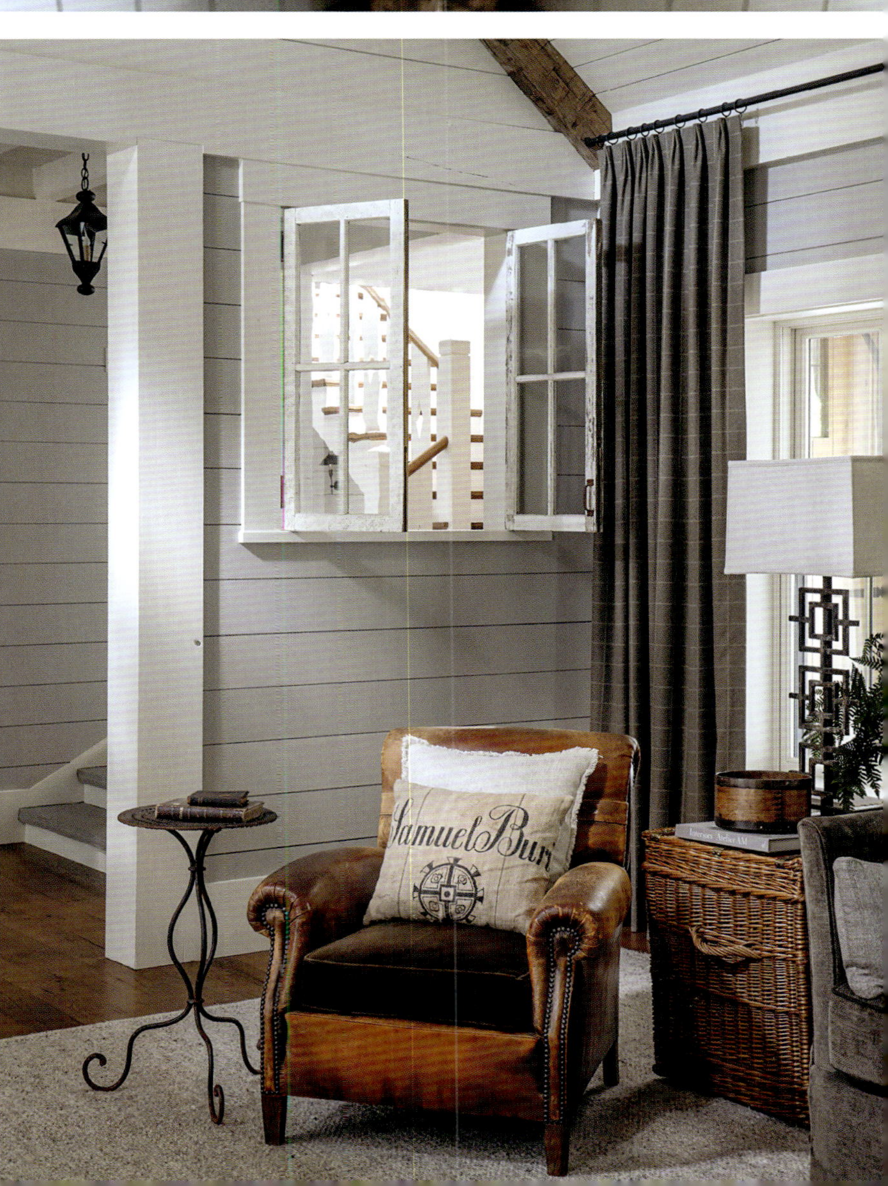

So, behind the entry loggia is a relatively small volume, containing the living room, that could conceivably have begun life as a single-room cabin, with a fireplace at one end. To its right is a larger two-story addition that could have been put on when the cabin's inhabitants needed more space. An ell in the rear holds the primary bedroom and bath suite and its own private sitting porch, mirrored on the far corner of the home by a bigger, taller screened porch suitable for social gatherings. A separate structure holding the garage and guest quarters is partially embedded in the earth off to one side and connected to the front of the main house by a breezeway running under the elegant swell of an eyebrow roof.

In keeping with the notion of growth over time, we worked in architectural features that are deliberately a little bit ad hoc: in one place, a dormer appears to have been added to shoehorn an extra bedroom or two beneath the roof; elsewhere, a window "remains" between two interior spaces, piercing what could have once been an exterior wall. The ceilings of main-level spaces, such as the kitchen and foyer, are formed of larger beams with planking laid on top, to look like the support structure of the floor above, and the breakfast room was built to look like it occupies a section of what was originally a wider rear veranda.

My clients wanted a house that would respond sensitively to its environment. Since Lake Keowee is only a few miles from the North Carolina border, we decided to pull aspects of the classic mountain style so prevalent in the Cashiers-Highlands region down to the foothills, if you will. Irregular chunks of fieldstone make up some of the home's walls; others are faced with dark-stained live-edge siding. Most of the window casings are very simple—four boards fitted together with wooden pegs—and the plank shutters are decorated with rustic diamond cutouts. The landscape architecture firm we partnered with did a great job of

OPPOSITE: The breakfast room is designed to look as if it were once a part of a back porch that was later enclosed. Hence, the structure of its ceiling matches the ceiling of the veranda outside, and a thicker mullion between two of the windows occurs where a column would have been placed to support the porch roof.

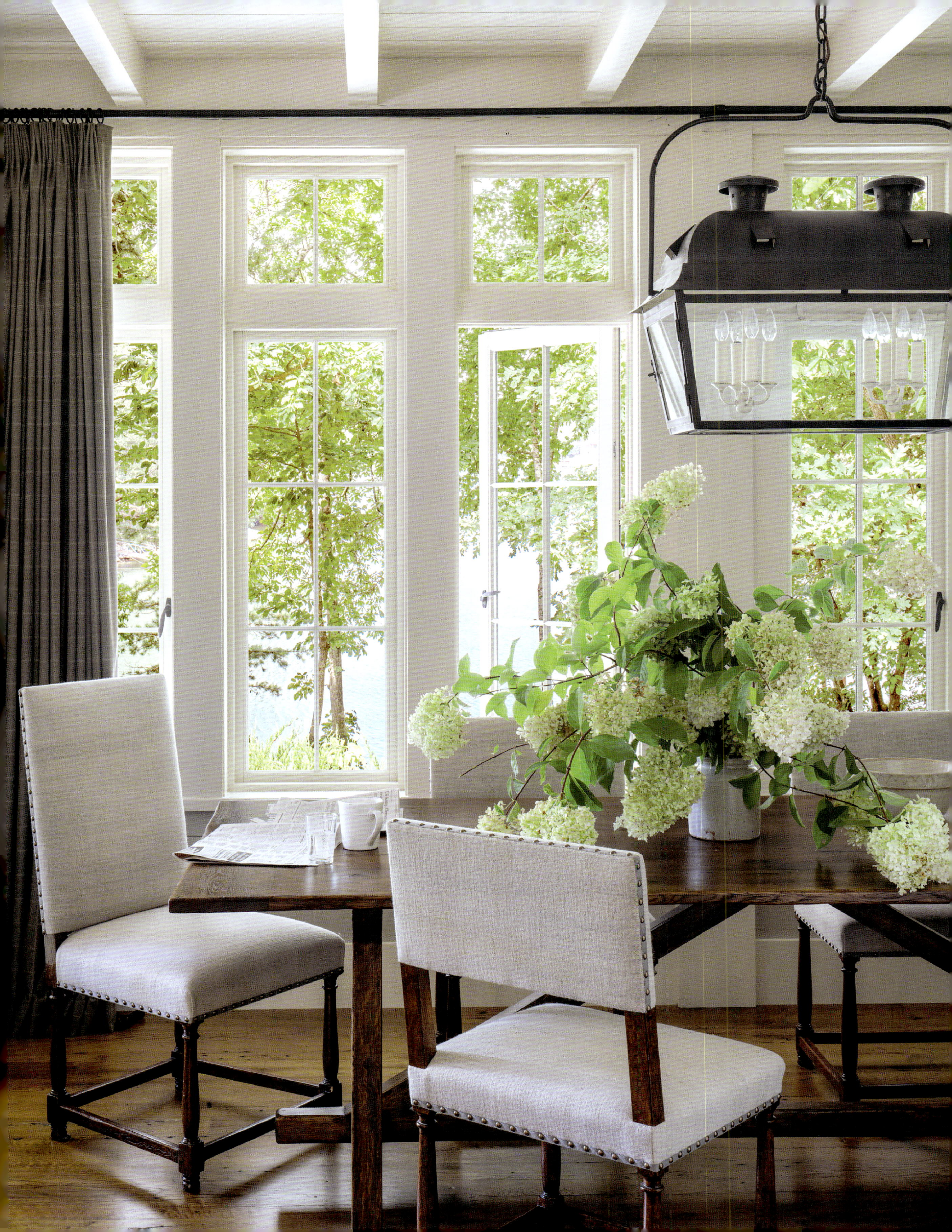

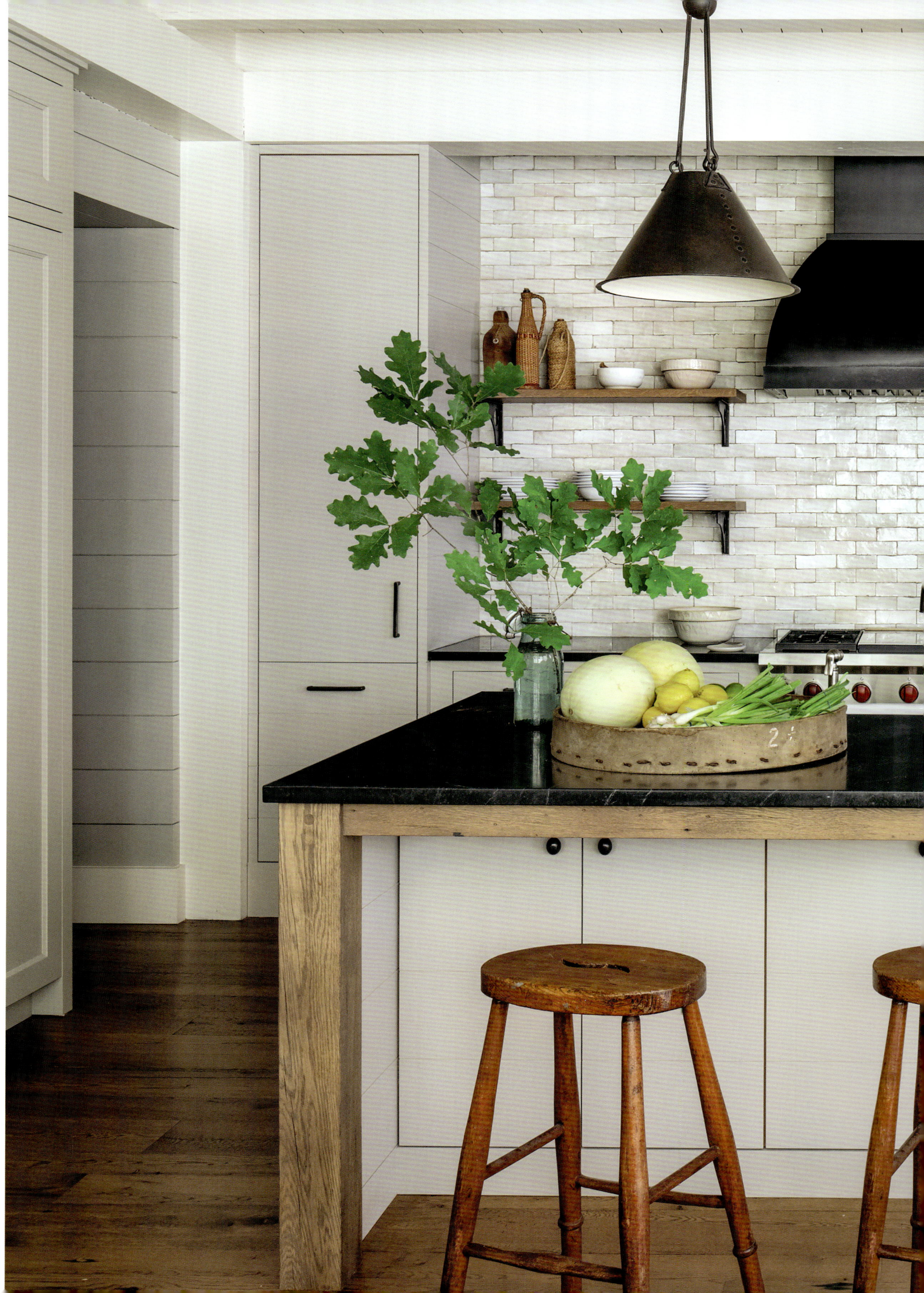

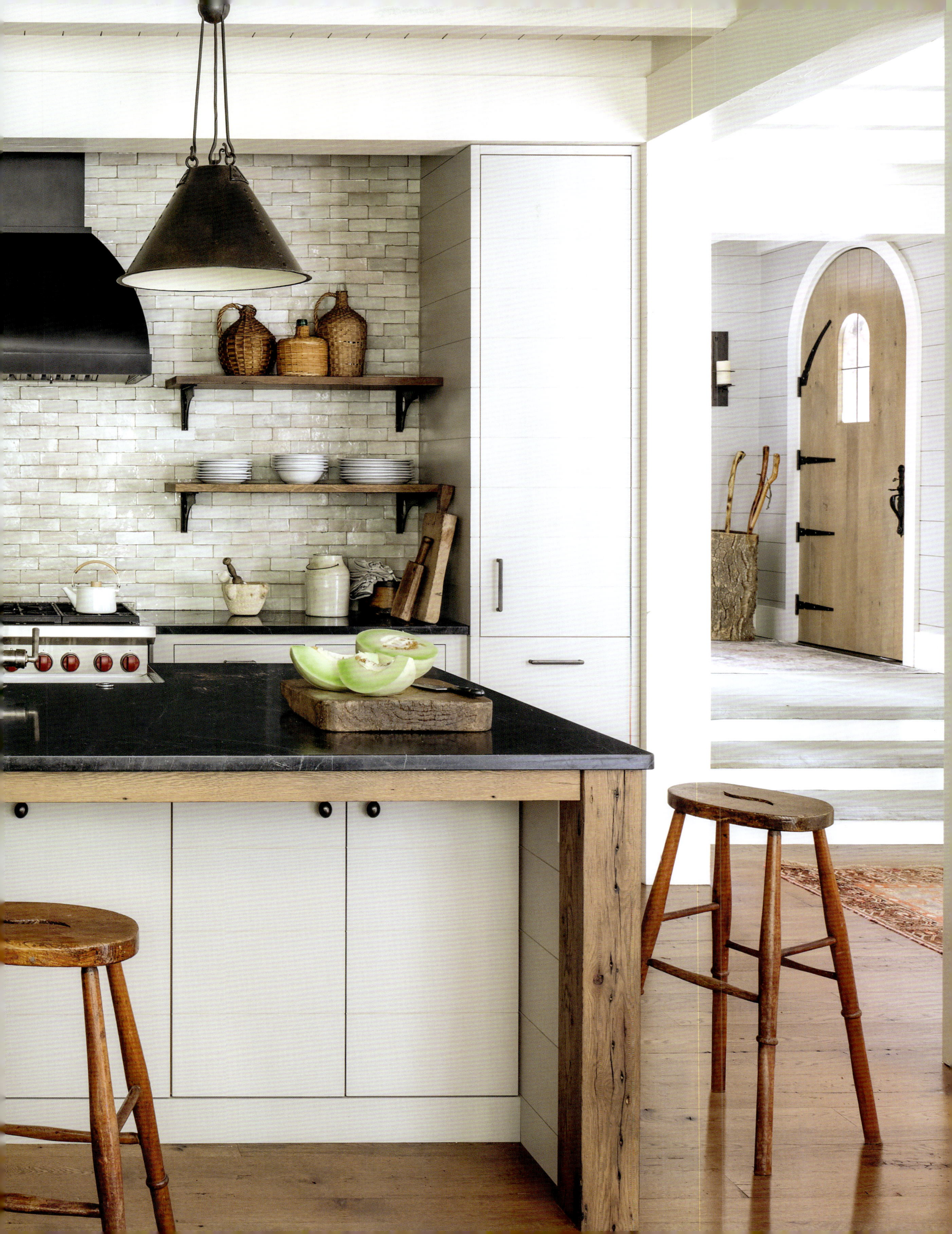

following suit, surrounding the house with retaining walls and stairs that integrate natural boulders and installing railings fashioned from black locust branches with the bark still attached.

Another advantage to the additive structure of this house is that it easily accommodates interior changes of elevation—a necessity on such a vertical property—and it allowed us to further play up our narrative of discovery and wayfinding. Entering the front door, you're faced with a choice of paths. Straight ahead is the home's main stair, whose flat-sawn balusters, with their diamond cutouts, recall the window shutters outside, while a leftward turn reveals three steps down to the living room and kitchen level and an open passage toward the back of the house. Beyond a set of French doors in the far wall, a prospect of water screened by trees beckons you forward to the covered veranda I mentioned earlier, lined with rocking chairs, and a final two-step drop to a spacious flagstone terrace. The house engages the land, continuing to work its way lower on the hill as you move through it.

It's not a terribly large home, yet with its winding driveway approach, the indirect circulation pattern inside, and the final backyard drop to the shore, it provides an unexpectedly dramatic experience. The whole point of lake houses is their relationship to the water—that's the reason people love them. Here, you get teased by portions of the view at several moments both before and after you enter the house, but the true payoff doesn't come until the end when you reach the lakeside itself, framed and focused by the progression you've just been guided through. This cozy cottage—comfortable, casual, not ostentatious, and made of simple materials simply shaped—works a bit differently to create a powerful impression.

PRECEDING SPREAD: Open shelves set against a backdrop of subway tiles reinforce the laid-back atmosphere of the kitchen. The island has the look of a simple table made of heavy timbers, with cabinets beneath. The metal range hood bears a notable resemblance to the vent hood built into the living room fireplace. OPPOSITE: The mudroom, which opens to the breezeway and garage, serves as a practical space to keep outdoor gear separate from the main flow of the home.

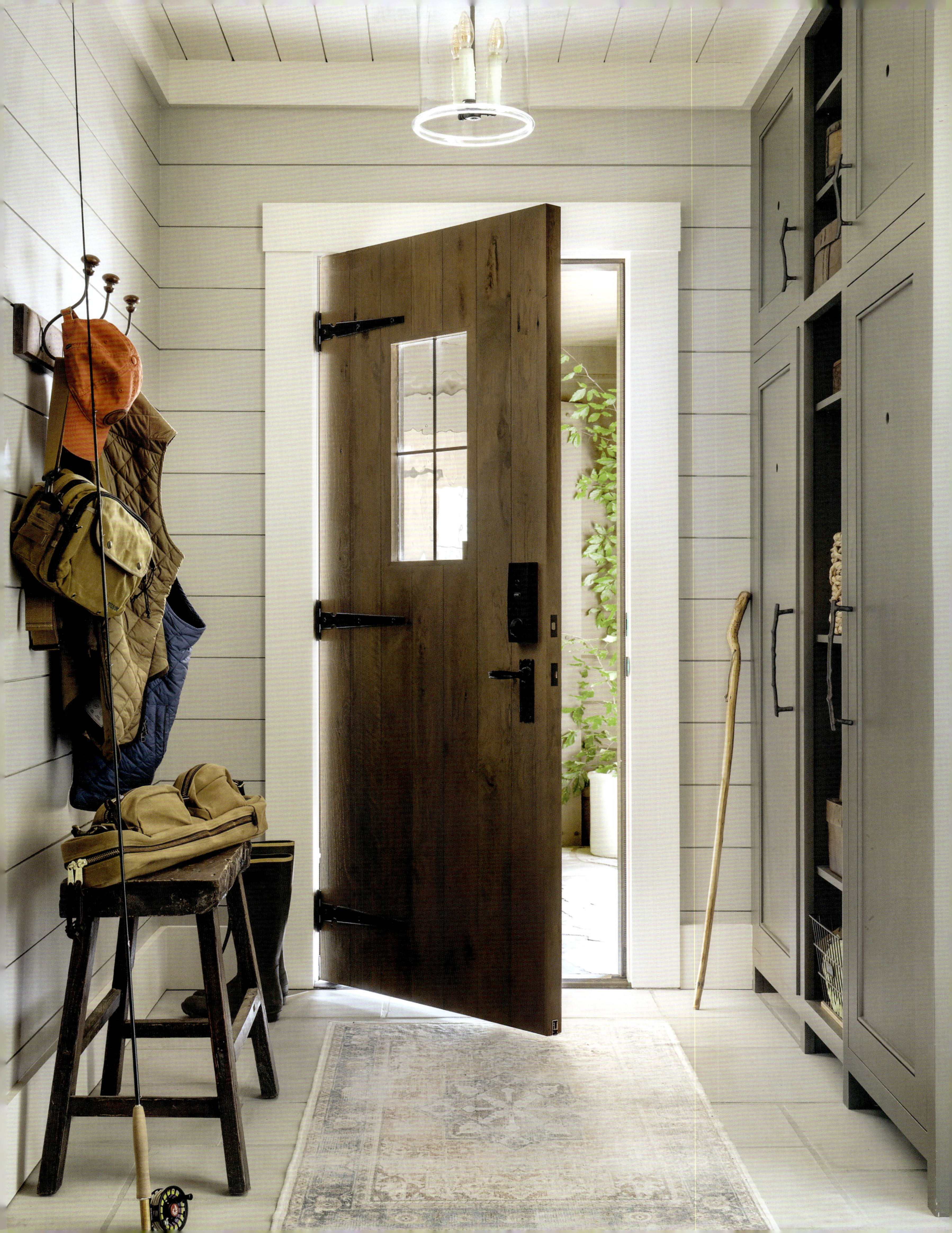

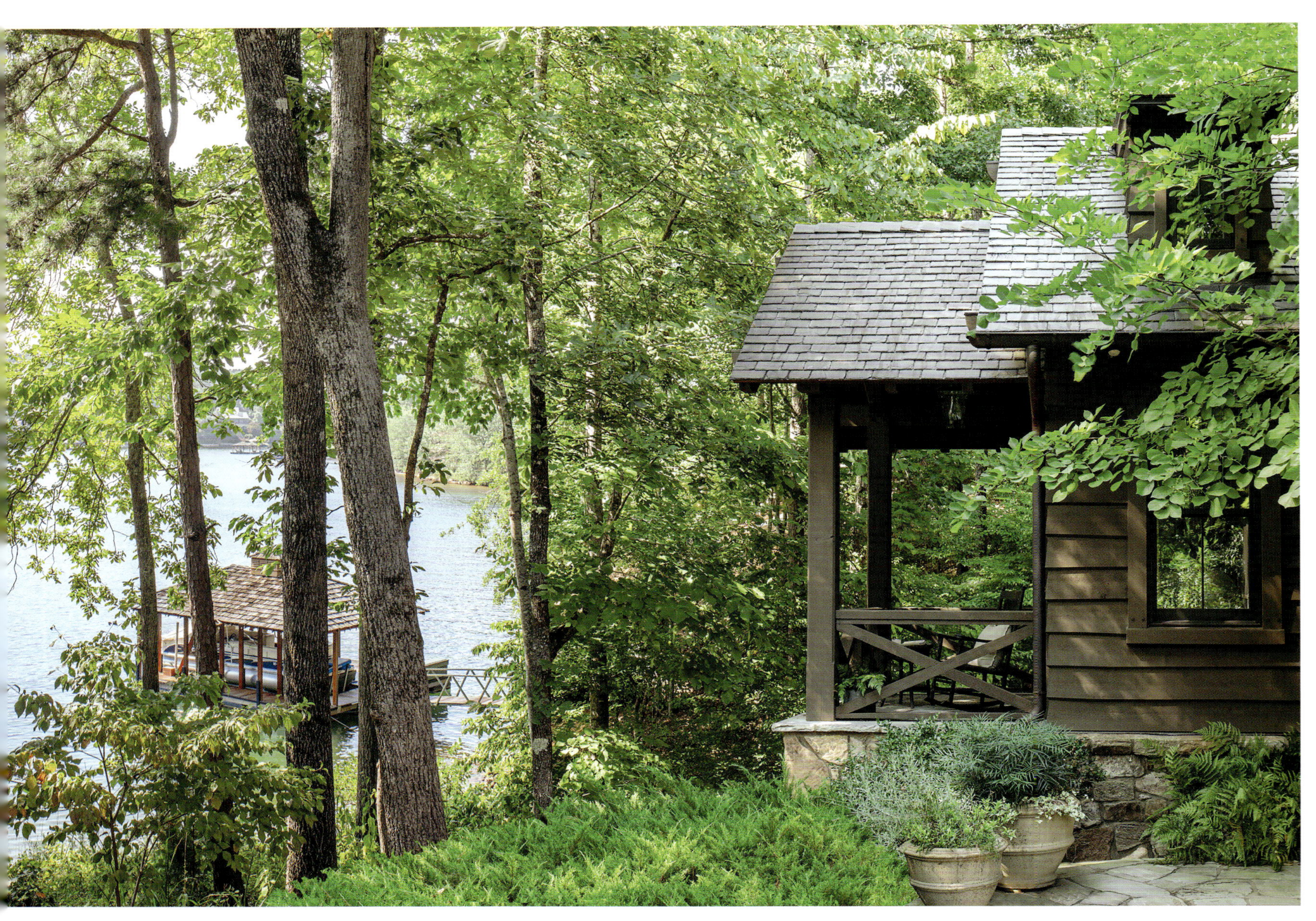

ABOVE AND OPPOSITE: The owners' suite features a private porch that provides a peaceful retreat with a bird's-eye view of the lake below. Their bedroom, an airy vaulted space, is bathed in natural light from roof dormers that mirror the configuration of dormers in the living room.

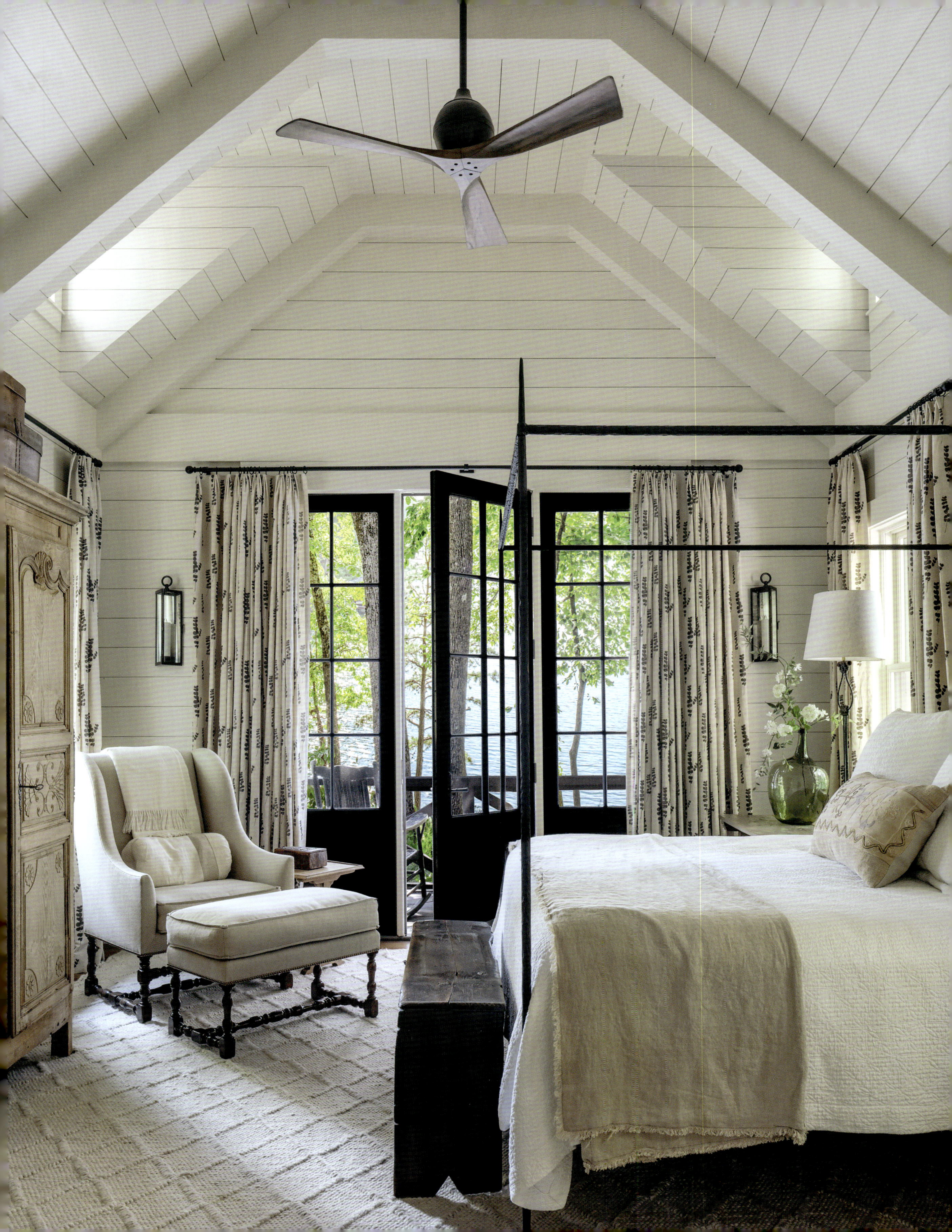

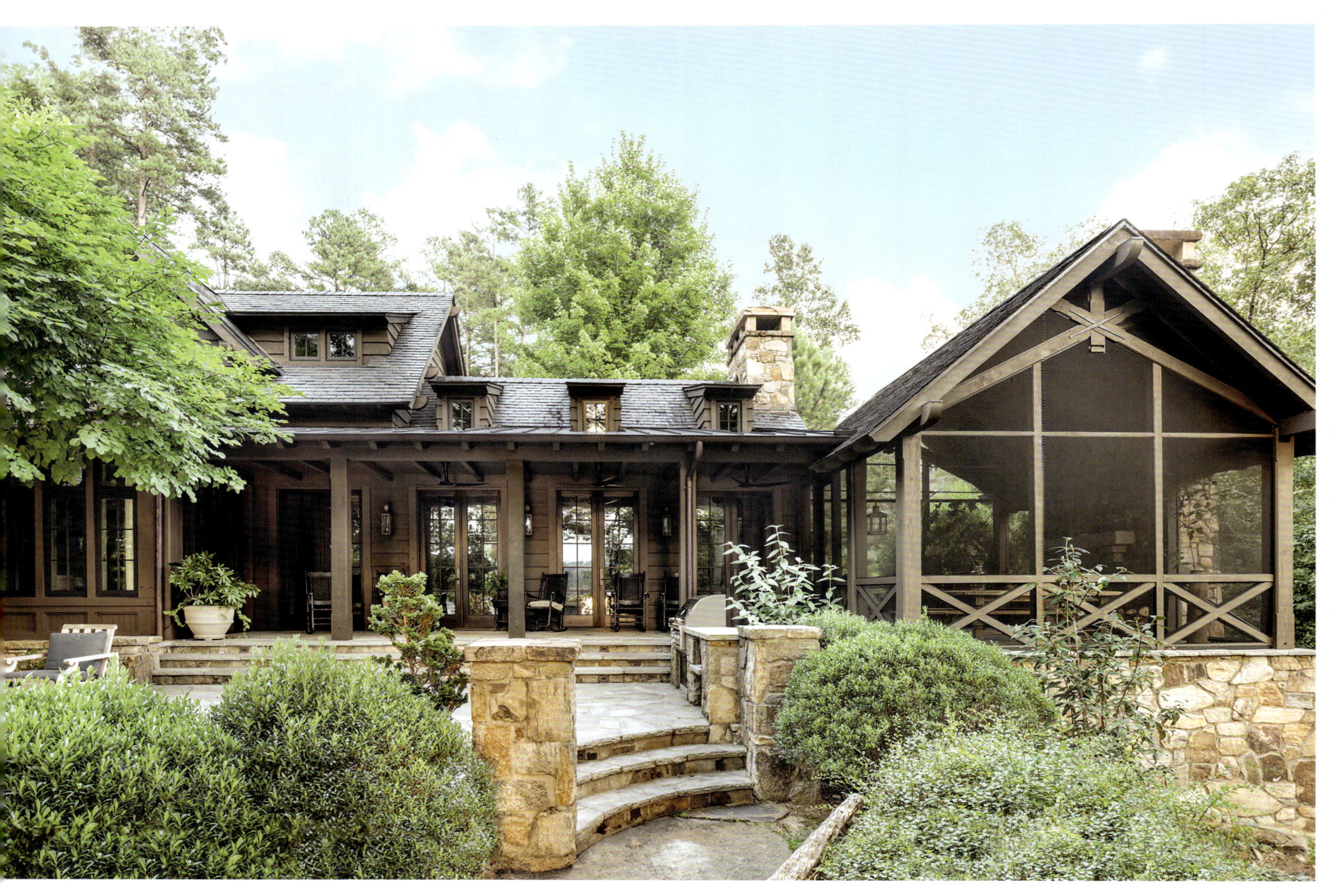

ABOVE: The lake side of the home is fully oriented toward the water, offering a variety of indoor and outdoor spaces designed to engage with nature in different ways. These spaces invite both tranquil reflection and lively interaction with the surrounding landscape. OPPOSITE: The screened porch overlooking the lake soars upward, supported by elegant scissor trusses and metal tie rods. FOLLOWING SPREAD, LEFT: Stairways on the property are fashioned from irregular natural stones, with slightly more finished piers marking the ends. FOLLOWING SPREAD, RIGHT: A stone fireplace with a contrasting granite mantel warms the screened porch on chilly days.

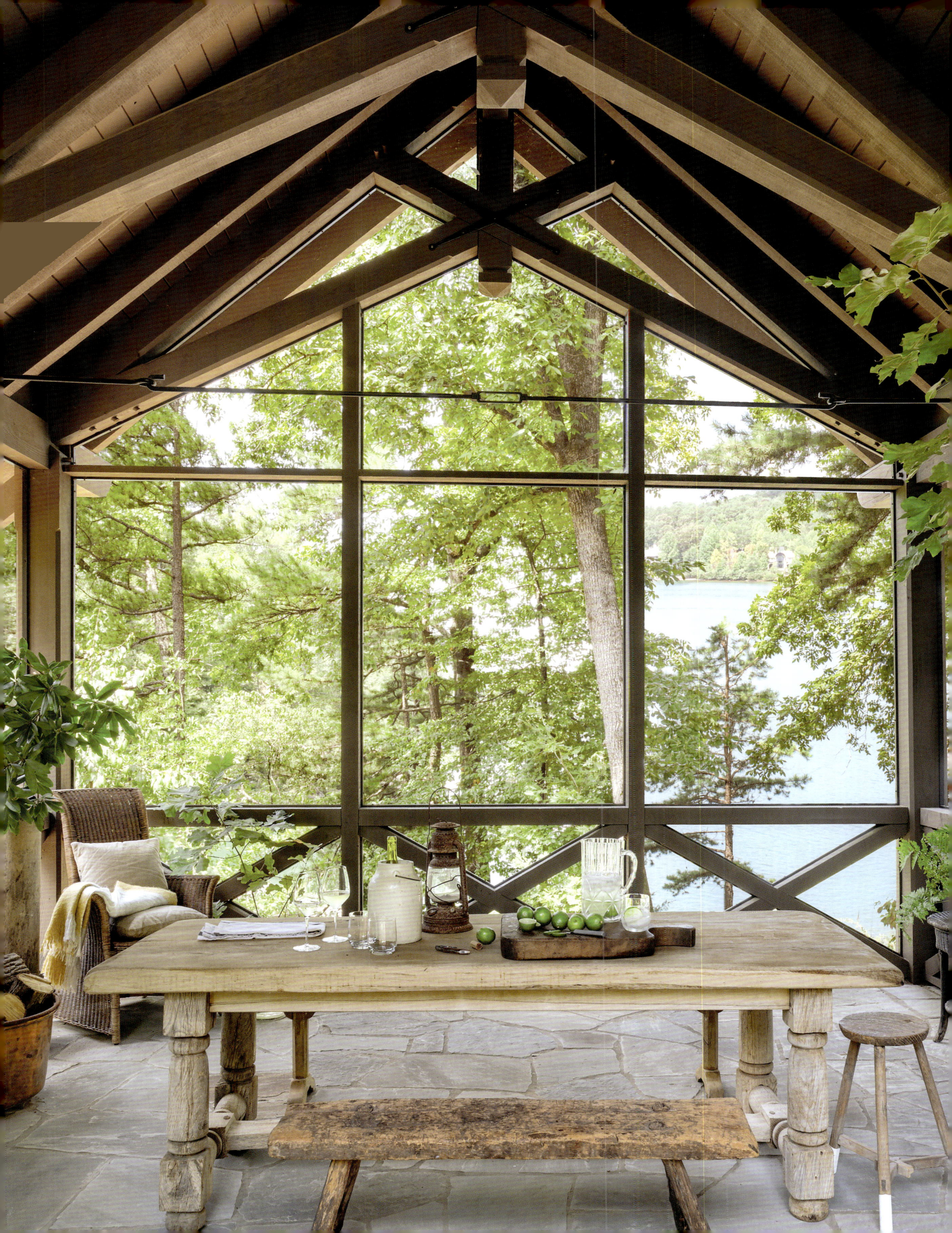

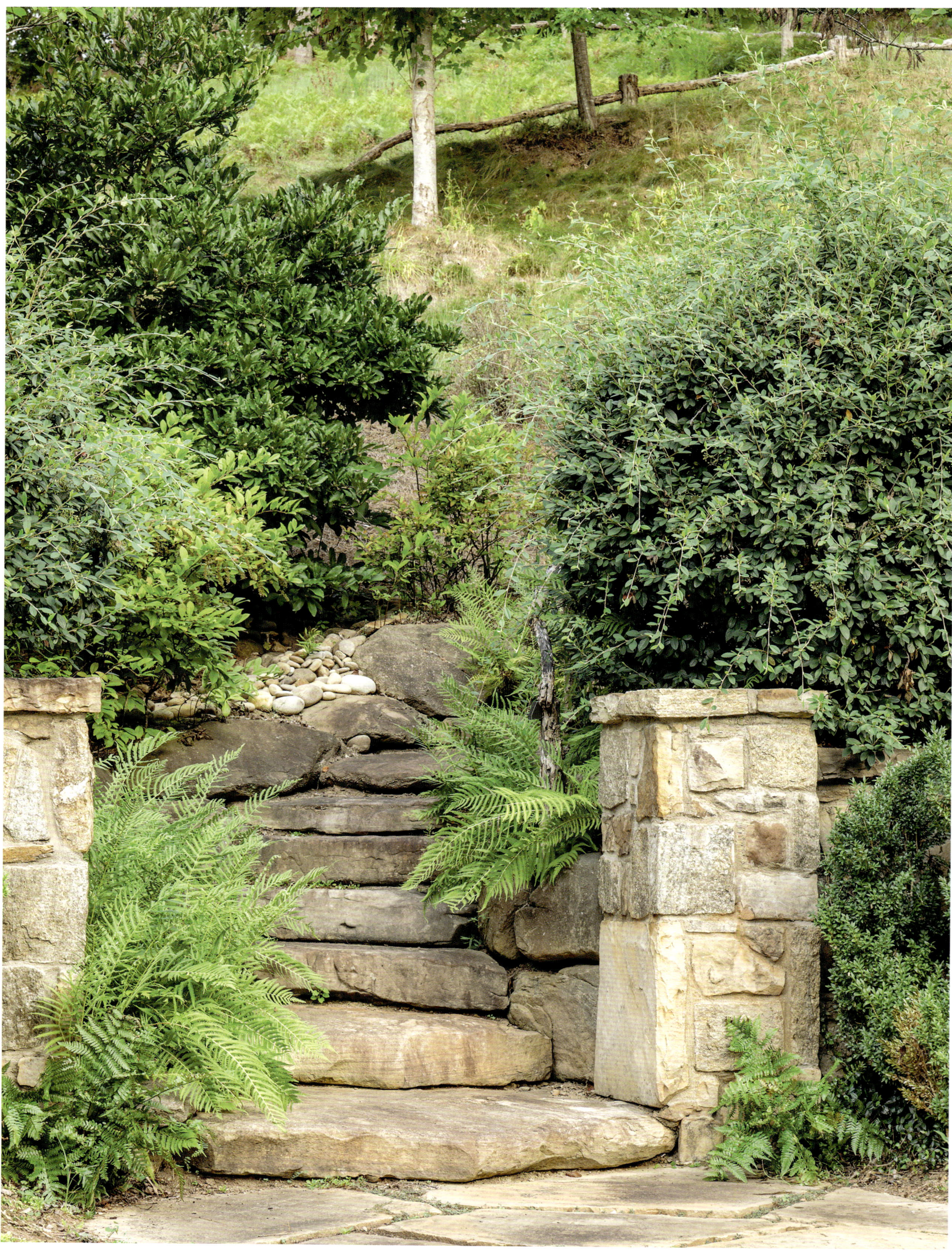

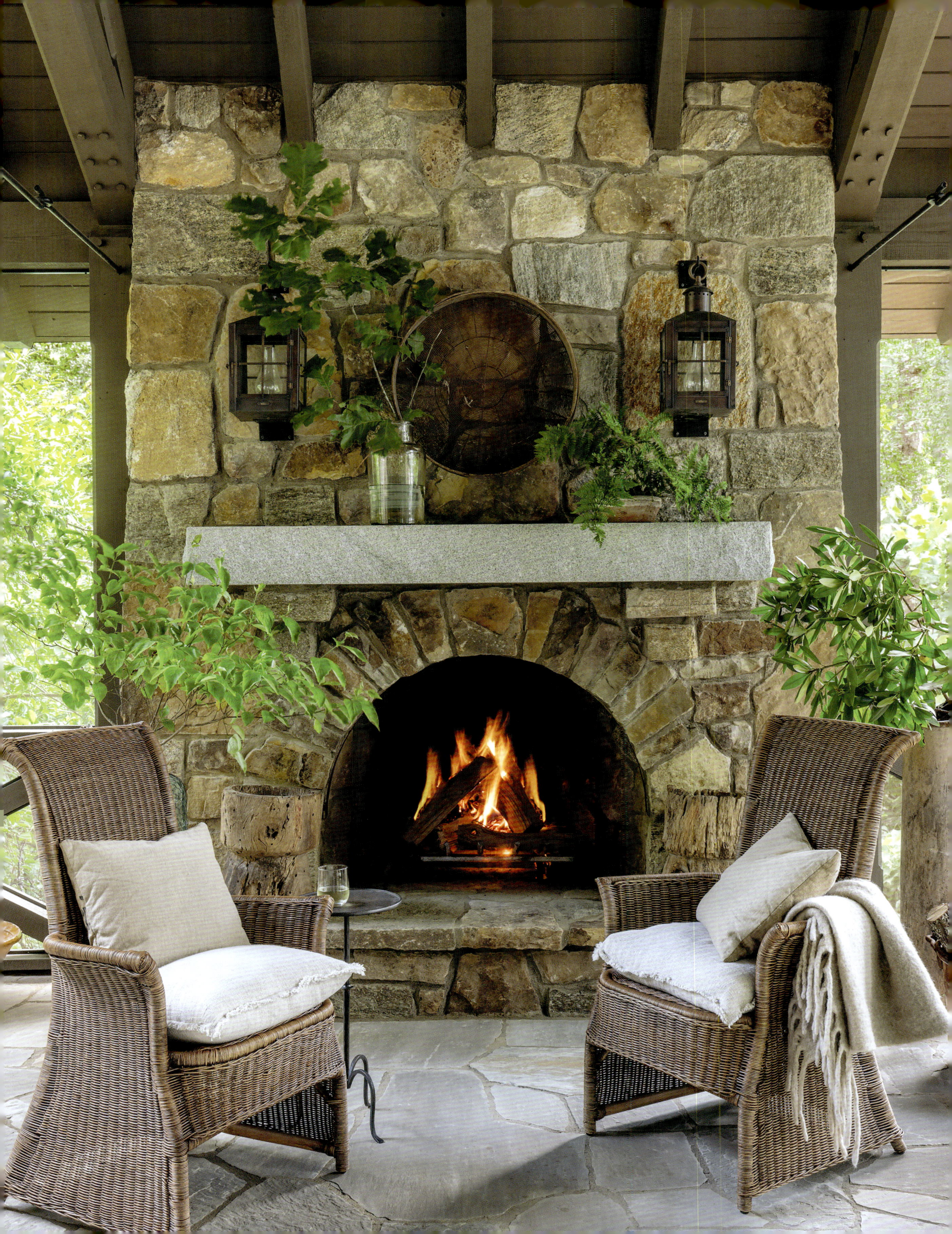

PROJECT CREDITS

MEADOW'S EDGE
Chloe Flaharty, *project architect*
Amanda Wyatt, *interior design*
Alex Smith Garden Design, *landscape design*
Harris Custom Homes, *builder*

VILLA ON THE BLUFF
Noah Speights, *project manager*
Cynthia Nunez & Courtney Dickey, *interior design*
Viator and Associates, *landscape design*
Mark Laborde Builders, *builder*

UNDER THE OAKS
Justin Bell, *project architect*
Beth Webb Interiors, *interior design*
Planters, *landscape design*
Macallan Construction, *builder*

THE OVERLOOK
Chloe Flaharty, *project architect*
Catherine Brown Paterson Interior Design, *interior design*
Byrd Landscape Design, *landscape design*
Harris Custom Homes, *builder*

SEVEN STONES FARM
Paul Geary, *project architect*
Ashley Gish, *interior design*
Land Plus, *landscape design*
Kendall Hart Contracting, *builder*

OASIS HOUSE
Noah Speights, *project manager*
Chelsea Robinson Interiors, *interior design*
Horton Land Works, *landscape design*
Gulfview Construction, *builder*

STONECOURT MANOR
Noah Speights, *project manager*
Cheryl Smith Associates, *interior design*
Land Plus, *landscape design*
Bill Grant Homes, *builder*

HARDWOOD RIDGE
Noah Speights, *project manager*
Westbrook Interiors, *interior design*
Land Plus, *landscape design*
Rob Marett Custom Homes, *builder*

BEACHVIEW RETREAT
Paul Geary, *project architect*
Beth Webb Interiors, *interior design*
Land Plus, *landscape design*
Davis Dunn Construction, *builder*

HICKORY BANK
Campbell Doughty, *project manager*
Westbrook Interiors, *interior design*
Planters, *landscape design*
Ken Berry Construction, *builder*

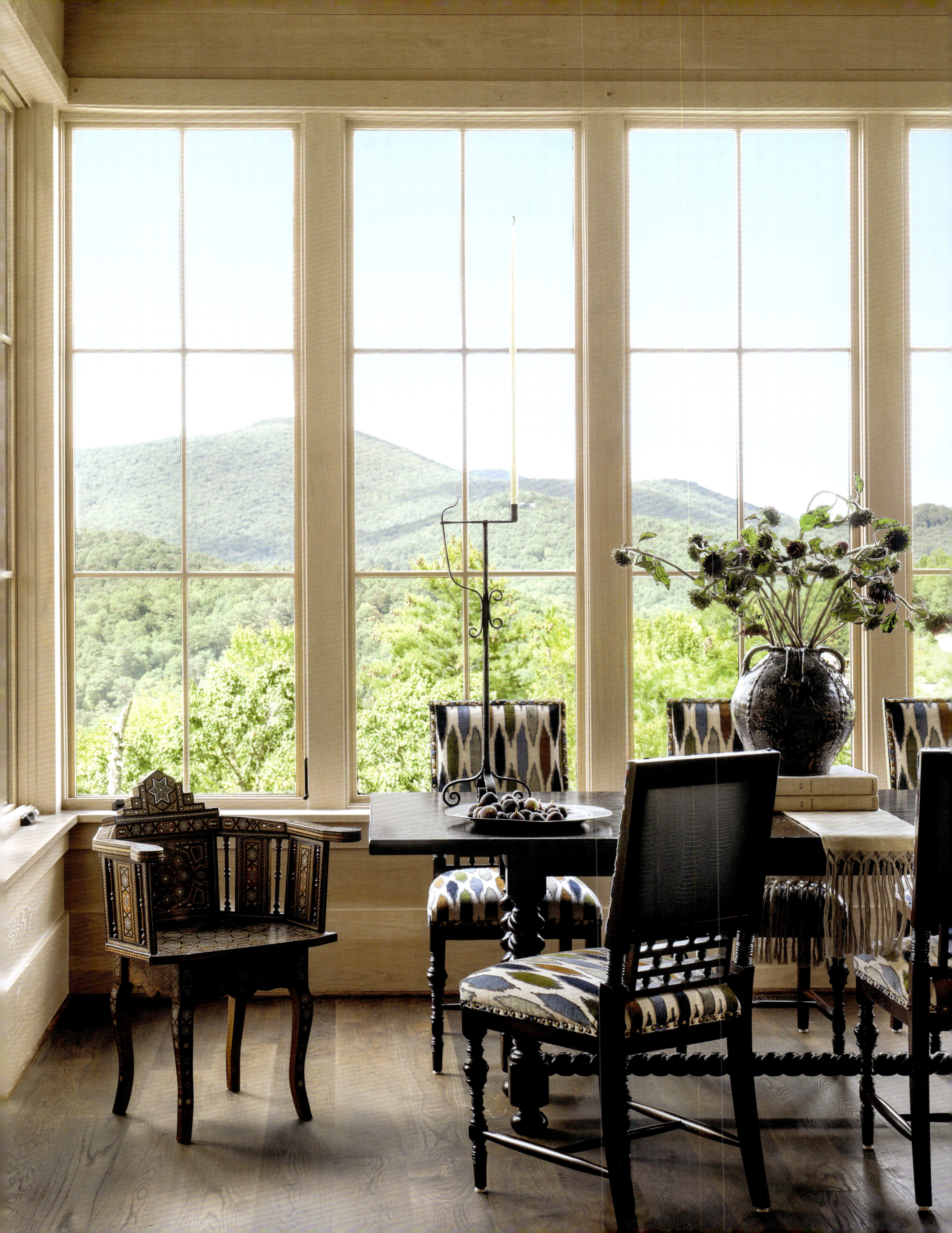

ACKNOWLEDGMENTS

Since the inception of T.S. Adams Studio, Architects twenty-five years ago, I feel as though I have been on a continued sprint. Venturing down this path to put this book together forced me to reflect on this journey. It would be foolish of me to think that this adventure is all my own doing. In fact, it has so much less to do with me and more to do with the countless people who have stepped in and out of my life over these years. I have been blessed beyond my own comprehension by the good Lord and I am eternally grateful for the talents He has blessed me with, the individuals He has placed in my life, and the many opportunities He has gifted to me. No matter how hard I try, I feel I will be negligent in acknowledging everyone, but I will do my best. To begin with, my family. My wife, Kelli, who has endured all my "I have an idea" moments, supported me through thick and thin, and has always been by my side since we said "I do" twenty-nine years ago. My kids—Will, Ben, and Caroline—for being my biggest fans and cheerleaders. My mother, who endowed me with creativity, encouraged me to dream big, and opened my eyes to the world of architecture at an early age. My father, who modeled hard work, shared his love for construction, and taught me how to work with my hands. Tom Bridges, architect and family friend, who mentored me and guided my path with wisdom throughout my high school years, when I needed it most. Finally, Mike Gullett for helping me see my potential in the early years of my career.

The talent pool of professionals, designers, and craftspeople that has been required to assemble this body of work is beyond measure, each one leaving their own fingerprint. Thank you to the incredibly talented interior designers Beth Webb, Barbara Westbrook, Ashley Gish, Catherine Paterson, Amanda Wyatt, and Chelsea Robinson for their thoughtful touch and creativity to finish each of the homes appropriately. Thank you to the landscape architects Land Plus, Planters, Alex Smith, Ted Viator, and Renee Byrd for carefully setting the scene for each home's environment. Finally, to all the contractors: Ben Harris, Mark Laborde, David Childers, Reynolds Hart, John Brown, Bill Grant, Bo Quinnelly, Rob Marett, Will Dunn, and Ken Berry for taking as much pride in our projects as we do.

Over the lifespan of T.S. Adams Studio, Architects, there have been so many talented individuals who shaped who we are today. Foremost, the leadership team: Noah Speights, Chloe Flaharty, Riley Tart, and Trent Miller, all of whom have taken our firm to the next level. Past project managers Paul Geary, Campbell Doughty, Justin Bell, Garrett Daniel, and Kent Thagard. Finally, thank you to all the staff members over the years who have meticulously drawn and detailed each of these homes.

Working side by side with each of the visionary photographers and stylists has been impactful. Thank you to Lisa Romerein, Emily Followill, Dean Courtois, Andrew Petrich, Eleanor Roper, and Helen Crowther for capturing these homes and bringing them to life in this book.

I am truly grateful to Jill Cohen for her confidence in me and unflappable honesty, Lizzy Hyland for her calm leadership through this process, Kathleen Jayes for her consistent guidance, Kyle Hoepner for bringing to life my incoherent thoughts, Melissa Wilson for always believing in me and putting me out there, and Doug Turshen and Steve Turner for their patience through all our edits and their visionary talent in designing this monograph.

Lastly, all these projects reflect our shared clients' dreams and would not have been possible without their unending commitment. I am thankful for each client and each opportunity afforded me over the past twenty-five years.

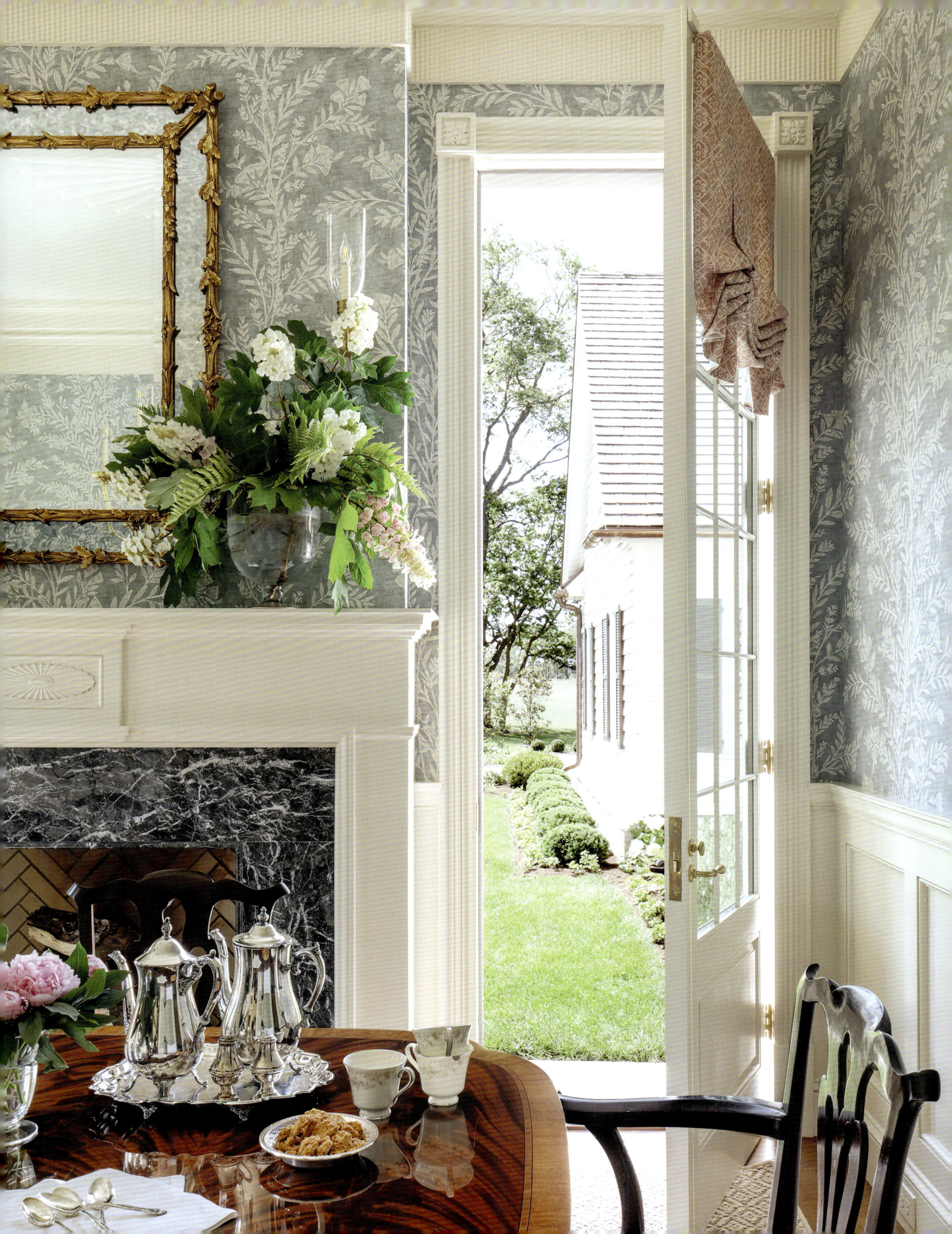

First published in the United States of America in 2025 by
Rizzoli International Publications, Inc.
49 West 27th Street
New York, NY 10001
www.rizzoliusa.com

Foreword: Beth Webb
Text: Kyle Hoepner

All photographs by Lisa Romerein except:
Courtesy of Tim Adams: 10–13 and all drawings
Emily Followill: 8, 50, 58, 64, 84, 86, 87, 88–89, 90,
91, 92–93, 94, 95
Aimée Mazzenga: 165–181

Publisher: Charles Miers
Senior Editor: Kathleen Jayes
Production Manager: Rebecca Ambrose
Managing Editor: Lynn Scrabis

Designed by Doug Turshen with Steve Turner

Developed in collaboration with Jill Cohen and Associates,
at Sandow Capital, LLC dba JCA

ISBN: 978-0-8478-7447-7
Library of Congress Control Number: 2025934305

Printed in China
2026 2027 2028 2029 / 10 9 8 7 6 5 4 3 2

The authorized representative in the EU for product safety and compliance is Mondadori Libri S.p.A., via Gian Battista Vico 42, Milan, Italy, 20123, www.mondadori.it

Visit us online:
Instagram.com/RizzoliBooks
Facebook.com/RizzoliNewYork
Youtube.com/user/RizzoliNY

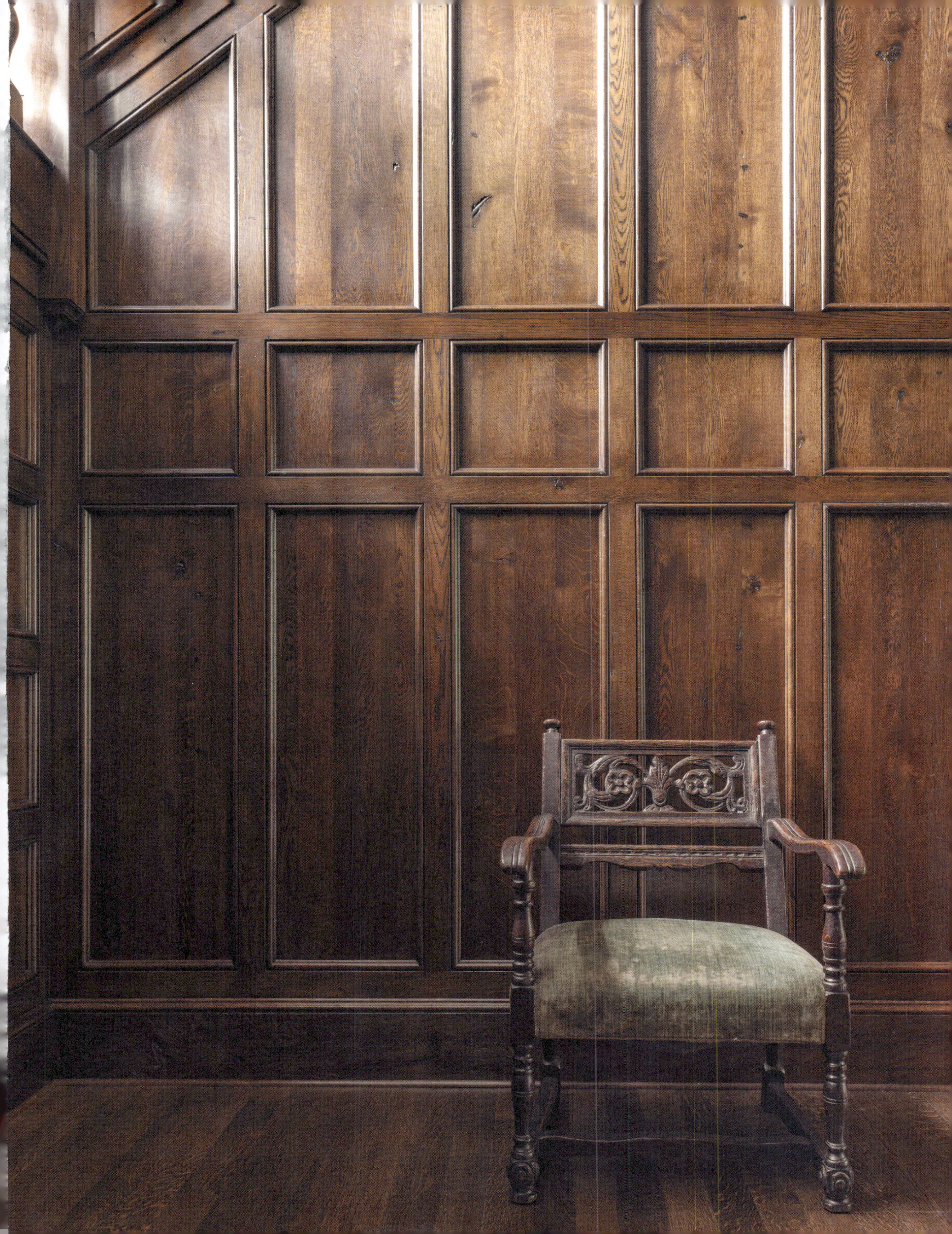

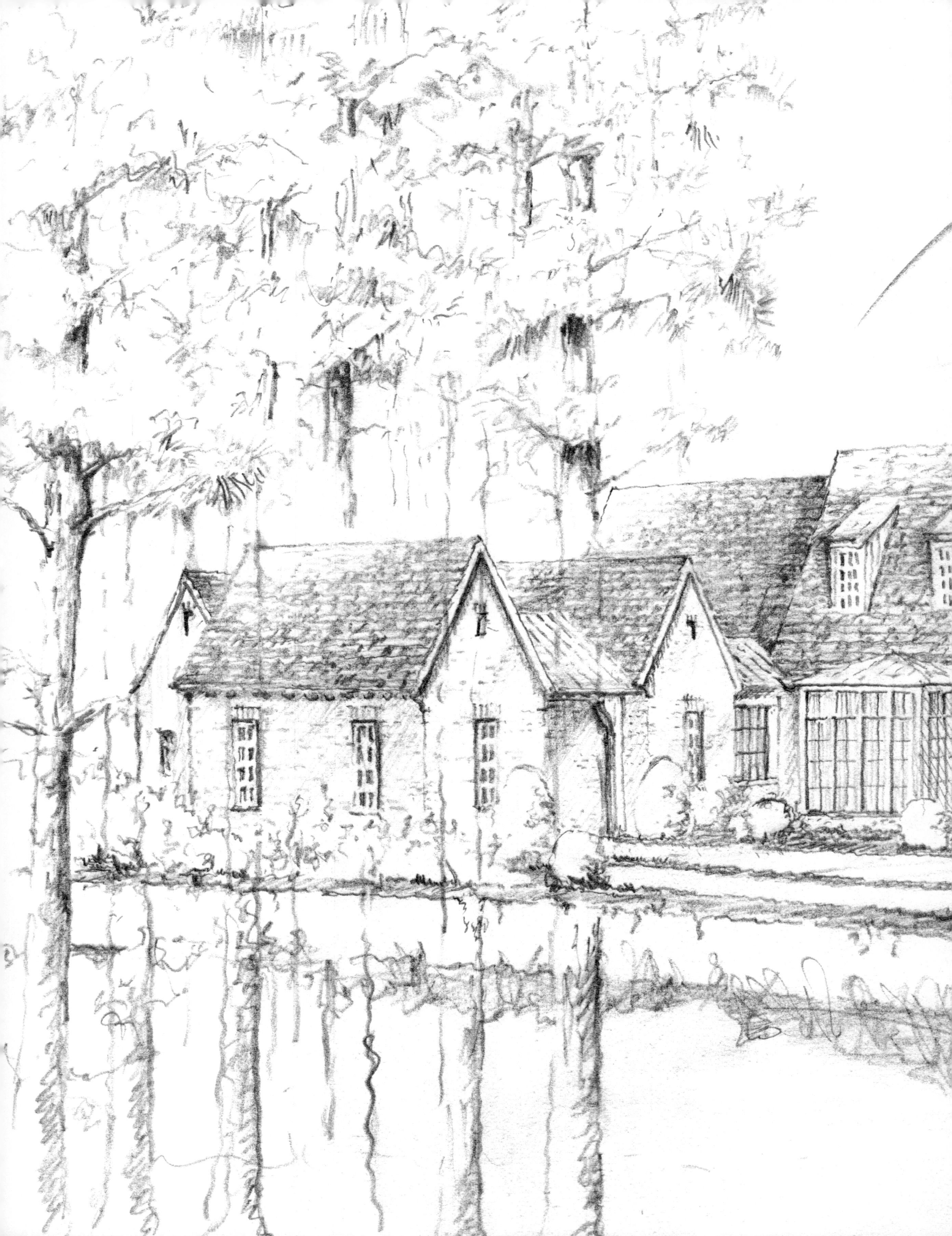